STUDENT SERVICES

STUDENT SERVICES

A Handbook for the Profession

SIXTH EDITION

John H. Schuh, Susan R. Jones, Vasti Torres
Editors

JOSSEY-BASS
A Wiley Imprint
www.josseybass.com

Published by Jossey-Bass
A Wiley Brand
One Montgomery Street, Suite 1000, San Francisco, CA 94104-4594—www.josseybass.com

Jossey-Bass books and products are available through most bookstores. To contact Jossey-Bass directly call our Customer Care Department within the U.S. at 800-956-7739, outside the U.S. at 317-572-3986, or fax 317-572-4002.

Wiley publishes in a variety of print and electronic formats and by print-on-demand. Some material included with standard print versions of this book may not be included in e-books or in print-on-demand. If this book refers to media such as a CD or DVD that is not included in the version you purchased, you may download this material at http://booksupport.wiley.com. For more information about Wiley products, visit www.wiley.com.

Library of Congress Cataloging-in-Publication Data
Names: Schuh, John H., editor of compilation. | Jones, Susan R., 1955- editor of compilation. | Torres, Vasti, 1960- editor of compilation.
Title: Student services : a handbook for the profession / John H. Schuh, Susan R. Jones, Vasti Torres, editors.
Description: 6th edition. | San Francisco, CA : Jossey-Bass, 2016. | Includes bibliographical references and index.
Identifiers: LCCN 2016018928 (print) | LCCN 2016021064 (ebook) | ISBN 9781119049593 (cloth) | ISBN 9781119051244 (ePDF) | ISBN 9781119051343 (ePub) | ISBN 9781119051244 (pdf) | ISBN 9781119051343 (epub)
Subjects: LCSH: Student affairs services—United States—Handbooks, manuals, etc. | College student development programs—United States—Handbooks, manuals, etc. | Counseling in higher education—United States—Handbooks, manuals, etc.
Classification: LCC LB2342.9 .K65 2016 (print) | LCC LB2342.9 (ebook) | DDC 378.1/97—dc23
LC record available at https://lccn.loc.gov/2016018928

Cover Design: Wiley
Cover Image: ©traffic_analyzer/iStockphoto

Printed in the United States of America
SIXTH EDITION
HB Printing   V006916_042718

CONTENTS

v

PART FIVE: ESSENTIAL COMPETENCIES 375

ABOUT THE AUTHORS

Elisa S. Abes is an associate professor in the student affairs in higher education program at Miami University in Oxford, Ohio. She earned her BA and PhD at The Ohio State University and her JD at Harvard Law School. Prior to teaching at Miami University she was an assistant professor at the University of South Florida and a practicing attorney. Abes's research focuses on critical approaches to student development, multiple social identities, and disability identity. She is a coauthor of the book *Identity Development of College Students* (with Susan R. Jones) and guest editor of a New Directions for Student Services volume *Critical Perspectives on Student Development Theory*. Abes is the recipient of ACPA's Emerging Scholar Award and the Annuit Coeptis award for an emerging professional. She is also on the editorial board for the *Journal of College Student Development*.

Jan Arminio is professor and director of the higher education program at George Mason University. She received her doctorate in college student personnel at the University of Maryland–College Park. From 2004 to 2008 she served as president of the Council for the Advancement of Standards in Higher Education (CAS). She also was appointed to and later chaired the Faculty Fellows of the National Association of Student Personnel Administrators and the Senior Scholars of the American College Personnel Association. Her most recent scholarship includes the coauthored books *Student Veterans in Higher Education* (2015) and the second edition of *Negotiating the Complexities of Qualitative Research* (2014). Also, she is the first editor of *Why Aren't We There Yet: Taking Personal Responsibility for Creating an Inclusive Campus* (2012). She is the 2011 recipient of the Robert H. Shaffer Award for excellence in graduate teaching.

Ellen M. Broido is an associate professor of higher education and student affairs at Bowling Green State University. She received an AB from Columbia College of Columbia University, an MSEd from Indiana University, and an EdD from Pennsylvania State University. Before Bowling Green State University, she had a joint appointment in student affairs and as a faculty member at Portland State, and she worked in residence life at the University of Massachusetts at Amherst. Her research focuses on social justice issues on college campuses and the experiences of underrepresented or marginalized groups in higher education. Her publications include the books *Disability in Higher Education: A Social Justice Approach* (in press, coauthored with Nancy Evans, Kirsten Brown, and Autumn Watts) and *Developing Social Justice Allies* (2005, with Robert Reason, Nancy Evans, and Tracy Davis). She has served on the governing board of ACPA and as the editor of ACPA's Books and Media board.

Brian A. Burt is assistant professor of higher education in the School of Education at Iowa State University. He held an academic and student affairs hybrid position at the University of Maryland–College Park. He earned his BS in secondary English education from Indiana University–Bloomington, his MA in educational policy and leadership studies (with a concentration in higher education administration) from the University of Maryland–College Park, and PhD in higher education from the University of Michigan. Burt's research draws on learning theories and critical theories to study institutional practices related to the educational and work force pathways of graduate students of color, particularly black males in engineering. A recipient of a National Academy of Education/Spencer Postdoctoral Fellowship, he regularly presents his work at national and international convenings, such as the American Educational Research Association (AERA), Association for the Study of Higher Education (ASHE), National Association of Student Personnel Administrators (NASPA), American Society of Engineering Education (ASEE), and International Colloquium on Black Males in Education (ICBME).

Jill Ellen Carnaghi is currently an assistant vice president for student development at Saint Louis University (SLU). Prior to working at SLU, she was associate vice chancellor for students and dean of campus life at Washington University in St. Louis. Carnaghi earned her BA from Purdue University, her MA in college student personnel administration from Michigan State University, and her PhD in higher education administration from Indiana University. She has held administrative positions at the University of Vermont and University of California–Davis as well. Among her involvements in professional associations, Jill served as president, treasurer, and vice president for commissions within ACPA, and she cochaired the ACPA-NASPA joint meetings in 1997 and 2007. Peter Magolda and Jill Carnaghi are coeditors of *Job One: Experiences of New Professionals in Student Affairs* (2004) and *Job One 2.0: Understanding the Next Generation of Student Affairs Professionals* (2014).

Nancy E. Chrystal-Green is the director of student activities and involvement at the University of Florida and an adjunct faculty member in the Department of Educational Administration and Policy. She earned her BA from McMaster

University, a master's degree from Georgia Southern University, and a doctorate from the University of Georgia. Chrystal-Green has spent her career working as an administrator in the fields of residence life, campus recreation, and student activities. She has held positions at Coastal Carolina University, Oxford College of Emory University, and the University of Georgia. She has been recognized for her service to national student affairs organizations in a variety of capacities including chairing the faculty for the School of Recreational Sports Management. She has served as an external reviewer and she coauthored a book on advising student organizations. Her research interests include staff supervision, leadership development, and experiential learning.

John P. Dugan is associate professor of higher education and director of the undergraduate minor in leadership studies at Loyola University Chicago. He earned his BA from John Carroll University and his master's degree and PhD from the University of Maryland. Dugan's research employs critical perspectives to examine theoretical and developmental considerations associated with leadership. He is the author of *Leadership Theory: Cultivating Critical Perspectives*. He also is coeditor of *Leadership Theory: A Facilitator's Guide for Cultivating Critical Perspectives* (with Natasha Turman, Amy Barnes, and Mark Torrez) and *The Handbook for Student Leadership Development* (with Susan Komives, Julie Owen, Wendy Wagner, and Craig Slack). To date he has authored and coauthored more than thirty-five books, book chapters, and peer-reviewed journal articles. John is a past recipient of the ACPA: College Educators International Burns B. Crookston Doctoral Research Award, Nevitt Sanford Award for Research in Student Affairs, and was named an Emerging Professional Annuit Coeptis.

Norbert W. Dunkel is associate vice president for student affairs at the University of Florida. Prior to his assignment at Florida, he held administrative positions at South Dakota State University and the University of Northern Iowa. Dunkel served as the president of the Association of College and University Housing Officers–International (ACUHO-I). He is the cofounder of the James C. Grimm National Housing Training Institute and is the founding codirector of the Student Housing Training Institute in South Africa. Dunkel has authored or edited nineteen books and more than forty articles and chapters. He recently completed a six-volume book set titled *Campus Housing Management* serving as coeditor and author. He has served as a consultant to more than twenty universities and has given numerous presentations and keynote speeches. He has twice testified before US Congressional committees in Washington. He is the recipient of the ACUHO-I Parthenon Award, ACUHO-I Research and Publication Award, and the James E. Scott Memorial Award for Outstanding Leadership and Service to the University of Florida.

Tara E. Frank is an assistant dean of students with student advocacy at Virginia Tech. Prior to Virginia Tech, she worked as an administrator in various functional areas including graduate student life, assessment and evaluation, student conduct, and student activities. She earned her BA and master's degrees from Shippensburg University of Pennsylvania and her PhD from Virginia Tech. Frank's research focuses on why student affairs administrators leave the field and how mattering influences their professional experience.

Ann M. Gansemer-Topf is an assistant professor of higher education and student affairs in the School of Education at Iowa State University. Prior to becoming a faculty member, Gansemer-Topf worked in several student affairs units such as admissions, academic advising, and residence life. She also worked in institutional research and assessment at Grinnell College in Grinnell, Iowa. She earned her BS from Loras College in Dubuque, Iowa, and her master's and doctoral degrees from Iowa State University. Her research interests focus on examining micro and macro factors affecting student success, and she has expertise in developing effective and sustainable institutional assessment practices. She has presented at several regional and national conferences, and her research has been published in journals such as *Research in Higher Education, Journal of the First-Year Experience and Students in Transition,* and *Journal of Student Affairs Research and Practice.*

Marybeth Gasman is a professor of higher education in the Graduate School of Education at the University of Pennsylvania. She holds secondary appointments in history and Africana studies. She also directs the Penn Center for Minority Serving Institutions (http://www.gse.upenn.edu/cmsi). Gasman's areas of expertise include the history of American higher education, historically black colleges and universities, minority-serving institutions, African American leadership, and fund-raising and philanthropy. She has written or edited twenty-one books, including *Envisioning Black Colleges: A History of the United Negro College Fund* and *Understanding Minority Serving Institutions* (with Benjamin Baez and Caroline Turner) and (with Clifton Conrad) titled *Educating a Diverse Nation: Lessons from Minority Serving Institutions* (2015). Eight of Gasman's books have won research awards. Gasman's articles have been published in the *American Education Research Journal, Educational Researcher, Teachers College Record,* the *Journal of Higher Education,* the *Journal of Negro Education, Research in Higher Education,* and *Journal of College Student Development,* among others. She is a regular contributor to *The Chronicle of Higher Education, Diverse Issues, Huffington Post, New York Times,* and *Washington Post.*

Kimberly A. Griffin is an associate professor of student affairs at the University of Maryland. She previously worked at Pennsylvania State University. She received her bachelor's degree in psychology from Stanford University, master's in higher education from the University of Maryland, and PhD from UCLA. Her research focuses on how the experiences and environments students and faculty members encounter on college campuses shape their outcomes, specifically their relationships, achievement, and career development. Her work has appeared in the *American Educational Research Journal,* the *Review of Higher Education, Journal of College Student Development,* and *Teachers College Record.* She sits on multiple editorial boards and is an associate editor of the *Journal of Diversity in Higher Education.* She has been recognized as an Emerging Scholar by ACPA, with the Promising Scholar/Early Career Award by ASHE, and as a Distinguished Alumni Scholar of Stanford University.

Florence A. Hamrick is professor and graduate program director of the PhD in higher education program at Rutgers University. Prior to Rutgers, she was a professor in the educational leadership and policy studies department at Iowa

State University. She earned her BA from the University of North Carolina at Chapel Hill, her master's degree from The Ohio State University, and her PhD from Indiana University–Bloomington. Hamrick's research emphasizes higher education equity, access, and success—particularly among members of traditionally underrepresented or nondominant populations. She is the author or editor of three books; more than seventy articles, chapters, and invited publications; and more than one hundred scholarly or professional presentations, invited lectures, and conference addresses. She is former editor of the *Journal of College Student Development*, the premier refereed journal of research on college students. Hamrick is active in scholarly and professional organizations, and she is currently a Senior Scholar of ACPA–College Student Educators International.

Ebelia Hernández is an associate professor in the Department of Educational Psychology at Rutgers, The State University of New Jersey. She earned her BA in English from California State University, Chico, MS in counseling from California State University, Northridge, and PhD in higher education and student affairs from Indiana University–Bloomington. Hernández's research agenda focuses on examining the interconnections between holistic development and engagement for Latina college women. Her publications include book chapters and articles on student development theory, college student activism, and the use of critical race theory in research design. She was selected as a Faculty Fellow by the American Association of Hispanics in Higher Education, was recognized as an ACPA Emerging Scholar and Annuit Coeptis Emerging Professional, and was a finalist for the NASPA Melvene D. Hardee Dissertation of the Year.

Amy S. Hirschy is an assistant professor in the College of Education and Human Development at the University of Louisville. She holds a BBA from Stetson University, an MEd from the University of South Carolina, and PhD from Vanderbilt University. Experiences at private liberal arts colleges and medium and large state institutions inform her research and teaching. Hirschy's research interests include college student persistence and retention theories, socialization to the student affairs profession, and normative structures in student affairs. Hirschy is a coauthor of the monograph *Toward Understanding and Reducing College Student Departure* (with John Braxton and Shederick McClendon) and the book *Rethinking College Student Retention* (with John Braxton, Will Doyle, Hal Hartley, Willis Jones, and Michael McLendon). She served as an academic fellow for the Institute for Higher Education Policy and received the Fred Rhodes Outstanding Service Award (Kentucky) and the University of Louisville's Distinguished University Teaching Professor Award.

Joan B. Hirt is a professor of higher education at Virginia Tech. She has also served as the interim director of the School of Education and interim dean of the College of Liberal Arts and Human Sciences at the university. She earned her BA in Russian studies from Bucknell University, her MAEd in college student personnel services from the University of Maryland–College Park, and her PhD in higher education policy and administration from the University of Arizona. Hirt's research focuses on specialization and professionalization of administration in the academy. In particular, she explores variations in administrative life at different types of colleges and universities. She authored *Where You Work Matters*, coedited *Becoming Socialized in Student Affairs*, and coauthored *Supervised Practice in Student Affairs*. Her work has been recognized through awards from the National Association of Student Personnel Administrators, the University of Maryland, ACPA–International, the American College and University Housing Officers–International, and the Association of Fraternity Advisors, among others.

Wayne Jacobson is assessment director in the Office of the Provost at the University of Iowa (UI) and also holds an adjunct faculty appointment in educational policy and leadership studies. He is responsible for coordinating learning outcomes assessment in academic programs, engaging departments in evidence-based examination of student experience and success in their programs, and coordinating campus surveys that provide opportunities to bring student voices into institutional assessment and decision making. Recent publications of his include "Sharing Power and Privilege through the Scholarly Practice of Assessment" (in Sherry Watt [Ed.], *Designing Transformative Multicultural Initiatives: Theoretical Foundations, Practical Applications and Facilitator Considerations*, 2015) and "Belonging and Satisfaction of Service-Minded Students at Research Universities" (with Teniell Trolian and Sarah SanGiovani, in Krista Soria & Tania Mitchell [Eds.], *Revisiting the Civic Mission of the American Public Research University*, 2016). He holds degrees in counseling (MS) and adult education (PhD) from the University of Wisconsin–Madison.

Susan R. Jones is professor of higher education and student affairs at The Ohio State University. Prior to Ohio State, she was an associate professor in the college student personnel program at the University of Maryland–College Park. She earned her BA from St. Lawrence University, her master's degree from the University of Vermont, and her PhD from the University of Maryland. Jones's research focuses on multiple social identities and intersectionality, psychosocial development, service-learning, and qualitative methodologies. She is also a coauthor of the books *Negotiating the Complexities of Qualitative Research in Higher Education* (2nd ed., with Vasti Torres and Jan Arminio) and *Identity Development of College Students* (with Elisa Abes). She is the coeditor of New Directions for Student Services and recipient of a number of awards including ACPA's Contribution to Knowledge Award, ACPA Senior Scholar, NASPA's Robert H. Shaffer Award for Academic Excellence as a Graduate Faculty Member, and Ohio State's Distinguished Teaching Award.

Reynol Junco is an associate professor of education and human computer interaction at Iowa State University, a faculty associate at the Berkman Center for Internet and Society, and a researcher who studies how technology use affects college students. Junco is particularly interested in using quantitative methods to assess the effects of social media on student development, engagement, learning, and success. His work has been cited in major news outlets such as the *New York Times, NPR, PBS, NBC, Time, US News & World Report, USA Today*, the *Guardian, The Atlantic, Huffington Post*, and *Mashable*. He holds a bachelor's degree in psychology from The University of Florida, where he studied and conducted research in neuroscience. He earned his master's degree in clinical psychology from Penn State, where he studied and conducted research in neuropsychology. He also earned his doctorate in counselor education from Pennsylvania State University.

Lance C. Kennedy-Phillips is vice provost for planning and assessment at Pennsylvania State University. Prior to joining Penn State, Lance was associate vice provost for institutional research at the University of Illinois at Chicago. In addition, he served as executive director of the Center for the Study of Student Life at The Ohio State University. He earned his BA from Eastern Illinois University and his MEd and PhD degrees from the University of Nebraska–Lincoln. Kennedy-Phillips has served in leadership roles for NASPA, ACPA, and AIR. He coedited the book *Quantitative and Qualitative Research: A Mixed Methods Approach in Higher Education* and a volume in the New Directions for Institutional Research sourcebook series titled, *Measuring Co-Curricular Learning: The Role of the IR Office.*

Adrianna Kezar is a professor of higher education at the University of Southern California and codirector of the Pullias Center for Higher Education. Kezar holds an MA and PhD in higher education administration from the University of Michigan. Kezar is a national expert of change, governance, and leadership in higher education, and her research agenda explores the change process in higher education institutions and the role of leadership in creating change. Kezar is well published with eighteen books or monographs, more than one hundred journal articles, and more than one hundred book chapters and reports. Recent books include *How Colleges Change, Enhancing Campus Capacity for Leadership,* and *Organizing for Collaboration.* She is an AERA Fellow, a TIAA-CREF Research Fellow, a Haynes Fellow, and has received numerous national awards, including from ASHE for her editorial leadership of the ASHE-ERIC and from ACE for developing a leadership development program for women in higher education.

Cindy Ann Kilgo is an assistant professor of higher education at the University of Alabama. Previously she was the lead research assistant for the Center for Research on Undergraduate Education at the University of Iowa. Kilgo earned a BS in psychology from Georgia Southern University, a master's degree in higher education and student affairs from the University of South Carolina, and a PhD from the University of Iowa in educational policy and leadership studies with an emphasis in higher education and student affairs. Kilgo's research centers on high-impact educational practices, practically in terms of the ways these practices are facilitated on college campuses and methodologically in terms of the ways higher education researchers study these practices. Kilgo has published in several journals, including the *Journal of College Student Development, Higher Education, New Directions for Institutional Research,* New Directions for Student Services series, *Journal of College Orientation and Transition,* and the *International Journal of Research on Service-Learning and Community Engagement.*

Patricia M. King is professor of higher education in the Center for the Study of Higher and Postsecondary Education at the University of Michigan.

She has held administrative and faculty appointments at the University of Iowa, The Ohio State University, and Bowling Green State University. She earned her BA from Macalester College and her PhD from the University of Minnesota in educational psychology. King's teaching and research focuses on the learning and development of college students and young adults. She is a co-principal investigator on the Wabash National Study of Liberal Arts Education and has coauthored three books, *Developing Reflective Judgment* (with Karen Strohm Kitchener), *Learning Partnerships: Theory and Models of Practice to Educate for Self-Authorship,* and *Assessing Meaning Making and Self-Authorship* (the latter two with Marcia Baxter Magolda). She served as a founding editor of *About Campus: Enriching the Student Learning Experience,* the national magazine sponsored by the American College Personnel Association. She is the recipient of a number of awards, including ACPA's Contribution to Knowledge Award, ACPA Senior Scholar, and NASPA's Robert H. Shaffer Award for Academic Excellence as a Graduate Faculty Member.

Jillian Kinzie is associate director at the Center for Postsecondary Research and the National Survey of Student Engagement (NSSE) Institute at Indiana University School of Education. She conducts research and leads project activities on effective use of student engagement data to improve educational quality, and she serves as senior scholar with the National Institute for Learning Outcomes Assessment (NILOA) project. She is coauthor of *Using Evidence of Student Learning to Improve Higher Education* (2015), *Student Success in College* (2005/2010), and *One Size Does Not Fit All: Traditional and Innovative Models of Student Affairs Practice* (2008/2014). She is coeditor of the series New Directions in Higher Education, a member of the editorial board of the *Journal of College Student Development,* and on the boards of the Washington Internship Institute, and the Gardner Institute for Excellence in Undergraduate Education. She was honored with a Student Choice Award for Outstanding Faculty at IU (2001), received the Robert J. Menges Honored Presentation by the Professional Organizational Development (POD) Network in 2005 and 2011, and in 2014 was named Senior Scholar by the American College Personnel Association (ACPA).

Marcia Baxter Magolda is Distinguished Professor Emerita, Miami University of Ohio (USA). She received a BA in psychology from Capital University and MA and PhD degrees in higher education from The Ohio State University. Her scholarship addresses the evolution of learning and self-authorship in college and young adult life. Her books include *Assessing Meaning Making and Self-Authorship: Theory, Research, and Application* (coauthored with Patricia King); *Authoring Your Life: Developing an Internal Voice to Meet Life's Challenges, Development and Assessment of Self-Authorship: Exploring the Concept across Cultures* (coedited with Elizabeth Creamer and Peggy Meszaros); *Learning Partnerships: Theory and Models of Practice to Educate for Self-Authorship* (coedited with Patricia King); *Making Their Own Way: Narratives for Transforming Higher Education to Promote Self-Development; Creating Contexts for Learning and Self-Authorship: Constructive-Developmental Pedagogy;* and *Knowing and Reasoning in College.* She received the ASHE Research Achievement Award, ACPA Lifetime Achievement and Contribution to Knowledge awards,

NASPA Robert H. Shaffer Award, and Miami University's Benjamin Harrison Medallion.

Peter Magolda, Professor Emeritus in the Department of Educational Leadership at Miami University, has focused his scholarship on ethnographic studies of college students and critical issues in qualitative research. He is coauthor of *It's All about Jesus: Faith as an Oppositional Collegiate Subculture.* His most recent scholarship (and soon-to-be published book) focuses on the lives and work experiences of campus custodians. Magolda has served on the editorial boards of *Research in Higher Education,* the *Journal of College Student Development,* and the *Journal of Educational Research.* He was an ACPA Senior Scholar and recipient of numerous awards including ACPA's Contribution to Knowledge Award and the Association for the Study of Higher Education's (ASHE) Mentoring Award. He also received Miami University's Richard Delp Outstanding Faculty Member Award, as well as an alumni award from The Ohio State University and Indiana University.

Kathleen Manning served as a professor in the University of Vermont's higher education and student affairs program from 1989 until her retirement in 2014. She has a BA in biology from Marist College, an MS in counseling and student personnel services from the University at Albany, and a PhD in higher education from Indiana University. Manning's professional interests include social justice, international higher education, leadership, and organizational theory. She published eight books including two editions of *Research in the College Context: Approaches and Methods* (with Frances K. Stage) and the well-received *Organizational Theory in Higher Education.* Manning was awarded the NASPA Outstanding Contribution to Literature/Research Award, the University of Vermont's Kroepsch-Maurice Award for Teaching Excellence, was named a NASPA Pillar of the Profession, and has received on-campus awards for LGBTQA, gender, and race-related advocacy. She has taught and consulted in several international contexts including three voyages on Semester at Sea, and she has received three Fulbright Awards.

Brian L. McGowan is an assistant professor of higher education at the University of North Carolina at Greensboro (UNCG). Prior to UNCG, he was an assistant professor in the student affairs and higher education program at Indiana State University. He earned his bachelor's degree from Old Dominion University, his master's degree from The Ohio State University, and his PhD from Indiana University. McGowan's work explores the identity development of college students, particularly the intersections of race and gender among black male undergraduate students and issues affecting professional preparation, teaching, and socialization experiences of graduate students and faculty members of color. His newest book project is titled *Black Men in the Academy: Narratives of Resiliency, Achievement, and Success* (with Robert T. Palmer, J. Luke Wood, and David F. Hibbler Jr.). His scholarship and professional practice have been recognized through awards including the ACPA Annuit Coeptis Emerging Professional Award, and the NASPA Melvene D. Hardee Dissertation of the Year.

Thomas Miller is the vice president for student affairs at the Tampa Campus of the University of South Florida. He is also an associate professor in the College of Education. He previously held student affairs positions at Eckerd College, Canisius College, Indiana University, and Shippensburg University. Miller holds a bachelor's degree from Muhlenberg College and master's and doctoral degrees from Indiana University. He received the Elizabeth Greenleaf Distinguished Alumnus Award from Indiana University's Higher Education and Student Affairs Program in 1989. He received the Scott Goodnight Award for Outstanding Performance as a dean from NASPA in 2001, was chosen as a Pillar of the Profession in 2004, and received the Robert H. Shaffer Award for Academic Excellence as a Graduate Faculty Member in 2015. His scholarly work has focused on student expectations, student attrition, and legal and risk management issues.

John A. Mueller is a professor in the Department of Student Affairs in Higher Education at Indiana University of Pennsylvania. He earned his BS and MS at Illinois State University and his EdD at Teachers College, Columbia University. He has worked in higher education for thirty years with practitioner and teaching experience at multiple institutions. He is an active member and leader in the American College Personnel Association and has received several association awards including Annuit Coeptis, Emerging Scholar, and Diamond Honoree. His publications, presentations, and service activities have focused primarily on issues of diversity, multiculturalism, and inclusion. He has served on the editorial boards of the *Journal of College Student Development*, the *College Student Affairs Journal*, and ACPA Books and Media. He is a coauthor of Jossey-Bass publications including *Multicultural Competence in Student Affairs* and *Creating Multicultural Change on Campus*.

Samuel D. Museus is associate professor of higher education and student affairs and serves as director of the Culturally Engaging Campus Environments (CECE) Project at Indiana University–Bloomington. He received his bachelor's and master's degrees from the University of Minnesota, Twin Cities, and his PhD from Pennsylvania State University. He has produced more than 180 publications and conference presentations on diversity and equity, campus environments, and college students' experiences and outcomes. He has published several books, including *Creating Campus Cultures: Fostering Success among Racially Diverse Student Populations*, and he is creator of the culturally engaging campus environments (CECE) model of college success among racially diverse populations. He has also received several national awards for his scholarship, including the Association for the Study of Higher Education's (ASHE) Early Career Award and the National Association of Student Personnel Administrators' (NASPA) Outstanding Contribution to Research and Literature Award.

Anna M. Ortiz is department chair and professor of educational leadership, California State University, Long Beach. Ortiz has been a student development educator in the classroom as a professor or as a practitioner in the field for more than twenty-five years. Her research interests center on college student development, primarily in the areas of ethnic identity development, multicultural education, and professional issues in student affairs. She has authored a range of publications including books, articles, and book chapters. Ortiz received her bachelor's from UC Davis, her master's from The Ohio State University, and her doctorate from UCLA and has served on the faculty at Michigan State University. She is an active member of the National Association of Student Personnel Administrators, the American College Personnel Association, the Association for the Study of Higher Education, and the American Educational Research Association, having held leadership positions in each of them. She most recently served as the founding director of the NASPA Faculty Division.

Laura Osteen is the director of Florida State University's Center for Leadership and Social Change. The center is a campus-wide endeavor to transform lives through leadership education, identity development, and community engagement. Before coming to FSU, Osteen worked with leadership, community, diversity, and experiential learning programs in student and academic affairs positions on the campuses of Kansas State University, University of Maryland, University of Missouri, and Stephens College. Osteen envisions a world where every student is enabled and empowered to create positive sustainable change. She received her undergraduate degree from Indiana University, her master's degree from Colorado State University, and her doctorate of philosophy degree from the University of Maryland.

Lori D. Patton is an associate professor of higher education and student affairs at Indiana University. She has been recognized nationally for research examining issues of identity, equity, and racial injustice affecting diverse populations in college. Her scholarship has been published in the *Journal of College Student Development,* the *Journal of Higher Education,* and several other highly regarded venues. She is a coauthor of the second edition of *Student Development in College* and a contributor to other Jossey-Bass publications including *Student Services: A Handbook for the Profession* (5th ed.) and *The Handbook of Student Affairs Administration* (3rd ed.). She is the editor of *Campus Culture Centers in Higher Education: Perspectives on Identity, Theory and Practice* (Stylus) and coeditor of the New Directions for Student Services monograph, *Responding to the Realities of Race.* She is actively involved in and has been recognized for her scholarly and service contributions to ACPA, NASPA, ASHE, and AERA. She earned her BS in speech communication (Southern Illinois University at Edwardsville), her MA in college student personnel (Bowling Green State University), and her PhD in higher education at Indiana University

Patricia "Patty" A. Perillo serves as the vice president for student affairs and assistant professor of higher education at Virginia Tech. Prior to her work at Virginia Tech, Perillo has served in a variety of leadership roles in academic and student affairs at a broad range of institutions including Davidson College, the University of Maryland–Baltimore County, the University of Maryland–College Park, the State University of New York at Plattsburgh and Albany campuses, and the University of Delaware. Patty served as the sixty-ninth president of ACPA–College Student Educators International, an international student affairs association. She earned her BA and MEd degrees from the University of Delaware and her PhD from the University of Maryland. She has received many awards, most notably the ACPA Esther Lloyd-Jones Professional Service and ACPA Diamond Honoree Awards.

Raechele L. Pope is an associate professor of higher education at the University at Buffalo. She earned her bachelor's at Indiana University of Pennsylvania, her MA in student affairs administration at Indiana University of Pennsylvania, and her doctorate from the University of Massachusetts at Amherst. Her scholarship has focused primarily on multicultural issues on campus, and she has published numerous journal articles and is the coauthor (along with Amy L. Reynolds and John A. Mueller) of *Creating Multicultural Change on Campus* and *Multicultural Competence in Student Affairs*. She has worked at several institutions in a variety of functional areas including residential life, academic advising, and diversity education and training. In the past several years she was selected as a Senior Scholar for ACPA and received the ACPA Annuit Coeptis Award and the NASPA Robert H. Shafer Award for Academic Excellence as a Graduate Faculty Member.

Stephen John Quaye is associate professor in the student affairs in higher education program at Miami University. He is a 2009 ACPA Emerging Scholar and was awarded the 2009 Melvene D. Hardee Dissertation of the Year Award from NASPA. Quaye's research and teaching focus on understanding how students can engage with difficult issues (for example, privilege, oppression, power) civilly and honestly as well as how storytelling is used as an educational tool to foster reflection and learning across differences. He also is interested in the strategies educators use to facilitate these dialogues and what they learn about themselves in the process. His work is published in different venues, including the *Review of Higher Education, Teachers College Record,* the *Journal of College Student Development,* and *Equity & Excellence in Education.* He is coeditor of the second edition of *Student Engagement in Higher Education: Theoretical Perspectives and Practical Approaches for Diverse Populations.* He holds degrees from the James Madison University (BS), Miami University (MS), and Pennsylvania State University (PhD).

Robert D. Reason is professor of higher education and student affairs at Iowa State University. Prior to Iowa State, he was associate professor and senior scientist at the Center for the Study of Higher Education at Pennsylvania State University. He earned a BA from Grinnell College, a master's degree from Minnesota State University Mankato, and a PhD from Iowa State University. Reason is currently an associate editor of the *Journal of College Student Development* and an ACPA Senior Scholar. His publications include *Developing Social Justice Allies* (2005, with Ellen Broido, Nancy Evans, and Tracy Davis) and *College Students in the United States: Characteristics, Experiences, and Outcomes* (2012, with Kristen Renn).

Kristen A. Renn is a professor of higher, adult, and lifelong education at Michigan State University, where she has also served as associate dean of undergraduate studies and director for student success initiatives. She earned her AB from Mount Holyoke College, her master's degree from Boston University, and her PhD from Boston College. Prior to her assignment at Michigan State University she was a dean in the Office of Student Life at Brown

University. Renn focuses her research and teaching on topics related to student learning, development, and success. In particular, she studies the experiences of students with minoritized racial, gender, or sexual orientation identities. She recently completed a study of women's colleges and universities worldwide and is co-principle investigator of the National Study of LGBTQ Student Success. Her books include *Mixed Race College Students: The Ecology of Race, Identity, and Community* and, as coauthor, *Student Development in College: Theory, Research and Practice* (second and third editions) and *College Students in the United States: Characteristics, Experiences, and Outcomes.*

Amy L. Reynolds is an associate professor in the Department of Counseling, School, and Educational Psychology at the University at Buffalo. She is also the director of training for the combined doctoral program in counseling psychology and school psychology. Reynolds received her bachelor's from Miami University and her master's degree in student personnel work and her doctorate in counseling psychology from The Ohio State University. Her work focuses on multicultural competence in counseling and student affairs as well as college mental health issues. She has published more than twenty-five journal articles and book chapters and has made more than forty presentations at regional or national conferences. She is one of the coauthors of *Multicultural Competence in Student Affairs* and *Creating Multicultural Change on Campus* and is the sole author of *Helping College Students: Developing Essential Skills for Student Affairs Practice.* She is recognized as a fellow in the American Psychological Association Division 17, Outstanding Contribution to the Profession of Higher Education and Significant Research/Publication in Higher Education (CSPA of NY), and Outstanding Contribution to Multicultural Education Award.

Jeffrey Rokkum is a PhD student in the School of Education at Iowa State University studying human computer interaction and social psychology. Prior to Iowa State University, he attended California State University, Dominguez Hills, where he received his BA in psychology and his MA in clinical psychology. His research interests cover a broad swath of topics: social media, technology use, big data, multitasking, and student outcomes. Among his publications are a scale that can be used to assess overall technology use as well as studies on sleep quality and media predicting ill health among children.

Larry D. Roper is a professor in the School of Language, Culture and Society at Oregon State University, where he serves as coordinator of the undergraduate social justice minor and coordinator of the college student services administration. Previously he served as vice provost for student affairs at Oregon State University from 1995 to 2014, during which he also served eighteen months as interim dean of the College of Liberal Arts. He has degrees from Heidelberg University, Bowling Green State University, and the University of Maryland. He currently serves as a commissioner with the State of Oregon's Higher Education Coordinating Commission, Board of Trustees of Heidelberg University, and on the Education Committee of the Oregon Community Foundation. He served a term as editor of the *NASPA Journal,* and for six years he was a commissioner with the Northwest Commission on Colleges and Universities. He writes a regular "Ethical Issues on Campus" column for the *Journal of College and Character.*

He coedited the book *Teaching for Change: The Difference, Power and Discrimination Model* (2007) and edited *Supporting and Supervising Mid-Level Professionals: Charting a Path to Success* (2011). He has also served on more than seventy-five thesis or dissertation committees, aiding as chair of more than thirty.

Sue A. Saunders is emeritus extension professor and was director of the higher education and student affairs program at the University of Connecticut. Prior to her work at UConn, she was an assistant professor in the college student affairs administration program at the University of Georgia. She has held senior administrative posts at Lycoming College (PA) and Longwood University (VA). Her bachelor's degree in journalism and a master's degree in counseling are from Ohio University. Her PhD in counseling and student personnel services is from the University of Georgia. Saunders's research focuses on socialization in student affairs administration and staff supervision. She has served the American College Personnel Association (ACPA) as a member of the governing board, on the editorial board of the *Journal of College Student Development*, and was chair of the 2008 ACPA National Convention. Her professional contributions have been recognized through the ACPA Diamond Honoree program and ACPA Senior Scholars.

John H. Schuh is director of the Emerging Leaders Academy and Distinguished Professor Emeritus at Iowa State University. He has held administrative and faculty assignments at Wichita State University, Indiana University–Bloomington, and Arizona State University. He earned his BA from the University of Wisconsin–Oshkosh and his master of counseling and PhD degrees from Arizona State. Schuh is the author, coauthor, or editor of more than 275 publications, including thirty-two books and monographs. Among his books are *Assessment in Student Affairs* (2nd ed., with Patrick Biddix, Laura A. Dean, and Jillian Kinzie), *One Size Does Not Fit All: Traditional and Innovative Models of Student Affairs Practice* (with Kathleen Manning and Jillian Kinzie), and *Student Success in College* (with George D. Kuh, Jillian Kinzie, and Elizabeth Whitt). He has received two Fulbright Awards as well as the Research Achievement Award from ASHE, ACPA's Contribution to Knowledge Award, the Contribution to Research or Literature Award, and the Robert H. Shaffer Award for Academic Excellence as a Graduate Faculty Member from NASPA.

Robert Schwartz is a professor of higher education and is currently school chair of the Department of Educational Leadership and Policy Studies at Florida State University. Prior to his assignment at Florida State, he was an assistant professor of higher education at the University of South Carolina, associate professor at Valdosta State University in Georgia, and served in a variety of administrative positions in student affairs at the University of North Dakota. He earned his BA in English at Hanover College (IN), his MA in student personnel work in higher education from Ball State University, and his PhD in higher education from Indiana University. He has written and presented research on women and minorities in higher education and the history of deans of men and women. His most recent book is *Deans of Men and the Shaping of Modern College Culture* (Palgrave, 2010).

Mahauganee D. Shaw is an assistant professor in the Miami University student affairs in higher education program. She received her BA and MA from the University of Missouri–Kansas City and her PhD in higher education and student affairs from Indiana University. Her research agenda focuses on organizational efficiency and leadership in higher education. This is accomplished through an exploration of crisis response and emergency preparedness as well as faculty and student affairs practices. She was a founding member of the ACPA Commission for Campus Safety and Emergency Preparedness in 2011 and has served as the commission's Vice Chair for Research, Scholarship, and Practice since 2012. This term will end in 2017.

Dafina-Lazarus Stewart is a professor of higher education and student affairs at Bowling Green State University where ze has taught since 2005. Previously, ze taught at The Ohio State University and Ohio University. Stewart completed hir undergraduate degree in sociology from Kalamazoo College and earned hir master's and doctoral degrees in higher education and student affairs from The Ohio State University. Stewart's research interests focus on issues of race, ethnicity, sexuality, gender, religion, spirituality, and faith as they are related to student identity, experiences, and outcomes, and institutional transformation through an intersectional framework. In 2011, Stewart published an edited volume on the practice of multicultural affairs, *Multicultural Student Services on Campus: Building Bridges, Re-visioning Community*, and is currently working to complete a historical narrative of racial desegregation and integration and the experiences of black collegians at private, elite, liberal arts colleges in the Great Lakes region between 1945 and 1965.

Kari B. Taylor is a PhD student in the higher education and student affairs program at The Ohio State University. Previously, she served as a senior associate director for Miami University's Honors Program. She also was a qualitative research team member for the Wabash National Study of Liberal Arts Education and an associate editor for *About Campus: Enriching the Student Learning Experience*. She received a bachelor's degree from the University of Missouri–Columbia and a master's degree in student affairs and higher education from Miami University. Her research interests include the assessment of student learning and development and sociocultural factors that influence learning.

John R. Thelin is a professor at the University of Kentucky with particular interest in the history of higher education and public policy. An alumnus of Brown University, he concentrated in history and was elected to Phi Beta Kappa. He received his MA and PhD from the University of California, Berkeley. Prior to joining the faculty at the University of Kentucky he was Chancellor Professor at the College of William & Mary and professor at Indiana University. He is author of *A History of American Higher Education* (Johns Hopkins University Press). Thelin has served as president of the Association for the Study of Higher Education (ASHE) and received the ASHE Outstanding Research Award. At the University of Kentucky he received the 2014 Provost Award for Outstanding Faculty Contribution to Graduate Studies.

Vasti Torres is a professor of higher education and student affairs and former dean of the College of Education at the University of South Florida (USF). Prior to her assignment at USF, Torres was professor at Indiana University–Bloomington and director of the Center for Postsecondary Research. She received her BA degree from Stetson University and her MEd and PhD degrees from the University of Georgia. Her research focuses on student success issues among underrepresented students and how the ethnic identity of Latino students influences their college experiences. She was the principal investigator for multiyear grants investigating the choice to stay in college for Latino students as well as a grant looking at the experiences of working college students. From 2011 to 2013 she served as a Fulbright Specialist in South Africa. From 2007 to 2008 she served as the first Latina president of a national student affairs association—ACPA. Among her awards are ACPA Senior Scholar, NASPA's Contribution to Literature and Research Award, Hispanic Scholarship Fund Alumni Hall of Fame, and Indiana University Trustees Teaching Award.

Sherry Watt is a professor of higher education and student affairs at the University of Iowa. She received a BA degree from University of North Carolina at Greensboro and MS and PhD degrees in counselor education, with an emphasis in student affairs, from North Carolina State University. Prior to becoming a faculty member, she worked as a residence life director and a career counselor. She is the editor of *Designing Transformative Multicultural Initiatives: Theoretical Foundations, Practical Applications and Facilitator Considerations,* which highlights her research on effective ways to design and implement multicultural initiatives. Her research on privileged identity exploration expands the understanding of the various reactions people have to difficult dialogues on race and other social issues. She is also the coeditor of the New Directions for Student Services series and recipient of a number of awards including ACPA Senior Scholar and Diamond Honoree, and University of Iowa's Collegiate Teaching Award in 2006 and 2013.

Elizabeth J. Whitt is vice provost and dean for undergraduate education and professor of sociology at the University of California, Merced. Whitt is past editor of the New Directions for Student Services sourcebook series. Her research and scholarship focus on institutional conditions for student success, academic and student affairs partnerships, and issues and trends in student affairs practice. In 2015, she received the George D. Kuh Outstanding Contribution to Literature and/or Research Award from NASPA: Student Affairs Professionals in Higher Education, and, in 2007, the Outstanding Contribution to Knowledge Award from ACPA–College Student Educators International. In addition, she has served on the governing boards of ACPA, NASPA, Division J (Postsecondary Education) of the American Educational Research Association, and the Association for the Study of Higher Education, and on the editorial boards of *Journal of College Student Development, NASPA Journal,* and the *Review of Higher Education.*

Christine M. Wilson is assistant vice president for student affairs and director of student activities at the University of Connecticut, where she also teaches in the higher education and student affairs program. Prior to her assignment at

UConn, she was the assistant director of student leadership in the Memorial Union at the University of Rhode Island. Wilson received her BA and MS degrees from Indiana State University and her PhD degree from the joint program at the University of Rhode Island/Rhode Island College. Her research focuses on the experiences of college student leaders from marginalized and oppressed identity groups, inclusive leadership and organizations, and student leader stress. She was the recipient of the NASPA Region 1 Outstanding Contribution to Higher Education Award in 2014.

Maureen E. Wilson is a professor and chair of the Department of Higher Education and Student Affairs at Bowling Green State University. She has also worked at Mississippi State University, the University of South Carolina, and the College of William & Mary. She received a BSBA from Aquinas College in Michigan, an MA from Michigan State University, and a PhD from The Ohio State University. Wilson's research focuses on professional identity, socialization, and preparation; behavioral norms in professional practice; and administrative practice in student affairs. Wilson edited the *ASHE Reader on College Student Development Theory*. She has contributed chapters to books including *Campus Housing Management* and *Campus Crisis Management*. She is associate editor for the *Journal of College Student Development* and served on the governing board for ACPA–College Students International. Her awards include the Association of College and University Housing Officers–International Research and Publication Award, ACPA Diamond Honoree, and National Association of Student Personnel Administrators Region IV–East Outstanding Contribution to Student Affairs through Teaching Award.

PREFACE

This book focuses on preparing people for careers as student affairs educators. Exactly when student affairs practice began is virtually impossible to measure, but our view is that an early version might have been the discussion a young student had with a tutor at one of the colonial colleges about meeting the challenges of preparing himself (the students of the day were young men) to take his place in colonial society, preparing for the ministry, or maybe dealing with homesickness. Although the work of today's student affairs educators is far more complex and sophisticated, the fact is that those engaged in student affairs work still care deeply about students, will do everything they can to assist them in achieving their educational goals, and see our postsecondary institutions as central to the success in building an educated citizenry.

Student affairs practice has changed dramatically since that first conversation between tutor and student, the tools available to student affairs educators have become more numerous and sophisticated, and research increasingly has been used to inform professional practice. But in the end, the relationship between educator and student has been the heart of student affairs going back, at least, to Tommy Arkle Clark (dean) and Fred Applegate (student) at the University of Illinois in 1890 (Becque, 2015). Since then the field of student affairs has founded professional organizations, developed professional literature and graduate degree programs, and played an important role in the education of college students.

Today, student affairs practice is challenging, complex, sophisticated, and touches students from before they apply for admission to when they graduate and beyond. Various titles have been used to characterize the work of student affairs professionals including, but not limited to, student personnel, student services, student development, student affairs administration, student affairs education, and just plain student affairs. The titles of the day are probably less important than to assert that it would be an unusual institution that does not have staff members who are dedicated to the growth and development of students outside of the formal curriculum. These staff members form the audience for this book, though we will be delighted if faculty members and administrators outside of the units that comprise student affairs on a given campus read the book or even parts of it. Although our primary audience consists of graduate students and student affairs staff members who are in the early stages of their careers, we also hope that this book will resonate with those who teach courses in the preparation of student affairs as well as senior leaders in student affairs practice and others who are concerned about the growth and development of college students.

The Green Book

Student Services: A Handbook for the Profession has become known as the "green book" over the years. Ursula Delworth and Gary R. Hanson edited the first edition in 1980, and revised editions of the "green book" were released in 1989, 1996, 2003, and 2011. Is there a need to release new editions of this book periodically? Our view is that because higher education in general, and student affairs in particular, continue to evolve and change rapidly, as will be asserted frequently by our authors, this book needs to be as contemporary as possible. More than twenty million students were enrolled in postsecondary institutions in 2012 (National Center for Education Statistics, 2015, table 304.10) at 4,726 institutions (table 303.90), an increase from more than fifteen million enrolled at 4,056 institutions in 2000 (table 303.90). In a dozen years five million more students enrolled at just about seven hundred more institutions. Other developments, such as the use of increasingly sophisticated technology, new budgeting models, and changing expectations for higher education, have led to what Allen and Cherrey (2003) have described as working in permanent white water (citing Vaill, 1996). Whether this pace of growth and change will continue in the future is impossible to predict, but if past is prologue, we believe that those who serve as student affairs educators will need to be able to adapt, change, and develop innovative solutions to circumstances that are increasingly difficult to anticipate.

Ursula Delworth and Gary R. Hanson were the pioneers of this series, editing the first two editions (*Student Services: A Handbook for the Profession*, 1980, and *Student Services, A Handbook for the Profession*, 2nd ed., 1989). They were trailblazers in other respects, too, also having served as the inaugural editors of the New Directions for Student Services sourcebook series. Susan R. Komives and Dudley B. Woodard Jr., also exceptional scholars, edited the third and fourth editions. Susan and Doug upheld the high standards set by Ursula and Gary. John H. Schuh, Susan R. Jones, and Shaun Harper edited the fifth edition of the "green book," and the editorial group continues to evolve with Vasti Torres serving as one of the coeditors of this edition.

The Title

The title of this book has been a concern of the editors over the years, and it continues to be a matter that needs to be addressed in this edition. *Student services* is yesterday's characterization of the work of student affairs educators and has been so for several decades. Clearly, some of the work of student affairs educators has to do with providing services, but the essence of student affairs education is far more complex than that. Nevertheless, we wish to be true to the roots of this series of books and we have retained the title for this edition. The focus of today's practice is much more on providing learning experiences for students than transactional services, but in the spirit of recognizing the quality of the work that has gone into the development of the previous editions of this book, we have chosen to sustain the title recognizing that the title acknowledges and honors our roots rather than characterizes the work of contemporary student affairs educators.

The Focus of the Sixth Edition

As was our approach to the fifth edition, we have reorganized this book, adding some chapters and deleting others. Among the new chapters are those that address campus climate, student retention, institutional success, social media, crisis management, and embracing difference through programming. Although these topics were addressed in part in the previous edition, we believe that they merit a more complete treatment, and as a consequence, we included them as the central foci of chapters in the book.

It is important to note that this book does not purport to be a complete treatise of all that needs to be known to engage in a successful career as a student affairs educator. We have conceptualized this book as a place to start one's education. Accordingly, the book's content can and should be explored in greater depth through additional readings, activities, and conversations. The reference list for each chapter is extensive, but additional readings are just a start. New to this edition is the inclusion of discussion questions and sometimes activities at the end of each chapter, which provide additional learning experiences to advance an understanding of the content of each chapter. These take the form of discussion questions and items, activities, and other learning experiences. All are designed to extend the conversation that has been developed in the chapter. Our view is that the additional learning experiences will help stimulate out-of-class learning, which could take the form of informal conversations, field trips, interviews, or other experiences that will add richness to those who read this book.

The Organization and Contents of the Sixth Edition

The organization of this edition is similar to previous editions. We begin with laying a foundation for student affairs practice in the first section by providing a historical overview of higher education in the United States and then trace the development of student affairs. Then we look at the philosophies and values that inform our work.

The second section provides the context for our work. We begin with a discussion of campus cultures and institutional varieties. Higher education institutions have become increasingly diverse over the years by governance, mission, and purpose. Campus climate and the increasingly diverse people who comprise our institutions are the focus of the next chapter. We continue with establishing the context for our work by examining the ethical principles and standards that frame our work and conclude the chapter with a discussion of selected legal foundations and practice that inform our work.

The third section provides a description and analysis of the theoretical bases of the profession. We begin with a discussion about the nature and uses of theory. Knowing how to apply theory to our work is essential to understanding the value of applying theory to student affairs practice. Building on this foundation are chapters devoted to holistic development, cognitive development, psychosocial and social identities, critical theoretical perspectives, organization theories and change, environmental theories, and theories that inform student retention and institutional success. We acknowledge that the curricula of many graduate programs include one or more courses on the theoretical aspects of student affairs practice. In this book we are providing a basis for further study and examination of theories that inform our work, and we encourage those who do not take courses on the theoretical aspects of student affairs practice to conduct independent reading on the topics introduced in this book. The growth of the theoretical basis of student affairs education has gone through a rapid development, and we expect that the theoretical foundation of our work will continue to evolve and develop in the future.

In the fourth part of this book we provide an introduction to elements of the professional practice of student affairs educators. This section focuses on selected organizational dimensions of student affairs, providing an introduction to important topics that we hope will lead to additional reading, study, and reflection on the part of our readers. Included in this section are issues related to the organization of student affairs, the financial dimensions of our work, selected topics related to assessment and evaluation of student affairs, using technology and social media, and developing partnerships with colleagues in academic affairs including faculty members.

The fifth part of this book includes what we believe are essential competencies for those who are engaged in professional student affairs practice. The content might also be referred to as the basic skill set required of student affairs educators, similar, but not quite identical, to the competencies identified in the document *Professional Competency Areas for Student Affairs Practitioners* (Joint Task Force on Professional Competencies and Standards, 2010). As is the case with the third section, we do not claim that we have provided all that a student affairs educator needs to know to be engaged in professional practice. The topics included in this section are professionalism, multicultural competence, leadership, staffing and supervision, teaching and facilitation, counseling and helping skills, advising, crisis management, embracing difference through programming, and applying theories and research to practice. Similar to the fourth section, our authors have provided a foundation for further reading, discussion, reflection, and investigation of these topics. Every topic is complex and merits additional focus on the part of student affairs educators.

We conclude the book with a look into the future of student affairs, beginning with a discussion of the professional development of student affairs educators. This new chapter challenges student affairs professionals to reenvision their thinking and approach to professional development. We conclude with our prognostications about the future of student affairs practice as well some ideas about how student affairs educators can shape the future of higher education. As higher education continues to change, so must student affairs professionals. Taken together, these chapters provide an introduction to the evolving challenges and research that drive our field. As editors we hope that reading this book will facilitate more student learning and a greater sense of cohesion about the work of student affairs.

References

Allen, K. E., & Cherrey, C. (2003). Student affairs as change agents. *NASPA Journal, 40*(2), 29–42.

Becque, F. (2015). Who was Thomas Arkle Clark, Dean of Men? Focus on fraternity history & more. Retrieved from http://www.franbecque.com/2015/04/02/who-was-thomas-arkle-clark-dean-of-men/

Delworth, U., Hanson, G. R., & Associates. (1980). *Student services: A handbook for the profession.* San Francisco: Jossey-Bass.

Delworth, U., Hanson, G. R., & Associates. (1989). *Student services: A handbook for the profession* (2nd ed.). San Francisco: Jossey-Bass.

Joint Task Force on Professional Competencies and Standards. (2010). *Professional competency areas for student affairs practitioners.* Washington, DC: ACPA and NASPA.

National Center for Education Statistics. (2015). *Digest of education statistics, 2013* (NCES 2015-011). Washington, DC: US Dept. of Education. Retrieved from http://nces.ed.gov/programs/digest/d13/

Vaill, P. (1996). *Learning as a way of being.* San Francisco: Jossey-Bass.

PART ONE

HISTORICAL CONTEXT

The purpose of this book is to provide basic information about student services to graduate students, young (in terms of experience) professionals, those new to the profession, and seasoned members of the academy who are not familiar with student affairs. We think it is important to offer a foundation for how student affairs practice has grown and developed to where it is today, as well as to develop a philosophical basis for our professional practice. As is the case with other aspects of higher education, the process of development for student affairs has taken decades, and it will continue to do so as long as there are people on college campuses whose primary focus has to do with the student experience outside the institution's curriculum.

Accordingly, this part of the book begins with a historical overview of American higher education. Chapter 1 by John R. Thelin and Marybeth Gasman highlights the periods of higher education development, from colonial

times when the first colleges were founded, to the beginning of the development of state universities, to the passage of the Morrill Act and the resulting rise of land-grant universities, to colleges that were founded to serve African Americans, and so on. They continue through several more periods to where higher education in the United States stands today—the envy of the world in many respects but not without serious problems, including access to higher education, the cost of attendance, disappointing graduation rates, and so on. This historical foundation is important to keep in mind in that although higher education faces serious problems today, it has almost always had challenges to be managed, sometimes because of internal conflict and other times resulting from political, social, or economic external forces.

From an overview of the history of higher education we move to the history of student affairs, guided by Robert Schwartz and Dafina-Lazarus Stewart in chapter 2.

Formal student affairs practice began in the twentieth century, picking up momentum just before and after World War II with the publication of the *Student Personnel Point of View* in 1937, which was updated in 1949. During the twentieth century professional organizations were founded, graduate curricula were developed, and a literature base for our professional practice was published. Our authors guide us through the growing pains experienced by student affairs and then focus on the consumer movement and passage of federal legislation that affected higher education as a new century approached. The chapter also addresses current issues and identifies future challenges and considerations for student affairs practice.

Chapter 3 defines, describes, and analyzes the profession's philosophy. Robert D. Reason and Ellen M. Broido identify the enduring principles and values of student affairs and then discuss the current influences on our professional philosophies and values. They conclude that multiple documents have provided strength for our professional heritage in student affairs practice.

As a set, these chapters provide a foundation for understanding the historical and philosophical bases of our work. We think that such an understanding is necessary before moving on to our professional and theoretical foundations as well as the more practical aspects of our work. Our authors have done a splendid job of guiding us along this path, and we invite you to learn from them.

CHAPTER 1

HISTORICAL OVERVIEW OF AMERICAN HIGHER EDUCATION

John R. Thelin and Marybeth Gasman

During a visit to the Midwest in 1910, an editor researching the growth of American colleges and universities noted that "the University of Chicago does not look its age. It looks much older. This is because it has been put through an artificial aging process, reminding one of the ways furniture is given an 'antique oak finish'" (Slosson, 1910, p. 429). Indeed, American universities' fondness for Gothic spires and Georgian-revival brick quadrangles reveals an essential feature about higher education in the United States: the American public expects its colleges and universities to be historic institutions with monumental architecture that invokes a sense of continuity and heritage. In fact, a historical profile of US higher education is in large part a story of structures, not just bricks and mortar but also the legal and administrative frameworks—products of US social and political history—that have made colleges and universities enduring institutions.

Our concern is with higher education's history, not its archaeology, so we need a theme to bring these skeletal structures to life. James Garfield, later president of the United States, praised his own alma mater's president by proclaiming, "The ideal college is Mark Hopkins on one end of a log and a student on the other" (Rudolph, 1962, p. 243). His tribute reminds us that despite the proliferation of magnificent buildings and elaborate facilities in American colleges and universities, ultimately the history of colleges and universities in this country is about teaching and learning. Although their relationship has continually evolved, students and faculty members remain the central characters in the higher education drama, without which the structures are nothing but inanimate stage props. Whether in the eighteenth, nineteenth, twentieth, or—now—early in the twenty-first century, the American tradition in higher education has espoused a strong commitment to undergraduate education. As historian Larry Cuban of Stanford

University concluded in his study of universities in the twentieth century, it often has been a story of "how research trumped teaching" (Cuban, 1999). This is not—and need not—always be the outcome. From time to time highly publicized commentaries have urged higher education leaders to reclaim the American education heritage by rediscovering the importance of "putting student learners first" (Wingspread Group on Higher Education, 1993, p. 1).

Structures and Students

A good way to chart the history of higher education in the United States is to keep in mind that quantitative changes have signaled qualitative changes. For example, from 1700 to 1900, less than 5 percent of Americans between the ages of eighteen and twenty-two enrolled in college. Between World Wars I and II, this figure increased to about 20 percent, rising to 33 percent in 1960, and dramatically expanding to more than 50 percent in the 1970s. These numbers accurately forecast the transformation of American higher education from an elite to a mass activity, a trend that continued during the final decades of the twentieth century when the prospect for universal access to postsecondary education emerged as part of the American agenda (Trow, 1970). According to one estimate, in 2015 more than twenty million students enrolled in postsecondary education in the United States.

To attempt to grasp the 370-year history of American higher education in a single glimpse is unwieldy and unwise. Therefore, the following pages first consider the legacy of the English influence on colonial colleges and then shift to how America wrestled with the question of creating a distinctive "American way" in higher education during the new national period. Next, the discussion highlights the emergence of the "university" model from 1880 to about 1914, with the reminder that other institutional forms also flourished during this period. After considering higher education in the three decades between World Wars I and II, the historical analysis moves to the problems of abundance and prosperity in the 1960s, whereas the decades from 1970 to 1990 are analyzed as an era bringing further adjustment and accountability. Finally, analysis of some of the demographic and structural trends since 1990 to the present provides a way to make sense from the transition into the twenty-first century. Having completed this narrative account, the chapter then aims to bring coherence to the history of American higher education by considering the implications for professional practices and policies brought on by trends in research and scholarship within a variety of related disciplines.

The Colonial Period: Sorting Out the English Legacy

Although the ideal of an intense undergraduate education by which young adults are prepared for leadership and service is a distinctively American tradition, it owes much to the example set by the English universities of Oxford and Cambridge in the sixteenth and seventeenth centuries. These institutions earned a reputation for their unique practice of arranging several residential colleges within a university structure, all located in a pastoral setting. This model, commonly known as the "Oxbridge" model, departed from the patterns of academic life and instruction found in the urban universities of the late middle ages on the European continent. At Paris, Salerno, Heidelberg, and Bologna, scholars banded together for protection and to set standards for teaching, pay, and tuition—but they gave little attention to building a permanent campus or supervising student life (Haskins, 1923). In sharp contrast, by the seventeenth century Oxford and Cambridge had developed a formal system of endowed colleges that combined living and learning within quadrangles. This model consisted of an architecturally distinct, landscaped site for an elaborate organizational culture and pedagogy designed to build character rather than produce expert scholars. The college was an isolated "total" institution whose responsibilities included guiding the social and academic dimensions of undergraduate life. The Oxbridge model not only combined these elements but also integrated them within a coherent philosophy of residential education. This approach eventually influenced college builders in the New World.

Rudolph (1962) called this adopted educational tradition the "collegiate way" (p. 87). Even when the realities of the American wilderness set in or when college officials ran out of money for building, the "collegiate way" persisted as an aspiration in the colonial and, later, national culture. The most telling legacy of the early college founders is their combination of optimism and caution in their quest to create what historian James Axtell (1974) has called the "school on a hill." The American colonists built colleges because they believed in and wished to transplant and perfect the English idea of an undergraduate education as a civilizing experience that ensured a progression of responsible leaders for church and state. The importance of colleges to colonial life is suggested by their proliferation and protection—starting with Harvard, founded in the Massachusetts Bay Colony in 1636, and followed by The College of William & Mary in Virginia in 1693, Yale in Connecticut in 1701, and six more colleges by the start of the Revolutionary War in 1775.

Tensions between students and faculty characterized colonial college life. Indeed, the residential college was as much a recipe for conflicts as for harmony. Numerous consumer complaints ranging from bad food in the dining commons to dissatisfaction with the curriculum often sparked student riots and revolts. Although relatively homogeneous in its restriction to white, Christian young men, the study body still institutionalized the nuances of social class. College rosters listed students by social rank. Furthermore, following the Oxford tradition, academic robes reflected socioeconomic position, delineating the "commoners" (those who dined at college commons) from the "servitors" (those who waited on tables).

Religion, of course, was an important part of the fabric of American culture, including in its colleges. Religious concerns and sectarian competition often fueled the creation of new colonial colleges. A majority of these institutions developed denominational ties, and most college presidents were men of the cloth. However, emphasis on Christian values and discipline (more specifically, Protestant values) did not preclude preparation for secular and civil life. As relatively young students matriculated, colleges embraced the role of in loco parentis, with the faculty members and president offering supervision of student conduct and moral development. Although colonial colleges did educate future ministers, that purpose was only one of many among the undergraduate bachelor of arts curriculum (Handlin & Handlin, 1974). Few written records are available to help reconstruct the colonial collegiate curriculum. The best estimate is that oral disputations provided the most rigorous hurdles, subject to the immediate critical evaluation of masters and fellow undergraduates. American higher education in the eighteenth century did include some precedents for diversity—and the associated challenges of that commitment. Periodically colonial colleges attempted to expand their missions but often encountered only weak or even disastrous results. For example, attempts to extend the collegiate education beyond the white population of the British colonies reflected noble intentions, but it relied on limited planning, and thereby generated extremely limited results. One of these episodes caused Benjamin Franklin (1784) to recount how after a group of Native American students returned from their scholarship studies at The College of William & Mary, their chieftain fathers complained that the sons had become unhealthy, lazy, and unable to make good decisions. As a result, tribal elders politely refused the college's offer to renew the scholarship program, suggesting instead that perhaps the colonial leaders would like to send *their* sons to the Native Americans for an education that would make the Anglo boys into strong and wise men.

The novelty (and high failure rate) of such experiments underscores the fundamental limits of the colonial colleges' scope and constituency. Enrollment in college courses was confined to white males, mostly from established, prosperous families and members of each colony's dominant Protestant denomination. College attendance tended to confirm existing social standing rather than provide social mobility. The curriculum primarily provided for an analytic or intellectual edge in the discourse and writing associated with public life, such as the practice of law (Handlin & Handlin, 1974). In plain terms, the college mission was to ensure the preparation and disciplined seasoning of a future leadership cohort.

The aim of the colonial college then was the rigorous education of the "gentleman scholar." If the colonial colleges were limited in their constituency and their mission, they were at least remarkably effective in their education of an articulate and learned leadership group, as suggested by the extraordinary contribution of their alumni (including Thomas Jefferson and James Madison) to the political and intellectual leadership of the American Revolution and the creation of the new United States.

Creating the "American Way" in Higher Education: The New National Period

During the new national period following American independence in 1776 and extending into the mid-nineteenth century, the small college persisted as the institutional norm, despite scattered attempts to create a modern comprehensive university. On closer inspection, continual innovations and experimentation in American higher education existed, as indicated by the curriculum proposed by Thomas Jefferson at the new University of Virginia. An undeniable fact of American life well into the late nineteenth century was that going to college was not necessary for "getting ahead" economically, although a college degree did confer some prestige. Colleges had to compete incessantly for the attention of donors and paying students. New state governments showed relatively little inclination to fund higher education, although granting college charters was a popular and easy way for legislators to repay political debts. State universities in Georgia, North Carolina, and South Carolina were chartered by the early nineteenth century, but they enjoyed only sparse support from their respective legislatures and often took years to get around to the business of actually enrolling students and offering instruction. That the American college was not universally supported—by legislators, donors, or paying students—did not mean it was unimportant. The fervor generated by the Second Great Awakening seemingly caused every religious group to want to build its own college for propagating its doctrines and for reinforcing its distinctive orthodoxy among members who were growing from adolescence into adulthood. The interesting result was a boom in college building in the first half of the nineteenth century: whereas in 1800 there were probably twenty-five colleges offering instruction and conferring degrees, by 1860 this number had increased almost tenfold to 240—not including numerous institutions that had opened and then gone out of business (Burke, 1982).

Between 1860 and 1900, such historically excluded constituencies as women, African Americans, and Native Americans gained some access to higher education. By the mid-nineteenth century, women in particular had become formal participants in advanced studies. One educational innovation was the founding of the "female academies" and "female seminaries"—institutions that offered a range of courses and instructional programs beyond elementary and secondary schooling. In part, curricula included home economics and, at some institutions, the social graces and deportment associated with a "finishing school." Important to keep in mind is that the curriculum also included formal instruction in the sciences, mathematics, foreign languages, and composition—subjects associated with undergraduate collegiate curricula. Even though such studies did not officially lead to the bachelor's degree for women, they often rivaled the academic excellence of the men's colleges of the era. Over time, especially by the 1860s and 1870s, many of the female seminaries became degree-granting colleges in their own right (Horowitz, 1984). In the late nineteenth century a few colleges, such as Oberlin and later Cornell, pioneered coeducation, enrolling men and women—a policy that would soon gain a wide following in the Midwest and on the Pacific Coast (Gordon, 1990).

Although a few Northern black colleges—Lincoln University (Pennsylvania), Cheyney University (Pennsylvania), and Wilberforce University (Ohio)—had been established by free blacks and white abolitionists prior to the end of the Civil War, between 1865 and 1910 additional provisions were made for African American students to pursue higher education, with the founding of many small black colleges in the South. The first impetus for financial support for these colleges came from Northern philanthropic groups such as the Peabody Foundation. The colleges also benefited from the financial support of black churches, state governments, and the federal government through the Freedmen's Bureau. Many of these institutions, such as Booker T. Washington's Tuskegee Institute, began as a combination of elementary and secondary schools that eventually offered a college-level curriculum. In this respect, newly established institutions for African Americans followed familiar patterns of American nineteenth-century colleges, displaying an array of curricular emphases—ranging from liberal arts at Fisk, Howard, Spelman, and Morehouse to industrial arts and normal schools at Hampton Institute in Virginia along with black state colleges in numerous Southern states (for example, Prairie View A&M University). The Land Grant Act of 1890 also provided funding for black colleges in sixteen states in the South, leading them to offer studies in agriculture and the mechanical arts. The black colleges and universities, despite differences in curricula, religious affiliation, and leadership, shared a widespread condition of uncertain and inadequate funding. Furthermore, well into the twentieth century many of these institutions were prohibited by state governments from offering graduate programs, advanced work, or first professional degree programs such as law (Wright, 1988). Illustrative of the impediments the black colleges and universities faced in the South was that they were not admitted to full membership in the Southern Association of Colleges and Schools until 1957 and even after admission there is considerable evidence that they were treated in discriminatory ways. Despite the double burden of not having large endowments or being able to charge more than modest tuitions, these colleges have been disproportionately effective in the enrollment and graduation of a large number and percentage of African American students (Drewry & Doermann, 2001). In effect, black colleges and universities are responsible for the education of the black middle class as we know it today. An often overlooked fact is that federal monies and private foundations of this era also support some higher education for Native Americans—whether as part of campuses such as Virginia's Hampton Institute or at distinct institutions such as California's Sherman School for Indians, Pennsylvania's famous Carlisle School for Indians (Jenkins, 2007), or the University of North Carolina at Pembroke.

The cumulative impact of the innovations and experiments in American higher education in the nineteenth century generated an interesting social change: by 1870, "going to college" had come to capture the American fancy. As one brash, ambitious (and perceptive) undergraduate candidly told historian Henry Adams in 1871, "A degree from Harvard is worth money in Chicago" (Adams, 1918, pp. 305–306). More precisely, to be a "college man" or a "college woman" lifted one to a social standing that had prestige and "scarcity value" (Canby, 1936, pp. 25–26). About 1890, popular national magazines started to run profiles of selected colleges and universities as a regular feature.

University Building and More: 1880 to 1914

As higher education became more and more popular, the emergence of the modern university in America dominated press coverage. At one extreme, the ideal of advanced, rigorous scholarship and the necessary resources of research libraries, laboratories, and doctoral programs were epitomized by the great German universities. Emulating and transplanting the German model to the United States became the passion of The Johns Hopkins University in Baltimore, Clark University in Massachusetts, and the University of Chicago. At the same time, a commitment to applied research and utility gained a following at the emerging land-grant institutions, ranging from the Midwestern, rural University of Wisconsin to the urban Massachusetts Institute of Technology. Between 1870 and 1910 America was the setting for a dramatic "university movement," which created a hybrid type of institution undergirded by large-scale philanthropy and widespread construction of new campus buildings (Veysey, 1965). On balance, the building of great universities in America contributed to the advancement of cutting edge scholarship. At the same time, however, this "cutting edge" remained marginal to the central purpose of undergraduate education. Although the ideals of research and utility were conspicuous, they were tempered to varying degrees by the value traditionally placed on a liberal education and, often, on piety. The best evidence of this claim is that no American university, including the pioneering examples of Johns Hopkins and Clark, was able to survive without offering an undergraduate course of study. Furthermore, in contrast to higher education in the twenty-first century, American universities of 1910 remained relatively underdeveloped and small. Only a handful of institutions, such as the urban universities of Harvard, Columbia, and Pennsylvania, enrolled more than five thousand students.

Sponsored research and graduate programs were limited in size and resources. One of the more substantial achievements of the university-building era was the annexation of professional schools such as medicine, law, business, theology, pharmacy, and engineering into the academic structure of the university. Equally important, American undergraduates displayed ingenuity and perseverance by creating a robust extracurricular world of athletics, fraternities, sororities, campus newspapers, humor magazines, and clubs. These vied successfully for attention with the official curriculum. Observers likened the student culture to a "primitive brotherhood" or, drawing an analogy from political science, the campus was a "state within a state" (Canby, 1936, p. 245).

The strength of the undergraduate culture gained added support from a new entity: organized alumni associations, which created an alliance of old and new students who worked tirelessly to ensure that presidents and professors did not encroach on the precious traditions of undergraduate life.

Higher Education after World War I: 1915 to 1945

Historian David Levine (1986) charted the rise of American colleges and the concomitant "culture of aspiration" (p. 14) in the three decades between World Wars I and II. The most salient feature of this period was the stratification of American higher education into institutional layers, indicating that distinctions were drawn between prestige and purpose in pursuing a college education. The emergence of public junior colleges, an increase in state normal schools and teachers colleges, and the creation of new technical institutes all represented this trend (Diener, 1986; Levine, 1986). The great state universities of the Midwest and West finally started to fulfill the promise of the Morrill Act to serve the statewide public, with enrollment at typical large campuses reaching fifteen thousand to twenty-five thousand.

Perhaps the greatest puzzle facing American higher education in the early twentieth century is what may be termed the dilemma of diversity. Individuals at the most heterogeneous institutions often encountered the most glaring conflicts, hostilities, and discrimination within the campus life. Coeducation, for example, deserves to be hailed as a positive change in promoting equity and access for women. At the same time, however, such celebration needs to be tempered with careful historical analysis of how female students were actually treated once admitted. Gordon (1990) found that at the University of California, the University of Chicago, and Cornell, women undergraduates encountered discrimination academically and in student activities. A comparable pattern of discrimination occurred at those universities that enrolled ethnic, racial, and religious minorities. Historian Helen Horowitz (1987) traced the effects of this discrimination, noting how student subcultures developed over time, with "insider" groups tending to dominate the rewards and prestige of campus life. Conversely, Horowitz's (1984) account of the founding of new women's colleges from 1860 to 1930 suggests that special-purpose colleges provided distinctive educational benefits for their students and alumni.

In the 1920s some colleges enjoyed the luxury of choice. For the first time they had more applicants than student places, enabling administrators to implement selective admissions policies. They looked to testing programs of the United States military for models and inspirations of how to administer and process standardized tests. Ultimately the Educational Testing Service (ETS) was developed as an appendage of the College Entrance Examination Board (CEEB). Creation and refinement of the Scholastic Aptitude Test (widely known as the "SAT") gained stature and infamy among education-minded young Americans as a rite of passage from high school to college (Lehman, 2000). Unfortunately, these various admissions tools and practices were often used to exclude some students on the basis of race, ethnicity, gender, or other criteria unrelated to academic merit (Karabel, 2005). Synnott's (1979) study of admissions at Harvard, Yale, and Princeton suggested selective admissions was at best a "half-opened door." On balance, American higher education's capacity to provide access ran ahead of its ability to foster assimilation and parity within the campus. The result was a complex dilemma for campus officials and policy analysts: how to best serve minority groups and new participants in higher education? More often than not, American higher education achieved diversity through colleges dedicated to serve a special constituency, whether defined by race, gender, or religious affiliation. Accommodation with segregation was in the American grain.

Higher Education's "Golden Age": 1945 to 1970

The dramatic changes in student recruitment after 1945 came from the federal government intent that the Servicemen's Readjustment Act, popularly known as the GI Bill, provide a short-term measure by which the federal government could mitigate the pressure of simply allowing hundreds of thousands of returning war veterans to become job seekers in a saturated national labor market. The strategy was to make federal scholarships for postsecondary education readily available to veterans. But the GI Bill had unexpected long-term consequences: first, it was far more attractive than legislators anticipated; second, it set a precedent for making portable government student aid into an entitlement; and, third, it provided a policy tool for increasing the diversity of students at American colleges and universities. In retrospect, the unexpected successes of the bill also revealed some dysfunctions in the ideals of expanded opportunity. First, even though thousands of women were veterans of war service, they were disproportionately underrepresented as recipients of the GI Bill's benefits. Second, the bill's well-intentioned provisions to provide GI scholarship recipients with a wide range of choices of programs and institutions exposed the lack of standards or accountability in matters of institutional quality and legitimacy. This latter weakness opened the gates for regional accreditation associations to provide legislators and taxpayers with some reasonable thresholds of academic integrity among institutions approved to receive federal scholarship funds. And third, the influx of new students on many campuses, including black colleges and universities, resulted in great stress on the physical plant of the campuses, causing institutions to create make-shift classrooms and residence halls.

The popularity of the GI Bill underscored the importance of higher education to the nation's long-term adjustment to a new economy and postwar democracy. A 1947 report authorized by President Harry S. Truman brought to Congress and the American public the bold proposition of permanently expanding access and affordability to higher education. This egalitarian impulse coincided with effective lobbying for the expansion of government- and foundation-sponsored research grants for scholars at universities. The convergence of the two trends resulted in what has been called higher education's "Golden Age," one marked by an academic revolution in which colleges and universities acquired unprecedented influence in American society (Freeland, 1992; Jencks & Riesman, 1968). The new commuter institutions often enrolled a large percentage of "first-generation" college attendees; the consequence was that those students probably most in need of academic support and immersion were less likely to receive it (Brint & Karabel, 1989). It also pointed to signs of "tracking" in the American higher education system, because community colleges showed a student profile skewed disproportionately toward enrollment of African American and Hispanic students. At worst, this ease of admission at community colleges was followed by ease of departure, because community college students who were underprepared or unfamiliar with navigating academic institutions were at risk and tended to have a high drop-out rate.

Problems during a Time of Prosperity: The 1960s

Ironically, the prosperity of the 1960s actually created new problems for higher education. Freeland's (1992) study of universities in Massachusetts during the years from 1945 to 1970 recounted an era of ruthless competition among colleges and universities, especially in the greater metropolitan Boston area, in pursuit of students, research grants, donors, and external funds. Most troubling for those concerned with the quality of undergraduate education was the strong temptation for all universities to use undergraduate enrollments as a convenient means of subsidizing new graduate programs and research institutes. In many states policy proposals included discussions between university officials and legislative subcommittees over teaching strategies.

The prestigious title used to describe the idealized institutions of the era was "multiversity," which connoted what Kerr (1964) called the "federal grant university" (p. 46). These institutions consisted of a flagship campus with advanced-degree programs, whose enrollment usually exceeded twenty thousand students and whose budgets relied heavily on the "soft money" of external research and development projects funded by the federal government and private foundations. Despite the predominance of these schools, enrollments in other kinds of institutions—small independent colleges, religious colleges, private universities, community colleges, regional campuses, and technical institutes—were also healthy, often beyond enrollment capacity. As sociologist Burton Clark (1970) documented, at the same time that the multiversity gained prominence, the private distinctive liberal arts colleges also flourished. Curricular innovations at all of these types of institutions added honors programs and freshman seminars. Testimony to the strength of the "collegiate ideal" for American educators of the late twentieth century was that even the large public universities came full circle to ponder ways in which mass higher education might provide a modern equivalent of the old New England hilltop college. Kerr (1964) summed up the challenge for undergraduate education at the prestigious, large state universities of the mid-1960s with the rhetorical question, "How do we make the university seem smaller as it grows larger?" (pp. 104–105). He then proceeded to answer his own query supporting an interesting innovation known as the "cluster college"—separate residential units within a large university that restored the colonial ideal of bring living and learning together within an Oxbridge model of higher education transplanted to the late twentieth-century United States.

The history of higher education is often a story of unexpected consequences. For college and university administrators of the 1960s, the boom in construction and enrollments tended to mask problems and tensions among students that would emerge between1963 and 1968 and violently erupt between 1968 and 1972. Two distinct yet related sources of undergraduate discontent existed. First, discontented students complained about large lecture classes, impersonal registration, crowded student housing, and the psychological distance between faculty members and students caused by the expanded size of campuses. Second, student concern about external political and societal events—notably the Vietnam War, the military draft, the counter-culture movement, and the civil rights movement—kindled a visible and eventually widespread student activism. This activism not only preoccupied but also strained the real and symbolic foundations of higher education, and it affected universities' internal and external conduct.

An Era of Adjustment and Accountability: 1970 to 1990

Years of student unrest contributed to several negative effects on American higher education, not the least of which was declining confidence on the part of state governments and other traditional sources of support. No longer did public officials assume that a university president or a dean of students could keep his or her "house in order." By 1972 the federal government's action emerged with large-scale entitlements for student financial aid—an alphabet soup of funding including Basic Educational Opportunity Grants (BEOG) (later known as Pell Grants) and the Supplementary Educational Opportunity Grants (SEOG). These generous programs embodied the ideal that affordability should not circumscribe students' choices in making college plans. During the same years, new legislation prohibiting discrimination in educational programs via the 1972 federal Title IX allowed women and other underrepresented constituencies to gain access gradually yet persistently to academic fields such as business, law, medicine, and a host of PhD programs. By 1990, Section 504 of the Vocational Rehabilitation Act had further encouraged diversity and access by providing guidelines and advocacy for students with disabilities who sought admission to higher education institutions.

The early 1980s was a period in which a succession of commission reports, including *A Nation at Risk*, criticized American public education as uncertain and incoherent. Initially the focus was on primary and secondary schooling—a focus that gave higher education a temporary reprieve. However, this changed in 1984 when the Study Group on the Conditions of Excellence in American Higher Education (sponsored by the National Institute of Education) released its report, *Involvement in Learning: Realizing the Potential of American Higher Education*. Its call for scrutiny and reform in higher education was reinforced by numerous other reports, especially periodic studies on the college curriculum, the college as a community, and reconsideration of scholarship that the Carnegie Foundation for the Advancement of Teaching published under the leadership of Ernest Boyer. Consequently, by 1985 colleges and universities, especially public institutions, were increasingly expected by governors and state legislators to demonstrate efficiency and effectiveness. One state strategy was to tie a portion of state appropriations to performance measures as part of a larger assessment movement that caught on in numerous states, including Tennessee, Arizona, Kentucky, and New York.

The problems were real, and the concerns were warranted, but American higher education demonstrated a great deal of innovation and resiliency. Enrollment declines were muted as colleges recruited new constituents, including older students and more students from traditionally underserved groups such as women and minorities. Campus administration underwent a managerial revolution in two ways. First, administrators increasingly relied on systematic data analysis from national and institutional sources, which helped them make informed decisions that promoted budget accountability. Second, new government-incentive programs prompted colleges to shift resources to marketing, fund-raising, and student recruitment in order to seek and retain new student constituencies—and to develop new programs to serve them.

History, however, always includes seasonal changes, and ultimately American colleges and universities could not evade financial problems. By 1990, reports from virtually every governor's office in the country indicated severe shortfalls in state revenues in addition to other sustained indications of a depressed economy. At the same time, federal support for university-based research tapered, making even the most prestigious universities vulnerable to budgetary problems and cutbacks. If an apt motto existed for the situation facing higher education in the final decade of the twentieth century, it was the admonition, "Do more with less."

The Twentieth to the Twenty-First Century, 1990 to 2015

Between 1990 and 2000 most colleges and universities were prosperous and had robust enrollments that erased the harsh memories of declining state appropriations and dismal endowment portfolios of 1989. K. Patricia Cross (1981), a pioneering dean of students and renowned researcher, forewarned her colleagues of the presence of a generation of "new learners" and of another constituency, "adults as learners." Developments at the end of the twentieth century reaffirmed her research findings and projections from the 1970s and 1980s. Furthermore, even though parents and institutions enjoyed prosperity in the 1990s, concerns about rising college costs and their subsequent high prices persisted (Ehrenberg, 2000). Vice presidents and deans of student affairs had to face the fact that the services for which they were responsible accounted for a substantial portion of rising college costs. Whatever luxuries American higher education of the 1950s or 1960s claimed, closer inspection finds them modest and frugal in comparison to contemporary expectations with regard to such obvious services as career planning, campus security, residence hall wiring to accommodate computers, health and wellness programs, and numerous new, expanded programs and facilities for students.

By 2000 the certainty and coherence of the undergraduate campus experience had been diffused and diluted. The diversity of students in American higher education eventually influenced the shape and structure of institutions. Also during this time, women became a decisive majority of student enrollments at numerous independent and public institutions. Nowhere was this change reflected more than in the character and composition of women's intercollegiate athletics and other student activities. Despite some gains, it appears that even by 2008 women in coeducational institutions still received less than their fair share of resources and opportunities in all activities. Within the campus at several state universities data indicated that first-generation college students, including women and students of color, participated in student government and campus elections. This participation had resulted in the emergence of new leadership groups among students—and in some cases, signs of decline of the influence of traditionally powerful groups such as fraternities in campus-wide activities. Adults, often placed in the category of "nontraditional students," continued to gain in numbers and as a percentage of enrollments at each and all levels of academic degree programs.

Some women's colleges that had resisted the invitation to adopt coeducation in the 1970s now enjoyed a resurgence of enrollments and revitalization of their special missions and constituencies. Tribal colleges and universities, especially in the far West, gained autonomy and funding after numerous deliberations with state and federal governments. And, Hispanic-serving institutions, which were established under the Higher Education Act of 1965, grew at enormous rates—a reflection of the increasing presence of Latinos in the United States population (Gasman, Baez, & Turner, 2008).

Finally, American consumerism combined with technological advances to provide a generation of students with opportunities to study via distance-learning courses, Internet curricula, "virtual universities," and off-campus sites. Each and all of these could be mixed and matched in conjunction with the traditional residential campus. These innovations led nontraditional students, especially adults, to show inordinate interest in a new segment of postsecondary education—the for-profit education sector. However, because the propriety institutions acquired eligibility for federal student financial aid, combined with their enterprising use of new electronic technologies, they became a substantial force within the ranks of degree-granting institutions nationwide.

Conclusion

Any attempt to present a brief survey of American higher education over four centuries risks superficiality. A good resolution to carry away is to see the history of American colleges and universities less as a compendium of facts and more as a description of the lively process by which each generation of college students, administrators, donors, and legislators has wrestled with the issue of who shall be educated and how. Clark (1970), for example, developed the notion of a "campus saga" to explain how some colleges acquired over time a sense of heritage and mission that they effectively transmit to new students, administrators, faculty members, as well as alumni. Much work remains to be done in order to apply Clark's concept to numerous understudied and unexamined community colleges, colleges, and universities. Intensive case studies of individual institutions are a good way for higher education professionals to make sense of their own experience and campus in terms of preceding generations and national trends.

This issue usually is played out in the media for students and their families with the rhetorical question, "Why does college cost so much?" Although this concern probably refers to all aspects of college and university operations, it has particular significance for this book because of its inordinate presence in the expenses associated with expanding a wide range of student services and support systems. According to a series of reports from the Delta Cost Project sponsored by the American Institutes of Research (AIR) in 2010 and 2012, most colleges and universities in all categories show a steadily increasing problem of various revenue streams not keeping pace with annual expenditures. Usually this means that students have been expected to bear an increasing proportion of this burden, as demonstrated through tuition charges that have risen annually more than various price indices (Desrochers & Wellman, 2010; Hurlburt & Kirshstein, 2012).

College student life and the numerous activities and services associated with it are part of this renegotiation because many of the professionals and services in this broad area cross boundaries. It is not always clear or consistent, for example, whether a study skills center falls under the auspices of an academic dean or, perhaps, is hosted and staffed by the vice president for student affairs. These permutations reflect a growing trend in recent years for the extracurricular activities often to be redefined and renamed as being "cocurricular."

Not surprisingly, most colleges and universities show great and growing concern about those offerings that tend to attract and retain academically able, motivated undergraduates who one hopes will complete their degrees in a timely manner. In fact, luxuries are outliers and even when they take place, they do not explain the larger, more serious question of institutional investment in learning—and where money comes from and then where money goes. A more thoughtful analysis comes from Scott Carlson, a feature writer for *The Chronicle of Higher Education,* whose summer 2014 lengthy analysis of spending on student services provides genuine insights into the prospects and problems many colleges face—and will continue to face in the twenty-first century.

Carlson (2014) found that the keen competition to increase the number of applications and then to enroll students has had a differential impact on a particular group of institutions, namely, those that are located in geographically isolated areas and that tend not to have the great financial and historic reservoirs of reputation in trying to attract good students. Translated into budgetary terms and decisions, this means that spending on a student center, recreation center, career planning office, and offering a generous slate of varsity teams is seen as an imperative. It means that residence life cannot run the risk of offering the austerity and obsolete technology of decades-old dormitories.

Hence, at every turn, the well-intentioned race to remain attractive and competitive tends to drive up spending—especially in student services and facilities. This is going to be the widespread situation facing colleges and universities—a peculiar, particular legacy of consumerism in the present and future era of highly sophisticated and high expectations, which students—and their parents—bring to the central matter of college choice. A college's decision to provide more services and facilities for students also raises the difficult question of whether such innovations are enhancing a college experience or simply making students more comfortable and entitled (Hoover, 2014).

The sobering, undeniable fact of institutional life is that it is a situation that most likely will increase the chasm between "haves" and "have-nots" among colleges and universities in an arms race that does not always acknowledge let alone reward the thoughtfulness and dedication of faculty and staff members to teaching and learning for students. This is a living tradition that truly connects past and present in American higher education's perennial quest to attract and serve students.

Discussion Questions

Identify a college or university with which you have had first-hand experience. It could be your undergraduate alma mater, perhaps your graduate school, or a campus where you have worked.

1. How does this living history shape the organizational life and culture in the present?
2. How might the campus saga be revised and reconsidered over time?
3. What are the distinctive legends and heroic events from the past that have helped shape or define this campus today to create its institutional saga?

References

Adams, H. (1918). *The education of Henry Adams: An autobiography.* Boston: Houghton Mifflin.

Axtell, J. (1974). *The school on a hill: Education and society in colonial New England.* New Haven, CT: Yale University Press.

Brint, S., & Karabel, J. (1989). *The diverted dream: Community colleges and the promise of educational opportunity in America, 1900–1985*. New York: Oxford University Press.

Burke, C. B. (1982). *American collegiate populations: A test of the traditional view*. New York: New York University Press.

Canby, H. S. (1936). *Alma mater: The gothic age of the American university*. New York: Farrar and Strauss.

Carlson, S. (2014). Spending shifts as colleges compete on students' comfort. *The Chronicle of Higher Education* (August 1), 20–23.

Clark, B. R. (1970). *The distinctive college: Antioch, Swarthmore, & Reed*. Chicago: Aldine.

Cross, K. P. (1981). *Adults as learners*. San Francisco: Jossey-Bass.

Cuban, L. (1999). *How scholars trumped teachers: Change without reform in university curriculum, teaching and research, 1890–1990*. New York: Columbia University, Teachers College Press.

Desrochers, D. M., & Wellman, J. V. (2010). *Trends in college spending, 1999–2009: Where does the money come from? Where does it go? What does it buy?* Washington, DC: Delta Cost Project of the American Institutes for Research.

Diener, T. (1986). *Growth of an American invention: A documentary history of the junior and community college movement*. New York: Greenwood Press.

Drewry, H. N., & Doermann, H. (2001). *Stand and prosper: Private black colleges and their students*. Princeton, NJ: Princeton University Press.

Ehrenberg, R. G. (2000). *Tuition rising: Why college costs so much*. Cambridge, MA: Harvard University Press.

Franklin, B. (1784). *Remarks concerning the savages of North America*. London.

Freeland, R. (1992). *Academia's golden age: Universities in Massachusetts, 1945–1970*. New York: Oxford University Press.

Gasman, M., Baez, B., & Turner, C. S. (2008). *Understanding minority-serving institutions*. Albany: State University of New York Press.

Gordon, L. (1990). *Gender and higher education in the progressive era*. New Haven, CT: Yale University Press.

Handlin, O., & Handlin, M. (1974). *The American college and American culture*. New York: McGraw-Hill.

Haskins, C. H. (1923). *The rise of the universities*. Ithaca, NY: Cornell University Press.

Hoover, E. (2014). The comfortable kid: Colleges walk a fine line between empowerment and entitlement. *The Chronicle of Higher Education* (August 1), 16–19.

Horowitz, H. L. (1984). *Alma mater: Design and experience in the women's colleges from their 19th century beginnings to the 1930s*. New York: Knopf.

Horowitz, H. L. (1987). *Campus life: Undergraduate cultures from the end of the eighteenth century to the present*. New York: Knopf.

Hurlburt, S., & Kirshstein, R. J. (2012). *Spending: Where does the money go? A Delta data update 2000–2010*. Washington, DC: AIR.

Jencks, C., & Riesman, D. (1968). *The academic revolution*. New York: Doubleday.

Jenkins, S. (2007). *The real all Americans: The team that changed a game, a people, a nation*. New York: Doubleday.

Karabel, J. (2005). *The chosen: The hidden history of exclusion at Harvard, Yale, and Princeton*. New York: Houghton Mifflin.

Kerr, C. (1964). *The uses of the university*. Cambridge, MA: Harvard University Press.

Lehman, N. (2000). *The big test: The secret history of American meritocracy*. New York: Farrar, Straus, and Giroux.

Levine, D. (1986). *The American college and the culture of aspiration, 1915–1940*. Ithaca, NY: Cornell University Press.

National Commission on Excellence in Education. (1983). *A nation at risk: The imperative for educational reform*. Washington, DC: US Government Printing Office.

Rudolph, F. (1962). *The American college and university: A history*. New York: Knopf.

Slosson, E. E. (1910). *Great American universities*. New York: Macmillan.

Study Group on the Conditions of Excellence in American Higher Education. (1984). *Involvement in learning: Realizing the potential of American higher education; Final report*. Washington, DC: National Institute of Education.

Synnott, M. G. (1979). *The half-opened door: Discrimination and admissions at Harvard, Yale, and Princeton, 1900–1970*. Westport, CT: Greenwood Press.

Trow, M. (1970). Reflections on the transition from elite to mass to universal higher education. *Daedalus, 99*, 1–42.

Veysey, L. R. (1965). *The emergence of the American university*. Chicago: University of Chicago Press.

Wingspread Group on Higher Education. (1993). *An American imperative: Higher expectations for higher education*. Racine, WI: Johnson Foundation.

Wright, S. (1988). Black colleges and universities: Historical background and future prospects. *Virginia Humanities, 14*, 1–7.

CHAPTER 2

THE HISTORY OF STUDENT AFFAIRS

Robert Schwartz and Dafina-Lazarus Stewart

As you have seen from chapter 1 on the history of higher education by John R. Thelin and Marybeth Gasman, the creation of colonial colleges in the northeastern section of what would become the United States of America occurred early in our history. The history of student affairs begins much later, not until the late 1800s by most accounts. Regardless, the history of the field now known as "student affairs" is a lively and fascinating story. We hope you read about our shared history with the same excitement we had in writing it.

Era of Paternalism: 1636 to 1850

As described in chapter 1, the early creation of Harvard in 1636 and the eight "colonial" colleges established before the Revolutionary War occurred was an important starting point for higher education. However, in reality, it was a very small start. The early colleges were tightly connected to religious groups and were primarily intended for the education of new ministers in the colonies. A very small number of men attended these colleges and the size of both faculty and student body was quite limited. As an example, between 1636 and 1689 Harvard College produced 368 graduates, a small number by today's standards but quite a few in the 1600s (http://library.harvard.edu/university-archives/using-the-collections/homepage). After the Civil War, colleges remained quite small and most students were white and male. There are exceptions, such as Lincoln and Cheyney, colleges that admitted African American men, as well as Oberlin in Ohio, where women were admitted but to a different academic track than men (Rudolph, 1990). Most colleges were run by the faculty members and often had strong ties to a religious denomination. Strict rules and regulations governed student conduct, and bad behavior often resulted in dismissal (Moore, 1976; Rudolph, 1990).

After the Civil War, women's higher education began to grow but slowly. Several women's colleges were established in the Northeast, and the best known was a group known as the "Seven Sisters" because of their proximity to each other. However, the oldest women's college is Wesleyan College in Macon, Georgia, chartered in 1836 (http://www.wesleyancollege.edu/about/). As the enrollment of women expanded, women's enrollments increased steadily. At the same time, the creation of new state colleges funded by the Morrill Acts of 1862 and 1890 accelerated enrollments significantly. New colleges in the Midwest were often coeducational, admitting women and men and prompting, in many cases, the need for greater oversight of the student population, especially the women students (Solomon, 1985).

Era of College Life: 1850 to 1913

For a long time after the establishment of Harvard in 1636 and the early colonial colleges, women were not permitted to attend college. It was not until after the Civil War had ended in 1864 that women in significant numbers were able to seek out a higher education. There were exceptions, such as Oberlin College, but in general, women's higher education opportunities did not exist.

Deans of Women

The first professionals to embrace the fundamental tenets of what would later become "student affairs" were women faculty members at several colleges and universities in the Middle West (Midwest) and Eastern United States. Nidiffer (2001) cites "lady principals" and "matrons" at several colleges in the middle of the nineteenth century; however, one of the earliest, if not the first, woman to be named officially as a dean of women was Alice Freeman Palmer, who held that position at the newly opened University of Chicago in 1892. She was hired by the university president, William Rainey Harper who wanted a woman of "national significance" to be in place when he opened the university as a coeducational institution. Palmer was dean of women and professor of history at Chicago (Schwartz, 1997).

Alice Freeman had attended the University of Michigan, personally admitted by president James Angell, one of a few university presidents who supported women's higher education. After graduating from Michigan, Freeman became a history professor at Wellesley College in Massachusetts in 1879 (Bordin, 1993). Freeman quickly enamored herself among the female undergraduates and many of the female faculty members at Wellesley so when the presidency opened in 1881, the Durant family, who had endowed Wellesley from its inception, hired Freeman as their new president. She "reigned supreme" for several years, introducing the "cottage system" to enable the young women to create "home-like" spaces for residential living and close friendships. She was a model of female leadership and integrity whose reputation spread quickly as she led Wellesley to be a premiere women's institution (Solomon, 1985).

A single woman for much of her adult life, Alice Freeman met Harvard philosophy professor, George Herbert Palmer at a friend's home in Boston in 1887 (Palmer, 1908). Palmer pursued Freeman vigorously and they married in 1889. As a married woman, Palmer was not expected to work outside the home, and she resigned her position as president of Wellesley. As a very active and self-sufficient woman, it is not surprising that Palmer was lured to Chicago by president Harper in 1892 to be an engaged academic again. Even so, she only agreed to take the position if she could return from Chicago to Boston on a regular basis to maintain her marriage. Harper agreed to these terms and Palmer moved to Chicago on a part-time basis. To assist in her supervision of the women undergraduates at the University of Chicago, Palmer persuaded Harper to hire Marion Talbot as her assistant. Palmer and Talbot had become close friends through their work in the Association of Collegiate Alumnae, a group of women in Boston who lobbied hard for the admission of women to college.

Marion Talbot came to Chicago as Assistant Dean of Women and Assistant Professor of Household Sanitation, an early version of home economics with a heavy emphasis on sciences, such as chemistry and physics. Talbot became the dean of women herself when, after three years in Chicago, Palmer resigned and moved back to Boston permanently (Schwartz, 1998). To collaborate with other deans of women, Talbot organized several meetings with such women in Chicago, the earliest occurring in 1901 and followed by another in 1903 (Gerda, 2004). At these meetings, the assembled deans shared concerns, policies, handbooks, and the latest developments on their respective campuses. Women attended from a variety of other institutions, from nearby states such as Wisconsin and as far away as New York. Many deans of women would travel by train to the annual meetings of the Association of Collegiate Alumnae (ACA), often arranging to ride on the same train to extend their time together. By 1916, the deans of women announced the formation of a professional association, the National Association of Deans of Women (NADW) in 1916.

Many deans of women would use their summers to travel to Teachers College, Columbia University in New York to further their educations. Although many deans had been faculty members prior to their administrative positions, others had not advanced beyond an undergraduate degree. Many deans believed a graduate education was critical. A number of deans lobbied Teachers College professor Paul Monroe for course work directly related to their work. He obliged by creating a department for deans of women (Schwartz, 1997). In the 1920s, the NADW quickly moved to establish its own journal that published studies and reports on their work (Nidiffer, 2000).

Deans of Men

This section examines the deans of men and their organizations: National Association of Deans of Men (NADM) to National Association of Deans and Advisors to Men (NADAM) to Student Affairs Administrators in Higher Education (formerly the National Association of Student Personnel Administrators; NASPA).

Unlike the deans of women, deans of men were not created to be "champions" for college men as the deans of women were for female undergraduates. In many respects, the deans of men were created in response to the deans of women. A key role for the deans of men was to alleviate the growing burden placed on college and university presidents by a rapidly increasing undergraduate population of young men. As the number of colleges expanded in the years following the Civil War, so did the number of new students. In the Midwest, in particular, many students came from farms or small towns. The land-grant universities created by the Morrill Acts of 1862 and 1890 provided states money in the form of land grants to build new or expand existing public institutions. Land-grant institutions were required to teach agriculture and related arts necessary for farming as well as training young men for service in the militia, comparable to the modern Reserve Officer Training Corps (ROTC). So although young men were eager to leave the farm, in college, they often faced a regimented life-style of book learning, constant supervision by the faculty members, and military training on a regular basis. Many young men, eager to embrace college, often found the rules and regulation confining and sought out any opportunity to buck the system.

By general consensus, one of, if not the first, official dean of men was Thomas Arkle Clark at the University of Illinois. (Clark himself attributed the title of "first" to a dean at the University of Oregon appointed in 1890.) Clark had attended Illinois as an undergraduate although he was considerably older by the time he began his college career. Orphaned at an early age and raised on a farm in central Illinois, Clark was committed to a college career and, similar to many other young men of the time, was determined to get off the family farm. After graduation from Illinois, he worked as a high school teacher and principal in a rough neighborhood near Urbana, Illinois, for two years. Eager to return to the university, he was hired to teach rhetoric and lower-level English classes.

Clark had a gift for working with difficult young men and often befriended them in his classes. Soon the university president, hearing of Clark's successes with recalcitrant youth, asked him to take on the son of a university benefactor. The young man was at the university to play baseball and enjoy himself, which did not include going to classes. At President Draper's direction, Clark kept the young man on the straight and narrow enough to avoid failing out of the university. Impressed, President Draper made Clark his assistant and moved Clark to a small office in the administration building in 1901.Within a few years, Clark was given the official title of "Dean of Men" in 1909 (Schwartz, 2010).

Clark quickly began to assemble what some called his "empire" because he was granted a great deal of latitude by a succession of Illinois presidents. Clark was an older initiate into Alpha Tau Omega fraternity and the experience convinced him that fraternities were a boon, not a bane, to deans of men. During his time as dean of men at Illinois, the fraternity system became one of the largest in the country and Clark himself was lauded by the National

Interfraternity Council and many alumni, including many wealthy and powerful men (Schwartz, 2010).

Clark expanded his roles broadly on campus including a campus clinic and organized many events and activities. He wrote newspaper columns in the student paper and gave radio addresses on the college radio station. Decades ahead of his time, Clark was well aware of the power of social media and its influence on students, so he used it to his advantage. Clark also became notorious among the students at Illinois for his "network of spies." To students, Dean Clark often seemed to know about mischief even before it happened. Many young men who violated the campus rules about drinking, driving automobiles, missing classes, gambling, or the like often found themselves on the "green carpet" in Clark's office. The worst offenders were escorted personally to the railroad station by Clark after expulsion from the university. Clark even authored books on the topic of being a dean of men, using such provocative titles as *Discipline and the Derelict* (1922).

As his reputation grew, Clark became known to his peers as "the dean of deans." As a pioneer, other deans of men sought his advice and sponsorship. In 1918, Scott Goodnight, dean of men at the University of Wisconsin, called for a meeting of the "big ten" deans about student conduct at athletic events. Goodnight hosted a meeting in January, 1918, in Madison, Wisconsin. Eight other deans attended, including Clark. Over two days, the assembled deans shared their stories and discussed rules and campus conduct. At the end of their meeting, they decided to meet again the following year in Champaign-Urbana on the Illinois campus. At this second meeting, the deans declared themselves to be the National Association of Deans of Men (NADM) and made Dean Clark their first president.

Walter Dill Scott and the "Student Personnel" Movement: 1914 to 1945

Although the deans of women and deans of men emerged slowly on their respective campuses, at Northwestern University, a different approach to student life emerged. The personnel movement, an effort driven by the use of the new social science of psychology, was the brainchild of Walter Dill Scott. Scott, similar to Thomas Arkle Clark, was an Illinois farm boy who had been raised in the rural countryside. Eager to escape the farm, Scott and his brother had made a pact to go to college and become teachers. Scott studied hard in high school and later accepted a scholarship to attend Northwestern University in Chicago in 1891 (Scott Hall Committee, 1939). He graduated from Northwestern and soon headed to Germany to pursue a doctoral degree in psychology with Wilhelm Wundt, an international scholar. Wundt was a pioneer in the development and application of behavioral psychology and saw learning as a conditioned response to the environment (Kim, 2006). Scott earned his PhD in educational administration and psychology under Wundt at the University of Leipzig.

After earning his doctorate, Scott returned to the United States and began teaching at Northwestern in 1902. He moved quickly through the ranks and was promoted to full professor in 1907. He authored two books, *Theory of Advertising* in 1903 and the *Psychology of Advertising* in 1908. In 1916, Scott was granted a leave of absence to work as the director of the Bureau of Salesmanship at the Carnegie Institute of Technology. He studied the psychology of salesmanship and applied psychological tests and measurements to business (Scott Hall Committee, 1939).

When World War I broke out, Scott offered to help the US Army with officer training and personnel classification. Initially rejected, Scott was allowed to try his system at Fort Myers in New Jersey. After great success, the Scott system was applied to officer training in many settings. Scott was so successful that the Army awarded him the Distinguished Service Medal in 1919 (Scott Hall Committee, 1939).

After the war, in February 1919, Scott and several army associates founded the Scott Company, Engineers and Consultants in Industrial Personnel with offices in several major US cities—a highly successful consulting firm (Ferguson, 1976). Scott and Robert Clothier (1923) saw the primary goal of their work as linking employee efficiency and satisfaction with management methods focusing on the individual (Biddix & Schwartz, 2012). In 1920, Scott was elected president of the American Psychological Association (APA). In the same year, his alma mater, Northwestern, asked him to become their president. Scott accepted both offers and began to reorganize the university campus that was desperate for leadership. When it came to student life, Scott saw an opportunity to apply his ideas from personnel psychology to higher education. It was clear to him that the same ideas and methods he had used so successfully in businesses, factories, and the US Army could also work on the college campus with students.

Scott's faith in the benefits of industrial psychology led him to reorganize the administrative staff at Northwestern to serve student needs. He dismissed the dean of men and the dean of women and replaced them with a campus personnel office. The personnel office would address enrollment management issues, help increase student satisfaction through the assessment of student needs, and even aid in the job placement of students after graduation (Biddix & Schwartz, 2012).

The personnel office staff members began their work by introducing the key steps in the personnel psychology approach—interviewing and classifying all the new students on campus. Scott and L. B. Hopkins also instituted an individual record, known as an "appointment card" for each new freshman student. Detailed information on each student was gathered and students were interviewed each year as they progressed at Northwestern. A staff member would meet with each student to inquire about each student's work, social activities, family characteristics, and other key elements of the student's background. The four key elements of personnel work were an interest in individuals; an appreciation of the methods of science, as opposed to unsupported personal convictions, feelings, or class prejudices; utilization of scientific methods and scientific knowledge in personnel pursuit; and the coordination of the work of all agencies within the institution participating in either personnel service or personnel research or both, so that service and research in the institution may not proceed on divergent paths, but rather work in a reciprocal relationship. (Lloyd-Jones, 1929, p. 19)

In campus interviews (Fry, c.a. 1924) and in articles (Hopkins, 1924), Scott's protégé, described the personnel office as a way of taking a "personal point of view" to help a large university operate like a smaller one in its individualized treatment of students. A 1926 pamphlet listed the motto of the personnel department on its cover: "Before all else . . . the individual, his welfare, his opportunity for self-development" (Scott, Northwestern Personnel Department brochure).

One missing element Scott and Hopkins noted was the lack of women on the staff who might better address the needs and interests of female students. Hopkins identified a young undergraduate, Esther McDonald, who had expressed strong interest in psychology and the personnel psychology of Hopkins and Scott in particular. McDonald had been an active undergraduate and an outstanding student at Northwestern. She understood the importance of connecting the student with the institution through not only academics but also student activities. After her graduation, McDonald was appointed to be the personnel department's first assistant director for women. She also arranged to complete her master's degree while serving in the personnel office. McDonald, better known to contemporary audiences as Esther (McDonald) Lloyd-Jones, served in her new position for two years, 1924–1926, before leaving to earn her doctorate and teach at Teachers College, Columbia. Her experiences at Northwestern eventually led to her dissertation, "Student Personnel Work at Northwestern University," the first comprehensive work on campus student personnel services published in 1929.

The work in the personnel office intentionally connected students with careers at graduation. Consequently, staff members in the personnel offices at Northwestern were known as "appointment secretaries" because many of the early workers in the areas were also women. Soon the appointment secretaries formed their own professional organization, the National Association of Appointment Secretaries (NAAS) in 1924. The NAAS later became the American College Personnel Association (ACPA), the name of the organization, ACPA, reflecting the work and the personnel movement created by Scott and his contemporaries. As the personnel movement spread to other campuses, the movement took on the term *student* and became known as the "student personnel movement."

All of these groups, the National Association of Deans of Women, the National Association of Deans of Men, and the Association of College Personnel Association, were represented as the country moved to a peak of college attendance in the 1920s. At the same time, historically black colleges had added deans to attend to their students as well. But often, the African American deans of men and women did not find common ground with their white counterparts. Some, such as Dean Lucy Sloan Diggs at Howard University, helped create separate organizations for black deans. It should be noted that Dean Sloan earned her master's degree at Teachers College and had a strong affiliation with the NADW in the 1930s (Solomon, 1985).

As colleges expanded and the numbers of men and women in college rose, the interest in college students became more pronounced. Some of the most focused attention came from the newly created American Council on Education, better known as the ACE. The ACE was headed from 1934 to 1951 by George Zook, former president of the University of Akron. In 1936, Zook organized a committee to examine students in higher education from a psychological perspective, following the same lines suggested earlier by Walter Dill Scott and his protégés. The committee published a monograph in 1937 appropriately titled, *The Student Personnel Point of View* (SPPV), which directed college presidents and others to pay particular attention to the experiences and needs of college students. This national prescription for working more intentionally with students has often been seen as the beginning of the modern student affairs profession because it outlined many of the key principles of the field.

Although the student personnel movement received a boost with the publication of the SPPV, much of the momentum for the movement was limited because the Great Depression that had begun in 1929 lingered and dramatically limited college attendance. Many federal programs were created to combat the economic problems of the country, but in reality, it was not until the United States entered World War II in December 1941 after the Japanese attack at Pearl Harbor in Hawaii that the United States began to move out of the Depression (Thelin, 2011).

Golden Age of Higher Education: 1945 to 1970

When the war ended in the mid-1940s, President Truman created a commission to study the economic status of the United States. The president's commission warned Truman that the country must return to a "peace-time" economy very slowly to avoid a second Great Depression. One way to slow the labor demands of returning veterans was to create government funding to encourage veterans of WWII to seek additional education including high school, college, or vocational training to become plumbers, electricians, or truck drivers. To incentivize the effort, the government would offer military veterans a monetary supplement to further their education.

The Serviceman's Readjustment Act of 1944, better known as the GI Bill, was very successful as shown by the fact that more than 2.2 million veterans had used the GI Bill to attend a college or university by 1956 (Thelin, 2011). The demand for college created a huge number of new students at existing colleges and universities. Many institutions doubled or tripled in size within a few years. Many states began authorizing new campuses and the access to higher education grew rapidly.

The huge numbers of new students created new demands for student services on college and university campuses as well. Accordingly, the number of student affairs workers grew as well. Because many, if not most, of the new students were men, the demand for more deans of men grew as did the need for more financial aid, housing, and other services. The deans of women, however, were not as necessary. Although women still attended colleges, their numbers declined rapidly. In turn, the numbers of deans of women began decline as well. More men were assigned to positions as deans of students or vice presidents for student personnel services. Even though many of the women serving as deans of women were often equally, if not better, prepared, they did not get promoted if a man was available (Schwartz, 1997).

In concert with this surge of new professionals, the deans of men voted in 1951 to change their association's name to the National Association of Student Personnel Administrators and to drop the term *deans of men* from their name. The deans of women maintained their association as the National Association of Deans of Women but later changed to the National Association of Women Deans, Administrators, and Counselors (NAWDAC), and much later, to NAWE, the National Association of Women in Education. Women joined the ranks of ACPA and then NASPA over time. As a result, the NAWE as an association ceased to exist altogether in 2000.

Because these changes occurred during the postwar period from the 1940s to the 1950s and beyond, the nature of student personnel work evolved into the more contemporary concept of student affairs. The expansion of responsibility for anyone in the field moved away from discipline and management of student behavior to all aspects of student life, such as financial aid and assistance, residence halls including design as well as supervision of student on-campus and off-campus housing, student activities, Greek life, career planning and placement, and more. One unintended or unanticipated outcome of the GI Bill was that the returning veterans were also incentivized to marry and have children. The government subsidies offered low-cost mortgages and provided additional monies to those who married and for every child produced as well.

The social phenomenon now known as the "baby boom" emerged in the postwar years as a direct result of government subsidies in the GI Bill to veterans to marry and have children. As those children grew, so did the demands on the educational system, starting with kindergartens and elementary education. By the 1960s, many of those children were ready for college and created an unprecedented demand for higher education. The boomers brought with them even greater demands for student affairs professionals. At the same time, the unpopular war in Vietnam and the civil rights movement were rising in social awareness. So it was that the baby boomers arrived on campuses with, at the least, three major social issues to confront: a war and the military draft for young men and the integration of American society by African Americans and others. The confluence of all of these issues occurred for many young people on the college campus.

Era of Consumerism: 1970 to 1995

As the protests over the Vietnam War and civil rights began to wane on some college campuses (Altbach, 1979), students' rights and expectations of colleges and universities began to take center stage. This era, beginning in the early 1970s and continuing into the mid-1990s, was highlighted by the passage of several pieces of legislation and the publication of documents outlining the roles and responsibilities of student affairs professionals (Evans & Reason, 2001), which centered on higher education's social responsibilities to its students. However, another impact of this era was the assertion of the managerial role of student affairs administrators and calls to professionalize the field.

Key Federal Laws and Judicial Decisions in the 1970s

Significant pieces of federal legislation and judicial decisions were passed and decided during this period that confirmed the status of students as their own agents, conclusively ending in loco parentis, set in motion by the decision against the university in *Dixon* v. *Alabama*. Many of these came in quick succession between 1972 and 1974.

The first of these laws was Title IX of the Educational Amendments passed in 1972. Title IX made it a violation of federal law for any educational institution receiving federal dollars to discriminate on the basis of sex in educational programs. Although the effects of Title IX have focused mainly on intercollegiate athletics over time, the bill's supporters and initiators were primarily concerned about women's access to academic programs and majors traditionally thought to be inappropriate for women to perform (for example, business and economics; science, technology, engineering, and mathematics [STEM] fields).

Allowing women equal access to any and all educational programs at co-educational institutions required that faculty members and administrators had the authority to steer particular students away from majors and fields deemed inappropriate for them based on patriarchal ideas about a woman's place. Systems and processes were instituted to oversee institutional compliance. Title IX coordinators and women's centers were created to serve in this role.

In the following year, 1973, Section 504 of the Rehabilitation Act was passed. This legislation demanded access for students with disabilities to education at all levels. Educational institutions were required to provide access to a quality education to students regardless of disability if students met the qualifications for admission. Section 504 also required the provision of accommodations for students so that their disability was not a deterrent to their success. Again, the needs of students seeking higher education trumped the barriers imposed by higher education institutions. Student affairs added offices of disability services as colleges and universities sought administrative means for complying with these new legal obligations to students. In 1990, the rights of people with disabilities would be extended under the Americans with

Disabilities Act (ADA). The ADA provided a legal definition for disability, extending rights to employees and students, thus putting freedom from discrimination on the basis of one's abilities on par with other civil rights legislation.

In 1974, the addition of the Buckley Amendment to the legislation, now known as the Family Educational Rights and Privacy Act (FERPA), would round out this era's legislative entrance. In conjunction with the 1971 ratification of the Twenty-Sixth Amendment to the US Constitution that lowered the age of enfranchisement to eighteen years old, the Buckley Amendment changed the age of majority for students from twenty-one to eighteen years old. This change effectively gave the vast majority of college students in the nation control over their educational records, including the right to withhold access from their parents. When institutional officials, particularly regarding student conduct and academic advising, may have been holding on to the last threads of in loco parentis, the Buckley Amendment completed the decimation of institutional paternalism set in motion by the court's decision in *Dixon*. Students now became consumers of their education and had the right to make certain demands of their educational institutions.

Federal legislation also served to widen access and bolster student choice during this decade. Originally passed in 1965, the Higher Education Act was amended in the early 1970s to include the Basic Educational Opportunity Grants program, which would later become known as the Pell Grants (Russo & Coomes, 2000). This grant was designed to be portable and follow students to the institutions they chose to attend (Russo & Coomes, 2000). With the availability of portable federal financial aid, college became accessible to many more students from low-income families, especially in the expanding community colleges.

In 1978, the US Supreme Court again transformed higher education regarding access and diversity. The five-to-four decision written by Justice Powell in *The Regents of the University of California* v. *Bakke* upheld the use of affirmative action in college admissions as educationally beneficial for the student body and mission of the institution, but it rejected the use of racial quotas to do so. Although the decision in *Bakke* found the University of California to be inappropriately applying federally mandated affirmative action, the Court opened the door for other highly selective institutions to implement affirmative action in admissions decisions. As a result, access to the elite tier of higher education to white women and members of underrepresented racial and ethnic groups was ceded. In response, colleges and universities had to create another set of offices and services to promote access and retention of women of all races and racially marginalized students across genders.

As students' rights and needs were validated by these new laws, particularly for underrepresented student populations, higher education and student affairs realized the need to redefine itself. Student affairs professionals were increasingly required to provide more services to increasingly diverse populations of students including offices of minority or multicultural affairs, disability services, women's centers, and so on. They were also expected to coordinate student activities beyond the classroom. To guide this expanding set of new responsibilities, new philosophical statements and guiding documents were published that reset the course of higher education and student affairs (Evans & Reason, 2001).

Student Affairs Documents

Three significant documents that laid out the guiding principles of student affairs as a profession were published in 1975: the Council of Student Personnel Associations in Higher Education (COSPA) publications *Student Development Services in Postsecondary Education, Tomorrow's Higher Education (T.H.E.) Phase II: A Student Development Model for Student Affairs,* and *The Future of Student Affairs.* These three documents ushered in the student development movement in student affairs, recommitting the profession to many of the foundational ideas and values that were first articulated in *The Student Personnel Point of View* (American Council on Education [ACE], 1937, 1949). Among these ideas were the fundamental value and dignity of each student as human beings, the development of the whole student, and the need for strong research and assessment to support the practice of student affairs practitioners (Evans & Reason, 2001).

In a related development, the Council for the Advancement of Standards for Student Services (CAS) was founded in 1979 with the mission to begin to codify and document effective practices in student services across colleges and universities. These discussions led to the first set of professional standards being published in 1986. Sixteen functional areas were included in the first edition of what would become the *CAS Standards* (Council for the Advancement of Standards, 2014). These standards, as well as processes and protocols for the review of student affairs programs, continued to professionalize the field (Carpenter & Stimson, 2007). The rapid growth of graduate-level preparation programs across the nation during the previous era (sixty-four programs began between 1945 and 1963) brought the total to ninety-one; Ewing & Stickler, 1964; Kruempel, 1990). A new professional literature of theories and models of learning, development, and persistence further confirmed the development of student affairs as a professional field.

Midway through the era, *A Nation at Risk* (National Commission on Excellence in Education, 1983) was authored by the Secretary of Education T. H. Bell. A conservative polemic, it quickly became a rallying cry for those dismayed by the sweeping changes in higher education resulting from the activism of the 1960s and the legislative actions of the 1970s. *A Nation at Risk* bemoaned the decline in student performance in standardized tests compared to students in other countries as well as decried the effects of multiculturalism and efforts to diversify the curriculum. *A Nation at Risk* called for a return to a common core of knowledge and the recentering of education for democracy, capitalism, and US exceptionalism. Soon after the publication of *A Nation at Risk,* Lynne Cheney led the publication of a report of a national commission, *50 Hours: A Core Curriculum for College Students* (Cheney, 1989). *50 Hours* argued for centering study on the achievements of the United States and Western Europe and emphasizing prescription over election in the core curriculum.

These two publications, *Nation at Risk* and *50 Hours*, challenged the values of diversity, multiculturalism, and inclusion that student affairs professionals had begun to assert and emphasize in their guiding documents of the period. These arguments also questioned the validity and necessity for the growing cadre of administrators, including student affairs professionals, on college and university campuses, while faculty ranks showed much slower growth (for example, National Association of Scholars, 2008).

Era of Student Learning: 1994 to 2010

Coomes and Wilson (2009) posit that the era of student learning took hold with the publication of ACPA's *Student Learning Imperative* in 1994. This document, as well as NASPA's *Learning Reconsidered* (2004) a decade later, sought to establish the centrality of student affairs professionals as educational partners with faculty members in promoting student learning on campus. These documents redefined learning to include the holistic development and growth of students inside and outside the classroom. Although this idea was contested by some faculty members (for example, National Association of Scholars, 2008), student affairs professionals asserted themselves as equal partners with faculty members and as contributors to the academic mission of colleges and universities.

Between the publications of the *Student Learning Imperative* (ACPA, 1994) and *Learning Reconsidered* (ACPA & NASPA, 2004), ACPA produced the *Principles of Good Practice for Student Affairs* (1998). In this document, the leading national associations for student affairs professionals outlined the general characteristics of effective practice in student affairs. Among the principles emphasized were to engage students in active learning, help students develop and clearly articulate their ethical values, encourage partnerships to advance student learning, and to use systematic inquiry to improve practice (ACPA, 1998). These ideas confirmed the stance taken in the *Student Learning Imperative*, which would be further enunciated in *Learning Reconsidered*.

Student affairs sought to align itself with the academic mission of higher education, instead of as "those people who plan parties and order pizza." The image of student affairs as cheerleaders and high-energy extraverts was replaced by a more serious approach to and engagement with the core mission of the academy—the education of students. In so doing, student affairs professionals and their publications considered how to better engage faculty members and get them to understand the purpose and value of student affairs for a liberal education (Coomes & Wilson, 2009). Defending the validity of student affairs' contributions to student learning was sometimes central (for example, Coomes & Wilson, 2009). Some student affairs scholars identified the conflict in professional values and socialization between faculty members and student affairs professionals (for example, Kuh, Shedd, & Whitt, 1987). Later scholars would encourage student affairs professionals to assert their expertise and enter conversations about faculty members and student affairs collaborations as equals (see Magolda, 2005).

As ACPA and NASPA continued to gain strength, the National Association for Women in Education (NAWE) closed its doors in 2000. Having grown out of the NADW, but now facing declining membership and attendance at its annual meetings, NAWE leaders considered that women no longer felt the need for an association devoted to their interests. Moreover, ACPA and NASPA had promoted the needs and interests of women in student affairs through the Standing Committee for Women and Women in Student Affairs, respectively. The most significant initiatives sponsored by NAWE found new homes in the other associations. For example, NAWE's quarterly journal *Initiatives* was taken on by NASPA as a biennial publication renamed as the *Journal about Women in Higher Education.*

Era of Professionalism: 2010 to the Present

Coomes and Wilson's (2009) eras end with identifying the era of student learning. We propose that student affairs since has entered another era. The joint publication by ACPA and NASPA of *Professional Competency Areas for Student Affairs Practitioners* (2010) marks a shift in focus from student affairs professionals' role in student learning and development to the status and accountability of the profession.

The era of professionalism currently reflects the profession's response to the adjustment and accountability that has affected much of higher education from the 1970s to the 2000s (Thelin, 2011; Thelin & Gasman, 2011) as well as recent calls for greater financial accountability as college costs skyrocketed. According to data reported in the *Digest of Education Statistics* (National Center for Education Statistics [NCES], 2015), the number of executive, administrative, and managerial employees as a group has increased by 57 percent between 2001 and 2011; faculty member ranks have also swelled during this period but only by 36.9 percent). Moreover, expenditures of public and private nonprofit higher education institutions on student services, as categorized by the NCES, have also steadily increased by 29.1 percent in public postsecondary institutions between 2006–2007 and 2012–2013, and by 71.9 percent in private nonprofit institutions during that same period. Calls for greater efficiency and production have pushed student affairs to focus more heavily on outcomes-based assessments in light of this increasing institutional financial investment, led by quantitative methodologies.

A greater focus on assessment is not limited to effectiveness in promoting student learning and development through interaction with student affairs cocurricular initiatives. Assessing student affairs professionals' own growth and development of knowledge, awareness, and skills necessary for effectiveness also took center stage. The professional competencies published by ACPA and NASPA (2010) have been incorporated by many graduate programs as capstone projects by which students self-assess their competence in each area. The competencies are now used consistently by both associations to build their annual convention and meeting programs.

As student affairs accumulated more of the evidence of a full-fledged profession (Carpenter & Stimson, 2007), discussions have emerged about the benefits and drawbacks of licensure and formal certification for student affairs professionals. These discussions are intimately connected to graduate-level preparation for careers in the field. To date, access to careers in student affairs has never been restricted to one avenue (Blimling, 2001). Entry-level opportunities for new professionals remain available, particularly at smaller institutions, and are often concentrated in residence life, admissions, and academic advising areas. Nevertheless, as knowledge of the canon of student affairs professional literature becomes increasingly required for professionals in the field, initial and continued graduate preparation for entry-level as well as mid- to senior-level professionals has been asserted, affirmed, and challenged.

Rifts within the profession have been manifested in other ways as well. Increased scrutiny on budgets across the academy and continued duplication of professional development activities have generated discussions about consolidating the two national associations, ACPA and NASPA, into one overarching association. The argument that such a consolidation would enable greater coherence inside and beyond the profession was promoted. Strategies to reconcile the different organizational styles and structures of the two associations were developed and presented, and many discussions were conducted by association leaders with members of both associations over an eighteen-month period. In a historic vote in 2009 that evidenced what appeared to be irreconcilable differences between the associations, the move to consolidate ACPA and NASPA into one association failed.

This outcome, bemoaned by some and heralded by others, leaves ACPA and NASPA concurrently competing and collaborating as professional entities that serve the same consumer base. Branding and marketing of professional development, networking, and volunteer leadership opportunities as "products" follow the same approaches that have come to characterize the intense competition among higher education institutions for a dwindling pool of traditional-age college students. Student affairs divisions have poured more money into middle-class, leisure amenities, such as new residence halls, recreation centers, and dining options, at the same time reducing the budgets of developmental programming and the staff members needed to deliver them. To be considered a professional student affairs division now carries a certain character, appearance, and price tag that continues to recycle and reproduce hegemony.

Future Challenges and Considerations

Several challenges confront the future of student affairs. These factors are likely to bring about the next era in the development of student affairs. The following six areas continue to demonstrate the role of student affairs in the larger system of higher education.

First, increasing enrollment in higher education by distance learners, online learners, and older adult learners will challenge the profession with how to translate student services and support for student learning and development beyond face-to-face interactions. What systems will student affairs develop to engage students beyond the classroom? Will the increasing population of nonresidential learners with jobs and family obligations off campus confirm the irrelevance of student affairs to its critics?

Second, the continued and increasing diversity of the student body along many dimensions, including race and ethnicity, nationality and immigration status, sexuality, gender, and convictional beliefs, will require student affairs professionals to develop better methods of getting students to go beyond superficial engagement with difference. Student affairs will have to answer its critics who charge it with thought policing and liberal indoctrination. How can its purported values in social justice, as articulated by ACPA and NASPA in their values and ethics statements, be espoused and enacted across lines of political and ideological difference?

Third, as college costs continue to rise and the availability of need-based grant and scholarship aid decreases, economic disparities among students attending the same institution and between students at different institutions will become more evident. What are the implications of these disparities for student access to "traditional" and normative student affairs experiences? How will the intersections of social class oppression with other systems of oppression (e.g., disability, gender identity, nationality and immigration status, race and ethnicity, and sexuality) segregate student engagement?

Fourth, social media has significantly altered how people communicate with each other and made evident the bullying and harassment that was previously hard to show. What are the implications of social media and new technologies for student codes of conduct policies and enforcement, the nature of campus community, and relationships between student affairs professionals and their students? What are the boundaries of the campus in this globally, technologically interconnected age?

Fifth, increased business applications of competition, commodification, as well as budgeting and management principles have implications for the long-standing, guiding philosophies of student affairs practice. The values and attitudes articulated in the *Student Personnel Point of View* (ACE, 1937, 1949) do not seem to align well with today's demands for efficiency and quantifiable, measurable outcomes of student affairs work. Will student affairs respond to these pressures, as it has in the past, by reaffirming its commitment to the holistic education of students?

Finally, the internalization of student affairs as a professional practice brings unique challenges and opportunities to the field. In our claims to support diversity and inclusion, will the US-centric nature of student affairs submit itself to introspection, inspection, and revision? Will the canonical theories and models of student learning, development, and persistence, built on predominantly white, middle-class, heterosexual, cisgender, and Christian samples (already not reflective of US diversity), continue to hold sway in an international student affairs arena? Will US-style student affairs professionalism simply become another one-way cultural commodity exported to an international marketplace? Our ability to think beyond and to function outside of the systems that have shaped the development of higher education in the United States will be a harbinger of how well student affairs is able to weather these future challenges.

Conclusion

As you can see from this brief history of our profession, student affairs has grown rapidly over the late nineteenth, twentieth, and early twenty-first centuries. Largely created in response to the wants of students and their multifaceted needs and concerns, as well as to advocate on their behalf, student affairs has become a very broad profession within higher education, ranging from orientation to residence life to career services and more. Student affairs has become intimately involved across all aspects of higher education.

As a profession that owes its earliest development to women faculty members who were concerned for the welfare of female students on male-oriented campuses in the late-nineteenth and early twentieth centuries, student affairs often appears to be focused on the affective domain of human development. As such, student affairs is sometimes perceived to be in conflict with the cognitive domain, which is the primary emphasis of academic life with its focus on the objective and detached search for "truth" and new knowledge. Some may contend that concern for the welfare and livelihood of students is misplaced and unnecessary. But as we have consistently seen in extensive research that began in the 1950s and has extended far beyond, the welfare and livelihood of students in general and in all its many aspects is critical to the success of our institutions of higher learning and to the success of all students.

Discussion Questions

1. Student activism has been essential to prompting change within student affairs over time. What current issues among student activists have the potential to initiate another shift in direction, focus, or concern for student affairs professionals?

2. Graduate preparation programs began with a focus on training deans of women. Is this early focus on a marginalized population among students manifested in the curriculum and philosophy of your graduate preparation program? If so, in what ways?

3. How has the relationship between colleges and universities and their students evolved over time?

4. What is your perception of the challenges facing the field in the current era?

References

ACPA. (1994). *The student learning imperative.* Washington, DC: Author.

ACPA. (1998). *Principles of good practice for student affairs.* Washington, DC: Author.

ACPA & NASPA. (2004). *Learning reconsidered.* Washington, DC: Authors.

ACPA & NASPA. (2010). *Professional competency areas for student affairs practitioners.* Washington, DC: Authors.

Altbach, P. G. (1979). From revolution to apathy: American student activism in the 1970s. *Higher Education, 8*(6), 609–626.

American Council on Education. (1937). *The student personnel point of view.* Washington, DC: Author.

American Council on Education. (1949). *The student personnel point of view.* Washington, DC: Author.

Biddix, J. P., & Schwartz, R. (2012). Walter Dill Scott and the student personnel movement. *Journal of Student Affairs Research and Practice, 49*(3), 285–298.

Blimling, G. S. (2001). Uniting scholarship and communities of practice in student affairs. *Journal of College Student Development, 42*(4), 381–396.

Bordin, R. (1993). *Alice Freeman Palmer: The evolution of a new woman.* Ann Arbor: The University of Michigan Press.

Carpenter, S., & Stimson, M. T. (2007). Professionalism, scholarly practice, and professional development in student affairs. *NASPA Journal, 44*(2), 502–521.

Cheney, L. (1989). *50 hours: A core curriculum for college students.* Washington, DC: National Endowment for the Humanities.

Clark, T. A. (1922). *Discipline and the derelict: Being a series of essays on some of those who tread the green carpet.* New York: Macmillan.

Coomes, M. D., & Wilson, M. E. (2009). The contributions of student affairs to a liberal education: Three imperative questions. *Journal of College and Character, 10*(3), 1–5.

Council for the Advancement of Standards. (2014). *CAS history.* Washington, DC: Author. Retrieved from http://www.cas.edu/history

Evans, N. J., & Reason, R. D. (2001). Guiding principles: A review and analysis of student affairs philosophical statements. *Journal of College Student Development, 42*(4), 359–377.

Ewing, J. C., & Stickler, W. H. (1964). Progress in the development of higher education as a field of professional graduate study and research. *Journal of Teacher Education, 15*(4), 397–403.

Ferguson, L. W. (1976). The Scott Company. In L. W. Ferguson, *The heritage of industrial psychology.* Hartford, CT: Finlay Press.

Fry, G. A. (c.a. 1924). The personnel department. Syllabus. General files (Record Group 7, HR Box. Board of Personnel Administration Folder). Evanston, IL: Northwestern University Archives. Retrieved May 15, 2015, from http://hul.harvard.edu/lib/archives/h1718/

Gerda, J. (2004). *History of the conferences of deans of women, 1903–1922.* Unpublished doctoral dissertation. Bowling Green State University, Bowling Green, OH.

Hopkins, L. B. (1924). The new personnel office: A glimpse at a new department where director Hopkins seems to match the men with the task. *N.U. Alumni News,* pp. 9–11. General files (Record Group 7, HR Box, Board of Personnel Administration Folder). Evanston, IL: Northwestern University Archives.

Kim, A. (2006). *Stanford encyclopedia of philosophy.* Retrieved from http://plato.stanford.edu/entries/wilhelm-wundt/

Kruempel, B. J. (1990). *Attitudes of academic and student affairs administrators toward student affairs preparation programs and their accreditation.* Doctoral dissertation. Iowa State University, Ames, IA.

Kuh, G. D., Shedd, J. D., & Whitt, E. J. (1987). Student affairs and liberal education: Unrecognized and (unappreciated) common law partners. *Journal of College Student Personnel*, pp. 252–260.

Lloyd-Jones, E. (1929). *Student personnel work at Northwestern University.* New York: Harper & Brothers.

Magolda, P. M. (2005). Proceed with caution: Uncommon wisdom about academic and student affairs partnerships. *About Campus, 9*(6), 16–21.

Moore, K. (1976). Freedom and constraint in 18th century Harvard. *Journal of Higher Education, 47,* 109–120. Retrieved from http://ed-share.educ.msu.edu/scan/ead/mabokela/document36.pdf

National Association of Scholars. (2008). *Rebuilding campus community: The wrong imperative.* New York: Author. Retrieved from http://www.nas.org/articles/Rebuilding_Campus_Community_The_Wrong_Imperative

National Center for Education Statistics. (2015). *Digest of education statistics* (Tables 314.20, 314.30, 334.10, and 334.30). Retrieved from https://nces.ed.gov/programs/digest/current_tables.asp

National Commission on Excellence in Education. (1983, April). *A nation at risk: The imperative for educational reform.* Washington, DC: US Department of Education. Retrieved from http://www2.ed.gov/pubs/NatAtRisk/index.html

Nidiffer, J. (2001). *Pioneering deans of women: More than a wise and pious matron.* New York: Teachers College Press.

Palmer, G. H. (1908). *The life of Alice Freeman Palmer.* New York: Houghton Mifflin.

Rudolph, F. (1990). *The American college and university.* Athens: University of Georgia Press.

Russo, J. A., & Coomes, M. D. (2000). Enrollment management, institutional resources, and the private college. In M. D. Coomes (Ed.), *The role student aid plays in enrollment management* (New Directions for Student Services, no. 89, pp. 33–46). San Francisco: Jossey-Bass.

Schwartz, R. A. (1997). How deans of women became men. *Review of Higher Education, 20,* 419–436.

Schwartz, R. A. (1998). Alice Freeman Palmer. In L. Eisenmann (Ed.), *Historical dictionary of women's education in the U.S.* (pp. 317–319). Westport, CT: Greenwood Press.

Schwartz, R. A. (2010). *Deans of men and the shaping of modern college culture.* New York: Palgrave.

Scott, W. D., & Clothier, R. C. (1923). *Personnel management: Principles, practices, and point of view.* Chicago: A. W. Shaw Co.

Scott Hall Committee. (1939, February 5). Biography of Walter Dill Scott prepared for the dedication of Scott Hall, Northwestern University. Reprinted from the *Northwestern Alumni News.* Personnel Department files (Box 2, Folder 4). Evanston, IL: Northwestern University Archives.

Solomon, B. A. (1985). *In the company of educated women: A history of women and higher education in America.* New Haven, CT: Yale University Press.

Thelin, J. R. (2011). *A history of American higher education* (2nd ed.). Baltimore: Johns Hopkins University Press.

Thelin, J. R., & Gasman, M. (2011). Historical overview of American higher education. In J. H. Schuh, S. R. Jones, & S. R. Harper (Eds.), *Student services: A handbook for the profession* (5th ed., pp. 3–23). San Francisco: Jossey-Bass.

CHAPTER 3

PHILOSOPHIES AND VALUES

Robert D. Reason and Ellen M. Broido

In 1984, Louis Stamatakos and Russell Rogers posed the question "Is the student affairs profession in need of a professional philosophy?" These authors presented a strong case for the practical importance of a professional philosophy. They argued that a professional philosophy would enable us as student affairs professionals to articulate what we believe, what we value, what we do, and, ultimately, who we are—four questions they believed could not be answered in the early 1980s.

A strong philosophy, widely understood within the academy, would discourage us and our faculty colleagues from questioning our professionalism (Stamatakos & Rogers, 1984). And, perhaps most important, a strong professional philosophy would enable purpose-driven work by student affairs professionals. It makes sense that if we know what we believe, what we value, what we do, and who we are, then it becomes easier to make a purposeful decision when forced to choose among multiple courses of action.

Complaints about the lack of a philosophical rationale for the work of student affairs have a long tradition; such criticism dates at least as early as 1938. That year Esther Lloyd-Jones and Margaret Smith, in the first edition of *A Student Personnel Program for Higher Education*, reviewed the debates within higher education as a whole about the purposes of higher education and, specifically, whether higher education should concern itself solely with intellectual development or with "intellectual, physical, emotional, spiritual" development (Wriston, 1930, as cited in Lloyd-Jones & Smith, 1938, p. 4). These tensions reflect, in part, the similarly long-standing conflict within higher education between "(a) Those who interpret 'preparation for life' predominantly in a vocational, professional, utilitarian sense [and] (b) those who interpret 'preparation for life' from a broader standpoint as including properly one's ability to function successfully in nonvocational activities and relationships; those who believe that there is an 'art of living' which is as important as the 'business of earning a living'" (Lloyd-Jones & Smith, 1938, p. 7).

Joined by Paul Bloland ten years after their initial discussion, Stamatakos and Rogers (Bloland, Stamatakos, & Rogers, 1994) concluded, "It is fair to say that we in the profession have been denied a Hegelian 'zeitgeist' through which to put our entire house into rational order because we have failed to resolve the essential question of which [philosophical] statement best represents the philosophy and foundations of the student affairs profession" (p. 18).

This chapter addresses the question "Is student affairs still a profession in search of a philosophy?" If, as Bloland and his colleagues implied, our profession requires a single, coherent, comprehensive statement to serve as our philosophy, then we are still in need. We do, however, have a series of documents that, taken together, address Stamatakos and Rogers's four questions. Building on the ideas of John Dewey, these thirteen documents, reviewed by Evans and Reason (2001), provide our philosophical foundation. Furthermore, the widely accepted idea of student development theory as the educational foundation of our profession, although not without critics, informs our principles and values. The same is true for the more recent "student learning" movement in student affairs. Although not neatly packaged in a single document, we conclude a shared sense of philosophy and values is not absent from student affairs.

A Framework for Understanding Philosophies

In their critique of student affairs, Stamatakos and Rogers (1984) argued that professional philosophies contain four essential elements: (1) an articulation of the basic principles that underlie the profession; (2) clarity about the values that arise from and sustain those basic principles; (3) statements of the roles, functions, and standards of practice of a profession "that are congruent with what the profession believes and values" (p. 401); and (4) an awareness of what the profession is and what it means to be a professional.

Basic Principles

Stamatakos and Rogers (1984) and later Bloland, Stamatakos, and Rogers (1994) applied these four criteria to student affairs, arguing that our basic or first principles were found in the answers to the three-part question "What does the student affairs field believe to be 'the role and purpose of institutions of higher education, the human nature of students, and the educational relationship between the two, i.e., learning'" (p. 19)? Without a shared understanding of the purpose of higher education, of students, and of how learning (or development) occurs, we lack the foundation for a professional philosophy. Although Bloland and his colleagues asserted that the answers to these particular questions would identify our first principles, there is no consensus within the student affairs profession as a whole that these are the questions with which we should be grappling. A review of the history of student affairs indicates that other questions and answers seem to have formed our foundational beliefs and that we do indeed have a well-defined set of basic principles that are widely shared.

Values

A profession's values derive from and are consistent with its basic principles. Whereas principles speak to what is, values speak to what should be. Bloland and his colleagues argued that our values must answer the following questions: "What do we believe the purpose of higher education should be?" "What aspects of human nature are desirable in students?" and "How should we best help students acquire those traits?" Other writers have identified different sets of values as fundamental to and commonly shared by student affairs practitioners. Young and Elfrink (1991), for example, found that student affairs practitioners with overwhelming consensus identified the following seven values as essential to the profession:

- *Altruism,* or concern for the welfare of others
- *Equality,* or [as]surance that all people have the same rights, privileges, or status
- *Aesthetics,* or qualities of objects, events, and persons that provide satisfaction
- *Freedom,* or the capacity to exercise choice
- *Human dignity,* or the inherent worth and uniqueness of an individual
- *Justice,* or the upholding of moral and legal principles
- *Truth,* or faithfulness to fact or reality (Young, 1993a, p. 1)

Adding to this list of seven, Young (1993a) and Roberts (1993) argued that *community* was and historically has been an additional, essential value of student affairs, a perspective shared by other writers.

Roles and Functions

Articulation of the roles and functions of the profession is the third aspect of a professional philosophy, according to Stamatakos and Rogers (1984). In a very pragmatic way, professionals must understand how their work has been carried out historically and currently as well as what standards and training are necessary to be effective. Common roles and functions of student affairs professionals are covered in parts 4 and 5 of this book. It should be noted here, however, that the influence of institutional types and contexts on what is under the purview of student affairs is strong (Dungy & Gordon, 2011). Admissions, academic advising, intercollegiate athletics, and campus safety, for example, may (or may not) fall under the auspices of the student affairs division at any particular institution. We would certainly argue that professionals in these areas undertake student affairs functions, regardless of their organizational placement.

Recent work within the profession (ACPA & NASPA, 2010) to identify essential competencies for all student affairs professionals, however, begins to provide some coherence to the skills necessary to be a student affairs professional, even if a common list of student affairs roles eludes us. This work, along with the commonly agreed-on criteria set forth by the Council for the Advancement of Standards in Higher Education (2012), identifies standards and training necessary to be an *effective* student affairs professional. Although the student affairs profession may never have the level of consensus about necessary professional competencies, roles, and functions that would enable certification or entry exams (similar to CPA exams and bar exams), an understanding of shared competencies moves us closer to the professional philosophy Stamatakos and Rogers (1984) envisioned.

A Profession's Identity

Stamatakos and Rogers (1984) noted that "the integration and well-developed congruence among what a profession believes, what it values, and what it does surely results in clarity and integrity—if not self-actualization—regarding who it is" (p. 401). They suggested that given clarity about the initial three questions, questions of professional identity in student affairs would be limited to those relating to admission to and criteria for membership in the profession. However, concerns and questions about whether student affairs is a *real* profession have plagued it from its start. Questions continue today in the form of concerns about whether it is necessary to have a degree in student affairs or higher education to be an effective practitioner or is some lesser form of certification sufficient. In part, questions and concerns about what constitutes a student affairs professional arise because we conduct our work in a setting in which another professional group, the faculty, sees itself as having the primary responsibility for students' education. Although at many institutions student affairs work is valued, this is often not the case, and questions about the value and importance of student affairs' contribution to student learning and success are an ongoing concern.

The Philosophical Legacy of Student Affairs

One of the strengths of student affairs has been its willingness to draw from a variety of sources for its ideas and practices, and the philosophical assumptions underlying our work share this eclecticism. Beliefs about the nature of people's capacities for and inclinations in work and learning shaped the measurement movement, perhaps the first philosophical influence on the student personnel profession in the years immediately following World War I (Caple, 1998). This focus on assessment and the use of data concerning students has been an ongoing theme in student affairs work.

By 1931, Clothier (1931/1986) laid out sixteen principles of student personnel work, the first of which stated, "Every student differs from every other student in aptitudes . . .; in interests . . .; [and] in character traits . . . The college must know these qualifications so far as it is possible to do so and must utilize that knowledge in planning his [sic] college course, both within and without the curriculum" (pp. 12–13). This first principle was an early indicator of our profession's ongoing concern with the uniqueness of each student; the other fifteen principles dealt with specific functions student personnel workers were to assume in ensuring that diverse students were to be successful.

Cowley (1936/1986) placed basic assumptions about students within a tradition dating back to the Greek philosophers, noting that student personnel's concern with the development of the whole student was not "the private concern of personnel workers." He argued instead that "personnel people are merely subscribing to the point of view of a long line of philosophers dating at least from Socrates and leading to John Dewey and his adherents" and that "the psychology of individual differences from which many personnel activities have directly grown is but a verification by science of an age-old philosophical insight" (pp. 69–70).

Many of the guiding principles and values of today's student affairs work can be traced back through our profession's historical documents, beginning with *The Student Personnel Point of View* in 1937 (NASPA, 1987), and prior to that to ideas advocated by the educational philosopher and theorist John Dewey (Evans & Reason, 2001). Although his major influence on higher education has been in debates about the nature of the curriculum (Thelin, 2004), and although his main focus was primary and secondary education (Fuhrman, 1997), Dewey's ideas also shaped the ideas of early student affairs practitioners.

Many authors (for example, Cowley, 1936/1986; Young, 1996) have noted Dewey's influence on early leaders in student affairs, specifically the significance of his philosophy of pragmatism. Although this claim may be overstated in that writers are vague about the specific links between ideas of pragmatism and Dewey's more general views about education that have been embraced by student affairs, there is no question that many of his ideas shaped student affairs practice.

Education for Democracy

Dewey believed that the primary function of education in a democratic society was to enable citizens to participate fully and effectively in that democracy. For Dewey, democracy was not merely a form of government but a way of living in community, a way of interacting that affected all aspects of life, a way of making decisions. Dewey believed that education was the primary means by which societies shape the values of their citizens, and he had a profound belief that education should promote particular democratic values: "cooperation, tolerance, critical mindedness, and political awareness" (Hlebowitsh, 2006, p. 74). Dewey (1916/1964) wrote, "A democracy is more than a form of government; it is primarily a mode of associated living, of conjoining communicated experience. The extension in space of the number of individuals who participate in an interest so that each has to refer his own action to that of others, and to consider the action of others to give point and direction to his own, is equivalent to the breaking down of those barriers of class, race, and national territory which kept men [sic] from perceiving the full import of their activity" (p. 87).

Dewey believed that students learned to be effective members of democratic societies by attending democratic schools. Noddings (2007) summarized Dewey's perspective, noting that "learning to participate in democratic life involves living democratically—students working together on common problems, establishing the rules by which their classrooms will be governed, testing and evaluating ideas for the improvement of classroom life and learning, and participating in the construction of objectives for their own learning" (p. 36). This belief in the importance of democracy meant that students should have a voice in the direction of their own education. Dewey wrote, "There is, I think, no point in the philosophy of progressive education which is sounder than its emphasis upon the importance of the participation of the learner in the formation of the purposes which direct his [sic] activities in the learning process" (Dewey, 1938, p. 77). The idea that students should direct their own learning is clearly echoed in early student affairs writings. Lloyd-Jones and Smith (1938) cited Dewey's 1933 book *How We Think* when they argued, "Only when a student is free to make choices is it possible to enlist his [sic] whole intelligence and his initiative in the situation" (p. 122).

Education for Everyone

Dewey also believed that everyone could and should benefit from education, and that education should be tailored for each student (Martínez Alemán, 2001). Writing about Dewey's educational philosophies, Robert Orrill (1997) stated, "The social purpose of genuinely democratic and liberal education . . . was not to convey that 'genius' is exceptional and far above the common lot, but rather . . . to bring to full realization the natural fact that resourcefulness and intelligence are widespread. If varied in their outward appearance, these human capacities nonetheless are possessions owned by all and are endowments from which each can contribute to the betterment of associated living and common enterprise" (p. xix).

Problem-Based Learning

The goal of education according to Dewey is the growth of people's capacity to solve problems, skills he called *inquiry*, not simply the transmission of existing knowledge—arguing for active, participatory pedagogies grounded in real-world problems of interest to and experienced by students. Dewey would have seen a student's experiences working in the university library or participating in a committee within a sorority or fraternity as having as much (if not more) educational potential as what she or he learned in the classroom. Dewey "believed that to be educative, an experience has to be built on or be connected to prior experience" (Noddings, 2007, p. 31), and "the experience itself must have meaning for students here and now" (p. 32).

Dewey's focus on grounding learning in students' lived experiences and on the importance of learning through problem-solving are constitutive elements of today's student affairs work. Grounding learning in students' experiences and treating knowledge as something that can be developed by all people are fundamental aspects of college students' growth and development (Evans, Forney, Guido, Patton, & Renn, 2010), and they are widely accepted principles of many statements of exemplary student affairs practice (for example, Keeling, 2004, 2006).

Dewey's ideas are most often seen in student affairs work in contemporary writing about service-learning (Kezar & Rhoads, 2001). Kezar and Rhoads tied the founding of service-learning to Dewey's emphasis on the importance of grounding learning in real experience, erasing the dualism of learning and doing. The Association of American Colleges and Universities (AAC&U, 2015) has more recently begun using the language of "integrative learning" (p. 1) to describe intentional efforts to blend learning and doing with an emphasis on civic well-being, often working with NASPA to further this cause through the efforts related to civic learning and democratic engagement (Sponsler & Hartely, 2014). Peter Hlebowitsh (2006) thought Dewey believed that "inculcating students in the attitudes, habits of mind and methods of scientific inquiry could not only give students, as Dewey phrased it, 'freedom from control by routine, prejudice, dogma, unexamined tradition, [and] sheer self-interest' but 'also the will to inquire, to examine, to discriminate, to draw conclusions only on the basis of evidence after taking pains to gather all available evidence' (Dewey, 1938)" (p. 75). This set of assumptions clearly leads to the view that education should be problem based, focusing on methods of inquiry rather than memorization of existing knowledge.

The profession of student affairs has a wide and varied philosophical framework, which is to be expected of a field with a history of more than one hundred years. Nevertheless, certain core principles have continued from our profession's origin through to the present day. Although the next section will cover values that arose as student personnel work entered its more formalized history, during which it has published several statements of philosophies and values, it is clear that early beliefs about students, how they learn, and to what ends that learning should be directed influence us to this day.

Enduring Principles and Values of Student Affairs

After reviewing thirteen philosophical documents of our profession, Evans and Reason (2001) concluded that the student affairs profession has consistently maintained four broad guiding principles: a focus on students as the primary purpose of our work; a recognition of the role of the environment in a student's collegiate experience; an acknowledgment of the importance of intentional, empirically grounded practice; and a belief that student affairs professionals are responsible to the broader society. These authors also acknowledged that social justice advocacy, an important student affairs principle, was noticeably absent from the philosophical literature.

The principles identified by Evans and Reason (2001) are reflected in and reinforced by the values of the profession and articulated by the two major professional associations, the American College Personnel Association (ACPA) and the National Association of Student Personnel Administrators (NASPA), and the work of other scholars (Young, 1993b; Young & Elfrink, 1991). If we accept the proposition that the values articulated by ACPA and NASPA are the overarching values of the student affairs profession, then by juxtaposing these values with the principles identified by Evans and Reason we see even more clearly the congruence within our professional philosophy and values.

Lest we leave the reader with any sense that philosophical principles and professional values are erudite matters for academics, the following discussion provides tangible examples of how each principle and value influences the daily functioning of student affairs professionals. In this way we agree with Stamatakos and Rogers (1984): a professional philosophy that comprises guiding principles and thoughtful values provides purpose for professionals and guides daily practice. We also enact Dewey's (1938) assertion that theory must guide and be informed by practice.

Focus on Students

The philosophical documents throughout our professional history call for a holistic view of students, a respect for individual differences, and an appreciation for the agency students bring to their own learning (Evans & Reason, 2001). These understandings focus our work directly on students and students' development and learning as the most prominent aspects of student affairs works.

These early and consistent understandings of our profession's focus on students hold true today. More recent works, such as *Learning Reconsidered* (Keeling, 2004, 2006), continue the call for a holistic view of students, emphasizing the importance of engaging students in their own learning processes. These principles are further reinforced by the values forwarded by the two major professional organizations. ACPA, for example, lists the "education and development of the total student" and "diversity, multicultural competence, and human dignity" as primary values (http://www.myacpa.org, n.d.). NASPA acknowledges a "commitment to diversity, inclusion, and equality" (http://www.naspa.org, n.d.). The connection between today's values and the historical focus on students is clear and consistent.

The Educative Role of the Environment and Context

Evans and Reason (2001) found that the philosophical documents of our profession contained a consistent call to harness the educational potential of campus environments. Lewin's *interactionist perspective* (1936), in which behavior is assumed to be the result of the interaction between a person and the environment, was an unstated assumption underlying each document reviewed by Evans and Reason and is a foundation for most student development theories that guide our profession (Evans, Forney, Guido, Patton, & Renn, 2010). Concurrent with Lewin, Dewey (1916/1964, 1933) suggested that most, if not all, of education was mediated through the environment. Our understanding of the importance of environment and the component parts of a positive learning environment have grown over the years since Lewin's and Dewey's work (Strange & Banning, 2001).

ACPA cites as a core value of the association the "free and open exchange of ideas in a context of mutual respect," a value that directly relates to the educative role of the college environment (http://www.myacpa.org, n.d.). This statement reveals the value student affairs professionals place on the education process and on educational environments.

Student affairs professionals influence the learning environment in many ways, and they take this role seriously. Environments, according to Strange and Banning (2001), can facilitate learning through physical structures, human aggregates, and organizational characteristics. For example, one needs to look only so far as the increase of living-learning communities (organizational characteristics) to recognize how student affairs professionals have adapted residence halls (physical structures) to encourage students and faculty members (the human aggregate) to engage with educational topics. We would argue that a resurgent focus on the educational potential of the environment is underway, citing recent works by Renn and her colleagues to push this conversation (Renn & Arnold, 2003; Renn & Reason, 2013).

Intentional, Empirically Grounded Work

Despite the long-held belief that the student affairs profession is anti-intellectual, our philosophical documents reveal a deep-rooted belief in the importance of research-driven, intentional practice. Careful reading of various histories of the student affairs profession (for example, Bashaw, 1999; Nidiffer, 2000) reveal a profession built on "scholar-practitioners." Even prior to the widespread development of student affairs graduate programs, the professional leaders of student affairs were making decisions based on disciplinary study and empirically grounded research.

This focus on intentional and empirically grounded work continues today, an emphasis that ACPA and NASPA reinforce through their values. NASPA upholds a "spirit of inquiry," supporting research and scholarly efforts to inform the practice of the administration of student affairs (http://www.naspa.org, n.d.); ACPA propounds the "continuous professional development" of student affairs practitioners. ACPA has assumed as one of its major roles the "advancement and dissemination of knowledge relevant to college students and their learning and to the effectiveness of student affairs professionals and their institutions" (http://www.myacpa.org, n.d.). ACPA's journal, the *Journal of College Student Development*, is considered a top journal within all of higher education.

Responsibility to Society

Student affairs professionals take seriously their role in preparing college students to be fully functioning members of a democratic society (Evans & Reason, 2001; Hamrick, 1998; Hamrick, Evans, & Schuh, 2002; Sponsler & Hartley, 2013). Although this was the least consistent principle identified by Evans and Reason, a sense of responsibility to society has been of growing importance in our professional literature for the last twenty years, often manifesting in a responsibility to educate engaged, democratic citizens. Dewey (1916/1964) wrote, "A society which makes provision for participation in its good of all members on equal terms and which secures flexible readjustment of its institutions through interaction of the different forms of associated life is insofar democratic. Such a society must have a type of education which gives individuals a personal interest in social relationships and control, and the habits of mind which secure social changes" (p. 95). Hamrick (1998) found further support for Dewey's call, citing at least three major philosophical documents that call for educating students to engage with a democratic society.

It is clear that our sense of responsibility to society translates into a value placed on civic engagement and learning (Hamrick, Evans, & Schuh, 2002). Facilitating civic engagement through programming, advising student leaders, and engaging students in service-learning activities are manifestations of this value in our professional practice (Sponsler & Hartley, 2013).

Social Justice Advocacy

Evans and Reason (2001) noted that social justice advocacy was conspicuously absent from the historical documents they reviewed. However, after comparing these documents with the stated values of the profession, Evans and Reason concluded that student affairs practitioners should consider social justice advocacy to be a guiding principle of the profession. As stated previously, ACPA and NASPA indicate a value placed on diversity. The shared competency document lists skills related to equity, diversity, and inclusion as essential to competence in a student affairs professional. Young's work (1993b; Young & Elfrink, 1991) on the values of our profession reinforces the focus on social justice advocacy. Young and Elfrink (1991), in a study of professional leaders and senior administrators, found almost unanimous support for eight professional values, which Young (1993a) later grouped into three broad categories: human dignity, equality, and community. The emerging influence of critical theories on our professional preparation and practice (discussed following in this chapter) is also evidence of the role of social justice advocacy.

Hamrick (1998) crafted a compelling argument that student affairs professionals should value social justice advocacy as a form of democratic engagement. Hamrick ties together the principles of responsibility to society and social justice advocacy with the values of democracy, human dignity, equality, and community. Understanding a citizen's responsibilities to include "critique, dissent, and reform of the status quo" also enables student affairs professionals to advise students about appropriate, peaceful activism (Hamrick, Evans, & Schuh, 2002, p. 187).

Current Influences on Our Professional Philosophies and Values

The previous discussion revealed long-held professional principles and values identified in several historical and contemporary documents. We turn now to contemporary influences on our profession in order to more fully refine our understanding of the philosophy and values of student affairs. We start with a discussion of the influence of the student development movement, which has been around for several decades, followed by the more recent emphasis on student learning. Two major influences on the broader academic culture also influence student affairs work: critical, postmodern, and poststructural theories coming out of the humanities and the growing internationalization of higher education.

The Student Development Movement

Bloland and others (1994) labeled the acceptance of student development theories as the foundation of the student affairs profession a "movement," implying that the wholesale acceptance of these theories was more closely related to a conversion experience than a reasoned decision. These authors went on to critique student development theories and their application to student affairs work, as if these theories constituted a new philosophical principle for the profession. Although we disagree with Bloland and his colleagues' assertion that the student development perspective constitutes a philosophical principle, we recognize that student development influences the constituent parts of a philosophy—what we believe in, what we value, what we do, and who we are as professionals.

Evolving since the early 1970s, the movement toward accepting student development as the theoretical foundation of the profession has its roots in the need for establishing legitimacy within the academy (Bloland, Stamatakos, & Rogers, 1994); the need to understand, anticipate, and address an increasingly complex set of student issues (Evans, Forney, Guido, Patton, & Renn, 2010); and the need to ground professional practice in disciplinary theory (Evans, Forney, Guido, Patton, & Renn, 2010). Student development theories guide the work of student affairs professionals, describing how students change and grow during college and what activities or experiences best influence that growth. Student development theories attempt to explain the process of human development in college students and, as such, do serve as the educational foundation of the student affairs profession.

Bloland, Stamatakos, and Rogers (1994) critiqued student development as a philosophy for the profession, claiming that "student development emphasizes the student to the exclusion of the other institutional purposes [and] ignores or deems as unimportant the collegiate institution's responsibilities for preserving, transmitting, and enriching the culture, for creating new knowledge, or for educating students toward being responsible participants in society" (p. 20).

Although Bloland and his colleagues (1994) base this conclusion on the review of a single document, *Student Development Services in Post-Secondary Education* (Council of Student Personnel Associations, 1975), limiting greatly their understanding of student development, it behooves us to examine their perspective closely.

In keeping with our professional principles and values, student development theories do emphasize a student's growth toward a more complex and integrated whole (Evans, Forney, Guido, Patton, & Renn, 2010). More recent theoretical developments integrate cognitive development with interpersonal and intrapersonal development (see, for example, Baxter Magolda, 2009) and build a holistic understanding of student development, inclusive of creating knowledge of and responsibility toward others. In this manner, student development reinforces the principles and values of the student affairs profession.

The student development movement also has enabled us as student affairs professionals to understand what we do and who we are professionally, the final two components of a professional philosophy (Stamatakos & Rogers, 1984). The student development movement has pushed us to see ourselves as educators concerned about holistic student growth and development (Evans, Forney, Guido, Patton, & Renn, 2010). We might argue that the educator identity that grew out of the student development movement foreshadowed the student learning movement in student affairs, to which we now turn.

The Student Learning Movement

Komives and Schoper (2006) suggested that, beginning in the 1980s, a series of reports calling for a renewed focus on learning and learning outcomes in higher education began the student learning movement in student affairs. The evolution of the movement from *student development* to *student learning* as the primary focus of student affairs work focused much attention on the concept of learning within and outside of student affairs. Student affairs scholars responded to this evolution with the *Student Learning Imperative* (ACPA, 1994), which clearly put learning in the forefront of our professional practices.

More recently, documents produced in collaboration among many student affairs professional organizations continued and furthered the profession's focus on learning. *Learning Reconsidered* (Keeling, 2004) and *Learning Reconsidered 2* (Keeling, 2006) serve as a call and a how-to manual to focus on learning in student affairs work, respectively. Learning, according to the authors in these two documents, is inseparable from development. Learning is also something larger and transformative, incorporating intellectual and personal growth and resulting in a qualitative change in the *identity* of the learner.

The student learning movement places student affairs practice in the center of the learning environment. According to the authors of *Learning Reconsidered,* "Student affairs, in this conceptualization, is integral to the learning process because of the opportunities it provides students to learn through action, contemplation, reflection and emotional engagement as well as information acquisition" (Keeling, 2004, p. 11). Student affairs professionals thus assume a proactive and co-primary role with faculty members in the education of college students.

The increased attention on learning emphasizes many of the previously held beliefs of student affairs professionals. In fact, we would argue that the student learning movement is congruent with all of the principles identified by Evans and Reason (2001). Interestingly, although some view the focus on student learning as new, we argue that it simply reinforces and recenters an emphasis on learning that has been part of student affairs since the beginning (Evans & Reason, 2001). The movement does, however, change what we do and how we see ourselves professionally. Student affairs professionals now focus on learning outcomes (Komives & Schoper, 2006) and creating curricula to guide the achievement of those outcomes.

Critical, Postmodern, and Poststructural Theories

Over the last fifteen years, our understandings of how power and privilege affect student experiences and organizational dynamics have been shaped by the influences of critical, postmodern, and poststructural theories (Martínez Alemán, Pusser, & Bensimon, 2015). These theories raise challenges for long-held tenants of student development theories, questioning the possibility "that identity of any sort is [ever] stable, singular, static" (Broido & Manning, 2002, p. 441). They offer lenses for a social justice–based critique of higher education institutions, seeking "to bring social science inquiry to identify the causes and causalities of inequitable access to higher education, as well as to craft a view of the discriminatory and unjust experiences of actors in higher education" (Martínez Alemán, Pusser, & Bensimon, 2015, p. 2). Although these theories are not interchangeable, they have similar foci on the influence of power on social institutions and individuals' experiences, ways of challenging oppression, and the ways in which multiple aspects of social identity interact.

Internationalization

Although student affairs work had its origins in the residential colleges of England, student affairs has been, as a profession, a distinctly US phenomenon. Indeed, histories of student affairs typically make no mention of student affairs work beyond the United States. There is, however, growing awareness across the globe that the holistic development of students is a desirable outcome of higher education and recognition that the academic success of students is dependent on their ability to meet basic needs (Dominguez-Whitehead, 2015), including food and shelter and physical and psychological safety. All of these are concerns of student affairs work, and thus, there is growing international interest in our profession and nascent awareness in the United States that we might benefit from strategies being used to support students in other countries.

Understanding the experiences of students in non-US contexts and the ways universities support their success can bring to awareness previously unrealized assumptions underlying practices in our own contexts. For example, most European and African universities have limited student affairs divisions, yet African and European students have much higher levels of political engagement than do US college students. How might these regions be developing political engagement in ways we have not considered? Awareness of this international diversity also enables us to question the perception that our ways of understanding and supporting students, of organizing our programs and services, and the outcomes we desire for our students are the only normal, natural, or right approaches (Schwartz, 2012). Finally, the growing numbers of international students attending US colleges and universities call us to be more conscious of the cultural norms and expectations and the political and social dynamics of their countries of origin and to consider how those influence their learning.

Conclusion

In this chapter we have drawn a connection between the philosophies and values of student affairs and the work we do on our campuses. But have we answered the initial question "Is the student affairs profession in need of a philosophy?" As a profession, we do not have a single document to "put our entire house into rational order" (Bloland, Stamatakos, & Rogers, 1994, p. 18), but we are not without a strong, coherent, and consistent professional heritage.

The philosophical roots of our profession, grounded in the guidance movement of the 1920s, the works of John Dewey in the 1930s, and other writings of the twentieth century, still inform our values in the twenty-first century. Our values inform our practice. We would argue that a single document is not needed to put our house in order, but rather the multiple documents, written over decades, add to the strength of our professional philosophy. Although our philosophy has evolved slightly with the changing times, our profession has held true to a coherent set of principles and values; we know what we believe, what we value, what we do, and who we are.

Activities

1. Visit websites of the two major professional organizations (ACPA and NASPA) and identify the values and philosophies of these two groups.
2. Answer Bloland, Stamatakos, and Rogers's (1994) four questions about professional philosophy, first for yourself and then for your understanding of student affairs.
3. Reflect on your values and philosophies. Identify specific areas in which your values and philosophies align with and diverge from the values and philosophies of student affairs. Think about how the interaction between your personal and our professional values and philosophies will affect your career.

References

American College Personnel Association (ACPA). (1994). *The student learning imperative: Implications for student affairs.* Washington, DC: Author.

ACPA & NASPA. (2010). *Professional competencies for student affairs practitioners.* Retrieved from http://www.myacpa.org/professional-competency-areas-student-affairs-practitioners

Association of American Colleges and Universities. (2015). *General education maps and markers: Designing meaningful pathways to student achievement.* Washington, DC: Authors.

Bashaw, C. T. (1999). *"Stalwart women": A historical analysis of deans of women in the South.* New York: Teachers College Press.

Baxter Magolda, M. B. (2009). *Authoring your life: Developing an internal voice to navigate life's challenges.* Sterling, VA: Stylus.

Bloland, P. A., Stamatakos, L. C., & Rogers, R. R. (1994). *Reform in student affairs: A critique of student development.* Greensboro, NC: ERIC Counseling and Student Services Clearinghouse.

Broido, E. M., & Manning, K. (2002). Contemporary philosophical and paradigmatic shifts in qualitative research. *Journal of College Student Development, 43,* 434–445.

Caple, R. B. (1998). *To mark the beginning: A social history of college student affairs.* Lanham, MD: University Press of America.

Clothier, R. C. (1986). College personnel principles and functions. In G. L. Saddlemire & A. L. Rentz (Eds.), *Student affairs: A profession's heritage* (pp. 9–20). Alexandria, VA: ACPA Media. (Reprinted from *The Personnel Journal,* 1931, pp. 9–17)

Council for the Advancement of Standards in Higher Education. (2012). *CAS professional standards for higher education* (9th ed.). Washington, DC: Author.

Council of Student Personnel Associations in Higher Education (COSPA). (1975). Student development services in post-secondary education. *Journal of College Student Personnel, 25,* 400–411.

Cowley, W. H. (1986). The nature of student personnel work. In G. L. Saddlemire & A. L. Rentz (Eds.), *Student affairs: A profession's heritage* (pp. 47–73). Alexandria, VA: ACPA Media. (Reprinted from *Educational Record,* 1936, pp. 3–27.)

Dewey, J. (1933). *How we think: A restatement of the relation of reflective thinking to the educative process.* New York: D. C. Heath.

Dewey, J. (1938). *Experience and education.* New York: Macmillan.

Dewey, J. (1964). *Democracy and education: An introduction to the philosophy of education.* New York: Macmillan. (Originally published in 1916.)

Dominguez-Whitehead, Y. (2015). Students' food acquisition struggles in the context of South Africa: The fundamentals of student development. *Journal of College Student Development, 56,* 292–307.

Dungy, G. J., & Gordon, S. A. (2011). The development of student affairs. In J. H. Schuh, S. R. Jones, S. R. Harper, & Associates (Eds.), *Student services: A handbook for the profession* (5th ed., pp. 61–79). San Francisco: Jossey-Bass

Evans, N. J., Forney, D. S., Guido, F. M., Patton, L. D., & Renn, K. A. (2010). *Student development in college: Theory, research, and practice* (2nd ed.). San Francisco: Jossey-Bass.

Evans, N. J., & Reason, R. D. (2001). Guiding principles: A review and analysis of student affairs philosophical statements. *Journal of College Student Development, 42,* 359–377.

Fuhrman, B. (1997). Philosophies and aims. In J. G. Gaff, J. L. Ratcliff, & Associates (Eds.), *Handbook of the undergraduate curriculum* (pp. 86–99). San Francisco: Jossey-Bass.

Hamrick, F. A. (1998). Democratic citizenship and student activism. *Journal of College Student Development, 39,* 449–460.

Hamrick, F. A., Evans, N. J., & Schuh, J. H. (2002). *Foundations of student affairs practice: How philosophy, theory, and research strengthen educational outcomes.* San Francisco: Jossey-Bass.

Hlebowitsh, P. S. (2006). John Dewey and the idea of experimentalism. *Education and Culture, 22,* 73–76.

Keeling, R. P. (Ed.). (2004). *Learning reconsidered: A campus-wide focus on the student experience.* Washington, DC: American College Personnel Association & National Association of Student Personnel Administrators.

Keeling, R. P. (Ed.). (2006). *Learning reconsidered 2: A practical guide to implementing a campus-wide focus on the student experience.* Washington, DC: American College Personnel Association, Association of College and University Housing Officers-International, Association of College Unions International, National Association for Campus Activities, National Academic Advising Association, National Association of Student Personnel Administrators, & National Intramural-Recreational Sports Association.

Kezar, A., & Rhoads, R. A. (2001). The dynamic tensions of service learning in higher education. *Journal of Higher Education, 72,* 148–171.

Komives, S. R., & Schoper, S. (2006). Developing learning outcomes. In R. P. Keeling (Ed.), *Learning reconsidered 2: A practical guide to implementing a campus-wide focus on the student experience* (pp. 17–41). Washington, DC: American College Personnel Association, Association of College and University Housing Officers-International, Association of College Unions International, National Association for Campus Activities, National Academic Advising Association, National Association of Student Personnel Administrators, & National Intramural-Recreational Sports Association.

Lewin, K. Z. (1936). *Principles of topological psychology.* New York: McGraw-Hill.

Lloyd-Jones, E., & Smith, M. R. (1938). *A student personnel program for higher education.* New York: McGraw-Hill.

Martínez Alemán, A. M. (2001). Community, higher education, and the challenge of multiculturalism. *Teachers College Record, 103,* 485–503.

Martínez Alemán, A. M., Pusser, B., & Bensimon, E. M. (2015). Introduction. In A. M. Martínez Alemán, B. Pusser, & E. M. Bensimon (Eds.), *Critical approaches to the study of higher education: A practical introduction* (pp. 1–6). Baltimore: Johns Hopkins.

NASPA. (1987). *A perspective on student affairs.* Washington, DC: Author.

Nidiffer, J. (2000). *Pioneering deans of women: More than wise and pious matrons.* New York: Teachers College Press.

Noddings, N. (2007). *Philosophy and education.* Boulder, CO: Westview.

Orrill, R. (1997). Editor's prologue. In *Education and democracy: Re-imagining liberal learning in America* (pp. xxi–xxvi). New York: College Entrance Examining Board.

Renn, K. A., & Arnold, K. A. (2003). Reconceptualizing research on peer culture. *Journal of Higher Education, 74,* 261–291.

Renn, K. A., & Reason, R. D. (2013). *College students in the United States: Characteristics, experiences, and outcomes.* San Francisco: Jossey-Bass.

Roberts, D. C. (1993). Community: The value of social synergy. In R. B. Young (Ed.), *Identifying and implementing the essential values of the profession* (New Directions for Student Services, no. 61, pp. 35–45). San Francisco: Jossey-Bass.

Schwartz, S. J. (Ed.). (2012). *Identity around the world.* (New Directions for Child and Adolescent Development, no. 138). San Francisco: Jossey-Bass.

Sponsler, L. E., & Hartley, M. (2013). *Five things student affairs professionals can do to institutionalize civic engagement.* Washington, DC: NASPA.

Stamatakos, L. C., & Rogers, R. R. (1984). Student affairs: A profession in need of a philosophy. *Journal of College Student Personnel, 25,* 400–411.

Strange, C. C., & Banning, J. H. (2001). *Educating by design: Creating campus learning environments that work.* San Francisco: Jossey-Bass.

Thelin, J. (2004). *A history of American higher education.* Baltimore: Johns Hopkins University Press.

Young, R. B. (1993a). Essential values of the profession. In R. B. Young (Ed.), *Identifying and implementing the essential values of the profession* (New Directions for Student Services, no. 61, pp. 5–14). San Francisco: Jossey-Bass.

Young, R. B. (Ed.). (1993b). *Identifying and implementing the essential values of the profession* (New Directions for Student Services, no. 61). San Francisco: Jossey-Bass.

Young, R. B. (1996). Guiding values and philosophy. In S. R. Komives, D. B. Woodard Jr., & Associates (Eds.), *Student services: A handbook for the profession* (pp. 83–105). San Francisco: Jossey-Bass.

Young, R. B., & Elfrink, V. L. (1991). Essential values of student affairs work. *Journal of College Student Development, 32*(1), 47–55.

PART TWO

PROFESSIONAL CONTEXT

Understanding the history presented in part 1 is important because historical vestiges continue to linger as well as to inform the contemporary context in which the profession of student affairs is practiced. In part 2 student affairs practice is explored in more depth through the examination of four specific contexts that greatly influence the ways in which student affairs educators approach their work and create environments that promote success for all students: institutional missions and campus culture, campus climate and diversity, ethical principles and standards, and legal foundations. Effective student affairs practice requires, at a minimum, a basic understanding of these four areas because they greatly affect the professional context in which student affairs is situated.

In chapter 4 Kristen A. Renn and Lori D. Patton introduce the landscape of higher education by focusing on the variety of institutional missions and types in American higher education. By highlighting the ways in which institutional missions reflect unique methods in which campus environments are constructed to promote student success, they link institutional missions to campus culture.

Their chapter then paves the way for a deeper understanding of campus climate and diversity, which Kimberly A. Griffin addresses in chapter 5. Unfortunately, there continues to be no shortage of incidents on college campuses that poignantly illustrate campus climates punctuated by hate crimes, incivility, racism, and intolerance. In this chapter several frameworks for studying and considering diversity and campus climate are introduced with an eye toward helping practitioners understand how varying groups of students experience campus climates differently. Further, the chapter emphasizes the critical leadership role student affairs educators must play in transforming campus climates into welcoming and inclusive ones for all students and provides specific strategies practitioners may use to this end.

In chapter 6 Sue A. Saunders and Christine M. Wilson address the question, "What is ethical professional practice?" To respond they introduce readers to ethical principles and standards, as well as those professional ethical statements that should guide the work of student affairs educators. They bring many of these principles and standards to life through the presentation of several ethical dilemmas, complex situations any one of us in student affairs may encounter, and help the reader work through the situation and resolve the dilemmas through the application of good ethical decision making.

Principles and standards provide an ethical scaffolding for professional practice, and so do legal principles and laws, as discussed by Thomas Miller in chapter 7. Although the legal environment is dynamic as new laws and mandates are implemented (for example, consider Title IX legislation), the litigious nature of US society is apparent in higher education. The presence of legal issues facing student affairs educators is enduring, which requires those who work with students and in higher education settings to have a cursory understanding of the law. In this chapter, key legal principles, sources of law, and areas in which the law is most influential in student affairs practice are introduced and applied to important campus-wide issues such as free speech and civility, guns on campus, and due process. Although student affairs practitioners cannot ever fully eliminate risk in their work with students and on college campuses, becoming knowledgeable about legal requirements and obligations will help inform practitioners and mitigate the legal consequences as particular situations arise. Of course most student affairs practitioners are not attorneys so knowing basic legal knowledge also helps one decide when consulting with legal counsel is necessary and appropriate.

The topical areas in this part are foundational for effective student affairs practice and also must be considered in relation to the chapters that follow. Student development theories, campus environments, organizational structures and functions, and core competencies are all influenced by institutional missions, campus climate and diversity, ethics, and the law. Without understanding the context in which it is situated, student affairs practice, at best, runs the risk of being misinformed and, at worst, threatens the essential purposes of our work.

CHAPTER 4

INSTITUTIONAL IDENTITY AND CAMPUS CULTURE

Kristen A. Renn and Lori D. Patton

The purpose of this chapter is to introduce the concepts of institutional mission and types as well as their relationship to campus culture. It lays a foundation for understanding subsequent chapters on campus climate and organizations. In chapter 1, John R. Thelin and Marybeth Gasman reviewed the history of colleges and universities in the United States, the culmination of which is a twenty-first-century landscape of higher education comprising thousands of institutions. Enormous diversity exists among colleges and universities in the United States. Every campus environment has a distinct identity based on a number of aspects ranging from student subcultures and history to geographical location and traditions. Of these, two key features are instrumental in understanding campus environments as a student affairs educator: institutional identity and campus culture. Institutional identity is heavily situated in institutional mission and type, both of which in turn influence campus culture. How individuals experience the campus environment has much to do with the role of culture and how it is fostered, as well as the climate that emanates through culture (see chapters 5 and 14, respectively, for discussion of campus climate and environmental theories).

Institutional Missions and Types

There are over four thousand accredited postsecondary institutions in the United States, and they vary by governance and funding (public, private, for-profit, denominational); degree programs (certificate, associate, undergraduate, graduate, professional); student populations; and curricula. Institutions have been categorized—and categorize themselves—in various ways by, for

example, the Carnegie Classification System (see www.carnegieclassifications
.iu.edu); affiliation with athletic conferences (for example, Ivy League, Big
Ten, National Junior College Athletic Association); and association memberships (for example, National Association of Independent Colleges and
Universities, Association of Public and Land-grant Universities, Association of
Private Sector Colleges and Universities). Yet these affiliations and classifications do not fully explain how students and others experience campus environments. We argue that institutional mission, institutional type, and institutional
identity are critical to campus culture and point to different ways to consider
education in and out of the formal curriculum.

Institutional Mission

In a statement often cited by student affairs scholars, Lyons (1993) posited,
"Each college or university is unique, and that uniqueness derives from a
distinctive mission" (p. 3). This mission serves as a public declaration of the
institution's identity (Meacham & Gaff, 2006). Institutional missions evolve
from a number of influences including but not limited to history, tradition,
heritage, geographical location, relationship to the state where it resides, and
culture, to name a few (Barr, 2000; Lyons, 1993).

Missions influence how university administrators facilitate the business of
the campus, shape the behaviors that permeate the daily interactions on campus, and serve as a philosophical and practical guide for carrying forth the
goals and objectives of the college or university. Institutional missions serve as
the crux of communal knowledge that responds to questions such as (1) Who
are we? (2) What do we value? (3) Where are we headed? and (4) How do
we get there? Answers to these questions rely heavily on an institution's type,
culture, history, and current context, which inform and play out across faculty
and administrative units. Upholding and contributing to accomplishing the
institutional mission is a critical component of effective student affairs practice
(Hirt, 2006; Manning, Kinzie, & Schuh, 2014).

Institutional Types

To set the stage for understanding our discussion of campus culture and subsequent chapters in this book, we describe ten institutional types here. This list
is not exhaustive, and there are institutions that fall into more than one type
or that are hybrids of two or more types. There will likely be additional types
and modifications that evolve during the current period of disruption of traditional higher education by new technologies.

Community Colleges Community colleges provide a disproportionate number of adult learners, women, and racially underrepresented populations
with an opportunity to pursue postsecondary education (Hirt, 2006; National
Center for Education Statistics [NCES], 2015; Schuetz, 2005). They are an

essential point of entry to higher education for students who may have few or no alternatives. For many students, "the choice is not between the community college and a senior residential institution; it is between the community college and nothing" (Cohen & Brawer, 2003, p. 53). A major mission of community colleges is to create access to higher education for anyone who desires the opportunity. They also provide a pathway for students wishing to pursue vocational education, take remedial courses, or transfer to four-year institutions. Community colleges educate substantially more diverse student populations than four-year residential institutions; for example, there are more immigrant students at community colleges than at any other type (Teranishi, Suárez-Orozco, & Suárez-Orozco, 2011). Schuetz (2005) contended that studies of community colleges rarely account for the role the campus environment plays in student success and attrition. Although community colleges are "open-access" environments and live out their mission by providing access to affordable higher education for millions of students, they still face the task of sharing the responsibility to ensure that students achieve their educational goals (Shuetz, 2005). Contemporary movements for college completion focus on community colleges as critical locations for increasing access, managing costs, augmenting academic preparation for bachelor degrees, and enhancing student success (for example, see Complete College America [http://www.Completecollege.org]).

Comprehensive Institutions   The use of the term *comprehensive institution* has changed over time, though there remains a category of universities that offer master's degrees in science, humanities, social sciences, and professional fields such as business, education, and social work. Hundreds of these institutions were founded as public normal schools or state teachers colleges; often they serve a region within a state, and some offer a few doctoral programs, such as an EdD. Some private colleges that formerly offered only undergraduate degrees have expanded into comprehensive institutions in efforts to diversify their offerings and appeal to new audiences of adult learners and professionals seeking master's degrees. Hirt (2006) noted, "They mix the traditional focus of liberal arts education with the research focus of a campus that offers graduate education" (p. 61). The majority have fewer than five thousand students, though they may have up to thirty thousand. Comprehensive institutions educate roughly 20 percent of all undergraduates in the United States. Admissions selectivity ranges, though historically these institutions have been only modestly selective, maintaining a commitment to upward mobility through postsecondary education for first-generation students. Some scholars argue that faculty members at comprehensive universities have a special role to play in the scholarship of teaching and learning, in which they may contribute to literature about teaching in the disciplines, such as chemistry education or college composition instruction (Henderson & Buchanan, 2007). The emphasis on undergraduate education at these institutions may support opportunities for student affairs professionals to partner with faculty members on matters of teaching, learning, and student development.

Research Universities Research universities emerged in the United States in the latter part of the nineteenth century as stand-alone institutions (for example, Clark, Johns Hopkins, and Chicago); as transformations of elite private colleges (such as Yale and Princeton); or as knowledge-creation engines at public flagship and land-grant institutions (for example, University of California, Berkeley, or Iowa State University) (Geiger, 2014). Nearly all research universities—public and private—in the twenty-first century include undergraduate education in their mission, though the overall institutional culture may be one that seeks to balance undergraduate success with knowledge production through the research enterprise. Tenure track and tenured faculty members at research universities typically must include scholarly productivity among their other responsibilities related to teaching and service, which may result in a campus culture that seemingly places undergraduate education and outcomes in competition with graduate education and research (Lee & Rhoads, 2004; O'Meara & Braskamp, 2005). Yet research universities are also home to substantial numbers of undergraduate students who can avail themselves of rich resources in the curriculum and cocurriculum, including a number of opportunities for high-impact practices such as undergraduate research, faculty-led study abroad, internships, and service-learning (see Kuh, 2009).

Liberal Arts Colleges The first colleges in the United States (Harvard, William & Mary, and Yale) were what we now recognize as liberal arts colleges. Committed to a well-rounded liberal arts curriculum of classics, literature, natural philosophy, and the emerging areas of science and then social science, they retained a commitment to holistic intellectual and character development. Although those early colleges evolved into research universities, thousands of other small colleges, many founded by Christian denominations, opened in the nineteenth and early twentieth centuries (Thelin, 2011). Today, most liberal arts colleges are private, residential in nature, and located in more rural settings that serve a particular region (Hartley, 2003). In addition, liberal arts colleges place significant value on tradition and have smaller campuses that serve a primarily undergraduate population (Hirt, 2006). Liberal arts colleges are known for providing substantial faculty-student contact and interaction, which has been shown to enhance student engagement (Pascarella, Wolniak, Seifert, Cruce, & Blaich, 2005). These colleges also emphasize students' holistic development by facilitating seamless learning environments rooted in sound practices in undergraduate education (Seifert and others, 2008; Seifert, Pascarella, Goodman, Salisbury, & Blaich, 2010). Moreover, given the burgeoning importance of diversity on college campuses, some scholars argue that liberal arts colleges are quite successful in their efforts to expose students to campus diversity, despite having limited structural diversity and being in settings that lack diversity (Umbach & Kuh, 2006). Astin (1999) summed up this institutional type well when he stated, "residential liberal arts colleges in general, and highly selective liberal arts colleges in particular, produce a pattern of consistently positive student outcomes not found in any other type of American higher-education institution" (p. 77). What Astin and other scholars have noted is consistent in recent studies stemming from the Wabash National Study of Liberal Arts Education (http://www.liberalarts.wabash.edu/study-overview/) and other scholarship produced by the Center of Inquiry into the Liberal Arts (http://www.liberalarts.wabash.edu). Residential liberal arts colleges distinguish themselves in outcomes related to critical thinking and civic engagement.

Women's Colleges   Women's colleges have a reputation for creating educationally rich environments that are central to empowering and supporting the unique needs of women college students. Most of the remaining forty-five women's colleges are small and private; some offer a limited number of coeducational graduate programs. Collectively they are recognized for learning effectiveness, educational gains, and leadership development, especially in comparison to peer coeducational institutions (Hardwick-Day, 2008; Kinzie, Thomas, Palmer, Umbach, & Kuh, 2007; Renn & Lytle, 2010). In their classic text, Tidball, Smith, Tidball, and Wolf-Wendel (1999) identified two enduring characteristics that are largely responsible for women's colleges' ability to promote success: the student population they serve and their institutional mission. Women's voices are heard and respected, issues important to women are unapologetically grounded in women's experiences, and students gain experience by serving in leadership roles on campus, many of which are traditionally held by men on coeducational campuses. There is also a strong press toward positive peer influence. Finally, the mission of women's colleges is deeply interwoven, linking history to a current context in which the education of women remains at the core and intersects with every aspect of the campus environment. In the context of changing social understanding of gender, some women's colleges have reconsidered their historic "single-sex" mission to include a wider range of gender diversity, admitting transgender and gender queer students (see Elfman, 2015).

Minority-Serving Institutions (MSIs)   MSIs may be any type of institution we describe here, from private liberal arts institution (for example, Bennett College or Tougaloo University) to public research university (University of California, Santa Barbara, or Southern University); denominational comprehensive university (California Lutheran University); or community college (De Anza College or Keweenaw Bay Ojibwa Community College). The US Department of Education designates different types of MSIs based on varying criteria, including historical foundations and contemporary enrollment of students from certain racial or ethnic categories and with threshold levels of students with high financial need. One type—historically black colleges and universities—is a fixed group of institutions designated in the Higher Education Act of 1965. A second, tribal colleges and universities, must be founded and controlled by American Indian tribes (see Gasman, Baez, & Turner, 2008). The other two types, however, are dynamic categories into which a nonprofit predominantly white institution (PWI) may evolve if it reaches a designated proportion of students from the relevant group, 10 percent AANAPI students or 25 percent Hispanic/Latino students. It is important to note that "minority serving" has different meanings on different campuses; some scholars point to negative campus racial climates at some PWIs that are eligible for MSI funding, calling them "minority enrolling" rather than "minority serving" (Johnston & Yeung, 2014). Still, the institutional mission and culture at MSIs tends to support students of color in ways that many PWIs do not (Gasman, Baez, & Turner, 2008).

Tribal Colleges and Universities (TCUs)   Thirty-six tribal colleges and universities educate thirty thousand Native American/American Indian college students, about 9 percent of all Native American/American Indian students (Tribal Colleges and Universities, n.d.). All TCUs grant associates degrees, a handful offer bachelor degrees, and a few offer master degrees. Tribal college missions are similar to community colleges in that they exist to serve students and the surrounding communities. However, what makes tribal colleges unique is their service to reservation communities and strong emphasis on tribal culture, customs, and ways of knowing (González, 2008). The American Indian Higher Education Consortium (1999) asserted that "tribal colleges are different from mainstream community colleges in their cultural identities, which are reflected in virtually every aspect of college life" (p. B-1). Tribal colleges have a mission of preserving their heritage while providing a quality education. Every aspect of these campuses is rooted in Native American culture including artwork, physical structures, and the curriculum. Though they suffer from an extreme lack of resources, their presence is essential to cultural preservation, education, and economic development on reservations (González, 2008; Pavel, Inglebret, & VanDenHende, 1999). TCUs are also critical sources for Native American/American Indian transfer students to PWIs (Makomenaw, 2014).

Historically Black Colleges and Universities (HBCUs)   The mission of historically black colleges and universities (HBCUs) ensures that African Americans receive access to higher education, support in their academic endeavors, and racial empowerment and uplift in a setting that values African American culture, history, and identity (Abelman & Dalessandro, 2009; Harper, Patton, & Wooden, 2009). Abundant literature (for example, Gasman, Baez, Drezner, Sedgwick, Tudico, & Schmid 2007; Gasman, Baez, & Turner, 2008; Kim & Conrad, 2006; Perna & others, 2009) provides evidence that HBCUs exert a substantial positive impact on students, specifically that African American students have more overall positive experiences at these institutions in comparison to peers at predominantly white institutions. Whereas African American students at PWIs often experience feelings of isolation and discrimination, those attending HBCUs thrive because of opportunities to interact one-on-one with faculty members and administrators (many of whom serve as mentors), engage in educationally meaningful activities, develop the academic and intellectual skills to succeed toward graduation, and remain consistently satisfied with their experiences despite the lack of resources available on some campuses. Outcalt and Skewes-Cox (2002) specifically named the human environment—a critical component of campus culture—as a contributor to HBCU student success.

Hispanic-Serving Institutions (HSIs)   HSIs are postsecondary institutions that meet two criteria in order to qualify for federal support: (1) a 25 percent enrollment of Hispanic students and (2) at least 50 percent of students have eligibility for federal student aid. The HSI designation allows institutions to seek federal support through various programs if their student population includes Latino/a students from low-income households (Contreras & Contreras, 2015). There are HSIs in many states across the United States. Altogether, over 50 percent of their student population is Latina/o and they comprise roughly 8 percent of colleges and universities (Garcia, 2012). The largest HSI presence is in California, Texas, and Puerto Rico, and many of these institutions are community colleges (Contreras & Contreras, 2015). Doran (2015) explained that HSIs tend to serve a primarily undergraduate population, and their curriculum is more vocational in nature than at other institutional types.

Although many institutions meet the federal criteria to be considered an HSI, they may not view this designation to be a central distinguishing characteristic. Contreras and Contreras (2015) explained, "The literature on HSIs frames HSI status as largely accidental or due to state and regional Chicano/Latino demographic growth" (p. 152). As a result an institution may be considered an HSI based on demographics rather than on a firm commitment to serving Latino/a students. However, given their large Latino/a population HSIs are well positioned to enhance the educational experiences of Latino/a college students. Researchers have taken an interest in HSIs to study their impact on Latino/a students (Arbelo-Marrero & Milacci, 2015; Contreras & Contreras, 2015; Contreras, Malcom, & Bensimon, 2008; Garcia, 2012; Hagedorn, Chi, Cepeda, & McLain, 2007). Findings from these studies indicate that despite the HSI designation, Latino students often struggle in these environments with outcomes that include high attrition and low completion rates. One reason for these disappointing outcomes, scholars suggest, is a lack of focus on using HSI-specific federal funding to benefit Latino/a students (Hurtado & Ruiz, 2012). Contreras and Contreras (2015) noted, "Yet, in many of these institutions, targeted efforts to raise Latino academic performance is unclear, and those most likely to benefit from these student support grants are low-income White and Asian American students" (p. 154).

Asian American and Native American Pacific Islander–Serving Institutions (AANAPISIs)   Asian American and Pacific Islander (AAPI) students represent a diverse array of ethnicities and cultures. The model minority myth, which has historically been attached to AAPI groups, fails to account for students within AAPI subpopulations who are more recent immigrants, have limited income, or are first-generation students (Conrad & Gasman, 2015; Teranishi, 2012; Teranishi, Maramba, & Ta, 2013). Furthermore, several ethnic groups within the AAPI population are less likely to complete college (Conrad & Gasman, 2015). Given the diverse needs and circumstances of AAPI populations, the US Department of Education established a program in support of Asian American and Native American Pacific Islander–serving institutions (AANAPISIs) (http://www2.ed.gov/programs/aanapi/index.html). AANAPISIs are composed of federally designated two- and four-year colleges and universities "with at least a 10 percent enrollment of AAPI full-time equivalent students, a minimum threshold of low-income students, and lower than average educational and general expenditures per student" (Teranishi, 2011, p. 151). AANAPISIs are significant in that they challenge the model minority myth, highlight the need for more concentrated attention to the access and retention needs of Asian American and Pacific Islander (AAPI) students, and signify a sustained investment of federal and institutional support to assist economically disadvantaged AAPI students to enter and graduate from college (Laanan & Starobin, 2004; Teranishi, 2011, 2012). Since being authorized in 2007, AANAPISIs have used their federal funding to enhance academic offerings, leadership development, and research opportunities, all focusing on AAPI students (Conrad & Gasman, 2015; Teranishi, 2011). Similar to HSIs, AANAPISIs are primarily located in areas with a high concentration of AAPI populations and serve first-generation, low-income students (Conrad & Gasman, 2015).

Online Institutions   There are some online and hybrid learning experiences at all of the previously mentioned institutional types, but there are also fully online institutions that enroll substantial numbers of students in the United States and around the world. These institutions, too, have missions and cultures. Often, but not always for-profit entities, fully online colleges and universities offer a range of curricula, degrees, and course formats. Student services such as financial aid and registration may be key means to convey mission and support to students (Yadgir, 2011), who may respond to their experience of institutional culture by persisting at the institution, stopping out, transferring, or departing higher education (Shefsky & Sutton, 2015). Adopting a customer service approach to online instruction and resources to meet the needs of, for example, students who are also working full-time means providing instruction and services that students need to make the most of the time that they devote to education (Lechuga, 2008). The symbols and artifacts of campus culture that we describe in the next section may not be as easy to locate in an online environment, but an online institution can convey a culture of student-centered education and services through the timeliness of communication and the format and architecture of its online presence. The number of mouse clicks—or time waiting on hold on a telephone call—it takes to get to someone who can help resolve a problem, for example, communicates a culture of support or indifference to the student.

◆ ◆ ◆

The range of diverse colleges and universities exemplifies institutional types committed to creating campus environments focused on student success. Through their missions they convey their institutional identities as distinct from thousands of other colleges and universities in the United States. Through their educational programs, they aim to create campus climates that align with their missions and identities. Though diverse in their missions and educational offerings, at their core, these institutions represent a commitment to student success in college. How institutions communicate their commitment is embedded within their respective campus culture.

Campus Culture

Regardless of institutional mission or type, campus cultures are powerful forces that shape—and are shaped by—postsecondary constituents. Campus culture can be a difficult element to define and assess on a college or university campus (Kuh & Whitt, 1988), but even so they wield substantial influence in the lives of students and faculty and staff members (Kuh, 2001/2002; Museus, 2008). For example, Museus, Nichols, and Lambert (2008) found that campus racial climate, a component of campus culture, can directly and indirectly affect persistence and degree completion of racially minoritized populations. Kuh and Whitt (1988) referred to culture as the "invisible tapestry" of an institution: "persistent patterns of norms, values, practices, beliefs, and assumptions that shape the behavior of individuals and groups in a college or university and provide a frame of reference within which to interpret the meaning of events and actions on and off the campus" (p. iv).

Each institution, regardless of institutional type, has its own unique culture. Individuals within a particular setting become familiar with "the way things are done" on campus and interpret observations in a similar fashion. Conversely, those new to a given institution might interpret the same observations in a different way because they lack familiarity with campus norms. Although campus culture may often be perceived as static, the opposite is true. Campus culture is ever changing, influenced by time and the diverse people who inhabit the campus environment. Drawing on the work of Schein (1985), Kuh and Whitt (1988) described three levels of campus culture: artifacts, values, and basic assumptions and beliefs.

Artifacts refer to symbolic aspects of campus culture as well as tangible evidence of how culture is practiced. Artifacts might come in the form of rituals such as first-year convocation or graduation and signify tradition, community standards, and expectations. Artifacts might also be embedded in the language used or stories told to communicate campus values that are often passed down for generations.

Values, the second level of culture, represent ideals that are espoused and enacted on campus. Values such as diversity, intellectual freedom, and critical thinking are often explicitly mentioned in institutional mission statements as well as value statements. They also shape the belief systems and underlying assumptions individuals hold within their respective campus environments. Values embody what institutions hold dear. In times of crises institutional leaders often rely on values and subsequently make value-driven decisions about the future of their college or university.

The third level of culture deals with basic assumptions and beliefs. These assumptions and beliefs are not stated explicitly, but they are highly influential in shaping thoughts, ideas, perceptions, and feelings of those on campus, particularly in "responses to threats to institutional survival" (Kuh & Whitt, 1988, p. 25). Basic assumptions and beliefs are deeply embedded and shape how people view reality. They reveal the implicit, unquestioned nature of human interactions on campus, but they may be difficult to articulate because of their implicit, entrenched nature. Senior campus leaders, for example, may hold loyalty to the institution as one of these assumptions; in a crisis, such as a student death from alcohol consumed on campus or alleged hazing, they may assume that any public or private questioning of policies, practices, or handling of the incident constitutes unforgivable disloyalty to them and the institution. Beliefs about the meaning of a shared identity as a Spartan, Hoosier, or other mascot seen in social media campaigns such as #WeAreAll[Mascots] are another example of unarticulated assumptions about a presumed collective identity.

Institutional type, characteristics, and mission combine to exert a cultural milieu on campuses that set an institution apart from others. Culture is present in classrooms, the student union, and human interactions. For example, various subcultures exist on campuses among students, faculty members, and administrators. Social identities, academic disciplines, administrative functions (such as academic advising, residence life, counseling, or admissions) may influence the formation of subcultures. Each group will view the campus based on their respective role and status in that environment. Moreover, the functioning of subcultures and the larger institutional culture are mutually shaping phenomena. It is important to understand that culture is a driving force on college and university campuses that can shape broader understanding of institutional type and the characteristics that make each institution unique, despite larger categorizations.

Application of Research and Theory to Student Affairs Practice

Two books—Hirt's (2006) *Where You Work Matters* and Manning, Kinzie, and Schuh's (2014) *One Size Does Not Fit All*—remind student affairs professionals that institutional mission, type, size, and culture matter in designing and working within various higher education environments (see chapter 16 for a further discussion of aligning student affairs practice with institutional mission and culture). They present compelling cases for why and how educators can maintain commitments to core professional principles, values, and theories in the context of very different institutions. We share their conviction that research and theory can inform practice in any professional setting. To illustrate, we provide the following example of diversity-related services in higher education.

Diversity-related services have existed on campuses since the late 1960s. In their earlier establishment, diversity programming focused primarily on race, but it soon expanded to include women and LGBT groups. How these programs and services are realized likely differs from campus to campus. For example, at large research institutions, it would not be surprising to find race-specific culture centers with missions designed to address the four primary racially minoritized populations in the United States (that is, African American/Black, Asian American, Latino/a, and Native American/American Indian). At a small liberal arts college or comprehensive institution, culture centers might exist in the form of a multicultural center or office. Most often, culture centers are located within the student affairs division, though a few are organizationally situated in academic affairs. Regardless of the diversity effort, their existence signifies an institutional commitment to valuing diversity. In contemporary higher education, diversity, or at least the pursuit of it, has become a normalized value that can shift culture and climate on campus prompting campus inhabitants to view diversity as institutionalized or embedded in the overall function and structure of campus. More important, student affairs educators also understand the value and role of diversity services and programs and work to provide a campus experience in which students are exposed to diverse people, perspectives, and ideas. Thus, as campus contexts may change, enduring values such as diversity and respect for others are longstanding, supported by research, and should inform student affairs practice.

Conclusion

The provision of programs and services consistent with institutional mission and type is paramount to maintaining high-quality student affairs and services. Aligning priorities, activities, and assessment to the mission and to campus culture provides a foundation and a context through which to advance student as well as institutional needs. A hallmark of US higher education is the diversity of institutional identities, from small private women's colleges to large public research universities, that are also MSIs. Yet this diversity calls on educators to align their work with the institutional mission and culture. Whether in the area of serving diverse students or in any one of a number of the areas discussed in this book, knowing how mission, type, and culture affect students and student affairs is essential to good practice.

Discussion Questions

1. Choose an institution from among the types described in this chapter. How much can you learn online about its mission? Its culture? What evidence (for example, curriculum, faculty members, student body, activities) do you observe that aligns with the institutional mission? What do you observe that seems counter to or unrelated to the mission? As a newcomer to that community, or someone considering joining it as a student or employee, what elements of the mission and apparent culture stand out to you?

2. What institutional types did we *not* describe in this chapter? What makes them distinct from and similar to some of the types we did describe? What elements of institutional mission and culture at these types would influence the provision of student affairs and services?

3. What institutional types do you believe may disappear from US higher education? Are there emerging institutional types that you believe will become more prominent or relevant? Why will these institutional types disappear or become more relevant? Are there adaptations that some institutions could make to survive or to make themselves even more relevant?

References

Abelman, R., & Dalessandro, A. (2009). The institutional vision of historically black colleges and universities. *Journal of Black Studies, 40*(2), 105–134.

American Indian Higher Education Consortium. (1999, Feb.). *Tribal colleges: An introduction.* Retrieved from http://www.aihec.org/colleges.cfml

Arbelo-Marrero, F., & Milacci, F. (2015). A phenomenological investigation of the academic persistence of undergraduate Hispanic nontraditional students at Hispanic-serving institutions. *Journal of Hispanic Higher Education.* Advance online publication. doi:10.1177/1538192715584192

Astin, A. W. (1999). How the liberal arts college affects students. *Daedalus, 128*(10), 77–100.

Barr, M. J. (2000). The importance of institutional mission. In M. J. Barr, M. K. Desler, & Associates (Eds.), *The handbook of student affairs administration* (2nd ed., pp. 25–36). San Francisco: Jossey-Bass.

Cohen, A. M., & Brawer, F. B. (2003). *The American community college* (4th ed.). San Francisco: Jossey-Bass.

Conrad, C., & Gasman, M. (2015). *Educating a diverse nation: Lessons from minority-serving institutions.* Cambridge, MA: Harvard University Press.

Contreras, F., & Contreras, G. J. (2015). Raising the bar for Hispanic-serving institutions: An analysis of college completion and success rates. *Journal of Hispanic Higher Education, 14*(2), 151–170.

Contreras, F. E., Malcom, L. E., & Bensimon, E. M. (2008). Hispanic-serving institutions: Closeted identity and the production of equitable outcomes for Latino/a students. In M. Gasman, B. Baez, & C. Turner (Eds.), *Understanding minority-serving institutions: Interdisciplinary perspective* (pp. 71–90). Albany: State University of New York Press.

Doran, E. E. (2015). Negotiating access and tier one aspirations: The historical evolution of a striving Hispanic-serving institution. *Journal of Hispanic Higher Education*. Advance online publication. doi:10.1177/1538192715570638

Elfman, L. (2015). Women's colleges address transgender admission policies. *Women in Higher Education, 24*(4), 6.

Garcia, G. A. (2012). Does percentage of Latinas/os affect graduation rates at 4-year Hispanic-serving institutions (HSIs), emerging HSIs, and Non-HSIs? *Journal of Hispanic Higher Education, 12*(3), 256–268.

Gasman, M., Baez, B., Drezner, N. D., Sedgwick, K. V., Tudico, C., & Schmid, J. M. (2007). Historically black colleges and universities: Recent trends. *Academe, 93*(1), 69–77.

Gasman, M., Baez, B., & Turner, C.S.V. (2008). *Understanding minority-serving institutions.* Albany: State University of New York Press.

Geiger, R. L. (2014). *The history of American higher education: Learning and culture from the founding to World War II.* Princeton, NJ: Princeton University Press.

González, R. G. (2008). From creation to cultural resistance and expansion: Research on American Indian higher education. In J. C. Smart (Ed.), *Higher education: Handbook of theory and research* (Vol. 28, pp. 299–327). Dordrecht, The Netherlands: Springer Netherlands.

Hagedorn, L. S., Chi, W., Cepeda, R. M., & McLain, M. (2007). An investigation of critical mass: The role of Latino representation in the success of urban community college students. *Research in Higher Education, 48*(1), 73–91.

Hardwick-Day. (2008). *What matters in college after college: A comparative alumnae research study.* West Hartford, CT: Women's College Coalition. Retrieved from http://www.womenscolleges.org/sites/default/files/report/files/main/2012hardwickdaycomparativealumnaesurveymarch2012_0.pdf

Harper, S. R., Patton, L. D., & Wooden, O. S. (2009). Access and equity for African American students in higher education: A critical race historical analysis of policy efforts. *Journal of Higher Education, 80*(4), 389–414.

Hartley, M. (2003). "There is no way without a because": Revitalization of purpose at three liberal arts colleges. *The Review of Higher Education, 27*(1), 75–102.

Henderson, B. B., & Buchanan, H. E. (2007). The scholarship of teaching and learning: A special niche for faculty at comprehensive universities? *Research in Higher Education, 48*(5), 523–543.

Hirt, J. B. (2006). *Where you work matters: Student affairs administrators at different types of institutions.* Lanham, MD: University Press of America.

Hurtado, S., & Ruiz, A. (2012). *Realizing the potential of Hispanic-serving institutions: Multiple dimensions of institutional diversity for advancing Hispanic higher education.* Los Angeles: University of California, Higher Education Research Institute. Retrieved from http://www.hacu.net/images/hacu/OPAI/H3ERC/2012_papers/Hurtado%20ruiz%20-%20realizing%20the%20potential%20of%20hsis%20-%20updated%202012.pdf

Johnston, M. P., & Yeung, F. P. (2014). Asian Americans and campus climate: Investigating group differences around a racial incident. *Journal of Student Affairs Research and Practice, 51*(2), 143–156.

Kim, M. M., & Conrad, C. F. (2006). The impact of historically black colleges and universities on the academic success of African-American students. *Research in Higher Education, 47*(4), 399–427.

Kinzie, J., Thomas, A. D., Palmer, M. M., Umbach, P. D., & Kuh, G. D. (2007). Women students at coeducational and women's colleges: How do their experiences compare? *Journal of College Student Development, 48*(2), 145–165.

Kuh, G. D. (2001/2002). Organizational culture and student persistence: Prospects and puzzles. *Journal of College Student Retention: Research, Theory, & Practice, 3*(1), 23–39.

Kuh, G. D. (2009). What student affairs professionals need to know about student engagement. *Journal of College Student Development, 50*(6), 683–706.

Kuh, G. D., & Whitt, E. J. (1988). The invisible tapestry: Culture in American colleges and universities. *ASHE-ERIC Higher Education Report, 17*(1). Washington, DC: The George Washington University, Graduate School of Education and Human Development.

Laanan, F., & Starobin, S. S. (2004). Defining Asian American and Pacific Islander–serving institutions. In B. Vigil Laden (Ed.), *Serving minority populations* (New Directions for Community Colleges, no. 127, pp. 49–59). San Francisco: Jossey-Bass.

Lechuga, V. M. (2008). Assessment, knowledge, and customer service: Contextualizing faculty work at for-profit colleges and universities. *The Review of Higher Education, 31*(3), 287–307.

Lee, J. J., & Rhoads, R. A. (2004). Faculty entrepreneurialism and the challenge to undergraduate education at research universities. *Research in Higher Education, 45*(7), 739–760.

Lyons, J. W. (1993). The importance of institutional mission. In M. J. Barr & Associates, *The handbook of student affairs administration* (pp. 3–15). San Francisco: Jossey-Bass.

Makomenaw, M. (2014). Goals, family, and community: What drives tribal college transfer student success. *Journal of Student Affairs Research and Practice, 51*(4), 380–391.

Manning, K., Kinzie, J., & Schuh, J. H. (2014). *One size does not fit all: Traditional and innovative models of student affairs practice* (2nd ed.). New York: Routledge.

Meacham, J., & Gaff, J. G. (2006). Learning goals in mission statements: Implications for educational leadership. *Liberal Education, 92*(1), 6–13.

Museus, S. (2008). Focusing on institutional fabric: Assessing campus cultures to enhance cross-cultural engagement. In S. R. Harper (Ed.), *Creating inclusive campus environments for cross-cultural learning and student engagement* (pp. 205–234). Washington, DC: NASPA Student Affairs Administrators in Higher Education.

Museus, S. D., Nichols, A. H., & Lambert, A. D. (2008). Racial differences in the effects of campus climate on degree completion: A structural equation model. *The Review of Higher Education, 32*(1), 107–134.

National Center for Education Statistics. (2015). *Condition of education 2015.* Washington, DC: US Department of Education.

O'Meara, K. A., & Braskamp, L. A. (2005). Aligning faculty reward systems and development to promote faculty and student growth. *Journal of Student Affairs Research and Practice, 42*(2), 369–386.

Outcalt, C. L., & Skewes-Cox, T. E. (2002). Involvement, interaction, and satisfaction: The human environment at HBCUs. *The Review of Higher Education, 25*, 331–347.

Pascarella, E. T., Wolniak, G. C., Seifert, T. A., Cruce, T. M., & Blaich, C. F. (Eds.). (2005). Liberal arts colleges and liberal arts education: The evidence on impacts. *ASHE Higher Education Report, 31*(3), 1–148. San Francisco: Jossey-Bass.

Pavel, D. M., Inglebret, E., & VanDenHende, M. (1999). Tribal colleges. In B. Townsend (Ed.), *Two-year colleges for women and minorities* (pp. 113–149). New York: Falmer.

Perna, L., Lundy-Wagner, V., Drezner, N. D., Gasman, M., Yoon, S., Bose, E., & Gary, S. (2009). The contribution of HBCUs to the preparation of African American women for STEM careers: A case study. *Research in Higher Education, 50*(1), 1–23.

Renn, K. A., & Lytle, J. H. (2010). Student leaders at women's postsecondary institutions: A global perspective. *Journal of Student Affairs Research and Practice, 47*(2), 212–229.

Schein, E. H. (1985). *Organizational culture and leadership: A dynamic view.* San Francisco: Jossey-Bass.

Schuetz, P. (2005). UCLA community college review: Campus environment: A missing link in studies of community college attrition. *Community College Review, 32*, 60–80.

Seifert, T. A., Goodman, K. M., Lindsay, N. K., Jorgensen, J. D., Wolniak, G. C., Pascarella, E. T., & Blaich, C. F. (2008). The effects of liberal arts experiences on liberal arts outcomes. *Research in Higher Education, 49*, 107–125.

Seifert, T. A., Pascarella, E. T., Goodman, K. M., Salisbury, M. H., & Blaich, C. F. (2010). Liberal arts colleges and good practices in undergraduate education: Additional evidence. *Journal of College Student Development, 51*, 1–22.

Shefsky, E., & Sutton, R. (2015, March). Stop-outs: A new variable in online student retention. *Society for Information Technology & Teacher Education International Conference, 2015*(1), 7990–7997.

Teranishi, R. T. (2011). Asian American and Native American Pacific Islander–Serving Institutions: Areas of growth, innovation, and collaboration. *AAPI Nexus: Asian Americans & Pacific Islanders Policy, Practice and Community, 9*(1&2), 151–155.

Teranishi, R. T. (2012). Asian American and Pacific Islander students and the institutions that serve them. *Change: The Magazine of Higher Learning, 44*(2), 16–22.

Teranishi, R. T., Maramba, D. C., & Ta, M. H. (2013). Asian American and Native American Pacific Islander–serving institutions: Mutable sites for science, technology, engineering, and math (STEM) degree production. In R. T. Palmer, D. C. Maramba, & M. Gasman (Eds.), *Fostering success of ethnic and racial minorities in STEM: The role of minority-serving institutions* (pp. 168–180). New York: Routledge.

Teranishi, R. T., Suárez-Orozco, C., & Suárez-Orozco, M. (2011). Immigrants in community colleges. *The Future of Children, 21*(1), 153–169.

Thelin, J. R. (2011). *A history of American higher education.* Baltimore: Johns Hopkins University Press.

Tidball, M. E., Smith, D. G., Tidball, C. S., & Wolf-Wendel, L. E. (1999). *Taking women seriously: Lessons and legacies for educating the majority.* Phoenix, AZ: Oryx.

Tribal Colleges and Universities. (n.d.). *Tribal colleges and universities.* White House Initiative on American Indian and Alaska Native Youth. Retrieved from http://www.ed.gov/edblogs/whiaiane/tribes-tcus/tribal-colleges-and-universities/

Umbach, P. D., & Kuh, G. D. (2006). Student experiences with diversity at liberal arts colleges: Another claim for distinctiveness. *Journal of Higher Education, 77*(1), 169–192.

Yadgir, S. A. (2011). Leading in a technological age. *Educational Research and Reviews, 6*(10), 664–670.

CHAPTER 5

CAMPUS CLIMATE AND DIVERSITY

Kimberly A. Griffin

Many colleges and universities strive to offer their students inclusive campus environments, where all feel welcomed and accepted. But during spring 2015, social media and national news outlets prominently displayed the many ways institutions continue to struggle with this goal. A video surfaced in March, documenting white Oklahoma University students singing, "There Will Never be a N***r in SAE" to the tune of "If You're Happy and You Know It." Later that month, an e-mail from a male fraternity student at the University of Maryland was released that dismissed the notion of needing consent before engaging in sexual activity and used racial slurs to describe black, Indian, and Asian women. Additionally, Muslim students protested showings of the film *American Sniper*, which tells the story of a US Navy SEAL during the Iraq War, arguing the film perpetuates stereotypes and lends to unsafe campus environments for Middle Eastern and Muslim students. Student veterans and others argued that the film should be showed, expressing concern about students' development of the ability to engage those with different points of view and violations of the First Amendment.

Students often aggregate these kinds of incidents with their own experiences and observations about campus dynamics to form general impressions of their campus environment and culture. Researchers widely report how students' perceptions of hostility, conflict, and marginalization in their campus communities can have negative implications for development, learning, achievement, and persistence (for example, Chang, Eagan, Lin, & Hurtado, 2011; Johnson, Wasserman, Yildirim, & Yonai, 2014; Tetreault, Fette, Meidlinger, & Hope, 2013). Conversely, more welcoming and hospitable campus environments can create opportunities for students to be their authentic selves, develop a sense of belonging in the campus community, and gain access to social support, outcomes that are all related to learning, development, and persistence (see, for examples, Locks, Hurtado, Bowman, & Oseguera, 2008; Lundberg, 2014;

Museus & Maramba, 2011). The question then becomes, how do institutions create campus environments that welcome students from all backgrounds and foster students' abilities to embrace perspectives different from their own, and what role can we, as student affairs educators, play in this process?

To foster better understandings of the challenges college and university campuses face as they seek to maximize students' access to safe and supportive campus communities, this chapter examines multiple aspects of the study of diversity and campus climate. The evolution in our understanding of these constructs is presented, along with an overview of multiple theoretical frameworks developed to explore and improve the climates students' experience. After an overview of key themes in climate research, I offer suggestions regarding what student affairs professionals can do individually and collectively to promote more hospitable campus environments that increase and welcome diversity.

Defining Diversity

How do we know when an environment is diverse? What does diversity actually mean? When discussing diversity, we perhaps think most often in terms of numbers, examining how many individuals from various groups are represented in a campus community (Hurtado, Milem, Clayton-Pedersen, & Allen, 1999). Although representation is important, what makes a campus diverse goes beyond numbers. Mitchell Chang and Erica Yamamura (2006) suggested that simply examining the enrollments of white students or students of color can mask the nuances in a campus environment. For example, is a community that is 10 percent black, 12 percent Latino, and 8 percent Asian American more or less diverse than one that is 22 percent Asian American, 5 percent Latino, and 3 percent black? Both campuses could report that 30 percent of the student body comprises people of color, but would both campuses be equally diverse?

Diversity can also be defined in terms of actions and educational experiences. Gurin, Dey, Hurtado, and Gurin (2002) and Milem (2003) argued structural diversity, campus initiatives, and diverse interactions all must be considered in assessing campus diversity. Structural diversity is the actual number of individuals from different racial and ethnic groups present on campus. Diversity-related initiatives are activities inside and outside of the classroom that address the experiences of marginalized populations or lead to the development of cultural competence. Finally, diverse interactions represent engagement with those from different backgrounds. Each of these dimensions may positively influence educational outcomes, and the effect is amplified by the strength and weakened by the absence of other dimensions (Milem, 2003).

Definitions are also distinguished by who is considered "diverse." As institutions began to discuss diversity in the 1970s and 1980s, conversations often focused on how to address the needs and increase the success of students from racial or ethnic groups underrepresented in higher education (Native

Americans, blacks, and Latinos) (Smith, 2009). In addition, legal challenges levied against the use of affirmative action in college admissions pushed the conceptualization of diversity as largely linked to race and ethnicity. As the Supreme Court considered the continued need and constitutional basis for affirmative action policies, the arguments that gained the most traction were rooted in the "diversity rationale," which claims that increasing the number of individuals from diverse backgrounds leads to gains in learning and enhances students' abilities to engage in our increasingly diverse democracy.

Consistent with this argument, a generation of researchers clearly established the positive learning outcomes stemming from exposure and opportunities to engage with those from different racial and ethnic backgrounds (for examples, see antonio, Chang, Hakuta, Kenny, Levin, & Milem, 2004; Chang, Denson, Saenz, & Misa, 2006; Gurin, Dey, Hurtado, & Gurin, 2002; Milem, 2003). Milem's (2003) comprehensive review documented a wide range of outcomes associated with increased exposure to diversity, including racial understanding and awareness, critical thinking skills, and overall satisfaction with one's college experience. According to Hu and Kuh (2003), students generally experience learning and developmental gains when they interact with individuals from a different racial or ethnic background. Interestingly, although white students were less likely to engage with individuals from different racial or ethnic backgrounds, in most cases, they reported the greatest gains. Further, engagement with individuals from different racial and ethnic backgrounds can have a long-term influence on outcomes. Jayakumar (2008) found that exposure to diversity in college was related to more diverse friends and living in more diverse neighborhoods postcollege as well as the development of competencies necessary for success in an increasingly diverse work force (for example, perspective taking, openness to challenge). Bowman (2011) reported that participation in ethnic studies courses and diversity workshops in college could have an indirect, but significant, effect on individuals' self-assessments of personal growth and the ability to recognize racism thirteen years after they completed college.

In the mid-1990s and into the 2000s, demographic shifts and increasing attention to multiple marginalized social identity groups, as well as legal challenges calling for broader conceptualizations of diversity, pushed institutions to think beyond race and ethnicity. Current definitions implemented by many institutions attend to a wide range of social identities, including race and ethnicity, gender, sexual orientation and identity, ability, class, religion, and region of origin (Smith, 2009). These shifts have been met with mixed interpretations and complex emotions. Increasingly broad definitions of diversity can promote inclusion, enabling institutions to leverage new opportunities for students to learn from one another and embrace perspectives different from their own (Smith, 2009). For example, Park, Denson, and Bowman (2012) examined the relationship among socioeconomic diversity, racial diversity, and engagement across multiple forms of difference. Although there was no direct relationship between socioeconomic diversity and participation in diversity activities or cross-racial interaction, there was an indirect influence of socioeconomic diversity and engagement. However, some have expressed concern that the definition of diversity may be getting too broad (White, 2015). If everyone is from a diverse background, what does diversity really mean? Does engaging with a student from a different geographic location who plays a musical instrument or has a different political ideology produce the same educational and social outcomes as engaging with someone from a different racial background or who embraces a different sexual identity? These are questions many campuses will continue to wrestle with as scholars, practitioners, and institutional leaders seek to understand learning across difference.

Frameworks for Studying Diversity and Campus Climate

Assessments of campus diversity offer insights into who is present in a campus community; however, assessments of campus climate can help us gain a more comprehensive image of how diversity is engaged and experienced. Climate is defined as the current patterns of behavior in a campus community and how those behaviors are perceived (Peterson & Spencer, 1990). Thus, in relation to issues of diversity, campus climate can be understood as attitudes, beliefs, behaviors, and perceptions of community members about issues of difference (Hurtado, Milem, Clayton-Pederson, & Allen, 1999).

The models that follow capture several of the frameworks advanced by scholars for understanding and assessing the campus climate for diversity. Although they share key characteristics, such as the incorporation of a multidimensional framework and attention to internal and external factors shaping climate, each offers a unique perspective on how campus climate is shaped and subsequently can be transformed.

The Campus Climate Framework

Hurtado, Milem, Clayton-Pedersen, and Allen (1999) developed a campus racial climate (CRC) model based on a review of extant literature on the experiences of people of color in higher education. Within this framework, climate is a multidimensional phenomenon that is uniquely constructed on each campus through a convergence of external forces (governmental policy and sociohistorical factors) and an institution's specific racial context. Institution-specific forces shaping climate can be assessed across four dimensions: (1) structural diversity, (2) historical legacy of inclusion or exclusion, (3) psychological climate, and (4) behavioral climate (Hurtado, Milem, Clayton-Pederson, & Allen, 1999). These four dimensions influence one another and shape attitudes, beliefs, behaviors, and perceptions about race and diversity in a specific community.

Hurtado and colleagues (1999) argued that colleges and universities are most aware of the campus's structural diversity, or the numerical representation of people of color. Many may try to improve campus climate through structural diversity, increasing their efforts to recruit a diverse student body.

Although critical to creating opportunities for engagement across difference, increasing structural diversity without emphasizing the other dimensions of climate creates conflict, competition, and separation across groups (Hurtado, Milem, Clayton-Pederson, & Allen, 1999). For example, although history cannot be changed, an institution's legacy or history of inclusion and exclusion can continue to have implications. An institution's legacy of inclusion or exclusion captures whether a campus's past treatment of marginalized groups is acknowledged and perceived as something that continues to need to be addressed. The psychological dimension reflects the perceived hostility, racism, and racial tension among community members. The psychological dimension is emphasized in many assessments of CRC, because students are often asked about their perceptions of the campus environment (Hurtado, Griffin, Arellano, & Cuellar, 2008). Finally, the behavioral dimension captures the frequency and quality of interaction between diverse peers (Hurtado, Milem, Clayton-Pederson, & Allen, 1999). This dimension reminds institutional leaders to consider with whom students study, eat, and live and whether interactions between students of different backgrounds are open and friendly or tense and hostile.

In recent years, the scholars who originally developed the model proposed adjustments, which have resulted in two new versions. In their revision, Milem, Chang, and antonio (2005) acknowledged the importance of thinking about diversity broadly, but they continue the model's emphasis on racial and ethnic diversity. Perhaps the most notable changes were to the CRC model itself, where the *structural diversity dimension* was renamed *compositional diversity*. A new organizational-structural diversity dimension was added, representing how institutional structures, policies, and procedures may benefit dominant groups.

Hurtado, Alvarez, Guillermo-Wan, Cuellar, and Arellano (2012) also offered a revision to the campus racial climate framework: the multicontextual model for diverse learning environments (DLE). Although previous iterations of this climate model focused largely on racial and ethnic diversity, the DLE embraces a broader definition. This model centers students, their multiple identities, and learning outcomes as a result of the climates they encounter. The DLE incorporates the five internal and external dimensions of climate presented in Milem, Chang, and antonio's (2005) model, but they are presented in a three-dimensional, layered format. Students' experiences in curricular and cocurricular contexts lie at the center of the model and are linked to their identities, the identities of faculty and staff members, and course and programmatic content. This model also explicitly incorporates a link to three kinds of outcomes: habits of mind and lifelong learning (for example, critical thinking, motivation, willingness to accept feedback); the competencies necessary to navigate in a multicultural world; and academic achievement.

The Framework for Diversity

Smith's framework for diversity (2009) highlights four dimensions of campus diversity: access and success, climate and intergroup relations, education and scholarship, and institutional viability and vitality. Smith argued that because of colleges' decentralized nature, conversations about diversity and climate happen in multiple locations across and from multiple perspectives within institutions. This necessitates an integrated strategy, bringing multiple stakeholders to the table and acknowledging the importance of monitoring indicators of progress (Smith, 2009). Institutions must be assessed across all four dimensions of the model to facilitate change and diversity in their campus communities (Garcia, Hudgins, Musil, Nettles, Sedlacek, & Smith, 2001; Smith, 2009).

The dimensions of Smith's (2009) model are complementary and interconnected. Access and success are defined as how much students from various backgrounds are included and succeeding in higher education. Often assessed through campus representation and completion rates, Smith noted that this is where many diversity efforts begin and unfortunately end. How students experience campus and relate to one another across difference is captured in the climate and intergroup relations dimension, addressing the ways sense of belonging and community are fostered. Education and scholarship reflects the presence of diverse perspectives in the curriculum and learning goals, considering whether and how students are being prepared to engage in a pluralistic society. Institutional viability and vitality focuses on institutional resources and capacity to support a diverse campus community. In other words, how are diversity goals and initiatives incorporated in the institutional mission, reflected in the culture, incorporated into institutional processes, or addressed in staff member training and development?

The Transformational Tapestry Model

The transformational tapestry model was developed to guide assessment, planning, and, ultimately, action fostering more inclusive climates and organizational change (Rankin & Reason, 2008). The focus of this model is on the social climate, or the quality of social interactions on a given campus. The model embraces a power and privilege lens, in which individuals in dominant groups have unearned privilege and experience benefits that those from marginalized groups do not. Similar to Smith's (2009) model, the transformational tapestry model aims to transform campus communities for all marginalized groups, rather than focusing on one specific population.

The four dimensions of the transformational tapestry model are the current climate, assessment procedures, transformation interventions, and the transformed climate (Rankin & Reason, 2008). The first dimension, current climate, is influenced by six different factors: access and retention, research and scholarship, inter- and intra-group relations, curriculum and pedagogy, institutional policies and services, and external relations. The level of support and validation, inclusion of diverse perspectives, and effort to promote equitable outcomes for all across each of these dimensions shapes the way campus climate is experienced by members of the community.

Assessment of the multiple aspects of climate, the second dimension of the model, occurs through a multistep process. First, there is a level of preparation and strategies to encourage community members to take ownership of the process through convening a social equity team, fact-finding interviews, and a comprehensive systems analysis of institutional guiding documents and data. Second, the institutional climate is assessed using survey research methodology, followed by dissemination of the results and recommendations to the community. In phase three, the social equity team formulates a diversity strategic plan, incorporating the data from the internal assessment and feedback from their constituency groups. This plan should include strategies addressing the six factors influencing campus climate. In the final phase, the plan is implemented, along with strategies to engage in longitudinal assessment of institutional progress in transforming campus climate.

The climate assessment drives the third dimension of the model: transformation interventions. The social equity team develops a strategic plan based on the findings, addressing the six factors influencing climate. In addition to identifying immediate, short-term, and long-term actions, the plan should articulate specific goals and assign responsibilities to various units across the institution. In the final dimension of the model, the transformed climate, the plan is widely shared, and plans are developed for ongoing assessment.

Comparing the Models

Institutional leaders and student affairs professionals may find any one or all three of these climate models useful as they aim to improve students' experiences on their respective campuses. All three models move beyond a reliance on "the numbers," offering leaders ways to understand the dynamics that can make their campuses more equitable and comfortable spaces in which to learn and develop. All three models remind that the recruitment and retention of a diverse student body must move beyond admissions or graduation rates; they reinforce the need to examine campus dynamics and interactions across groups to better understand the nature of the environment students' enter.

Although each model offers an important multidimensional perspective of campus climate, each also offers a somewhat unique perspective. The various versions of the CRC model turn attention toward whether and how people are interacting and whether institutional structures are conducive to fostering such interactions. Further, the CRC model more directly incorporates an institution's history and external factors such as national policies, social movements, and sociohistorical patterns, acknowledging the larger context within which an individual campus's climate exists. Interestingly, Smith's (2009) model for diversity focuses perhaps more directly on promoting equitable outcomes than climate itself; understanding and addressing climate issues is part of a larger institutional project to promote more equitable outcomes. The transformational tapestry model is grounded in assessment and organizational change. Although the CRC and framework for diversity can also guide research and assessment, the transformational tapestry model is unique in its articulation of a set of steps leaders can take to better understand their climates and develop strategies for institutional transformation. Thus, although all three models offer useful insights, careful consideration must be given to which model may be best suited to the user's needs.

How Students Experience Climate

Consistent with earlier models framing campus climate that emphasized racial and ethnic diversity, much of the work assessing students' experiences with campus climate focuses on the experiences of students of color. Students of color report more direct and indirect experiences with racism than their white peers, leading to more negative assessments of the campus environment (Pewewardy & Frey, 2002; Rankin & Reason, 2005; Suarez-Balcazar, Orellana-Damacela, Portillo, Rowan, & Andrews-Guillen, 2003). Three decades of research have examined the ways in which Asian American, black, Latina/o, and Native American students have experienced racism and isolation at predominantly white institutions, documenting the ways they have been subject to and experienced stereotypes about their ability, exclusion from spaces inside and outside of the classroom, harassment, and unfair treatment (see reviews by Harper & Hurtado, 2007; Smith, 2009).

Traditionally, researchers have found that white students often view the campus climate for students of color more favorably than their peers and are less likely to recognize the marginalization or racism students of color face (Harper & Hurtado, 2007; Rankin & Reason, 2005). Some may endorse perspectives informed by color-blind racism, rooted in beliefs that race does not matter, that merit drives all decision making, and any differences in experiences or outcomes across race are because of class, culture, or personality (Cabrera, 2014; Reason & Evans, 2007). Although being less likely to see racism and marginalization against people of color, white students may be increasingly likely to claim that they are being oppressed and are subject to "reverse" racism because of affirmative action and targeted student support programs (Cabrera, 2014). These trends remind student affairs professionals and scholars about the importance of disaggregating climate data and including questions about climate for specific groups.

More recent research highlights the subtle ways in which students experience marginalization. For example, scholars have increasingly examined microaggressions, or verbal and nonverbal "unconscious, subtle forms of racism" (Solorzano, Ceja, & Yosso, 2000, p. 60), which can become increasingly debilitating over time and are related to negative academic and psychological outcomes (Nadal, Wong, Griffin, Davidoff, & Sriken, 2014). Microaggressions can come in multiple forms, including racial jokes, social avoidance and exclusion, expectations that one person can represent the perspectives of his or her whole social group, minimization of racist experiences, or assumptions about an individual's academic skills and abilities based on group membership. The experience of microaggressions appears common across students of color; however, specific expectations, stereotypes, and interactions appear to vary. Some may embrace the "model minority stereotype" of Asian Americans that frames them as more academically able and not subject to racism and oppression because of their own hard work (Museus, 2014; Trytten, Lowe, & Walden, 2012). McCabe's work (2009) suggested that black men were assumed to be more hostile and aggressive, whereas Latinas were exoticized and subsequently more subject to unwanted sexual advances.

A robust body of literature examines the campus climate for women, noting that they are more likely to perceive campus environments as exclusionary and unwelcoming (Allan & Madden, 2006; Hall & Sandler, 1982). Although women have experienced success with gaining access to higher education and are well represented on most campuses, there are significant differences in their college experiences and outcomes (Jacobs, 1996). Hall and Sandler (1982) are early scholars who described a "chilly" academic climate for women marked by professors who perceive women as less able, use sexist language, minimize or ignore women's contributions, and offer women fewer opportunities for meaningful engagement, critical thinking, and development. More recent work emphasizes the experiences of women in science, documenting the ways in which women feel silenced in the classroom, excluded from social and academic groups, and subject to stereotypes and low expectations about their abilities (Blickenstaff, 2005; Carlone & Johnson, 2007; Hill, Corbett, & St. Rose, 2010; Ong, Wright, Espinosa, & Orfield, 2011).

Extensive research also documents students' experiences with harassment and unwanted sexual contact. In one study over 60 percent of women reported experiences with unwanted sexual contact or harassment, most often from peers, although some had experiences with faculty members and administrators (Hill & Silva, 2005). Although widely experienced, sexual harassment and assault are underreported, masking the magnitude of the problem on most campuses. Lundy-Wagner and Winkle-Wagner (2013) noted that this literature is often discussed outside the context of wider campus climate issues, and they urge a more structural approach to harassment research and interventions that go beyond remedies at the individual level.

Finally, there is a growing body of research documenting how members of the LGBT community experience the campus climate. Similar to other marginalized groups, sexual minorities view their campus environments as less welcoming. According to Brown, Clarke, Gortmaker, and Robinson-Keilig (2004), lesbian, gay, bisexual, and transgender (LGBT) students perceived more anti-LGBT attitudes on campus and demonstrated the greatest interest in learning more about LGBT communities and issues than students outside of the LGBT community, residence assistants, faculty members, and student affairs professionals. Similarly, Rankin's (2005) national data suggested that although most participants identified their campus environments as homophobic, they perceived the climate as friendly and respectful to those who are not members of the LGBT community. Transgender college students participating in another study painted a generally negative picture of their institutions, citing a lack of resources and structures, counseling support, and informed faculty and staff members (McKinney, 2005). Beemyn and Rankin's (2011) national study of transgender people revealed that experiences with harassment were widespread and that individuals hid their gender identities in an effort to avoid negative experiences.

This body of research suggests that there are similarities and distinctions across the experiences of those who embrace identities that are marginalized in the academy. Multiple groups recount experiences with hostility and discrimination; however, the specific ways in which students are marginalized may vary. Scholars are increasingly exploring the climate for students with disabilities, from religious minority groups, and from less affluent or low-income socioeconomic backgrounds. Thus, scholars and practitioners must be increasingly aware of how students' multiple social identities may shape their experiences and perceptions of climate in unique ways, distinct from others with marginalized identities. Strategies to create supportive climates can and should vary to meet students' distinct encounters with oppression.

The Role of Student Affairs in Supporting Diversity and Improving Campus Climate

Student affairs professionals play critical roles in the process of creating more welcoming campus climates (Gaston Gayles & Kelly, 2007; Pope, Reynolds, & Mueller, 2004; Rankin, 2005; Reason & Broido, 2005). Student affairs professionals are perhaps in closest proximity as students engage with those who embrace different social identities and come from different backgrounds. Consequently, they are well positioned to help students make meaning of these experiences, facilitating the link between engagement across difference and learning. Further, as key parts of the established structure and leadership of the institution, student affairs professionals are in positions to support and encourage (or silence and further marginalize) those who are lacking power (Rankin, 2005). Thus, rather than relying on specialists to manage any issues that may arise, it is advisable that all student affairs professionals possess a baseline level of knowledge about campus climate and diversity to offer students holistic support and foster more inclusive communities (Pope, Reynolds, & Mueller, 2004). Chapters 22 and 23 of this text offer guidance on the development of cultural competence and professionalism, and they should be reviewed and deeply considered for how these topics should be applied to issues of diversity and climate.

Consider the example offered in the introduction: multiple campuses struggled with whether or not to show the film *American Sniper*. Decisions to show the film left Muslim students feeling unwelcome and marginalized. Decisions to cancel screenings drew critiques and challenges from student veterans and others. Based on extant theory and research, student affairs professionals may use multiple strategies and competencies in order to successfully navigate these kinds of situations, simultaneously promoting more welcoming campus environments:

1. *Campus climate assessment:* It can be helpful to systematically examine the climate for diversity and inclusion on your campus. If Muslim students report that the showing of this film will expose them to greater

levels of hostility and oppression, it may be helpful to gain a deeper understanding of how they currently experience the climate. What is their numerical representation? How do Muslim students describe the extent and quality of their interactions with students from backgrounds different than their own? How has the institution incorporated religious diversity into the curriculum? Similar questions could and should be asked to assess the climate for student veterans. A full assessment of the climate can provide insight into the needs and concerns of multiple student populations.

2. *Listen and learn:* It can be difficult to understand students' perceptions of the campus environment or beliefs about institutional decision making without deeper knowledge about their culture and experiences. Student affairs professionals would be well served to take an active role in exploring and learning about communities with which they are less familiar through conferences and workshops on the experiences of marginalized populations, intergroup dialogue, and reading popular literature and research. Learning about a community can often begin simply with authentic conversations with students about their experiences. In this case, taking the time to develop deeper personal understanding about the ways in which Muslim and veteran students may feel marginalized or the challenges they generally face can increase your sensitivity and ability to respond with empathy.

   Further, it may also be useful to consider the ways in which you may be unintentionally perpetuating students' marginalization on campus. Reason and Broido (2005) recommended that student affairs professionals critically consider their own power and privilege, struggle through acknowledging their own role in the maintenance of structural inequality, and understand their own identities as they engage in justice-oriented work and support their students. It is important to take the opportunity to critically reflect on your own beliefs and how they may be shaping your interactions and perceptions of whether or not the film should be shown.

3. *Facilitate engagement across difference:* Some of the differences between student veterans and Muslim students' perspectives on *American Sniper* and what it would mean to show it on campus may be rooted in a lack of understanding of each other's perspectives. Facilitating opportunities for intergroup dialogue between these populations may create new opportunities for understanding and reconciliation. Engaging in difficult or intergroup dialogues has been related to students' openness to diversity and appreciation of multiple perspectives (Nagda & Zúñiga, 2003); however, faculty and staff members, and students may be reluctant to engage in these conversations for fear of conflict, feeling attacked, or being in a position that is too vulnerable (Quaye, 2012; Watt, 2007). Student affairs professionals must adequately prepare for these dialogues, developing knowledge about the steps necessary to ready themselves for these conversations as well as pedagogy to help students navigate difficult moments and learn in the midst of conflict (Quaye, 2012).

4. *Creating spaces for community support and celebration:* Ensuring that there are spaces and organizations that provide opportunities for Muslim students and student veterans to congregate and that these organizations are well resourced and supported is an important strategy to promote a sense of inclusion for these student populations. Although engagement across difference can promote important learning outcomes, development, and understanding, researchers have also noted the importance of students having the opportunity to spend time with those who share their identities (Harper & Quaye, 2007). Student groups, programs, and campus-wide events that celebrate diversity and students' identities can offer important avenues for support and learning (Griffin, Nichols, Perez, & Tuttle, 2008). Student affairs professionals can play an important role in supporting these groups, providing them with guidance on programming, resources, and opportunities for leadership development and training.

Conclusion

According to the Higher Education Research Institute's *The American Freshman: National Norms Fall 2014,* 80 percent of incoming students perceived their tolerance of others with different beliefs and ability to work with diverse people as a strength (Eagan, Stolzenberg, Ramirez, Aragon, Suchard, & Hurtado, 2014). As compared to their predecessors, they are more likely to want to study abroad and anticipate engaging with individuals different from themselves. Overall, they report high rates of support for same-sex marriage, college access for undocumented students, and admissions policies that give additional consideration to students from disadvantaged backgrounds.

Although these trends are promising, the research presented in this chapter and current events suggest students also have much "room to grow" (Eagan, Stolzenberg, Ramirez, Aragon, Suchard, & Hurtado, 2014, p. 15) when it comes to their ability to engage with diversity and difference. Although students report great confidence in their skills when entering college, many have little experience engaging with those from different backgrounds or who embrace distinctive worldviews (Jayakumar, 2008; Saenz, 2010). Engaging campus diversity has potential to foster cognitive development, critical thinking, perspective taking, and civic engagement; however, without guidance and support, increases in campus heterogeneity will translate to hostility, tension, and greater distance between groups. Developing a deeper understanding of diversity and campus climate arms student affairs professionals with important insights into the source of these conflicts and how to engage in meaningful ways as institutional leaders generate solutions.

Discussion Questions and Activities

1. Research a climate-related incident that has taken place at your institution. Share the details of the incident, the campus response, and any strategies used to address the issue. What do you think student affairs professionals on that campus could have done to address the issue or the larger climate issues on campus? What climate model would have been most useful in guiding their work?

2. Consider your current institution and one other institution at which you have either attended or worked. How did each institution define diversity, address climate issues, and assess students' perceptions of climate? What would you suggest that each institution do differently across these three dimensions?

3. *Case Study:* You are the director of student activities at a medium-sized (about ten thousand students) comprehensive institution. The vice president of student affairs asks to meet with you about a recent editorial in the student newspaper, which criticizes the multiple organizations for marginalized groups as promoting self-segregation and limiting opportunities for student growth and learning. The vice president is concerned and wants to know what your office is doing or can possibly do to address the issues raised by the editorial. What are your thoughts about these assertions, what can your office do to support students as they engage across difference, and how do you respond as an individual and an office?

References

Allan, E. J., & Madden, M. (2006). Chilly classrooms for female undergraduate students: A question of method? *Journal of Higher Education, 77*(4), 684–711.

antonio, a. l., Chang, M. J., Hakuta, K., Kenny, D. A., Levin, S., & Milem, J. F. (2004). Effects of racial diversity on complex thinking in college students. *Psychological Science, 15*(8), 507–510.

Beemyn, B. G., & Rankin, S. (2011). *The lives of transgender people.* New York: Columbia University Press.

Blickenstaff, J. C. (2005). Women and science careers: Leaky pipeline or gender filter? *Gender and Education, 17*(4), 369–386.

Bowman, N. A. (2011). Promoting participation in a diverse democracy: A meta-analysis of college diversity experiences and civic engagement. *Review of Educational Research, 81*(1), 29–68.

Brown, R. D., Clarke, B., Gortmaker, V., & Robinson-Keilig, R. (2004). Assessing the campus climate for gay, lesbian, bisexual, and transgender (GLBT) students using a multiple perspectives approach. *Journal of College Student Development, 45*(1), 8–26.

Cabrera, N. L. (2014). Exposing whiteness in higher education: White male college students minimizing racism, claiming victimization, and recreating white supremacy. *Race Ethnicity and Education, 17*(1), 30–55.

Carlone, H. B., & Johnson, A. (2007). Understanding the science experiences of successful women of color: Science identity as an analytic lens. *Journal of Research in Science Teaching, 44*(8), 1187–1218.

Chang, M. J., Denson, N., Saenz, V., & Misa, K. (2006). The educational benefits of sustaining cross-racial interaction among undergraduates. *Journal of Higher Education, 77*(3), 430–455.

Chang, M. J., Eagan, M. K., Lin, M. H., & Hurtado, S. (2011). Considering the impact of racial stigmas and science identity: Persistence among biomedical and behavioral science aspirants. *Journal of Higher Education, 82*(5), 564–596.

Chang, M. J., & Yamamura, E. (2006). Quantitative approaches to measuring student body diversity: Some examples and thoughts. In W. Allen, M. Bonous-Hammarth, & R. Teranishi (Eds.), *Higher education in a global society: Achieving diversity, equity and excellence* (pp. 369–386). Oxford, UK: Elsevier.

Eagan, K., Stolzenberg, E. B., Ramirez, J. J., Aragon, M. C., Suchard, M. R., & Hurtado, S. (2014). *The American freshman: National norms fall 2014.* Los Angeles: Higher Education Research Institute, UCLA.

Garcia, M., Hudgins, C., Musil, C. M., Nettles, M. T., Sedlacek, W. E., & Smith, D. G. (2001). *Assessing campus diversity initiatives: A guide for campus practitioners.* Washington, DC: Association of American Colleges and Universities.

Gaston Gayles, J., & Kelly, B. T. (2007). Experiences with diversity in the curriculum: Implications for graduate programs and student affairs practice. *Journal of Student Affairs Research and Practice, 44*(1), 193–208.

Griffin, K. A., Nichols, A. H., Perez, D., & Tuttle, K. D. (2008). Making campus activities and student organizations inclusive for racial/ethnic minority students. In S. R. Harper (Ed.), *Creating inclusive campus environments for cross-cultural learning and student engagement* (pp. 121–138). Washington, DC: NASPA.

Gurin, P., Dey, E. L., Hurtado, S., & Gurin, G. (2002). Diversity and higher education: Theory and impact on educational outcomes. *Harvard Educational Review, 72*(3), 330–367.

Hall, R. M., & Sandler, B. R. (1982). *The classroom climate: A chilly one for women?* Washington, DC: Association of American Colleges.

Harper, S. R., & Hurtado, S. (2007). Nine themes in campus racial climates and implications for institutional transformation. In S. R. Harper & L. D. Patton (Eds.), *Responding to the realities of race on campus* (New Directions for Student Services, no. 120, pp. 7–24). San Francisco: Jossey Bass.

Harper, S. R., & Quaye, S. J. (2007). Student organizations as venues for black identity expression and development among African American male student leaders. *Journal of College Student Development, 48*(2), 127–144.

Hill, C., Corbett, C., & St. Rose, A. (2010). *Why so few? Women in science, technology, engineering, and mathematics.* Washington, DC: American Association of University Women.

Hill, C., & Silva, E. (2005). *Drawing the line: Sexual harassment on campus.* Washington, DC: American Association of University Women.

Hu, S., & Kuh, G. D. (2003). Diversity experiences and college student learning and personal development. *Journal of College Student Development, 44*(3), 320–334.

Hurtado, S., Alvarez, C. L., Guillermo-Wann, C., Cuellar, M., & Arellano, L. (2012). A model for diverse learning environments. In J. C. Smart & M. B. Paulsen (Eds.), *Higher education: Handbook of theory and research* (pp. 41–122). New York: Springer.

Hurtado, S., Griffin, K. A., Arellano, L., & Cuellar, M. (2008). Assessing the value of climate assessments: Progress and future directions. *Journal of Diversity in Higher Education, 1*(4), 204.

Hurtado, S., Milem, J. F., Clayton-Pederson, A. R., & Allen, W. R. (1999). Enacting diverse learning environments: Improving the campus climate for racial/ethnic diversity in higher education. *ASHE-ERIC Higher Education Reports Series, 26*(8). San Francisco: Jossey-Bass.

Jacobs, J. (1996). Gender inequality and higher education. *Annual Review of Sociology, 22,* 153–185.

Jayakumar, U. (2008). Can higher education meet the needs of an increasingly diverse and global society? Campus diversity and cross-cultural workforce competencies. *Harvard Educational Review, 78*(4), 615–651.

Johnson, D. R., Wasserman, T. H., Yildirim, N., & Yonai, B. A. (2014). Examining the effects of stress and campus climate on the persistence of students of color and white students: An application of Bean and Eaton's psychological model of retention. *Research in Higher Education, 55*(1), 75–100.

Locks, A. M., Hurtado, S., Bowman, N. A., & Oseguera, L. (2008). Extending notions of campus climate and diversity to students' transition to college. *The Review of Higher Education, 31*(3), 257–285.

Lundberg, C. A. (2014). Institutional support and interpersonal climate as predictors of learning for Native American students. *Journal of College Student Development, 55*(3), 263–277.

Lundy-Wagner, V., & Winkle-Wagner, R. (2013). A harassing climate? Sexual harassment and campus racial climate. *Journal of Diversity in Higher Education, 6*(1), 51–68.

McCabe, J. (2009). Racial and gender microaggressions on a predominantly white campus: Experiences of black, Latina/o and white undergraduates. *Race, Gender & Class, 16*(1/2), 133–151.

McKinney, J. S. (2005). On the margins: A study of the experiences of transgender college students. *Journal of Gay and Lesbian Issues in Education, 3*(1), 63–76.

Milem, J. F. (2003). The educational benefits of diversity: Evidence from multiple sectors. In M. J. Chang, D. Witt, J. Jones, & K. Hakuta (Eds.), *Compelling interest: Examining the evidence on racial dynamics in higher education* (pp. 126–169). Palo Alto, CA: Stanford University Press.

Milem, J. F., Chang, M. J., & antonio, a. l. (2005). *Making diversity work on campus: A research-based perspective.* Washington, DC: Association of American Colleges and Universities.

Museus, S. D. (2014). *Asian American students in higher education.* New York: Routledge.

Museus, S. D., & Maramba, D. C. (2011). The impact of culture on Filipino American students' sense of belonging. *The Review of Higher Education, 34*(2), 231–258.

Nadal, K. L., Wong, Y., Griffin, K. E., Davidoff, K., & Sriken, J. (2014). The adverse impact of racial microaggressions on college students' self-esteem. *Journal of College Student Development, 55*(5), 461–474.

Nagda, B.R.A., & Zúñiga, X. (2003). Fostering meaningful racial engagement through intergroup dialogues. *Group Processes & Intergroup Relations, 6*(1), 111–128.

Ong, M., Wright, C., Espinosa, L., & Orfield, G. (2011). Inside the double bind: A synthesis of empirical research on undergraduate and graduate women of color in science, technology, engineering, and mathematics. *Harvard Educational Review, 81*(2), 172–209.

Park, J. J., Denson, N., & Bowman, N. A. (2012). Does socioeconomic diversity make a difference? Examining the effects of racial and socioeconomic diversity on the campus climate for diversity. *American Educational Research Journal, 50*(3), 466–496.

Peterson, M. W., & Spencer, M. G. (1990). Understanding academic culture and climate. In W. Tierney (Ed.), *New Directions for Institutional Research* (no. 68, pp. 3–18). Hoboken, NJ: Wiley.

Pewewardy, C., & Frey, B. (2002). Surveying the landscape: Perceptions of multicultural support services and racial climate at a predominantly white university. *The Journal of Negro Education, 71*(1/2), 77–95.

Pope, R. L., Reynolds, A. L., & Mueller, J. A. (2004). *Multicultural competence in student affairs.* San Francisco: Jossey-Bass.

Quaye, S. J. (2012). Think before you teach: Preparing for dialogues about racial realities. *Journal of College Student Development, 53*(4), 542–562.

Rankin, S. R. (2005). Campus climate for sexual minorities. In R. Sanlo (Ed.), *Gender identity and sexual orientation: Research, policy, and personal* (New Directions for Student Services, no. 111, pp. 17–23). San Francisco: Jossey-Bass.

Rankin, S. R., & Reason, R. D. (2005). Differing perceptions: How students of color and white students perceive campus climate for underrepresented groups. *Journal of College Student Development, 46*(1), 43–61.

Rankin, S., & Reason, R. (2008). Transformational tapestry model: A comprehensive approach to transforming campus climate. *Journal of Diversity in Higher Education, 1*(4), 262.

Reason, R. D., & Broido, E. M. (2005). Issues and strategies for social justice allies (and the student affairs professionals who hope to encourage them). In R. Reason, E. Broido, T. Davis, & N. Evans (Eds.), *Developing social justice allies* (New Directions for Student Services, no. 110, pp. 81–89). San Francisco: Jossey-Bass.

Reason, R. D., & Evans, N. J. (2007). The complicated realities of whiteness: From color blind to racially cognizant. In S. R. Harper & L. D. Patton (Eds.), *Responding to the realities of race on campus* (New Directions for Student Services, no. 120, pp. 67–75). San Francisco: Jossey-Bass.

Saenz, V. B. (2010). Breaking the segregation cycle: Examining students' precollege racial environments and college diversity experiences. *The Review of Higher Education, 34*(1), 1–37.

Smith, D. G. (2009). *Diversity's promise for higher education: Making it work.* Baltimore: Johns Hopkins University Press.

Solorzano, D., Ceja, M., & Yosso, T. (2000). Critical race theory, racial microaggressions, and campus racial climate: The experiences of African American college students. *Journal of Negro Education, 69*(1/2), 60–73.

Suarez-Balcazar, Y., Orellana-Damacela, L., Portillo, N., Rowan, J. M., & Andrews-Guillen, C. (2003). Experiences of differential treatment among college students of color. *Journal of Higher Education, 74*(4), 428–444.

Tetreault, P. A., Fette, R., Meidlinger, P. C., & Hope, D. (2013). Perceptions of campus climate by sexual minorities. *Journal of Homosexuality, 60*(7), 947–964.

Trytten, D. A., Lowe, A. W., & Walden, S. E. (2012). "Asians are good at math. What an awful stereotype." The model minority stereotype's impact on Asian American engineering students. *Journal of Engineering Education, 101*(3), 439–468.

Watt, S. K. (2007). Difficult dialogues, privilege and social justice: Uses of the privileged identity exploration (PIE) model in student affairs practice. *College Student Affairs Journal, 26*(2), 114–126.

White, G. B. (2015). The weakening definition of diversity. *The Atlantic.* Retrieved from http://www.theatlantic.com/business/archive/2015/05/the-weakening-definition-of-diversity/393080/?utm_source=SFFB

CHAPTER 6

WHAT IS ETHICAL PROFESSIONAL PRACTICE?

Sue A. Saunders and Christine M. Wilson

Every day student affairs professionals negotiate tricky ethical situations. Sometimes those situations involve simply obeying an ethical code that provides clear direction, but more often professionals are called on to make judgments among choices in situations in which ethical principles are in conflict and there is no clear delineation between right and wrong (Dalton, Crosby, Valente, & Eberhardt, 2009; Kidder, 1995).

Developing one's facility with ethical practice guides action in thinking how to respond to such practical questions as these:

- How can I balance consistency and understanding with students who violated policies?
- How can I be loyal to my supervisors when I disagree with their actions?
- How can I support an individual while not sacrificing the needs of the community?
- How can I help a troubled supervisee while still trying to meet the productivity requirements of my office?
- When should I divulge a confidence?

Ethics, Values, Professionalism, Legal Imperatives, and Codes of Conduct

Determining what is "good" or "right" is influenced, even without our explicit awareness, by our own values and those of our cultures, societies, and institutions (Fried, 2003). Ethics are connected to and different from values, professional behavior, societal norms, legal imperatives, and institutional codes of conduct.

It is easy to confuse values and ethics. Values describe what a person believes is important in life, whereas ethical principles and standards prescribe what is considered good or bad and right or wrong behavior.

A particular behavior in the workplace can be inconsistent with professional norms but not necessarily unethical (Winston & Saunders, 1991). For example, failure to arrive promptly at meetings, slowness in responding to e-mails, lack of proofreading an internal memo, or communicating with slang rather than more formal language often are considered unprofessional behaviors, but they may not rise to the level of being unethical.

Similarly, although legal requirements are typically consistent with what is ethical, distinctions exist. For example, although it would be unethical to give a totally positive letter of recommendation to a subordinate who exhibited immature behavior, that action would not be illegal. Conversely, the 1960s civil rights movement points out the importance of challenging laws that are discriminatory, unfair, and fundamentally unethical.

Ethical principles rely on cultural and societal norms and assumptions that privilege certain perspectives and diminish others. The connections between prevailing norms and ethical decision making are often tacit, beneath the realm of conscious, everyday awareness. Therefore, it becomes increasingly important to develop the competency to "identify and articulate the influence of various cultures in the interpretation of ethics" (ACPA/NASPA, 2010, p. 12).

There are situations in which ethical behavior is codified into institutional "codes of ethical conduct." Employees of the institution most often are required to make their agreement to abide by the explicit code by signing a document or affirming an oath. Determining compliance with such ethical conduct codes is relatively straightforward. For example, many institutions have, as part of their ethical codes, rules that prohibit nepotism—hiring or supervising a relative. To abide by the code then one would simply not hire or supervise a relative.

Purpose of This Chapter

In this chapter we will discuss those ethical dilemmas in which the choices are more complex than applying a prescribed set of rules. Developing skills in ethical decision making involves an ability to carefully analyze a problem, reflect on past experience and possible future implications, craft a resolution, consult ethical standards and principles, summon the moral courage to actually enact the chosen action, and make corrections in light of changing circumstances and emerging understanding (Saunders & Lease Butts, 2011). The purpose of this chapter is to foster ethical skill development. The authors will explain student affairs philosophical concepts that undergird professional ethics, describe influences of modern-day ethical practice, discuss the ethical principles along with several ethical standards or frameworks adopted by student affairs professional associations, and provide a decision-making model with multiple examples.

Philosophies That Undergird Professional Ethics

As student affairs professionals, it is important to know and to question the philosophies that undergird our practice. (See chapter 3 for further information about student affairs philosophies.) Since the beginning of student affairs there have been more than a dozen documents that describe beliefs about the nature of students, the purpose of student affairs, and the functions of professionals.

An analysis of these documents by Evans and Reason (2001) revealed several common philosophical themes, all of which have connections to ancient wisdom about what constitutes virtue and to twentieth-century educational philosophers such as Dewey (1985). These four themes—holism, individualism, student agency, and contributions to a democratic society—shape the more-specific principles and standards that guide ethical practice. Holism, as described in the 1937 *Student Personnel Point of View* (SPPV) (American Council on Education, 1994a), emphasizes development of students as persons rather than narrowly focusing on the intellectual or any other single aspect of their identities. Holism requires that professionals assume that the student life cannot be subdivided into learning and development, but instead these two processes are "intertwined and inseparable elements of the student experience" (Keeling, 2004, p. 3). Holism encourages ethical decision making that promotes student development and leverages the collaborative efforts of all units to promote student learning.

A second important construct is a belief that individuals can be responsible if offered the right conditions of freedom and discipline. One commonly assumed role of student affairs practitioners is to help students and colleagues "develop a sense of agency" (Evans & Reason, 2001, p. 373). As far back as 1949, the second "SPPV" (American Council on Education, 1994b) asserted that students were responsible participants in their development, rather than passive recipients of knowledge.

A third important philosophical tenet is respect for individual differences. Persons are regarded to be unique individuals, with distinct backgrounds, goals, interests, and characteristics that may or may not be aligned with particular classifications or identities. A crucial aspect of this value is to "respect individuality and promote an appreciation of human diversity" (NASPA Standards of Professional Practice, 1990, n.p.).

A final common value of the student affairs profession involves the principled citizenship necessary for a productive democracy (Evans & Reason, 2001). According to the ACPA "Statement of Ethical Principles and Standards" (2006), "professionals, both as citizens and practitioners, have a responsibility to contribute to the improvement of the communities in which they life and work and to act as advocates for social justice for members of those communities" (p. 7). In 2012, NASPA's Ethics Task Force (NASPA) raised important questions about the relevance of the traditional student affairs philosophies and values for determining ethical practice in current, global, and diverse contexts. This task force asserted that "every culture and every belief system has an ethical framework, but when many of these frameworks rub together on our campuses, conflicts may occur when decisions need to be made because each perspective represented embodies a different idea of 'the Good'" (NASPA, 2012, n.p.). To manage the complexity of twenty-first-century ethical practice, professionals need to know their history well enough to affirm and question its foundational assumptions and also to consider more modern perspectives about the responsibilities of universities and professionals.

Modern-Day Ethical Considerations

Today's student affairs professionals meet a variety of student needs, from the most basic food and shelter to the more complex desires, to craft a principled identity or contribute to the campus. However, all staff members have one important thing in common: they care about student needs, student development, and student success.

Ethic of Care

Noddings (2007) asserted that caring is the foundation for ethical decision making. In order for student affairs professionals to help students assert their rights and freedoms and to help them live up to their responsibilities, staff members must have caring relationships with students. "The ethic of care rejects the notion of a truly autonomous moral agent and accepts the reality of moral interdependence" (Noddings, 2007, p. 234). In other words, professionals are partners with students in their own development. This call for positive, productive relationships with students to meet their basic and developmental needs is the foundation of our ethical practice in student affairs.

One ethical caution about relationships with students concerns the concept of dual relationships (Janosik, Cooper, Saunders, & Hirt, 2014). In these situations, professionals regard students as egalitarian friends or confidants rather than relationships that are more professional. When these dual relationships occur, students and professionals can be damaged by unrealized expectations for support and agreement as well as by missed opportunities to receive critical feedback.

Cultural Competence   Mueller and Broido (2012) comment that diversity on campus requires that professionals must possess the knowledge, skills, and dispositions to create affirming campuses. Multicultural competence is "essential for efficacious student affairs work" (Pope, Reynolds, & Mueller, 2004, p. 9). Because caring is based on trusting relationships with students, and because each student is different personally and culturally, caring will look different, depending on the nature of students and their groups (Noddings, 2007,

p. 223). Culturally competent practice is fundamentally ethical practice requiring deep reflection about the students for whom we are caring:

- What do our students need? This could mean any individual student or any community of students, or group of students with something in common, such as race, gender, sexual orientation, religion, disability, class, or other groups with common experiences such as veterans, returning adults, students with children, students in recovery, sexual assault survivors.
- What is the effect of filling any need on other groups of students?
- What is the effect of filling any need on other programs and services? Who is best suited to fill any given need?

In many cases, we must collaborate with students to help them articulate their needs, because not all students have the self-awareness or even the vocabulary to do so (Noddings, 2007).

Social Justice Sometimes our work goes beyond meeting the needs of students or groups of students. Professionals are called on to address policies and practices that may not be serving all students well or programs and services that are not supporting the value of equity prized by our profession and institutions. According to Noddings (2007) a sense of justice is important in creating a positive environment for those whom we care about. So, at times, professionals must engage in social change.

Social change can be best achieved through caring relationships based on the long-standing values of our profession—agency, collaboration, dignity, and fairness (Young, 2011). Part of being a multiculturally competent professional involves advocating for social change by working to address structural diversity (the gender, gender identity and expression, sexual orientation, racial, and ethnic composition of the population) and also to ensure that all constituents are treated fairly and included in decision making. By doing this "institutions are more able to create an institutional culture and climate that embraces diversity at every level" (Pope & LePeau, 2012, p. 122).

Risk Management Laws such as the Jeanne Clery Act (Disclosure of Campus Security Policy and Campus Crime Statistics Act, 20 USC § 1092(f), 1990), a federal statute that evolved from a crime-reporting bill to call for promoting student safety on campus (Lake, 2013), and directives from the Office of Civil Rights in the Department of Education regarding sexual assault prevention and reporting, have affected student affairs practice. Care is expressed as engagement in "risk management" for student programs and services. This increased responsibility for student safety includes describing potential risks, educating students about foreseeable risks, and developing systems of reporting, as well as supporting victims and affected communities. Student affairs fulfill these duties not just to reduce liability.

They educate students about risk so that they can be safe, to treat students as individuals who can make reasoned choices, and to address human dignity and community—all ethical principles of student affairs practitioners (Young, 2011).

Ethics and the "Corporatization" of Higher Education

There has been a great deal of public commentary about the problems with the corporatization of higher education. Nicolaus Mills (2012), a professor at Sarah Lawrence College, states that less tax support for higher education and recent slow economic growth have led to corporatization; this development has not led to greater efficiency but to a focus of students as customers. Derek Bok (2000), former president of Harvard, asserted that the profit motive, which is now so present in all aspects of university life, undermines the fundamental mission of the university and compromises academic values. Bernard Beins, a professor at Ithaca College, warns that "giving students [consumers] what they want could sometimes come at the expense of what they actually need" (Clay, 2008, p. 50).

Student affairs work with students, in which we partner with students for their own development, is transformational. The concept of "customers" is more transactional and is not focused on what they need for development but what they want. A focus on customer wants and profit motives can cause ethical dilemmas for student affairs professionals. For example, charging students a fee to attend a campus event or belong to student organization may enhance the funding of the university, but it will likely exclude students with financial challenges. Working with students to advocate for changing institutional policies on sexual assault, for example, can empower students to problem-solve and affect issues at their institutions, but this initiative could be worrisome for staff members who manage public perceptions (typically a more corporate concern).

The imperative to care for others, multiple and often conflicting perspectives of what students need, and the increasing corporatization of universities can easily cause difficult ethical dilemmas, especially when public perception is so quickly solidified through social media. This modern context calls for increased attention to ethical principles and decision making.

Fundamental Ethical Principles and Standards

For the past forty years, most student affairs professional associations have written, debated, reviewed, and rewritten statements about ethical principles and standards or rules. Principles are the more aspirational concepts on which specific professional association standards or rules are built. In 2012, the Council for Advancement of Standards in Higher Education (CAS), representing more than thirty-five active professional associations, reviewed ethics codes promulgated by their member associations (CAS, 2012). This review concluded that the majority of these associations had developed specific ethical standards or rules that should be followed, along with strategies to hold members accountable. Rather than establish another set of obligatory ethical standards, the leadership of CAS decided to explicate shared ethical principles that are foundational to all member codes (CAS, 2012). In this section we will cover general ethical principles established by CAS as well as review the ethical decision-making frameworks or standards statements of several professional associations.

Ethical Principles

The seven principles identified by CAS include autonomy, beneficence, non-malfeasance, justice, fidelity, veracity, and affiliation. These principles encompass and expand on the five traditional ethical principles used within the profession that were articulated by Kitchener (1985).

Autonomy means respecting an individuals' right to choose and expecting all to be responsible and accountable for their own behavior and learning. Additionally, autonomy carries with it the obligation to respect the rights and welfare of others.

Beneficence means doing good, being altruistic, and contributing to the health and welfare of others. In the day-to-day work with students there is frequently a conflict between respecting autonomy and beneficence. When sorting through these types of dilemmas, it is important to consider whether a particular approach will promote long-term or short-term benefits. Although courtesy is a part of this principle (CAS, 2012), one should not assume that doing good involves only the positive or pleasant. Doing good may require confrontation, giving negative feedback, or standing up to change a practice that is not working.

Nonmalfeasance means that professionals avoid doing harm to others. For example, there are many instances when harm can be caused by comments made unintentionally, and professionals have the obligation to be careful enough to refrain from such action. Making assumptions about limitations based solely on a category could be demeaning and could limit motivation and self-esteem. Microaggressions and stereotyping have the potential, over time, to negatively affect psychological health (Torres, Driscoll, & Burrow, 2010). Therefore, to be an ethical professional, one needs to be educated about and committed to using inclusive language.

Justice means treating people equitably regardless of personal opinion. Being just goes beyond simply providing equal access. Because our profession values individualism, being just with a student who has a particular need means giving special treatment such as extra coaching for a student who has time management difficulties.

Fidelity means being faithful in terms of meeting obligations and honoring commitments. This principle is seemingly straightforward, but the nature of one's commitments can change because of changing circumstances.

Veracity means telling the truth and sharing all relevant information while respecting privacy and confidentiality of students. A typical ethical dilemma involving veracity is how much to share in a reference for employment when the student or colleague would be harmed by failure to get this job. In such situations when veracity conflicts with nonmalfeasance, it is important to consider the risks and benefits to the individual student, the community being served, and one's own credibility.

Affiliation means promoting connectivity and fostering community. This is probably the most ambiguous of all of the CAS shared ethical principles. However, this principle encourages empathy, teaching others about the value of community, and mutual respect.

Professional Association Ethical Standards and Frameworks

Ethical standards statements developed by professional associations often provide specific rules or behavioral expectations, which are more concrete than the abstract and aspirational principles. Some ethical statements provide advice about how to confront instances of behavior that violate the standards and others do not. Other associations focus on the process of making effective ethical decisions and refrain from offering specific rules. Even though CAS was able to determine general ethical principles across its diverse associations, there are nuanced differences between the association standards reflecting the culture, history, and emphasis of the particular organization (Dalton, Crosby, Valente, & Eberhardt, 2009). Professionals should be conversant with the professional association standards or frameworks with which their office or functional area aligns. For illustration purposes, this chapter will review the differences and similarities between the two "umbrella" student affairs associations, ACPA (College Student Educators International) and NASPA (Student Affairs Administrators in Higher Education). In subsequent sections of this chapter, the authors also make reference to the standards of the NODA (Association for Orientation, Transition, Retention in Higher Education) and NACA (National Association for Campus Activities).

ACPA The ACPA (2006) "Statement of Ethical Principles and Standards" highlights the association's historic roots emphasizing student development and learning. The statement affirms the association's commitment to "comprehensive education of students, protecting human rights, advancing knowledge of student growth and development, and promoting effectiveness of institutional programs, services, and organizational units" (p. 1). It also reinforces that the primary purpose of the document is to help professionals monitor their own actions in ethically problematic areas and to be ethical role models for others.

The ACPA statement contains sixty-four actions required of ethical professionals that are organized in four ethical standards areas. The four standards are professional responsibility and competence, student learning and development, responsibility to the institution, and responsibility to society. Given the evolution and origin of the ACPA ethical standards (Winston & McCaffrey, 1981), it is not surprising that the most comprehensive and specific standard is about student learning and development. This standard requires such actions as these:

2.5 Inform students of the conditions under which they may receive assistance.

2.6 Inform students of the nature and/or limits of confidentiality. They will share information about the students only in accordance with institutional policies and applicable laws, when given permission, or when required to prevent harm to themselves or others.

2.7 Refer students to appropriate specialists before entering or continuing a helping relationship when the professional's expertise or level of comfort is exceeded. (Winston & McCaffrey, 1981, p. 2)

The ACPA statement acknowledges that implementing ethical standards is challenging because of the need to consider differences in such contextual issues as culture, individual perspectives, and community norms. The perspective advocated in this document requires complexity in thinking and problem-solving, recognizing that in many situations there are valid and varied interpretations of the standards.

NASPA In 2006, the NASPA board of directors voted to use the CAS "Statement of Ethical Principles" as the guiding ethical statement for the association. In 2012, the NASPA board appointed a task force that reviewed the CAS ethics statement and a number of other documents to create an ethical framework for the association (personal communication, Stephanie Gordon, June 19, 2015).

The ethics task force focused on an approach to ethical decision making that emphasized content and dialogue rather than universal principles (NASPA, 2012). The task force endeavored to create a process that acknowledged the fundamental challenges of preventing the hegemony of a single culture, recognizing the potential conflicts between a global context and one's own ideas of ethical behavior, and accepting ambiguity and disagreement. The task force provided guidance to professionals in the form of the three following reflection questions that can be used when facing an ethical dilemma:

1. What would the greater good, benevolence, or compassion look like in this situation?

2. What thoughts, ideas, behaviors, and relationships will be expanded from what is created by my decision? What will be reduced?

3. Does the decision respect my individual values and the integrity of all people being affected by it? (NASPA, 2012, n.p.)

Making Ethical Decisions

In this section, we offer a model for making ethical decisions and examples of how this model might be used to examine dilemmas. To begin the decision-making process, a professional must recognize that there is an ethical decision to be made. The scope of the dilemma must be defined as well as the reason(s) why there is a dilemma. What are the facts of the situation? What are assumptions? Is there any second guessing (imagining scenarios that haven't happened yet), which could mean that there actually isn't a decision to be made yet?

Next, a professional should first look for local guidance. Is there an institutional policy or legal guidance that may inform the decision? What does the relevant professional organization advise?

At this point, the professional may have enough information to make a decision. Sometimes, though, the situation stems from a lack of clear direction from a policy or standard or a conflict with a policy or an ethical standard. In this case additional steps are necessary.

Vaccaro, McCoy, Champagne, and Siegel (2013) created a framework for decision making in student affairs. They describe the importance of considering context: professional, campus, and external. Who or what are the relevant parties? Relevant parties could be internal, such as the professional's supervisor, students, staff, and the institution, or external, such as families, donors, politicians, or any combination of individuals or institutions.

Nash (2002) asserted that time, place, and manner should be considered when an educator is considering a matter of integrity. Would this be a dilemma at all, or a different dilemma, if it were happening at a different time? Location? Or in a different way? These may also be relevant factors because any one or a combination may affect the available options.

Listing the relevant parties and determining how time, place, and manner inform the next step create options for resolving or addressing the dilemma. One must work diligently to generate as many ideas as possible. Once options are outlined, the professional should imagine consequences of each for the relevant parties.

The next step is to consider the options and consequences in light of ethical principles, such as those identified by CAS (2012). Do any of these principles apply more than the others? In most cases, it is important to engage an appropriate colleague and share one's thinking at any stage of this process but definitely before a final choice is made. This colleague may be a supervisor or a trusted colleague from another institution, or the person could be someone in a formal position, such as an ombudsperson. The purpose of this consultation is to expand the perspective of the decision maker.

At this point, it should be clear what the better choices are, even if it will be difficult to implement. Stadler (1986) suggested professionals employ several questions to aid in making a final decision: the test of publicity (would I be confident in my decision if it were reported in the press?) and the test of universality (would I recommend this decision to another professional in the same situation?).

It takes fortitude to implement a difficult decision. If the professional is thoughtful and goes carefully through the steps, then he or she should confidently implement the decision. Later, the professional can reflect on the decision-making process and the actual consequences of the choice. This reflection will inform future decision making.

The next section of this chapter will focus on the application of this model. These scenarios reflect issues with multiple right answers, clear answers that do not seem right, and choices that demonstrate conflicting ethical principles. The analyses are not meant to be complete but are broad examinations to facilitate further discussion.

Leslie, Sam, and the Campus Climate Event

Leslie is director of the Gender Diversity Office and often supervises independent study (IS) interns who implement special projects. One of the interns, Sam, has publicly criticized the administration regarding the racial campus climate. Sam has proposed holding an open forum to collect feedback from students about the climate and to invite politicians and media to the event. The university's media office is concerned about negative publicity; office staff members are also concerned about campus climate, but they would prefer the issue be handled in a more private way. Leslie's supervisor tells her to tell Sam not to have the event.

Ethical Dilemma

Leslie must decide whether or not to tell Sam to have the open forum. She is also wondering if there is another way for Sam to collect the information.

Guidance from the Profession

ACPA's (2006) "Statement of Ethical Principles and Standards" does give Leslie some guidance. Standard 2.1 tells professionals to treat students with respect as persons who possess dignity, worth, and the ability to be self-directed. Standard 3.1 states that professionals contribute to their institution by supporting its mission, goals, policies, and abiding by its procedures. Standard 3.3 asks professionals to recognize that conflicts among students, colleagues, or the institution should be resolved without diminishing respect for or appropriate obligations to any party involved.

Context: Relevant Parties and Time, Place, and Manner

The relevant parties are Leslie, her supervisor, the media and government relations office, and Sam. All have an interest in campus climate at the university. The academic department that awards credit for the IS students could also be helpful, because there might

(continued)

be guidance about types of student projects or ways to manage conflicts about student independent studies. Government officials are also likely relevant, given that climate issues are often governed by state and federal regulations.

Time, place, and manner may also be important. Is the issue the format that Sam proposes (open forum)? Or is it that Sam wants to collect the information at all? Does the fact that this is a credit-bearing experience have any impact on the manner of Sam's actions?

Leslie's feelings about campus climate, and her interest in collecting climate information from students, are also relevant. She may believe that the climate is not positive for students, and therefore Sam's efforts are necessary to improve it.

Options

Leslie can disobey her supervisor and let Sam hold the open forum or she can tell Sam not to hold the event. She could also help Sam find a way to collect campus climate information from students in a different way. It may be helpful for Sam to meet with campus administrators (including media staff members) to hear more about their concerns. If there are other campus climate efforts, Leslie can make sure Sam is aware of those and connect him to the staff members involved.

Application of Principles and Consequences

Leslie cares deeply about students realizing their goals. She could let Sam hold the open forum because she believes in supporting the principles of student autonomy; she believes he has freedom of choice in his education. She may also feel this project may help lead to campus climate improvement. In this case, she is considering beneficence, because she is part of Sam's efforts to promote the welfare of others.

However, Leslie has a responsibility to her supervisor, and her supervisor has given her direction. She is also beholden to institutional policies. Therefore, she can apply the principle of fidelity (to her institution) and tell Sam that he cannot hold the forum as part of his IS.

Leslie has another choice. If she is able to help Sam find a different way to collect the information, particularly by connecting him with others in the campus community who are interested in the topic, she is employing the principle of affiliation. There would still be a risk that she would be violating the principle of fidelity to her workplace, but not if she obtains the agreement of her supervisor for an alternate information-collection strategy.

Tomas, Dwayne, and the Student Leader Grade Policy

Tomas is advisor to multiple student organizations. He is also responsible for implementing the department's student leader grade policy. Student leaders must earn at least a 2.5 each semester to keep their positions.

Dwayne is the president of the Brothers United group and Tomas is their advisor. Last semester was hard for Dwayne. There was a racist incident on campus, and his group was involved in many follow-up initiatives. Dwayne became exhausted, and his health and grades were negatively affected. After some rest during break, Dwayne is looking forward to a productive new semester.

Tomas looks at the grades of the student leaders. He sees that Dwayne earned a 2.45, but his cumulative GPA is still above a 3.0. Dwayne assures Tomas that the low grades were an anomaly and he is committed to improving. He asks Tomas to give him a chance, but there are no exceptions to this policy.

Tomas's supervisor reminds him of his responsibility to officially inform students whose grades are below the limit so that that they resign their positions. The supervisor does not monitor the names of students who do not meet the grade requirements nor is she copied on the communication.

Ethical Dilemma

Tomas wants Dwayne to keep his position, and he wonders if there could be an exception. But he understands the purpose of the policy: to make sure that students focus on academics. Dwayne could stay involved; he would just have to give up his position.

Guidance from the Profession

The National Association for Campus Activities (NACA) "Statement of Business Ethics and Standards" encourages professionals to "assist students in development and practicing appropriate balance between curricular, co-curricular and extra-curricular involvements" (2015, p. 2). Dwayne is striving to find that balance, and focus on classes may be a good course of action. By upholding the policy, Tomas is upholding the NACA guideline to "teach students to be accountable" (p. 2). The NACA guideline that calls for practicing "active commitment to the student development and to the co-curricular educational process" (p. 2) may also be relevant, not only for assisting Tomas as he works with Dwayne but also as he thinks about the policy, its purpose, and its effects on students who identify their leadership positions as important elements of their educational experiences.

Context: Relevant Parties and Time, Place, and Manner

Dwayne and Tomas are relevant parties, as are Tomas's supervisor and the other students affected by this policy. Dwayne's instructors and academic advisor are also interested in the intersection of Dwayne's classes and extracurricular activities. Tomas's knowledge of Dwayne, his situation, and his potential are also relevant.

If a policy is applied the same way, each semester, to all students, then the policy will likely avoid questions of time, place, and manner. This consistency may not be fair, though. Time is a factor, given that what happened occurred during a certain time period (last semester). Manner (what happened and what Dwayne had to deal with logistically and emotionally) is also relevant. The manner in which the policy is also applied matters. Is a policy that is applied without exception appropriate for all students?

Options

Tomas could simply not send a communique to Dwayne and let Dwayne keep his position. He could uphold the policy and let Dwayne know he no longer holds his position. He could tell his supervisor about Dwayne's situation and ask for an exception for Dwayne; he might suggest in that he worked with Dwayne and his academic advisor to map out a success plan for the upcoming semester. He could tell his supervisor that he thinks they should create a process for students to seek exceptions.

(continued)

Application of Principles and Consequences

Tomas knows that Dwayne has been through a very tough situation, and he wants to support Dwayne's wishes. He believes this would be fair and respectful (principle of justice) and acknowledging of Dwayne's autonomy. He also believes that it is important for the institution to have strong, visible student leaders, such as Dwayne (affiliation). He also knows he needs to support Dwayne's academic career and that the policy is designed to promote the welfare of students (beneficence). Tomas has a duty to uphold the policies of the institution (fidelity), and even though his supervisor has not asked for the names of the students who have fallen below the grade threshold, if he does not tell her about Dwayne's grades, he will be omitting truth (veracity). Tomas also has a responsibility to address issues that are unfair. By collaborating to create a procedure for exceptions, he may be working toward respect and fairness in the future for other students (justice).

Anya and Scotti, and the Student Determined to Stay Focused

Anya is the director of the orientation office and Scotti is a student worker. Scotti is a high-achieving student and intends to attend medical school. Scotti also works to pay for college. Last semester, Scotti used over-the-counter substances to stay awake and to sleep, and he is worried about not being able to manage without these substances. His grades did not suffer, but he is afraid that they might, and he wants to break this habit before medical school. Anya, Scotti's academic advisor, and Scotti's recovery counselor met with Scotti at his request. At the meeting Scotti shared that, next semester, he would be involved in only two things: his student job and his classes. He asked for their support as he implemented his new plan.

Anya's supervisor, the vice president, tells Anya about a new task force that is going to work to improve orientation. The VP tells Anya that the task force chair appointed Scotti as the representative of the students and asks Anya to share the good news with Scotti.

Ethical Dilemma

Anya has agreed to support Scotti's plan, and his plan includes not getting overly involved. But the task force is a great opportunity for Scotti. Should Anya tell Scotti about the opportunity? Should Anya tell her supervisor that Scotti cannot serve?

Guidance from the Profession

Anya uses the NODA ethical standards (http://www.nodaweb.org/?page=ethical_standards). NODA directs members to "respect confidentiality in relationships with students" (2015, n.p.). This standard relates to whether or not, and how, Anya discusses Scotti's situation with her supervisor. NODA also states that professions should "provide feedback on performance and other issues in a timely and fitting manner." Although there is not a performance issue, Scotti's plan for restricted involvement and the new opportunity could fall under "other issues." This could help Anya decide whether or not to tell Scotti about the opportunity. NODA advises professionals to "recognize their own limits/boundaries in helping relationships with students." This could steer Anya to reviewing the situation with Scotti's academic advisor and recovery counselor.

Context: Relevant Parties and Time, Place, and Manner

Scotti is the central party. This issue could affect his current situation and long-term goals. Anya, Scotti's academic advisor, the recovery counselor, and Anya's supervisor are also relevant parties. All have an interest in Scotti's success. The new task force is also relevant, because student perspectives are being sought, Scotti's in particular. Time and manner are relevant. Scotti has asked for support at a crucial time in his academic career. This new opportunity has come when Scotti wants to restrict his involvements.

Options

Anya can honor Scotti's request for support in his involvement-restriction plan, not tell him about the opportunity, and tell her supervisor that Scotti cannot serve. Anya could tell Scotti and let Scotti decide what to do. The academic advisor and recovery counselor could also be helpful as Anya decides what to do. Perhaps the three of them could meet with Scotti and work through the pros and cons of the new opportunity.

Application of Principles and Consequences

Anya could uphold the principle of "fidelity" and not tell Scotti about the opportunity. Scotti has a plan, and Anya agreed to support him. In this case, she would be faithful to her word and duty. But she would have to tell her supervisor that Scotti cannot serve. This could be risky; Anya has a responsibility to be truthful and accurate to her supervisor (veracity), but also to respect a confidential matter with Scotti (nonmalfeasance).

She could honor the principle of "autonomy" and respect Scotti's freedom of choice, tell him about the opportunity, and let him decide what to do. This might worry Anya, because Scotti has asked for help to deal with an issue that is difficult for him to manage on his own, and she does not want to make this more difficult (nonmalfeasance).

The principle of "beneficence" is also a consideration, as Anya, the academic advisor, and the recovery counselor are all involved in promoting Scotti's welfare. Autonomy and beneficence can be applied if Anya and the others meet with Scotti to consider the opportunity.

Conclusion

Applying the principles discussed in this chapter requires a deep personal commitment to continued growth as an ethical practitioner. Throughout the history of student affairs, ethical practice has never been simple or straightforward, but with increasing complexity in higher education administration and the intricacy of challenges faced by students, enhancing our ethical integrity requires even more diligence and careful considerations of morally ambiguous situations.

Each of us must devote time and effort to maintaining and enhancing our ethical fitness. Trusted colleagues who discuss and debate the ethical implications of our policies and approaches provide much needed support. Further, a foundation for growth is unflinching honesty as we reflect on our decisions—critically examining our actions from various professional ethical frameworks and understanding the subtle influence, positive and negative, of our personal values.

Finally, enhancing capacity as an ethical practitioner requires courage and action. We must discern the best ethical response and implement it. We must strive for congruence between our knowledge of professional ethics and our actions. In the end, lived ethical practice is practice that maintains the credibility of our field and best serves our students.

Activities

The multiple and conflicting interests in higher education make it impossible to have a simple recipe for ethical practice that can be consistently applied. However, engaging in the following reflective and discussion activities can be helpful:

1. Frequently reread and question ethical principles and frameworks. When thinking about established ethical guidelines, pay special attention to the influence of one's own values and assumptions about others who may possess different identities, cultural backgrounds, and life experiences.
2. Develop and discuss actual or potential ethical dilemmas with colleagues and mentors. It is especially helpful to work through scenarios that involve feeling pressured by upper-level administrators to make exceptions or act in less principled ways. Doing the right thing in these types of situation requires risk-taking, quick analysis, and fundamental courage that take time to develop. Without practice, it is all too easy to simply make the exception because of the power of the person asking or to indignantly confront the administrator making the request. Frequent analysis discussions about how to respond to troublesome hypothetical dilemmas are essential to enhancing one's ethical fitness.

References

American College Personnel Association (ACPA). (2006). *Statement of ethical principles and standards.* Washington, DC: Author.

American College Personnel Association (ACPA)/National Association of Student Personnel Administrators (NASPA). (2010). *Professional competency areas for student affairs practitioners.* Washington, DC: Authors.

American Council on Education. (1994a). The student personnel point of view. In A. L. Rentz (Ed.), *Student affairs: A profession's heritage* (American College Personnel Association Media Publication no. 40, 2nd ed.). Lanham, MD: University Press of America. (Original work published 1937)

American Council on Education. (1994b). The student personnel point of view. In A. L. Rentz (Ed.), *Student affairs: A profession's heritage* (American College Personnel Association Media Publication no. 40, 2nd ed.). Lanham, MD: University Press of America. (Original work published 1949)

Bok, D. (2000). *Universities in the marketplace: The commercialization of higher education.* Princeton, NJ: Princeton University Press.

Clay, R. (2008). The corporatization of higher education. *Monitor on Psychology, 39*(11), 50.

Council for Advancement of Standards in Higher Education (CAS). (2012). Statement of shared ethical principles. *CAS Professional Standards for Higher Education* (8th ed.). Washington, DC: Author.

Dalton, J., Crosby, P. C., Valente, A., & Eberhardt, D. (2009). Maintaining and modeling everyday ethics in student affairs. In G. McClelland & J. Stringer (Eds.), *The handbook of student affairs administration* (3rd ed.). San Francisco: Jossey-Bass.

Dewey, J. (1985). *Democracy and education.* Carbondale: Southern Illinois University Press. (Original work published in 1916)

Evans, N. J., & Reason, R. D. (2001). Guiding principles: A review and analysis of student affairs philosophical statements. *Journal of College Student Development, 42,* 359–377.

Fried, J. (2003). Ethical standards and principles. In S. R. Komives & D. B. Woodard Jr. (Eds.), *Student services: A handbook for the profession* (4th ed.). San Francisco: Jossey-Bass.

Janosik, S., Cooper, D., Saunders, S., & Hirt, J. (2014). *Learning through supervised practice* (2nd ed.). New York: Taylor-Francis.

Keeling, R. (2004). *Learning reconsidered: A campus-wide focus on the student experience.* Washington, DC: National Association for Student Personnel Administrators and American College Personnel Association.

Kidder, R. M. (1995). How good people make tough choices. New York: HarperCollins.

Kitchener, K. (1985). Ethical principles and ethical decisions in student affairs. In H. J. Canon & R. D. Brown (Eds.), *Applied ethics in student affairs* (New Directions for Student Services, no. 30, pp. 17–30). San Francisco: Jossey Bass.

Lake, P. J. (2013). *The rights and responsibilities of the modern university: The rise of the facilitator university* (2nd ed.). Durham, NC: Carolina Academic Press.

Mills, N. (2012). The corporatization of higher education. *Dissent, 59*(4), 6–9.

Mueller, J. A., & Broido, E. M. (2012). Who we are is part of who we are. In J. Arminio, V. Torres, & R. Pope (Eds.), *Why aren't we there yet?* Sterling, VA: Stylus.

Nash, R. (2002). *Real world ethics: Frameworks for educators and human services professionals* (2nd ed.). New York: Teachers College Press.

National Association of Campus Activities. (2015, Sept. 3). *NACA statement of business ethics and standards.* Retrieved from https://www.naca.org/ABOUT/Documents/NACA%20Statement%20of%20Business%20Ethics.pdf

National Association of Student Personnel Administrators. (1990). *NASPA standards of professional practice.* Washington, DC: Author. Retrieved June 5, 2015, from https://www.naspa.org/about/student-affairs

National Association of Student Personnel Administrators. (2102). *Ethical framework for NASPA.* Unpublished document. NASPA Ethics Task Force. Washington, DC: Author.

NODA. (2015, June 19). *Statements of ethical standards 2002.* Retrieved from http://www.nodaweb.org/?page=ethical_standards

Noddings, N. (2007). *Philosophy of education* (2nd ed.). Boulder, CO: Westview Press.

Pope, R., & LePeau, L. (2012). The influence of institutional context and culture. In J. Arminio, V. Torres, & R. Pope (Eds.), *Why aren't we there yet?* Sterling, VA: Stylus.

Pope, R., Reynolds, A., & Mueller, J. (2004). *Multicultural competence in student affairs.* San Francisco: Jossey-Bass.

Saunders, S. A., & Lease Butts, J. (2011). Teaching integrity. In R. Young (Ed.), *Advancing the integrity of professional practice* (New Directions for Student Services, no. 135, pp. 67–77). San Francisco: Jossey Bass.

Stadler, H. A. (1986). Making hard choices: Clarifying controversial ethical issues. *Counseling and Human Development, 19,* 1–10.

Torres, L., Driscoll, M. W., & Burrow, A. L. (2010). Racial microaggressions and psychological functioning among highly achieving African-Americans: A mixed-methods approach. *Journal of Social and Clinical Psychology, 29*(10), 1074–1099.

Vaccaro, A., McCoy, B., Champagne, D., & Siegel, M. (2013). *Decisions matter.* Washington, DC: National Association of Student Personnel Administrators.

Winston, R. B., & McCaffrey, S. A. (1981). Development of ACPA ethical and professional standards. *Journal of College Student Personnel, 22,* 183–189.

Winston, R. B., & Saunders, S. A. (1991). Ethical professional practice in student affairs. In T. K. Miller & R. B. Winston (Eds.), *Administration and leadership in student affairs: Actualizing student development in higher education* (2nd ed.). Muncie, IN: Accelerated Development.

Young, R. B. (2011). The virtues of organizational integrity. In R. B. Young (Ed.), *Advancing the integrity of professional practice* (pp. 5–14), San Francisco: Jossey Bass.

CHAPTER 7

LEGAL FOUNDATIONS AND ISSUES

Thomas Miller

The law as it relates to higher education continues to develop in its complexity, and student affairs professionals need to be alert to practices and activities that manage risk. As our society has become increasingly immersed in legal issues, student affairs staff members at public and private institutions must be equipped to help modify practices that create risk and protect their institutions, the students they serve, and their resources from unintended consequences. There is every reason to believe that the management of legal issues and associated risk will become an increasingly central aspect of the work in student affairs in the future. This chapter is intended to help future student affairs professionals see the basic principles of legal issues from a broad perspective rather than in great detail. It focuses on a few general groupings of legal issues that address the matters that are most useful to those learning about student affairs work. The chapter will address how the United States Constitution affects student affairs practice, the ways in which the law interacts differently with public universities than with private institutions, and how federal regulations affect what student affairs professionals do.

There are many forms of risk that student affairs professionals face. The most obvious type of risk is associated with lawsuits in the form of liability for perceived wrongful acts or broken promises. Risk can also be associated with loss of or damage to property. Another form of risk is associated with actions that may have the effect of damaging the reputation of the institution through negative relations or damaging publicity. Additionally, risk can arise that is associated with the health or safety of students and other members of the campus community. Student affairs administrators also can find risk associated with enrollment management. Some activities or events could jeopardize student recruitment or persistence. The attentive student affairs staff member will be sensitive to all of these forms of risk and the strategies for managing each.

A uniform approach to understanding legal issues does not exist. The context in which a student affairs professional works, including state and even the local government and norms, can set the tone for the best approach. Therefore, a factor associated with discussing legal issues is the variation in culture and perspective between states. These differences often prompt citizens in those states to elect very different sorts of legislators who write different kinds of laws and select unlike sorts of judges. As a result, laws and judicial decisions may vary as one considers the complexity of the United States of America.

The United States Constitution

The United States Constitution frames basic duties for public universities and colleges. It also sets the stage for many practices at private institutions. A portion of the latter condition is related to public image. Many private schools would generally wish to adhere to the rights of citizens protected by the Constitution, even though if they chose to implement a particular practice or policy associated with the goals or purposes of the institution—but was unconstitutional in a public institution setting—it could well stand the test of law.

Religious Expression

The first clause of the First Amendment, related to the expression of religion, is important to student affairs professionals on two key tenets (Kaplin & Lee, 2009). First, what is commonly referred to as the establishment clause prohibits government from creating religion or forcing religion on citizens. Case law has established that public institutions cannot force persons to pray, partake in religious services, or be subjected to religious readings. A number of decisions by the United States Supreme Court have provided useful context for this aspect of the Constitution, including findings of clarity regarding school prayer.

The second part of this clause prohibits government from preventing the expression of religion, and this is where student affairs professionals at public universities might become confused. The casual understanding of this aspect of the Constitution has commonly been characterized as the "separation of church and state." Some student affairs administrators might believe that the Constitution does not allow religious expression on public university campuses. To the contrary, case law rather firmly establishes that a public institution that prohibits students from gathering to express religion or religious beliefs is acting in a way that is contrary to the First Amendment. Such restrictions are, in effect, restrictions of speech based on content. Not only should public institutions avoid prohibiting students from expressing religion but also they should not fail to fund activities associated with the practice of religion. Some public institutions have misinterpreted this issue in fear of violating the establishment clause of the First Amendment, but failing to permit or fund religious expression is a violation of the free exercise clause.

The following example demonstrates the two aspects of legal interpretations of the First Amendment on religious expression. If a group of students at a public institution wants to use a residence hall lounge that is otherwise available for a Bible study meeting, it should be permitted. Failing to allow them to would be prohibiting their free expression of religion. However, if the Bible study is organized by a resident director, a professional employee of the institution, and student attendance is expected, it may be subject to challenge. Similarly, if a student is assigned Bible readings as part of a disciplinary sanction at a public institution, it probably entangles the institution with forced religious practice.

Free Speech

The second clause of the First Amendment prohibits government from unreasonable restrictions of freedom of speech. This aspect of the First Amendment has received much attention from the courts over the years, and case law has helped to form standards and clarify rights that are associated with free speech (Kaplin & Lee, 2009). An important aspect for student affairs professionals to understand is the principle of a "public forum." A public forum is a place where government does not regulate speech, and a key condition of speech regulation is that it cannot be content based. In other words, a student affairs administrator cannot permit one form of speech outside of the student union building, such as student election campaigning, and regulate against another form of speech, such as a pro-life protest, without placing the institution at risk. By permitting the student election campaigning, the administrator has created a "public forum" at that location and would be wise to not prohibit other forms of speech based on content at that same place.

Some challenges have arisen in which students have acted as though their First Amendment rights were restricted by their institutions because they were forced to express things they did not wish to say (Kaplin & Lee, 2007). A student in the theater department, for example, may be required to speak words in a performance that she finds offensive. Courts have indicated that in this particular instance acting necessarily involves saying or doing things that one might not naturally say or do, although the student's right to freely express religion may prevail over the argument about acting.

Although this second clause of the First Amendment permits citizens to protest in public places, the right of expression does not extend to the right to disrupt the fundamental purposes of universities. The courts have determined that reasonable restrictions on free expression can be made in the form of time limitations, place designations, and manner of speech. For example, institutions may govern when and where amplified speech may be allowed. Institutions may also restrict speech that is inside of or near classroom buildings and any other speech that interferes with the purpose of the university. A regulation that requires speech or printed work to be "wholesome" risks a constitutional challenge, as might one that prohibits "offensive speech." Further, restrictions of time, place, and manner must be reasonable. An administrator who directs a group of protesters to a remote part of campus so they do not disturb or disrupt the normal traffic in a busy part of campus may be imposing an unreasonable restriction that, in effect, is based on content.

Although this practice has recently become less common, a number of institutions have created what are referred to as "free speech zones." The notion of such a designation is that there are no content restrictions in those spaces. A complication is that any other space that becomes by designation or default a public forum would also have no content restrictions. Some have argued that free speech zones have the effect of regulating the content of speech, and, of course, one might wonder about the openness of speech at all places that are not free speech zones.

Student affairs professionals face requests from students to organize about a cause or belief. Colleges and universities usually encourage social activism and student expression of opinion or values (Pavela, 2014). Free expression has been so highly valued on college campuses that institutions are referred to as "marketplaces of ideas." Some university leaders have attempted to restrict students from organizing about subjects or in affiliation with groups that are believed to be supportive of violence or at least disruptive behavior. Courts have determined that the suspicion or fear associated with some risk of future disruption is not sufficient reason to not allow students to organize. The standard that courts have imposed is greater than "suspicion." That is, courts have said that institutions must reasonably forecast that a disruption or illegal behavior is imminent before they can prevent activity that would cause it (Pavela, 2014).

Universities may have policies that require student organizations to open their memberships to all students in order to be eligible for funding. Such a requirement may restrict some types of organizations from accessing funds and may result in complicated tests of free association and free expression. It is not clear at this time whether such a restriction is a failsafe approach to guide the funding of student organizations. However, a decision by the United States Supreme Court allowed a restriction of the funding for a student organization that was open to only students who subscribed to the group's beliefs.

Court decisions have indicated that the rights of visitors on college campuses may be different than those of members of the university community, such as faculty members and students. Many institutions have set limits on time and place restrictions for visitors that are different than those restrictions on student or faculty member speech. Those limitations are most likely seen by courts as permissible, as long as they are not based on content. There are colleges that have required persons to receive prior approval before an event or public expression is allowed. The potential challenge to these prior-approval restrictions would probably be based on prior restraint on free expression, motivated by a content restriction, so that in some jurisdictions, prior approval may be impermissible. In other words, particularly at public institutions (because of their role as agents of government), a policy that requires permission before an activity or an expression can take place could be interpreted as a restriction of expression and be subject to contention.

Among the foundational principles of student affairs work are those that emphasize civility and respect for others (Young, 1997). Possibly as a result of this sort of thinking and in an effort to protect students and others from harm, some institutions have attempted to regulate speech with rules that limit the kinds of expression that are allowed. These speech codes can be risky because they can be seen as an unreasonable restriction of speech based on content. A code that regulates against speech that is harmful or hurtful obligates the speaker to know when harm or hurt might take place. A code that regulates against speech that is "offensive" or speech that is "upsetting" may be overly broad and not supported in a court test. A code that regulates against speech that is disruptive might seem on its face to be contradictory with the fundamental principles of the First Amendment, which at its core protects unpopular speech and minority viewpoints.

For similar reasons, to promote civility student affairs administrators may be inclined to restrict actions by students or others that disrupt programs or speeches. Heckling or interrupting speakers may be seen as uncivil or discourteous, but courts may determine that the behavior advances the purposes of the First Amendment. It can be difficult to know where the line is between the right to express disagreement with the speaker's position and the rights of audience members to hear the expressed views. At public institutions, in particular, student affairs staff members need to be sensitive to the rights of those who wish to express opposition to a viewpoint.

Hate speech is difficult to regulate because it is defined as speech that has the purpose of humiliating or causing hurt more than communicating ideas. Establishing a motive or purpose for such speech may be a very challenging enterprise. Hate speech that is not directly threatening nor falling under the doctrine of "fighting words" (addressed later in this section) is probably best left unregulated. An additional context is that courts have determined that emotional content is as much protected by the First Amendment as is cognitive content, and the offensiveness of speech is no reason to restrict it.

An institution of higher education may be challenged if it regulates against obscenity or cursing. The challenge associated with obscenity is that it is hard to define and regulate, and cursing is a form of speech that exists in the public forum, in media, and in many aspects of communication between adults. There may be some sites on college campuses where obscenity can be regulated, such as a chapel or an elementary school located on campus property.

Universities can reasonably limit expression in a variety of conditions (Pavela, 2014). Commercial speech, for example, does not enjoy the same level of protection as does the communication of ideas or opinions about issues. Universities are not obligated to permit commercial speech at the same level and under the same conditions as other speech. As described previously, institutions are also not obligated to allow speech that disrupts the academic environment or the fundamental purposes of the university. Commercial speech is limited, for example, in the classroom, because this is the fundamental teaching and learning environment.

Further, universities are not required to permit speech that encourages or has the direct result of unlawful behavior (Pavela, 2014). The test for limiting this type of speech, however, is rigorous. Lawlessness must be immediately imminent before the provoking speech can be prohibited. A form of expression that falls in this category is that of "fighting words," expression that has a tendency to provoke an immediate violent reaction. Courts rarely apply this doctrine. Another form of speech that can be limited is a true threat of violence. The threat must be genuine and an expression of a serious intent to commit harm.

An additional point that the courts have made clear is that expression may be in the form of the spoken word or the written word, but it may also be symbolic in nature. A black armband, a Confederate flag, and a Nazi swastika are all symbolic forms of expression. Though many may object, those examples of symbolic expression are as closely protected by the First Amendment as are spoken and written words.

Besides having the capacity to regulate forms of speech as described previously, institutions may also establish regulatory conditions that limit expression in other ways. For example, although such regulations cannot be based on content, institutions can clearly regulate against graffiti or the defacing of buildings and interior walls. Again, these regulations must be viewpoint neutral, so it might be risky for an institution to permit sidewalk chalking for some purposes and not for others. Of course, institutions can regulate against expression that causes harm to people or property, so the reader can see that institutions are not required to permit every form of expression in every setting. Viewpoint neutrality is essential, and speech cannot be regulated based on content, except as previously detailed.

The First Amendment applies to public institutions as it protects speech rights of employees. Generally, those employed by public higher educational institutions are free to criticize governmental entities, including their employing institutions, as long as they speak as private citizens (Pavela, 2013). However, they may be subject to consequences including dismissal if their speech is as employees or associated with their official duties.

College students are a very diverse collection of people, and they often gravitate to argument and dispute. Some have deeply held religious beliefs and some have none at all. Almost every campus has some students who might be considered activists or dissenters who impose their views on others in ways that some might consider annoying. The views and expressions of extremists are afforded as much protection as the positive, agreeable messages some might prefer. The values of those in the student affairs field often revolve around harmony, civility, and agreement; but we need to value more highly the freedom for the expression of unpopular ideas that fuel debate and discussion and help students refine their own beliefs. What better place than a college or university campus to provide appropriate opportunities for such activities to occur! Student affairs staff members should recognize that dispute and disagreement, even when it is disturbing and upsetting, is usually protected by the United States Constitution, particularly at public institutions.

Religious expression is similarly protected, as is the freedom of the student press. Those at private institutions operate under slightly different conditions, and they need to be aware of how their published policies inform practice and decision making.

Weapons on Campus

The Second Amendment of the United States Constitution relates to the right to bear arms. Although the amendment is in the federal Constitution, interpretation of it has been in the hands of the states, and there is great variation in how the states have responded, particularly in the past several years. States have varying cultures, and state lawmakers hold varying ideological beliefs in regard to protecting the welfare of their citizens. There are many states with laws that ban guns from college campuses, and quite a few other states permit colleges to develop their own policies regarding firearms on campus. Some states have passed or are considering legislation that ensures that citizens can possess guns on public property. States have passed or will consider legislation that allows guns on public property in locked trunks of cars or that permit guns in the hands of employees but not students. As legislation and litigation associated with these matters will surely unfold over the coming years, student affairs professionals are encouraged to stay informed about associated state law that can affect the rights of students and employees regarding the possession of firearms.

Search and Seizure

The Fourth Amendment of the United States Constitution protects citizens from government intrusion when individuals have an expectation of privacy. That expectation clearly extends to residence halls on college campuses and also to other places where privacy is assumed. Where the expectation might exist, ". . . persons, houses, papers, and effects . . ." can be clarified. "Persons" has been interpreted by the courts to include an individual's clothing, materials and pockets, and bodily fluids. "Houses" includes rental property, such as an apartment, a porch, and a mobile home or camper in which one lives. "Papers" include a diary, a journal, a book, and letters. "Effects" would typically include a backpack, a purse, an MP3 player, a personal computer, and mobile communication devices (for example, a smartphone or tablet).

The key legal test for Fourth Amendment challenges is the matter of what is reasonable as opposed to unreasonable. One of the primary tests of reasonableness relates to the expectation of privacy. If an individual is in an environment where privacy might reasonably be expected, an intrusion into that environment may be seen as a violation of her rights. However, an expectation of privacy isn't necessarily a binding aspect of this matter. For example, an individual may have an expectation of privacy, but an objective assessment of that may find the expectation may not be reasonable.

Due Process

The Fifth Amendment to the United States Constitution obligates government, including state institutions, to provide "due process of law" in the
student conduct setting as well as in the review of employee performance.
Due process has been defined in case law over the years. Its fundamental
requirement is twofold: provide notice of allegations about violations of
regulations and provide the accused with a hearing as an opportunity to respond to the allegations (Kaplin & Lee, 2009). There are some jurisdictions
where courts have expanded the obligations associated with due process, but
notice and hearing apply throughout the United States. Although the Fifth
Amendment provides the context for due process in public institutions, the
direct definition of due process is located in their published materials and
codes of conduct. However, few public institutions limit their procedures
to simply notice and hearing. Many public institutions have several levels
of appeal or review regarding student conduct, and many permit students
accused of misconduct to be accompanied by attorneys. It is also common
for those accused of rule violations to be allowed to hear and respond to
those who initiate the charges.

Student Affairs Practice at Public Compared with Private Institutions

The practice of student affairs at different types of institutions has great
variance (Hirt, 2006). A principle difference between public institutions and
private ones relates to the areas of law that largely govern their relationships
with students (Kaplin & Lee, 2009). Public institutions are, effectively, arms
of state government. They are established by state authority, funded by state
resources, and governed by state organizations. The United States Constitution
establishes what government can and cannot do, including public colleges and
universities.

Because private institutions are not agencies of the state, the United States
Constitution does not directly establish standards for how they interact with
students. The fundamental area of law that governs the relationships between
private colleges and universities and their students is contract law. The forms
of contracts between institutions and students are largely related to published materials and other ways in which services or programs are promised
to students. Contract law also has significant application to public institutions,
because all of their published materials establish the nature of the relationship
between universities and their students.

Government may establish limits for its exposure to liability, which is
referred to as sovereign immunity. It serves to protect government and state
entities from unlimited risk. The specific standards for sovereign immunity
vary from state to state. Individual states have passed legislation to provide
definitions of immunity, and judicial decisions have further defined sovereign

immunity in individual states. Many states have passed legislation that establishes specific financial limits of exposure by state institutions to claims of liability. Private institutions are not insulated at all by sovereign immunity, unless, in special circumstances, they are acting as agents of the state as determined by courts that are reviewing their claim of sovereign immunity.

In addition to the protections associated with sovereign immunity, many states have passed laws insulating government employees, including employees of public universities and colleges, from personal liability. This usually applies to employees performing their functions within the scope of their assigned responsibilities.

The Fourth Amendment of the United States Constitution provides a context for the rights of students attending public universities with regard to freedom from searches (Kaplin & Lee, 2009). The Fourth Amendment restricts the rights of government officials to search the property of individuals or to search their person without a properly executed warrant. Government officials, in this case, would include the employees of public colleges and universities. Conducting a search in violation of a student's Fourth Amendment rights could expose employees and public institutions to liability for damages.

Employees of private institutions have more leeway in conducting searches in the absence of law enforcement personnel. However, even in those instances in which Fourth Amendment or state law constraints do not apply, a room search that is conducted outside of the parameters of the housing contract between the institution and the student may generate litigation associated with a violation of contract. The purpose for searching a student's room is the test for legal determination. When it is for the purpose of enforcing the law, Fourth Amendment limits apply. When it is for the purpose of protecting institutional interests, such as suspicion of a fire hazard, constitutional limitations are less applicable.

Federal Regulations

The next section examines selected federal regulations that have an important influence on student affairs practice at public and private colleges and universities.

Title IX

The original intent of Title IX of the Educational Amendments of 1972 was to eliminate sex discrimination in higher education, particularly in admission. As it has unfolded, it further obligates institutions to provide opportunity to either gender that is underrepresented in a particular activity. Much of Title IX legal activity has hovered around intercollegiate athletics, but it applies to cocurricular programs, academic programs, and so forth. Title IX is enforced by the United States Office of Civil Rights.

Originally, institutions measured their compliance with Title IX based on a three-part test. The elements of the test were having the percentage of male and female participants substantially proportionate to the percentage of male and female students enrolled at the institution, having a history in continuing practice of expanding participation opportunities for the under-represented gender and demonstrating the accommodation of interests and abilities of the underrepresented gender (Kaplin & Lee, 2009).

Title IX liability has recently been extended to colleges when they have shown "deliberate indifference" to a student's grievance associated with sexual assault or harassment. In order for an institution to be held liable the following conditions must apply: the harassment is so significant that it can prevent the victim from accessing educational opportunity, the college has control over the circumstances in which the harassment took place, the college has control over the perpetrator of harassment, and the college was notified of the harassment and did not respond in an appropriate fashion.

The application of Title IX to sexual assault changes the landscape for such matters for colleges and universities (Pavela, 2010). It brings the federal government and its attorneys into the dispute and makes for a much more challenging circumstance than a simple, private lawsuit might. In recent years the federal government has been much more aggressive in the application of Title IX to sexual assault matters. High-profile cases have raised awareness of the usefulness of Title IX in the pursuit of resolution of sexual assault charges; it is predictable that more cases of this nature will occur.

The duty to report cases of sexual discrimination, including sexual assault, fall on many student affairs staff members, from resident assistants to deans of students. The regulations refer to them as "responsible employees" and give them the reporting duty because they have oversight responsibility for the student experience.

The responsible student affairs administrator will evaluate assault cases that have a Title IX element carefully and make sure to pursue facts diligently and thoroughly. Initiating a Title IX investigation is a serious matter, and the institution is best advised to proceed quickly and not wait for resolution of any associated criminal investigation or proceeding. Those involved in the investigation should have training and experience in responding to complaints of sexual violence, and they should understand the grievance procedure and requirements associated with confidentiality.

Jeanne Clery Act

Through the Jeanne Clery Act, in its original form and after several amendments and clarifications, institutions are required to report crimes that occur on and near campus and to provide an annual security report that summarizes crimes, safety steps the institution employs, and practices that help students to understand ways to protect their safety.

The law requires certain employees, called campus security authorities, to report to those responsible for responding to crime on campus, usually campus police, any allegation of a student being victimized by crime. Campus security authorities are those persons with oversight of or supervisory duties for students. That would include most student affairs administrators and many graduate assistants who work with students. More information about the details associated with the law can be found at the Clery Center website: http://clerycenter.org/.

Violence against Women Reauthorization Act

The Violence against Women Reauthorization Act (VAWA) was signed into law by President Obama in 2013, and it gives institutions of higher education substantial responsibility (http://www.whitehouse.gov/sites/default/files/docs/vawa_factsheet.pdf). One of them is the obligation to report incidents of domestic violence, dating violence, and stalking. This duty to report these classifications of crime goes beyond those required by the Clery Act.

Another set of responsibilities associated with VAWA pertains to the student conduct process. Institutional policy must include information on the rights of victims to seek assistance from law enforcement and campus authorities. Policy also must make clear the rights of victims regarding judicial no-contact, restraining, and protective orders, which serve to isolate victims from the accused. VAWA also prescribes standards for student conduct proceedings in domestic violence, dating violence, sexual assault, and stalking cases.

Under VAWA, institutions are obligated to offer prevention and awareness programs that promote awareness of rape, domestic violence, and associated behaviors. Such training programs are expected to include definitions of the offenses and of consent regarding sexual offenses as well as a statement that the institution prohibits the offenses. Programs also must include information on bystander intervention in the recognition of signs of abusive behavior. Institutions are expected to provide prevention and awareness campaigns on an ongoing basis; these programs must be made available to new students and new employees. Much of the responsibility for compliance with VAWA will fall on student affairs professionals, and they must be alert to the law and its requirements.

Family Educational Rights and Privacy Act of 1974 (FERPA)

FERPA gives college students the right to control the disclosure of their education records, to inspect those records, and to seek amendment to their records if they wish (Ramirez, 2009). Students, not parents, hold these rights irrespective of their age. The law has the effect of protecting the privacy of college students. There are several exceptions to FERPA that permit disclosure to parents, including a health or safety emergency, a violation of alcohol or controlled substance laws, and financial reporting for income tax purposes in the case of dependency. The enforcement of FERPA is the responsibility of the Family Policy Compliance Office of the Department of Education. Although the consequences for FERPA violations are potentially grave, that is, the loss of all federal aid, the compliance office seeks to help institutions adjust policies and practices and fix problems associated with violations rather than punish institutions.

FERPA is frequently misunderstood and it may sometimes be misrepresented. For example, when student affairs staff members tell parents that federal law prevents them from answering the parents' questions about the student, it is often not true. For example, students who are under twenty-one years of age and dependents of their parents for tax purposes may find that educational information may be shared with their parents in no violation of FERPA. The truth is that many student affairs staff members do not want to share information with parents, seeing the student as the primary constituent. In emergencies or when a student is in some risk of harm or injury, parents can certainly be informed. In any event, falsely hiding behind FERPA is not the best practice. The responsible administrator will know what the purpose of FERPA is and also what its limitations are and will treat student educational records, as defined by the law, appropriately.

Conclusion

We live in litigious times, and lawsuits will occur with increasing frequency. Being sued is an unpleasant experience. It is adversarial and contentious, and it can take a great amount of time and emotional energy from the life of a busy student affairs professional. Even the threat of a lawsuit is unpleasant, but, sadly, it is not uncommon. Concern for potential litigation, however, should not dominate an innovative, educationally sound student affairs administrative division. Focusing on students and their welfare and their success is the primary purpose of work in student affairs. The driving force in our lives should not be avoiding lawsuits.

Working with college students, whose values, beliefs, and place in society are taking shape, is a noble undertaking. However, it has inherent risks on an everyday basis. Many students in their late adolescence are risk-takers. We know this, and that knowledge arms us with the warning that we may need to look out for the students for whom we are responsible. Student safety or welfare is a significant liability risk. Activity that puts students in harm's way or threatens their good health must be avoided. Irrespective of litigation, activity that threatens the welfare of students should not take place.

Another form of risk is associated with the ownership of property. Universities own great amounts of land and buildings. With that ownership comes the duty to keep it safe, and the diligent student affairs professional will be alert to unsafe condition and let the proper authorities know so that people can be warned of the condition and it can be repaired.

It will remain the burden of college attorneys to defend student affairs administrators and their employing institutions in the event of litigation. Although those attorneys will remain the best equipped individuals to represent an institution in a lawsuit, student affairs administrators are the persons best equipped to manage the risk of liability for their own actions. Good planning, intentional and farsighted staff training, policies that are well grounded and clear, and, when appropriate, advice from legal counsel will help student affairs administrators craft intelligent strategies for risk management. In addition, conducting their duties in a prudent and reasonable fashion and in good faith with an understanding of the principles of law as they relate to higher education is sound practice. Student affairs administrators need to be tolerant of the ambiguity associated with legal issues. Best practice will depend on what is learned from case law, the nature of government regulation and policy, and the specific facts associated with the issue being measured.

Not all crises can be anticipated, but a carefully developed crisis plan is an essential tool in responding to a crisis. A crisis plan that is associated with one type of event can be used to react to a different type of event. For example, student affairs practitioners can use their resourcefulness to apply the principles of a hurricane evacuation plan to respond to a student health epidemic on campus.

There is one aspect of legal issues management that merits attention because it relates to the establishment of good relationships with students and student organizations. A student affairs administrator whose connections to students are characterized as trusting and fostering mutual respect is more likely to be informed on a timely basis about campus conditions or activities from which risk may evolve. When students trust administrators, they are more apt to alert them in advance to situations from which risk will evolve. Having the opportunity to engage a situation proactively, rather than reacting to an unfortunate event, is always a better strategy for risk management.

A consequence of a legal misstep is associated with bad public relations outcomes. Damaging publicity, whether accompanied by other forms of risk or not, can be hard to recover from or almost impossible to refute. When our mistakes or criticisms become public it can put us in an untenable position. A secondary effect of negative public relations can be an adverse effect on enrollment and student recruitment. Many times, bad publicity cannot even be rebutted. If the issue is associated with an unhappy former employee or a student, a student affairs staff member might be in a position to be unable to respond to questions or challenges if it is a confidential employment or student record matter at hand.

The field of student affairs is a challenging one. It is populated by persons who genuinely care about students in the institutions they serve. Valuing learning above all other purposes of higher education, the profession celebrates diversity, inclusion, and a culture of excellence. Student affairs staff members see their campuses as very special places where people come to develop their talent and realize their potential for the future. Student affairs administrators do not shrink from challenges or fear difficult circumstances. They are planners, they are problem-solvers, and they are decision makers. They do what they must in order to manage the risks with which they are presented.

Clearly, the law is dynamic, and future court decisions, legislative initiatives, and practices in higher education will alter details associated with best practices for risk management in student affairs administration. The nature of the future is hard to predict, and well-informed student affairs professionals must assume responsibility for staying current on the law and risk management.

Discussion Questions

1. What are some ways in which the First Amendment rights of students might challenge the traditional thinking of a student affairs administrator regarding how students should treat each other?
2. What are some arguments for (and against) the rights of students to carry concealed weapons on a public college campus?
3. Under what circumstances would a public university be required to permit a neo-Nazi student organization to demonstrate? What restrictions could be applied? How would it be different at a private institution?
4. What are some typical student affairs positions that would be apt to be considered "responsible employees" for the purpose of Title IX?
5. Under what circumstances would FERPA regulations permit a student affairs administrator to speak with the parent of a student?

References

Hirt, J. B. (2006). *Where you work matters: Student affairs administration at different types of institutions* (pp. 185–209). Lanham, MD: United Press of America.

Kaplin, W. A., & Lee, B. A. (2007). *The law of higher education* (4th ed., pp. 306–310). San Francisco: Jossey-Bass.

Kaplin, W. A., & Lee, B. A. (2009). *A legal guide for student affairs professionals* (4th ed., pp. 23–49, 365–371, 456–474, 478–508, 735–738). San Francisco: Jossey-Bass.

Pavela, G. (2010). The April 4, 2011 OCR "dear colleague" letter. In *The Pavela Report, 16*(12). St. Johns, FL: College Administration Publications.

Pavela, G. (2013). *The Pavela Report, 18*(29). St. Johns, FL: College Administration Publications.

Pavela, G. (2014). *The Pavela Report, 19*(4). St. Johns, FL: College Administration Publications.

Ramirez, C. A. (2009). *FERPA: Clear and simple* (pp. 27–62). San Francisco: Jossey-Bass.

Young, R. B. (1997). *No neutral ground* (pp. 71–85). San Francisco: Jossey-Bass.

PART THREE

THEORETICAL BASES OF THE PROFESSION

Long ago, social psychologist Kurt Lewin declared that there is "nothing so practical as a good theory"; and, indeed, the theories that constitute the theoretical bases for student affairs practice continue to provide conceptual and practical guidance to the field. Although these theories have evolved over time and new theoretical perspectives have developed, those in student affairs remain concerned with understanding the whole student, that is, how individual students develop holistically and come to construct their identities, the role of environment in promoting or deterring development, the influence of organizations and campus climate on student experiences and outcomes, and what contributes to student success.

The chapters in part 3 discuss foundational theories with which all those practicing in student affairs should be familiar as well as more contemporary theoretical perspectives that provide a lens for understanding

college student development, students' experiences, and their environments. It is impossible in a book of this nature to cover all theories in great depth. Instead, we tried to strike an artful balance in discussing those foundational theories that have not only served the profession well over time but also have been extended to broaden the focus, be more inclusive, or have been reconceptualized to pose new theorizations of important concepts integral to student affairs practice.

We also provide an updated and revised table III.1, "Theories about College Students, Environments, and Organizations," initially developed by Marylu McEwen for the fourth edition and revised here from the one that appeared in the fifth edition by Susan R. Jones, Elisa S. Abes, and Zak Foste. This table, which appears at the end of this part opener, is not intended to be exhaustive, nor is it representative of all the possibilities for understanding college students. In revising this table, we erred in the direction of including theories or frameworks grounded in empirical research and those drawn on by the chapter authors included in this section. We hope this table will be a useful reference for those interested in a guide that includes foundational theories as well as newer work contributing to the development of theory as well as to theoretical understandings of college students and their experiences. It may also serve as an impetus for additional research because the table makes more obvious those areas in which theory is underrepresented and thus little is known (for example, social class, disability). Organizing theories in the way we have in this table also points to the limitations of placing theories into particular categories because some groupings cross boundaries or require a more integrative approach. For this reason, we begin the presentation of theories in the chapters that follow with holistic development so as to affirm the commitment to understanding the whole student found in foundational theories as well as more contemporary conceptualizations that put the pieces of development back together in more complex and integrated ways (Torres, Jones, & Renn, 2009). What follows is a brief overview of the theory chapters included in this section, which, taken together, provide an introduction to the theoretical foundation of the field.

TABLE III.1 THEORIES ABOUT COLLEGE STUDENTS, ENVIRONMENTS, AND ORGANIZATIONS

Theory Family	Subcategory	Focus of Theory	Specific Theories
Holistic Development (see chapter 9)		Maturity	Heath, D. H. (1968). *Growing up in college.* San Francisco: Jossey-Bass.
		Self-evolution	Kegan, R. (1982). *The evolving self: Problem and process in human development.* Cambridge, MA: Harvard University Press.
			Kegan, R. (1994). *In over our heads: The mental demands of modern life.* Cambridge, MA: Harvard University Press.
		Self-authorship	Barber, J. P., King, P. M., & Baxter Magolda, M. B. (2013). Long strides on the journey toward self-authorship: Substantial developmental shifts in college students' meaning making. *The Journal of Higher Education, 84*(6), 866–896.
			Baxter Magolda, M. B. (2009). *Authoring your life: Developing an internal voice to navigate life's challenges.* Sterling, VA: Stylus.
			Baxter Magolda, M. B., & King, P. M. (2012). Assessing meaning making and self-authorship: Theory, research, and application. *ASHE Higher Education Report, 38*(3). San Francisco: Jossey-Bass.

Theory Family	Subcategory	Focus of Theory	Specific Theories
			Jones, S. R., Kim, Y. C., & Cilente Skendall, K. (2012). (Re)Framing authenticity: Considering multiple social identities using autoethnographic and intersectional approaches. *The Journal of Higher Education, 83*(5), 689–723.
			Pizzolato, J. E. (2010). What is self-authorship? A theoretical exploration of the construct. In M. B. Baxter Magolda, E. G. Creamer, & P. S. Meszaros (Eds.), *Development and assessment of self-authorship: Exploring the concept across cultures* (pp. 187–206). Sterling, VA: Stylus.
			Torres, V., & Hernandez, E. (2007). The influence of ethnic identity on self-authorship: A longitudinal study of Latino/a college students. *Journal of College Student Development, 48*(5), 558–573.
Psychosocial Development (see chapter 11)	General psychosocial development	Foundational theory	Erikson, E. H. (1968). *Identity: Youth and crisis.* New York: Norton.
		Challenge and support	Sanford, N. (1962). *The American college.* New York: Wiley.
			Sanford, N. (1967). *Why colleges fail: A study of the student as a person.* San Francisco: Jossey-Bass.
		Vectors of development	Chickering, A. W., & Reisser, L. (1993). *Education and identity* (2nd ed.). San Francisco: Jossey-Bass.
		Crisis and commitment	Marcia, J. E. (1966). Development and validation of ego-identity status. *Journal of Personality and Social Psychology, 3,* 551–559.
		Women's development	Josselson, R. (1987). *Finding herself: Pathways to identity development in women.* San Francisco: Jossey-Bass.
			Josselson, R. (1996). *Revising herself: The story of women's identity from college to midlife.* New York: Oxford University Press.
		Career development	Super, D. E. (1990). A life-span, life-space approach to career development. In D. Brown, L. Brooks, & Associates, *Career choice and development: Applying contemporary theories to development* (2nd ed., pp. 197–261). San Francisco: Jossey-Bass.
	Adult development	Life stage	Levinson, D. J. (1978). *The seasons of a man's life.* New York: Ballantine.
			Levinson, D. J. (1996). *The seasons of a woman's life.* New York: Ballantine.
			Neugarten, B. L. (1979). Time, age, and the life cycle. *American Journal of Psychiatry, 136,* 887–894.
			Vaillant, G. (1977). *Adaptation to life.* Boston: Little, Brown.

(*continued*)

TABLE III.1 (*continued*)

Theory Family	Subcategory	Focus of Theory	Specific Theories
		Life transitions	Anderson, M. L., Goodman, J., & Schlossberg, N. K. (2012). *Counseling adults in transition: Linking Schlossberg's theory with practice in a diverse world* (4th ed.). New York: Springer.
		Emerging adulthood	Arnett, J. J. (2011). Emerging adulthood(s). In L. Arnett Jensen (Ed.), *Bridging cultural and developmental approaches to psychology: New syntheses in theory, research, and policy.* New York: Oxford University Press.
			Arnett, J. J. (2015). *Emerging adulthood: The winding road from the late teens through the twenties* (2nd ed.). New York: Oxford University Press.
			Kroger, J. (2004). *Identity and adolescence the balance between self and other* (3rd ed.). London: Routledge.
Development of Social Identities (see chapter 11)	General identity development		Deaux, K. (1993). Reconstructing social identity. *Personality and Social Psychology Bulletin, 19,* 4–12.
			Tajfel, H. (Ed.). (1982). *Social identity and intergroup relations.* Cambridge, UK: Cambridge University Press.
	Racial identity	Black racial identity	Cross, W. E. (2001). Encountering nigrescence. In J. G. Ponterotto, J. M. Casas, L. A. Suzuki, & C. M. Alexander (Eds.), *Handbook of multicultural counseling* (pp. 371–393). Thousand Oaks, CA: Sage.
			Helms, J. E., & Cook, D. A. (1999). *Using race and culture in counseling and psychotherapy: Theory and process.* Boston: Allyn and Bacon.
			Jackson, B. W., III. (2012). Black identity development: Influences of culture and social oppression. In C. L. Wijeyesinghe & B. W. Jackson III (Eds.), *New perspectives on racial identity development: Integrating emerging frameworks* (2nd ed., pp. 33–50). New York: New York University Press.
		White racial identity	Frankenberg, R. (1993). *White women, race matters: The social construction of whiteness.* Minneapolis: University of Minnesota Press.
			Hardiman, R., & Keehn, M. (2012). White identity development revisited: Listening to white students. In C. L. Wijeyesinghe & B. W. Jackson III (Eds.), *New perspectives on racial identity development: Integrating emerging frameworks* (2nd ed., pp. 121–137). New York: New York University Press.
			Helms, J. E., & Cook, D. A. (1999). *Using race and culture in counseling and psychotherapy: Theory and process.* Boston: Allyn and Bacon.

Theory Family	Subcategory	Focus of Theory	Specific Theories
		Asian American racial identity	Kim, J. (2012). Asian American racial identity development theory. In C. L. Wijeyesinghe & B. W. Jackson III (Eds.), *New perspectives on racial identity development: Integrating emerging frameworks* (2nd ed., pp. 138–160). New York: New York University Press.
			Kodama, C. M., McEwen, M. K., Liang, C.T.H., & Lee, S. (2002). An Asian American perspective on psychosocial student development theory. In M. K. McEwen, C. M. Kodama, A. Alvarez, S. Lee, & C. T. H. Liang (Eds.), *Working with Asian American college students* (New Directions for Student Services, no. 97, pp. 45–59). San Francisco: Jossey-Bass.
		Native American racial identity	Horse, P. G. (2012). Twenty-first century Native American consciousness: A thematic model of Indian identity. In C. L. Wijeyesinghe & B. W. Jackson III (Eds.), *New perspectives on racial identity development: Integrating emerging frameworks* (2nd ed., pp. 108–120). New York: New York University Press.
			LaFromboise, T. D., Trimble, J. E., & Mohatt, G. V. (1990). Counseling intervention and American Indian tradition: An integrative approach. *The Counseling Psychologist, 18*(4), 628–654.
		Latino racial identity	Gallegos, P. I., & Ferdman, B. M. (2012). Latina and Latino ethnoracial identity orientations: A dynamic and developmental perspective. In C. L. Wijeyesinghe & B. W. Jackson III (Eds.), *New perspectives on racial identity development: Integrating emerging frameworks* (2nd ed., pp. 51–80). New York: New York University Press.
			Torres, V. (2004). Familial influences on the identity development of Latino first year students. *Journal of College Student Development, 45*(4), 457–469.
		Biracial identity	Kerwin, C., & Ponterotto, J. G. (1995). Biracial identity development: Theory and research. In J. G. Ponteretto, J. M. Casas, L. A. Suzuki, & C. M. Alexander (Eds.), *Handbook of multicultural counseling* (pp. 199–217). Thousand Oaks, CA: Sage.
			Khanna, N. (2011). *Biracial in America: Forming and performing racial identity.* Lanham, MD: Lexington Books.
			Kich, G. K. (1992). The developmental process of asserting a biracial, bicultural identity. In M.P.P. Root (Ed.), *Racially mixed people in the America* (pp. 304–417). Newbury Park, CA: Sage.
			Poston, W.S.C. (1990). The biracial identity development model: A needed addition. *Journal of Counseling and Development, 69,* 152–155.

(continued)

TABLE III.1 (*continued*)

Theory Family	Subcategory	Focus of Theory	Specific Theories
		Multiracial identity	Renn, K. A. (2004). *Mixed race students in college: The ecology of race, identity, and community.* Albany: State University of New York Press.
			Renn, K. A. (2008). Research on biracial and multiracial identity development: Overview and synthesis. *Biracial and multiracial students* (New Directions for Student Services, no. 123, pp. 13–21). San Francisco: Jossey-Bass.
			Root, M.P.P. (Ed.). (1996). *The multiracial experience: Racial borders as the new frontier.* Thousand Oaks, CA: Sage.
			Wijeyesinghe, C. L. (2012). The intersectional model of multiracial identity: Integrating multiracial identity theories and intersectional perspectives on social identity. In C. L. Wijeyesinghe & B. W. Jackson III (Eds.*), New perspectives on racial identity development: Integrating emerging frameworks* (2nd ed., pp. 81–107). New York: New York University Press.
	Ethnic identity	Crisis and commitment	Phinney, J. S. (1993). A three-stage model of ethnic identity development in adolescence. In M. E. Bernal & G. P. Knight (Eds.), *Ethnic identity formation and transmission among Hispanic and other minorities* (pp. 61–79). Albany: State University of New York Press.
			Ruiz, A. S. (1990). Ethnic identity: Crisis and resolution. *Journal of Multicultural Counseling and Development, 18*(1), 29–40.
	Sexual identity	Gay and lesbian identity	Abes, E. S., & Jones, S. R. (2004). Meaning-making capacity and the dynamics of lesbian college students' multiple dimensions of identity. *Journal of College Student Development, 45*(6), 612–632.
			Bilodeau, B. L., & Renn, K. A. (2005). Analysis of LBGT identity development models and implication for practice. In *Gender identity and sexual orientation: Research, policy, and personal perspectives* (New Directions for Student Services, no. 111, pp. 25–39). San Francisco: Jossey-Bass.
			Cass, V. C. (1979). Homosexual identity formation: A theoretical model. *Journal of Homosexuality, 4,* 219–235.
			D'Augelli, A. R. (1994). Identity development and sexual orientation: Toward a model of lesbian, gay, and bisexual development. In E. J. Trickett, R. J. Watts, & D. Birman (Eds.), *Human diversity: Perspectives on people in context* (pp. 312–333). San Francisco: Jossey-Bass.

Theory Family	Subcategory	Focus of Theory	Specific Theories
			Fassinger, R. E., & Arseneau, J. R. (2007). "I'd rather be wet than be under that umbrella": Experiences and identities of lesbian, gay, bisexual, and transgender people. In K. J. Bieschke, R. M. Perez, & K. A. DeBord (Eds.), *Handbook of counseling and psychotherapy with lesbian, gay, bisexual, and transgender clients* (pp. 19–49). Washington, DC: American Psychological Association.
			McCarn, S. R., & Fassinger, R. E. (1996). Revisioning sexual minority identity formation. *The Counseling Psychologist, 24*(3), 508–534.
			Peña-Talamantes, A. E. (2013). Empowering the self, creating worlds: Lesbian and gay Latina/o college students' identity negotiation in figured worlds. *Journal of College Student Development, 54*(3), 267–282.
			Stewart, D.-L., Renn, K. A., & Brazelton, G. B. (2015). *Gender and sexual diversity in U.S. higher education: Contexts and opportunities for LGBTQ college students* (New Directions for Student Services, no. 152). San Francisco: Jossey-Bass.
		Bisexual identity	Klein, F., Sepekoff, B., & Wolf, T. J. (1990). Sexual orientation: A multi-variable dynamic process. In T. Geller (Ed.), *Bisexuality: A reader and sourcebook* (pp. 64–81). Ojai, CA: Times Change Press.
			Parker, B. A., Adams, H. L., & Phillips, L. D. (2007). Decentering gender: Bisexual identity as an expression of a non-dichotomous worldview. *Identity: An International Journal of Theory and Research, 7*(3), 205–224.
		Heterosexual identity	Mueller, J. A., & Cole, J. C. (2009). A qualitative examination of heterosexual consciousness among college students. *Journal of College Student Development, 50*(3), 320–336.
			Worthington, R. L., Savoy, H. B., Dillon, F. R., & Vernaglia, E. R. (2002). Heterosexual identity development: A multidimensional model of individual and social identity. *The Counseling Psychologist, 30,* 496–531.
		Queer identity	Abes, E. S., & Kasch, D. (2007). Using queer theory to explore lesbian college students' multiple dimensions of identity. *Journal of College Student Development, 48,* 619–636.
	Gender identity	Feminist identity	Downing, N. E., & Roush, K. L. (1985). From passive acceptance to active commitment: A model of feminist identity development for women. *Counseling Psychologist, 13,* 695–709.

(continued)

TABLE III.1 (*continued*)

Theory Family	Subcategory	Focus of Theory	Specific Theories
		Womanist identity	Ossana, S. M., Helms, J. E., & Leonard, M. M. (1992). Do "womanist" identity attitudes influence college women's self-esteem and perceptions of environmental bias? *Journal of Counseling and Development, 70*, 402–408.
		Men's identity	Davis, T. L. (2002). Voices of gender role conflict: The social construction of college men's identity. *Journal of College Student Development, 43*, 508–521.
			Edwards, K. E., & Jones, S. R. (2009). "Putting my man face on": A grounded theory of college men's gender identity development. *Journal of College Student Development, 50*(2), 210–228.
			Harris, F. (2010). College men's conceptualizations of masculinities and contextual influences: Toward a conceptual model. *Journal of College Student Development, 51*(3), 297–318.
			Kimmel, M. (2008). *Guyland: The perilous world where boys become men.* New York: Harper Collins.
		Transgender identity	Beemyn, B. Curtis, B., Davis, M., & Tubbs, N. J. (2005). Transgender issues on college campuses. In *Gender identity and sexual orientation: Research, policy, and personal perspectives* (New Directions for Student Services, no. 111, pp. 49–60). San Francisco: Jossey-Bass.
			Carter, K. A. (2000). Transgenderism and college students: Issues of gender identity and its role on our campuses. In V. A. Wall & N. J. Evans (Eds.), *Toward acceptance: Sexual orientation issues on campus* (pp. 261–282). Lanham, MD: University Press of America.
			Rankin, S., & Beemyn, B. (2008). *The lives of transgender people.* New York: Columbia Press.
	Social class and background		Liu, W. M. (2011). *Social class and classism in the helping professions: Research, theory, and practice.* Thousand Oaks, CA: Sage.
			Martin, G. L. (2015). "Always in my face": An exploration of social class consciousness, salience, and values. *Journal of College Student Development, 56*(5), 471–487.
			Mullen, A. (2010). *Degrees of inequality: Culture, class, and gender in American higher education.* Baltimore: John Hopkins University Press.

Theory Family	Subcategory	Focus of Theory	Specific Theories
	Religious identity		Mayhew, M. J., & Bryant, A. N. (2013). Achievement or arrest? The influence of the collegiate religious and spiritual climate on students' worldview commitment. *Research in Higher Education, 54,* 63–84.
			Peek, L. (2005). Becoming Muslim: The development of a religious identity. *Sociology of Religion, 66*(3), 215–242.
	Abilities and disabilities		Gibson, J. (2006). Disability and clinical competency: An introduction. *The California Psychologist, 39,* 6–10.
			Jones, S. R. (1996). Toward inclusive theory: Disability as a social construction. *NASPA Journal, 33,* 347–354.
			Kimball. E. W., Wells, R. S., Ostiguy, B. J., Manly, C. A., & Lauterbach, A. A. (2016). Students with disabilities in higher education: A review of the literature and an agenda for future research. In M. B. Paulsen (Ed.), *Higher education: Handbook of theory and research* (Vol. 31, pp. 91–56). Cham, Switzerland: Springer International Publishing.
			Sherry, M. (2004). Overlaps and contradictions between queer theory and disability studies. *Disability & Society, 19*(7), 769–783.
	Multiple identities	Multiple oppressions	Reynolds, A. L., & Pope, R. L. (1991). The complexities of diversity: Exploring multiple oppressions. *Journal of Counseling and Development, 70,* 174–180.
		Multiple identities	Jones, S. R. (2009). Constructing identities at the intersections: An autoethnographic exploration of multiple dimensions of identity. *Journal of College Student Development, 50*(3), 287–304.
			Jones, S. R., & Abes, E. S. (2013). *Identity development of college students: Advancing frameworks for multiple dimensions of identity.* San Francisco: Jossey-Bass.
			Jones, S. R., & McEwen, M. K. (2000). A conceptual model of multiple dimensions of identity. *Journal of College Student Development, 41,* 405–414.
			Stewart, D. L. (2009). Perceptions of multiple identities among black college students. *Journal of College Student Development, 50*(3), 253–270.
Cognitive-Structural Development (see chapter 10)	Cognitive Development	Foundational theory	Piaget, J. (1950). *The psychology of intelligence.* San Diego: Harcourt Brace Jovanovich.
			Piaget, J. (1977). *The moral judgment of the child* (M. Gabain, Trans.). Harmondsforth, UK: Penguin. (Original work published in 1932)
		Intellectual and ethical development	Perry, W. G., Jr. (1970). *Forms of intellectual and ethical development in the college years: A scheme.* New York: Holt, Rinehart, & Winston.

(continued)

TABLE III.1 (*continued*)

Theory Family	Subcategory	Focus of Theory	Specific Theories
		Women's ways of knowing	Belenky, M. F., Clinchy, B. M., Goldberger, N. R., & Tarule, J. M. (1986). *Women's ways of knowing: The development of self, voice, and mind.* New York: Basic Books.
		Reflective judgment	King, P. M., & Kitchener, K. S. (2002). The reflective judgment model: Twenty years of research on epistemic cognition. In B. K. Hofer & P. R. Pintrich (Eds.), *Personal epistemology: The psychology of beliefs about knowledge and knowing* (pp. 37–61). Mahwah, NJ: Erlbaum.
		Epistemological reflection	Baxter Magolda, M. B. (1992). *Knowing and reasoning in college: Gender-related patterns in students' intellectual development.* San Francisco: Jossey-Bass.
	Moral development	Justice and rights	Kohlberg, L. (1976). Moral stages and moralization: The cognitive-developmental approach. In T. Lickona (Ed.), *Moral development and behavior: Theory, research, and social issues* (pp. 31–53). New York: Holt, Rinehart, & Winston.
		Care and responsibility	Gilligan, C. (1982). *In a different voice: Psychological theory and women's development.* Cambridge, MA: Harvard University Press.
		Moral reasoning	Rest, J. R., Narvaez, D., Bebeau, M. J., & Thoma, S.J. (1999). *Postconventional moral thinking: A neo-Kohlbergian approach.* Mahwah, NJ: Erlbaum.
	Faith development	Faith	Bryant, A. N. (2008). The developmental pathways of evangelical Christian students. *Religion & Education, 35*(2), 1–26.
			Fowler, J. (2000). *Becoming adult, becoming Christian: Adult development and Christian faith* (rev. ed.). San Francisco: Jossey-Bass.
		Spirituality	Parks, S. D. (2000). *Big questions, worthy dreams: Mentoring young adults in their search for meaning, purpose, and faith.* San Francisco: Jossey-Bass.
			Rockenbach, A. B., Walker, C. R., & Luzader, J. (2012). A phenomenological analysis of college students' spiritual struggles. *Journal of College Student Development, 53*(1), 55–75.
			Stewart, D. L. (2002). The role of faith in the development of an integrated identity: A qualitative study of black students at a white college. *Journal of College Student Development, 43*(4), 579–596.

Theory Family	Subcategory	Focus of Theory	Specific Theories
Typologies and Student Learning	Personality	Temperament and development	Heath, R. (1964). *The reasonable adventurer.* Pittsburgh, PA: University of Pittsburgh Press.
			Jung, C. (1923/1971). *Psychological types* (Vol. 6): *The collected works of C. G. Jung.* Princeton, NJ: Princeton University Press.
		Psychological type	Myers, I. B. (1980). *Gifts differing.* Palo Alto, CA: Consulting Psychologists Press.
		Vocational personality types	Holland, J. L. (1985). *Making vocational choices: A theory of vocational personalities and work environments* (2nd ed.). Englewood Cliffs, NJ: Prentice Hall.
		Learning style	Kolb, D. (1976). *Learning styles inventory technical manual.* Boston: McBer.
	Learning	Transformative	Mezirow, J. (Ed.). (2000). *Learning as transformation: Critical perspectives on a theory in progress.* San Francisco: Jossey-Bass.
		Intercultural learning	King, P. M., & Baxter Magolda, M. B. (2005). A developmental model of intercultural maturity. *Journal of College Student Development, 46*(6), 571–592.
			Perez, R. J., Shim, W., King, P. M., & Baxter Magolda, M. B. (2015). Refining King and Baxter Magolda's model of intercultural maturity. *Journal of College Student Development, 56*(8), 759–776.
Organizational Approaches (see chapter 13)			Baldridge, J. V. (1971). *Power and conflict in the university: Research in the sociology of complex organizations.* New York: Wiley.
			Berquist, W. (1992). *The four cultures of the academy.* San Francisco: Jossey-Bass.
			Bolman, L., & Deal, T. (2008). *Reframing organizations: Artistry, choice, and leadership.* San Francisco: Jossey-Bass.
			Cohen, M., & March, J. (1974). *Leadership and ambiguity.* Boston: Harvard Business School Press.
			Morgan, G. (1997). *Images of organization.* Thousand Oaks, CA: Sage.
			Weick, K. E. (1991). Educational organizations as loosely coupled systems. In M. W. Peterson, E. E. Chaffee, & T. H. White (Eds.), *Organization and governance in higher education* (4th ed.). Needham Heights, MA: Ginn Press.
Campus Environments (see chapter 14)	Human aggregates	Environmental press	Moos, R. H. (1979). *Evaluating educational environments: Procedures, measures, findings, and policy implications.* San Francisco: Jossey-Bass.

(continued)

TABLE III.1 (*continued*)

Theory Family	Subcategory	Focus of Theory	Specific Theories
	Organized environments	Campus culture	Kuh, G. D., & Whitt, E. J. (1988). The invisible tapestry: Culture in American colleges and universities. *ASHE-ERIC Higher Education Report* (1). Washington, DC: Association for the Study of Higher Education.
			Museus, S. D., & Jayakumar, U. M. (Eds.). (2014). *Creating campus cultures: Fostering success among racially diverse student populations.* New York: Routledge.
	Constructed environments	Inclusion and safety, involvement, community	Astin, A. W. (1984). Student involvement: A developmental theory for higher education. *Journal of College Student Development, 25,* 297–308.
			Museus, S. D. (2014). The culturally engaging campus environments (CECE) model: A new theory of college success among racially diverse student populations. In M. B. Paulsen (Ed.), *Higher education: Handbook of theory and research* (pp. 189–227). New York: Springer.
			Strange, C. C. (2003). Dynamics of campus environments. In S. R. Komives, D. B. Woodard Jr., & Associates (Eds.), *Student services: A handbook for the profession* (4th ed., pp. 297–316). San Francisco: Jossey-Bass.
			Strange, C. C., & Banning, J. H. (2015). *Designing for learning: Creating campus environments for student success.* San Francisco: Jossey-Bass.
	Design for educational success		Banning, J. H., & Kaiser, L. (1974). An ecological perspective and model for campus design. *Personnel and Guidance Journal, 52,* 370–375.
			Bronfenbrenner, U. (1993). The ecology of cognitive development: Research models and fugitive findings. In R .H. Wozniak & K. W. Fischer (Eds.), *Development in context: Aging and thinking in specific environments* (pp. 3–44). Hillsdale, NJ: Erlbaum.
			Moos, R. H. (1986). *The human context: Environmental determinants of behavior.* Malabar, FL: Krieger.
	Environmental impact		Armstrong, E. A., & Hamilton, L. T. (2013). *Paying for the party: How college maintains inequality.* Cambridge, MA: Harvard University Press.
			Astin, A. (1993). *What matters in college? Four critical years revisited.* San Francisco: Jossey-Bass.
			Mayhew, M. J., Rockenbach, A. N., Bowman, N. A., Seifert, T. A., Wolniak, G. C., Pascarella, E. T., & Terenzini, P. T. (2016). *How college affects students: 21st century evidence that higher education works* (Vol. 3). San Francisco: Jossey-Bass.

Theory Family	Subcategory	Focus of Theory	Specific Theories
			Pascarella, E. T., & Terenzini, P. T. (2005). *How college affects students: A third decade of research.* San Francisco: Jossey-Bass.
	Mattering and marginality		Schlossberg, N. K. (1989). Marginality and mattering: Key issues in building community. In D. C. Roberts (Ed.), *Designing campus activities to foster a sense of community* (New Directions for Student Services, no. 48, pp. 5–15). San Francisco: Jossey-Bass.
Student Success (see chapter 15)	Student departure	Organizational	Braxton, J. M., Hirschy, A. S., & McClendon, S. A. (2004). Understanding and reducing college student departure. *ASHE-ERIC Higher Education Report, 30*(3). Washington, DC: School of Education and Human Development, The George Washington University.
	Student persistence		Braxton, J. M., Doyle, W. R., Hartley, H. V. III, Hirschy, A. S., Jones, W. A., & McLendon, M. K. (2014). *Rethinking college student retention.* San Francisco: Jossey-Bass.
			Habley, W. R., Bloom, J. L., & Robbins, S. (2012). *Increasing persistence: Research-based strategies for student success.* San Francisco Jossey-Bass.
			Hirschy, A. S. (2015). Models of student retention and persistence. In D. Hossler, J. P. Bean, & Associates (Eds.), *The strategic management of college enrollments* (pp. 268–288). San Francisco: Jossey-Bass.
			Milem, J. F., & Berger, J. B. (1997). A modified model of college student persistence: Exploring the relationship between Astin's model of student involvement and Tinto's theory of student departure. Journal of College Student Development, 38(4), 387–400.
			Museus, S. D., & Quaye, S. J. (2009). Toward an intercultural perspective of racial and ethnic minority college student persistence. *The Review of Higher Education, 33*(1), 67–94.
			Tinto, V. (1993). *Leaving college: Rethinking the causes and cures of student attrition* (2nd ed.) Chicago: University of Chicago Press.
			Tinto, V. (2012). *Completing college: Rethinking institutional action.* Chicago: University of Chicago Press.

(continued)

TABLE III.1 (*continued*)

Theory Family	Subcategory	Focus of Theory	Specific Theories
		Student success	Kuh, G. D. (2008). *High-impact educational practices: What they are, who has access to them, and why they matter.* Washington, DC: Association of American Colleges and Universities.
			Kuh, G. D., Kinzie, J., Schuh, J. H., Whitt, E. J., & Associates (2005). *Student success in college: Creating conditions that matter.* San Francisco: Jossey-Bass.
			Perna, L. W., & Thomas, S. L. (2008). Theoretical perspectives on student success: Understanding the contributions of the disciplines. *ASHE-Higher Education Reader Report.* San Francisco: Jossey-Bass.
Critical Theoretical Perspectives (see chapter 12)	Critical race theory		Delgado Bernal, D. (2002). Critical race theory, Latino critical theory, and critical raced-gendered epistemologies: Recognizing students of color as holders and creators of knowledge. *Qualitative Inquiry, 8*(1), 105–126.
			Delgado, R., & Stefancic, J. (2012). *Critical race theory: An introduction* (2nd ed.). New York: New York University Press.
			Ladson-Billings, G. (1998). Just what is critical race theory and what's it doing in a nice field like education? *Qualitative Studies in Education, 11*(1), 7–24.
			Ladson-Billings, G., & Tate, W. F. (2009). Toward a critical race theory of education. In A. Darder, M. P. Baltodano, & R. D. Torres (Eds.), *The critical pedagogy reader* (2nd ed., pp. 167–182). New York: Routledge.
	Queer theory		Butler, J. (1990). *Gender trouble: Feminism and the subversion of identity.* New York: Routledge.
			Sedgwick, E. K. (1990). *Epistemology of the closet.* Berkeley: University of California Press.
			Sullivan, N. (2003). *A critical introduction to queer theory.* New York: New York University Press.
	Intersectionality		Dill, B. T., McLaughlin, A. E., & Nieves, A. D. (2007). Future directions of feminist research: Intersectionality. In S. N. Hesse-Biber (Ed.), *Handbook of feminist research* (pp. 629–637). Thousand Oaks, CA: Sage.
			Dill, B. T., & Zambrana, R. E. (Eds.). (2009). *Emerging intersections: Race, class, and gender in theory, policy, and practice.* Piscataway, NJ: Rutgers University Press.
			Mitchell, D., Jr., Simmons, C. Y., & Greyerbiehl, L. A. (Eds.). (2014). *Intersectionality & higher education: Theory, research, & praxis.* New York: Peter Lang Publishing.

Theory Family	Subcategory	Focus of Theory	Specific Theories
			Nash, J. C. (2008). Re-thinking intersectionality. *Feminist Review, 89*, 1–15.
	LatCrit		Villalpando, O. (2003). Self-segregation or self-preservation? A critical race theory and Latino/o critical theory analysis of a study of Chicano college students. *Qualitative Studies in Education, 16*, 619–646.
	Critical race feminism		Wing, A. K. (Ed.). (2003). *Critical race feminism* (2nd ed.). New York: New York University Press.
Theoretical Critiques (see chapter 8)	Multiple theoretical perspectives		Abes, E. S. (2009). Theoretical borderlands: Using multiple theoretical perspectives to challenge inequitable power structures in student development theory. *Journal of College Student Development, 50*, 141–156.
			Abes, E. S. (2012). Constructivist and intersectional interpretations of a lesbian college students' multiple social identities. *Journal of Higher Education, 83*(2), 186–216.
			Abes, E. S. (Ed.) (2016). *Critical perspectives on student development theory* (New Directions for Student Services, no. 154). San Francisco: Jossey-Bass.
			Lather, P. (2007). *Getting lost: Feminist efforts toward a double(d) science.* Albany: State University of New York Press.
			Lincoln, Y. S., & Guba, E. G. (2000). Paradigmatic controversies, contradictions, and emerging confluences. In N. K. Denzin & Y. S. Lincoln (Eds.), *Handbook of qualitative research* (2nd ed., pp. 163–188). Thousand Oaks, CA: Sage.
			Tanaka, G. (2002). Higher education's self-reflexive turn: Toward an intercultural theory of student development. *The Journal of Higher Education, 73*(2), 263–296.

Source: Adapted and updated by Susan R. Jones, Elisa S. Abes, and Zak Foste with permission from Jones, Abes, and Cilente (2011) and McEwen (2003).

In chapter 8 Susan R. Jones and Elisa S. Abes set the context for the chapters that follow by discussing the nature of theory in student affairs. They explore the question "What is theory?" and discuss the paradigmatic influences on theory construction and how different worldviews yield different results. Introducing the conceptualization of families of theories, they emphasize key constructs and concepts central to understanding the theoretical foundation in higher education and student affairs.

In chapter 9 Marcia Baxter Magolda and Kari B. Taylor discuss holistic development by addressing the evolution of meaning making along three integrated developmental domains: cognitive, interpersonal, and intrapersonal. Drawing on six holistic longitudinal models they present the phases and nuances of the process of self-authorship.

In chapter 10 Patricia King addresses the mechanisms that promote development in the cognitive domain and introduces key models of cognitive development. She also presents several other models that include elements of cognitive development, such as moral development, intercultural sensitivity, and self-authorship.

In chapter 11 Vasti Torres and Brian L. McGowan present foundational psychosocial theories of development as well as theories that focus specifically on social identities, such as racial identity, ethnic identity, gender identity, and sexual identity. Taken together, these theories address the psychosocial tasks facing college students generally as well as the unique developmental patterns and issues that emerge when social identities are considered.

In a paradigmatic move, Ebelia Hernández discusses the contributions of critical theoretical perspectives in chapter 12. In particular, she highlights how these perspectives, such as critical race theory, intersectionality, and queer theory, elevate the role and significance of structures of inequality. These theories are not developmental but do shed light on developmental tasks and the influence of power and privilege on student development.

In chapter 13 Adrianna Kezar moves the focus from primarily individuals to organizations, providing an overview of several influential theories that address organizations and organizational change in addition to characteristics of higher education as organizations. This chapter addresses how to understand changes occurring in organizations as well as how to create change.

In chapter 14 campuses as environments and the interaction of students with their environments is explored by Samuel D. Museus through the lens of environmental theories and frameworks. The strategies for the intentional design of campus environments to promote safety, inclusion, and success are emphasized.

Finally, in chapter 15 Amy S. Hirschy discusses what is considered a primary outcome associated with higher education, that is, student success and retention. In this chapter, several disciplinary approaches (sociological, psychological, economic, and organizational) to understanding the student departure process are presented while also examining student success and educational attainment.

Despite a primary emphasis on theories in the chapters in this section, every chapter reinforces the integral relationship between theory and practice. In this age of accountability and documenting outcomes, it behooves those more comfortable in the world of theories to ground their theoretical knowledge in the realities of practice, and for those more at ease in the world of practice to guide their practice using theories generated from a quest to understand student development, students' experiences with higher education, and student outcomes. The chapters in part 3 provide an excellent foundation for effective practice.

References

Jones, S. R., Abes, E. S., & Cilente, K. (2011). The nature and uses of theory. In J. H. Schuh, S. R. Jones, & S.R. Harper (Eds.), *Student services: A handbook for the profession* (5th ed., pp. 138–148). San Francisco: Jossey-Bass.

McEwen, M. (2003). The nature and uses of theory. In S.R. Komives, & D. B. WoodardJr. (Eds.), *Student services: A handbook for the profession* (4th ed., pp. 153–178). San Francisco: Jossey-Bass.

Torres, V., Jones, S. R., & Renn, K. A. (2009). Identity development theories in student affairs: Origins, current status, and new approaches. *Journal of College Student Development, 50,* 577–596.

CHAPTER 8

THE NATURE AND USES OF THEORY

Susan R. Jones and Elisa S. Abes

- Students who participate in service-learning and study abroad programs increase their critical thinking skills and appreciation of diversity as a result.
- African American students who attend historically black institutions are more likely to graduate from STEM majors than their counterparts at predominantly white institutions.
- College campuses are not set up well to meet the needs of students with disabilities.
- Living on campus, especially in living-learning communities, improves overall satisfaction with the college experience.

"Nothing So Practical as a Good Theory"

The preceding statements all represent a point of view that a student affairs educator may have about students. But are they theories? Student affairs educators may hold perspectives grounded in their own experiences that clearly influence their practice. Indeed, we all carry with us, whether explicitly stated or implicitly implied, ideas, beliefs, and prior experiences that directly influence how we make sense of ourselves and the students with whom we interact. Do these constitute theories? What "theories" do you have about college students? And where do these "theories" come from? What questions about college students do your "theories" address—are they questions about college student development, about campus environments, about institutions and organizations? These are all questions for which there may be theoretical considerations. And although well-known social psychologist Kurt Lewin (1952) suggested that there is "nothing so practical as a good theory" (p. 169), theories represent more than common sense or a particular point of view based on one's own experiences, assumptions, and beliefs.

Theories have long served and equipped the field of student affairs and provide what Knefelkamp (1982) referred to as a "common language" (p. 379). Whether focused on individual college student development, campus environments, student learning, student engagement, or organizational functioning, "knowledge of theory in student affairs helps student affairs professionals develop habits of mind that define how to think about the educational needs of students" (Blimling, 2011, p. 47). However, it is important to note that theories have evolved over the years. Although many of the early theories of the 1950s and 1960s continue to serve as guiding foundations, newer theories have emerged that shift the discourse of theory in student affairs and influence how we understand the process and content of student development and the student experience.

An important distinction when evaluating the theoretical relevance of the statements introducing this chapter is that between formal theories and informal theories. Formal theories (for example, theories based on empirically generated generalizations) and informal theories (for example, individual observations and assumptions grounded in experiences) influence practice in student affairs; however, they are at once different and mutually reinforcing. That is, use of formal theory without the grounding of the realities of practice runs the risk of missing a particular context, although applying informal theories, based on one's own assumptions and experiences, risks inaccuracy and limited understanding (Evans & Guido, 2012). Returning to the opening statements with theory in mind, we see that these statements may in fact be theoretically grounded, but they may also be based solely on individual perceptions and observations. Knowing and understanding the formal theories that define the field of student affairs serves "as a corrective . . . to ensure that a practitioner's actions are effective and proactive in nature" (Evans & Guido, 2012, p. 199).

In this chapter we present the more traditional approaches to theory, focusing on families of theories in particular, while also introducing readers to newer theoretical conceptualizations that extend or reconceptualize foundational theoretical perspectives. More specifically, in this chapter we provide the foundation for the theory chapters that follow by (1) defining theory, distinguishing formal theory from those informal assumptions we use in our daily practice; (2) discussing paradigmatic influences on theory development and the evolution of theories; (3) introducing the umbrella of families of theories and exploring theoretical concepts central to understanding theories that influence student development and current conceptualizations of theories; and (4) considering the relationship between theories and student affairs practice.

What Is Theory?

Noted author Robert Coles recounts an anecdote about himself as a young medical resident eager to treat a patient with a psychiatric illness (Coles, 1989). After spending a short amount of time with the patient and asking questions about her medical history, he quickly diagnosed her condition. Still, the patient did not respond to him or improve. Under the tutelage of a supervisor, Coles learned the importance of not only using medical shorthand to diagnose the condition of his patient but also listening to the patient's story in order to understand her and relate to her experiences. When he understood her unique stories, the patient became more than a medical category, and he developed a caring connection that enabled him to more effectively help her.

Through this anecdote, Coles illustrates the relationship between a theory and a story. How often do student affairs professionals quickly try to make sense of students by assigning theoretical language based on brief observations or experiences rather than listening to stories? By doing so, are we "diagnosing" students and categorizing them with theories rather than honoring their individuality? Is it possible to learn, plan for, and respond to numerous and diverse students' individual stories without the benefit of theories to inform us? Coles's anecdote asks us to think about the meaning of theory. What is a theory? How do we honor individual stories and apply the theories on which they are based? These questions are woven throughout this chapter, but it is up to each of us to determine how to strike this artful balance.

Theories help to simplify and make sense of the complexities of life and represent "an attempt to organize and integrate knowledge and to answer the question 'why?'" (Patterson, 1986, p. xix). Although this is generally also true of our informal assumptions, the theories we describe in this text are different from the informal assumptions we carry about students and student affairs practice. Formal theory is defined as "a set of propositions regarding the interrelationship of two or more conceptual variables relevant to some realm of phenomena. It provides a framework for explaining the relationship among variables and for empirical investigations" (Rodgers, 1980, p. 81). Related, theory is characterized as "an abstract representation based on a potentially infinite number of specific and concrete variations of a phenomenon" (Strange & King, 1990, p. 17).

Starting with the Greek origin of *theory*, meaning "I behold," Coles (1989) explained that just as we behold a scene at a theater, when working with people we "hold something visual in our minds; presumably the theory is an enlargement of observation" (p. 20). Theory also offers a framework for understanding more than what is obvious from our observations. As Rabbi Abraham Heschel (n.d.) illuminated, "It is far easier to see what we know than to know what we see." Theories help us to know what we see, even when our own reality might otherwise blind us to a reality different from our own. In essence, theories in student affairs are grounded in the particularities of individual stories and serve as a way to make sense of the diverse and complex nature of phenomena by reducing many aspects of a phenomenon into an integrated representation (McEwen, 2003).

Although we try to construct theories that are true to the stories on which they are based, empirical research does not mean the objective creation of theory. Coles (1989) recollected: "Remember, what you are hearing . . . is to some considerable extent a function of *you*, hearing" (p. 15). Indeed, Knefelkamp suggested that all theory is autobiographical—that is, "theory represents the knowledge, experience, and worldviews of the theorists who construct it" (McEwen, 2003, p. 165). As socially constructed ideas, theories are developed within changing sociological, historical, and political contexts (McEwen, 2003). Depending on the worldview of the theorist, theory can therefore reinforce the status quo or societal power relationships, such as racism, heterosexism, and classism, or it can serve to expose and critique these relationships.

When applied with the understanding that theories are socially constructed, shaped by researchers' identities and worldviews, and do not capture all stories, theories serve multiple purposes. Theory is used to describe, explain, predict, influence outcomes, assess practice, and generate new knowledge and research (Abes, 2016; Knefelkamp, Widick, & Parker, 1978; McEwen, 2003). Theories also serve to deconstruct, critique, and transform power structures. Sometimes one theory can serve multiple purposes. For example, Cross's (1995) theory of black racial identity, an example of a student development theory, *describes* stages that African American students experience as they develop a complex understanding of their racial identity. Through its description of developmental stages, this theory also *explains* why students might behave in certain ways, for instance why the African American students might seek out black cultural centers or prefer to sit together in a classroom. Through this description and explanation, student affairs professionals can *predict* behavior and provide educational contexts that enable this intentional self-segregation that Cross's theory espouses as integral to black identity development. In this way, the theory can also be used to *influence outcomes* by encouraging educational contexts that foster racial identity development. The theory can then be used to *assess* the educational contexts that are intended to foster development by determining whether or not educational contexts are promoting development toward the more complex stages. Scholar-practitioners might see limitations to the stages Cross uses to describe black racial identity development and choose to conduct research that builds on his theory, thus *generating new knowledge and research*. For instance, Cross's theory does not critique racism but rather foregrounds the individual, explaining student development in light of racism. Building on Cross's theory using a critical worldview, for instance, foregrounds and *critiques* racism, adding a praxis component that seeks to *deconstruct and transform* racism.

Theory Creation and Paradigmatic Influences

How is it that we move from the particularities of individual stories to the construction of the formal theories used in student affairs practice, and how do our worldviews influence this process? Unlike our informal assumptions, empirical research, qualitative and quantitative, is used to generate and validate formal theories. For instance, grounded theory methodology is one qualitative approach to constructing theory (Corbin & Strauss, 2008). The art and science of grounded theory, which is an inductive approach to theory creation using stories gathered through interviews, is to create a theory that is general enough to describe the experiences of all of the participants but also true to the particularities of the individual stories. Quantitative research, which relies on statistical analysis of large samples of numerical data typically accessed through surveys, is a deductive approach and can also be used to generate theory. Derived from large samples, these theories offer a broad perspective on college students.

Regardless of the research method used to create theory, our identities, experiences, and worldviews influence theory construction. To the extent possible, theorists should be aware of this influence. Although they cannot entirely know the influence of their subjectivities, because we are all often unaware of perspectives beyond our field of vision (much like a fish is unaware of the water in which it swims), there are certain subjectivities about which it is important to be explicit. Specifically, it is important to make clear the research paradigm that guided the theory construction. In addition to reviewing paradigms that have traditionally been used in the creation of student affairs theories, we emphasize in this section paradigms that address social inequities in student affairs.

A paradigm, often referred to as a worldview, is a "set of interconnected or related assumptions or beliefs" that guides thinking and behavior (Jones, Torres, & Arminio, 2014, p. 3). Every research paradigm consists of assumptions about the nature of reality (ontology), knowledge (epistemology), and how knowledge is accessed (methodology) (Guba & Lincoln, 2005). Depending on the nature of these assumptions, a paradigm influences the research questions that lead to theory creation, whose stories are included in the research, and how the researcher hears and retells the stories. In his notable work, *The Structure of Scientific Revolutions*, Kuhn (1962) described how new paradigms emerge as the limitations of previous ones become apparent. New paradigms diversify the assumptions behind theory construction, resulting in more inclusive theories that challenge normative understandings of students and student affairs practice.

Whether creating theory, applying theory in practice, or developing one's professional philosophy, it is important to be aware that the worldviews that guide theory creation are not merely scholarly terms saved for research but philosophical beliefs that shape our practice as we apply theory to understand diverse student populations. Theory construction is a dynamic process that informs and is informed by practice and therefore matters to all who work with college students. Here we briefly review and provide examples of some of the basic elements of traditional and emerging paradigms that have been used to create theories about college students as well as strengths and limitations.

Positivism

Positivism assumes the existence of one reality and that knowledge is objectively knowable, measurable, and predictable through inquiry in which the researcher is removed from the object of study (Lincoln & Guba, 2000). For instance, in the early phases of her longitudinal study, Baxter Magolda (2004) used a positivist framework as she began her investigation into epistemological development. She assumed an objective stance separate from the participants to categorize students into developmental stages. She put the theory in the foreground and students in the background, seeking to fit the participants into an unchanging theory. Although this framework offers predictability and consistency, it does not enable differences in interpretation based on changing contexts and diverse identities and perspectives.

Constructivism

In later phases of her longitudinal research, Baxter Magolda (2001) transitioned to a constructivist paradigm. Constructivism is grounded in the notion that multiple realities exist and that knowledge is co-constructed between the researcher and participants (Lincoln & Guba, 2000). Using a constructivist approach, Baxter Magolda put the students' stories before existing theories, enabling her to see multiple possibilities in how to interpret students' stories based on their individuality, changing contexts, and her own subjectivities. She was able to reshape existing theory rather than only test it. Much of the contemporary research in student affairs is grounded in constructivist perspectives.

Although constructivism enables participants' voices to more prominently make their way into theory, this paradigm does not intentionally address how power structures, such as racism, classism, heterosexism, and ableism, have shaped theory. When thinking about Rabbi Heschel's quotation cited previously, theories that intentionally bring power structures to the forefront empower us to see inequities often made invisible through the way they have been normalized into society, enabling us to better "know what we see." Here we review two paradigms that make visible how power structures shape student experiences.

Critical Theory

Critical perspectives uncover how invisible power structures shape whose stores are told and how they are heard in the construction of student affairs theories. Critical theory calls for a "radical restructuring [of] society toward the ends of reclaiming historic cultural legacies, social justice, the redistribution of power and the achievement of truly democratic societies" (Lincoln & Denzin, 2000, p. 1056). An important element of critical theory is its praxis component, meaning that research should be tied into action that changes society in a socially just way. An example of a critical theory taking hold in student affairs is critical race theory. Critical race theorists seek to make visible how racism shapes reality and to transform this reality in part by centering the narratives of people of color (Delgado & Stefancic, 2012).

Poststructural Theories

Poststructural theories deconstruct reality to explore how reality has been shaped by power structures, most of which are invisibly woven into society (Lather, 2007). Unlike critical theorists, who seek to transform society in a particular way, poststructuralists question the creation of "normality" without assuming one way in which society ought to be structured. Poststructural theories perceive reality as a fluid process (Sullivan, 2003) and suggest that a singular story is impossible to tell and that, in fact, "refusing definition is part of the theoretical scene" (Lather, 2007, p. 5). Queer theory is one example of a poststructuralist theory gaining some traction in student affairs research. Queer theory brings poststructural concerns to sexuality studies, challenging identity constructions grounded in heteronormativity, which is the unexamined assumption that heterosexuality defines normal (for example, Denton, 2016; Sullivan, 2003).

How Theories Evolve

Representing one worldview, all paradigms are incomplete (Kuhn, 1962). The use of emerging paradigms or even multiple paradigms is therefore one way in which theories evolve to more effectively help us understand college students (Abes, 2009). As the nature of college students evolve, so, too, must student affairs theories (Jones & Stewart, 2016). New research questions must be asked and new methodological approaches used as critiques of the limitations of existing theories and as ways to build on these theories as new insights are generated. For instance, as increasing numbers of students with disabilities are attending college (Brown & Broido, 2014), theorists need theories inclusive of their experiences (Peña, Stapleton, & Schaffer, 2016). Merging ideas from disability studies (Linton, 1998) and critical disability studies (Pothier & Devlin, 2006) with student affairs literature shifts the nature of theory about students with disabilities and the college environments in which they are situated. Further, not only are students and student affairs practice changing but also so are the identities of the theorists and practitioners. The subjectivities of the person asking the research questions drive the nature of the questions, and the changing nature of who is applying the theories in practice reveals personal strengths and limitations.

Theories in Student Affairs

A diverse array of theories provide the foundation for student affairs practice and are typically grouped together in what is referred to as "families" of theories or "theory clusters" (Knefelkamp, Widick, & Parker, 1978, p. xi). This umbrella term incorporates those theories that are developmental and focus on the individual, including individuals' social identities; those that examine students in the collegiate context such as student success, engagement, and learning; theories that explain the relationship of campus environments to student development and success; those focused on organizations and institutions of higher education; and theories considered more holistic or integrative of multiple domains of development and context. Although this conceptualization of theories as families is useful as an organizing heuristic, critical and poststructural theories provide different theoretical explanations for understanding students.

These newer theoretical frameworks push the boundaries of the traditional heuristic and offer deconstructing and transformative lenses through which to interpret student development, environments, and experiences. These theoretical frameworks challenge or can be infused with the foundational theory families, changing the nature of those theories to reflect systems of inequality. The chapters that follow detail these theory families and newer conceptualizations of theory, providing readers with a theoretical knowledge base for professional practice.

In the following discussion, we highlight several core ideas underlying theories of student development. The emphasis on student development reflects the central role of student development in the evolution of theories in student affairs and the intersections of student development with other families of theories, such as campus environments, student success, and organizations. This emphasis also signifies the importance of promoting the development of students as a core aim of higher education and the ways in which environments and organizations have an effect on the ability to advance this goal. A central organizing premise is that student *development* theories focus on the growth and change that occurs for individuals while they are in higher education contexts. What follows is a discussion of several concepts relevant to a contemporary consideration of the perspectives that enable a rich theoretical understanding of college students.

Developmental Approaches

Rooted in their disciplinary origins of psychology, many of the early student development theories focused explicitly on a developmental process and a developmental trajectory in the direction of positive change. One of the earliest contributors to the scholarship on student development, Sanford (1967), defined development as the "organization of increasing complexity" (p. 47); Rodgers (1990) extended this definition to focus on students, defining student development as "the ways that a student grows, progresses, or increases his or her developmental capabilities as a result of enrollment in an institution of higher education" (p. 27). The focus of developmental theories gives us a lens for examining the content of development (for example, psychosocial theories) and the process of development (for example, cognitive-structural theories), and the interaction of content, process, and context (holistic, environmental, and critical theories).

A central characteristic of developmental theories is that they typically describe development occurring along a trajectory of simple to complex. Many of the theories most often used in student affairs practice include terminology that suggests a placement or location along a continuum. The differential language used for these placements conveys underlying ideas about the process of development. For example, Helms (1995) revised the terminology she used for her racial identity theories from stage to status in order to more adequately capture the fluid and dynamic nature of development. Further, poststructural theorists abandon the use of terminology that suggests the possibility of categorizing something as fluid as identity.

Regardless of the terminology used, the intent of these theorists was never to posit that the totality of a student's experiences and development could be captured through knowledge only of one's stage or dimension. Each is intended to capture some defining feature of an individual among others. Newer theoretical frameworks for understanding student development, particularly the influence of structures of privilege and oppression, question the centrality of a trajectory, who names the trajectory, and the role of context in defining progress (Jones & Stewart, 2016).

Challenge and Support

One of the most fundamental theories to student development is Sanford's (1966) theory of challenge and support. Sanford suggested that students need an optimal balance of challenge and support for development to occur. That is, too much support and students are able to stay comfortable with what they know and too much challenge and the student becomes overwhelmed. In articulating the need for challenge and support, Sanford implied that the campus environment interacts with the individual student in putting into place people, policies, and programs that support students' development or impede it with the creation of too much challenge. As the scholarly base of student development theory evolved, we now understand that what constitutes challenge and support for different populations of students may be very different. For example, what constitutes support for first-generation college students may be distinct from those with parents who attended college and may also vary among first-generation students by cultural backgrounds.

Dissonance

Nearly all student development theories suggest that for development to occur, the individual must experience dissonance or "crisis" or disequilibrium. In psychosocial terms, this crisis "is not a time of panic or disruption: It is a decision point—that moment when one reaches an intersection and must turn one way or the other" (Widick, Parker, & Knefelkamp, 1978, pp. 3–4). In theories emphasizing cognitive development, dissonance represents an impetus for changing one's way of thinking and worldview (King, 2009). The resulting interest in resolving the dissonance or disequilibrium creates the conditions for development to occur. Dissonance may emerge from environmental forces, internal processes, or a combination of these. Evident in the results of research on the ethnic identity development of Latino students by Torres (for example, 2003, 2004) is the central encounter with dissonance when trying to make sense of stereotypes that existed about Latinos. In another study with students of color and investigating self-authorship development, two kinds of dissonance were delineated: identity dissonance and relationship dissonance, noting that the kind of dissonance influenced developmental pathways for individuals (Pizzolato, Nguyen, Johnston, & Wang, 2012).

Meaning Making

The process of making meaning is also central to student development theories as a theoretical anchor to theories that describe specific patterns in the activity of meaning making (for example, movement toward more-complex structures of meaning making) as well as portrayals of the meaning students make of their own experiences (for example, the meaning students make of their experiences as gay Latinos). As Robert Kegan (1982) noted, "The activity of being a person is the activity of meaning-making. There is no feeling, no experience, no thought, no perception, independent of a meaning-making context in which it *becomes* a feeling, an experience, a thought, a perception, because we *are* the meaning-making context" (p. 11).

Meaning making as a structured evolution of more simplistic to complex ways of thinking draws on Piaget's constructivist developmental tradition and emphasizes cycles of differentiation (stepping back and pulling a problem apart) and integration (putting the problem back together in a new way) (King, 2009). What emerges are revisions to ways of thinking that are new, and more complex, structures for meaning making.

In addition to an understanding of meaning making as structural and patterned, the student development literature includes studies focused on the *meaning* students make of experiences (for example, their identity development, their participation in a service-learning program, their involvement in a STEM major). These studies are rarely developmental in nature, nor are researchers necessarily assessing changes in meaning making. Instead, what these theories illuminate are sources of interest and concern, particularities concerning lived experiences, and environmental and contextual influences on a student's development. This distinction is important because a focus on one or the other will yield different knowledge about student development and experiences.

Context and the Role of Power

The influence of *context* has always been considered important in student development theories. However, what constitutes context has shifted over time. For example, Erikson's (1959/1980) psychosocial theory explicitly addressed the interaction of the individual in a social world, though prioritizing internal psychological processes in development and a societal context that is quite different from contemporary times. An important distinction that emphasizes the reciprocal relationship of individuals with contexts, developmental contextualism "is not the study of person in context, but rather study of the interaction among many individual and contextual systems and their influences on one another" (Kroger, 2004, p. 5). Recognition of context in developmental theories foregrounds the role of context in an individual's development, rather than the particulars of the context itself.

Critical and poststructural theories elevate the role of context in understanding student development. They provide insights into *how* context influences development, especially the ways in which the power structures that shape context mediate development. These theories are not developmental as such, but they shed light on the nature of development. For example, critical race theory foregrounds the role of race and racism and suggests that racism is ever present in an individual's life, regardless of whether or not the individual perceives it as such (Jones, Abes, & Quaye, 2013). Racism therefore interacts with development. Further, investigating the influence of context necessarily brings to light intersecting structures of inequality and the ways in which privilege and oppression pattern development (Jones, Kim, & Skendall, 2012). In fact, the framework of intersectionality, now prevalent in the theoretical discourse in higher education, insists on a structural analysis rather than sole attention to individual narratives and experiences (Collins, 2009). Considered from a poststructural perspective on context, queer theory, for instance, deconstructs the normative power structures that ground developmental trajectories, opting instead for fluidity as central to "development" (Abes & Kasch, 2007). The queer perspective suggests that identity is performed through behaviors that resist power structures, such as heterosexism and genderism. As a performative grounded in action, identity is constantly changing and therefore defies categories that can be assessed for complexity along a trajectory (Abes & Kasch, 2007).

Relationships of Theories to Student Affairs Practice

Student affairs educators are frequently faced with complex decisions in their daily practice. Resolving complicated issues and making good decisions requires professional judgment, which Blimling (2011) defined as "the result of merging experience and theory to guide practice" (p. 45). Further, our roles often include overlapping responsibilities and obligations to promote student development, design campus environments that are educationally purposefully, and understand higher education as an organization (McEwen, 2003). Theories provide an important and necessary lens through which to engage our roles and responsibilities and make decisions. Theories do not inform us about what exactly to do, but they do provide student affairs educators with a way to make professional judgments about how to interpret individuals, environments, and organizations. When applying theory to practice in student affairs it is important to remember, as Perry (1981) cautioned, students always remain larger than their categories. Theories are meant to provide an interpretive lens for what a student affairs educator is anticipating, witnessing, or planning. Let's look at an example.

Scenario

During resident assistant training, one session on "appreciating diversity" used the well-known "privilege walk" activity. The facilitator, a white woman and new residence hall director, believed it was a great way to help students understand the concepts of privilege, racism, and oppression. Lining up the RAs, she instructed the group to take a step forward or backward to represent their responses to a series of statements. She begins:

> If your ancestors were forced to come to the United States take one step back.
> If you were raised in a rented apartment, or house, take one step back.
> If you were ever called names because of your race, ethnicity, or sexual orientation, take one step back.
> If you were taken to plays or art galleries by your parents, take one step forward.

As she moved through her list, the resident director noticed that the RAs who were members of underrepresented racial-ethnic groups appeared to not be paying attention anymore and chatting about other things. Meanwhile, the white males were competing with one another for "first place." At the conclusion of the activity, the resident director began processing the privilege walk when conflict in the group erupted.

An American Indian male began:

> I don't know why we need yet another activity to remind students of color of "their place" in this world. This activity seems designed to reinforce all kinds of stereotypes and assumptions about who I am and where I come from.

To which a white female RA responded:

> I think you are taking this way too personally. I think it is so good that we are talking about these issues.

And a Latina student retorted:

> Well, this is easy for you to say. You have the luxury of obliviousness. I do take this personally, because it is personal, it is my life! (Jones, 2008)

How might a student affairs educator use theories to make sense of what took place in this scenario and develop an appropriate response? First, it is important for a practitioner to evaluate the assumptions brought to an interpretation of a particular situation. When thinking about identifying and applying theories to practice, it behooves student affairs educators to look inward and consider how their own experiences, biases, and assumptions may predispose them to one set of theories over others. This scenario might be interpreted through the theoretical lens of racial or ethnic identity theory. However, an emphasis given to individuals alone may miss the larger consideration of the organizational culture in residence life that perpetuates training activities that promote learning for some at the expense of others.

Second, because of the complexity of much of our work it is rare that one theory will carry enough explanatory power for a particular phenomenon so that when applying theory to practice, theories often are used in combination. In this scenario, a student affairs educator might begin by considering the racial identity of each individual, as well as the other social identities that may be salient. This might help explain why the white woman was not attuned to the emotional impact of the privilege walk activity and why the American Indian man was perceived as lashing out. Further understanding may be gleaned from adding a cognitive theory dimension because the white woman appears to be viewing this situation in a less cognitively complex way than the students of color. In addition, an organizational analysis provides another lens as this activity may also be reflective of a particular organizational culture and affect the climate of the RA staff. Drawing from a critical race theory interpretation necessitates an analysis of this situation in relation to the omnipresence of racism and discrimination in US society. It is important to recognize that in this scenario, as in practice, student affairs educators rarely possess all there is to know about a particular situation or individual. Therefore, theories guide us toward potential and plausible interpretations, but these should never be viewed as *the* one way to understand what is going on. Consulting with trusted colleagues is helpful in applying theories to practice, especially when doing so with someone who might not share your social identities or background experiences.

Third, applying theories to practice takes practice. Because no situation or individual is ever exactly the same, no precise recipes exist for which theories to use under which set of circumstances. Surely, there are clear indicators of fit and mismatch, but each theory applied to a particular phenomenon will illuminate a different part of the story. Staying current with theory evolution and scholarly literature is important to applying theory to practice. Student affairs educators now have a far greater and deeper repertoire of theories from which to choose than before the new millennium.

Conclusion

The chapters that follow provide more in-depth descriptions of those theories that scaffold the theoretical foundation for the field of student affairs. We have a rich and varied body of theory from which to draw, and it is important to read primary sources rather than to rely only on summaries of these theories. As noted, theories continue to evolve because of new questions, new students, new methodological approaches, and in relation to who is developing and applying theories. However, those early theories that guided the field need not be discarded completely. As you continue to study, understand, and apply theories and theoretical perspectives that inform student affairs research and practice you will discern those constructs and themes that are enduring as well as important points of departure. Finally, as your knowledge of theories becomes more robust, you will see that, indeed, there is nothing so useful as a good theory.

Discussion Questions and Activity

1. What "theories" do you have about college students and their development? Where did these theories come from? How do you describe your subject-ivities and worldview that might influence these theories?
2. What do you think about the relationship between story and theory?
3. What sense do you make of the relationship between foundational and critical or poststructural theories? What does each framework or theory contribute? What are the limitations?
4. How do you envision the relationship between student affairs practice and the evolution of theory? Interview several student affairs practitioners about how they apply theory to their practice contexts.

References

Abes, E. S. (2009). Theoretical borderlands: Using multiple theoretical perspectives to challenge inequitable power structures in student development theory. *Journal of College Student Development, 50,* 141–156.

Abes, E. S. (2016). Situating paradigms in student development theory. In E. S. Abes (Ed.), *Critical perspectives on student development theory* (New Directions for Student Services, no. 154). San Francisco: Jossey-Bass.

Abes, E. S., & Kasch, D. (2007). Using queer theory to explore lesbian college students' multiple dimensions of identity. *Journal of College Student Development, 48,* 619–636.

Baxter Magolda, M. B. (2001). *Making their own way: Narratives for transforming higher education to promote self-development.* Sterling, VA: Stylus.

Baxter Magolda, M. B. (2004). Evolution of a constructivist conceptualization of epistemological reflection. *Educational Psychologist, 39*(1), 31–42.

Blimling, G. S. (2011). How are dichotomies such as scholar/practitioner and theory/practice helpful and harmful to the profession? In P. M. Magolda & M. B. Baxter Magolda (Eds.), *Contested issues in student affairs* (pp. 42–53). Sterling, VA: Stylus.

Brown, K., & Broido, E. M. (2014). Engaging students with disabilities. In S. R. Harper & S. J. Quaye (Eds.), *Student engagement in higher education: Theoretical perspectives and practical approaches for diverse populations* (2nd ed., pp. 187–207). New York: Routledge.

Coles, R. (1989). *The call of stories: Teaching and the moral imagination.* Boston: Houghton Mifflin.

Collins, P. H. (2009). Foreword: Emerging intersections—Building knowledge and transforming institutions. In B. T. Dill & R. E. Zambrana (Eds.), *Emerging intersections: Race, class, and gender in theory, policy, and practice* (pp. vii–xiii). New Brunswick, NJ: Rutgers University Press.

Corbin, J., & Strauss, A. (2008). *Basics of qualitative research: Techniques and procedures for developing grounded theory* (3rd ed.). Thousand Oaks, CA: Sage.

Cross, W. E., Jr. (1995). The psychology of Nigrescence: Revising the Cross model. In J. G. Ponterotto, J. M. Casas, L. A. Suzuki, & C. M. Alexander (Eds.), *Handbook of multicultural counseling* (pp. 93–122). Thousand Oaks, CA: Sage.

Delgado, R., & Stefancic, J. (2012). *Critical race theory: An introduction* (2nd ed.). New York: New York University Press.

Denton, J. M. (2016). Critical and poststructural perspectives on sexual identity development. In E. S. Abes (Ed.), *Critical perspectives on student development theory* (New Directions for Student Services, no. 154). San Francisco: Jossey-Bass.

Erikson, E. H. (1980). *Identity and the life cycle.* New York: W. W. Norton & Company. (Original work published 1959)

Evans, N. J., & Guido, F. M. (2012). Response to Patrick Love's "informal theory": A rejoinder. *Journal of College Student Development, 53,* 192–200.

Guba, E. G., & Lincoln, Y. S. (2005). Paradigmatic controversies, contradictions, and emerging confluences. In N. K. Denzin & Y. S. Lincoln (Eds.), *The Sage handbook of qualitative research* (pp. 191–215). Thousand Oaks, CA: Sage.

Helms, J. E. (1995). An update of Helms's white and people of color racial identity models. In J. G. Ponterotto, J. M. Casas, L. A. Suzuki, & C. M. Alexander (Eds.), *Handbook of multicultural counseling* (pp. 181–198). Thousand Oaks, CA: Sage.

Jones, S. R. (2008). Student resistance to cross-cultural engagement: Annoying distraction or site for transformative learning? In S. R. Harper (Ed.), *Creating inclusive campus environments* (pp. 67–85). Washington, DC: NASPA.

Jones, S. R., Abes, E. S., & Quaye, S. J. (2013). Critical race theory. In S. R. Jones & E. S. Abes, *Identity development of college students: Advancing frameworks for multiple dimensions of identity* (pp. 166–190). San Francisco: Jossey-Bass.

Jones, S. R., Kim, Y. C., & Skendall, K. C. (2012). (Re-)framing authenticity: Considering multiple social identities using autoethnographic and intersectional approaches. *Journal of Higher Education, 83,* 698–724.

Jones, S. R., & Stewart, D.-L. (2016). Evolution of student development theory. In E. S. Abes (Ed.), *Critical perspectives on student development theory* (New Directions for Student Services, no. 154). San Francisco: Jossey-Bass.

Jones, S. R., Torres, V., & Arminio, J. (2014). *Negotiating the complexities of qualitative research in higher education: Fundamental elements and issues* (2nd ed.). New York: Routledge.

Kegan, R. (1982). *The evolving self: Problem and process in human development.* Cambridge, MA: Harvard University Press.

King, P. M. (2009). Principles of development and developmental change underlying theories of cognitive and moral development. *Journal of College Student Development, 50,* 597–620.

Knefelkamp, L. L. (1982). Faculty and student development in the 80s: Renewing the community of scholars. In H. F. Owens, C. H. Witten, & W. R. Bailey (Eds.), *College student personnel administration: An anthology* (pp. 373–391). Springfield, IL: Charles C. Thomas.

Knefelkamp, L., Widick, C., & Parker, C. (1978). *Applying new developmental findings* (New Directions for Student Services, no. 4). San Francisco: Jossey-Bass.

Kroger, J. (2004). *Identity in adolescence: The balance between self and other* (3rd ed.). New York: Routledge.

Kuhn, T. S. (1962). *The structure of scientific revolutions.* Chicago: University of Chicago Press.

Lather, P. (2007). *Getting lost: Feminist efforts toward a double(d) science.* Albany: State University of New York Press.

Lewin, K. (1952). *Field theory in social science: Selected theoretical papers by Kurt Lewin.* London: Tavistock.

Lincoln, Y. S., & Denzin, N. K. (2000). The seventh movement: Out of the past. In N. K. Denzin & Y. S. Lincoln (Eds.), *Handbook of qualitative research* (2nd ed., pp. 1047–1065). Thousand Oaks, CA: Sage.

Lincoln, Y. S., & Guba, E. G. (2000). Paradigmatic controversies, contradictions, and emerging confluences. In N. K. Denzin & Y. S. Lincoln (Eds.), *Handbook of qualitative research* (2nd ed., pp. 163–188). Thousand Oaks, CA: Sage.

Linton, S. (1998). *Claiming disability: Knowledge and identity.* New York: New York University Press.

McEwen, M. K. (2003). The nature and uses of theory. In S. R. Komives, D. B. Woodard Jr., & Associates (Eds.), *Student services: A handbook for the profession* (4th ed., pp. 153–178). San Francisco: Jossey Bass.

Moore, L. V., & Upcraft, M. L. (1990). Theory in student affairs: Evolving perspectives. In L. V. Moore (Ed.), *Evolving theoretical perspectives on students* (New Directions for Student Services, no. 51, pp. 3–23). San Francisco: Jossey-Bass.

Patterson, C. H. (1986). *Theories of counseling and psychotherapy* (4th ed.). New York: Harper & Row.

Peña, E. V., Stapleton, L. D., & Schaffer, L. M. (2016). Critical perspectives on disability identity. In E. S. Abes (Ed.), *Critical perspectives on student development theory* (New Directions for Student Services, no. 154). San Francisco: Jossey-Bass.

Perry, W. G., Jr. (1981). Cognitive and ethical growth: The making of meaning. In A. W. Chickering & Associates (Eds.), *The modern American college: Responding to the new realities of diverse students and a changing society* (pp. 76–116). San Francisco: Jossey-Bass.

Pizzolato, J. E., Nguyen, T.-L. K., Johnston, M. P., & Wang, S. (2012). Understanding context: Cultural, relational, and psychological interactions in self-authorship development. *Journal of College Student Development, 53,* 656–679.

Pothier, D., & Devlin, R. (Eds). (2006). *Critical disability theory: Essays in philosophy, politics, policy, and law.* Vancouver, BC: UBC Press.

Rodgers, R. F. (1980). Theories underlying student development. In D. G. Creamer (Ed.), *Student development in higher education* (pp. 10–95). Cincinnati, OH: American College Personnel Association.

Rodgers, R. F. (1990). Recent theories and research underlying student development. In D. G. Creamer & Associates, *College student development: Theory and practice for the 1990s* (pp. 27–79). Alexandria, VA: American College Personnel Association.

Sanford, N. (1966). *Self and society.* New York: Atherton Press.

Sanford, N. (1967). *Where colleges fail: A study of the student as a person.* San Francisco: Jossey-Bass.

Strange, C. C., & King, P. M. (1990). The professional practice of student development. In D. G. Creamer (Ed.), *College student development: Theory and practice for the 1990s* (pp. 9–24). Alexandria, VA: American College Personnel Association.

Sullivan, N. (2003). *A critical introduction to queer theory.* New York: New York University Press.

Torres, V. (2003). Influences on ethnic identity development of Latino college students in the first two years of college. *Journal of College Student Development, 44,* 532–547.

Torres, V. (2004). Familial influences on the identity development of Latino first-year students. *Journal of College Student Development, 45,* 457–469.

Widick, C., Parker, C., & Knefelkamp, L. L. (1978). Erik Erikson and psychosocial development. In L. L. Knefelkamp, C. Widick, & C. A. Parker (Eds.), *Applying new developmental findings* (New Directions for Student Services, no. 4, pp. 1–17). San Francisco: Jossey-Bass.

CHAPTER 9

HOLISTIC DEVELOPMENT

Marcia Baxter Magolda and Kari B. Taylor

In today's increasingly diverse, globalized world, demands to make meaning in complex ways abound. Colleges and universities expect students to develop critical thinking skills, take responsibility for their own learning, collaborate among diverse teams, and articulate their own perspectives on problems with no clear-cut answers. Similarly, in work settings, individuals face the challenge of evaluating multiple perspectives to make well-informed decisions and implement effective solutions (AAC&U, 2015; Baxter Magolda & King, 2004; Kegan, 1994). As Daloz Parks (2009) explained, "The difficult and glorious reality is that becoming an adult requires finding and including your own voice in the arena of authority—developing an inner sense of your own truth and authority that you (and others) can trust" (p. xvi).

Becoming an adult in contemporary society also requires negotiating a wide array of choices about who one wants to be and how to build and sustain meaningful relationships (Arnett, 2006; Baxter Magolda, 2001). Within personal relationships, choices ranging from what career opportunities to pursue to how to balance personal and professional commitments call for mature forms of agency as well as mutuality. These characteristics are also essential for engaging with others in diverse communities. Addressing social issues such as educational inequality, immigration, and poverty requires community members to listen to one another, identify common ground, and work through tough choices (Carcasson & Sprain, 2012). Living, learning, and working within diverse communities further require individuals to gain awareness of their social identities and navigate systems of privilege and oppression (Abes & Jones, 2004; McIntosh, 2004; Torres & Hernández, 2007). Ultimately, today's diverse society demands intercultural maturity, which encompasses the ability to use multiple cultural frames, openly engage challenges to one's views and beliefs, and build interdependent relationships that reflect an appreciation for human differences (King & Baxter Magolda, 2005).

These demands to make meaning in complex ways represent demands for self-authorship—what Baxter Magolda (2001) defined as the developmental capacity to internally define one's own beliefs, identities, and relationships. By allowing individuals to reflect on and decide how to filter external expectations, self-authorship enables individuals to think critically, act authentically, and interact mutually. Yet, as Daloz Parks (2009) explained, "learning how to listen to 'our own insides' and how to consciously and responsibly make meaningful sense of self and world is a kind of journey" (p. xvi). Understanding the nuances of this journey and the ways to help students with diverse backgrounds navigate this passage are key responsibilities of college educators.

Understanding the whole student has been a mainstay of the student affairs profession from its inception. Research on college student and adult development, however, historically separated developmental dimensions. A long-standing psychosocial theoretical base foregrounds identity and relational development (see chapter 11 in this book). A long-standing cognitive theoretical base foregrounds ways of knowing (see chapter 10 in this book). Both address dynamics of person-environment interactions, yet a separate environmental theoretical base foregrounds the role of the environment (see chapter 14 in this book). Kegan (1982, 1994) integrated these strands into a holistic perspective of self-evolution from which self-authorship theory emerged. One of the core assumptions of Kegan's (1982, 1994) theory of self-evolution is that the essence of being human lies in making meaning. Thus, although his theory includes self-authorship as a specific way of making meaning—which is particularly relevant to college students (Baxter Magolda, 2001)—his theory as a whole focuses on meaning-making capacities.

In this chapter, we focus on the evolution of meaning making as a holistic framework that integrates three developmental dimensions: cognitive (which addresses ways of knowing), intrapersonal (which addresses ways of seeing oneself), and interpersonal (which addresses ways of relating with others); we also focus on the evolution of meaning making because of its emphasis on dynamic interactions between individuals and their environments. Because self-authorship is a way of making meaning that enables college students to meet the demands they face in and beyond college, we examine in particular how individuals gain the meaning-making capacities of self-authorship. We explore this journey using six key holistic longitudinal models—all of which describe how students' cognitive, intrapersonal, and interpersonal development intertwine and evolve over multiple years. We selected longitudinal models because following the same participants over time is the most effective way to trace the developmental process (Kegan, 1994). Five of these models are explicit models of meaning making; one (the reconceptualized model of multiple dimensions of identity, RMMDI) integrates meaning making as an element of identity development. We map these multiple models onto one another to show connections among the models and highlight nuances of the journey toward self-authorship.

Key Holistic Models

For each of the six holistic longitudinal models, we describe the key concepts the model contributes to an understanding of college students' journeys toward self-authorship. We explain how each model's unique contribution expands the overall portrait and process of the journey. Table 9.1 synthesizes the key elements of each model, which are further described in the following sections, and illustrates the overarching journey toward self-authorship. This journey begins with students relying on external authority to make meaning of their beliefs, identities, and relationships. When students encounter dissonance with relying on external authority, they enter the crossroads, which is characterized by a tension between following others' versus their own expectations. They shift to self-authorship when they use their own perspectives to coordinate external expectations.

Kegan's Theory of Self-Evolution

Kegan's (1982, 1994) theory of self-evolution moved the intersection of person and environment to the center of the developmental process. He argued that moving away from dichotomies such as affect versus cognition or individual versus social toward a focus on the intersection of such dichotomies offered a more powerful view of developmental evolution. Thus, he integrated the cognitive, intrapersonal, and interpersonal developmental dimensions to focus on their intersections across the life span. Kegan (1982) described the activity of meaning making as the context in which person and environment intersect, noting that people make meaning in "the place where the event is privately composed, made sense of, the place where it actually *becomes* an event for that person" (p. 2). Kegan articulated the key organizing principle through which this meaning making occurred as the combination of elements over which people have control (object) and elements that have control over people (subject). People stand outside of, and can reflect on, elements over which they have control; they are embedded in or fused with elements that have control over them. For example, college students who are subject to their peers' perceptions find themselves giving in to peer pressure even if their peers' opinions make them uncomfortable or conflict with their own beliefs and values. Others' approval is an element with which they are fused. When peers' perceptions become object, students are able to stand back and reflect on peer pressure and determine how to respond to it in a way that aligns with their beliefs and values. As experiences challenge a particular way of making meaning, the elements that were subject become object, and more complex meaning-making structures evolve that reconstruct the relationship between self and other. As Baxter Magolda (2009) explained, we interpret our experiences through rules we have formed based on prior experience:

TABLE 9.1. SIX LONGITUDINAL MODELS

	External	Crossroads				Internal or Self-Authorship
	Third Order[1]	Third (Fourth)	Third/Fourth	Fourth/Third	Fourth (Third)	Fourth Order
Kegan (1994)	Subordinate own interests on behalf of greater loyalty to maintaining bonds of friendship, team, or group participation; define self via loyalty to external expectations	Perceive fourth order, but only from lens of third	Third and fourth orders exist; third predominates	Third and fourth orders exist; fourth predominates	Fourth order working not to fall back on third	Stand apart from external expectations to take a perspective on them; internally create values, beliefs, identity, relationships
Baxter Magolda (2009)	Uncritically rely on external authorities to define beliefs, identity, relationships	Tension between external influence and internal voice	Begin to identify and listen to internal voice	Use internal voice to sort out beliefs, identity, relationships		Trust internal voice to shape reaction to reality — Use internal voice to build philosophy of life — Live out internal commitments
Baxter Magolda and King (2012)	Ea Eb Ec • Ea: Unquestioningly rely on external authorities • Eb: Tensions with relying on external authorities • Ec: Recognize shortcomings of relying on external authorities	E(I) • E(I): Awareness of need for internal voice	E-I • E-I: Actively work on constructing internal voice	I-E • I-E: Listen to internal voice	I(E) • I(E): Cultivate internal voice to mediate most external sources	Ia Ib Ic • Ia: Trust internal voice to refine beliefs, identity, relationships • Ib: Use internal voice to build philosophy of life • Ic: Live out internal commitments
Torres (Torres and Hernández, 2007)	Identity defined by family; dichotomous view of culture; may believe negative stereotypes	Recognize racism; understand positive and negative cultural choices; manage family influence				Informed Latino/a identity; integrate cultural choices into daily life — Contextual decisions include cultural choices; live interdependent life that maintains cultural values in diverse contexts
Abes, Jones, and McEwen (2007)	External influences strongly shape social identities	Growing awareness of ability to make meaning of contextual influences		Understand identity as more consistent with internal voice		Determine for oneself the meaning and salience of social identities
Olson and Pizzolato (2016)	Relationships with extended family, social, or government agencies require following external formulas for survival; begin to see truth as a perspective	Recognize role in meaning making and repurpose formulas to identify possibilities		Recognize agency in deciding identity and purpose		No data available

[1]Kegan uses these combinations to illustrate the gradual transition from third to fourth order.

> [W]e do not consciously think about these rules unless something
> unexpected happens that surprises us. When we have an experience that
> contradicts our rule, we usually see it as an exception rather than seriously
> questioning the rule we have come to trust. Only when we have encountered
> a number of exceptions do we stop to consider whether our rule needs to be
> changed . . . It is this ability to extract ourselves from how we operate in the
> world to analyze it that reflects movement along the developmental journey.
> (p. 3)

Of the five meaning-making structures Kegan identified across the life
span, two are particularly relevant to college and adult populations. In the
third order, or the socializing mind, people are subject to or fused with others'
expectations of them. As a result they accept others' knowledge uncritically,
sacrifice their interests and needs to please others, and are unable to take a
perspective on these relationships. For example, Mike, a white college student
in Boes's (2006) study, shared his dilemma in choosing between two summer
internships:

> Working [with the advance team that prepares for political candidates' visits]
> is like concert promotion and is more fun, and certain people have said it
> would even be better to do. But everyone says that field work [to organize
> voter turnout] is a better way up the [political] ladder. (Boes, 2006, p. 162)

By contrast, in the fourth order, or using a self-authoring mind, people are
able to take others' expectations as object and stand apart from relationships
to construct their own internal voice to coordinate external expectations. The
self-authoring person has "an internal identity, a *self-authorship* that can coordinate, integrate, act upon, or invent values, beliefs, convictions, generalizations,
ideals, abstractions, interpersonal loyalties, and intrapersonal states. It is no
longer *authored by* them, it *authors them*" (Kegan, 1994, p. 185). Neil, a white college student in Boes's study, reveals this perspective in describing his decision
to leave a community project:

> For the project to be successful I had to be plausible to myself as well as
> others; whether or not I was plausible to others, I was never able to convince
> myself that this was something I should be directly invested in, and as a
> result, I had difficulty marshaling a sense of passion to the work. (Boes, 2006,
> p. 150)

Neil relied on his internal values and beliefs to guide his actions. In contrast, Mike relied on what others thought he should do.

Movement from third to fourth order occurs gradually (depicted in table
9.1) as individuals encounter and reflect on experiences that challenge their
existing meaning-making structures. Although Kegan (1994) initially developed these orders by integrating existing theoretical conceptualizations, a nine-
year longitudinal study involving twenty-two adults supports this evolution of

meaning making. Kegan's holistic portrait of self-evolution strongly influenced longitudinal studies of college students' journey toward self-authorship. Because Kegan's theory was initially applied to studies primarily involving white college students, scholars have increasingly worked to study self-authorship among more diverse racial and ethnic groups of college students.

Baxter Magolda's Theory of Self-Authorship

Baxter Magolda's (2009) twenty-nine-year longitudinal, constructivist study of adult development refined the journey toward self-authorship by following participants from the age of eighteen to forty-seven. Of the 101 traditional aged, predominantly white collegians who participated in the study, 80 participated in interviews annually through their college years when the study focused on cognitive development. In the postcollege phase of her study, Baxter Magolda broadened her focus to include Kegan's holistic perspective and followed seventy participants as they pursued a range of career paths and advanced educational opportunities. Currently, thirty individuals continue to participate in the study. Although this study includes three individuals with nondominant racial and ethnic identities, we use examples from white participants to emphasize the primary context from which this theory emerged.

Based on her participants' lives in their twenties, Baxter Magolda (2001) identified two prevalent phases in participants' developmental journeys: uncritically following external formulas and navigating the crossroads. During the college experience, many participants *uncritically followed external formulas*; they relied on authorities to define their beliefs, identities, and relationships. Dawn, a white participant in this study, described learning as "tak[ing] everything in" and "plant[ing] it in [her] head." Near the end and after college, many participants encountered a *crossroads* characterized by tension between following others' versus their own visions. For Dawn this occurred as she was challenged to bring her own voice to characters she played in her theater work and to publicly acknowledge that she is gay.

The crossroads became increasingly prevalent for participants throughout their thirties, leading Baxter Magolda (2009) to identify nuances of the crossroads. Participants started the process of *listening to internal voice* and began work to identify it. Dawn shared that it took her five years to feel solid in listening to her internal voice:

> Now, I don't care if you know if I'm gay. It doesn't matter and this is who I am . . .

> That has contributed a great deal to how I see things and how I think . . . you know you have the inner strength to stand apart from the mainstream. (Baxter Magolda, 2001, pp. 182–183)

Cultivating internal voice involved using the internal voice to sort out beliefs, identities, and relationships. Dawn worked on cultivating her internal voice, spurred in part by being diagnosed with multiple sclerosis (MS) at age thirty-three:

> The whole thought process of just taking stock of where you are in your life. It's like putting your life through a sieve, getting the big awkward chunks out of your life, getting the nice finely sifted residue—it is kind of sorting it all out. What is the essence of you and what isn't? (Baxter Magolda, 2009, p. 51)

Although a few participants developed self-authorship late in college, the majority did so in their thirties and forties. Self-authorship is the capacity to internally define one's beliefs, identities, and relationships. Baxter Magolda identified three components of self-authorship. *Trusting internal voice* began when participants realized that reality was beyond their control but they could control their reactions to it. For Dawn, this meant "finding the balance between [going with the flow] and me saying I have control over myself, not letting this condition get the best of me. Knowing how to make things happen and let things happen" (Baxter Magolda, 2009, p. 53).

Once they began to use their internal voices to shape their reactions, participants used those voices to make internal commitments and *build an internal foundation,* or philosophy of life, to guide their actions. Dawn described this as "building this whole network and infrastructure for myself" (Baxter Magolda, 2009, p. 57). Living out those commitments in everyday life helped *secure internal commitments* as central to their identities. Dawn described it like this:

> To me knowledge is an awareness of when you know things. You know them as facts; they are there in front of you. When you possess the wisdom, you've lived those facts, that information so fully that it takes on a whole different aspect than just knowing. It is like you absorbed that information into your entire being . . . the knowledge has a deeper level—internal, intuitive, centered in entire being, the essential part of you that just—makes the basic knowledge pale by comparison. (Baxter Magolda, 2009, pp. 59–60)

Self-authoring participants were able to navigate effectively the complexity of their work and personal lives. Baxter Magolda's long-term longitudinal study surfaced more detailed descriptions of the major phases of the journey toward self-authorship, deepened understanding of the intersections of person and context, and clarified intersections of the three developmental dimensions over time.

Baxter Magolda and King's Model of the Journey toward Self-Authorship

The Wabash National Study (WNS), a mixed-method study designed to explore how student experiences and meaning-making capacities affect growth toward liberal arts outcomes and self-authorship (Baxter Magolda & King, 2012), is a second large-scale study of college students' journey toward self-authorship. This study began twenty years after Baxter Magolda's longitudinal study and intentionally sought a more racially and ethnically diverse sample of participants. Baxter Magolda and King (2012) conceptualized the qualitative portion of the WNS to focus on recursive relationships between experiences and meaning making. The interview portion of this study began in 2006 with 315 traditional-age students, including thirty-four who identified as African American, twenty-nine as Latino/a, twenty-seven as Asian/Pacific Islanders, and seven as mixed racial heritage, from six campuses. Of this sample, 228, 204, and 177 participated in the annual interviews in 2007, 2008, and 2009, respectively.

Two major contributions to self-authorship theory emerged from this study. First, a ten-position model of the journey toward self-authorship (depicted in table 9.1) emerged from constant-comparative analysis of the longitudinal data (Baxter Magolda & King, 2012). This model refined external meaning making by identifying three positions within it: *Trusting external authority (Ea)* without question, experiencing *tensions with trusting external authority (Eb)*, and *recognizing shortcomings of trusting external authority (Ec)*. Gavin, a white participant in the WNS, demonstrated trusting external authority in describing his college-selection process: "My mom actually pointed me toward [this college] . . . I hadn't even thought about it" (Baxter Magolda & King, 2012, p. 55). By his sophomore year, he demonstrated tensions with trusting external authority. Gavin reported having encountered "a lot of gray all the time" and said, "It's important for me to have mentor figures who I trust and who I believe in give me their opinions in terms of black and white instead of gray" (Baxter Magolda & King, 2012, p. 60). Sara, a participant who identified as Latina and white, demonstrated recognizing the shortcomings of trusting external authority her sophomore year as she described her art history experience: "I mean everything's up for interpretation, and it's kind of neat to hear all sides" (Baxter Magolda & King, 2012, p. 63).

This model further refined the crossroads meaning-making structure by identifying two positions in the early part of the crossroads: *questioning external authority [E(I)]*, in which awareness of the need for an internal voice emerged, and *constructing the internal voice (E-I)*, in which active work on constructing a new way of making meaning began. Diana, an African American participant in the WNS, began questioning external authority when her English professor challenged her to disagree with him and find her own style. She began constructing her internal voice by working to find her own style, saying "I will read other writers . . . and then take a little bit out of each one and figure out my own writing style" (Baxter Magolda & Taylor, 2016). Baxter Magolda's descriptions of *listening to (I-E)* and *cultivating internal voice [I(E)]* were also evident in the WNS data as two positions in the later part of the crossroads. The final three positions within self-authoring meaning making are Baxter Magolda's *trusting the internal voice (Ia), building an internal foundation (Ib),* and *securing internal commitments (Ic)* because the WNS data did not contain extensive examples of self-authorship for these positions.

Second, a model of the interaction among elements involved in the evolution of meaning making emerged from the data analysis. The interactionist learning model (King & Baxter Magolda, 2016) portrays cyclical, reciprocal relationships among four elements: meaning making, personal characteristics, experiences, and effects of experiences. The data support the activity of meaning making as the core element. Personal characteristics (such as family history, previous educational experiences, salient identities, health status, and preferred learning styles) often affect what experiences appeal to students or their interpretation of experiences. Experiences include curricular, cocurricular, personal, and societal events. The model considers not only the content or nature of the experience but also its context, how it unfolded, and whether it challenged or supported the student to develop more complex meaning making. Effects of experiences include general effects (such as an emotional reaction); content learning effects (including knowledge, skill, and liberal arts outcomes); and developmental effects (that is, effects associated with developing more complex meaning-making structures and moving toward self-authorship). Each element of the model interacts with each of the other elements in a bidirectional manner and can evolve over time. This large-scale study with a diverse population not only refines the journey toward self-authorship and how it evolves but also clearly links development and learning within contemporary collegiate contexts.

Torres's Matrix of Holistic Development

Torres's four-year longitudinal study enriched understanding and diversified the portrait of the journey toward self-authorship by exploring the influence of ethnic identity on students' development. Her study included twenty-nine Latino/a collegians who began college between 2000 and 2003 in four different urban universities (Torres & Hernández, 2007). Her annual interviews revealed that participants made meaning through external formulas, the crossroads, becoming the author of their lives, and building internal foundations. Yet Torres and Hernández (2007) identified important additional developmental tasks as participants became authors of their lives, which included "recognizing their cultural reality, . . . integrating an informed Latino/a identity into their daily lives, . . . and renegotiating their relationships with others based on their Latino/a identity" (p. 569). Those using external formulas accepted negative messages about their ethnic identity. For example, Sagi said, "I feel ashamed . . . because I have an accent, if I am confused, people judge me more, because you have accent . . . It affects me because when I have an accent, I see myself as not being well prepared [educated]" (Torres & Baxter Magolda, 2004, p. 338). Those in the crossroads recognized racism and made deliberate choices about how it affected their sense of identity. Nora recognized racism when she transferred to a predominantly white institution. She shared:

> [P]eople have told me, friends of mine, that there are still people that don't like Mexicans or any other culture. I guess they think Mexicans are all the same . . . I got to appreciate more of who I am and my family back home and the whole Mexican American thing. (Torres & Hernández, 2007, p. 565)

These insights led participants to craft their own informed cultural identity and integrate it into their lives and relationships. Araceli came to understand her Chicana identity by participating in political rallies and learning her history. She concluded, "Even though we're a minority doesn't mean it's a bad thing. And I now feel like that applies to me and I say it with pride" (Torres & Hernández, 2007, p. 566). Some participants made meaning from an internal foundation in which they included cultural choices in their decisions and maintained their cultural values. For Vanessa, an adult student and a parent, making meaning from an internal foundation enabled her to be comfortable with her own ethnicity and, in turn, be comfortable speaking with her children about language and culture. As Torres and Hernández (2007) explained, "There was no longer intimidation in being different or being around others who were different" (p. 566).

Torres used a grounded theory approach to enable the portrait of Latino/a students' development to emerge from their own stories instead of existing theory; Torres and Hernández (2007) clarified that "the use of self-authorship as a framework was not a priori, rather it emerged as a plausible lens during the coding process" (p. 560). Torres's work deepens our understanding of the intersection of culture and meaning making by identifying the unique tasks that her participants faced within each developmental dimension. The influence of systemic oppression included the need to recognize and manage racism, develop trust in authorities outside of the family, sort out positive and negative cultural choices, and construct an informed Latino/a identity (Torres & Hernández, 2007).

Abes, Jones, and McEwen's Reconceptualized Model of Multiple Dimensions of Identity (RMMDI)

The RMMDI emerged from Abes's longitudinal, constructivist narrative inquiry exploring ten lesbian students' multiple social identities (Abes & Jones, 2004). With the aim of understanding how social identities influence holistic development, this study integrated the external-to-internal meaning-making framework from Kegan (1994) and Baxter Magolda (2001) with the existing model of multiple dimensions of identity (Jones & McEwen, 2000), which highlighted the intersections among personal attributes (such as being compassionate or being hard-working); social identities (such as race, social class, sexual orientation, gender, religion, and ability); and contextual influences (such as peers, family, cultural norms, stereotypes, and sociopolitical conditions). Based on this research, Abes, Jones, and McEwen (2007) created the RMMDI, which integrates relationships among students' multiple social identities, students' meaning-making capacities, and contextual influences.

Describing the RMMDI, Jones and Abes (2013) explained that meaning-making capacity functions as a filter between context and identity:

The wider the screen openings, the more permeable the filter. Contextual, external influences more easily move through a highly permeable filter (representing less complex meaning making), thereby having a stronger influence on a person's perceptions of identity than they would if the filter were less permeable (representing more complex meaning making). (p. 104)

KT, a white participant in Abes's study, initially made meaning of her sexual orientation as a lesbian with a highly permeable filter in which "most everything she knew about what it meant to be a lesbian was based on negative stereotypes she heard from her mother" (Jones & Abes, 2013, pp. 107–108). For example, she believed she could not be Catholic, feminine, or professionally successful as a lesbian. Moving into the crossroads, she began to filter out heterosexist messages. She noted, "Although I sometimes struggle to freely express my sexual orientation, my sexual orientation need not affect my religious beliefs and practices, my professional success, or my appearance and for the most part it does not" (Jones & Abes, 2013, p. 112). As KT approached self-authorship, the filter between her external environments and her multiple identities became increasingly fine-grained, which enabled her "true self to evolve" (Jones & Abes, 2013, p. 111) rather than be defined or constrained by others.

The meaning-making filter between contextual influences and multiple social identities links the RMMDI to the journey toward self-authorship and resonates with Kegan's placing the activity of meaning making at the center of the developmental process. Similar to Baxter Magolda's and Torres's participants, Abes's participants who used internal meaning making managed external influences more effectively as they constructed their beliefs, identities, and relationships (Abes & Jones, 2004). Although the RMMDI incorporates meaning making, its primary focus continues to be the intersection of multiple social identities. Jones and Abes (2013) further described the RMMDI from three critical perspectives—intersectionality, critical race theory, and queer theory—to explore possibilities for how these perspectives might reshape the nature of the RMMDI. Overall, the RMMDI provides a nuanced portrait of how meaning-making capacities intersect with context and multiple social identities. In particular, the RMMDI shows that some contexts such as those characterized by oppressive structures are more difficult to filter and that the permeability of an individual's meaning-making filter may vary across different social identities. Yet, the RMMDI aligns with other holistic models in terms of showing that more complex meaning-making filters can enhance students' abilities to integrate their multiple identities and deal with negative stereotypes.

Pizzolato's Theory of Self-Authorship

Pizzolato's research on the relationship of the three developmental dimensions and the intersections of self and cultural context resonates with King and Baxter Magolda's interactionist learning model and Torres's matrix of holistic development. Pizzolato (2010) conducted numerous cross-sectional studies with participants from diverse populations that led her to articulate the role of cultural self ways, or the "socialization of individual selves toward the culturally agreed-upon ways of being and knowing" (p. 192), in meaning making. Pizzolato linked meaning making and identity development to the larger context of privilege and oppression, identified culture and psychological contexts as part of the interperso nal dimension, and described the role that personal characteristics such as coping skills play in the meaning-making process. A longitudinal study exploring these dynamics with twenty-five diverse community college students revealed the strength of context in mediating their evolution from uncritical reliance on external formulas to the crossroads (Olson & Pizzolato, 2016). These students, ages twenty to fifty-one and with an average of two children, relied on extended family (for example, for childcare) and public assistance. Relationships with these crucial groups often required following external formulas. Community college experiences prompted students to see themselves as having a role in meaning making; yet, they were unable to safely extract themselves from external formulas. For example, Cynthia's initial external formula involved earning a college degree to get off welfare. Then, after realizing that she needed to find a career path that suited her interests, she adopted a new external formula that involved using a career assessment to explore possible career paths. Those moving into the crossroads either adjusted existing formulas or used new ones to navigate these environments whereas those who were unable to do so regressed in their development. No participants were identified as self-authoring. This study confirms Jones and Abes's (2013) suggestion that some contexts, welfare systems in this case, are more challenging to filter in complex ways. This study also demonstrates that academic and personal contexts can place conflicting demands on students, which in turn complicates how cognitive, intrapersonal, and interpersonal dimensions evolve and intersect.

Intersections with Additional Theoretical Perspectives

Mapping additional theoretical perspectives including those from different research paradigms (see chapter 8 in this book) onto the six holistic perspectives previously described can further expand the portrait of college students' development. Through the holistic perspectives, we have synthesized aspects of psychosocial and cognitive theories; yet, further mapping the theories from chapters 10 and 11 onto the holistic perspectives could help refine the cognitive, intrapersonal, and interpersonal dimensions. For example, one could map social identity theories onto the holistic models in table 9.1 to deepen understanding of the intrapersonal and interpersonal dimensions for particular student populations. Critical perspectives (chapter 12 in this book) can further enrich understanding of developmental possibilities by including social forces such as racism, power, and oppression. Considering the tensions among critical, queer, intersectional, and constructivist perspectives enables deeper exploration of the intersections of person and context (Jones & Abes, 2013). As Jones and Abes (chapter 8 in this book) note, theory is an enlargement of observation. The six models we have highlighted in this chapter are possibilities of how development occurs based on the participants and researchers associated with each model. Thus educators need to determine whether or how each model transfers to students in their particular contexts. We remind readers that this is our construction of how these models map together; it is educators' responsibility to select and organize multiple theoretical perspectives to understand development of the whole student in the contexts in which they work.

Practice: Supporting Young Adults in Growing toward Self-Authorship

As the longitudinal models illustrate, college students' evolution toward self-authorship is neither automatic nor swift. Yet, given the demands students face in and beyond college, gaining the capacity for self-authorship remains essential. In the previous section and through table 9.1, we have focused on helping you as a student affairs educator see an overarching portrait of the evolution of meaning making among college student populations. Now we turn our attention to helping you work with students to foster their development toward increasingly complex, more adaptive meaning making.

Kegan (1994) used the metaphor of building a bridge to describe how to foster development. Addressing educators and including himself among this group, he stated,

> We cannot simply stand on our favored side of the bridge and worry or fume about the many who have not yet passed over. A bridge must be well anchored on both sides, with as much respect for where it begins as for where it ends. (p. 62)

To anchor the bridge at the starting point, you need to listen carefully to how students are making meaning of their identities, relationships, and beliefs and negotiating influences from the various layers of context with which they interact. To facilitate such conversations, you can draw on and adapt aspects of the interview protocols Baxter Magolda and King (2012) identified as designed to assess self-authorship. These interview protocols focus on asking open-ended questions to allow students to discuss what they deem significant and following up with probing questions as the conversation unfolds to further understand and refine your interpretation of a student's meaning-making capacities. The main goal is to "encourage deep reflection about students' experiences," which will allow you to know where students are beginning their journey (Baxter Magolda & King, 2012, p. 120).

To continue building the bridge and ensure it is anchored on the other side, you need to create a balance of challenge and support. That is, you need to combine challenges that require students to stretch beyond their current ways of making meaning toward more complex ways of making meaning with supports that validate their ability to develop and use their internal voice.

Baxter Magolda's (2009) learning partnerships model (LPM) provides a set of three challenges and three accompanying supports to foster growth toward self-authorship. The challenges include dealing with complex decisions, developing personal authority, and collaborating to solve issues. In turn, the supports include respecting students' thoughts and feelings, helping students sort through their experiences, and collaborating with students to solve problems. For example, educators can implement the LPM by first identifying a complex decision students face related to the context in which they work—agreeing how to live together with roommates, addressing the effects of racism on campus, or choosing a major (to name but a few). Then, educators can invite students to explore and evaluate multiple solutions, along the way asking questions such as "What is at stake for you in this decision? From your perspective, what does a good solution entail? How do you see the benefits and limitations of each solution stacking up against one another?" The focus of such questions is for students themselves to make sense of the multiple solutions. The LPM can be and has been used in multiple contexts including individual advising appointments, course design, leadership experiences, residential life communities, orientation, learning assistance, cultural immersion programs, and departmental curricula (see Baxter Magolda and King's [2004] *Learning Partnerships* and Taylor, Haynes, and Baxter Magolda's [2010] *Learning Communities Journal, Special Issue* for detailed examples). Again, listening carefully to students is essential to understand how to tailor the LPM to your students' specific developmental needs and particular contexts.

Finally, first-hand experience with traversing the bridge toward self-authorship will help you build a bridge for others. Thus, fostering your own development is important. See Magolda and Carnaghi's chapter (chapter 32) for strategies for designing challenges and supports for yourself.

Conclusion

The value in understanding the journey toward self-authorship lies in being able to intentionally guide young adults toward acquiring the developmental capacities required to succeed in adult life. Effective student affairs educators forge learning partnerships tailored to particular contexts that welcome students' backgrounds and experiences and give them responsibility for cultivating their beliefs, identities, and relationships.

Discussion Questions and Activities

1. Describe a significant learning experience you have had. How did this learning experience involve the three dimensions of development (cognitive, intrapersonal, and interpersonal)? How did it involve interactions with your particular context?
2. Compare your developmental story with the holistic perspectives described

here. In what ways does your story overlap with these perspectives? In what ways does your story differ from them? Consider whether and how the latter offer new possibilities that are not captured by current models of meaning making.

3. Take a development theory from chapter 10, 11, or 12 that you find particularly useful and map it onto the holistic perspectives we described in table 9.1. How does mapping this theory onto the holistic ones help you gain an even deeper understanding of development?

4. One of your roles as a professional is to be aware of your own assumptions and biases so that you can listen carefully to students. Make a list of assumptions or biases you hold about development and make notes about how you will manage these assumptions and biases. Reflect on how systemic oppression and privilege influence your biases.

5. Reflect on a time when students with whom you worked faced challenges they struggled to meet. How did the nature of the challenge relate to their meaning making? How could you use learning partnerships to help them address the challenges?

References

Abes, E. S., Jones, S. R., & McEwen, M. K. (2007). Reconceptualizing the model of multiple dimensions of identity: The role of meaning-making capacity in the construction of multiple identities. *Journal of College Student Development, 48*(1), 1–22.

Abes, E. S., & Jones, S. R. (2004). Meaning-making capacity and the dynamics of lesbian college students' multiple dimensions of identity. *Journal of College Student Development, 45*(6), 612–632.

Arnett, J. J. (2006). Emerging adulthood: Understanding a new way of coming of age. In J. J. Arnett & J. L. Tanner (Eds.), *Emerging adults in America: Coming of age in the 21st century* (pp. 3–19). Washington, DC: American Psychological Association.

Association of American Colleges & Universities (AAC&U). (2015). *Liberal Education & American's Promise essential learning outcomes.* Retrieved from http://www.aacu.org/leap/essential-learning-outcomes

Baxter Magolda, M. B. (2001). *Making their own way: Narratives for transforming higher education to promote self-development.* Sterling, VA: Stylus.

Baxter Magolda, M. B. (2009). *Authoring your life: Developing an internal voice to navigate life's challenges.* Sterling, VA: Stylus.

Baxter Magolda, M. B., & King, P. M. (Eds.). (2004). *Learning partnerships: Theory & models of practice to educate for self-authorship.* Sterling, VA: Stylus

Baxter Magolda, M. B., & King, P. M. (2012). Assessing meaning making and self-authorship: Theory, research, and application. *ASHE Higher Education Report, 38*(3). San Francisco: Jossey-Bass.

Baxter Magolda, M. B., & Taylor, K. B. (2016). Developing self-authorship in college. In J. J. Arnett (Ed.), *The Oxford handbook of emerging adulthood* (pp. 299–315). New York: Oxford University Press.

Boes, L. M. (2006). *Learning from practice: A constructive-developmental study of undergraduate service-learning pedagogy.* Doctoral dissertation. Harvard University, Cambridge, MA.

Carcasson, M., & Sprain, L. (2012). Deliberative democracy and adult civic education. In L. Muñoz & H. Spruck Wrigley (Eds.), *Adult civic engagement in adult learning* (New Directions for Adult and Continuing Education, no. 135, pp. 15–23). doi:10.1002/ace/20022

Daloz Parks, S. (2009). Foreword. In M. B. Baxter Magolda, *Authoring your life: Developing an internal voice to navigate life's challenges* (pp. xv–xvii). Sterling, VA: Stylus.

Jones, S. R., & Abes, E. S. (2013). *Identity development of college students: Advancing frameworks for multiple dimensions of identity.* San Francisco: Jossey-Bass.

Jones, S. R., & McEwen, M. K. (2000). A conceptual model of multiple dimensions of identity. *Journal of College Student Development, 41*(4), 405–413.

Kegan, R. (1982). *The evolving self: Problem and process in human development.* Cambridge, MA: Harvard University Press.

Kegan, R. (1994). *In over our heads: The mental demands of modern life.* Cambridge, MA: Harvard University Press.

King, P. M., & Baxter Magolda, M. B. (2005). A developmental model of intercultural maturity. *Journal of College Student Development, 46*(6), 571–592.

King, P. M., & Baxter Magolda, M. B. (2016). *Integrating individual and contextual factors in college student learning and development: A conceptual framework.* Manuscript in preparation.

McIntosh, P. (2004). White privilege: Unpacking the invisible knapsack. In M. Anderson & P. H. Collins (Eds.), *Race, class, and gender: An anthology* (5th ed., pp. 103–107). Belmonth, CA: Wadsworth.

Olson, A., & Pizzolato, J. E. (2016). Exploring the relationship between the three dimensions of self-authorship. *Journal of College Student Development.*

Pizzolato, J. E. (2010). What is self-authorship? A theoretical exploration of the construct. In M. B. Baxter Magolda, E. G. Creamer, & P. S. Meszaros (Eds.), *Development and assessment of self-authorship: Exploring the concept across cultures* (pp. 187–206). Sterling, VA: Stylus.

Taylor, K. B., Haynes, C., & Baxter Magolda, M. B. (Eds.). (2010). *Learning Communities Journal, Special Issue* (Vol. 2). Oxford, OH: Miami University.

Torres, V., & Baxter Magolda, M. B. (2004). Reconstructing Latino identity: The influence of cognitive development on the ethnic identity process of Latino students. *Journal of College Student Development, 45*(3), 333–347.

Torres, V., & Hernández, E. (2007). The influence of ethnic identity development on self-authorship: A longitudinal study of Latino/a college students. *Journal of College Student Development, 48*(5), 558–573.

CHAPTER 10

COGNITIVE DEVELOPMENT

Patricia M. King

And the day came when the risk to remain tight in a bud was more painful than the risk it took to blossom.

ELIZABETH APPELL

There are few greater joys than watching someone you care about blossom. Whether it is a child learning to read or an advisee proudly explaining how she had applied principles of logic learned in a philosophy class to her advocacy for first-generation students, watching learning develop and seeing individuals blossom gives pleasure and satisfaction to educators. More important, these accomplishments illustrate to the individual that she or he is capable of learning and mastering new tasks by taking the risk to change. This, of course, is the promise of education: with opportunity and guidance, students will learn to navigate increasingly complex tasks by learning the knowledge and skills required to address life's changing and unknown demands. Colleges and universities often communicate this promise through the learning outcomes they endorse; these outcomes are embedded in the courses, programs, and services they offer, and they also provide a standard against which institutional success is subsequently measured, such as through strategic plans and accreditation reviews. The achievement of learning outcomes reflects the successful integration of individuals' knowledge and skills, guided by their understanding of the world and their place in it. In this way, the aim of education is to help students develop complex capacities through their learning experiences (American Association of Colleges & Universities [hereafter, AACU], 2002; Baxter Magolda, 2001), and to transform who they are as learners and how they can use their knowledge and skills when facing adult responsibilities (Drago-Severson, 2010; Heifetz, 1998; Mezirow, 2000).

This requires transformative learning, which Mezirow (2000) defines as "the process by which we transform our taken-for-granted frames of reference (meaning perspectives, habits of mind, mind-sets) to make them more inclusive, discriminating, open, emotionally capable of change, and reflective so that they may generate beliefs and opinions that will prove more true or justified to guide action" (pp. 7–8). This kind of learning applies to a wide range of learning outcomes and contexts. For example, employers of college graduates rate as most important "written and oral communication skills, teamwork skills, ethical decision-making, critical thinking, and the ability to apply knowledge in real-world settings" (AACU, 2015, p. 1). All of these outcomes call for the capacity to construct defensible beliefs to guide actions, which is at the heart of cognitive educational outcomes.

This chapter focuses on one aspect of human development—cognitive development in late adolescents and adults—and its implications for learning. It focuses on foundational theories that describe cognitive development and reflect transformative learning. Although brain development continues through the mid-twenties (Jetha & Segalowitz, 2012) and is an important facet of cognitive development, this research is beyond the scope of this chapter. Here, I first briefly introduce developmental constructs, discuss and synthesize major models of cognitive development, then introduce several models in other developmental domains that include a strong cognitive component. I conclude with activities for helping you understand these models and use them to promote student development.

The Nature and Mechanisms of Development

In order to promote development, it is important to understand what development is (and is not) and how it occurs. In this section, I discuss several terms and concepts that provide the basis for the developmental models discussed in this chapter. I divide this section into two parts, the first of which introduces key concepts that serve as distinguishing features of development. The second introduces factors affecting development (which supplement and extend those introduced in chapter 8).

First, it is important to differentiate development from the related concepts of change and growth. *Change* refers to becoming different in some way (such as changing your mind) and includes positive and negative changes (such as becoming more independent or becoming a binge drinker). *Growth* refers to gaining more of something (such as developing more confidence or holding a point of view more strongly). By contrast, *development* is a transformation in the form, organization, or structure of one's understanding and response that reflects increased complexity of understanding (such as understanding the basis for two points of view rather than just one and being able to compare abstract concepts such as democracy and justice rather than just citing definitions or concrete examples). More complex cognitive skills enable people to understand multiple perspectives and layers of interpretation, and they are associated with possessing a broader repertoire of skills and increased adaptability to changing contexts. Complex cognitive skills are reflected in the nuanced complexities associated with a wide variety of collegiate outcomes, including integration of learning (Barber, 2009); intercultural maturity (King, Baxter Magolda, & Massé, 2011); decision making (Drobney, 2012); leadership (Christman, 2013; Shim, 2013); and well-being (Wakefield, 2013); and a variety of prosocial civic behaviors (King & Mayhew, 2002).

As discussed by Jones and Abes in chapter 8, theories posit descriptions of and explanations for observed phenomena. Theories and models describing development focus on key clusters of characteristics that signal developmental transitions in individuals' habits of mind, that is, how their ways of knowing, being, and interacting transform from simpler to more complex forms. Rather than thinking of theories that map out people's life journeys as identifying specific routes through life (after all, variability is inevitable because of environmental and cultural factors), it is more helpful to think of these theories as reports of common *milestones* that reflect general patterns across individuals. Theories backed by robust evidence (such as showing that these milestones have been observed among populations that differ by factors such as background and region and that account for relevant personality characteristics and behaviors) are considered to have higher explanatory power than those with weaker evidentiary bases. In addition, longitudinal evidence supporting the posited change in patterns over time is essential for demonstrating the validity of theories mapping development.

These milestones (also called *meaning-making structures* by Baxter Magolda and Taylor in chapter 9) generally change in orderly and sequential ways; common examples are learning to crawl and walk before running and learning to count objects using simple number skills before solving algebra problems using the abstract skills called for by algebraic equations). Interestingly, although individuals retain the ability to access skills and approaches associated with the forms of earlier milestones, they typically turn to earlier forms only under conditions of high stress, temptation, or challenge. Although these clusters of characteristics go by many names (such as position, perspective, order, level, and stage) depending on the author's purpose and intention, all refer to qualitatively different forms of understanding. And even though developmental change mapped by these models is typically portrayed as sequential in order to show the transformations over time, this is not to say that development follows a strictly linear progression; instead it is "more accurately portrayed as wavelike than linear" (King & Kitchener, 2016, p. 5). This is because people follow many routes between milestones (and sometimes within milestones, depending on the specificity of the model). This variability contributes to the richness of human experience, even within observed common contours of cognitive development. Comparing the forms across general levels for each model, it is important to remember that these evolving forms reflect development, not growth or simple change: they are qualitatively different, transformational changes in ways of understanding the world and interpreting one's experience. (For additional information about the nature of development, see King, 2015, and Overton, 2010.)

The second set of concepts needed to understand development relate to factors affecting development. What makes these forms evolve over time? What triggers development? Although our understanding of specific mechanisms is not yet well developed, a major tenet of developmentalism (Overton, 2010) is *interactionism:* development occurs as individuals interact with their environments. Thus, development is understood as resulting from a combination of individual readiness (including the maturation of neural connections in the brain) and opportunity (the conditions under which an individual learns and is challenged to adapt). Individual characteristics (such as curiosity or tolerance for ambiguity) can render a person open or closed to opportunities to learn. Similarly, opportunities to learn new approaches vary greatly across contexts, along with the presence or absence of encouragement and the expectation to think in more rigorous and complex ways.

Another tenet of developmentalism is that development is often triggered by feelings of *dissonance*, which sometimes occur when individuals are confronted with the limitations of their ways of understanding. This type of discomfort can be disconcerting or overwhelming, especially if it is experienced under conditions of low cognitive support, such as lack of scaffolding for increasingly complex tasks or modeling or conditions where emotional support is absent. Sanford (1966) suggested that institutions should present students with strong *challenges*, appraise their abilities to cope with these challenges, and "and offer . . . *support* when they become overwhelming" (p. 46; no italics in original). Support may take the form of scaffolding information, tasks, and expectations (knowing that what is perceived as a challenge and a support depends on developmental level), as well as providing emotional support. More recently, scholars have discussed the nature of a *demand* within an experience (Barber & King, 2014; Drago-Severson, 2010; Kegan, 1994), which is "a task that requires a meaning-making structure beyond the one the individual currently uses, and thus stretches an individual's capacity to respond" (King & Baxter Magolda, 2015, p. 15). Heifetz (1998) refers to these as adaptive challenges; both require a transformation in how one makes meaning about an experience and understands the world. In summary, dissonance that triggers the recognition that one's current form of understanding is no longer sufficient can result from exposure to tasks that developmentally stretch the individual's capacity to respond, especially when they occur within cognitively and emotionally supportive environments. We turn now to models that are based on these concepts and tenets of development.

Models of Cognitive Development

In order to promote development, it is also important to understand what you are promoting. Most models of cognitive development attempt to describe what cognitive capacities develop over time, as I show next. At the end of this section, I also include theories that address other dimensions of development that include a strong cognitive component. Each of the models described here is developmental as previously defined and is based on a body of empirical evidence that demonstrates the developmental progression it describes.

A major focus of theory and research on young adult and adult cognitive development is epistemology (the origin, nature, and limits of knowledge) and how people's assumptions about knowledge change over time. Hofer and Pintrich (2002) provided comprehensive and insightful reviews of research on what they call *personal epistemology*. They noted that although there are many similarities across epistemological theories, there is no consensus about the construct and its dimensions, a point illustrated in the following overview. All but one of the models described in what follows were inspired (at least in part) by Perry's (1970) seminal observations of how college students "construe the nature and origins of knowledge, of value, and of responsibility" (p. 1). Acknowledging that no brief summary can adequately capture the insightful nuances about cognitive development that each of these models provides, I present thumbnail sketches of each of these models, comment on the distinctive perspective of each model, and summarize how these have been synthesized.

Perry's Scheme of Intellectual and Ethical Development

Perry (1970) was an astute observer of how the college students seeking "study counsel" (the name of the office he led) thought about their college experiences, noting that "people tend to 'make sense,' that is to interpret experiences meaningfully" (p. 41). He was keenly aware of students' vantage points and how they positioned themselves in the world; this led to his selection of the word position for the milestones of his scheme. He developed his model from annual interviews with 139 students (including eighty-four complete four-year sets); his sample was composed primarily of undergraduate men attending Harvard College, along with a smaller sample (20 percent) of female students at Radcliffe College; all were enrolled in the 1950s and 1960s.

The resulting nine-position model starts with a bifurcated (we-they, right-wrong) view of knowledge that he called *dualism*, as follows: "When I came here I didn't think any question could have more than one answer" (Perry, 1970, p. 64). This evolves into the acknowledgment that a *multiplicity* of opinions exists, which sets the stage for the emergence of *relativism*, which reflects the discovery that points of view can be weighed for their validity and that they depend on the context: "You find yourself thinking in more complex terms: weighing more than one factor in trying to develop your own opinion . . . Somehow what I think about things now seems to be more . . . sensible" (p. 113). His final positions reflect the development of personal *commitments*, acts that affirm one's values and reflect what he called "the ultimate welding of epistemological and moral issues" (p. 202). Although this welding is a distinctive feature of Perry's scheme, it resulted in the portrayal of an epistemological dimension that extends from positions 1 to 5 and then a shift to a personal responsibility dimension (identity and ethical issues) in positions 6 to 9. Although strong relationships across developmental domains (such as cognitive and moral development) are well documented (Kegan, 1994; King & Kitchener, 1994; Moshman, 2015), virtually all research on the Perry scheme is based on only the first five cognitively focused positions, and we know relatively little about the development of identity and ethics described in Perry's commitment positions. In light of this and the fact that these latter positions do not reflect increasing structural complexity (King & Kitchener, 2016; Moshman, 2015; West, 2004), table 10.1 includes descriptions of only the first half of the Perry scheme. I organized the table into three sections, unequivocal knowing, radical subjectivism, and generative knowing, following Love and Guthrie's (1999) use of these terms in their synthesis of this literature. Each section captures distinct modes of meaning making that are apparent across models.

TABLE 10.1.   OVERVIEW OF COGNITIVE DEVELOPMENT MODELS

Perry: Intellectual and Ethical Development	King and Kitchener: Reflective Judgment Model	Belenky, Clinchy, Goldberger, and Tarule: Women's Ways of Knowing	Baxter Magolda: Epistemological Reflection	Kuhn, Cheney, and Weinstock: Levels of Epistemological Understanding
Unequivocal Knowing				
Position 1: <u>Dualism</u> Sees the world in polar terms of we-right-good and other-wrong-bad; answers are known to Authorities.	<u>Pre-reflective</u> Stage 1: Knowledge absolute and concrete; no justification necessary.			<u>Realist:</u> Assertions are copies of external reality.
Position 2: <u>Multiplicity Pre-legitimate</u> Accounts for differences of opinion and uncertainty as unwarranted confusion.	<u>Pre-reflective</u> Stage 2: Right answers are coordinated with wrong answers via authority; justification via authority.	<u>Received Knowing</u> Truth is absolute and unambiguous; right versus wrong, black or white.	<u>Absolute Knowing</u> Knowledge is certain or absolute and received from authorities (mastery and received patterns).	<u>Absolutist</u> Assertions are facts that can be right or wrong in representation of reality.
Radical Subjectivism				
Position 3: <u>Multiplicity Subordinate</u> Diversity and uncertainty are accepted as legitimate but temporary in areas where authority hasn't found the answer yet.	<u>Pre-reflective</u> Stage 3: When authorities don't know the truth with certainty, truth is temporarily inaccessible and knowledge is limited to personal impressions.	<u>Subjectivism</u> Knowledge is uncertain. All opinions are equally valid and personal.	<u>Transitional Knowing</u> Knowledge is partially certain and partially uncertain (impersonal and interpersonal patterns).	

Perry: Intellectual and Ethical Development	King and Kitchener: Reflective Judgment Model	Belenky, Clinchy, Goldberger, and Tarule: Women's Ways of Knowing	Baxter Magolda: Epistemological Reflection	Kuhn, Cheney, and Weinstock: Levels of Epistemological Understanding
Position 4: Multiplicity Correlate or Relativism Subordinate Perceives extensive legitimate uncertainty, hence opinions are judged as equal.	Quasi-reflective Stage 4: Accepting uncertainty enables the differentiation of well- and ill-structured problems. The process of knowing is confusing, but the role of evidence is emerging as a criterion.	Procedural Knowing Perceives legitimate uncertainty to be extensive, hence opinions are judged as equal; begins to discern contextual relativistic reasoning.	Independent Knowing Knowledge is uncertain thus everyone has his or her own beliefs and knowledge is relative (individual and interindividual patterns).	Multiplist Assertions are opinions, chosen and accountable only to owners.

Generative Knowing

Perry: Intellectual and Ethical Development	King and Kitchener: Reflective Judgment Model	Belenky, Clinchy, Goldberger, and Tarule: Women's Ways of Knowing	Baxter Magolda: Epistemological Reflection	Kuhn, Cheney, and Weinstock: Levels of Epistemological Understanding
Position 5: Relativism Correlate, Competing, or Diffuse All knowledge and values are contextual and relativistic; right-wrong becomes a special case.	Quasi-reflective Stage 5: Knowledge is contextual and people know via individual filters. Justification is based on evidence and seen as a reflection of perspectives.	Constructed Knowing All knowledge and values are contextual and relativistic; right-wrong becomes a special case.	Contextual Knowing Knowledge is contextual; judge on the basis of evidence in context, not all solutions are equally valid.	
	Reflective Stage 6: Knowledge and justification are coordinated; knowledge can be justified by evidence from several perspectives and contexts.			
	Reflective Stage 7: Knowledge is seen as the outcome of considering legitimate alternatives and justifying the most compelling view of an issue based on available evidence.			

Note. Adapted from table 1 of King, P. M., & Kitchener, K. S. (2016). Cognitive development in the emerging adult: The emergence of complex cognitive skills. J. Arnett (Ed.), *The Oxford handbook of emerging adulthood,* (pp. 109–111). New York: Oxford University Press.

The Reflective Judgment Model

Following Dewey's (1933) concept of reflective thinking and drawing on the work of several theorists (including Perry), King and Kitchener (1994) sought to describe intellectual development in ways that explicitly focused on epistemology. We sought to identify how people resolved "ill-structured" problems (that is, those that cannot be described with a high degree of completeness and solved with a high degree of certainty) without resorting to purely relativistic approaches in which all solutions are judged as equal and to differentiate the capacity to make a reflective judgement (RJ) from other intellectual abilities. We conducted semi-structured interviews with a sample of eighty participants (starting with high school, college, and graduate students) for ten years. Our research revealed seven distinct developmental levels (milestones), each of which is associated with increasing capacity to engage in reflective thinking and reflects a cluster of assumptions about knowledge, how it is gained, and the certainty with which one can know. We chose the word stage to reflect this cluster of assumptions guiding meaning making—not to portray development as linear but to capture the coherence of the underlying assumptions within levels. This progression evolves from simple reliance on the word of an authority figure (pre-reflective thinking) to the use of evidence and whim in reasoning (quasi-reflective thinking) to the ability to relate different perspectives to each other and apply considered criteria when resolving problems (reflective thinking). For a more detailed description of the model and its theoretical grounding, see King (2000) and King and Kitchener (1994).

The RJ interview has been administered to more than 1,700 individuals from fourteen to sixty-five; several reviews of the RJ literature (King & Kitchener, 1994, 2002, 2004) document significant increases in reflective thinking from high school students (predominantly stage 3) to college students (stages 3 and 4; stage 4 for seniors) through early graduate students (stages 4 and 5) to advanced graduate students (stage 5 and 6). Unfortunately, stage 4 reasoning does not provide students with the capacity to demonstrate collegiate learning outcomes (for example, complex critical thinking) associated with college graduation or entry to graduate programs; however, it nevertheless represents an advance over stage 3 reasoning in the ways evidence is used to inform judgments and in the acknowledgment of uncertainty in the knowing process.

Women's Ways of Knowing

Belenky, Clinchy, Goldberger, and Tarule (1986) began their influential study with the goal of helping institutions better serve the needs and interests of women. Their sample of 135 women who varied widely in education, ethnicity, and social class reflected their desire to address issues raised by the homogeneity of Perry's (1970) sample. Although Perry was interested in intellectual and ethical development, these authors conducted semi-structured interviews that focused on topics that included epistemology, self, morality, education, and relationships. They also focused on participants' relationship to what they know and how they saw themselves as knowers, which yielded a revealing and informative dimension of learning, the development of one's own voice. These authors identified five perspectives on truth, knowledge, and authority: silence; received knowing (the new preferred term; Clinchy, 2002); subjectivism; two kinds of procedural knowing (separate and connected); and constructed knowing. Despite its structural similarity with related models, the authors make no claim that their model describes a developmental sequence. The new perspectives they identified, especially the exploration of the relationships across "the development of self, voice, and mind" (the book's subtitle), sparked new lines of inquiry on gender differences and the creation of educational practices that were more attuned to women's voices; both significantly expanded our understanding of each of these three aspects of development.

Epistemological Reflection Model

Baxter Magolda's (1992) study was inspired by the work of Perry (1970) and Belenky, Clinchy, Goldberger, and Tarule (1986). This original five-year longitudinal study sought to document the evolution of ways of knowing on an annual basis with an eye toward possible gender differences. She used a large sample (relative to most longitudinal qualitative studies) of 101 traditional-age college students who started college in 1986, 70 of whom continued all five years. This work culminated in the epistemological reflection model, which consists of four structurally different ways of knowing (positions), each of which is characterized by a core set of epistemic assumptions that became more complex over time. Baxter Magolda observed gender-related stylistic patterns for the first three positions. (In the following list, women used the first pattern more often and men used the second pattern more often.) The four positions are absolute knowing (receiving and mastery), transitional knowing (interpersonal and impersonal), independent knowing (interindividual and individual), and contextual knowing (which had too few examples to confidently identify gender-related patterns). For each position, the patterns provided different paths leading to the same developmental end.

Baxter Magolda's (1992) study not only identified these gender-related patterns but also documented shifts toward the use of more complex epistemic assumptions over this five-year span of time. These positions evolved in an order that was consistent with the longitudinal trends observed by Perry (1970) and King and Kitchener (1994) and with Belenky and others' (1986) cross-sectional research.

Epistemological Understanding

Kuhn's (1991) work on the development of thinking and reasoning beyond childhood is well known. The model of epistemological understanding (Kuhn, Cheney, & Weinstock, 2000) displays a similar but more simplified progression of beliefs about knowing and knowledge from early childhood through adolescence than earlier models. A distinguishing feature is that the ages at which developmental levels emerge is much earlier than discussed in the prior models. The first two levels are called *realist* (assertions copy external reality) and *absolutist* (assertions are factual representations of reality). In the third level, *multiplist,* individuals acknowledge the legitimacy of conflicting representations or opinions, which signals a shift from the domination of objective dimensions to subjective dimensions. At the fourth level, *evaluativist,* objective and subjective positions are coordinated: despite being able to see and respect other's points of view, an individual can also recognize that criteria can be used to evaluate some viewpoints as having more merit than others. This study also documented differences in epistemological understanding across domains (personal taste, aesthetics, values, truth about the social world, and truth about the physical world). They also reported that "no more than half of the adults of any background and in any judgment domain" (p. 324) reasoned at the evaluativist position.

In a creatively designed study based on this model (Weinstock & Cronin, 2003), prospective jurors who were awaiting assignment to trials first solved an ill-structured problem about a fictitious war to determine epistemological level and then viewed audiotaped reenactments of the highlights of two criminal trials and were asked to make and justify a verdict about each trial. Evaluativists were more likely to use evidence and to link this to the chosen verdict; although "muliplists have informal reasoning skills, [they were] disinclined by their epistemological beliefs to use them" (p. 178). In light of the social implications of having jurors arrive at well-reasoned and defensible verdicts, this study shows the practical importance of understanding and promoting epistemological understanding.

Synthesis of Cognitive Development Models

This brief description of these models is intended to provide an introduction to the epistemological foundations of young adult cognitive development. Deeper understanding will likely require reading the primary works and thinking critically about the purposes, samples, research, and claims of each model. An overarching observation among this group of models is the emergence of increasingly complex, integrated, and coordinated cognitive structures (King & Kitchener, 2016). For example, a common theme is that an early form of reasoning is absolutistic and characterized by bifurcated either-or thinking. In their synthesis of cognitive development theories, Love and Guthrie (1999) called this unequivocal knowing; I used their labels in table 10.1 in recognition of their useful synthesis of this literature. A second theme that cuts across models is that as individuals realize the limitations of this absolutistic approach, their thinking evolves to some form of skepticism (radical subjectivism). There is more divergence across models in the next general level, but these models share the feature that context and quality of judgments are now salient and relevant. This subjective approach is seen to have its own weaknesses as well as strengths, and individuals begin to acknowledge their own role in constructing what they know (hence, generative knowing). In recognition of the important developmental advance it reflects, Love and Guthrie (1999) acknowledged that development to this level requires a "great accommodation" (p. 78) to reframe one's assumptions about the source and certainty of knowledge. Given the authors' different purposes, research questions, perspectives, samples, and data-gathering techniques, this consistency across models is quite remarkable, suggesting they are robust observations. As noted, the nature of the last level is less well understood; for example, the reflective judgment model is the only one among these models of cognitive development to propose a structurally different way of knowing that resolves the dilemma of strictly relativistic thinking.

The Role of Cognitive Development in Other Developmental Models

Several other developmental models include descriptions of cognitive development but position this component of development within other areas of focus. In this section, I introduce three models in which cognitive development is a central component but does not define the model. The first of these theories is moral development. Morality is inherently a relational construct because it addresses issues of what people can expect of each other, whether interacting in dyads, groups, or social institutions. College students who negotiate roommate contracts, make decisions about academic integrity, or are accused of violating a campus judicial code are involved in relational issues that have a moral dimension, especially questions of fairness. Scholars such as Kohlberg (1984) and Rest (1986; Rest, Narvaez, Bebeau, & Thoma, 1999) engaged in extensive study of morality and of the factors affecting the production of moral (and nonmoral) behavior. Their work has guided hundreds of studies about moral judgment development among college students (King & Mayhew, 2002, 2004).

The cognitive component of morality is reflected in research in the field of moral cognition (Padilla-Walker, 2016) and in the structural similarities between arguments about intellectual and moral issues (King & Kitchener, 1994, table 8.1). In addition, Rest and others (1999) used cognitive schema theory as an interpretive lens on the major developmental levels identified by Kohlberg, showing how approaches to reasoning about moral dilemmas evolved from being guided by personal interest; to maintaining norms (such as social rules and systems, role expectations, rules); to postconventional schema, where moral decisions are guided by moral principles (such as respect for human rights). King (2009) argued that cognitive and moral development are linked by "the construction of meaning . . ., processes of development, and similarities in patterns of changes over time (from simple to complex, from one dimension to multiple dimensions, from authority-based to criteria-based judgments)" (p. 617).

The second model that includes a central cognitive component is Bennett's (1993) model of intercultural sensitivity, which describes development in how people make meaning of cultural differences. This model includes three entho-centric stages in which one's own culture is seen as central to reality and three ethno-relative stages in which one's own culture is increasingly seen in the context of other cultures. Each stage reflects a qualitatively different cognitive structure that is reflected in intercultural attitudes and behaviors. Development culminates in the ability to effectively move in and out of different cultural worldviews and by actively constructing an intercultural identity.

King and Baxter Magolda (2005) also proposed a multidimensional framework of intercultural maturity that includes cognitive, intrapersonal, and interpersonal dimensions across three developmental levels. For example, for an individual who operates at an early developmental level, the cognitive characteristics include "resists challenges to one's own beliefs and views different cultural perspectives as wrong" (p. 575). By contrast, at the mature level of development, the cognitive capacities include "ability to consciously shift perspectives and behaviors into an alternative cultural worldview and to use multiple cultural frames" (p. 575). Perez, Shim, King, and Baxter Magolda (2015) have recently empirically tested and refined this model. This example demonstrates the role of cognitive complexity in intercultural development and its effects on reasoning about intercultural issues.

The third and last model in this section is the development of self-authorship (discussed at length in chapter 9), in which the cognitive dimension is one of three interwoven strands (along with intrapersonal and interpersonal dimensions). This construct was introduced by Kegan (1994) and refined and applied to the development of college students by Baxter Magolda (2001). This holistic model of life-span development describes the shifting balance between two aspects of knowing: according to Kegan, the first is the "object" of our knowing, those aspects we can examine, take responsibility for, reflect on, and internalize; the second type includes those aspects to which we are "subject," that is, those that are so fused with who we are that we can't reflect on or exert control over because we are embedded in this way of knowing. This balance shifts over time as adults develop the capacity to initiate and take responsibility for more and more aspects of their lives. Baxter Magolda (2009) captured this phenomenon by expressing it as a continuum of evolving meaning-making structures that extend from an external orientation (following external formulas) to the crossroads (a mixture of external and internal) to an internal orientation (self-authoring). As a model for which the central construct is the evolution of meaning-making structures, it is tempting to categorize this as a cognitive model (such as how cognition guides meaning making about knowledge, identity, and relationships). However, doing so would again privilege the cognitive domain, and the empirical evidence is mixed as to whether the cognitive dimension is an equal or the strong partner (King, 2010). Because this model is discussed in depth in chapter 9, my focus here is on its holistic integration of domains, showing how the cognitive dimension can be interwoven with other dimensions of development. As was true for the cognitive models, this additional collection also shows the important role of perspective taking and the ability to see relationships across elements, which I call "connective complexity" (King, 2010, p. 182).

Conclusion

The saying with which I opened this chapter reminds us that stasis and development involve risk, and that every day, students weigh the risks as they grapple with dissonance and consider opportunities. For this reason, it is quite fitting that this saying was written by an educator to inspire and motivate adult learners to enroll in classes at her university (Appel, 1979). It may seem odd to conclude a chapter on cognitive development by reflecting on a saying about a bud blossoming. Nevertheless, I consider it an apt and eloquent metaphor for the transformational changes that occur in the course of cognitive development. Rich learning experiences not only make it possible for students to learn the content, methods, and problems within curricular and cocurricular settings but also they help students develop the capacities to engage with these topics in ways that give them better cognitive tools for understanding the world and the multiple roles they may play in the future.

Discussion Questions and Activities

1. Write your own intellectual autobiography. How has your own way of knowing developed? What were the characteristics of important experiences that affected your cognitive development? Did you feel that this required intellectual risks? What were your support systems?

2. Learning about others' frames of reference and ways of thinking can be difficult because it requires suspending your own preferred approach ("making your own thinking object" in Kegan's words). It can help to be aware that you need to get inside someone else's head in order to understand these models. Identify a way of knowing that you find implausible (such as the unequivocal knowing of a first-year student or the radical subjectivism of a coworker), then try to construct the internal logic of this approach. Based on these models, what assumptions about knowledge and knowing might be guiding this person's approach? How are these assumptions similar to and different from your own assumptions about knowledge and knowing?

3. Interview a college student using general questions ("Describe a time when your opinion was challenged or when you changed your mind about an issue.") Interpret the student's responses using one or more of these models of cognitive development, noting how his or her responses illustrate a given developmental level. If the model didn't adequately capture the student's response, note how you might revise the model to accommodate this response. Listen to ways the developmental level

influenced how the student interpreted his or her experiences. What factors (such as educational level, gender, race and ethnicity, academic major, geographic region) do you think affected how this student views knowledge and knowing?

4. Critique institutional-level initiatives designed to promote student learning for the ways they take student development levels into account. For example, consider Indiana University–Purdue University Indianapolis's (n.d.) principles of undergraduate learning, the AACU (n.d.) VALUE rubrics, or other institution-wide initiatives with which you are familiar. To what degree do these initiatives reflect the content and processes of students' cognitive development as described in these models? Where are they underdeveloped, and how would you suggest taking these considerations into account?

References

Appell, E. (1979). *Who wrote "Risk"? Is the mystery solved?* Retrieved May 8, 2015, from http://anaisninblog.skybluepress.com/2013/03/who-wrote-risk-is-the-mystery-solved

Association of American Colleges and Universities (AACU). (2002). *Greater expectations: A new vision for learning as a nation goes to college.* Washington, DC: Author.

Association of American Colleges and Universities (AACU). (2015). *Falling short: College learning and career success.* Washington, DC: Author. Retrieved May 8, 2015, from http://www.aacu.org/leap/public-opinion-research/2015-survey-falling-short

Association of American Colleges and Universities (AACU). (n.d.). *Valid assessment of learning in undergraduate education (VALUE) rubrics.* Retrieved May 22, 2015, from https://www.aacu.org/value-rubrics

Barber, J. P. (2009). Integration of learning model: A grounded theory analysis of college students' learning. *American Educational Research Journal, 49*(3), 590–617. doi:103102/0002831212437854

Barber, J. P., & King, P. M. (2014). Pathways toward self-authorship: Student responses to the demands of developmentally effective experiences. *Journal of College Student Development, 55*(5), 433–450.

Baxter Magolda, M. B. (1992). *Knowing and reasoning in college: Gender-related patterns in students' intellectual development.* San Francisco: Jossey-Bass.

Baxter Magolda, M. B. (2001). *Making their own way: Narratives for transforming higher education to promote self-development* (pp. 3–36). Sterling, VA: Stylus.

Baxter Magolda, M. B. (2009). *Authoring your life: Developing an internal voice to navigate life's challenges.* Sterling, VA: Stylus.

Belenky, M., Clinchy, B., Goldberger, N., & Tarule, J. (1986). *Women's ways of knowing: The development of self, voice, and mind.* New York: Basic Books.

Bennett, M. (1993). Towards ethnorelativism: A developmental model of intercultural sensitivity. In M. Paige (Ed.), *Education for the intercultural experience* (pp. 21–71). Yarmouth, ME: Intercultural Press.

Christman, H. (2013). *Connections between leadership and developmental capacities in college students.* Unpublished doctoral dissertation. Miami University, Oxford, OH.

Clinchy, B. (2002). Revising *Women's Ways of Knowing.* In B. K. Hofer & P. R. Pintrich (Eds.), *Personal epistemology: The psychology of beliefs about knowledge and knowing* (pp. 63–87). Mahwah, NJ: Lawrence Erlbaum.

Dewey, J. (1933). *How we think: A restatement of the relations of reflective thinking to the educative process.* Lexington, MA: Heath.

Drago-Severson, E. (2010). *Leading adult learning: Supporting adult development in our schools.* Thousand Oaks, CA: Corwin Press.

Drobney, K. L. (2012). *Decision-making processes and developmental capacities of high-risk college students.* Unpublished doctoral dissertation. Miami University, Oxford, OH.

Heifetz, R. (1998). *Leadership without easy answers.* Cambridge, MA: Harvard University Press.

Hofer, B. K., & Pintrich, P. R. (2002). *The psychology of beliefs about knowledge and knowing.* Mahwah, NJ: Lawrence Erlbaum.

IUPUI. (n.d.). *Principles of undergraduate learning.* Retrieved May 8, 2015, from http:// studentaffairs.iupui.edu/about/assessment/learning-outcomes.shtml

Jetha, M. K., & Segalowitz, S. J. (2012). *Adolescent brain development: Implications for behavior.* Oxford, UK: Elsevier.

Kegan, R. (1994). *In over our heads: The mental demands of modern life.* Cambridge, MA: Harvard University Press.

King, P. M. (2000). Learning to make reflective judgments. In M. B. Baxter Magolda (Ed.), *Teaching to promote intellectual and personal maturity: Incorporating students' worldviews and identities into the learning process* (New Directions for Teaching and Learning, no. 82, pp. 15–26). San Francisco: Jossey-Bass.

King, P. M. (2009). Principles of development and developmental change underlying theories of cognitive and moral development. *Journal of College Student Development, 50*(6), 597–620.

King, P. M. (2010). The role of the cognitive dimension of self-authorship: An equal partner or the strong partner? In M. B. Baxter Magolda, E. G. Creamer, & P. S. Meszaros (Eds.), *Development and assessment of self-authorship: Exploring the concept across cultures* (pp. 167–185). Sterling, VA: Stylus.

King, P. M. (2015). Developmental theory. In J. Bennett (Ed.), *Encyclopedia of intercultural competence* (pp. 225–229). Thousand Oaks, CA: Sage.

King, P. M., & Baxter Magolda, M. B. (2005). A developmental model of intercultural maturity. *Journal of College Student Development, 46*(6), 571–592.

King, P. M., & Baxter Magolda, M. B. (2015). *Integrating individual and contextual factors in college student learning and development: A conceptual framework.* Manuscript in preparation.

King, P. M., Baxter Magolda, M. B., & Massé, J. (2011). Maximizing learning from engaging across difference: The role of anxiety and meaning making. *Equity & Excellence in Education, 44*(4), 468–487.

King, P. M., & Kitchener, K. S. (1994). *Developing reflective judgment: Understanding and promoting intellectual growth and critical thinking in adolescents and adults.* San Francisco: Jossey-Bass.

King, P. M., & Kitchener, K. S. (2002). The reflective judgment model: Twenty years of research on epistemic cognition. In B. K. Hofer & P. R. Pintrich (Eds.), *Personal epistemology: The psychology of beliefs about knowledge and knowing* (pp. 37–61). Mahwah, NJ: Lawrence Erlbaum.

King, P. M., & Kitchener, K. S. (2004). Reflective judgment: Theory and research on the development of epistemic assumptions through adulthood. *Educational Psychologist, 39*(1), 5–18.

King, P. M., & Kitchener, K. S. (2016). Cognitive development in the emerging adult: The emergence of complex cognitive skills. In J. Arnett (Ed.), *The Oxford handbook of emerging adulthood* (pp. 105–125). New York: Oxford University Press.

King, P. M., & Mayhew, M. J. (2002). Moral judgement development in higher education: Insights from the defining issues test. *Journal of Moral Education, 33*(3), 247–270.

King, P. M., & Mayhew, M. J. (2004). Theory and research on the development of moral reasoning among college students. *Higher education: Handbook of theory and research, XI,* (pp.375–440). Dordrecht, The Netherlands: Kluwer Academic Publishers.

Kohlberg, L. (1984). *The psychology of moral development: The nature and validation of moral stages.* San Francisco: Harper & Row.

Kuhn, D. (1991). *The skills of argument.* Cambridge, UK: Cambridge University Press.

Kuhn, D., Cheney, R., & Weinstock, M. (2000). The development of epistemological understanding. *Cognitive Development, 15*(3), 309–328.

Love, P. G., & Guthrie, V. L. (1999). (Eds.). *Understanding and applying cognitive development theory* (New Directions for Student Services, no. 88). San Francisco: Jossey-Bass.

Mezirow, J. (2000). Learning to think like an adult: Core concepts of transformation theory. *Learning as transformation: Critical perspectives on a theory in progress* (pp. 3–32). San Francisco: Jossey-Bass.

Moshman, D. (2015). *Epistemic cognition and development: The psychology of justification and truth.* New York: Psychology Press.

Overton, W. F. (2010). Life-span development: Concepts and issues. In W. F. Overton (Ed.), *Handbook of life-span development. Vol. 1, Cognition, biology and methods* (pp. 1–29). Hoboken, NJ: John Wiley and Sons.

Padilla-Walker, L. M. (2016). Moral development during emerging adulthood. In J. Arnett (Ed.), *Handbook of Emerging Adulthood* (pp. 449–463). New York: Oxford University Press.

Perez, R. J., Shim, W., King, P. M., & Baxter Magolda, M. B. (2015). Refining King and Baxter Magolda's model of intercultural maturity. *Journal of College Student Development, 56*(8), 759–776.

Perry, W. G., Jr. (1970). *Forms of intellectual and ethical development in the college years: A scheme.* New York: Holt, Rinehart & Winston.

Rest, J. R. (1986). *Moral development: Advances in research and theory.* New York: Praeger Press.

Rest, J. R., Narvaez, D., Bebeau, M. J., & Thoma, S. (1999). *Postconventional thinking: A neo-Kohlbergian approach.* Hillsdale, NJ: Lawrence Erlbaum.

Sanford, N. (1966). *Self and society.* New York: Atherton Press.

Shim, W. (2013). *Understanding college students' leadership engagement.* Unpublished doctoral dissertation. University of Michigan, Ann Arbor.

Wakefield, K. (2013). *Meaning making of adversity: Coping and self-authorship in undergraduate students.* Unpublished doctoral dissertation. University of Michigan, Ann Arbor.

West, E. J. (2004). Perry's legacy: Models of epistemological development. *Journal of Adult Development, 11,* 61–70.

Weinstock, M., & Cronin, M. (2003). The everyday production of knowledge: Individual differences in epistemological understanding and juror-reasoning skill. *Applied Cognitive Psychology, 17*(2), 161–181.

CHAPTER 11

PSYCHOSOCIAL AND IDENTITY DEVELOPMENT

Vasti Torres and Brian L. McGowan

As the field of student affairs emerged, much of the research about how college can influence student changes came from psychosocial theories that focused on foundational life-span development of individuals. This all-encompassing approach, which provided common sequences to human development, set the foundation for college student development; yet these theories were limited because they evolved from observations of homogeneous populations (Arnold & King, 1997). In spite of their origins, the concepts of these foundational theories influenced later social identity theories that better explain the diverse populations with whom we currently work in higher education and student affairs. In order to provide context for the evolutions of theories, this chapter begins with a broad overview of the purpose and goals of foundational psychosocial theories and then moves into identities theories that describe the developmental theories among a diversity of students during their college experiences.

Psychosocial Development

Psychosocial theories primarily focus on the issues that can arise at various points during the life span (Evans, 2011). There are several important principles to understanding psychosocial theories. These principles suggest that psychosocial development (1) is continuous in nature and part of the maturation process, (2) is cumulative in nature and results from life experiences, (3) occurs progressively from simpler to more complex understandings, and (4) tends to be sequential and stage-related (Miller & Winston, 1990).

The best known of the psychosocial theorists is Erik Erikson, who sought to investigate the manner in which individuals change throughout their life span with his observations of ego identity development (Sneed, Whitbourne, & Culang, 2006). Erikson (1959/1994) defined development as the formation of an ego identity that has "certain comprehensive gains which the individual, at the end of adolescence, must have derived from all of his[/her] pre-adult experience in order to be ready for the tasks of adulthood" (p. 108). These gains are often associated with the concept of identity because they describe how individuals organize and resolve conflicts between self and their own environment (Erikson, 1959/1994; Jones & Abes, 2013). Ego identity tends to focus on three interacting elements: biological characteristics, psychological needs, interests and defenses, and also the cultural environment (Kroger, 2000). Early theorists defined the various points in the life span that generate development as providing "the means by which we differentiate ourselves from other people in our lives" (Kroger, 2004, p. 10). The early work of Erikson placed development as the resolution of different conflicts dependent on age. This approach often was seen as sequential, in which individuals successfully resolved dichotomous conflicts (for example, identity versus identity diffusion) in order to gain new skills that contribute to success. Individuals who are less successful in resolving conflicts could regress to previous stages as they recycle developmental issues that frequently arise during the life span (Evans, 2011). Recent research on the life span focuses on conceptualizing these developmental tasks as a matrix (Whitbourne, Sneed, & Sayer, 2009) or as a helix with "re-formational periods" within each status (Marcia, 2002, p. 15).

From Erikson's adolescent stage of identity resolution, Chickering (1969) conducted research on the impact of the curriculum on students' development. From this research he conceived seven vectors of development that influenced the formation of identity in college students and later revised the order and names of some vectors to reflect more current research on college students (Chickering & Reisser, 1993). In the revision, the vectors were depicted as progressions through life and not necessarily linear (Chickering & Reisser, 1993). An overview of the changes from the 1969 revisions is depicted in table 11.1.

TABLE 11.1. ARTHUR CHICKERING'S VECTORS

	Chickering (1969) Vectors	Chickering and Reisser (1993) Vectors
Vector 1	Developing competence	Developing competence
Vector 2	Managing emotions	Managing emotions
Vector 3	Developing autonomy	Moving through autonomy toward interdependence
Vector 4	Establishing identity	Developing mature interpersonal relationships
Vector 5	Freeing interpersonal relationships	Establishing identity
Vector 6	Developing purpose	Developing purpose
Vector 7	Developing integrity	Developing integrity

Psychosocial theories set the foundation for more specific theories in order to understand how individuals develop. The focus on the general content of development in psychosocial theories is what limits their applicability for understanding in-depth individual development. For this reason, this chapter will now focus on more current theories that influence how students develop a sense of self.

Links between Psychosocial and Identity Theories

From these earlier psychosocial theories three major themes influenced the development of identity theories in recent years. The first is the role of late adolescence, specifically the college years and developmental tasks associated with that period in life. Second are the historical and cultural aspects that influence identity (Erikson, 1994). The final theme is the act of revisiting statuses throughout the life span. The theories covered here will include elements of all these themes.

The role of late adolescence prompted Marcia to ground his stage theory on Erikson's ideas of development in this period. Marcia initially described identity development among four statuses: foreclosure, identity diffusion, moratorium, and identity achievement (Marcia, 1966, 2002). In his later work, Marcia (2002) recognized that in adults there can be an "identity reconstruction" process (p. 15). This process typically entails an experience that produces disequilibrium and prompts the individual to enter a re-formation period that then results in reconstruction of one's identity. This reconstruction process does not create a disintegration of identity; rather, it is a revisiting of previous developmental tasks, as adults experience changes in their lives. The more recent research illustrates that developmental statuses are not static and accomplished; instead, there is a moratorium-achievement-moratorium-achievement (MAMA) reformation cycle that occurs within each status (Marcia, 2002).

The second theme illustrates the unique history and cultural values that influence identity development in the United States and are formed mainly by the societally dominant group. Tatum (1997) explained, "The dominant group holds the power and the authority in society relative to the subordinates and determines how that power and authority may be acceptably used" (p. 23). Because historically subordinate groups were seen as inferior to the dominant group, oppression of the subordinate group was acceptable. As a result, for those in the minority, the influence of oppression on how they organize their experiences becomes a more complex developmental task (Abes & Kasch, 2007; Jones & Abes, 2013; Torres, 2009; Torres, Howard-Hamilton, & Cooper, 2003).

The final theme focuses on the processes that extend beyond the adolescent years and the process of revisiting identity statuses, suggesting that identity should not be seen as linear and completed at a certain point. As the average age of college students continues to increase, it is important to consider how the years beyond adolescence can influence identity. Understanding the grounding of identity within psychosocial foundational theories assists in comprehending the links between self and others. The theories covered within this chapter are listed in table 11.2 and grouped into their common themes or populations.

TABLE 11.2. CHAPTER THEORIES AND MODELS*

Theoretical Cluster	Construct	Theorist or Scholar
Psychosocial		Erikson (1959/1994)
		Chickering (1969); Chickering and Reisser (1993)
	Identity	Marcia (1966, 2002, 2009)
Racial	Black	Cross (1971, 1995); Cross and Vandiver (2001)
		Jackson (1976, 2012)
	People of Color	Helms and Cook (1999)
	White	Helms (1990, 1994)
		Rowe, Behrens, and Leach (1995)
		LaFleur, Rowe, and Leach (2002)
	Multiracial	Renn (2004)
		Wijeyesinghe (2012)
Ethnic		Phinney (1990, 1993)
		Ruiz (1990)
	Asian	Kim (2001, 2012)
	Latino/a	Ferdman and Gallegos (2001)
		Torres and Hernández (2007)
		Gallegos and Ferdman (2012)
	American Indian	LaFromboise, Trimble, and Mohatt (1990)
		Choney, Berryhill-Paapke, and Robbins (1995)
Gender	Women	Gilligan (1982)
		Belenky, Clinchy, Goldberger, and Tarule (1986)
		Josselson (1996)
	Men	Harris (2010)
		Edwards and Jones (2009)
	Transgender	Bilodeau (2005)
Sexual Orientation	Heterosexual	Worthington (2004)
	Lesbian, Gay, Bisexual	D'Augelli (1994)
		Cass (1996)
		Fassinger (1998)
	Quare Theory	Johnson (2005)

*This table presents the theories discussed in this chapter. It is not intended to be an exhaustive list of psychosocial, racial, ethnic, gender, and sexual orientation theories and models.

The Evolution of Identity Development Theories

The formation of identity is defined at various stages of life as a balance between self and others (Kegan, 1982; Kroger, 2004). The "other" can be interpreted to include people, societal norms, and cultural expectations. It is this interplay between the self and others that sets the foundation for identity as socially constructed and vulnerable to the sociocultural influences within the context (environment) in which the individual interacts (Kroger, 2004).

The endeavors involved in creating an identity require that college students make informed decisions about vocation, relationships, influence from family, and meaningful values, which enables them to enter adult life (Kroger, 2000). The need to help students through these critical developmental tasks requires student affairs practitioners to understand how this interplay is seen when students are drawn to different organizations, courses, or events based on their feelings about the interaction between self and the campus context (Torres, Jones, & Renn, 2009). To assist in viewing commonalities and differences among the theories, table 11.3 illustrates some of the overlapping concepts.

Social Identity Theories

Many of the early theories on identity development did not account for social identities. Social identities influence who we are, how we see ourselves, and how we relate to other aspects of our lives. Within the student affairs literature, social identities are often viewed as an individual's "personally held beliefs about the self in relation to social groups (e.g., race, ethnicity, religion, sexual orientation) and the ways one expresses that relationship" (Torres, Jones, & Renn, 2009, p. 577). Table 11.3 is provided to illustrate some commonalities among racial and ethnic identity theories offered in this chapter. The next section offers an overview of racial, ethnic, gender, and sexual identity and sexual orientation theories.

Racial Identity Theories Racial identity development theories explore how individuals view themselves and others through racialized lenses. These theories are "bounded in cultural and historical meanings attached to racial categories and identities" (Renn, 2012, p. 25). Racial identity development models typically consist of developmental stages or factors that make up an individual's identity. Embedded within racial identity models is how people recognize and make meaning of racism (Cross, 1995; Kim, 2012; Torres, 2003; Torres & Hernández, 2007). Another importance aspect of these theories is identity salience—the level of importance a person places on one's race as being essential (Cross, 1995). Given the significance of racial identity salience in the identity development of diverse populations, Hurtado, Alvarado, and Guillermo-Wann (2015) encouraged institutions to recognize and understand how racial identity salience is "fostered or diminished during the college years" (p. 129).

TABLE 11.3. COMMONALITIES AMONG RACIAL AND ETHNIC IDENTITY DEVELOPMENTAL THEORIES

	Identity diffusion	Foreclosure		Moratorium		Identity achievement	
Marcia (1966)	Identity diffusion	Foreclosure		Moratorium		Identity achievement	
Women Josselson (1996)	Drifters	Guardians		Searchers		Pathmakers	
Theory of Nigrescence (Cross, 1971, 1995)		Pre-Encounter	Encounter	Immersion-emersion		Internalization	Internalization-commitment
People of Color Racial Identity (Helms & Cook, 1999)	Status 1: Conformity		Status 2: Dissonance	Status 3: Immersion	Status 4: Emersion	Status 5: Internalization	Status 6: Integrated awareness
Kim (2001)	Ethnic Awareness/ white identified		Awakening to social political awareness	Redirection to an Asian American consciousness		Incorporation	
Ruiz (1990)	Causal		Cognitive	Consequences	Working through	Successful resolution	
Phinney (1993)	Unexamined ethnic identity		Ethnic identity search (moratorium)			Achieved ethnic identity	
Jackson (2012)	Naive		Acceptance	Resistance		Redefinition	Internalization
Torres & Hernández (2007)	Defined by external formulations (geography, family, stereotypes)		Understanding of positive and negative cultural choices	Integration of cultural choices into an informed Latino identity		Illustrates culture in behaviors and choices	

Black Identity Theories   Theories centered on black identity describe process-es that explain the way a person thinks, feels, and acts in reference to being black (Cross & Vandiver, 2001). Cross originally conceived his nigrescence theory with five stages; in 1995 he revised his theory to better incorporate cultural, social, psychological, and historical changes that occurred since his initial conception of the theory. Cross's revised theory also considers issues of race salience, reference group orientation, and social identity awareness by ex-panding the nigrescence model as themes of various exemplars of black racial identity attitudes—pre-encounter, immersion-emersion, and internalization—instead of developmental stages (Cross & Vandiver, 2001). Pre-encounter de-scribes individuals with attitudes or low racial identity salience attributed to being black. Immersion-emersion depicts individuals with an identity in a state of transition. Internalization occurs when an individual is comfortable being black and views race as being positive. In the expanded nigrescence model, individuals can hold multiple attitudes concurrently and to varying degrees across the three thematic categories (Cross & Vandiver, 2001). Helms (1990) also created a theory of black racial identity development by modifying and extending Cross's original nigrescence model resulting in four statuses (pre-encounter, encounter, immersion/emersion, internalization), with each one having two bimodal forms of expression. Jackson (1976, 2012) extended the conversation by creating a black identity development (BID) model. The BID stages are naive, acceptance, resistance, redefinition, and internalization. This newer version of the BID model offers important insights on racial identity development and conceptualizes it as "an interweaving of both the effects of racism and elements that are part of a heritage of Black culture that exists in-dependently, to varying degrees, of the primary influence of racism" (Jackson, 2012, p. 39). For instance, in the internalization stage, Jackson emphasizes the role of intersectionality in the conceptualization of BID. Of note, although developed independent of one another, Cross's and Jackson's models share many of the same concepts.

One common theme among these theories is the process of changing from low race salience to more complex understandings of race. Despite the linear processes embedded in these theories, they help student affairs educa-tors understand the dynamics of black identity development and the reasons black students may or may not group with other students who look like them for support when navigating the campus, some of which could be linked to their racial identity development (see table 11.3).

White Identity Theories   Whiteness is a privileged identity rooted within centu-ries of oppression of nonwhite groups (McDermott & Samson, 2005). White identity theories focus on the attitudes that whites possess regarding people of color rather than attitudes about their own race (Rowe, Behrens, & Leach, 1995). The developmental process that needs to occur is the understand-ing and acknowledgment of privilege that comes from being in the majority (Helms, 1990). Helms's white racial identity theory (1990, 1994) illustrates two phases, each of which has three statuses. Essentially, Helms argued that a healthy white racial identity involves overcoming the influence of racism, embracing the sociopolitical nature of whiteness, and identifying as a racial being while understanding the value of racial diversity.

Another way of thinking about the racial outlook of white people is through the white racial consciousness approach (LaFleur, Rowe, & Leach, 2002; Leach, Behrens, & LaFleur, 2002). The conceptual model of white racial consciousness categorizes the racial attitudes whites possess toward people of color. This approach emerged in response to concerns about previous white racial identity development models that were deemed as "being prescriptive and highly abstract" (LaFleur, Rowe, & Leach, 2002, p. 148). The original model conceived white racial consciousness through four types of attitudes: dominative, pro-white ethno-centric attitudes; conflictive, attitudes based on individualistic values but not supportive of overt discrimination; integrative, pragmatic, positive racial attitudes; and reactive strong pro-minority attitudes (Rowe, Behrens, & Leach, 1995). The revised white racial consciousness approach has a social justice orientation and consists of two basic constructs: racial acceptance and racial justice (LaFleur, Rowe, & Leach, 2002). White racial identity development models and approaches are helpful to student affairs educators seeking to engage white students in conversations about race and privilege in a meaningful way.

Multiracial Identity Theories   Increased attention has been devoted to the growing population of students who enter postsecondary institutions identifying with more than one racial group (Osei-Kofi, 2012; Wijeyesinghe, 2012). Despite this increased attention to multiraciality (Osei-Kofi, 2012), higher education research and scholarship tends to ignore multiracial students' experiences resulting in unanswered questions about how these students experience college. A potential explanation for this oversight can be linked to the social construction of race and how it is typically constructed within monoracial categories (Delgado & Stefancic, 2011).

Educators have begun using various approaches to understand the identity development for multiracial college student populations. Renn (2004) used an ecological approach to develop five patterns of biracial and multiracial identity among college students—monoracial identity, multiple monoracial identities, multiracial identity, extraracial identity, and situational identity. The context of college peer culture was found to be a critical aspect of multiracial students' identity development. Even though some students in Renn's study moved easily among identity-based social groups, there was a clear delineation among groups for others, and membership in one group precluded membership in another.

Extending the research on multiracial students, Wijeyesinghe (2001) offered a factor model of multiracial identity development that included racial ancestry, early experience and socialization, physical appearance, other social identities, religion, cultural attachment, political awareness and orientation, and social and historical context. Within this model, individuals may decide to change their identity "based on which factor or set of factors underlies this choice at any given point" (Wijeyesinghe, 2012, p. 92). Student affairs educators should move beyond thinking of multiracial students as a monolithic group and recognize how institutional policies and practices may be designed to marginalize these students. For instance, institutional documents often ask for demographic information that forces students to check a box that may not completely capture their multiracial identity.

Ethnic Identity Theories   Research focused on ethnic identity highlights three elements that assist in understanding the experiences of individuals. These elements are social identity, acculturation and cultural conflict, and identity formation (Phinney, 1990). Although social identity theory would interpret membership in the group as sufficient for a positive sense of belonging, issues of power and oppression associate some groups with potentially negative images. These negative images may encourage individuals from ethnic groups to seek out being part of the majority. The acculturation and cultural conflict element focuses on how the minority (or immigrant) relates to the dominant majority culture. This includes the concept of the "tension between how an individual is expected to be and how the person wants to be perceived as an ethnic being" (Kim, 2012, p. 139). The third element more explicitly addresses ethnic identity formation, which acknowledges the dynamic nature of ethnic identity and the influences that occur as a result of time and context (Phinney, 1990).

Asian American Identity Theories   The division between race and ethnicity is not always clear with groups such as Asian Americans. The diversity within this pan-ethnic category enables many Asian Americans to fit the definition of race as an "externally ascribed reference group" (Helms, 1990), yet other members of this group are more likely to resemble definitions of ethnicity.

Asian American identity revolves around the resolution of racial conflicts faced as "Americans of Asian ancestry in a predominantly White society" (Kim, 2001, p. 67). To further clarify the differences between race and ethnic identity Kim changed the name of her theory from the Asian American identity development theory (AAID) to Asian American racial identity development (AARID) (Kim, 2012) to describe the process used for Asian Americans to achieve a positive identity. There are five stages in this theory with stage 1 focused on level of ethnic awareness. Family and the racial composition of the community around the person is the main influence in this stage. Stage 2 is white identification and there are two variations that can occur within this stage—active or passive white identified. The third stage focuses on awakening to social political consciousness, which indicates a shifting worldview and understanding that the Asian American is not responsible for the racism against

Asians. Stage 4 is redirection to an Asian American consciousness, and the final stage is incorporation (see table 11.3).

A research study found that Asian Americans had a "relatively high level of color-blind racial attitudes and low racism-related stress" (Chen, LePhuoc, Guzmán, Rude, & Dodd, 2006, p. 474). Though this finding was unexpected, it does highlight the various ways individuals can view their racial or ethnic identity.

Latino/a Identity Development   Several models of Latino ethnic identity use a strong acculturation framework and therefore provide categorical types in which to place Latinos' cultural orientation (Felix-Ortiz de la Garza, Newcomb, & Myers, 1995; Ferdman & Gallegos, 2001; Gallegos & Ferdman, 2012; Keefe & Padilla, 1987; Torres, 1999). These theories describe Latinos in categories by level of acculturation to the majority culture and pride in their ethnic culture of origin (Torres & Delgado-Romero, 2008) and represent orientations such as bicultural (cultural blending), Latino oriented (Latino identified), American identified (Anglo oriented), or marginal (not fitting in) (Torres & Delgado-Romero, 2008). The recent thinking by Gallegos and Ferdman (2012) frames the ethno-racial identity orientations as adaptive strategies and incorporate external forces that "highlight the dynamic and adaptive utility of each orientation" (p. 64).

The more developmental theories focus on the influences Latinos' experience in their ethnic identity formation such as how family influences sense of identity. Ruiz (1990) conceptualized five stages from case studies in his counseling practice. The stages include causal, cognitive, consequence, working through, and successful resolution. These stages have some similarity (see table 11.3) to other racial and ethnic theories because the person moves from negative images of being Latino to a greater acceptance of self, Latino culture, and his or her ethnicity (Torres & Delgado-Romero, 2008).

Extending the research about the journey toward self-authorship, Torres and Hernández (2007) found that Latino/a college students face additional developmental tasks during the college years. Perhaps the most important of these tasks is the recognition of racism and the ability to make meaning of how racism influences Latino identity development. Although Latinos may understand that racism exists, it is not until an individual has to face racism against himself or herself (or his or her culture) that the reality of oppression truly influences his or her identity (Torres & Hernández, 2007). In their matrix of holistic development the intrapersonal dimension is focused on identity and views the developmental process as moving from external formulations through a process of understanding how stereotypes and cultural choices come together to create an informed Latino identity (Torres & Hernández, 2007) (see table 11.3). Understanding the conditions described in the theories (for example, environment in hometown, family composition, generation in the United States, or experiences with racism [Torres, 2003]) can help student affairs practitioners initiate conversations with students that are culturally sensitive and focused on what is happening with the student.

American Indians and Native American Identity   In spite of attempts to assimilate and destroy native culture, American Indians "insist on surviving on their own terms" (Lomawaima & McCarty, 2002, p. 281). This includes maintaining their native culture, language, and values. At the core of Indian values are communal concerns (adherence to tradition), responsibility for family and friends, cooperation, and tribal identification (LaFromboise, Heyle, & Ozer, 1990). These values can at times be in conflict with the majority values of individualism, competitiveness, and amassing property and titles.

American Indians possess varying degrees of acculturation to the majority culture that influences the self-identification and the development of American Indian college students. Horse (2012) discusses American Indian identity by identifying factors that influence individual and group identities. There are two models that can help practitioners understand the factors that influence American Indian college students. The first is the five categories of Indianness: traditional, transitional, marginal, assimilated, and bicultural (LaFromboise, Trimble, & Mohatt, 1990). Similar to the Latino identity models, these categories focus on the level of acculturation and maintenance of ethnic identity the individual exhibits. The second is the health model conceptualization of acculturation, which represents four areas of human personality that are in harmony "with the domains of the medicine wheel (a uniquely Indian means of conceptualizing the human condition based on four essential elements)" (Choney, Berryhill-Paapke, & Robbins, 1995, p. 85). The four areas of human personality are behavioral, social and environmental, affective and spiritual, and cognitive. Within these areas are concentric circles, with each perimeter of the circle representing a different level of acculturation: traditional, transitional, bicultural, assimilated, and marginal. There is no value judgment "placed on any level of acculturation, nor is any dimension of personality emphasized more than another" (p. 85). Understanding the categories of Indianness without placing a value on them can help student affairs practitioners engage American Indian students in conversations about their interactions.

Gender Identity

Beginning at birth, human beings learn to understand themselves in gendered ways that inform how they engage one another in their daily lives. Most individuals are socialized to understand gender as a binary identity (man or woman) with stereotypical traits, expressions, norms, and behaviors attached to each. Educators are learning that this binary thinking on gender draws from and contributes to sexism, genderism, and homophobia (Gilbert, 2009). Given the complexities of gender, it is helpful for educators to understand the multiple ways individuals identify, including cisgender, agender, trans*gender, and genderqueer, to name a few. Understanding these complexities is essential in order to foster inclusive and welcoming environments for people of all/no gender identities within higher education. This section will review the extant literature on gender identity development among women, men, and trans* students.

Women's Identity Development   Scholars have raised questions regarding the developmental trajectories of women. Josselson's longitudinal study (1996) revealed the ways that women develop their identities during the college years and beyond. Based on the reformulation of Marcia's (1966) work, Josselson (1996) created a theory of identity development in women that places them in four identity categories—drifters, guardians, searchers, and pathmakers. Josselson found in her work that the degree to which the women deviated from or remained connected to the value systems of their parents—especially their mothers—largely determined their identities. In Gilligan's text, *In a Different Voice: Psychological Theory and Women's Development* (1982), she proposed a model of moral development composed of three levels and two transition periods. Within this work, Gilligan revealed that women perceive care and responsibility to others as their moral foundation and define themselves within the context of their intimate relationships. Based on Gilligan's (1982) influence, Belenky, Clinchy, Goldberger, and Tarule, (1986) examined the epistemological beliefs and meaning-making capacities of women from diverse socioeconomic backgrounds and identified five knowledge perspectives "ways of knowing"—silence, received knowledge, subjective knowledge, procedural knowledge, and constructed knowledge.

What these models have in common is their emphasis on women's development from accepting societal norms about being women, to experiencing crises that enable them to question traditional roles, and eventually to growing toward a final truce between societal gender expectations and the individuals' desire to actively change the way women are seen in society. Though these theories contribute to our early understandings and sensemaking of women's identity development, scholars have critiqued these works for their lack of attention to the experiences of women of color.

Men's Identity Development   Although much of the early student development theories were centered on the experiences of heterosexual, middle-class, white men, it is important to note that these early scholars did not consider them as gendered beings in their empirical investigations (Harper & Harris, 2010). However, in the last two decades, scholarship on college men's identity development has grown considerably (Harper & Harris, 2010). Harris (2010) developed a conceptual model that included college men's meanings of masculinities (participants' gender-related attitudes, beliefs, and assumptions); contextual influences (influences that shape, reinforce, and challenge participants' meanings); and male-gendered norms (norms that represent the outcomes of the interactions between variables of the model). Harris's findings reveal that masculinities had obvious influences on men's friendship decisions and overall college experiences. This is consistent with Edwards and Jones's (2009) grounded theory study of men's gender-identity development, which is conceptualized as "a process of interacting with society's expectations by learning these expectations, putting on a mask to conform with these expectations, wearing the mask, and struggling to begin to take off the mask" (p. 214). Harris and Edwards (2010) acknowledged the consequences associated with external pressures and expectations shaping how men perform hegemonic masculinity in their respective studies. More recent investigations have explored the gendered experiences of men of color (Dancy, 2012; Harris, Palmer, & Struve, 2011) across multiple institutional types, which offer key insights into how they conceptualize and perform gender in college.

Trans* Student Identity Development   Despite increased scholarly attention to gender identity development in the higher education literature, trans* student identities and experiences are often neglected and ignored. Trans* identities are frequently grouped with sexual orientation as the lesbian, gay, bisexual, and transgender (LGBT) moniker implies. However, *transgender* "describes a broad range of individuals whose gender identity differs from their biological sex assignment and societal norms for gender expression" (Renn & Bilodeau, 2011, p. 59). The term *trans** is used to include "a wide range of identities, appearances, and behaviors that blur or cross gender lines" (Marine & Catalano, 2014, p. 136). To date, few frameworks and empirical studies on transgender students are available and there is a dire need for more scholarship that raises important questions about their collegiate experiences. Based on D'Augelli's lesbian, gay, and bisexual identity framework (1994), Bilodeau (2005) created a framework for trans* college student identity development, which involves exiting a traditionally gendered identity to entering a trans* community. Beemyn and Rankin's (2011) study on transgender diversity offers important insights into the experiences and perspectives on transgender life. Based on nearly 3,500 participants, Beemyn and Rankin discovered distinct differences in how participants experienced their gendered identities and how they came to see themselves as transgender.

Given institutional barriers and challenges facing trans* students, understanding the appropriate terminology coupled with adopting policies, procedures, and practices that are inclusive of individuals of all gender identities and expressions are paramount. It is important for educators to help reduce gender inequities while transgressing binaries in higher education practice. A helpful resource to help student affairs educators understand legal and policy issues is the Transgender Law and Policy Institute (www.transgenderlaw.org/).

Sexual Identity and Sexual Orientation

Scholars have increasingly acknowledged the complexity and multidimensional nature of sexual identity development among heterosexual and lesbian, gay, and bisexual (LGB) identified individuals. Though earlier writings in student affairs treated the terms *sexual identity* and *sexual orientation* interchangeably, it is important to differentiate these two constructs. Sexual identity is a broader construct that does include sexual orientation but that also "reflect a person's sexual values, sexual needs, preferred modes of sexual expression, preferences for characteristics of sexual partners and preferences for sexual activities" (Worthington, 2004, p. 742).

Heterosexual Identity In the United States, heterosexuality is the privileged sexual orientation and is assumed from birth. Given the assumption of heterosexuality coupled with the fact that heterosexuals constitute the majority, scholarship on heterosexual identity development is scant (Worthington, Savoy, Dillon, & Vernaglia, 2002). Worthington, Savoy, Dillon, and Vernaglia (2002) proposed a model that explores psychological and social factors that influence the heterosexual identity development process. This model has two interactive process components (internal and external sexual identity process) that occur within five identity development statuses ranging from *unexplored commitment* to *synthesis* (Worthington, Savoy, Dillon, & Vernaglia, 2002). *Unexplored commitment* reflects familial and societal gender roles and sexual behaviors that are assumed as part of the privileged identity. *Active exploration* is when an individual is involved in purposeful exploration, evaluation, and experimentation (processes that can be cognitive or behavioral). *Diffusion* occurs when a person does not engage in either commitment or exploration. *Deepening and commitment* occurs when an individual moves toward making a committed choice. *Synthesis* occurs when an individual demonstrates congruence among all aspects of his or her identity. This model should be thought of as "flexible, fluid descriptions of statuses that people may pass through as they develop their sexual identity" (Worthington, Savoy, Dillon, & Vernaglia, 2002, p. 512).

Worthington's work has been criticized for insufficiently considering gender processes that are contextually based and that shape men and women differently in relation to how heterosexual identity develops (Gilbert & Rader, 2002). Morgan (2011) used Worthington, Savoy, Dillon, and Vernaglia's (2002) model to classify and describe college students' narratives on heterosexual identity development and found variations and systematic gender-based differences in college students' heterosexual identity development. Most participants in Morgan's study described identity commitment with passive exploration, and few described active exploration without commitment, unexplored commitment, and identity diffusion.

Lesbian, Gay, and Bisexual (LGB) Identity Over the past three decades, a burgeoning body of research has begun delineating lesbian, gay, and bisexual (LGB) college students' experiences and identities. One common theme embedded in this literature is the discrimination and marginalization these students continue to face when negotiating the campus environment (Rankin, Weber, Blumenfeld, & Frazer, 2010). Furthermore, Renn and Bilodeau (2011) revealed that "the integration of LGB identity may also be more complicated for individuals who are in racial and ethnic minority groups, participate in conservative religious traditions, are from working-class families, or are people with disabilities" (p. 57). In 1996, Cass revised her identity development model and introduced potential pathways leading to either movement to the next stage or foreclosure at the current stage. In contrast to the stage models, D'Augelli (1994) employed a life-span approach to LGB identity that considers cultural and individual differences. Specifically, D'Augelli offered three sets of interrelated variables involved in identity formation—personal actions and subjectivities, interactive intimacies, and sociohistorical connections—and six interactive identity processes that include exiting heterosexuality to entering an LGB community. Fassinger (1998) extended the conversation in her model of lesbian and gay identity development, which represents two parallel processes of identity formation: one involving an internal process of awareness and identification and one involving group membership identity relating to one's role in the lesbian or gay community.

Newer empirical studies have adopted critical approaches to understand the experiences of students of color across multiple institutional contexts. For instance, using queer theory, Patton (2011) found that African American men at a historically black institution encountered challenges when publicly expressing their sexual identities. Similarly, Means and Jaeger (2013) used quare theory (Johnson, 2005) to investigate the experiences of black gay men attending historically black colleges and universities and found that these students internalized homophobia during their coming-out processes (Means & Jaeger, 2013). These studies illustrate how gay and bisexual men face significant challenges negotiating the college environment. If postsecondary educators aim to support LGB students, having knowledge of sexual identity theories is essential.

Conclusion

Since the early theories of psychosocial development, more current identity theories have emerged to provide interpretations of how diverse students develop their sense of self. Although new thinking on student development theory is moving away from a developmental emphasis to focus on systemic oppressions and inequitable power structures, understanding the early theories of psychosocial and identity development is both necessary and important as they undergird the student affairs profession. Through these theories, educators and practitioners are better able to understand the experiences of students and assist them in the meaning-making process critical to development.

Discussion Questions

1. What developmental tasks influence your sense of self?
2. Are your tasks similar or different from others who have a different background?
3. How could psychosocial and identity development theories influence how you do your work?

References

Abes, E. S., & Kasch, D. (2007). Using queer theory to explore lesbian college students' multiple dimensions of identity. *Journal of College Student Development, 48*, 619–636.

Arnold, K., & King, I. C. (1997). *College student development and academic life psychological, intellectual, social, and moral issues.* New York: Garland Publishing.

Beemyn, G., & Rankin, S. (2011). *The lives of transgender people.* New York: Columbia University Press.

Belenky, M., Clinchy, B. M., Goldberger, N. R., & Tarule, J. M. (1986). *Women's ways of knowing: The development of self, voice, and mind.* New York: Basic Books.

Bilodeau, B. (2005). Beyond the gender binary: A case study of two transgender students at a Midwestern research university. *Journal of Gay & Lesbian Issues in Education, 3*(1), 29–44.

Cass, V. (1996). Sexual orientation identity formation: A western phenomenon. In R. P. Cabaj & T. S.Stein (Eds.), *Textbook of homosexuality and mental health* (pp. 227–251). Washington, DC: American Psychiatric Press.

Chen, G. A., LePhuoc, P., Guzmán, M. R., Rude, S. S., & Dodd, B. G. (2006). Exploring Asian American racial identity. *Cultural Diversity and Ethnic Minority Psychology, 12*(3), 461–476.

Chickering, A. (1969). *Education and identity.* San Francisco: Jossey-Bass.

Chickering, A., & Reisser, L. (1993). *Education and identity* (2nd ed.). San Francisco: Jossey-Bass.

Choney, S. K., Berryhill-Paapke, E., & Robbins, R. R. (1995). The acculturation of American Indians: Developing frameworks for research and practice. In J. G. Ponterotto, J. M. Casas, L. A. Suzuki, & C. M.Alexander (Eds.), *Handbook of multicultural counseling* (pp. 73–92). Thousand Oaks, CA: Sage.

Cross, W. E. (1971). Toward a psychology of black liberation: The negro-to-black conversion experience. *Black World, 20*(9), 13–27.

Cross, W. E. (1995). The psychology of nigrescence: Revising the Cross model. In J. G. Ponterotto, J. M. Casas, L. A. Suzuki, & C. M. Alexander (Eds.), *Handbook of multicultural counseling* (pp. 93–122). Thousand Oaks, CA: Sage.

Cross, W. E., & Vandiver, B. J. (2001). Nigrescence theory and measurement: Introducing the Cross racial identity scale (CRIS). In J. G. Ponterotto, J. M. Casas, L. A. Suzuki, & C. M. Alexander (Eds.), *Handbook of multicultural counseling* (pp. 371–393). Thousand Oaks, CA: Sage.

Dancy, T. E. (2012). *The brother code: Manhood and masculinity among African American men in college.* Charlotte, NC: Information Age Publishing.

D'Augelli, A. R. (1994). Identity development and sexual orientation: Toward a model of lesbian, gay, and bisexual development. In E. J. Trickett, R. J. Watts, & D. Birman (Eds.), *Human diversity perspectives on people in context* (pp. 312–333). San Francisco: Jossey-Bass.

Delgado, R., & Stefancic, J. (2011). *Critical race theory: An introduction* (2nd ed.). New York: New York University Press

Edwards, K. E., & Jones, S. R. (2009). "Putting my man face on": A grounded theory of college men's gender identity development. *Journal of College Student Development, 50,* 210–228.

Erikson, E. H. (1994). *Identity and the life cycle.* New York: W. W. Norton & Company. (Originally published in 1959)

Evans, N. J. (2011). Psychosocial and cognitive-structural perspectives on student development. In J. H. Schuh, S. R. Jones, & S. R. Harper (Eds.), *Student services a handbook for the profession* (5th ed., pp. 168–186). San Francisco: Jossey-Bass.

Fassinger, R. E. (1998). Lesbian, gay, and bisexual identity and student development theory. In R. L. Sanlo (Ed.), *Working with lesbian, gay, bisexual, and transgender college students: A handbook for faculty and administrators* (pp. 13–22). Westport, CT: Greenwood Press.

Felix-Ortiz de la Garza, M., Newomb, M. D., & Myers, H. F. (1995). A multidimensional measure of cultural identity for Latino and Latina adolescents. In A. M. Padilla (Ed.), *Hispanic psychology: Critical issues in theory and research* (pp. 30–42). Thousand Oaks, CA: Sage.

Ferdman, B. M., & Gallegos, P. I. (2001). Racial identity development and Latinos in the United States. In C. L. Wijeyesinghe & B. W. Jackson III (Eds.), *New perspectives on racial identity development: A theoretical and practical anthology* (pp. 32–66). New York: New York University Press.

Gallegos, P. I., & Ferdman, B. M. (2012). Racial identity development and Latinos in the United States. In C. L. Wijeyesinghe & B. W. Jackson III (Eds.), *New perspectives on racial identity development: Integrating emerging frameworks* (2nd ed., pp. 51–80). New York: New York University Press.

Gilbert, M. A. (2009). Defeating bigenderism: Changing gender assumptions in the twenty-first century. *Hypatia, 24*(3), 93–112.

Gilbert, L. A., & Rader, L. (2002). The missing discourse of gender? *The Counseling Psychologist, 30,* 567–574.

Gilligan, C. (1982) *In a different voice: Psychological theory and women's development.* Cambridge, MA: Harvard University Press.

Harper, S. R., & Harris, F., III (Eds.). (2010). *College men and masculinities: Theory, research and implications for practice.* San Francisco: Jossey-Bass.

Harris, F., III (2010). College men's conceptualizations of masculinities and contextual influences: Toward a conceptual model. *Journal of College Student Development, 51*(3), 297–318.

Harris, F., III, & Edwards, K. (2010). College men's experiences as men: Findings from two grounded theory studies. *Journal of Student Affairs Research and Practice, 47*(1), 43–62.

Harris, F., III, Palmer, R. T., & Struve, L. E. (2011). Cool posing on campus: A qualitative study of masculinities and gender expression among black men at private research institution. *Journal of Negro Education, 80*(1), 47–62.

Helms, J. E. (1990). *Black and white racial identity theory, research, and practice.* Westport, CT: Praeger.

Helms, J. E. (1994). The conceptualization of racial identity and other "racial" constructs. In E. J. Trickett, R. J. Watts, & D. Birman (Eds.), *Human diversity perspectives on people in context* (pp. 285–311). San Francisco: Jossey-Bass.

Helms, J. E., & Cook, D. A. (1999). *Using race and culture in counseling and psychotherapy: Theory and process.* Boston: Allyn & Bacon.

Horse, P. G. (2012). Twenty-first century Native American consciousness. In C. L. Wijeyesinghe & B.W. Jackson III (Eds.), *New perspectives on racial identity development: Integrating emerging frameworks* (2nd ed., pp. 108–120). New York: New York University Press.

Hurtado, S., Alvarado, A. R., & Guillermo-Wann, C. (2015). Thinking about race: The salience of racial identity at two- and four-year colleges and the climate for diversity. *Journal of Higher Education, 86*(1), 127–155.

Jackson, B. W., III (1976). Black identity development. In L. H. Golubchick & B. Persky (Eds.), *Urban social and educational issues* (pp. 158–164). Dubuque, IA: Kendall Hunt.

Jackson, B. W., III (2012). Black identity development: Influences of culture and social oppression. In C. L. Wijeyesinghe & B. W. Jackson III (Eds.), *New perspectives on racial identity development: Integrating emerging frameworks* (2nd ed., pp. 33–50). New York: New York University Press.

Johnson, E. P. (2005). "Quare" studies, or (almost) everything I know about queer studies I learned from my grandmother. In E. P. Johnson & M. G. Henderson, *Black queer studies* (pp. 124–157). Durham, NC: Duke University Press.

Jones, S. R., & Abes, E. S. (2013). *Identity development of college students: Advancing frameworks for multiple dimensions of identity.* San Francisco: Jossey Bass.

Josselson, R. (1996). *Revising herself: The story of women's identity from college to midlife.* New York: Oxford University Press.

Keefe, S. E., & Padilla, A. M. (1987). *Chicano ethnicity.* Albuquerque: University of New Mexico Press.

Kegan, R. K. (1982). *The evolving self: Problem and process in human development.* Cambridge, MA: Harvard University Press.

Kim, J. (2001). Asian American identity development theory. In C. L. Wijeyesinghe & B. W. Jackson III (Eds.), *New perspectives on racial identity development: A theoretical and practical anthology* (pp. 67–90). New York: New York University Press.

Kim, J. (2012). Asian American racial identity development theory. In C. L. Wijeyesinghe & B. W. Jackson III (Eds.), *New perspectives on racial identity development: Integrating emerging frameworks* (pp. 138–160). New York: New York University Press.

Kroger, J. (2000). *Identity development adolescence through adulthood.* Thousand Oaks, CA: Sage.

Kroger, J. (2004). *Identity and adolescence: The balance between self and other* (3rd ed.). London: Routledge.

LaFleur, N. K., Rowe, W., & Leach, M. M. (2002). Reconceptualizing white racial consciousness. *Journal of Multicultural Counseling and Development, 30,* 148–152.

LaFromboise, T. D., Heyle, A. M., & Ozer, E. J. (1990). Changing and diverse roles of women in American Indian cultures. *Sex Roles, 22*(7/8), 455–476.

LaFromboise, T. D., Trimble, J. E., & Mohatt, G. V. (1990). Counseling intervention and American Indian tradition: An integrative approach. *The Counseling Psychologist, 8*(4), 628–654.

Leach, M. M., Behrens, J. T., & LaFleur, N. K. (2002). White racial identity and white racial consciousness: Similarities, differences, and recommendations. *Journal of Multicultural Counseling and Development, 30,* 66–80.

Lomawaima, K. T., & McCarty, T. L. (2002). When tribal sovereignty challenges democracy: American Indian education and the democratic ideal. *American Educational Research Journal, 39*(2), 279–305.

Marcia, J. E. (1966). Development and validation of ego identity status. *Journal of Personality and Social Psychology, 3,* 551–558.

Marcia, J. E. (2002). Identity and psychosocial development in adulthood. *Identity: An International Journal of Theory and Research, 2*(1), 7–28.

Marine, S. B., & Catalano, D.C.J. (2014). Engaging trans* students on college and university campuses. In S. J. Quaye & S. R. Harper (Eds.), *Student engagement in higher education: Theoretical approaches and practical approaches for diverse populations* (pp. 135–148). New York: Routledge.

McDermott, M., & Samson, F. L. (2005). White racial and ethnic identity in the United States. *Annual Review of Sociology, 31,* 245–261.

Means, D. R., & Jaeger, A. J. (2013). Black in the rainbow: "Quaring" the black gay male student experience at historically black universities. *Journal of African American Males in Education, 4*(2), 124–140.

Miller, T. K., & Winston, R. B., Jr. (1990). Assessing development from a psychosocial perspective. In D. G. Creamer (Ed.), *College student development: Theory and practice for the 1990s* (pp. 99–126). Lanham, MD: University Press of America and American College Personnel Association.

Morgan, E. M. (2011). Not always a straight path: College students' narratives of heterosexual identity development. *Sex Roles, 66*(1–2), 79–93.

Osei-Kofi, N. (2012). Identity, fluidity, and groupism: The construction of multiraciality in education discourse. *Review of Education, Pedagogy, and Cultural Studies, 34*(5), 245–257.

Patton, L. D. (2011). Perspectives on identity, disclosure and the campus environment among African American gay and bisexual men at one historically black college. *Journal of College Student Development, 52*(1), 77–100.

Phinney, J. S. (1990). Ethnic identity in adolescents and adults: Review of research. *Psychological Bulletin, 108*(3), 499–514.

Phinney, J. S. (1993). A three-stage model of ethnic identity development in adolescence. In M. E. Bernal & G. P. Knight (Eds.), *Ethnic identity formation and transmission among Hispanic and other minorities* (pp. 61–79). Albany: State University of New York Press.

Rankin, S., Weber, G., Blumenfeld, W., & Frazer, S. (2010). *2010 state of higher education for lesbian, gay, bisexual & transgender people.* Charlotte, NC: Campus Pride.

Renn, K. A. (2004). *Mixed race students in college: The ecology of race, identity, and community.* Albany: State University of New York Press.

Renn, K. A. (2012). Creating and re-creating race: The emergence of racial identity as a critical element in psychological, sociological, and ecological perspectives on human development. In C. L. Wijeyesinghe & B. W. Jackson III (Eds.), *New perspectives on racial identity development: Integrating emerging frameworks* (2nd ed., pp. 11–22). New York: New York University Press.

Renn, K. A., & Bilodeau, B. L. (2011). LGBT identity development theories. In B. J. Bank (Ed.), *Gender and higher education* (pp. 55–62). Baltimore: Johns Hopkins University Press.

Rowe, W., Behrens, J. T., & Leach, M. M. (1995). Racial/ethnic identity and racial consciousness: Looking back and looking forward. In J. G. Ponterotto, J. M. Casas, L. A. Suzuki, & C. M. Alexander (Eds.), *Handbook of multicultural counseling* (2nd ed., pp. 218–235). Thousand Oaks, CA: Sage.

Ruiz, A. S. (1990). Ethnic identity: Crisis and resolution. *Journal of Multicultural Counseling and Development, 18*, 29–40.

Sneed, J. R., Whitbourne, S. K., & Culang, M. E. (2006). Trust, identity, and ego integrity: Modeling Erikson's core stages over 34 years. *Journal of Adult Development, 13*, 148–157.

Tatum, B. D. (1997). *Why are all the black kids sitting together in the cafeteria?* New York: Basic Books.

Thompson, C. E., & Carter, R. T. (1997). *Racial identity theory applications to individual, group, and organizational interventions.* Mahwah, NJ: Lawrence Erlbaum.

Torres, V. (1999). Validation of a bicultural orientation model for Hispanic college students. *Journal of College Student Development, 40*(3), 285–299.

Torres, V. (2003). Influences on ethnic identity development of Latino college students in the first two years of college. *Journal of College Student Development, 44*, 532–547.

Torres, V. (2009). The developmental dimensions of recognizing racism. *Journal of College Student Development, 50*(5), 504–520.

Torres, V., & Delgado-Romero, E. (2008). Defining Latino/a identity through late adolescent development. In K. L. Kraus (Ed.), *Lifespan development theories in action: A case study approach for counseling professionals* (pp. 363–388). Boston: Lahaska Press Houghton Mifflin.

Torres, V., & Hernández, E. (2007). The influence of ethnic identity on self-authorship: A longitudinal study of Latino/a college students. *Journal of College Student Development, 48,* 558–573.

Torres, V., Howard-Hamilton, M., & Cooper, D. L. (2003). Identity development of diverse populations: Implications for teaching and practice. *ASHE/ERIC Higher Education Report, 29.* San Francisco: Jossey Bass.

Torres, V., Jones, S. R., & Renn, K. A. (2009). Identity development theories in student affairs: Origins, current status, and new approaches. *Journal of College Student Development, 50,* 577–596.

Whitbourne, S., Sneed, J., & Sayer, A. (2009). Psychosocial development from college through midlife: A 34-year sequential study. *Developmental Psychology, 45*(5), 1328–1340.

Wijeyesinghe, C. L. (2001). Racial identity in multiracial people: An alternative paradigm. In C. L. Wijeyesinghe & B. W. Jackson III (Eds.), *New perspectives on racial identity development: A theoretical and practical anthology* (pp. 129–152). New York: New York University Press.

Wijeyesinghe, C. L. (2012). The intersectional model of multiracial identity: Integrating multiracial identity theories and intersectional perspectives on social identity. In C. L. Wijeyesinghe & B. W. Jackson III (Eds.), *New perspectives on racial identity development: Integrating emerging frameworks* (2nd ed., pp. 81–107). New York: New York University Press.

Worthington, R. L. (2004). Sexual identity, sexual orientation, religious identity, and change: Is it possible to depolarize the debate? *The Counseling Psychologist, 32,* 741–749.

Worthington, R. L., Savoy, H. B., Dillon, F. R., & Vernaglia, E. R. (2002). Heterosexual identity development: A multidimensional model of individual and social identity. *The Counseling Psychologist, 30,* 496–531.

CHAPTER 12

CRITICAL THEORETICAL PERSPECTIVES

Ebelia Hernández

How can we best understand the development of our students? An important consideration is determining the extent to which social forces (such as power and privilege) should be studied as an influential factor. Foundational student development theories, many of which are based on psychology (see chapters 9, 10, and 11 in this book), center the study of development on the individual's meaning-making processes—thus, the role of context is examined in terms of how an individual makes meaning of his or her environment and the external formulas endorsed by others. Later work has applied sociological, postmodern, poststructural, and critical theoretical perspectives to examine how individuals manage and make meaning of their environment. These theories, such as queer theory, critical race theory, and intersectionality, provide frameworks that consider how power, privilege, and oppression influence and constrain experiences, meaning making, and the ways in which individuals manage these social forces in their day-to-day interactions with others.

In addressing the contemporary diversity of college students, some scholars employ a multicultural perspective in which differences regarding race, ethnicity, religion, or gender expression, for example, are addressed with inclusion, respect, and tolerance (Ladson-Billings & Tate, 2009). This approach may result in diversifying voices represented in student development studies to ensure representation of various identities and lived experiences, but it could be criticized as merely "coloring" a sample. A multicultural perspective may limit the examination of how, and to what extent, culture, values, and community may influence student development, especially of minoritized populations, because it does not consider systemic issues of power and oppression. Critical race theorists Ladson-Billings and Tate (2009) challenged this multicultural approach and concluded that it is not enough because "the tensions between and among these differences is rarely interrogated" (p. 178), nor is there an agenda to critique the status quo or a plan to create new models that are socially just and do not continue to perpetuate privileging of those in power. They "unabashedly reject a paradigm [that supports a multicultural perspective] that attempts to be everything to everyone and consequently becomes nothing for anyone" (Ladson-Billings & Tate, 2009, p. 178).

The use of critical race theory, intersectionality, and queer theory is creating new directions in how student development is studied and understood. Although these theoretical perspectives are not developmental in the sense that they do not explain how meaning making may develop and evolve, they are used to expose developmental processes that foundational student development theories do not have the language or concepts to capture (Abes & Kasch, 2007). These theoretical directions provide new understandings about the students with whom we work in our roles as student affairs educators that fully recognize their racialized, gendered, classed, and political realities. The goal in using critical theories is not to ultimately create a new "family" of student development theory. Rather, the principles and concepts reviewed in this chapter may be used to take a second look at existing developmental theories in ways that expose the strengths and limitations of these theories relative to explaining the development of marginalized and privileged populations, as well as the extent to which power and oppression are considered a part of the developmental process.

The purpose of this chapter is to review these newer theoretical perspectives and how they influence how we understand developmental pathways for individuals when privilege and marginalization are recognized as an influence on meaning making and sense of self. It should be noted that although these theories are referred to in this chapter as "critical," they are grounded in critical and post-structural paradigms that seek to identify how power is perpetuated in society, but they have different aims and tenets. First, the critical theories of critical race theory, intersectionality, and queer theory are introduced. Then, findings from scholarship that applies these critical theories to the study of student development are reviewed. Last, implications for student affairs work are addressed.

Critical Race Theory

Considering student development using a critical race theory (CRT) perspective, which is grounded in a critical paradigm, produces new ways of thinking about how racial realities inform our meaning making and sense of self. Drawing from the basic insight that racism is normal, not aberrant, in American society (Delgado & Stefancic, 2000), CRT's central focus is to uncover how racism is perpetuated and explain the effects of it in the lives of minoritized individuals. CRT "has become an important intellectual and social tool for . . . deconstruction of oppressive structures and discourses, reconstruction of human agency, and construction of equitable and socially just relations of power" (Ladson-Billings, 1999, p. 10). The tenets of CRT have been extended and branched out to focus on particular minoritized groups through creating sub-theories such as

AsianCrit, TribalCrit, and LatCrit (Solórzano & Yosso, 2001). Each of these critical theories centers the investigation of race and racism, and also seeks to illuminate how other forms of oppression particular to that group (for example, based on language, cultural values, identity, phenotype, and sexuality) are perpetuated and affect the individual.

Five elements or core tenets define the perspective, methods, and pedagogy of CRT in education (Solórzano, 1998; Solórzano & Delgado Bernal, 2001; Solórzano, Villalpando, & Oseguera, 2005). The first element characterizing CRT, the centrality of race and ethnicity and racism, and its intersectionality of other forms of subordination, explains that in order to understand the experiences and meaning making of marginalized populations, one must place the examination of identities and their positioning of power and marginalization at the center of the analysis. The second element is the challenge to ideologies of objectivity, meritocracy, color-blindness, race neutrality, and equal opportunity (Solórzano & Delgado Bernal, 2001). These often unspoken and unrecognized ideologies perpetuate beliefs that fail to account for the advantages that privilege provide, and the negative effects of marginalization, racism, and discrimination. The third element is the commitment to social justice. The aim of scholars who use CRT is to transform an understanding of student development into one that incorporates an analysis of power and marginalization; and in creating this new knowledge, it may cause people to think differently about marginalized groups and act in more socially aware and just ways. The fourth element is the centrality of experiential knowledge, which is endorsed by giving people an opportunity to speak about their experiences via storytelling, biographies, and interviews, often referred to as counter-storytelling in CRT. The fifth element is an interdisciplinary perspective, which requires studying the effects of racism by placing them in historical context and using different disciplines, such as sociology or political science, to guide the analysis.

The advantages of using CRT to inform student development theory is that it can provide the framework and language to investigate how the racialized experiences of students of color may affect their development. In particular, CRT's focus on race and ethnicity can illuminate how power and oppression is experienced by students of color, how they make meaning of their racialized realities, and how these students manage such social forces in acts of resistance. For example, CRT was used in the study of self-authorship for Mexican American women who were engaged in political activism in their Latino student communities (Hernández, 2012, 2016). This work highlights how increasing awareness of political and racialized realities may affect the journey toward self-authorship. For example, the women's cognitive development included their increasing knowledge of Latino politics, culture, and social norms. When the women were asked to describe how they made meaning of their ethnic identity (intrapersonal development), they responded with understandings of not only what being Latina meant to them but also how their collegiate peers perpetuated racist stereotypes. Interpersonal development was reconsidered beyond the romantic, familial, or friendship relationships considered in earlier work (Baxter Magolda, 2001) to take into account political relationships developed from membership in student organizations. This included how the women developed leadership skills, learned how to collaborate with other organization representatives, and worked with university administration. All of these developmental findings contributed to the developing political consciousness model, which connected how involvement in a political, culturally based student organization may have promoted developing political and social consciousness while on the journey toward self-authorship (Hernández, 2012).

Intersectionality

Rather than examine singular identities at a time, intersectionality considers the intersections of identities, such as the intersections of race and ethnicity and social class, and places these identities in larger structures of inequality (Jones & Abes, 2013). This theoretical lens recognizes that privileged and marginalized identities are experienced simultaneously, shifting the focus to understanding how these identities connect, influence, and clash with each other. Intersectionality is difficult to attach to a singular paradigm because it draws from critical theory's social justice agenda and objective to examine power and oppression, and also poststructuralism's rejection of identity categories and endorsement of identity being intersectional and fluid (Jones, Torres, & Arminio, 2014). For intersectional scholars, the study of identities is a means to the end of examining how privilege and marginalization function and is perpetuated in society (Dill & Zambrana, 2009). Intersectionality research includes (1) centering the focus of the study on the lived experience of marginalized people; (2) recognizing that identity is individual and group; (3) exploring identity salience and how it is influenced by social forces, such as power, privilege, and inequality; and (4) promoting a social justice agenda (Dill & Zambrana, 2009). Similar to CRT, intersectionality seeks to reveal how power and oppression are manifested in social policies, practices, and cultural ideologies (Dill & Zambrana, 2009).

Jones (2009) recognized a growing body of scholarship suggesting that self-authorship theory alone is incomplete in understanding the complex, multiple identity development of individuals that includes race, gender, social class, sexuality, and so on. Instead, researchers chose to use intersectionality to "break out of the boundaries of traditional student development research by exploring the complexities of the lived experience that rarely fall into neat categories and by situating individuals within the structures of power and oppression that influence the lived experience" (Jones, 2009, p. 289).

Findings from the analysis of autoethnographies of individuals who examined how their multiple identities intersected and clashed supported the findings of prior self-authorship studies (Abes & Kasch, 2007; Torres, 2009; Torres & Baxter Magolda, 2004; Torres & Hernández, 2007). These studies asserted that context plays a significant role in how minoritized individuals make meaning of themselves, their experiences, and how they choose to navigate their social spaces (Jones, 2009, 2010; Jones, Kim, & Skendall, 2012). However, unlike these previous studies, which placed a particular marginalized identity (race and ethnicity, sexual identity) as central, in Jones (2009) intersectionality enabled individuals to make meaning of their privileged and marginalized identities at the same time. Participants articulated how they could easily recognize their marginalizing identities and admitted how they had difficulty recognizing their privileged identities and making meaning of how they intersected and influenced their marginalized identities (Jones, 2009). Privilege, or lack of it, affected why some identities gained salience in certain contexts whereas others would be pushed to the background.

Using developmental meaning making to frame this analysis, the participants recognized how external forces constantly influenced how they performed identity, regardless of how internalized and self-authored their identities may be. Although self-authorship suggests that self-authored individuals live out their identities in a way that reflects their internalized sense of self, this work challenges such an assumption by indicating how identity performance is context specific. This can be used as a strategy to manage others' perceptions in order to influence how others treat them and the level of privilege they are afforded in a particular context (Jones, 2009). These findings suggest that the developmental goal of identity development is not the achievement of stable, well-defined identities but rather an ability to have "authenticity . . . in the day-to-day, moment-to-moment negotiations and decisions about managing who we are, given the current context" and to become "more aware of the intersection of privileged and oppressed identities and the ways in which larger structures of inequality patterned the ways in which these intersections [are] expressed" (Jones, Kim, & Skendall, 2012, p. 711). That is, the use of intersectionality to examine and make meaning of development has resulted in a different way of conceptualizing identity that is profoundly more fluid and responsive to perceived power, oppression, and social location. Jones and colleagues (2012) concluded that intersectionality enabled the critical exploration of how privilege provided choices in identity performance, whereas oppression constrained and required strategies to minimize harm.

Queer Theory

At the heart of queer theory is the assertion that categorizations based on gender and sexual identity do not accurately represent the realities of people who may not fit neatly into categories, especially those who are nonconforming or may identify with several categories. Abes and Kasch (2007) highlighted three concepts from queer theory to inform their examination of the development of lesbian college women: (a) *heteronormativity*, which privileges heterosexuality as the norm and all other sexual identities as the "other," and fails to recognize the social structures that uphold this privileging; (b) *performativity*, which describes identity not as predetermined or inherent but rather as created and enacted through everyday actions; and (c) *liminality*, which is illustrated by individuals who do not fall into neat identity categories but are in between identities, not quite fitting into one category or another, and engaged in the process of becoming. These concepts challenge the normed, easily categorized, binary notion of sexual identity and exemplify that identity is constantly developing and changing (Abes & Kasch, 2007).

Applying queer theory to student development theory challenges and questions assumptions held in foundational theories. Queer theory resists essentializing a particular group's experiences to a common denominator (or developmental pathway); therefore, the use of a model to define development is antithetical to queer theory's resistance to categorizations. Tenets of queer theory assert that identity is formed through performance, is not predetermined or innate, and is ever-changing because performances are never exactly the same. It challenges the assumption prevalent in student development theory (including the scholarship that uses CRT or intersectionality as theoretical frameworks reviewed in this chapter) that there is an internalized core self that processes meaning making and holds internalized values and identities (Abes, Jones, & McEwen, 2007; Jones & Abes, 2013). Queer theory proffers that no core self exists; rather, identity is a result of how one performs, expresses, and embodies identities. Because of these essential differences, one might conclude that there is incompatibility between queer theory and student development theory as it currently is understood. Abes (2009) acknowledged these issues but recognized that it is worthwhile to apply concepts from queer theory to reconsider identity development and to challenge our thinking about what student development may be. In doing so, a richer story can be captured that is "more complex than what the language of self-authorship allows" (Abes & Kasch, 2007, p. 631).

Abes's (2009; Abes & Kasch, 2007) research on lesbian college women applied a theoretical borderlands approach, which is the use of a constructivist paradigm and queer theory to tell a more expansive story than what each perspective could tell on its own. Performativity and self-authorship helped explain how the study participants made meaning of their identities and lived experiences. Self-authorship offered a framework to describe their internal struggle of challenging external formulas. Queer theory, however, provided greater significance to how they enacted their identities than what self-authorship theory could acknowledge by recognizing the value of a performative identity, growing consciousness and resistance to heteronormativity, and the extent to which time, place, and community affected identity expression.

Queer theory challenges the notion that developmental processes are universal, or in other words, that everyone follows the same general developmental pathway regardless of lived experiences, context, or identities. Abes and Kasch (2007) asserted that "the developmental process looks different for lesbian college students . . . [which may suggest that] the developmental process might also be reexamined for other dimensions of identity, such as social class, race, and ethnicity" (p. 630). That is, in using the lens of queer theory, there is evidence that social forces, such as heteronormativity, affect the development of queer students in such a profound way that not only the path toward self-authorship may be different but also the markers of developmental maturity. Their findings resulted in the idea of queer-authorship, which departs from self-authorship by describing development as fluid, nonlinear, and involving the process of identifying and deconstructing heteronormativity (Abes & Kasch, 2007).

Reconsidering Student Development

The first part of this chapter described the values, assumptions, and aims endorsed by critical race theory, intersectionality, and queer theory that guide scholars' efforts to understand the human condition. In applying these critical theories to the study of student development, scholars reconsidered the developmental process in ways that highlight the role of social forces on the developmental process and have challenged and departed from foundational student development theories. In this section, student development theory's purpose and structure are reconsidered, and new developmental processes and pathways are proposed.

Shifting the Purpose and Focus of Student Development Theory

Although foundational theories aim to uncomplicate student development by creating generalizable theories that can be useful for a large group of students, critical perspectives embrace complexity by examining how race, gender, sexuality, and other identities intersect and influence each other in ways that are often messy and complicated (Patton & Chang, 2011). By reducing differences in backgrounds, identities, and lived experiences of students for the purposes of creating a one-size-fits-all model for the sake of simplicity, we run the risk of diminishing, invalidating by omission, and making invisible the developmental pathways and tasks of those who are nonconforming, minority, or different. Several scholars concluded that although earlier models are often noted as limiting in understanding the role of power and oppression on the developmental process, student affairs has not quite embraced other ways of understanding the experiences of college students in general, LGBTQ students in particular, via the incorporation of critical theories into our work (Abes & Kasch, 2007; Patton & Chang, 2011; Patton, Kortegast, & Javier, 2011; Torres, Jones, & Renn, 2009).

The danger of creating one-size-fits-all models of student development is that such models may perpetuate the conclusion that the particular developmental process it illustrates is "normal," thereby relegating those processes and experiences not included as not normal, deviant, or "other." Kegan (1994) recognized the power student development theories have in privileging one group's developmental pathways as "normal," particularly those of majority white, heterosexual, traditionally aged college students whose pathways are the basis for our oldest and most recognized developmental theories. Kegan (1994) warned that "any time a theory is normative, and suggests that something is more grown, more mature, more developed than something else, we had all better check to see if the distinction rests on arbitrary grounds that consciously or unconsciously unfairly advantage some people (such as those people who create the theory and people like them) whose preferences are being depicted as superior" (p. 229).

Queer theory challenges normative categorizations because such categorizations can constrain, oppress, and fail to recognize the variety, uniqueness, and fluidity that college students exemplify in their everyday lives. Queer theory urges scholars to study sexual identity, for example, rather than focus on gay, lesbian, bisexual, or heterosexual development because doing so may be more inclusive of nonconforming individuals who do not fit neatly in any of these identity categories (Jones & Abes, 2013). Categorization seeks to simplify something that can indeed be fluid, complex, and changing. As one participant in Abes's (2007) study explained, her nonconforming sexual identity was difficult for her to deal with because she felt marginalized and misunderstood in the identity categories she tried to take on, until she finally realized that "there is no normal!" (p. 65).

Reconsidering Identity as Changing and Fluid

As noted previously, many foundational theories depict development as linear, where the end point of development is an "authentic" self, and an individual's sense of self and values are lived out in their everyday life. This is likened to a self-authored individual who has internally defined his or her gendered, racialized, sexual identities, and is making life choices that reflect these beliefs and values (Baxter Magolda, 2001). The authentic self reflects the values, beliefs, and sense of self derived from the inner core where meaning making is processed.

Jones and colleagues (2012) suggested that identity development may not only involve the process of developing a stable sense of self but also the process of meaning making of multiple identities and managing identity representations that are increasingly cognizant of context and for which "there is no location of arrival. Individuals' identities are endlessly transforming into some new form, meaning, or interpretation of identity" (p. 203). Jones's (2010) prior intersectional examination of self-authorship considered how context, specifically the influence of power and oppression within that context, affected how one presented multiple identities. She concluded, "what made authenticity troubling was the influence of different contexts, some of which were supportive of one's whole self, but others were not, and this resulted in decision making about how (and who) to present oneself in these different contexts" (p. 233). Being authentic by clearly displaying one's personal sense of self was not always safe, welcomed, or encouraged in spaces where such identities were not privileged or valued (Jones, Kim, & Skendall, 2012). The notion of living authentically can be difficult and dangerous, but should the decision to not be "authentic" be considered as less developed or more sophisticated in awareness of social forces?

Further supporting the notion of identity as not stable but fluid and constantly changing is Malcolm and Mendoza's (2014) study of Afro-Caribbean international students' choice to represent their identities as international students, Caribbean, and/or black in different ways according to context and desired response by others. This study, which applied intersectionality and CRT, affirmed "the conceptualizations of identity development as a process between the person, and their [sic] environment that is fluid, contingent, and negotiated, constantly shifting and transforming. In this process, students perform their intersecting identities based on their agency and the stage [of development] in which they find themselves" (p. 611).

Decoupling Internalized Identity from Identity Performance

Butler's (1990) concept of performativity is nondevelopmental and dismisses student development theory's prevalent conceptualization of an inner core guiding choices and identity, concluding that there is no core sense of self reflected in our identity representations and performances. Butler suggested that identities, specifically gender and sexual, are produced in our performances in which "we do not choose our gendered identity; our gender is produced as we repeat ourselves. We do not take on roles to act out as in a performance; we become subject through repetition" (p. 25). The inner core is conceptualized in self-authorship, and the inner voice is considered to be the voice of our inner conscience guiding our decision making and sense of self (Baxter Magolda, 2001). The concept of an inner core is also reflected in the model of multiple dimensions of identity (Jones & McEwen, 2000), in which the core consists of personal attributes, characteristics, and identity that are consistent, stable, and less susceptible to eternal influence. The inner voice and core share a similar purpose of housing one's essence as a human being.

Student development scholars who have incorporated the concept of performativity do not necessarily fully embrace the notion that there is no core self. Rather these theorists have challenged the conclusion that identity representation constantly mirrors our inner sense of self or that such congruence is a characteristic of a more authentic, developmentally mature individual (Jones, Kim, & Skendall, 2012). These scholars have examined the meaning and intent behind these identity performances to understand developmental processes and how privilege and oppression may also play a role in these performances. In the study of college men's gender identity development, Butler's notion of performativity was used to examine masculine gender performance (Edwards & Jones, 2009). The men in the study likened being a man to putting on a mask that included a "set of social behaviors, including feelings, thoughts, and actions" and recognized how these performances were contingent on time and place" (p. 222). The recognition of this mask and the choice to put it on or take it off included developmental meaning-making processes in the conscious and unconscious construction of identity.

Recentering the Study of Development to "Individual + Social Location"

Zaytoun (2006) asked the question, "How is the self and [developmental processes] defined within an individual's social and cultural context?" (p. 58). Drawing from the work of feminist scholars Anzaldúa (1999) and Collins (1998), she concluded that how we define self is inextricably linked to our social world, which includes social groups, communities, and spiritual entities we deem important to our lives. Although student development theories have always considered the role of context as a factor that may influence development, critical theories take the importance of context a step further to examine context itself (Jones & Abes, 2013). Patton and Chang (2011) cited this shortcoming in foundational student development theories, specifically in the study of sexual identity development, in which social location is often not included to examine how power structures affect how LGBTQ identities may define themselves personally and in particular spaces.

Hernández's (2012) study of Mexican American women also examined the role of location and community on ethnic identity development. Hernández's (2013) critical race theory examination of historical legacy of race relations at a university and the cultural politics of the time enabled recognition of unique environmental factors that played significant roles in ethnic identity development. The women in the study were strongly influenced by extreme cultural isolation and racist campus incidents that caused their Latina identities to be very salient in their day-to-day lives as undergraduates. Results also suggested that as their location changed, the meaning and social norms of Latina/o identity changed. The women responded to changing contexts (their hometowns to the university) by enacting their identities differently and choosing to self-identify as Latina. One participant commented she stopped identifying as Hispanic because it was socially unacceptable among her peers and started to use the popular term *Latina* in order to fit in with the group.

Recognizing the Intersections of Privilege and Marginalization

As explained previously, intersectionality seeks to understand how identities intersect and influence each other, so multiple identities are examined simultaneously to examine how these identities may clash, complement each other, or become salient depending on the power dynamics of a particular social location. Foundational theories tend to focus on singular identities, and many identity development models focus on those that are marginalized in our society. This can lead to the tendency to not consider certain developmental processes, such as how individuals make meaning of multiple identities, consider how these identities intersect in their lives, or how they manage privileged and oppressed identities simultaneously.

In Jones's (2009) autoethnographic study, the power of context in determining which identities were most salient was illustrated in the participants' narratives when they described how their marginalized identities, especially the visible ones, were often the most salient. This resulted in a feeling of "otherness" that remained a persistent part of their lives and began during early childhood. The participants also came to acknowledge their privileged identities, but with difficulty. They realized that although it was easier to name their oppressed identities than their privileged ones, they could not engage in discussion about how they made meaning of their identities without discussing social forces of power and marginalization. That is, how they made meaning of their identities was strongly influenced and shaped by external forces of social context and social forces (racism, privilege, oppression, invisibility) regardless if they had strong, internalized identities or were self-authoring. Ever-changing contexts of moving from one social location to another, they realized, made one identity privileged in one space and marginalized in another, salient in one relationship and not so in others. This process was described as a "push" and "pull" process in identity (Jones, Kim, & Skendall, 2012).

The Development of Political Consciousness

Activists have long held the belief that the growing awareness of social injustices and the political realities of one's own communities will lead to motivation for action. Zaytoun (2006) considered how the cognitive development complexity required to make meaning of racism, privilege, and oppression may lead to motivation to resistance to the status quo and engagement in activism. Zaytoun cited Collins's (1998) conclusion that "a changed consciousness encourages people to change the conditions of their lives" (p. 117). In other words, the more an individual learns of social injustices affecting her community, the more she is motivated to act to change her community's circumstances.

In Hernández's (2012) study of Mexican American women activists, the connection between development of political consciousness and its influence to motivate women toward advocacy and activism for one's cultural community was evidenced—the more aware a Latina was about her social world, the more likely she would be personally motivated to advocate for the Latino community. The developing political consciousness model was designed to demonstrate the ways that political consciousness affected development along all three dimensions of self-authorship. The model illustrates the development of social knowledge, which includes an understanding of political issues and power and oppression (cognitive), the shift of the motivation to engage in activism and advocacy for one's community from external expectations to an internalized value (intrapersonal), and development of political strategies and representing one's community for political purposes (interpersonal).

Conclusion

In this chapter I reviewed how the incorporation of critical theories to the study of student development contributes new perspectives and directions to illuminate developmental processes that are directly affected by the social forces of power and oppression. These new directions pose questions and concerns that scholars are challenged to answer. Some scholars have considered the applicability of foundational theories to explain the developmental processes that they have uncovered in their studies. Indeed, the findings reviewed here, such as the fluid, constantly transforming nature of identity that may or may not reflect individual's internalized sense of self "suggests a point of departure from student development theories . . . that posit a trajectory of movement from external influences to internal foundations by accenting the importance of ongoing external influences to self-definition" (Jones, 2009, p. 299). Furthermore, these critical perspectives suggest that some developmental theories may perpetuate the privileging and maintenance of social norms at the cost of further marginalizing minoritized groups and assessing their developmental processes as less mature or developed (Abes & Kasch, 2007). Another direction to take is to ask different questions to assess students' development that invites them to discuss their racialized, gendered, political realities, their understanding of racism and other forms of oppression, and their relationships to their communities (Hernández, 2016).

In the continued use of critical theories to examine the development of college students, several questions will propel scholars into digging deeper into the messiness and complexity that is the developmental process of individuals who hold multiple identities, straddle privileged and marginalized statuses simultaneously, and live their lives moving from one context to another. Is the developmental process substantially different for minoritized individuals that they require a very different developmental model to depict the substantive impact that oppression plays in their meaning making, identity, and relationships with others? Or could existing theories be revised to be more inclusive of the different developmental pathways revealed in these critical studies? There are no clear answers to these questions, but they are questions that are worthy of our time to consider.

An understanding that welcomes complexity and encourages examination of the ways that power and oppression may affect the college experience will go a long way in creating campus spaces that are inclusive and empowering. As educators, we must walk toward complexity and challenging conversations, not avoid them. The new directions in student development theory that emerged from empirical studies have demonstrated that making meaning of the messiness of intersectionality, letting go of identity categories and embracing individuality, and exposing and addressing racism, sexism, and other forms of oppression are critical components in development.

Discussion Questions and Activities

The recommended activities here are aimed toward developing awareness of the often-invisible ways that power and privilege are prevalent in society.

1. Journal or engage in dialogue with a peer to answer the following questions: What are your privileged identities? What are your marginalized identities?

How could you validate and support the struggle of identifying privileged and oppressed identities of others? This assignment could be useful to introduce intersectionality's focus on examining the intersections of privileged and marginalized identities.

2. Before creating dialogues on power and oppression with students, it is critical to honestly assess your own knowledge, comfort level, and skill to do so. A good resource to help understand the process and necessary components of facilitating difficult dialogues is Quaye's (2012) article, "Think before You Teach: Preparing for Dialogues about Racial Realities." Consider employing his suggestions to facilitate dialogues on race and ethnicity, including assessing your ability to gauge students' comfort levels and their development of intercultural maturity

3. For those who work with student leaders, encourage activities that promote development of politically informed, knowledgeable members to increase their motivation for advocacy work and social change efforts. The body of work reviewed here demonstrates that the more students learn about the politics, culture, and racial realities of their communities, the more they become intrinsically motivated to create change. For example, challenge community service leaders to research the needs of their community, the demographics of those they wish to serve, and seek out research that may inform their work.

References

Abes, E. S. (2007). Applying queer theory in practice with college students: Transformation of a researcher's and participant's perspectives on identity, a case study. *Journal of LBGT Youth, 5*(1), 57–77.

Abes, E. S. (2009). Theoretical borderlands: Using multiple theoretical perspectives to challenge inequitable power structures in student development theory. *Journal of College Student Development, 50*(2), 141–156.

Abes, E. S., Jones, S. R., & McEwen, M. K. (2007). Reconceptualizing the model of multiple dimensions of identity: The role of meaning-making capacity in the construction of multiple identities. *Journal of College Student Development, 48*(1), 1–22.

Abes, E. S., & Kasch, D. (2007). Using queer theory to explore lesbian college students' multiple dimensions of identity. *Journal of College Student Development, 48*(6), 619–636.

Anzaldúa, G. (1999). *Borderlands/La frontera: The new mestiza* (2nd ed.). San Francisco: Aunt Lute Books.

Baxter Magolda, M. B. (2001). *Making their own way: Narratives for transforming higher education to promote self-authorship.* Sterling, VA: Stylus.

Butler, J. (1990). *Gender trouble: Feminism and the subversion of identity.* New York: Routledge.

Collins, P. H. (1998). *Fighting words: Black women and the search for justice.* Minneapolis: University of Minnesota Press.

Delgado, R., & Stefancic, J. (Eds.). (2000). *Critical race theory: The cutting edge.* Philadelphia: Temple University Press.

Dill, B. T., & Zambrana, R. E. (2009). *Emerging intersections: Race, class, and gender in theory, policy, and practice.* New Brunswick, NJ: Rutgers University Press.

Edwards, K. E., & Jones, S. R. (2009). "Putting my man face on": A grounded theory of college men's gender identity development. *Journal of College Student Development, 50,* 210–228.

Hernández, E. (2012). The journey towards developing political consciousness through activism for Mexican American women. *Journal of College Student Development, 53*(5), 680–702.

Hernández, E. (2013). Mexican American women's activism at Indiana University during the 1990s. *Journal of Higher Education, 84*(3), 397–416.

Hernández, E. (2016). Utilizing critical race theory to examine race/ethnicity, racism, and power in student development theory and research. *Journal of College Student Development, 57,* 168–180.

Jones, S. R. (2009). Constructing identities at the intersections: An autoethnographic exploration of multiple dimensions of identity. *Journal of College Student Development, 50*(3), 287–304.

Jones, S. R. (2010). Getting to the complexities of identity: The contributions of an autoethnographic and intersectional approach. In M. B. Baxter Magolda, E. G. Creamer, & P. S. Meszaros (Eds.), *Development and assessment of self-authorship: Exploring the concept across cultures* (pp. 223–243). Sterling, VA: Stylus.

Jones, S. R., & Abes, E. S. (2013). *Identity development of college students: Advancing frameworks for multiple dimensions of identity.* San Francisco: Jossey-Bass.

Jones, S. R., Kim, Y. C., & Skendall, K. C. (2012). (Re-)framing authenticity: Considering multiple social identities using autoethnographic and intersectional approaches. *Journal of Higher Education, 83*(5), 698–724.

Jones, S. R., & McEwen, M. K. (2000). A conceptual model of multiple dimensions of identity. *Journal of College Student Development, 41*(4), 405–414.

Jones, S. R., Torres, V., & Arminio, J. (2014). *Negotiating the complexities of qualitative research in higher education: Fundamental elements and issues* (2nd ed.). New York: Routledge.

Kegan, R. (1994). *In over our heads: The mental demands of modern life.* Cambridge, MA: Harvard University Press.

Ladson-Billings, G. (1999). Just what is critical race theory, and what's it doing in a nice field like education? In L. Parker, D. Deyhle, & S. Villenas (Eds.), *Race is . . . race isn't: Critical race theory and qualitative studies in education* (pp. 7–30). Boulder, CO: Westview Press.

Ladson-Billings, G., & Tate, W. F. (2009). Toward a critical race theory of education. In A. Darder, M. P. Baltodano, & R. D. Torres (Eds.), *The critical pedagogy reader* (2nd ed., pp. 167–182). New York: Routledge.

Malcolm, Z. T., & Mendoza, P. (2014). Afro-Caribbean international students' ethnic identity development: Fluidity, intersectionality, agency, and performativity. *Journal of College Student Development, 55*(6), 595–614.

Patton, L. D., & Chang, S. (2011). Identity makeover millennial edition: Using contemporary theoretical frameworks to explore identity intersections among LGBTQ millennial populations. In F. A. Bonner, A. F. Marbley, & M. F. Howard-Hamilton (Eds.), *Diverse millennial students in college: Implication for faculty and student affairs* (pp. 193–209). Sterling, VA: Stylus.

Patton, L. D., Kortegast, C., & Javier, G. (2011). LGBTQ millennials in college. In F. A. Bonner, A. F. Marbley, & M. F. Howard-Hamilton (Eds.), *Diverse millennial students in college: Implication for faculty and student affairs* (pp. 175–192). Sterling, VA: Stylus.

Quaye, S. J. (2012). Think before you teach: Preparing for dialogues about racial realities. *Journal of College Student Development, 53*(4), 542–562.

Solórzano, D. G. (1998). Critical race theory, race and gender microaggressions, and the experience of Chicana and Chicano scholars. *Qualitative Studies in Education, 11*(1),

121–136.

Solórzano, D. G., & Delgado Bernal, D. (2001). Examining transformational resistance through a critical race and LatCrit theory framework. *Urban Education, 36*(3), 308–342.

Solórzano, D. G., Villalpando, O., & Oseguera, L. (2005). Educational inequities and Latina/o undergraduate students in the United States: A critical race theory analysis of their educational progress. *Journal of Hispanic Higher Education, 4*(3), 272–294.

Solórzano, D. G., & Yosso, T. J. (2001). Critical race and LatCrit theory and method: Counter-storytelling. *International Journal of Qualitative Studies in Education, 14*(4), 471–495.

Torres, V. (2009). The developmental dimensions of recognizing racism. *Journal of College Student Development, 50*(5), 504–520.

Torres, V., & Baxter Magolda, M. (2004). Reconstructing Latino identity: The influence of cognitive development on the ethnic identity process of Latino students. *Journal of College Student Development, 45*(3), 333–347.

Torres, V., & Hernández, E. (2007). The influence on ethnic identity on self-authorship: A longitudinal study of Latino/a college students. *Journal of College Student Development, 48*(5), 558–573.

Torres, V., Jones, S. R., & Renn, K. A. (2009). Identity development theories in student affairs: Origins, current status, and new approaches. *Journal of College Student Development, 50*(6), 577–593.

Zaytoun, K. (2006). Theorizing at the borders: Considering social location in rethinking self and psychological development. *NWSA Journal, 18*(2), 52–72.

CHAPTER 13

ORGANIZATION THEORY AND CHANGE

Adrianna Kezar

Similar to many professionals on campus, student affairs staff members now face the challenge of addressing unprecedented changes—assessing student learning, collaborating with academic affairs, helping diverse students succeed, cutting costs and doing more with less, innovating and trying new practices, integrating technology and social media. In this chapter, I introduce some of the most important authors and concepts related to organizational theory that help explain how to create change. I review the following key organizational theories that broadly introduce readers to well-known concepts: (1) Bolman and Deal's (2013) four frames—a synthesis of organizational theories related to change, (2) a summary of unique college characteristics that make it hard to change and innovate, and (3) specific theories of cultural change that also explain the challenges faced when working to implement something new.

Student affairs practitioners sometimes seek leadership roles because they identify changes they think would be important for the campus; perhaps they have a vision to help more first-generation college students. However, having a vision is much different from being able to achieve change, one of the most elusive practices on college campuses. Often, campuses move at a glacial pace. They are long-standing institutions with traditions that are not easily altered. Given this difficult environment, understanding how to create change is an important skill. In order to make concrete the organizational theories presented, I apply them to a case of creating change—building a learning community on campus, a task many student affairs staff members are currently working on. Learning communities are interdisciplinary teaching environments that are structured so that students learn in cohorts together and often live in a similar space, blending their in- and out-of-classroom experience. They are particularly helpful for first-generation students because they help build sense of belonging, community, and academic self-efficacy. After I present each theory I will describe how that theory helps to address the challenge of moving the campus from traditional forms of lecture and individualistic learning toward learning communities.

Making Sense of Organizations and Change: The Four Frames

Bolman and Deal (2013) provide one of the most comprehensive overviews of organizational theory and its implications for leaders. Their book, *Reframing Organizations,* synthesizes thousands of studies about organizational behavior and theory and describes four major frames (or schools of thought) that help to understand how organizations operate: structural, human resource, political, and symbolic. The term *frame* could also be called *mental model, mind-set,* or *cognitive lens* and refers to a set of ideas or assumptions that guide behavior. Frames are important because they help leaders to understand and negotiate a particular issue. Bolman and Deal also liken frames to a road map; if a leader is able to effectively understand the four frames, he or she will be better able to navigate and address organizational problems.

Structural Frame

The structural frame is perhaps the most commonly used framework among leaders and the most familiar to those in the general public. The structural frame is often epitomized by the notion of the organizational chart from which people understand how the organization functions through a definition of a variety of roles and the relationship among those roles (see chapter 17 for examples). The organizational chart is the underlying architecture or structure of the organization. Although people often mistake the notion of hierarchy as synonymous with the structural frame, the structural frame is much broader than hierarchy, which is merely one concept within this broad understanding of the way organizations can be structured to achieve their goals. For example, organizations may take on a matrix structure, network organization, or team structure.

Bolman and Deal (2013) identify six assumptions that underlie the structural frame:

1. Organizations exist to achieve establish goals and objectives.
2. Organizations increase efficiency and enhance performance through specialization and a clear division of labor.
3. Appropriate forms of coordination and control ensure that diverse efforts of individuals and units mesh.
4. Organizations work best when rationality prevails over personal preferences and extraneous pressures.
5. Structures must be designed to fit in organization's circumstances (including its goals, technology, work force, and environment).
6. Problems and performance gaps arise from structural deficiencies and can be remedied through analysis and restructuring.

The structural lens is important because it helps to identify ways that the organization might be restructured in order to maximize performance or better meet a goal. As a leader might decide to differentiate or integrate work, work might become more autonomous or more controlled, and work might need more or less coordination, rules, or policies.

Human Resource Frame

Many student affairs administrators may find themselves conceptualizing organizations through the human resource frame because of their counseling or psychology background. Not surprisingly, the human resource frame emphasizes the human subsystem of the organization, focusing on the motivation, needs, commitment, training, hiring, and socialization of people within the organization and how this affects organizational functioning. This framework may be more intuitive to student affairs leaders who are trained in psychological and humanistic theories and provide a source of bias that they might need to be aware of as it relates to the ways they view organizations.

The human resource frame is built on four basic assumptions:

1. Organizations exist to serve human needs rather than the reverse.
2. People and organizations need each other. Organizations need ideas, energy, and talent; people need careers, salaries, and opportunities.
3. When the fit between individual and system is poor, one or both suffer. Individuals are exploited or exploit the organization, or both become victims.
4. A good fit benefits both. Individuals find meaningful and satisfying work, and organizations get the talent and energy they need to succeed. (Bolman & Deal, 2013)

Leaders with a human resource frame are more likely to understand the importance of supporting human capital, encouraging participation, hiring the right people, and promoting from within. Furthermore, they provide leadership that brings out the best in others and make sure to invest in and reward individual's commitment and effort. And, leaders promote diversity that helps make the human resource subsystem operate more smoothly.

Political Frame

Bolman and Deal's (2013) research identified that many people, particularly educators and often women, downplayed the political framework for understanding organizational challenges and developing solutions. Politics often gets a negative image, such as ambitious people climbing to the top willing to engage in unscrupulous activities in order to move their agenda forward, but this is a very limited view of politics. Instead, the political frame can help leaders to understand the important ways that they can build an agenda or common vision for change, mobilize people, use persuasion to influence others, identify sources of power and use them to leverage change, and use the power of networks in order to create organizational direction and change. The political frame also helps many conflict-adverse leaders to see the value in conflict because it demonstrates where people have competing interests and where negotiation and solutions can be identified. The political frame also challenges leaders with a highly rational approach to their work to think about other conditions that are shaping organizational behavior, such as differing interests or beliefs.

The five major assumptions of the political frame are as follows:

1. Organizations are coalitions of diverse individuals and interest groups.
2. There are enduring differences among coalition members in values, beliefs, information, interests, and perceptions of reality.
3. Most important decisions involve allocating scarce resources—who gets what.
4. Scarce resources and enduring differences make conflict central to organizational dynamics and underlie power as the most important asset.
5. Goals and decisions emerge from bargaining, negotiation, and jockeying for position among competing stakeholders. (Bolman & Deal, 2013)

Leaders using a political frame are adept at developing an agenda that garners attention from multiple interest groups. They are able to map power relations and easily develop coalitions and influential allies in support of a change initiative.

Symbolic Frame

Perhaps the most underused frame is the symbolic perspective of the organization. Research and theory about the cultural and symbolic aspects of organizations did not emerge until the 1980s. Its recent emergence into academic research reflects the way that the symbolic subsystem (for example, mission, vision, values) of organizations has been downplayed and not capitalized on in the past. People inherently need meaning and the symbolic frame helps to provide avenues for people to establish meaning through their work. This frame also demonstrates why mission and vision are important for providing a sense of purpose for members of the organization and an image of the future for people to aim. Leaders can communicate meaning through rituals and ceremonies that help people to collectively remember their purpose. An example of an important ritual that most campuses have that reminds them of their purpose is the beginning-of-the-year convocation, which centers people on their work again. Overall, the symbolic subsystem of organizations sheds light on the values that undergird activities, practices, and policies that typically go unnoticed. Bolman and Deal (2013) point out how the symbolic frame, more so than any others, moves leaders beyond thinking in a highly rational or only strategic manner and highlights the importance of faith, purpose, emotions, values, and spirit for organizational functioning.

The five major assumptions of the symbolic frame are as follows:

1. What is most important is not what happens but what it means.
2. Activity and meaning are loosely coupled; events have multiple meanings because people interpret experience differently.
3. In the face of widespread uncertainty and ambiguity, people create symbols to resolve confusion, increase predictability, find direction, and anchor hope and faith.
4. Many events and processes are more important for what is expressed than what is produced. They form a cultural tapestry of secular myths, heroes and heroines, rituals, ceremonies, and stories that help people find purpose and passion in their personal and work lives.
5. Culture is the glue that holds an organization together and unites people around shared values and beliefs. (Bolman & Deal, 2013)

Symbolic leaders are able to tell stories that help others within an organization to find meaning and connect to the institutional mission and vision. Leaders within this frame are also skilled at communicating so others can contribute to developing a shared vision as well as understanding a collectively developed mission. And they help create rituals, ceremonies, and symbols to help guide and connect people to institutional culture.

Multi-frame Thinking: Pulling the Frames Together

Empirical research on the four frames suggests that leaders are more successful and effective when they use multi-frame thinking for conceptualizing issues within organizations. The research also suggests that leaders tend to use a single or a couple of frames in order to understand and analyze issues within an organization. Furthermore, studies demonstrate that leaders tend to overrate their use of frames. For example, they might perceive using the symbolic frame, but none of the people with whom they work perceive them using this frame. Leaders are biased toward relying on the one right answer or the one best way and, as a result, are often faced with resistance and turmoil.

For example, if a vice president of student affairs establishes a task force to address retention issues on campus and several months later that task force is experiencing significant problems in addressing their charge, the leader will likely assume that the problem can be found within his or her own personal way of viewing the organization. Therefore, if this vice president of student affairs tends to approach the organization through a human resource frame, she will believe that she put the wrong people on the task force and work to put new people on the committee. If she comes from a structural frame, she might believe that the charge was not clear enough and develop clearer instructions for the task force. Research on the four frames demonstrates that leaders who look at the task force from multiple perspectives (that is, that the wrong people might be on the task force, that they might need a clearer charge, that politics have emerged that are hindering interaction, or that common values are missing) are more likely to correctly diagnose problems and develop appropriate solutions. Last, it is important to note that each frame has strengths and weaknesses. Any frame taken to the extreme can jeopardize a leader's success. No frames are necessarily better in understanding or addressing problems, but leaders who use multiple frames increase their effectiveness.

In thinking about our case of organizational change, how can the four frames help? First, from a structural perspective the campus will need to be significantly restructured to support a set of residentially based learning communities. The initiative should likely report to academic and student affairs so that open communication between the units is established. New faculty roles will need to be established, such as faculty members in residence, and new responsibilities and roles developed for these individuals. From the human resource perspective, staff members will need to be recruited and trained to work in and support the learning communities. These employees will need to be socialized to the value of in- and out-of-classroom learning and of interdisciplinary approaches to teaching and knowledge construction. From a political perspective, disciplinary and departmental resistance to the idea of interdisciplinary teaching will need to be addressed. Various coalitions that support interdisciplinary teaching across campus can be mobilized to provide support for the initiative. From a symbolic perspective, leaders need to describe how the identity of the campus is changing and create new rituals and ceremonies that celebrate the move toward interdisciplinary teaching and learning on campus. The way the mission and values of the campus support the move toward a learning community should be emphasized, whether it be the liberal arts orientation, beliefs in collaboration, or the importance of developing the whole student. These values can be used to create buy in from people across campus for the notion of learning communities.

Distinctive Features of Higher Education Organizations

Scholarship suggests that higher education has some unique features that, when bundled together, define campuses as unique from other organizations (for example, businesses, hospitals). It is important to understand these features in order to lead change within them. In this section, I elaborate on the distinctive features that organizational scholars have described that are important to consider when making decisions, approaching organizational processes, and working to create change. These distinctive features include loosely coupled structures, shared governance, values-driven culture, referent and expert power basis, competing authority structures, conflicting faculty and administrative value systems, limited employee turnover, and image-driven culture. Research demonstrates that leaders who are cognizant of the unique organizational features and create strategy based on those features are more successful in decision making, change, and daily operations (Bastedo, 2012; Kezar, 2001).

Loosely Coupled Structures and Shared Governance

Weick (1991) coined higher education institutions as "loosely coupled systems." Tightly coupled organizations are centralized, non-differentiated, and highly coordinated, with strict division of labor, whereas loosely coupled systems are decentralized, have greater differentiation among components, are uncoordinated, and feature high degrees of specialization among workers. Because higher education institutions are loosely coupled systems, decision making is decentralized through the shared governance processes. Trustees or boards of regents have ultimate governance authority with certain areas of the institution such as finances, but the major functions and decisions of the institution are shared between the faculty members and administrators (Birnbaum, 1988). Members interact as equals, minimizing status differences to enable greater collective voice and involvement. Power also tends to be informal, through networks of influence. Broad buy in is necessary; veto power occurs by a small group if they perceive that all voices have not been heard (Baldridge, Curtis, Ecker, & Riley,1977). Shared governance is an area that varies by institutional type, because community colleges with collective bargaining systems tend to have less involvement in institutional governance (Bastedo, 2012).

Values-Driven Culture

Commentators of the higher education system have noted that the system is strongly values driven (Bastedo, 2012; Birnbaum, 1988; Clark, 1983). Although all organizations have belief systems that guide them, colleges and universities are noted for the complex and contrasting system of beliefs that have been developed to guide and shape the culture and structures (Clark, 1983). For example, each disciplinary culture has distinctive beliefs and reflects socialization to a particular profession; mathematicians stress logic and consistency of numbers and art historians stress perspective and interpretation. Faculty members (professional) and administrators (bureaucratic) hold vastly different values set. Some values and beliefs tend to be shared across the enterprise, such as integrity in research, freedom to teach what is considered appropriate, the significance of shared governance and academic freedom, the belief in access to higher education, and the value in specialization, but generally there are distinctive values.

Power Structures: Referent versus Expert Power and Competing Authority Structures

Birnbaum (1988) noted that normative organizations, such as colleges and universities, rely on referent and expert power rather than coercive (prisons), reward (increased salary), or legitimate power (businesses). Referent power results from the willingness to be influenced by another, because of one's identification with that person. Meanwhile, expert power is reflected when one person allows him- or herself to be influenced because the other person has some special knowledge. In particular, faculty members are likely to be influenced by referent power through other members of their community whom they trust, colleagues with shared values, or appeals to principles such as ethics, rather than salary increases or administrative sanctions (Birnbaum, 1988). In addition, autonomous faculty members are unlikely to be influenced by other means of administrative influence and power such as control and strategy. It is not just that academic institutions have unique power structures but that they also have competing authority structures. Authority is the right of a person or office in an organization to demand action of others and expect those demands to be met (Birnbaum, 1988).

Clark (1991) identified four kinds of competing authority systems: academic authority, enterprise-based authority, system-based authority, and charisma. Academic authority is maintained by the faculty members and is broken up into various subgroups such as disciplinary societies, associations, and collective bargaining units, all with varying power. By contrast, enterprise-based authority, which includes trustees or institutional authority, is the legal right to act on behalf of the institution. It is essentially a position-based authority. Enterprise power also encompasses bureaucratic authority based on hierarchical power (reward or legitimate). System-based authority comprises governmental authority, political authority, and academic oligarchy (for example, statewide governing boards). Systems-based authority tends to operate on reward and legitimate power as well. Last, charisma, which refers to the ability to garner willingness of a group to follow you because of unusual personal characteristics, is often associated with a particular president, trustee, or faculty member. This occurs from time to time on campuses. Clark (1991) noted another authority that is imposed on the system and is growing in importance—the market. Market forces cannot be ignored by institutions nor can they shape institutions because of their resource dependency to operate. Bess (1999) provided the following example of the market force: "while faculty may wish to maintain a strong curriculum in, say, aeronautical engineering, if there are too few students willing to major in that subject, the voice of the market will win out over the voice of the faculty" (p. 9).

Conflicting Faculty and Administrative Values System

Another unique characteristic of higher education institutions is that the two main employment groups tend to have differing values systems (Bastedo, 2012; Birnbaum, 1988; Sporn, 1999). Administrative power is based on hierarchy and it values bureaucratic norms and structure, power and influence, rationality, control, and coordination of activities; professional authority is based on knowledge and the values system emphasizes collegiality, dialogue, shared power, autonomy, and peer review. Faculty members also have divided loyalty among disciplinary societies, professional fields, and other external groups in which they participate (Sporn, 1999). Currently, faculty and administrative values are becoming increasingly divergent. Several studies have illustrated the increased bureaucratization and corporatization of administrative staff members (Gumport, 1993; Rhoades, 1995), who are increasingly coming from the business or legal professions rather than the ranks of faculty, and they are suggesting strategies from the corporate sector such as privatization and outsourcing.

Longevity of Employment

There is minimal employee turnover in higher education. Faculty members tend to stay in their job for their entire careers because of the tenure system. Yet, this is one characteristic that is rapidly changing as faculty members move from tenure track to mostly contingent appointments (Kezar & Sam, 2010). There are few organizations with this type of employee stability. In addition, even part-time and contract faculty members, noted as a rising percentage in the faculty, also tend to stay at institutions for a long period of time (Finklestein, Seal, & Schuster, 1999). Administrative staff members have more turnover, but compared to administrative staff in some other sectors their tenure is lengthy (Donofrio, 1990).

Image- and Reputation–Driven Organizations

Image drives behavior in higher education institutions because there are few bottom line measures, such as profit or return on investment, for assessing an institution's standing or establishing its competitive advantage (Astin, 1993; Gioia & Thomas, 1996; Pusser, 2012). Image is generally defined as how members believe others view their organization—and ultimately how others view individuals within the organization (Gioia & Thomas, 1996). This means that benchmarking, peer evaluations, and other comparative systems and ranks tend to influence behavior.

Returning to our example of the learning community, how can these unique organizational characteristics help shape our strategy? Knowing that shared governance is an important structure on many campuses, leaders can make sure to engage key stakeholders in the shared governance process through discussions about creating a learning community. Although in businesses, leaders can hire new people and easily fire people who no longer fit a certain role, in higher education staff and faculty members are less expendable, and training and development of longtime employees is required. Therefore, in starting up a learning community, the center for teaching and learning might offer a course on developing interdisciplinary courses and staff members might be trained on how their role will change as a result of developing learning communities. Because most campuses are not fashioned in a way to support collaborative work, and therefore people more often work autonomously, the campus likely will have to be restructured in order for the learning community to be effectively implemented, including the development of a cross-campus team representing different institutional units and decisions that are often siloed from each other. Because influential longtime employees have great powers of persuasion, longtime and respected faculty members on campus can be recruited to support the learning community idea and promote the idea among various disciplines. Also, because of the loose coupling of campus operations, it will take multiple efforts at persuasion and influence among a variety of different groups throughout the system in order to implement the change in learning communities.

Organizational Change as Challenging: Culture and Sensemaking

With a better understanding of the unique features of higher education as a long-standing organization, with complex and multiple goals, competing authority structures, and entrenched longtime employees, new professionals can better understand why change might entail persistence and determination. In this section, I explore two other theories or frameworks that help to explain change processes as potentially long term and challenging: organizational culture and sensemaking (Kezar, 2013). Organizational culture is the perspective that institutions are primarily driven by underlying values and assumptions that become tacit. Because they are tacit, institutional actors are not conscious of their beliefs and typically act more on impulse and routine. When staff and faculty members (and even students) operate from routines, change can be challenging. Imagine trying to persuade faculty members to move from lectures to active learning. Their underlying belief is that good teaching involves delivery of content. Asking them to move to a mode where they don't deliver content violates their unarticulated beliefs about good teaching. Sensemaking is a theory that helps explain ways that people can change, especially in relationship to taken-for-granted notions such as "good teaching." Sensemaking includes processes that help people to surface and examine their underlying assumptions about any concept and therefore make it more open to alteration (Weick, 1995). Sensemaking is a strategy to address deep-seated cultural changes—one's that we are often confronted with in higher education.

Cultural Theories

Cultural theories of change emphasize the need to analyze and be cognizant of underlying systems of meaning, assumptions, and values that are often not directly articulated, but shape institutional operations and can prevent or facilitate change. Change within an organization entails the alteration of deeply embedded values, beliefs, myths, and rituals (Kezar, 2013; Schein, 2004). In this section, I review some of the key aspects that can be used to understand the often-elusive institutional culture as well as ways to change it. First, history and traditions are important to understand, because they represent the collective experience of change processes over time. Understanding how individuals and groups reacted to earlier efforts, as well as the barriers that emerged and values that surfaced, is critical to a change agent's success. Institutional history and traditions have been found to strongly influence change processes and the way people make sense. So, change agents must carefully analyze the history of an issue they are embarking to change. Clearly history is deeply embedded, so this theory emphasizes how change is likely not to emerge from superficial efforts.

Perhaps the most important drivers of change (and barrier to it) are values and underlying assumptions. Values can be elusive because they are sometimes unarticulated and other times aspirational or espoused. Values guide behavior but often in a way that happens unconsciously. Values are often not clearly expressed and are difficult for people to articulate. Behaviors of people on campus reflect a system of values, as do the artifacts (for example, a policy) and symbols (for example, an image) that exist—sometimes these are a better reflection of values. It is important to recognize that espoused values are not always the true values of an organization. In fact, espoused values, examples of which are found in campus mission and values statements, are often aspirational; they reflect what a campus would like to be. Espoused and aspirational values can be potentially significant levers for change because they represent specific areas where stakeholders across the campus might be willing to invest resources and effort to achieve goals. Altering values that are often held firmly and serve to guide action also points to the difficulty of change.

Institutional culture can also be captured in the language and symbols people use on campus. People may use metaphors to describe and articulate meaning within settings and that capture views about change or particular issues. For example, student affairs staff members describing a wall between them and faculty members suggests collaboration will be difficult. New language might be invoked to support collaboration. Although language can be changed, it certainly takes time to use language enough to reinforce new ways of practice.

Artifacts are tangible representations of the value system of the organization. They can include policies, particular programs, or practice such as a way a campus goes about hiring employees. Artifacts that signal collaboration would be welcome on the campus or new practices that could be established would include joint committees, policies, or staffing arrangements. Although structures and processes do not always reflect underlying values, because they are dynamic, they often are an indicator of underlying assumptions and values. Change in artifacts can help to solidify and make real the changes in values that are desired.

A key finding from research is that change agents are more successful when they align their strategies with the institutional culture (Kezar & Eckel, 2002). For example, on a very decentralized campus, trying to develop a universal policy for all divisions and units might be met with great resistance. However, change agents can work from the bottom up within their different units to advance policies that are supportive of change initiatives campus-wide. By working within the institutional culture, which is decentralized, change agents will experience greater success and support than is likely to come from pushing for universal policy at the campus level alone. That approach would likely face persistent barriers and result in little or no change occurring. Kezar and Eckel (2002) demonstrated how savvy change agents conduct a cultural assessment and align strategies with the institutional culture.

Sensemaking

As noted, although values, artifacts, symbols, and language can all be used as levers for change, sensemaking has also been identified as a strategy to reshape the way people are entrenched in a particular value system (Kezar, 2013). Sensemaking highlights the role of learning and development with regard to change (Kezar, 2005). Studies of resistance to change illustrated that people were often not resisting a change because they disagreed with it but because they did not truly understand its nature or how they might integrate it into their work and role. Other times people held unconscious views that shaped their worldview (that is, paradigms and mental models) and that itself prevented change among individuals. Sensemaking is about changing mind-sets, which in turn alters behaviors, priorities, values, and commitments (Eckel & Kezar, 2003). Studies demonstrate that sensemaking is facilitated by change agents who can create vehicles for social interaction, introduce new ideas into the organization, provide opportunities for social connection, and effectively use language and communication to help facilitate people's evolving thinking (Gioia & Thomas, 1996; Weick, 1995). Examples of sensemaking strategies include ongoing campus brown bags or speaker series, professional development, bringing in outside speakers, creating concept papers to guide thinking, and cross-functional teams that work together regularly.

Part of the difficulty of creating change is realizing that people interpret their environment so differently from one another (Kenny, 2006). Therefore, the focus of change strategies within sensemaking is on how leaders can shape an individual's thinking within the change process, through framing and interpretation, and how individuals within an organization interpret and make sense of change (Kenny, 2006). Examples of the social cognition perspective in higher education include the work of Bolman and Deal (2013), Morgan (1997), and Weick (1995), the last of which explores how individuals view organizations in very different ways, making change challenging.

The goal of creating change at a broader level through learning and reexamining assumptions has led to two concepts that are gaining recognition: organizational learning and communities of practice. Organizational learning is described in the next section, but here I briefly discuss communities of practice as a strategy to create and scale change. Communities of practice are people who have shared occupations such as faculty members or student affairs practitioners. Changes might be implemented by affecting a particular community of practice that works across many different institutions throughout the entire sector. Communities of practice have been used on many campuses as a way to get people to think about the nature of their work differently. This strategy involves bringing staff members together to read some common publications, describe work in a shared area of interest (for example, how to assess student learning), and meet regularly to report on changes in their work.

Organizational Learning: Applying the Theories

Applying organizational theory to another example may be helpful. In this section, I synthesize and demonstrate how the theories together create a powerful strategy for action. Many organizations are under pressure to become learning organizations so that they can operate more effectively day-to-day, even if they are not engaged in a major change process such as implementing a learning community. Rather than pursue changes one by one, leaders help build the capacity for the organization to change on an ongoing basis. Learning organizations are campuses that value ongoing examination of existing practices and underlying assumptions through review of data in order to improve functioning. How can organizational theory help to create a learning organization in which employees of the institution routinely see it as their responsibility to acquire, organize, and use information to make better decisions and work with others to challenge existing norms about the organization and ensure the best functioning? The following example can also be used as a teaching tool to understand how each concept can be applied to a specific case, in this situation developing a learning organization. Although the example is at the overall campus level, students can apply it to their individual work situation or unit by imagining using concepts from the three concepts reviewed in this chapter. I provide examples in the following of how they might go about this activity.

Four Frames

Using the four frames, leaders would first examine if structures exist for acquiring data within the organization, such as an effective institutional research office and support offices throughout campus. It would also be important to examine the way that information is distributed from institutional research offices to campus employees, enabling the greatest access. After a review of the structures in place for collecting and distributing data, leaders need to examine whether faculty and staff members have the skills to examine such data and to make meaning out of it. It may be important to provide some training and development about the use of survey instruments. From the political frame, it might be important to consider if the implications of examining data might affect a group and whether the group should be contacted first and apprised of the data activity and brought into the process because it affects them more deeply. For example, if data are being collected about faculty member and student interactions, it is important to bring faculty members into the data collection process. And next, from a symbolic perspective, it is important that people understand the value of reviewing data and how they affect teaching and learning. Leaders may need to provide some initial framing and speeches about way that collecting data has proven effective on other campuses. An annual "data day" can be created to symbolize the campuses' commitment to improvement through data.

Distinctive Features of Higher Education

In thinking about creating a learning organization, it is also important to understand some of the distinctive features of higher education. Because of the power of image, campus leaders may want to emphasize how other campuses are using data to improve performance. Leaders are also aware that postsecondary institutions have ambiguous goals, decentralized processes, and unclear decision-making processes; therefore, getting data to the right people may require some mapping of the organization and conversations with people about who works on the process. Conversations about data may be necessary to reach various diffuse stakeholders. Also, people may need to obtain data that are outside the normal chain of command. Data also are not self-evident, and differing values (administrative versus faculty, for example) systems need to be taken into account when moving toward organizational learning. Dialogues should be hosted to unravel the meaning of data according to different groups. Otherwise, people may believe that their single interpretation is accepted and understood across campus. Given the vastly different values and interests, this assumption would be unwise.

Organizational Culture and Sensemaking

In thinking about creating a learning organization, theories of culture suggest the need to examine the ways that the campus has already used data for decision making. What experiences have there been and how successful were they? Have faculty or staff members ever felt threatened by the use of data to create decisions and drive institutional strategy. This will reveal potential barriers. Change agents might also examine the existing strategic plans for references to data use but looking for ways it is used regularly rather than episodically. Also, using current decision making as a barometer, change agents can reflect on what appears to be driving decisions (anecdote, influential individuals, rather than data). In exploring language or artifacts about learning communities, it will be important to explore how people discuss decision making and whether they mention or invoke data as well as systems they have to support a learning community. Not having a robust institutional research office, a way to distribute data, or a capacity for data may suggest a larger hurdle in terms of culture because there is little support in place—not just in terms of the campus systems but also in terms valuing data use. Conducting a cultural assessment can help gauge campus readiness for change.

Creating an organizational learning approach can be facilitated through sensemaking. A change agent might first speak to the value of organizational learning in order for people to become familiar with the concept or term. Then, training or professional development about how to establish organizational learning approaches, such as learning communities, might be offered. A brown bag series bringing in speakers from other campuses that have used learning communities to facilitate changes would be offered to help faculty and staff members envision what it would be like to partake in a learning community. Through these culture and sensemaking vehicles, change agents can break through the often-difficult-to-uncover veil of hidden assumptions that serve as a barrier to change.

Conclusion

Organizational theory can help student affairs leaders to become complex thinkers using multiple frames, understanding the unique characteristics and cultures of higher education, and delving into the rational and irrational sides of organizations. It will take years of practice to be able to sophisticatedly apply this thinking as an individual. However, creating leadership teams with people who hold different perspectives—seeing the world through different frames, existing in different subcultures on campus, with strengths in emotional and cognitive orientations—can help staff members and administrators to more quickly capitalize on complex thinking within the organization to inform decisions. Although I hope that you will continue to practice and advance your skills as an individual leader, I encourage you to develop the strongest leadership teams that represent the best thinking from organizational theory.

Discussion Questions

1. What organizational features make change challenging in higher education?
2. What are the four frames? What frame might you (the reader) be biased toward? Which frame might you need to work on? What frames can you see in the way your coworkers behave?
3. What features of higher education make it distinctive from other types of organizations, such as businesses? Which ones can you see operating within your own division, unit, or campus?
4. Why is culture change important? How do cultures change?

References

Astin, A. (1993). *What matters in college? Four critical years revisited.* San Francisco: Jossey-Bass.

Baldridge, J., Curtis, D., Ecker, G., & Riley, G. (1977). Alternative models of governance in higher education. In G. L. Riley & J. V. Baldridge (Eds.), *Governing academic organizations.* Berkeley, CA: McCutchan.

Bastedo, M. (2012). (Ed.). *The organization of higher education: Managing colleges for a new era.* Baltimore: Johns Hopkins University Press.

Bess, J. L. (1999, Nov.). *The ambiguity of authority in colleges and universities: Why the new managerialism is winning.* Paper presented at the annual meeting of the Association for the Study of Higher Education, San Antonio, TX.

Birnbaum, R. (1988). *How colleges work.* San Francisco: Jossey Bass.

Bolman, L., & Deal, T. (2013). *Reframing organizations.* San Francisco: Jossey Bass.

Clark, B. R. (1983). *The higher education system: Academic organization in cross-national perspective.* Berkeley: University of California Press.

Clark, B. R. (1991). Faculty organization and authority. In M. Peterson (Ed.), *ASHE reader on leadership and governance* (pp. 449–458). Needham Heights, MA: Gin Press.

Donofrio, K. (1990). *Compensation survey.* Washington, DC: College and University Personnel Association.

Eckel, P., & Kezar, A. (2003). Key strategies for making new institutional sense. *Higher Education Policy, 16*(1), 39–53.

Finklestein, M., Seal, M., & Schuster, J. (1999). New entrants to the full-time faculty of higher education institutions. *Education Statistics Quarterly, 1*(4), 78–80.

Gioia, D. A., & Thomas, J. B. (1996). Identity, image, and issue interpretation: Sensemaking during strategic change in academia. *Administrative Science Quarterly, 41*, 370–403.

Gumport, P. (1993). Contested terrain of academic program reduction. *Journal of Higher Education, 64*(3), 283–311.

Kenny, J. (2006). Strategy and the learning organization: A maturity model for formulation of strategy. *Learning Organization, 13*(4), 353–368.

Kezar, A. (2001). Understanding and facilitating organizational change in the 21st century: Recent research and conceptualizations *ASHE-ERIC Report Series, 28*(4). San Francisco: Jossey-Bass.

Kezar, A. (Ed.). (2005). *Higher education as a learning organization: Promising concepts and approaches* (New Directions for Higher Education, no. 131). San Francisco: Jossey-Bass.

Kezar, A. (2013). *How colleges change.* New York: Routledge.

Kezar, A., & Eckel, P. (2002). The effect of institutional culture on change strategies in higher education: Universal principles or culturally responsive concepts? *Journal of Higher Education, 73*(4), 435–460.

Kezar, A., & Sam, C. (2010). *The new faculty majority.* San Francisco: Jossey Bass.

Morgan, G. (1997). *Images of organization.* Thousand Oaks, CA: Sage.

Pusser, B (2012). Ranking and reputation in higher education. In M. Bastedo, (Ed.), *The organization of higher education: Managing colleges for a new era.* Baltimore: Johns Hopkins University Press.

Rhoades, G. (1995). Rethinking and restructuring universities. *Journal of Higher Education Management, 10*(2), 17–23.

Schein, E. (2004). *Organizational culture and leadership.* San Francisco: Jossey Bass.

Sporn, B. (1999). *Adaptive university structures: An analysis of adaptation to socioeconomic environments of U.S. and European universities.* London: Jessica Kingsley.

Weick, K. E. (1991). Educational organizations as loosely coupled systems. In M. W. Peterson, E. E. Chaffee, & T. H. White (Eds.), *Organization and governance in higher education* (4th ed.). Needham Heights, MA: Ginn Press.

Weick, K. (1995). *Sensemaking in organizations.* Thousand Oaks, CA: Sage.

CHAPTER 14

ENVIRONMENTAL THEORIES

Samuel D. Museus

Decades ago, scholars acknowledged the important function of campus environments in shaping the student experience (Moos, 1979). Today, few would argue with the assertion that campus environments play a critical role in college. In fact, the arrangement of campus environments could be the most powerful tool for college educators to affect their students (Moos, 1986). Indeed, although colleges and universities possess limited control over students' precollege dispositions and academic preparation levels, their capacity to shape environments on their campuses is significant.

Existing empirical evidence suggests that campus environments exhibit a profound impact on the experiences of students in college and the outcomes that they achieve during their time in higher education (Kuh, Kinzie, Schuh, Whitt, & Associates, 2005; Museus, 2014). Given the important role of campus environments in determining student experiences and outcomes, it is critical for college educators to understand their institutional environments and the ways in which these milieus shape individual experiences. Such an understanding enables college educators to maximize the extent to which their institutional environments enable students to thrive and minimize the existence of campus settings that hinder or adversely affect development and success among students on their campuses (Strange & Banning, 2001, 2015).

College and university educators who wish to better understand the nature of their campus environments and how these environments shape the experiences and outcomes of college students have many different perspectives and frameworks at their disposal. For the purposes of the current chapter, I use the term *environmental perspective* to indicate a proposed viewpoint about a focal phenomenon. The term *environmental framework* refers to a conceptual lens that can be used to make sense of the nature and impact of organizational environments on an outcome. In addition, I use the terms *typologies* and *models* to signify specific types of frameworks, with *typologies* referring to a delineation of different types of a focal phenomenon (such a delineation of the various types or personalities) and conceptual *models* denoting a set of concepts and hypotheses that seek to explain a focal process (such as a model that explains the impact of environments on student success). In this chapter, I provide an overview of some useful environmental perspectives and frameworks and discuss their applicability to the work of college educators today. The underlying assumption is that the perspectives and frameworks discussed herein can guide evidence-based research, policy, or practice aimed at creating, understanding, assessing, and improving institutional environments.

In the next section, I offer some general perspectives regarding the nature of the relationship between campus environments and college students. Then, I provide an overview of typologies and models that explain the nature and complexity of campus environments and how they shape college students' experiences and outcomes. The chapter concludes with discussion questions and a case study for readers to apply these frameworks to the analysis of real problems in postsecondary education.

Relationship between Campus Environments and College Students

College educators can use a range of perspectives to understand the relationships between institutional environments and college students. Some of these perspectives provide views on the responsibility of campuses to affect student outcomes. Other perspectives seek to explain how the characteristics of campus environments and college students interact to shape one another. I review several of the most influential environmental perspectives in this section.

Role of Campus Environments in Serving Students

Banning and Kaiser (1974) outlined several perspectives that have informed understanding of the roles of campuses and students in shaping undergraduate outcomes. First, the *unenlightened perspective* suggests that some young people do not belong in higher education and the expectation should be that many of them should not succeed. Second, the *adjustment perspective* indicates that institutions should provide students who are unlikely to succeed with the proper supports to change and better fit the environment of their institution. Third, the *developmental perspective* suggests that students are undergoing a growth period and must go through a process of development in order to benefit from college. According to this third perspective, higher education institutions have a responsibility to support college students in their development so they can reach a point at which they can benefit from the environment that campuses provide.

Banning and Kaiser (1974) noted that, although each of the three aforementioned perspectives has strengths and limitations, none of them sufficiently acknowledges the process of institutional change and institutions' responsibility to adapt to students. A failure to adequately recognize institutional responsibility for creating the conditions for students to thrive can be highly problematic because it fuels assumptions that the crux of responsibility for success belongs to students themselves and allows institutional responsibilities to fade into the background. In response, Banning and Kaiser offered an *ecological perspective*, which is based on the assumption that campuses have a responsibility to design and cultivate environments that help students thrive.

It is important to note that a failure to understand and acknowledge the institutional responsibility to cultivate the conditions for *all* students to thrive is particularly detrimental for populations that have been historically marginalized by postsecondary institutions but comprise an increasingly larger proportion of students on today's campuses (including, but not limited to, indigenous, minoritized, low-income, and first-generation students). Because most campuses were not originally designed to serve these populations, they must navigate a greater level of adaptation to fit into their respective institutional environments and are likely to encounter greater challenges doing so (Museus & Quaye, 2009; Tierney, 1992, 1999). Therefore, it is imperative that college campuses assume responsibility for all students' success. In the following sections, I discuss environmental perspectives that have been offered to help understand the relationship between postsecondary campuses and their undergraduate populations and can be used to guide efforts to construct campus environments that best serve today's diverse college students.

Relationship between Campus Environments and College Student Characteristics

Throughout the twentieth century, many researchers studied the relationship between environmental settings and the orientations of individual students (Barker, 1968; Clark & Trow, 1966; Holland, 1973; Stern, 1970). For example, Barker (1968) argued that behavioral settings attract and influence the behaviors of people who inhabit them. As a result, despite individual differences, people tend to behave in substantially similar ways when they inhabit the same environments. Thus, Barker argued that human environments exhibit a seemingly coercive impact on human behaviors (Walsh, 1973). In addition, Stern (1970) proposed a need-press model, which suggests that environments (presses) and people (needs) have a significant impact on individual behaviors. Environmental press places demands on people who exist within the environment, and individuals will gravitate toward environments that fulfill their needs. For example, the need-press model suggests that students who value diversity but attend campuses that lack enacted institutional diversity values might feel pressure to de-emphasize their appreciation for diversity. Moreover, the model suggests that students who value diversity and attend institutions that do not enact such values will be inclined to seek out subcultures that incorporate diversity into their spaces, discourse, policies, programming, practices, and interactions in a more meaningful way.

Clark and Trow (1966) shed light on the ways in which environments influence individual behavior. They offered a typology of four kinds of student subcultures most prevalent in higher education. First, *academic* subcultures are composed of serious students who work hard, exhibit high rates of academic achievement, and are engaged. Second, *nonconformist* subcultures are composed of students who identify in opposition to and express hostility toward the administration. Third, *collegiate* subcultures are loyal to their institutions but resistant to intellectual demands of college life while placing the premium on social, extracurricular, and athletic activities. Finally, *vocational* subcultures include students who care less about ideas or engagements in college but are focused on training to advance career opportunities. Clark and Trow emphasized the notion that people are attracted to and engaged in environments that are congruent with their own existing personal characteristics.

Finally, Holland (1973) also recognized the role of the environment and individual in determining human behavior. He outlined a typology of six dominant personalities: (1) *realistic* people who prefer ordered and systematic activities; (2) *investigative* persons who prefer observational and creative activities; (3) *artistic* personalities who favor ambiguous and unsystematic activities to create art; (4) *social* people who prefer activities that include manipulation of others to inform and enlighten or use of materials and tools; (5) *enterprising* persons who favor activities involving manipulation of others to achieve organizational goals or economic gain; and (6) *conventional* personalities who prefer ordered and systematic activities to operate machines and process data to attain organizational goals. Holland also suggested that there are six types of environments, reflecting the six personality types. Holland asserted that greater congruence between personalities and their environments leads to outcomes that are comprehensible from the perspective of the environment and individual. In the context of higher education, this framework suggests that students will choose environments or academic majors that are congruent with their personalities, and the level of congruence that exists between these environments and individual personalities is related to positive outcomes.

The aforementioned perspectives and frameworks vary in terms of their emphases and nuances. For example, some of these perspectives and frameworks stress the role of environments in influencing the individual (for example, Barker, 1968), and others foreground the impact of individual characteristics on their environments (for example, Clark & Trow, 1966; Holland, 1973). They also provide different typologies to understand the characteristics of individuals that comprise environments (for example, Clark & Trow, 1966; Holland, 1973). However, a key commonality across these perspectives and frameworks is that they all suggest that environmental and individual characteristics play a crucial role in determining students' behaviors. In addition, all of them underscore the importance of congruence between environments and persons in establishing a good fit and fostering positive outcomes. In the following sections, I provide an overview of frameworks that seek to further explain the nature and key components of campus environments as well as their impact on students.

Understanding the Elements of Campus Environments

Researchers have offered frameworks that can help better understand the nature of campus environments and their impact on students. In this section, I discuss three existing frameworks that, together, highlight key elements of campus environments, illuminate the complexity of campus milieus, and offer an understanding of how aspects of the campus environment can be adapted to respond to today's diverse college students.

Critical Elements of Campus Environments

In 1979, Rudolf Moos identified four key components of environments, including the physical setting, organizational factors, human aggregate, and social climate. Strange and Banning (2015) slightly adapted this framework to underscore four critical aspects of the campus environment in college: physical, organizational, human aggregate, and constructed environments.

First, *physical environments* refer to the physical features of campuses that stimulate, limit, or otherwise influence individual behaviors (Ellen, 1982; Moos, 1979). The physical features of campuses are often the most critical factors in shaping initial impressions of postsecondary institutions (Sturner, 1973). In addition, the physical features of college campuses stimulate some behaviors while rendering others less probable (Strange & Banning, 2015). For example, the placement of a cultural center on the first-floor of a building in a high-traffic area at the center of campus, rather than at the periphery of campus, might make it more likely that students will view the center as a valued entity on campus and access the services provided by that office.

Second, *organizational environments* of campuses emerge from the patterns of organization, structure, and process that evolve within institutions to achieve goals (Etzioni, 1964; Moos, 1979; Strange & Banning, 2001, 2015). Organizational environments include divisions of labor, power, and communication responsibilities. In other words, the ways in which responsibilities for managing academic programs, administrative support services (such as human resources), student support services (such as counseling and academic advising), and student activities are divided among various units partially determine the nature of the organizational environment. In addition, power centers that control behaviors directed toward the achievement of organizational goals, such as divisions of student affairs controlling leadership programs that contribute to the university's goals of developing society's future leaders, play a major role in shaping the environment. Finally, movement within or across organizational boundaries—such as hiring, termination, transfer, or promotion—shapes the organizational environment. For instance, if divisions or departments make a commitment to hire diverse peoples and are successful at it, such actions can function to reshape the environments on their campuses in significant ways. It is also important to acknowledge that organizational environments vary along a wide range of dimensions (Strange & Banning, 2001, 2015):

- **Complexity:** Postsecondary institutions vary in size and number of units that exist within their organizations.
- **Centralization:** More centralized institutions might be required to make decisions that are driven more heavily by executive administrators, whereas the decision making at decentralized campuses is concentrated in departments and programs dispersed across their institutions.
- **Formalization:** Campuses differ in the extent to which rules are formalized in institutional policies and norms, such as variation in the degree to which individuals are expected to be physically present during business hours.
- **Morale:** Institutions vary in the level of morale that exists within the environment, with some institutions engendering more enthusiasm and commitment to be part of the campus community among its members than others.

Third, *human aggregate environments* have to do with the dominant characteristics of individuals in a given setting (Moos, 1986; Strange & Banning, 2001, 2015). Specifically, a human aggregate view suggests that environments are transmitted through people, and the dominant characteristics of an environment are, in part, a function of the individuals who comprise it (Holland, 1973; Moos, 1986). Indeed, as previously discussed, scholars documented that students' characteristics, such as their demographic characteristics and personality types, shape their respective environments (Astin, 1993; Clark & Trow, 1966; Holland, 1973). For example, in many cases, students create and recreate subcultures that are defined by their races, ethnicities, sexual orientations, religions, academic and professional goals, civic attitudes, or athletic interests (Museus, 2008; Rhoads, 1997). And, the degree of congruence between the characteristics of human aggregate and individual students is positively related to the latter's attraction to, satisfaction in, and success in their respective environments. For example, students who enter college with a passion for leadership might be more likely to seek out, find, and engage in leadership programs and activities on their campuses. Although it is important to acknowledge that such views have been critiqued for being somewhat reductionistic in their categorization of students into various trait types, these perspectives can be useful in better understanding the (in)congruence between the dominant characteristics of human aggregates and individuals within an environment (Strange & Banning, 2015). An understanding of human aggregates can also inform the design and construction of more beneficial institutional environments.

Finally, *constructed environments* emphasize the socially constructed elements of organizational environments and acknowledge that a consensus of individuals constitutes an important environmental press that exerts direct influence on human behavior (Moos, 1986; Strange & Banning, 2015). Constructed environments focus on the subjective views and experiences of students on college campuses.

This point is important because the same human aggregates can be perceived as welcoming and friendly to one person while simultaneously cold or hostile to another. This point is illustrated by the results of campus climate studies, which show that minoritized racial and ethnic student populations often perceive the environment as less friendly and more hostile than their majority counterparts (Museus, Nichols, & Lambert, 2008). Moreover, the notion of constructed environments suggests that dominant institutional characteristics pressure students to conform to these dominant features. For example, postsecondary campuses with a strong tradition in athletics exert an environmental press that encourages students to participate in athletic life of the college or university regardless of whether they have a desire for such participation on matriculation. In sum, physical, organizational, human aggregate, and constructed environments all play a powerful role shaping human behavior, experiences, and outcomes in college.

Ecological Nature of Campus Environments

Although Moos (1974, 1979) wrote about the different critical elements of campus environments, Bronfenbrenner (1979) expressed concerns that developmental theorists were not giving sufficient attention to the role of environments in human development processes. He noted that "the understanding of human development demands more than the direct observation of behavior on the part of one or two persons in the same place; it requires an examination of multiperson systems of interaction not limited to a single study that must take into account aspects of the environment beyond the immediate situation containing the subject" (p. 21).

This assertion prompts educators to view campus systems in more complex ways by transcending socially constructed divisions, such as dichotomies between curricular and extracurricular settings or peer culture and administrative faculty spheres (Renn, 2003).

Bronfenbrenner's (1979) ecological model of human development illuminates the ecological nature of environments with greater complexity. The ecological model suggests that person, process, context, and time mutually shape the environment and development that takes place within it. The *person* element of the ecological model refers to individuals who exist within an environment and, in the context of higher education, includes the individual backgrounds, experiences, and characteristics that students bring with them into the environment. The *process* component of the model encompasses the interactions of people with an environment and their responses to it.

The Bronfenbrenner model places the student at the center of an ecological system, embedded within four nested layers of environmental *context*. First, *microsystems* are immediate settings that the individual navigates and constitute the location of proximal developmental processes. These microsystems include, but are not limited to, spaces such as classrooms, extracurricular spaces, and living quarters. Second, *mesosystems* refer to cases in which multiple microsystems interact and focus on the synergy that results from such interactions.

For example, the model suggests that students' families, communities, curricular, social, and work mesosystems might interact to shape their developmental processes. Third, *exosystems* underscore instances in which environments to which the individual does not belong influence her development. An example of exosystem influences could be faculty and administrative decisions to require diversity courses in the general education curriculum influencing the development of students who must fulfill that requirement. Finally, *macrosystems* involve the overarching interactions of microsystems, mesosystems, and exosystems, as well as the development of opportunities that emerge from those patterns (Bronfenbrenner, 1993).

Throughout Bronfenbrenner's life, the ecological model was constantly evolving and he included or excluded *time* as an essential element of the environmental ecology depending on the iteration of his work. Bronfenbrenner (1979) did assert that development involves individual change that is not bound by short durations of time but instead continues over time and space. In later iterations of his work, Bronfenbrenner (1995) added the *chronosystem* as an important component of the ecological model:

> The individual's own developmental life course is seen as embedded in and powerfully shaped by conditions and events occurring during the historical period through which the person lives . . . A major factor influencing the course and outcome of human development is the timing of biological and social transitions as they relate to the culturally defined age, role expectations, and opportunities occurring throughout the life course. (p. 641)

Therefore, the chronosystem suggests that individual developmental processes are partially a function of history, culture, and society. For example, the ways in which college students who do not feel welcome on campus experience the environment might shift in a positive direction after their institution conducts a climate assessment and makes efforts to cultivate more inclusive and welcoming environments. The chronosystem also suggests that the timing of events throughout the life span influences the ways in which human developmental processes unfold. For instance, it could be argued that older students who have accumulated a wider range of experiences in personal and professional spheres will go through different developmental processes than adolescent students who have had less extensive life experiences. In sum, the ecological model underscores the complex ways in which different elements of environmental systems interact to shape students' experiences and development in college.

Relevance and Responsiveness of Campus Environments

Since 2000, a significant amount of empirical research has been generated on the ways in which campus environments shape experiences of diverse student populations (Museus, 2014). Much of this research focuses on how specific aspects of the environment, such as campus climate or campus culture, influence the experiences and outcomes of college students and is reviewed in other chapters within this book. However, Museus's (2014) culturally engaging campus environments (CECE) model offers a broader framework that accounts for climate, culture, and other types of campus environments (such as organizational environments) to explain the impact of institutional environments on the outcomes of diverse student populations.

The CECE model highlights the role of institutions in constructing environments that shape students' experiences and outcomes. The model assumes that physical settings, organizational structures, human aggregates, and constructed environments all play a role in determining the degree to which campus environments are relevant and responsive to college students' backgrounds, communities, and identities. It also assumes that microsystems, mesosystems, and exosystems all play a role in determining the extent to which campus environments are relevant and responsive to students. Therefore, it implies that campuses have the capacity to construct environments that are relevant and respond to college students and maximize their engagement, development, and success.

The CECE model acknowledges that external influences (financial factors, employment, and family influences) and precollege inputs (academic preparation and academic dispositions at the time of entry) shape college experiences and outcomes (learning, satisfaction, persistence, and degree completion). However, the core of the CECE model emphasizes that college students' access to culturally engaging campus environments is positively correlated with individual influences on success (sense of belonging, academic self-efficacy, motivation, intent to persist, and academic performance) and ultimately an increased likelihood of success. The CECE model delineates nine indicators of the extent to which campus environments are culturally engaging for diverse students. These indicators can be divided into two subgroups of cultural relevance and responsiveness.

Relevance Five indicators focus on the ways that learning environments are relevant to the backgrounds, identities, and communities of college students:

1. **Cultural familiarity:** Availability of campus spaces for undergraduates to connect with faculty and staff members and peers who understand their backgrounds and experiences
2. **Culturally relevant knowledge:** Access to opportunities to learn about students' own communities via culturally relevant curricular and cocurricular activities
3. **Cultural community service:** Availability of mechanisms for students to give back to and positively transform their home communities (such as via problem-based research or service-learning)
4. **Meaningful cross-cultural engagement:** Degree to which programs and practices facilitate educationally meaningful cross-cultural interactions

among their students that focus on solving real social and political problems

5. **Culturally validating environments:** Extent to which campuses validate the cultural backgrounds, knowledge, and identities of diverse students

Responsiveness   The remaining four indicators focus on the degree to which campus support systems respond to the norms and needs of communities from which diverse students come:

1. **Collectivist cultural orientations:** Degree to which campuses emphasize a collectivist, rather than individualistic, cultural orientation that is characterized by teamwork and pursuit of mutual success
2. **Humanized educational environments:** Availability of opportunities to develop meaningful relationships with faculty and staff members who care about and are committed to students' successes
3. **Proactive philosophies:** Extent to which proactive philosophies lead faculty and staff members and administrators to go beyond making resources available and bring important information, opportunities, and support services to students
4. **Holistic support:** Degree of students' access to at least one faculty or staff member whom they are confident will provide the information they need, offer the help they seek, or connect them with the information or support they require regardless of the issue they face

In sum, the CECE framework offers one conceptual lens to understand how postsecondary campuses can and do cultivate environments that maximize congruence between institutional environments and individual students' lives, thereby potentially enhancing positive student outcomes.

Critical Contemporary Contexts

An informed understanding of campus environments must include a consideration of critical contemporary trends affecting the environments of postsecondary institutions and their students. It can be argued that three larger contemporary social trends, in particular, most profoundly affect college campuses and students: diversification, globalization, and digitization (Museus, 2011).

As a result of the change of US society, the domestic undergraduate population also is becoming rapidly more diverse (Prior, Hurtado, Saenz, Santos, & Korn, 2007). At the same time, forces of globalization are also contributing to undergraduate diversity through the expansion of international student populations across the United States (Institute of International Education, 2014). It could be argued that the increasing complexity of student bodies renders it more challenging for educators to foster environments that maximize positive outcomes for all. However, these developments also make it urgent for educators to assume responsibility to cultivate optimal environments for increasingly diverse students, produce the new generation of leaders who can function in an increasingly global society, and contribute to solutions to the nation's most pressing social problems, such as war, poverty, and inequality.

In recent decades, the expansion of digital technology has transformed the lives of students and campuses. Indeed, computers, smartphones, text messages, mobile applications, video chatting, and social networking are just a few digital mechanisms that today's students use to communicate and collaborate, search for information, and access online courses (Strange & Banning, 2015). Similarly, institutions now regularly use digital tools, such as websites to convey information about their campuses, online course management systems to facilitate learning, and electronic security systems to alert students to dangers on campus. It is important to note that, left unchecked, digital environments can negatively affect students by, for example, providing students with unlimited access to prejudicial or hostile digital content (Museus & Truong, 2013). At the same time, many educators are using digital pedagogies and social media to build community and engage students (Strange & Banning, 2015). Thus, it is critical that educators understand how to engage these environments in ways that enhance the quality of students' college experiences.

Implications for Student Affairs Educators

In the previous sections, I outlined a variety of perspectives and frameworks that help shed light on the nature of campus environments and their relationship to college students' experiences and outcomes. In this section, I build on that discussion to offer a few general recommendations for student affairs educators who are engaging or will engage in the difficult work of (re)designing and (re)constructing their campus environments.

In order to (re)design and (re)construct optimal campus environments to maximize positive student outcomes, it is important that educators use research and evidence to guide their efforts. Failure to engage research and evidence can lead to institutions investing an immense amount of resources in efforts that do not necessarily enhance their institutions' capacity to serve their respective students. By contrast, engaging research and evidence in such endeavors enables college educators to target resources toward efforts that facilitate the meaningful transformation of campus environments and improve students' experiences and outcomes.

The perspectives and frameworks discussed herein inform several recommendations for student affairs educators working to foster and improve environments that facilitate student learning, development, and success. They include, but are not limited to, the following:

Focus on the environment: As mentioned in the previous sections, many educators espouse views that students either are or are not college material.

Some educators also view college success as the sole or primary responsibility of the student. Such perspectives limit the capacity of educators to foster success among the individuals whom they serve. Therefore, it is prudent for educators to focus on how they can cultivate optimal environments so that all students have the *opportunity* to learn, grow, and succeed regardless of their levels of preparation or where their educational and professional trajectories may lead.

Recognize the power of spaces and structures: Some of the aforementioned perspectives and frameworks, such as Strange and Banning's (2015) aspects of campus environments, highlight the power of physical settings and organizational structures on the overall environment. For example, inclusive physical spaces can be created to empower people, artwork can send signals of exclusion or inclusion to members of various identity groups, and the organization of campus units can facilitate or hinder educators' abilities to provide students with holistic support. These aspects of the environment sometimes can be easy to ignore, because many physical settings and organizational structures are long-standing and not easy to change. Nevertheless, these elements of the environment must be engaged in efforts to (re)design and (re)construct campus environments in meaningful ways.

Consider multiple levels of context: When college educators design and implement programs and practices, it may seem intuitive to focus on microsystems in which tangible and intentional interactions often take place. However, a failure to also consider mesosystems, exosystems, and macrosystems when constructing programs and services can contribute to a myopic view that fails to take into account the ways in which policies, practices, and interactions in other parts of their campuses are affecting the students whom they serve. For example, decisions to hire counselors from minoritized populations might make it more likely that students from those communities will access counseling services (see Suzuki, 2002), which might subsequently influence the likelihood that these students will succeed academically and develop in healthy ways. In sum, to holistically understand how the environment is shaping students' experiences, campuses must be viewed through a more multifaceted lens that accounts for the complexity of the systems that students are required to navigate.

Account for diversity and the differential impact of environments: Campus environments are socially constructed, and different people can experience the same environment in disparate ways. It is, therefore, essential that educators continually examine their campuses through a critical lens to understand how environments that positively affect the experiences of some groups might further alienate other populations. Such critical analysis is especially important for institutions to adequately serve historically marginalized and underserved groups, who are at greater risk of being disadvantaged by campus environments that are designed to support the student populations that are most visible and have the loudest voices at their institutions (Museus & Jayakumar, 2012). Engaging in continual critical analysis of campus milieus can enable postsecondary educators to design and construct environments that are optimally relevant, responsive, and empowering to all students whom they serve.

These are just a few examples of how the aforementioned perspectives and frameworks can be applied to the analysis and transformation of campus environments. It is important to acknowledge, however, that specific recommendations regarding how to transform or enhance an institution's environments must be informed by an understanding of its unique history, culture, and region. Nonetheless, the recommendations offered herein are intended to catalyze discussions and thinking about how the information offered in the previous sections might be applied within those varied contexts.

Conclusion

Few would deny that the intentional design of environments is one powerful mechanism that college educators have at their disposal to create the conditions to maximize student learning, development, and success. In this chapter I discussed several environmental perspectives and frameworks offered to guide college educators in the evidence-based understanding, assessment, cultivation, and improvement of their respective institutional environments. Also underscored is the reality that contemporary social trends, such as the increasing diversification of US society, internationalization of higher education, and digitization of educational processes, must also be understood in order to most thoughtfully cultivate optimal environments for today's college students. Campus leaders can use the perspectives and frameworks discussed in this chapter to focus their success efforts on the environment, understand the power of physical structures in their efforts, use multiple levels of the environment to inform their strategies, and keep in mind the subjective nature of institutional environments.

Discussion Questions and Activity

1. In what ways might the four critical elements of campus environments inform assessment at your institution?
2. How might an understanding of the more complex and multilayered ecology of environments inform efforts to facilitate student development on your campus?
3. In what ways can student affairs educators rethink their cocurricula, programs, and spaces to make them more culturally relevant and responsive?
4. In efforts to enhance student learning, which aspects of the environment do you believe are most critical to engage? How would those aspects of the environment be engaged to increase student learning at your institution?
5. How might some aspects of the campus environment, such as physical settings or constructed environments, affect different groups in disparate ways?

Crisis at Midwestern University

Midwestern State University (MSU) is an urban public research university located in a state that recently passed a performance funding bill that declares that the allocation of public funds to state colleges and universities will now be based on institutions' persistence and graduation rates. Unfortunately, MSU has historically had relatively low graduation rates. Approximately 70 percent of MSU's first-time, full-time students return in the second year, and only 55 percent of their students graduate with a bachelor's degree within six years of matriculation. Moreover, racial and socioeconomic disparities exist, with the six-year graduation rate for undergraduates of color, first-generation students, and low-income college students hovering around 40 percent. As a result, MSU is in jeopardy of losing a substantial portion of its state funding.

The MSU campus recently conducted an assessment to explore some of the reasons why students are not persisting and completing their degrees on time. The assessment revealed that students at MSU exhibit relatively low levels of engagement, struggle to find a sense of belonging on campus, and are generally dissatisfied with the campus environment. Moreover, the assessment findings suggest that students of color, first-generation undergraduates, and low-income students all exhibit lower levels of engagement, belonging, and satisfaction. Executive administrators at MSU believe that the campus historically has failed to strategically design and construct environments to maximize engagement, belonging, and satisfaction on campus among its diverse students. In response, the administration initiated a task force with the charge of developing a strategic plan to redesign the campus environment with the long-term vision of improving their students' experiences and outcomes. Use the environmental perspectives discussed in this chapter to answer the following questions:

1. How can the environmental perspectives discussed in this chapter help explain the current situation at MSU? Are some perspectives more useful than others?
2. Use one or more of the frameworks discussed in the proceeding sections to develop an action plan that is aimed at leveraging campus environments to increase engagement, belonging, and satisfaction at MSU. What would such a plan look like? How would the frameworks inform this plan?

References

Astin, A. W. (1993). *What matters in college? Four critical years revisited.* San Francisco: Jossey-Bass.

Banning, J. H., & Kaiser, L. (1974). An ecological perspective and model for campus design. *The Personnel and Guidance Journal, 52*(6), 370–375.

Barker, R. G. (1968). *Ecological psychology: Concepts and methods for studying the environment of human behavior.* Palo Alto, CA: Stanford University Press.

Bronfenbrenner, U. (1979). *The ecology of human development: Experiments by nature and design.* Cambridge, MA: Harvard University Press.

Bronfenbrenner, U. (1993). The ecology of cognitive development: Research models and fugitive findings. In R. H. Wozniak & K. W. Fischer (Eds.), *Development in context: Acting and thinking in specific environments* (pp. 3–44). Hillsdale, NJ: Lawrence Erlbaum.

Bronfenbrenner, U. (1995). Developmental ecology through space and time: A future perspective. In P. Moen & G. H. Elder Jr. (Eds.), *Examining lives in context: Perspectives on the ecology of human development* (pp. 619–647). Washington, DC: American Psychological Association.

Clark, B. R., & Trow, M. (1966). The organizational context. In T. M. Newcomb & E. K. Wilson (Eds.), *College peer groups: Problems and prospects for research.* Chicago: Aldine.

Ellen, R. (1982). *Environment, subsistence and system: The ecology of small-scale social formations.* New York: Cambridge University Press.

Etzioni, A. (1964). *Modern organizations.* Englewood Cliffs, NJ: Prentice-Hall.

Holland, J. L. (1973). *Making vocational choices: A theory of careers.* Upper Saddle River, NJ: Prentice-Hall.

Institute of International Education. (2014). *Open doors report on international educational exchange.* New York: Author.

Kuh, G. D., Kinzie, J., Schuh, J. H., Whitt, E. J., & Associates (2005). *Student success in college: Creating conditions that matter.* San Francisco: Jossey-Bass.

Moos, R. H. (1974). *Family environment scale—Form R.* Palo Alto, CA: Consulting Psychologists Press.

Moos, R. H. (1979). *Evaluating educational environments.* San Francisco: Jossey-Bass.

Moos, R. H. (1986). *The human context: Environmental determinants of behavior.* Malabar, FL: Krieger.

Museus, S. D. (2008). Understanding the role of ethnic student organizations in facilitating cultural adjustment and membership among African American and Asian American college students. *Journal of College Student Development, 59*(6), 568–586.

Museus, S. D. (2011). Asian American millennials college in context: Living at the intersection of diversification, digitization, and globalization. In F. Bonner & V. Lechuga (Eds.), *Diverse millennial students in college: Implications for faculty and student affairs* (pp. 69–88). Sterling, VA: Stylus.

Museus, S. D. (2014). The culturally engaging campus environments (CECE) model: A new theory of college success among racially diverse student populations. In M. B. Paulsen (Ed.), *Higher education: Handbook of theory and research* (pp. 189–227). New York: Springer.

Museus, S. D., & Jayakumar, U. M. (Eds.). (2012). *Creating campus cultures: Fostering success among racially diverse student populations.* New York: Routledge.

Museus, S. D., Nichols, A. H., & Lambert, A. (2008). Racial differences in the effects of campus racial climate on degree completion: A structural model. *The Review of Higher Education, 32*(1), 107–134.

Museus, S. D., & Quaye, S. J. (2009). Toward an intercultural perspective of racial and ethnic minority college student persistence. *The Review of Higher Education, 33*(1), 67–94.

Museus, S. D., & Truong, K. A. (2013). Racism and sexism in cyberspace: Engaging stereotypes of Asian American women and men to facilitate student learning and development. *About Campus, 18*(4), 14–21.

Prior, J., Hurtado, S., Saenz, V., Santos, J. L., & Korn, W. (2007). *The American freshman: Forty year trends.* Los Angeles: Higher Education Research Institute.

Renn, K. A. (2003). Understanding the identities of mixed-race college students through a developmental ecology lessons. *Journal of College Student Development, 44*(3), 383–403.

Rhoads, R. A. (1997). A subcultural study of gay and bisexual college males: Resisting developmental inclinations. *Journal of Higher Education, 68*(4), 460–482.

Stern, G. G. (1970). *People in context.* New York: Wiley.

Strange, C. C., & Banning, J. H. (2001). *Educating by design: Creating campus learning environments that work.* San Francisco: Jossey-Bass.

Strange, C. C., & Banning, J. H. (2015). *Designing for learning: Creating campus environments for student success.* San Francisco: Jossey-Bass.

Sturner, W. F. (1973). College environment. In D. W. Vermilye (Ed.), *The future in the making* (pp. 71–86). San Francisco: Jossey-Bass.

Suzuki, B. H. (2002). Revisiting the model minority stereotype: Implications for student affairs practice and higher education. *Working with Asian American college students* (New Directions for Student Services, no. 97, pp. 21–32). San Francisco: Jossey-Bass.

Tierney, W. G. (1992). An anthropological analysis of student participation in college. *Journal of Higher Education, 63*(6), 603–618.

Tierney, W. G. (1999). Models of minority college-going and retention: Cultural integrity versus cultural suicide. *The Journal of Negro Education, 68*(1), 80–91.

Walsh, W. B. (1973). *Theories of person-environment interaction: Implications for the college student.* Iowa City: The American College Testing Program.

CHAPTER 15

STUDENT RETENTION
AND INSTITUTIONAL SUCCESS

Amy S. Hirschy

Widespread calls to increase the educational attainment in the United States identify the need for examining and improving access to and success in colleges and universities (The White House, 2015). Policy leaders connect educational attainment rates to economic competitiveness, and public and private sector leaders deem education important to individual and societal growth. Meanwhile, state funding shifts and the concern about student loan debts create uncertainty for students and institutions. Given the political press and fiscal reality to do more with less, leaders of postsecondary institutions seek efficient, effective ways to recruit and retain students who are likely to succeed. The purpose of this chapter is to describe the landscape of student success and retention theories and to examine them in relation to individual and institutional success. I will briefly discuss access to and outcomes of postsecondary education, as well as the policy context for educational attainment, but will primarily focus on student success within colleges and universities. Beginning with definitions of terms, retention theories that reflect perspectives from various academic disciplines are then presented. Recommendations for practice follow, and the chapter concludes with future directions.

Postsecondary Enrollment and Outcomes

Overall US postsecondary enrollment increased between 2002 and 2012, for full-time (up 28 percent) and part-time (up 19 percent) college students (NCES, 2016a), signaling the value placed on educational advancement and the opportunities it may bring. Though students invest in higher education for many reasons, an important motivator is the potential to improve one's career options. Individuals who earn an academic credential beyond high school have higher lifetime earnings and better employment prospects than those who attended college but left without a certificate or diploma (Carnevale, Rose, & Cheah, 2011).

Just as individuals gain from educational attainment, society benefits. Educated work forces attract business investments in the community, and higher levels of education are associated with greater employment rates, more economic activity, and more tax revenue. Meanwhile, an educated populace places fewer demands on social services, welfare, and corrections (Barton, 2008). Thus, investments in higher education provide advantages to individuals and the community.

Unfortunately, increased postsecondary enrollment does not always mean higher completion rates. Compared to thirty-three countries, US educational attainment rates lag, and the rate of US tertiary attainment increased by just 7 percent from 2000 to 2012, slower than the average 11 percent (OECD, 2014). Accordingly, federal, state, and local communities target efforts to increase college readiness, enrollment, retention, and completion. Meanwhile, long-term state financial support to higher education institutions has waned, causing colleges and universities to rely more than ever on strong retention rates. From 2005 to 2014, the national average of state support dropped from 61.7 percent to 51.1 percent, and the net tuition revenue (funded by students and their families) increased by 10.7 percent (State Higher Education Executive Officers, 2014, p. 9).

Given the tectonic shifts in postsecondary funding, stable enrollments drive the fiscal health of most institutions, because operating budgets usually hinge on tuition dollars. In a competitive market to attract the best students, some consider retention and completion rates to be a proxy for institutional quality, because they offer a common metric to compare institutions in a way that students, families, and other stakeholders understand. Performance-driven financing models often apply additional pressure to college and university leaders to attend to student retention (Dougherty & Reddy, 2013). Though the responsibility for student success is shared throughout the campus, student affairs professionals play key roles in assisting students in their transitions to and through college life. To competently perform their roles, student affairs professionals need to develop and maintain expertise about students and their collegiate environments (CAS, 2015), such as understanding theories of college student retention. Empirically based theories inform what institutional professionals can do to promote student success.

Definition of Terms

A review of terms related to postsecondary student success provides a common reference for readers. *Retention* refers to an institution's goal for students to continue their enrollment to the following term or successfully complete their program. Colleges and universities aim programs and policies to promote students' progress toward earning academic credentials, such as certificates or diplomas. Often the missions of two-year colleges also include preparing students for successful transfer to a four-year institution. *Persistence* indicates a student's continued enrollment in the postsecondary system, which may be at a single or multiple institutions. In other words, institutions retain and students persist (Hagedorn, 2005). Reflecting myriad enrollment paths some students traverse, *reverse-transfer* students start at four-year institutions yet shift their enrollment to community colleges (Townsend & Dever, 1999), and *swirling* students earn credits at more than two institutions before earning a certificate or degree (Renn & Reason, 2013). *Completion* reflects a student's attainment of a credential (NCES, 2016b).

Educational stakeholders sometimes define student success differently, presenting a conundrum (Davenport, Martinez-Saenz, & Rhine, 2012). For example, students may evaluate success as the achievement of an educational goal that may or may not include degree completion. Indicators of student success for faculty members and administrators may focus on student learning, development, and engagement. Colleges and universities, states, and accrediting bodies may define success outcomes as retention and completion rates, though some attrition is expected and may be in the best interests of the student or the institution (Tinto, 1982). Despite the different indicators of student success, the shared goal for most students and other educational stakeholders is academic progress. For the purpose of this chapter, *student success* refers to persistence within a particular institution, a primary concern of student affairs professionals.

Student Success and Retention Theories

A solitary retention theory cannot capture the experience of all students. Because college student departure is a complex, ill-structured problem that defies a single solution (Braxton & Mundy, 2001–2002), scholars develop theories from various academic disciplines. Sociological, psychological, economic, and organizational lenses provide a variety of ways to view the student departure process (Braxton, 2000; Melguizo, 2011; Tinto, 1993).

Sociological Approaches

Sociological theories center on the role of social forces and structures on the college student experience. Because of its paradigmatic status (Braxton, Hirschy, & McClendon, 2004), reviews of college student retention theory frequently address Tinto's theory of student departure (1975, 1987, 1993). Building on Durkheim's classic theory to explain differential suicide rates in various cultures in which individuals who were more connected to their communities experienced less isolation (and lower suicide rates), Tinto applied the idea of integration to the modern problem of college student departure. With more than five thousand citations since 1975, Tinto's original 1975 article has been referenced, lauded, critiqued, tested, and revised by higher education scholars worldwide. His subsequent publications have garnered even more attention by practitioners and scholars.

Tinto (1993) described his theory as interactionalist, underscoring the important interplay a student has with the college environment. Such experiences shape an individual's voluntary decision to stay or leave a single postsecondary institution. Tinto (1975) postulated that students enter college with a variety of personal, family, and academic characteristics and skills that influence their commitments to the goal of getting a college degree and their commitment to the institution. Each of these individual characteristics influences the interactions the student has with the college community as well as the student's decisions to stay in or leave college. Central to Tinto's theory is the degree to which a student becomes integrated into the academic and social realms of the institution. Academic and social integration refer to the "character of the individual's social and intellectual experiences within the college" (Tinto, 1993, p. 50) based on interactions and normative fit. Student interactions inside and outside the classroom with faculty members about academic matters and the perceived fit with the institution's intellectual values promote academic integration. Students whose social experiences in the institution (day-to-day informal interactions with peers and staff and faculty members and the behaviors of the campus community) match with the students' social values display higher levels of social integration. A student's perceived isolation and poor fit (or incongruence) with the institution indicate weak integration and represent "distinct roots of student departure" (p. 50). Levels of integration influence a student's subsequent commitment to the institution and to the personal goal of college graduation. Finally, Tinto postulated that the greater the student's levels of commitment to the institution and commitment to the goal of college graduation, the more likely the individual will persist in college.

Tinto's initial (1975) article offered several contributions to the study of college student retention. First, he underscored the role of the institution in creating an environment that is more or less conducive to student success. Previous research implicitly blamed students for attrition decisions without acknowledging that institutions share responsibility for retaining students. Second, earlier empirical student departure research lacked theoretical explanations. Third, he broadened the understanding of students who leave institutions. Those who withdraw are not all dropouts; some may stop out for a period of time and return to college.

Several critiques of Tinto's theory exist. A review of empirical studies based on Tinto's theory concluded that the theory needs revision (Braxton, Sullivan, & Johnson, 1997). Building on this idea, scholars (including Tinto) challenged the theory to reflect more recent demographical and institutional perspectives.

Regarding demographics, though Tinto considers individual characteristics in his theory, some believe it could better reflect the cultural backgrounds and perspectives of students. Practitioners and scholars are cautioned to not assume that all students experience the academic and social arenas of the college environment in the same ways; ethnic, racial, gender, and economic characteristics should be considered (Kuh & Love, 2000; Quaye & Harper, 2015; Rendón, Jalomo, & Nora, 2000). If Tinto's interactionalist model is based on an acculturation-assimilation perspective, then minority students may be pressured to separate from their cultural communities to successfully integrate into the college environment. Such separation as a rite of passage may hold harmful consequences for racial and ethnic minorities (Tierney, 1992). Next, Tinto's original theory focused too much on the integration of students into the college environment to the exclusion of important external influences on students such as family, work, and community. In his 1993 revision, Tinto added financial resources as a background characteristic and included the role that a student's world outside of the institution plays in educational decisions.

Related to the institution, scholars note that there should be greater acknowledgment of the influence of institutional characteristics on the student experience, given the interactionalist model (Braxton, Sullivan, & Johnson, 1997; Melguizo, 2011). Modest empirical support of Tinto's theory led to revisions to explain departure decisions of students enrolled in residential institutions (Braxton, Hirschy, & McClendon, 2004; Braxton & others, 2014). Regarding commuter institutions, a lack of empirical support of Tinto's theory in studies at commuter campuses prompted Braxton and colleagues to abandon Tinto's model and create a different theory (Braxton, Hirschy, & McClendon, 2004; Braxton & others, 2014), one that acknowledges the internal college atmosphere (for example, academic communities and campus environment) and students' off-campus lives. Additionally, demographic, technological, and market forces have altered institutional processes since Tinto's theories and revisions were published (Melguizo, 2011).

In another example of a sociological approach to examine student persistence, Berger (2000) applied Bourdieu's (1973, 1977) concept of cultural capital to college student persistence. Cultural capital refers to a symbolic resource that can be used by an individual to maintain and advance one's social status. Examples include informal interpersonal skills, manners, linguistics, and educational credentials (Bourdieu, 1973, 1977). Students demonstrate varying levels of cultural capital and attempt to optimize this resource as part of the social reproduction process. At the organizational level, educational institutions also possess cultural capital, demonstrated by selectivity in the admissions process and perceived success of graduates. The extent to which a student's cultural capital and the level of cultural capital at the particular college or university match can affect persistence. For example, students from a working class background or who are among the first generation in their families to attend college may not have had the exposure to the same cultural resources as the dominant student population at some elite colleges, and thus they may experience alienation or incongruence with their peers (Ostrove & Long, 2007; Walpole, 2003).

Psychological Approaches

Theories with a psychological orientation focus on individual abilities, dispositions, and personalities (Tinto, 1993). These characteristics may influence how a student perceives and responds to the campus environment, such as interactions with peers and faculty members, academic stress, and balancing life responsibilities.

Bean and Eaton (2000) proposed a retention theory that examined several psychological processes leading to academic and social integration: attitude-behavior theory, coping behavioral theory (approach-avoidance), self-efficacy, and attribution (locus of control) theory. Through their interactions with campus individuals (such as peers and staff and faculty members) and people outside the institution (such as family and high school friends), students assess their decision to stay in school. Interactions positively related to persistence promote individuals' beliefs that they are capable (self-efficacy), encourage active problem-solving to deal with challenges (approach coping mechanisms), and foster students' senses of responsibility for their actions and beliefs that they can take actions to affect outcomes (internal locus of control) (Bean & Eaton, 2000).

Related to students' self-efficacy, Rendón (1994) found that students who felt validated by someone else (on or off campus, in or out of class) were more likely to believe that they could be successful in college. When validating agents (for example, a parent, advisor, instructor, or peer) communicate active encouragement for students in academic and social settings, the student feels more capable of learning and more accepted as a member of the campus community (Rendón, 1994).

Sedlacek (2004) proposed that eight noncognitive variables correlate with college student persistence and educational attainment: positive self-concept, realistic self-appraisal, successfully handling the system, preference for long-term goals, availability of a strong support person, leadership experience, community involvement, and knowledge acquired in a field (p. 37). Combined with academic preparation, noncognitive characteristics can contribute to college student success (Melguizo, 2011).

Economic Approaches

Economic perspectives reflect the student's analysis of the costs of attending college versus the opportunities or potential benefits. Some individuals are willing to bear considerable financial hardship if they deem their experiences are valuable enough to persist (Tinto, 1993). Conversely, if the expenses exceed the perceived value, a student is more likely to withdraw from the institution. A student's ability to pay and perceptions of the cost of attendance influence enrollment decisions (Chen & DesJardins, 2010; St. John, Cabrera, Nora, & Asker, 2000).

Organizational Approaches

Organizational lenses address the structure, policies, and practices of the institution, including student perceptions of interactions with and actions by faculty and staff members and administrators. The effectiveness of various processes (such as admission, academic advising, registration, and financial aid policies) can also influence student success. Based on employee turnover in organizations, Bean's (1983) theoretical model suggested that organizationally based influences on student satisfaction with the institution include participation, communication, and distributive justice. Similarly, Braxton and others (2014) found that college and university communities that communicate their strong commitment to the welfare of students and display institutional integrity promote student success. Examples of organizational approaches that demonstrate commitment to the welfare of students include demonstrating care, respect, and fair treatment. Institutional integrity indicates congruence between the day-to-day actions of faculty and staff members and administrators and the mission and values of the institution.

Recommendations for Practice

Institutional leaders seek effective interventions and approaches that can be implemented on their campuses with current students. Many of the recommendations relate to concepts of engagement, involvement, or integration. Engagement involves two components that relate to student success: the amount of time and energy that students devote to educationally purposeful activities and the ways that the institution supports student learning opportunities that contribute to the effort students exert to participate in such activities (Kuh, Kinzie, Schuh, Whitt, & Associates, 2005). Involvement refers to the "amount of physical and psychological energy a student devotes to the academic experience" (Astin, 1984, p. 297). Some student affairs practitioners and researchers who study the college student experience use the terms *engagement, involvement,* and *integration* interchangeably, yet others draw distinctions between them (Wolf-Wendel, Ward, & Kinzie, 2009). In each definition of the terms, the student interacts with the institutional environment.

Because recent compendia of recommendations for practice are easily available (for example, see Braxton & others, 2014; Chambliss & Takacs, 2014; Habley, Bloom, & Robbins, 2012; Kuh, Kinzie, Schuh, Whitt, & Associates, 2005; Perna, 2010; Quaye & Harper, 2015; Reason, 2009; Reason & Kimball, 2012; Tinto, 2012), a concise discussion of empirically based recommendations follows. Each set of recommendations calls for a coherent institutional approach to support student success and offers principles to apply to student experiences in and out of the classroom.

Tinto's Framework for Institutional Action

Meaningful contacts and connections students shared with others in the campus community not only promote integration and persistence but also learning (Tinto, 1993). In his framework for institution actions, Tinto (2012) underscored the institutional obligation to help students succeed and elevated the classroom as the most promising site for effective practice. Institutional conditions for student success include clear and high expectations of students, especially in the classroom; high levels of academic, social, and financial support for students; frequent assessment and feedback to help students gauge their progress and make adjustments; and the most important, involvement or engagement in the academic and social realms of the campus.

Documenting Effective Educational Practices: DEEP Project

The Documenting Effective Educational Practices (DEEP) Project examined twenty institutions with better-than-predicted student engagement scores on the National Survey of Student Engagement (NSSE) and graduation rates. Kuh, Kinzie, Schuh, Whitt, and Associates (2005) identified six common educational practices high-performing institutions used to promote student success (p. 24): (1) a "living" mission and "lived" educational philosophy, (2) an unshakeable focus on student learning, (3) environments adapted for educational enrichment, (4) clearly marked pathways to student success, (5) an improvement oriented ethos, and (6) shared responsibility for educational quality and student success.

These six practices helped create conditions for success even when the institutions differed by mission, history, type, and size. The authors shared specific recommendations for student affairs professionals, including building cross-campus collaborations with students, faculty members, and academic administrators to share responsibility for educational quality and student success. At DEEP schools, such partnerships hinge on a common commitment to student learning and achievement. In addition to the communal concern for the student experience, each DEEP school identified noteworthy individuals who stood out as champions for student success. Acknowledging the "power of one," Kuh, Kinzie, Schuh, Whitt, and Associates (2005, p. 170) underscored the potential that each person on campus has to make a difference in students' lives.

Nine Imperatives for Institutional Policy and Action

In addition to specific recommendations for residential campuses, commuter campuses, and policy makers, Braxton and others (2014, pp. 39–41) offered nine imperatives to support student success, followed by an example of each:

1. All campus community members should embrace a commitment to safeguard the welfare of students as clients of the institution. *Example:* Threats to campus safety should be communicated in a timely manner with sufficient detail so that community members can evaluate the level of risk.
2. Students should be treated equitably and fairly by institutional actors and policies and procedures. *Example:* Student appeal processes should

be communicated clearly, and institutional leaders should consider designating an ombudsperson to investigate student claims of unfair treatment by academic or administrative processes.

3. Campus community members should display respect for students as individuals. *Example:* Retention coordinators can conduct exit interviews with departing students and faculty and staff members with significant student contact.

4. Campus administrators should ensure that policies and procedures align with the mission, goals, and values espoused by the institution. *Example:* Incongruent policies and practices should be discontinued or modified in a way that supports the mission, goals, or values of the institution.

5. The day-to-day actions of campus community members should support the mission, goals, and values of the institution. *Example:* Performance appraisal forms for administrators, staff members, and clerical workers should include items that assess the congruence of their actions with the mission, goals, and values of the institution.

6. The reward structure for campus community members should recognize the individuals who highly value students, treat students equitably, and demonstrate respect for students as individuals. *Example:* Clerical staff members with frequent student contact should be provided opportunities to develop strategies of assisting others with difficult personalities.

7. Publications and documents should communicate the institution's abiding concern for the growth and development of its students. *Example:* Materials used in the recruitment of students should receive careful scrutiny to ensure that the college or university portrays itself accurately to prospective students.

8. Public speeches by institutional leaders (including student affairs professionals) should communicate the high value their college or university places on students as members of the academic community. *Example:* Speeches should also resonate with the mission, goals, and values of the college or university.

9. Ongoing assessments of the student experience should inform improvements in policies and practices to communicate the commitment of the institution to the welfare of students. *Example:* Administrative offices and academic departments should conduct periodic reviews to determine what information or procedures are in place that confuses students. Once identified, student consultants can recommend changes and improvements.

Considerations for Evaluating Theories and Recommendations for Practice

The recommendations for practice summarized in this section are supported by theoretical grounding or research findings, typically both. Using such empirically based recommendations provides a helpful way to sort through the massive information available related to improving retention, but it is insufficient. Examining retention recommendations with a keen, critical eye helps student affairs professionals wisely invest their often-limited resources of time, staffing, and money. Using professional judgment that integrates academic study, professional practice, and other forms of professional engagement, such as conversations with colleagues, can help determine the relevance of theory to practice (Blimling, 2011). Student affairs professionals will benefit from actively using their professional judgment and knowledge of their particular campuses and students in determining the applicability of these and other recommendations (Hirschy, 2015).

Future Directions for College Student Success

Approaches to understanding student departure have shifted from student deficit models to identifying more effective institutional strategies. They also reflect broader diversity of student and institutional characteristics, yet more research is needed. Further research to understand diverse student populations, their needs, and how they interact with their respective campus environments will inform future student affairs professionals and increase their ability to support all students in their academic endeavors. Retention theories have traditionally focused on individual institutions, not the broader postsecondary system. Future directions in retention theory and policy are likely to view the student experience through a wide-angled lens (Hossler & Bean, 1990), looking at access, transition, persistence, and completion. Advances in partnerships across educational sectors will foster a better understanding of the transitions students experience as they forge their educational paths. Examples of future directions for retention scholarship aimed at the individual, institutional, and policy levels follow.

Individual Level

Increasingly diverse student populations (Jones, 2015) and new technologies offer opportunities to learn innovative ways to support college students in achieving their educational goals. More recent and emerging scholarship acknowledges the complexity of individuals' multiple, intersecting identities, such as race, ethnicity, gender, sexuality, class, ability status, and nation, yet much more is needed (Dill & Zambrana, 2009; Jones & Abes, 2013; Josselson & Harway, 2012). The experiences of student subpopulations, such as military and veteran students, student athletes, working students, and transgender students, also warrant more exploration in empirical studies. Student affairs administrators need to understand how to support individuals on campus as their students navigate across various social and cultural worlds.

Institutional Level

Nearly all the theory and resulting student retention literature has been built on a single institutional perspective of success. Although this perspective fits a traditional, linear progression model of student enrollment and degree attainment, it does not capture the various paths now forged by many students. By expanding the definition of success beyond the single institution, the study of student retention research shifts from an institutionally focused perspective to one that is more student-centered (Jones, Radcliffe, Huesman, & Kellogg, 2010, p. 172) and inclusive of multiple sectors and institutions. Similarly, a more thorough investigation of student experiences in various types of academic programs and institutions is needed.

Policy Level

Many educational practitioners, researchers, and policy leaders now work toward creating a seamless educational pipeline that leads to a well-educated citizenry, composed of individuals prepared for meaningful roles in a complex society (Bragg, 2011; Kirst & Venezia, 2004). Two examples of policy approaches that blend the boundaries between secondary and postsecondary sectors include creating more integrated data systems and partnerships with college-readiness programs.

Integrated Data Systems   State and federal policies aim to tighten the linkages among secondary education, postsecondary education, and an economically viable work force (Conley, 2010, p. 154). Taking a P–16 (preschool to college graduation) or P–20 (extended through graduate education) view of the educational pipeline often includes integrating the data systems among the segments to enable better tracking of student progress. No small task, such alignment requires members of each sector to coordinate their efforts in the midst of already demanding reporting requirements for accreditation and accountability, yet the potential is great to identify what works well and what needs adjustment. Currently individual college and university staff members report data to the federal government via the Integrated Postsecondary Education Data System (IPEDS) by completing eleven annual data surveys (Alexander, 2015).

The nonprofit organization National Student Clearinghouse (NSC) tracks student-level educational outcomes, such as current national enrollment and completion by institutional sector, state, enrollment intensity, age group, and gender. In contrast to IPEDS, NSC data include public high school to college transition rates and transfers between postsecondary institutions. Using student-level data enables individuals to be counted just once, even if they are enrolled in multiple institutions. Thus, the educational paths of reverse transfer and swirling students can be better understood.

Federal incentives urged states to develop and implement comprehensive P–20 longitudinal datasets to track individuals from preschool through the work force (NCES, 2016c). Nearly all states received at least one grant to support their efforts (forty-seven of fifty), but the complex implementation takes time. Presently, federal graduation rates exclude transfer and part-time students as well as long-term student outcomes for academic programs or institutions, such as postcollege earnings (Alexander, 2015). Omitting such information limits a comprehensive understanding of postsecondary students and their educational pathways (Shapiro & Dundar, 2015). Higher education stakeholders carefully consider their strategies to create a manageable, integrated, comprehensive, student unit record data system (Janice, 2015). Issues of concern include meeting simultaneous goals to increase transparency and accuracy, protecting students from privacy violations, reducing redundancy, and increasing efficiency in data collection and reporting.

Partnerships for College Readiness   Trends point toward increasing college readiness programs in primary and secondary schools, with many high schools requiring students to take college entrance exams and complete the Free Application for Federal Student Aid (FAFSA). Advanced Placement courses and International Baccalaureate programs offer college-like experiences at the high school level, but not all schools offer them and for those that do, not all students qualify (Conley, 2010). Many states adopt common college readiness standards composed of standardized tests and placement tests. Meanwhile, not-for-profit organizations such as the Lumina Foundation, the Bill and Melinda Gates Foundation, and the College Board lead boundary-spanning projects that promote college readiness and success. Wider curricular reform to enhance articulation with college and universities, including aligning high school assessments with college-level placement exams (Braxton & others, 2014), may be a useful long-term strategy. These shifts to form closer partnerships to promote college attainment extend already stretched secondary school and postsecondary university resources. Theory-driven, empirically based approaches may offer the most promise to invest the limited resources.

Conclusion

This chapter acknowledges the beginning and the end of the postsecondary educational pipeline, but it focuses primarily on student success within colleges and universities. Student affairs professionals serve all students, so knowing and applying retention theories and empirically based student success strategies improves our ability to approach situations from multiple perspectives. Student affairs professionals can seek out useful, empirically based resources from academic journals and books, professional associations, foundations, research centers, institutional websites, and various levels of government publications and websites. Despite vast student retention literature, much remains unknown.

Trends in the research reflect a shift toward employing a variety of disciplinary lenses (Braxton, 2000; Melguizo, 2011; Perna & Thomas, 2008); testing existing theories more thoroughly, especially concerning the experiences of a diverse student population (Jones, 2015); considering institutional variables (such as type and academic program differences); and broadening and deepening awareness of various student characteristics, such as intersectionality. To paraphrase poet Maya Angelou: when we know better, we do better, and we need to know more.

Discussion Questions and Activities

1. Discuss common problematic disconnects between P–12 and higher education and offer two recommendations for both sectors (for a total of four) to make the transition to college more seamless for students.
2. What types of students struggle on your current campus? What data are available about student retention at your institution? In your state? Nationally? Internationally? How do the educational attainment levels compare to others?
3. Locate and recommend two useful electronically accessible resources on college access and retention (one each). Create a one-page summary of each source that describes the information available, the web address, and your short critique of the source (including your assessment of its usefulness for various audiences).
4. Locate and read one of the compendia of recommendations for practice referenced in the chapter. What specific recommendations are most relevant to your particular campus? For a particular student subculture?

References

Alexander, L. (2015). *Federal postsecondary data transparency and consumer information concepts and proposals*. Washington, DC: United States Senate Committee on Health, Education, Labor, and Pensions (HELP). Retrieved April 19, 2016, from http://www.help.senate.gov/imo/media/Consumer_Information.pdf

Astin, A. W. (1984). Student involvement: A developmental theory for higher education. *Journal of College Student Personnel, 25*, 297–308.

Barton, P. E. (2008, Jan./Feb.). How many college graduates does the U.S. labor force really need? *Change, 40*, 16–21.

Bean, J. P. (1983). The application of a model of turnover in work organizations to the student attrition process. *Review of Higher Education, 6*, 129–148.

Bean, J. P., & Eaton, S. (2000). A psychological model of college student retention. In J. M. Braxton (Ed.), *Reworking the departure puzzle: New theory and research on college student retention* (pp. 48–61). Nashville, TN: Vanderbilt University Press.

Berger, J. B. (2000). Optimizing capital, social reproduction, and undergraduate persistence: A sociological perspective. In J. M. Braxton (Ed.), *Reworking the student departure puzzle* (pp. 95–124). Nashville, TN: Vanderbilt University Press.

Blimling, G. S. (2011). Developing professional judgment. In P. M. Magolda & M. B. Baxter Magolda (Eds.), *Contested issues in student affairs: Diverse perspectives and respectful dialogue* (pp. 42–53). Sterling, VA: Stylus.

Bourdieu, P. (1973). Cultural reproduction and social reproduction. In R. Brown (Ed.), *Knowledge, education, and cultural change* (pp. 189–207). London: Collier Macmillan.

Bourdieu, P. (1977). *Outline of a theory of practice* (R. Nice, Trans.). Cambridge, UK: University Press.

Bragg, D. D. (2011). Examining pathways to and through the community college for youth and adults. In J. C. Smart & M. B. Paulson (Eds.), *Higher education: Handbook of theory and research,* (Vol. 36, pp. 355–393). Dordrecht, The Netherlands: Springer.

Braxton, J. M. (2000). *Reworking the student departure puzzle.* Nashville, TN: Vanderbilt University Press.

Braxton, J. M., Doyle, W. R., Hartley, H. V., III, Hirschy, A. S., Jones, W. A., & McLendon, M. K. (2014). *Rethinking college student retention.* San Francisco: Jossey-Bass.

Braxton, J. M., Hirschy, A. S., & McClendon, S. A. (2004). Understanding and reducing college student departure. *ASHE-ERIC Higher Education Report, 30*(3). San Francisco: Jossey-Bass.

Braxton, J. M., & Mundy, M. (2001–2002). Powerful institutional levers to reduce college student departure. *Journal of College Student Retention, 3,* 91–118.

Braxton, J. M., Sullivan, A. S., & Johnson, R. M., Jr. (1997). Appraising Tinto's theory of college student departure. In J. Smart (Ed.), *Higher education: Handbook of theory and research* (Vol. 12, pp. 107–164). New York: Agathon.

Carnevale, T. P., Rose, S. J., & Cheah, B. (2011). *The college payoff: Education, occupations, lifetime earnings.* Washington, DC: The Georgetown University Center on Education and the Workforce.

Chambliss, D. F., & Takacs, C. G. (2014). *How college works.* Cambridge, MA: Harvard University Press.

Chen, R., & DesJardins, S. L. (2010). Investigating the impact of financial aid on student dropout risks: Racial and ethnic differences. *Journal of Higher Education, 81,* 179–208.

Conley, D. T. (2010). *College knowledge: What it really takes for students to success and what we can do to get them ready.* San Francisco: Jossey-Bass.

Council for the Advancement of Standards in Higher Education (CAS). (2015). *CAS professional standards for higher education* (9th ed.). Washington, DC: Author.

Davenport, Z., Martinez-Saenz, M., & Rhine, L. (2012). The student success conundrum. In B. Bontrager, D. Ingersoll, & R. Ingersoll (Eds.), *Strategic enrollment management: Transforming higher education* (pp. 25–50). Washington, DC: American Association of Collegiate Registrars and Admissions Officers.

Dill, B. T., & Zambrana, R. E. (Eds.). (2009). *Emerging intersections: Race, class, and gender in theory, policy, and practice.* Piscataway, NJ: Rutgers University Press.

Dougherty, K., & Reddy, V. (Eds.). (2013). Performance funding for higher education: What are the mechanisms? What are the impacts? *ASHE Higher Education Report, 39*(2). San Francisco: Jossey-Bass.

Habley, W. R., Bloom, J. L., & Robbins, S. (2012). *Increasing persistence: Research-based strategies for student success.* San Francisco: Jossey-Bass.

Hagedorn, L. S. (2005). How to define retention: A new look at an old problem. In A. Seidman (Ed.), *College student retention: Formula for student success* (pp. 89–105). Westport, CT: Praeger.

Hirschy, A. S. (2015). Models of student retention and persistence. In D. Hossler, J. P. Bean, & Associates (Eds.), *The strategic management of college enrollments* (pp. 268–288). San Francisco: Jossey-Bass.

Hossler, D., & Bean, J. P. (1990). Principles and objectives. In D. Hossler, J. P. Bean, & Associates (Eds.), *The strategic management of college enrollments* (pp. 3–20). San Francisco: Jossey-Bass.

Janice, A. (2015). *Consensus builds on need for high-quality postsecondary data: A review of comments on senate HELP committee white paper on consumer information.* Washington, DC: Institute of Higher Education Policy. Retrieved April 19, 2016, from http://www.ihep.org/sites/default/files/uploads/postsecdata/docs/data-at-work/responses_to_help_committee._update._6.9.15.pdf

Jones, D. R., Radcliffe, P. M., Huesman, R. L., Jr., & Kellogg, J. (2010). Redefining student success: Applying different multinomial regression techniques for the study of student graduation across institutions of higher education. *Research in Higher Education, 51,* 154–174.

Jones, S. R., & Abes, E. S. (2013). *Identity development of college students: Advancing frameworks for multiple dimensions of identity.* San Francisco: Jossey-Bass.

Jones, W. A. (2015). The persistence of students of color. In D. Hossler, B. Bontrager, & Associates (Eds.), *Handbook of strategic enrollment management* (pp. 311–332). San Francisco: Jossey-Bass.

Josselson, R., & Harway, M. (2012). The challenges of multiple identity. In R. Josselson & M. Harway (Eds.), *Navigating multiple identities: Race, gender, culture, nationality, and roles* (pp. 3–11). New York: Oxford University Press.

Kirst, M. W., & Venezia, A. (Eds.). (2004). *From high school to college: Improving opportunities for success in postsecondary education.* San Francisco: Jossey-Bass.

Kuh, G. D., Kinzie, J., Schuh, J. H., Whitt, E. J., & Associates. (2005). *Student success in college: Creating conditions that matter.* San Francisco: Jossey-Bass.

Kuh, G. D., & Love, P. G. (2000). A cultural perspective on student departure. In J. M. Braxton (Ed.), *Reworking the student departure puzzle* (pp. 192–212). Nashville, TN: Vanderbilt University Press.

Melguizo, T. (2011). A review of theories developed to describe the process of college persistence and attainment. In J. C. Smart & M. B. Paulson (Eds.), *Higher education: Handbook of theory and research* (Vol. 36, pp. 395–424). Dordrecht, The Netherlands: Springer.

National Center for Education Statistics (NCES). (2016a). *Fast facts.* Washington, DC: US Department of Education, Institute of Education Sciences. Retrieved April 19, 2016, from http://nces.ed.gov/fastfacts/display.asp?id=98

National Center for Education Statistics (NCES). (2016b). *Glossary.* Washington, DC: US Department of Education, Institute of Education Sciences. Retrieved April 19, 2016, from http://nces.ed.gov/ipeds/glossary/?charindex=R

National Center for Education Statistics (NCES). (2016c). *Statewide longitudinal data system.* Washington, DC: US Department of Education. Institute of Education Sciences. Retrieved April 19, 2016, from https://nces.ed.gov/programs/slds/

Organisation for Economic Co-operation and Development (OECD). (2014). *Education at a glance 2014: OECD indicators.* Retrieved April 19, 2016, from http://www.oecd.org/edu/Education-at-a-Glance-2014.pdf

Ostrove, J. M., & Long, S. M. (2007). Social class and belonging: Implications for college adjustment. *Review of Higher Education, 30,* 363–389.

Perna, L. W. (Ed.). (2010). *Understanding the working college student: New research and its implications for policy and practice.* Sterling, VA: Stylus.

Perna, L. W., & Thomas, S. L. (2008). Theoretical perspectives on student success. *ASHE Higher Education Report, 34*(1). San Francisco: Jossey-Bass.

Quaye, S. J., & Harper, S. R. (Eds.). (2015). *Student engagement in higher education: Theoretical perspectives and practical approaches for diverse populations* (2nd ed.). New York: Routledge.

Reason, R. D. (2009). An examination of persistence research through the lens of a comprehensive conceptual framework. *Journal of College Student Development, 50,* 659–682.

Reason, R. D., & Kimball, E. W. (2012). A new theory-to-practice model for student affairs: Integrating scholarship, context, and reflection. *Journal of Student Affairs Research and Practice, 49,* 359–376.

Rendón, L. I. (1994). Validating culturally diverse students: Toward a new model of learning and student development. *Innovative Higher Education, 19*(1), 33–51.

Rendón, L. I., Jalomo, R. E., & Nora, A. (2000). Theoretical considerations in the study of minority student retention in higher education. In J. M. Braxton (Ed.), *Reworking the departure puzzle* (pp. 127–156). Nashville, TN: Vanderbilt University Press.

Renn, K. A., & Reason, R. D. (2013). *College students in the United States: Characteristics, experiences, and outcomes.* San Francisco: Jossey-Bass.

Sedlacek, W. E. (2004). *Beyond the big test: Noncognitive assessment in higher education.* San Francisco: Jossey-Bass.

Shapiro, D., & Dundar, A. (2015). New context for retention and persistence. In D. Hossler, B. Bontrager, & Associates (Eds.), *Handbook of strategic enrollment management* (pp. 249–267). San Francisco: Jossey-Bass.

State Higher Education Executive Officers (SHEEO). (2014). *State higher education finance (SHEF): FY 2014.* Boulder, CO: Author. Retrieved April 19, 2016, from http://sheeo .org/projects/shef-state-higher-education-finance

St. John, E. P., Cabrera, A. F., Nora, A., & Asker, E. H. (2000). Economic influences on persistence reconsidered: How can finance research inform the reconceptualization of persistence models? In J. M. Braxton (Ed.), *Reworking the departure puzzle* (pp. 29–47). Nashville, TN: Vanderbilt University Press.

Tierney, W. (1992). An anthropological analysis of student participation in college. *Journal of Higher Education, 63,* 603–618.

Tinto, V. (1975). Dropout from higher education: A theoretical synthesis of recent research. *Review of Educational Research, 45,* 89–125.

Tinto, V. (1982). Limits of theory and practice in student attrition. *Journal of Higher Education, 53,* 687–700.

Tinto, V. (1987). *Leaving college: Rethinking the causes and cures of student attrition.* Chicago: University of Chicago Press.

Tinto, V. (1993). *Leaving college: Rethinking the causes and cures of student attrition* (2nd ed.). Chicago: University of Chicago Press.

Tinto, V. (2012). *Completing college: Rethinking institutional action.* Chicago: University of Chicago Press.

Townsend, B. K., & Dever, J. T. (1999). What do we know about reverse transfer students? In B. Townsend (Ed.), *Understanding the impact of reverse transfers on the community college* (New Directions for Community Colleges, no. 106, pp. 5–14). San Francisco: Jossey-Bass.

Walpole, M. (2003). Socioeconomic status and college: How SES affects college experiences and outcomes. *The Review of Higher Education, 27,* 45–73.

The White House. (2015). *Higher education.* Retrieved April 19, 2016, from https://www .whitehouse.gov/issues/education/higher-education

Wolf-Wendel, L., Ward, K., & Kinzie, J. (2009). A tangled web of terms: The overlap and unique contribution of involvement, engagement, and integration to understanding college student success. *Journal of College Student Development, 50,* 407–428.

PART FOUR

ORGANIZATIONAL ASPECTS OF PROFESSIONAL PRACTICE

Divisions of student affairs and the units that compose them have a variety of organizational aspects that provide a foundation for its mission, goals, and objectives. This is true no matter what the mission and characteristics are of the institutions in which the student affairs units are located, where student affairs units are located organizationally, how they are financed, or how the collaborate with other units in the institution. Typically, people do not decide to engage in the work of student affairs because they are interested in the intricacies of finance, organizational charts, strategic planning, or assessment and evaluation. Yet, these elements and others are central to providing a foundation for student affairs educators so that they can engage in their professional practice. In this section of this book we focus on the organizational aspects of student affairs.

A book of this type would be incomplete without addressing the administrative and managerial elements of student affairs practice. As a consequence, we have identified six chapters that are foundational to the organization and administration of student affairs. The chapters address how student affairs is organized, the units that often are included in a division of student affairs, strategic planning and financing student affairs, assessment and evaluation of student affairs programs, services and experiences that are provided for students, elements of social media and technology and how they apply to student affairs, and forming partnerships with academic affairs. This section is more complex than its counterpart in the fifth edition. Whether that reflects a reorganization of this edition or that student affairs organizations have become more complex over the years is unknown. What we are sure of is that the environment in which higher education operates has become more complicated, with increasing oversight being provided by entities external to higher education, as will be discussed in chapter 33, and that the future will lead to increasing organizational complexity.

In chapter 16 Kathleen Manning, Jillian Kinzie and John H. Schuh introduce a number of models that provide for the organization of student affairs. They emphasize that institutional values, missions, and goals will have a great influence on the organization of the division of student affairs. Then, they provide models of student affairs practice that are found in higher education, recognizing that hybrids of the models are in place at many colleges and universities.

Building on chapter 16, Maureen E. Wilson in chapter 17 identifies potential reporting lines and functional areas that are found in student affairs. Challenges for higher education and student affairs also are identified in this chapter.

Chapter 18 examines the related issues of strategic planning and finance as they relate to student affairs. Strategic planning is introduced first, and then the authors, Brian A. Burt and John H. Schuh, examine conceptual ways of thinking about higher education finance. The chapter concludes with a discussion of revenues and expenses that are found in student affairs units, and budgeting models are introduced.

In chapter 19 Ann M. Gansemer-Topf and Lance C. Kennedy-Phillips explore issues related to assessment and evaluation in student affairs. They ask penetrating questions about the efficacy of student affairs programs, experiences, and services in their chapter that student affairs educators must explore to sustain their work.

The use of technology in student affairs education is explored in chapter 20 by Jeffrey Rokkum and Reynol Junco. They urge student affairs educators to use various forms of social media to meet students on their electronic turf and to embrace the exciting dimensions of social media to enhance the student experience. They believe that the use of social media will enable student affairs educators to provide learning experiences more effectively in the future.

In chapter 21 Elizabeth J. Whitt examines academic and student affairs partnerships. She describes the advantages and disadvantages of such partnerships and provides suggestions that make for good practice in developing effective working relationships across organizational boundaries. She reminds us that student learning should be a central reason for developing partnerships.

CHAPTER 16

FRAMING STUDENT AFFAIRS PRACTICE

Kathleen Manning, Jillian Kinzie, and John H. Schuh

Student affairs was not conceived as part of student life when the earliest colonial colleges were founded. But the intervening years of activity since the publication of the American Council on Education's (1937) *Student Personnel Point of View,* often considered the birth date of student affairs, have seen tremendous growth in the field. During that time, theory and practice have developed so that standards for practice and measures of quality have advanced.

A hallmark of the development of the student affairs field has been practice designated for particular institutional contexts. In other words, student affairs theory and practice cannot be implemented in generic ways, as if all colleges and universities have the same founding values, missions, and goals. Different institutional types demand more nuanced approaches to student affairs practice than a one-size-fits-all approach. The purpose of this chapter is to describe eleven models of student affairs practice and discuss the ways that student affairs educators can use these models to maximize student engagement and success.

In 2003, Kathleen Manning, Jillian Kinzie, and John Schuh used research from the Documenting Effective Educational Practices (DEEP) study, knowledge from the literature, and their experience as student affairs educators and faculty members to outline eleven different approaches to student affairs practice. These models are fully depicted in *One Size Does Not Fit All: Traditional and Innovative Models of Student Affairs Practice* (Manning, Kinzie, & Schuh, 2014). In the next sections, we briefly introduce the DEEP study and then summarize the eleven approaches including definitions from Project DEEP to provide context.

Project DEEP Research

A team of higher education researchers, practitioners, and faculty members was recruited by George Kuh of the National Survey of Student Engagement (NSSE) Institute to conduct research on a sample of NSSE institutions with higher-than-predicted student engagement and student success. The purpose of Project DEEP was "to discover what a diverse set of institutions does to promote student success so other colleges and universities that aspire to enhance the quality of the undergraduate experience might learn from their example" (Kuh, Kinzie, Schuh, Whitt, & Associates, 2005, p. 18). For Project DEEP, the following definition of student engagement was used. "Student engagement represents two key components. The first is the amount of time and effort students put into their studies and activities that lead to the experiences and outcomes that constitute student success. Second is how institutions of higher education allocate their human and other resources as well as how they organize learning opportunities and services to encourage students to participate in and benefit from such activities" (Manning, Kinzie, & Schuh, 2014, p. 19). Student success was defined in Project DEEP as "retention, graduation, and educational attainment" (p. 21). Manning, Kinzie, and Schuh discovered that the DEEP institutions had various approaches to student affairs. For example, several visited institutions were academically focused and took one approach; others focused on the out-of-classroom experience and took a different approach. We compiled eleven models categorized according to whom or what was at the center of the effort expended. The models are listed by category in table 16.1.

The models provide student affairs educators (and graduate students preparing for their careers) an opportunity to reflect on the characteristics of student affairs practice and consider the extent of the emphasis on

TABLE 16.1. TRADITIONAL AND INNOVATIVE MODELS OF STUDENT AFFAIRS PRACTICE

Traditional	Innovative
Out of Classroom-Centered	**Student-Centered**
Extracurricular	Ethic of Care
Cocurricular	Student-Driven
Administrative-Centered	Student Agency
Functional Silos	**Academic-Centered**
Student Services	Academic-Student Affairs Collaboration
Learning-Centered	Academic-Driven
Competitive and Adversarial	
Seamless Learning	

Source: Manning, Kinzie, and Schuh (2014).

student engagement and success. To make use of the models, student affairs professionals are encouraged to (1) determine the model or models that characterizes their institution and (2) decide if a different model would increase student engagement and success. (The inventory at the end of this chapter provides insight when determining your institution's model.) There is no right or wrong selection regarding the models. Each model has it strengths and weaknesses. That said, the high-performing DEEP schools were the inspiration for the innovative models.

Models of Student Affairs Practice

The models of student affairs practice are divided into traditional and innovative categories. They represent ways that student affairs can be organized on a campus, depending on the mission of the institution and goals of the student affairs division. The following descriptions review the models with the hope that practitioners can choose from a diversity of ways to achieve the goals of student affairs.

Traditional Models

The traditional models of student affairs practice are grouped into three areas: out-of-classroom-centered, administrative-centered, and learning-centered. The out-of-classroom-centered models include extracurricular and cocurricular. The administrative-centered approaches include functional silos and student services. The learning-centered models include competitive-adversarial and seamless learning.

Extracurricular Model   When using the extracurricular model, student affairs professionals focus on student development in the out-of-classroom environment. Infinite settings exist outside the classroom for student development and learning, thereby creating countless opportunities for student growth. In institutions characterized by the extracurricular model, student and academic affairs are separated within the organizational structure, reporting to different vice presidents or other executives at the institutions. This separation makes it difficult for the two divisions to collaborate on student learning and success. In this model, student engagement activities are predominantly initiated by student affairs professionals. Faculty members emphasize intellectual development and are less involved in noncognitive student development.

The strengths of the extracurricular model include the discrete budgeting and resources providing a level of freedom that enables the division of student affairs to create innovative and extensive programs. These expanded opportunities create various learning in leadership, personal development, and areas beyond academics. The separation of student and academic affairs enables faculty members to concentrate their efforts on teaching, research, and service. The weaknesses of the model include the lack of integration that makes collaboration among faculty members and student affairs educators challenging. This weakness means that the whole student philosophy, so prominent in the 1937 *Student Personnel Point of View* (American Council on Education, 1937) cannot be fully achieved. An additional weakness is the confusion about college purposes that can occur when the academic and student affairs missions are separate, lacking ready connections for students.

Cocurricular Model In the cocurricular model, the academic and student affairs missions are separated in ways similar to the extracurricular model. Boundaries characterize the work environment with distinct lines between academic and student affairs. The difference between the models is that the two missions complement each other to enhance the in-classroom and out-of-classroom learning environments for students. The difference from the innovative models described in the following is that the contributions to student learning from student affairs is within their sphere of influence and learning from faculty members is from their area. Students, however, do not draw these distinctions and see the entire campus as a learning environment.

The primary strength of the cocurricular model is the way that this approach depicts student affairs professionals as educators. As such, they determine learning goals and set their sights on the development of students albeit separate from the related academic mission (NASPA, 1987). The cocurricular model sets the stage for a lively campus life. The weaknesses of the model include the unfulfilled opportunities for learning that occur when the curricular and cocurricular missions are separate. The institutional community fails to come together in integrated, coordinated ways. The separation of academic and student affairs missions as determined by administration and faculty members can frustrate students who see the campus in more seamless ways.

Functional Silos Student affairs educators using the functional silos model believe that students are best served through discrete programs, services, and environments. These educators have extensive professional expertise from their area-specific literature and experience rather than from a broad-spectrum student affairs approach. In student affairs divisions employing a functional silos model, staff supervision, professional development, and goals are autonomous by department. This autonomy is often reflected in space, budgets, and resource allocations. Services, programs, and policies in this model are delivered without any or with minimal coordination. The worst-case scenario in the functional silos model is when the separation leads to competition among departments for resources and student attention.

Strengths of the functional silos model include the high level of professional expertise available to students. Departments have independent, standalone budgets that enable staff members to shape programs and services appropriate to their area. This model provides administrative and organizational clarity often missing from other models. A weakness of the model is its administrative rather than student-centered approach. Professional isolation can result when departments are so autonomous by function and space that little to no interaction occurs among professionals. Independent, stand-alone units are more easily eliminated during difficult budget times. Finally, exaggerated self-importance can result when units act independently rather than as a team.

Student Services Model   The second administrative-centered model is the student services approach. Student affairs professionals using this model believe that students are best served by accessing services through a customer-oriented, corporate approach. The unit's reputation for convenient, high-quality service is paramount. Services through this model are accessed by students and others on a periodic rather than frequent basis. Students, often seen as clients, rarely develop close, personal relationships with staff members but interact on a transactional level.

This model exhibits its strengths when institution-wide initiatives such as enrollment management are readily coordinated among departments. The student services model enables faculty members to be unimpeded by service demands and able to concentrate on teaching and research. First-generation students or others needing clear pathways for success may readily find helpful services through this model. Students with multiple demands, such as family and full-time work, would likely appreciate the clarity and convenience of the student services model. Institutions with complex processes for graduation, course requirements, and registration could benefit from the principles underlying this approach. Similar to other traditional models, a weakness of the student services approach is the lack of full integration of functions and services leading to lost opportunities for student learning and engagement. A second weakness is that administrators may group functions in ways illogical from a student perspective. This model fits well with financial aid, career services, and the registrar but less well with student activities, residence life, and offices in which personal relationships are the basis for student engagement.

Competitive-Adversarial Model   This model, the only negative one among the eleven types, is grouped with the learning-centered approaches. In the competitive-adversarial model, the academic and student affairs missions are separate and, at times, at odds. This model pits student affairs against academic affairs with a recognizable us-versus-them attitude between the two groups. Student experiences and opportunities are independently planned with the potential of unintended competition for students' time and attention. Duplication of effort and rivalry may force students to choose between equally worthy activities. Although academic and student affairs are concerned with student learning, growth, and development, albeit in different contexts, neither side approaches the other to create coordinated, complementary learning experiences.

Although the negative attitudes dominating the competitive-adversarial model give it little to commend, the model does have some strengths. There are high levels of expertise in both "sides of the house" with a strong commitment to student learning. This commitment can lead to a competitive approach if either student or academic affairs feels that its role is most crucial. Despite the lack of coordination and cooperation, high-quality learning through the separate environments is possible. Weaknesses include the familiar lack of coherent student experience and limited coordination. This feature can lead to extra costs because of inefficiencies and overlap of services, often confusing for students. The missed opportunity for student engagement is the most significant weakness of the competitive-adversarial model.

Seamless Learning Model   The next learning-centered model, seamless learning, is underscored with the philosophy that student learning can result from virtually all college experiences. Structures are in place so that academic and student affairs leaders are aware of the student engagement possible throughout the institution. Ideas for working together on issues related to student learning are suggested routinely, regardless of origin.

In the seamless learning model, faculty and student affairs staff members (and the leaders of the two divisions) tear down silos and develop integrated, complementary experiences for students. For everyone, students in particular, boundaries are indistinguishable. Programs and services are collaborative efforts between academic and student affairs. Through this collaboration, the whole student experience is conceived of as being greater than the sum of its parts because no one person or unit possesses sufficient expertise so that others cannot add value by working together. The student experience is best conceived of as an ongoing developmental process beginning when a student applies for admission and ends, in a formal sense, with graduation. Everyone on campus contributes to the student learning effort with the end results of blurred in-class and out-of-class learning.

The strengths of the seamless learning model are impressive in the ways that student learning is central to institutional goals, regardless of who initiates the effort. The belief that all members have the potential to add value to the student experience promotes the attitude that all are involved in student learning. This model better reflects how students see the institution because their lack of familiarity with the way institutions are organized prevents them from seeing boundaries and distinctions that may be obvious to faculty members and administrators. Weaknesses of the model emanate from the blurred boundaries that can lead to confusion about who is in charge of what. Similar to all traditional models, the collaboration that does occur falls short of maximizing the full range of student learning opportunities. The learning-centered models work well with full-time students, traditional-age students, and residential campuses.

Innovative Models

The innovative models are grouped into two categories, student- and academic-centered. The student-centered group includes ethic of care, student-driven, and student agency. The two academic-centered models are academic-student affairs collaboration and academic-driven.

Ethic of Care Model   The ethic of care model embodies the underlying belief that with proper support and caring, all students can succeed in college. It is not that these students lack social and cultural capital, but they may lack the specific type of capital that dominates college campuses. In the ethic of care model, services and programs are developed to maximize student success and engagement. Departments and units are organized so that services are interrelated and safety nets established. This model is most effective when student and academic affairs assume shared responsibility for student engagement and success.

The strengths of the ethic of care model include the level of service available to students; time devoted to students in need; assistance provided in sensitive, compassionate ways; and an underlying philosophy that every person and every student is valued. The model's weaknesses include the time and resources necessary to achieve the model's goals, its labor-intensive nature, the danger that students could be treated in paternalistic and maternalistic ways, and the possibility that care can turn into coddling.

Student-Driven Model   The second student-centered approach is the student-driven model, characterized by trust, empowerment, and leadership. This model assumes that students can manage their functions, programming, and activities with gentle and minimal guidance from student affairs professionals. The assumption is made that the college environment provides rich opportunities to teach student leadership and engender engagement. When students are empowered in ways that do not interfere with those opportunities, learning occurs. In institutions employing the student-centered model, widespread use of student paraprofessionals is common. Students are hired for positions and involved in activities usually reserved for full-time staff members: building design, program delivery, and committee leadership. Students engage in institutional governance through committee and task force membership. This membership is not perfunctory because students are viewed as integral institutional members with important opinions and insights to share.

The strengths of the student-driven model are impressive. Research shows that retention rates increase and student engagement is enriched when students participate in high-impact educational practices (Kuh, 2008; Kuh et al, 2005/2010). Under-resourced institutions can reframe financial necessity into educationally empowering experiences. Expanded services previously out of reach are enabled by student labor. But, readers can readily imagine the pitfalls of this model. There are ethical implications to be considered when students fill roles usually occupied by full-time staff members. Student affairs educators must take care not to meet their goals at the expense of the student workers' life goals. Historically underrepresented students with less familiarity with college campuses may not have access to the benefits of the model in the same ways that dominant-identified students do. Student employment has its challenges as students juggle classes and responsibilities never experienced in their young lives.

Student Agency Model   Some have used the words *quasi-chaotic, trust,* and *action* to describe the student agency model. In this approach, students are completely responsible for student life. They are viewed as equal partners to administrators and faculty and other campus staff members. As equals, students are human agents who intentionally make things happen through their actions. Students take ownership for and invest in creating, learning, and sharing knowledge and are responsible for activities, decisions, and programs. In the student agency model, faculty members and administrators create policies, climate, and administrative structures that empower students and facilitate learning. Through these structures, students are urged to take full responsibility for their education as student affairs educators take a hands-off approach. Training and support are provided to student leaders to enable their success.

Strengths of the student agency model include the ways students are invested in their learning and success. Through their efforts, they develop autonomy and responsibility. Similar to the student-driven model, the presence of student workers means that the institution can deliver a wider range of programs than if dependent on full-time staff members alone. A weakness of the model is the common effort on the part of students to reinvent the system with each new cohort. When students are completely in charge of student life, the results can be inefficient and messy as they learn and gain experience. The messiness of the resulting programs and services may be incongruent with stakeholders who expect professional, polished results. This model assumes that student mistakes are part of learning, an approach that may not satisfy boards of trustees, parents, and constituent groups. Problems can be difficult to resolve using this model. Roommate problems, budget deliberations, and other issues can become protracted because of the emphasis on process. Issues may arise because students may not understand their institution's fiduciary relationships with external agencies, such as law enforcement and state and federal regulatory organizations. Despite these difficulties, the educational value of this model cannot be overemphasized.

Academic–Student Affairs Collaboration Model The academic-student affairs collaboration model "emphasizes significant interactions between student and academic staff around the common purpose of enhanced student learning" (Manning, Kinzie, & Schuh, 2014, p. 158). Presidents and provosts have shown interest in this model because of their desire to see more cooperation between academic and student affairs. In this model, mutual territory is shared and combined efforts on engagement and success are forged. Boundaries between academic and student affairs are blurred or nonexistent. Student and academic affairs have reciprocal relationships and both groups are involved in each other's primary areas. The result is student affairs educators and faculty members jointly facilitating the intellectual mission while appreciating each other's strengths. An interesting outcome of this approach is that student life programs and policies emphasize intellectual growth and challenge, often the domain of faculty. Conversely, faculty members are engaged in areas traditionally viewed as the purview of student affairs.

The strengths of the academic-student affairs collaboration model are notable. Institutions using this model can create high-quality learning environments for students. Creativity is encouraged and resources shared. Research from Project DEEP indicated that student affairs staff members in institutions with this model reported a high degree of satisfaction. The weaknesses are similarly noteworthy. The burden of initiation of the collaboration often falls to student affairs. Particular effort may need to be made by student affairs professionals to meet faculty members more than halfway. The collaborations may be lopsided or perhaps even unfair until both parties understand their mutual cultures. The goal of high-quality student learning should remain at the forefront as relationships are built and structures formed.

Academic-Driven Model The last innovative model is the academic-driven model. This model exists in institutions that are organized around the academic core. Without apology, these institutions privilege the academic experience over traditional student life activities. Academic and student affairs staff members at these institutions share responsibility for student success and engagement. They understand the ways they can collaborate with faculty members and students to develop a rich intellectual community. Student affairs educators in these institutions are highly sensitive to curricular rigors and have signed on to the limitations and benefits of this approach. The role of student affairs at academic-driven institutions is to provide structural support in an intense intellectual environment. Student affairs professionals play supporting and sustaining roles in achieving goals related to the academic mission. Students understand the roles of student and academic affairs and share in the promotion of the educational mission. Balance is created as student affairs staff members collaborate in ways that support yet do not distract from the academic environment. They understand that student involvement in intense educational mission trumps activities unrelated to the academic mission.

The strengths of this model include the presence of a clear and well-understood role for student affairs, one that enhances the formal academic environment. Student affairs staff members are educators who teach and contribute directly to the educational mission. Student affairs goals are based on student-learning outcomes, goals closely related to the academic mission. Weaknesses of the model include the fact that faculty members may not understand or appreciate the potential of student affairs to enhance the campus environment through nonacademically oriented programs and services. The academic-driven model depends heavily on faculty member–student interaction outside classroom, interaction that is not always possible given faculty member demands regarding teaching, research, and service. Faculty members are increasingly pressured to produce more research and scholarship with resulting higher and higher expectations for tenure. The time available for club and organization advising, academic advising, and other out-of-classroom activities is diminishing.

Theory to Practice

The models described in this chapter can be used by student affairs educators at all levels of professional experience as a means to shape their practice. The models, however, should be combined with a solid understanding of student affairs theory to gain full benefit from their use. Familiarity with the theories that guide student affairs work is essential to understanding how the models apply to practice. Table 16.2 summarizes likely theories that can be used to understand the reasoning behind each model. This is not an all-inclusive list and many theories not in the table can serve as a foundation for the models of student affairs practice.

TABLE 16.2.   THEORIES UNDERLYING THE MODELS OF STUDENT AFFAIRS PRACTICE

Model of Student Affairs Practice	Underlying Theories
Traditional Models	
Extra-Curricular and Co-Curricular	• Psychosocial Student Development (Evans, Forney, Guido, Patton, & Renn, 2009) • Leadership Theory (Komives, Longerbeam, Owen, Mainella & Osteen, 2006) • Organizational Theory (Manning, 2013)
Functional Silos and Student Services	• Bureaucracy (Manning, 2013)
Competitive and Adversarial and Seamless Learning	• Learning Theory • Student Learning Imperative (ACPA, 1996)
Innovative Models	
Ethic of Care	• Women's Psychological Development (Gilligan, 1982; Gilligan, Rogers, & Tolman, 2014) • Gender-related development (Baxter Magolda, 1992) • Spiritual Development (Rendón, 2009)

(continued)

TABLE 16.2 (*continued*)

Model of Student Affairs Practice	Underlying Theories
Student-Driven	• Student Involvement (Astin, 1993) • Student Engagement (Kuh et al., 2001; Harper & Quaye, 2014)
Student Agency	• Human agency (Bandura, 2001, 2015)
Academic-Student Affairs Collaboration	• The Student Learning Imperative (ACPA, 1996) • Academic-student affairs collaborations (Kezar, Hirsch, & Burack, 2001)
Academic-Driven	• Cognitive Development Theory (Evans, Forney, Guido, Patton, & Renn, 2009)

In addition to the underlying theories, the choice of model is heavily dependent on the senior student affairs leader(s). As divisional or department leaders, these individuals are charged with shaping the mission and vision. Their experience, theoretical orientation, personal characteristics, and background will heavily influence the model chosen for the campus. In addition to leadership, several other factors can influence the choice of model, particularly when a division is attempting to change from one model to another. Possible internal change motivators include senior leadership change, mission and vision evolution, organizational structure adaptations, strategic planning activities, and enrollment shifts. External change factors include shifting demographics, economic changes, government initiatives, catastrophes, and disasters. These factors, some planned, others unplanned, can be viewed as windows of opportunity when change from one model to another is desired. The research underlying the models and experience with practitioners show that it is possible to shift from one model to another.

Changing Your Model

The first step in the process of changing your model is to discover which model or models are currently in use. Although one model usually predominates, a second or even third model is often employed within various units in the student affairs division.

The next steps are to be explicit about the desired change and identify what might support or challenge the adoption of a new model. For example, to change from a cocurricular model to an academic-centered approach, student affairs educators are advised to find allies on the faculty and within academic affairs. These allies can advise student affairs educators on steps to take to achieve the shift. They can also speak to the value of the proposed model at faculty senates and other governance arenas. During any change in model, compromise is important. An important finding from Project DEEP was that the synergy possible when all areas of the campus work together results in significant educational outcomes for students. Compromise and collaboration are important approaches to cultivate.

Students are an essential constituent group in any proposed change. They are aware of the nuances of student life from a perspective that only they can fully understand. Their insights can save countless hours of effort as they suggest ways to make any model of practice work for their benefit.

Student affairs professionals are advised to attend to the infrastructure (for example, policies, training, staffing, budgeting) so fellow administrators, faculty members, and students can build programs, services, and policies. Higher education resources have always been scarce. As student affairs educators use resources to achieve student learning and engagement, strategic use of money, space, human power, and other resources is essential. Finally, research shows that programs and services intended to influence student engagement and learning cannot be successful without assessment (Schuh, 2011). Assessment can help student affairs educators understand the outcomes of their work, craft desired future initiatives, and discover ways to optimize available resources.

Summary

As student affairs staff members consider a model to employ on their campus, it is crucial that fit to the campus be a primary consideration. The choice of model is heavily dependent on institutional mission and must be congruent with the academic and other initiatives within the institution. As we conceived of the models, ways to identify existing campus models, and options to change existing campus models, our emphasis was always on how student engagement and learning can best be achieved at the institution. With an emphasis on student engagement and success at the center of student affairs, learning can be achieved in ways that best benefit students.

The models summarized in this chapter represent a snapshot in time, conceived by the authors of *One Size Does Not Fit All: Traditional and Innovative Models of Student Affairs Practice* (Manning, Kinzie, & Schuh, 2014). Over time, we expect the models to evolve as the priorities and issues within the field of student affairs change. We encourage others to expand and refine the models in ways that keep them relevant to student affairs practice.

Readers are directed to Manning, Kinzie, and Schuh's *One Size Does Not Fit All* (2014) and Kuh et al. *Student Success in College* (2005/2010) for additional discussion questions and activities to help graduate students, new professionals, and others learn about the options available regarding student affairs models for practice.

Discussion Questions and Activities

1. How does the model currently used by your division of student affairs enhance student engagement and learning?
2. How does your model complement and enhance the institutional mission? The academic mission?

3. What are the strengths and weaknesses of the model used by your division?
4. Who or what is at the center of your model? Whom does it serve? Who is left out?
5. How do students describe the model used by the division?
6. Does the model used help students navigate the campus environment and discover high-impact educational experiences?

References

American College Personnel Association (ACPA). (1996). *The student learning imperative.* Washington, DC: Author.

American Council on Education. (1937). *The student personnel point of view.* Washington, DC: Author.

Astin, A. W. (1993). *What matters in college? Four critical years revisited* (Vol. 1). San Francisco: Jossey-Bass.

Bandura, A. (2001). Social cognitive theory: An agentic perspective. *Annual Review of Psychology, 52,* 1–26.

Bandura, A. (2015). On deconstructing commentaries regarding alternative theories of self-regulation. *Journal of Management, 41*(4), 1025–1044.

Baxter Magolda, M. B. (1992). *Knowing and reasoning in college: Gender-related patterns in students' intellectual development.* San Francisco: Jossey-Bass.

Boyd, K., Robinson, K., & Cawthorn, T. (2015). The cultures of student affairs and academic collaboration: An examination of typology in higher education subcultures. *New York Journal of Student Affairs, 14*(2), 18–34.

Evans, N. J., Forney, D. S., Guido, F. M., Patton, L. D., & Renn, K. A. (2009). *Student development in college: Theory, research, and practice.* New York: John Wiley & Sons.

Gilligan, C. (1982). *In a different voice: Psychological theory and women's development.* Cambridge, MA: Harvard University Press.

Gilligan, C., Rogers, A. G., & Tolman, D. L. (2014). *Women, girls and psychotherapy: Reframing resistance.* New York: Routledge.

Harper, S. R., & Quaye, S. J. (Eds.). (2014). *Student engagement in higher education: Theoretical perspectives and practical approaches for diverse populations.* New York: Routledge.

Kezar, A., Hirsch, D. J., & Burack, C. (Eds.). (2001). *Understanding the role of academic and student a successful learning environment successful learning environment* (New Directions for Higher Education, no. 116). San Francisco: Jossey-Bass.

Komives, S. R., Longerbeam, S. D., Owen, J. E., Mainella, F. C., & Osteen, L. (2006). A leadership identity development model: Applications from a grounded theory. *Journal of College Student Development, 47*(4), 401–418.

Kuh, G. D. (2008). *High-impact educational practices: What they are, who has access to them, and why they matter.* Washington, DC: Association of American Colleges and Universities.

Kuh, G. D., Kinzie, J., Schuh, J., Whitt, E., & Associates. (2005/2010). *Student success in college: Creating conditions that matter.* San Francisco: Jossey Bass.

Manning, K. (2013). *Organizational theory in higher education.* New York: Routledge.

Manning, K., Kinzie, J., & Schuh, J. H. (2014). *One size does not fit all: Traditional and innovative models of student affairs practice* (2nd ed.). New York: Routledge.

NASPA. (1987). *A perspective on student affairs.* Washington, DC: Author.

Rendón, L. I. (2009). *Sentipensante (sensing/thinking) pedagogy: Educating for wholeness, social justice and liberation.* Sterling, VA: Stylus.

Schuh, J. H. (2011). *Assessment methods for student affairs.* San Francisco: John Wiley & Sons.

MODELS OF STUDENT AFFAIRS PRACTICE INVENTORY

Please check off the characteristics that apply to the student affairs division or department on your campus.

	1. Students are viewed as equals in the running of the institution.
	2. Academic affairs administrators "sound like" student affairs administrators and student affairs administrators "sound like" academic affairs administrators.
	3. Student development theory is the main theoretical underpinning for the division or department.
	4. Academic and student affairs cede responsibility for each other's experiences to the other and tend to stay out of the way.
	5. Student affairs staff members provide structural support for the intense academic environment.
	6. Academic and student affairs leaders are aware of developments in each other's areas.
	7. Student leadership is a major objective of the division or department.
	8. Activities, decisions, and programs are the responsibility of the students.
	9. Student affairs assumes that some students come to college inadequately prepared for academic work, and the institution is committed to providing that support.
	10. The complementary nature of academic and student affairs experiences is not recognized or acted on.
	11. Student and academic affairs missions are designed to contribute to the total student learning experience: from admission through graduation.
	12. Administrative and organizational clarity is present within the division.
	13. Significant interactions occur between student and academic affairs concerning the common purpose of enhanced student learning.
	14. Administrative silos are torn down in order to provide students with the best possible experience.
	15. There is an assumption that students require different programs, services, and environments that are best offered by distinct and separate offices.
	16. Services, programs, and policies are well and/or adequately delivered without or with minimal division-level coordination.
	17. An atmosphere of care and support is created.
	18. Attention of student affairs units is focused on areas where students are most in need of support.
	19. Student affairs possess a high level of trust in students, and they are intimately involved in running the majority of campus programs and services.
	20. Business and consumer orientations are prevalent.
	21. Student affairs and academic affairs programs, services, and activities compete for resources, student time, and mission priority.
	22. Competition for resources and student attention exists among student affairs offices and departments.

(continued)

MODELS OF STUDENT AFFAIRS PRACTICE INVENTORY

Please check off the characteristics that apply to the student affairs division or department on your campus.

	23. Student and academic affairs maintain their distinct functions but capitalize on the strengths of student learning from their unique perspective.
	24. Because of joint student-academic affairs efforts, students have increased opportunities for learning in in- and out-of-classroom settings.
	25. Duplication of effort by academic departments and student affairs is commonplace because of a lack of coordination between these two campus divisions.
	26. Efficiency and effectiveness are the main concerns in delivery of student affairs functions.
	27. Student affairs is organized based on the belief that students may need extra support to succeed in college.
	28. Faculty and student affairs staff members are divided into in- and out-of-classroom activities, respectively.
	29. Faculty members are free to concentrate their efforts on teaching, research, and service.
	30. Functions and services are clustered together.
	31. Growth and development come from out-of-class experiences that are independent from the formal academic curriculum.
	32. Students drive campus activities, programs, and services.
	33. High levels of professionalism and expertise are present within the departments and offices of the division of student affairs.
	34. Student affairs staff members work with faculty members to develop a rich intellectual community.
	35. Academic and student affairs are unaware of the contributions that each can make to the other.
	36. The highest priority is creating an intellectual environment.
	37. Student and academic affairs respect each other's professionalism and try not to interfere.
	38. Independent, stand-alone budgets characterize each student affairs office or department.
	39. *The Student Learning Imperative* and/or *Learning Reconsidered* form the philosophy of your on campus model.
	40. Individual relationships between students and student affairs educators are not as crucial as the overall reputation of the office.
	41. Campus programs and services are characterized by inefficient delivery because of the lack of awareness among academic units of student affairs goals and initiatives.
	42. Decentralization of supervision, professional development, and, oftentimes, goals exist within the division of student affairs.
	43. Student and academic affairs are independent though they do communicate with each other on important issues.

MODELS OF STUDENT AFFAIRS PRACTICE INVENTORY

Please check off the characteristics that apply to the student affairs division or department on your campus.

	44. Learning occurs everywhere in a seamless manner.
	45. Level of service available in the name of student support is very high.
	46. Student learning experiences offered by academic and student affairs are uncoordinated with one another's efforts.
	47. Student organizations are living laboratories to teach programming, budgeting, decision making, and conflict resolution.
	48. The main purpose of student affairs is to deliver services, not provide a developmentally oriented education to students.
	49. Departments within the division of student affairs operate independently of one another.
	50. Student affairs operationalizes the assumption that students are more satisfied when services are conveniently organized and provided.
	51. Only faculty members teach courses, including first-year experience, leadership, or other student affairs–oriented subject matter.
	52. Out-of-classroom learning is important but secondary to inside-the-classroom learning.
	53. Out-of-classroom learning is the main goal of the student affairs division or department.
	54. Planning between academic and student affairs is an effort to avoid conflicts, not to collaborate about student learning and engagement.
	55. Powerful partnerships are forged from the strengths of academic and student affairs.
	56. Student affairs staff members strategically and purposefully build student involvement into campus activities and programs.
	57. Programs and services may lack the polish of professionally managed experiences.
	58. Separate orientation and support services are tailored to the unique needs of particular students or student populations.
	59. Students run the institution.
	60. Services are accessed on a periodic rather than daily basis.
	61. Specialization and narrowness of focus in academic and student affairs are valued over coordination and cooperation.
	62. Student affairs activities are crafted to support, not compete with, the academic mission.
	63. Student affairs functions are to support the goals of education, not provide an education in and of itself.
	64. Student affairs is clear about its role as supporting the academic mission.
	65. Student affairs is often responsible for initiating collaborative efforts with academic affairs.

(continued)

MODELS OF STUDENT AFFAIRS PRACTICE INVENTORY

**Please check off the characteristics that apply to the student
affairs division or department on your campus.**

	66. Student affairs staff members are responsible for the choices made about the services, programs, and environment molded to advance student engagement.
	67. Student affairs staff members encourage and have high levels of expectation about the involvement of students in decision making and governance.
	68. Student affairs staff members often face ethical dilemmas over the extensive use of student employees.
	69. Student affairs staff members spends little energy on cocurricular programs that are not related to the academic mission.
	70. Student and academic affairs missions are distinct but each respects and acknowledges the contributions of the other to student learning.
	71. Student employees fill positions usually reserved for full-time staff.
	72. Student empowerment and leadership are at the center of the student affairs philosophy on campus.
	73. Student involvement and leadership are at the core of the student affairs philosophy.
	74. Student learning transcends administrative hierarchies and functional area boundaries.
	75. Student success and academic rigor are of primary importance.
	76. Students are highly invested in cocurricular life.
	77. Students are highly invested in the running of the institution because of their deep involvement.
	78. The academic mission is the highest priority at the institution.
	79. The emphasis is on student learning, regardless of where it is occurring.
	80. Student energies, time, and talents are channeled into activities shown to maximize student learning and development.
	81. The high level of service to students is labor intensive and expensive.
	82. The lines between in- and out-of-classroom activities are blurred.
	83. Through campus employment, students can develop skills that prepare them for postgraduation employment.
	84. Student learning has the potential to result from all student experiences—in and outside the classroom.
	85. The divisions of student and academic affairs are unwilling to work together.
	86. Programs, services, and policies in an out-of-classroom context are well developed.
	87. Student affairs may sometimes overprotect, coddle, or fail to adequately challenge students.
	88. Whole student development is maximized through well-integrated and coordinated student and academic affairs.

Source: Manning, Kinzie, and Schuh (2014).

SCORING

EXTRACURRICULAR	FUNCTIONAL SILOS	STUDENT SERVICES	COMPETITIVE-ADVERSARIAL
3. _____	12. _____	20. _____	21. _____
7. _____	15. _____	26. _____	25. _____
28. _____	16. _____	30. _____	35. _____
29. _____	22. _____	40. _____	41. _____
47. _____	33. _____	48. _____	46. _____
53. _____	38. _____	50. _____	51. _____
66. _____	42. _____	60. _____	61. _____
86. _____	49. _____	63. _____	85. _____
_____	_____	_____	_____ Totals

COCURRICULAR	SEAMLESS LEARNING	ETHIC OF CARE	STUDENT-DRIVEN
4. _____	6. _____	9. _____	32. _____
10. _____	11. _____	17. _____	56. _____
31. _____	14. _____	18. _____	68. _____
37. _____	39. _____	27. _____	71. _____
43. _____	44. _____	45. _____	73. _____
52. _____	79. _____	58. _____	76. _____
54. _____	82. _____	81. _____	80. _____
70. _____	84. _____	87. _____	83. _____
_____	_____	_____	_____ Totals

STUDENT AGENCY	ACADEMIC–STUDENT AFFAIRS COLLABORATION	ACADEMIC-CENTERED
1. _____	2. _____	5. _____
8. _____	13. _____	34. _____
19. _____	23. _____	36. _____
57. _____	24. _____	62. _____
59. _____	55. _____	64. _____
67. _____	65. _____	69. _____
72. _____	74. _____	75. _____
77. _____	88. _____	78. _____
_____	_____	_____ Totals

CHAPTER 17

ORGANIZATIONAL STRUCTURES AND FUNCTIONS

Maureen E. Wilson

There are more than 4,700 degree-granting colleges and universities in the United States alone, each with a unique organizational structure. Student affairs, with that name or another, is a key component of the institutional structure. However, the units that comprise the student affairs division vary from campus to campus. To whom does the senior student affairs officer (SSAO) report? How many direct reports does the SSAO have? What functional areas comprise the student affairs division? This chapter addresses the organizational structure of postsecondary institutions and student affairs, overviews common functional areas in student affairs, and concludes with a discussion of issues facing student affairs.

Several chapters in this text are good companions to this one. In chapter 4, Kristen A. Renn and Lori D. Patton discuss the wide variety of institutional types and role of campus culture on the organization of student affairs and the structures and functions found within it. Adrianna Kezar's discussion of organization theory and change in chapter 13 also contributes to an understanding of organizational structures and functional areas. In chapter 16, Kathleen Manning, Jillian Kinzie, and John H. Schuh detail the influence of institutional mission and culture on the conceptualization, organization, and operationalization of student affairs units. Finally, the essential competencies detailed in part 5 cut across the functional areas described in the following sections.

Organization of Higher Education and Student Affairs

Many stakeholders care deeply about the management of colleges and universities. Students want a good education and fair evaluation. Faculty members want to influence decisions regarding instructional content, how teaching occurs, and the conditions and facilities necessary for high-quality teaching and research. Academic leaders and trustees must administer the university and maintain its financial and academic viability. The public is rightly concerned about access; tuition; taxes paid to support higher education; and contributions of institutions to communities, states, and the nation (Bok, 2013). Increasingly, campuses pursue opportunities abroad to increase revenue and expand their reach. Satisfying all of these constituents simultaneously may be impossible.

Many factors influence organizational structures including institutional history and mission, governance systems, finances, strategic plans, preferences of the board and president, personnel, personalities, and politics. The top campus leader is the president or chancellor who reports to the institutional governing board, often called the *board of trustees*. Some states operate under a system model. In California, for example, chancellors at University of California campuses report to the system president, who reports to the board of regents.

Presidents have a number of direct reports. Although titles and organization charts vary from campus to campus, some patterns are typical. As illustrated in figure 17.1, the provost and vice president for academic affairs is the senior academic offer of the campus and reports directly to the president. At universities, the deans of the colleges or schools typically report to the provost. Vice provosts often oversee areas such as undergraduate studies, research, international affairs, and enrollment management. At small colleges, department chairs may report directly to the provost.

Other vice presidents reporting to the president may include those for alumni and development, administration, information and technology, and equity and diversity. The general counsel and athletic director may also report to the president, particularly at Division I schools.

In figure 17.1, student affairs reports to the provost and therefore is called the vice provost for student affairs. This puts the SSAO at the table with academic leaders, which should facilitate collaborative efforts to support student learning. As shown in figure 17.2, a more common model is for the vice president for student affairs (VPSA) to report directly to the president. In a recent survey, 72 percent of SSAOs reported directly to the president or chancellor, 16 percent to the provost or senior academic officer, and 6 percent to an executive or senior vice president. Regarding job titles for SSAOs, 48 percent were vice president, 20 percent dean, and 13 percent vice president and dean. Of those with the combined title, 83 percent were at four-year, private, not-for-profit institutions (National Association of Student Personnel Administrators [NASPA], 2014). Being a member of the president's cabinet gives the SSAO access to the institution's top leaders and ensures they consider student welfare and interests in decision making. Ultimately, the effectiveness of the SSAO is more critical than student affairs' placement on the organization chart (Sandeen & Barr, 2006). If the president, provost, and other campus leaders know little of the role of student affairs in student success, the SSAO must educate them and use strong assessment data to advocate for resources.

FIGURE 17.1. SAMPLE UNIVERSITY ORGANIZATION CHART

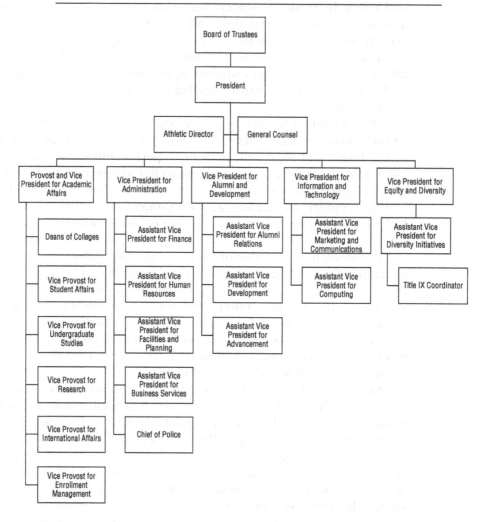

SSAO Educational and Professional Background and Salary

About two-thirds of SSAOs have a doctoral or professional degree. Of those with a doctorate, 70 to 75 percent earned the degree in education or higher education (Campbell, 2015; Lindsay, 2014; NASPA, 2014). Although one often hears the line, "Nobody goes into higher education to get rich," senior-level administrators often receive handsome salaries. In 2014–2015, the average salary for SSAOs was $137,484. The rate is higher at research universities ($212,665) than at associate's colleges ($110,335). The dean of students at research universities earns an average of $130,029 compared to $91,109 at associate's colleges (College and University Professional Association for Human Resources [CUPA-HR], 2015). With those salaries comes an enormous

FIGURE 17.2.   SAMPLE STUDENT AFFAIRS ORGANIZATION CHART—LARGE UNIVERSITY

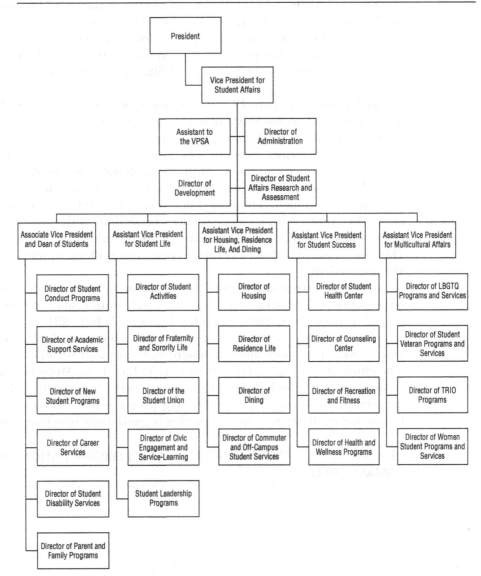

amount of responsibility and substantial time commitment, including nights and weekends. CUPA-HR also has salary data on a wide variety of student affairs positions.

Reporting Lines in Student Affairs

Beyond the SSAO, reporting lines and structures vary greatly from campus to campus. Figure 17.2 shows a sample student affairs organization chart for a large university. In this example, the VPSA reports directly to the president. One associate vice president and dean of students (DOS) plus four assistant vice presidents report to the VPSA and oversee a variety of functional areas headed by unit directors. Three directors plus an assistant to the VPSA also report to the VPSA. The assistant typically does not oversee specific functional areas or supervise other professionals but may manage the VPSA office, handle communications, and take responsibility for specific projects and tasks for the VPSA.

As illustrated in figure 17.3, the organizational hierarchy at small colleges is typically flatter so the SSAO may have a large number of direct reports. In this example, the VPSA-DOS supervises one associate dean, one assistant dean, and five unit directors. Student affairs professionals at small colleges may perform many roles simultaneously, have small staffs, and work as generalists across functional areas (Heida, 2006). Residence hall staff members may hold a collateral assignment, enabling them to work ten to fifteen hours per week in another unit such as career services or student activities. Small college professionals interact a great deal with students, individually and in groups. They also connect with faculty members via committees, campus events, and assisting students.

Institutional type and culture have a strong bearing on functional areas, organizational structures, reporting lines, and centralization or decentralization of services (Hirt, 2006; Manning, Kinzie, & Schuh, 2014). For example, some community colleges have residence halls, but most do not. Some campuses have a very large and prominent fraternity and sorority system, some have eliminated them, and others have never had them. Multicultural student services are apt to look different at minority-serving institutions than at predominantly white ones. A large housing program may have more residents than many small towns so these complex organizations may have hundreds of

FIGURE 17.3.   SAMPLE STUDENT AFFAIRS ORGANIZATION CHART— SMALL COLLEGE

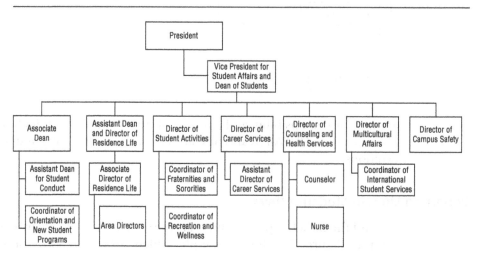

employees and therefore their own human resources, budgeting, mainte-nance, and housekeeping services. Smaller student affairs divisions may have one centralized human resources department or rely solely on the university's human resources unit. Using centralized processes may be more cost effective and facilitate the interdependence of various campus units.

Functional Areas for Student Affairs Professionals

The Council for the Advancement of Standards in Higher Education (2015) has developed forty-three sets of functional area standards for higher educa-tion programs and services (plus master's level student affairs professional preparation programs). The following list shows the current functional area standards, not all of which fall under the student affairs umbrella. However, most draw on skills and experiences typical of student affairs practitioners.

CAS Functional Area Standards for Higher Education Programs and Services

- Academic advising programs
- Adult learner programs and services
- Alcohol and other drug programs
- Assessment services
- Auxiliary services functional areas
- Campus activities programs
- Campus information and visitor services
- Campus police and security programs
- Campus religious and spiritual programs
- Career services
- Civic engagement and service-learning programs
- Clinical health services
- College honor society programs
- College unions
- Commuter and off-campus living programs
- Conference and event programs
- Counseling services
- Dining service programs
- Disability resources and services
- Education abroad programs and services
- Financial aid programs
- Fraternity and sorority advising programs
- Graduate and professional student programs and services
- Health promotion services
- Housing and residential life programs
- International student programs and services
- Internship programs
- Learning assistance programs
- Lesbian, gay, bisexual, and transgender programs and services
- Master's level student affairs professional preparation programs
- Multicultural student programs and services
- Orientation programs
- Parent and family programs
- Recreational sports programs
- Registrar programs and services
- Sexual violence-related programs and services
- Student conduct programs
- Student leadership programs
- Transfer student programs and services
- TRIO and other educational opportunity programs

- Undergraduate admissions programs and services
- Undergraduate research programs

- Veterans and military programs and services
- Women's and gender programs and services

Detailed in a survey conducted by NASPA (2014), the five functional areas that most commonly reported to student affairs were campus activities, student conduct, counseling, orientation, and student affairs assessment. However, organizational structures are not static; units may move in and out of the student affairs division. Veteran student services, student affairs assessment, and campus safety were the most common recent additions to student affairs divisions, and career services, financial aid, and intercollegiate athletics were the units most commonly removed from student affairs and placed elsewhere in the institution (NASPA, 2014).

Emerging specialist roles in student affairs include those for technology, development, communications, "assistant to" positions, human resources and professional development, director of administration, auxiliary services, and research and assessment (Tull & Kuk, 2012). These roles cut across functional areas and influence the entire student affairs division. Additionally, in a more coordinated effort to assist and manage students who present a threat of harm to themselves or others, cross-functional behavioral assessment teams composed of staff members from the dean of students office, residence life, campus police, student conduct, and the counseling center may meet regularly to discuss incidents, share information from various sources, connect students to available resources, and address ongoing problems. The increased presence of students on campus with serious mental health issues affects other students and faculty and staff members; it takes tremendous skill and resources to work effectively with these students.

Regardless of the specific organization chart and which functional areas fall in which areas, student affairs must build good working relationships and collaborate with colleagues in academic affairs, business affairs, and development to be truly successful in their roles. The following functional areas may be part of the student affairs division, employ student affairs professionals, or collaborate with student affairs to support student learning and promote students' holistic development.

Staff members in these areas may seek professional development opportunities through generalist professional organizations such as ACPA–College Student Educators International and NASPA–Student Affairs Administrators in Higher Education. Instead of or in addition to those organizations, they may join specialized organizations and enhance their practice by reading and contributing to scholarship sponsored by those associations.

Academic Advising

Academic advisors work with students to plan a course of study, achieve their goals, and promote their development. They play a key role in promoting student success, persistence, and retention; these are important individual, institutional, and societal outcomes. Academic advisors also work closely with faculty members and academic programs and may specialize in advising specific groups such as athletes, honors students, and students in STEM majors. Advising is often housed in academic affairs and may be co-ordinated centrally or be decentralized into individual colleges within a university. The National Academic Advising Association publishes the *NACADA Journal.*

Admissions

Often a function of enrollment management or student affairs, admissions professionals work to recruit and enroll students. Admission counselors or recruiters attend college fairs and visit high schools; they may or may not have a graduate degree. Higher-level positions likely require an advanced degree, often in student affairs or related disciplines. The National Association for College Admission Counseling publishes the *Journal of College Admissions.*

Assessment

Decreasing budgets and increased calls for accountability have amplified the need for assessment to evaluate programs, support student learning and devel-opment, set priorities, and make data-driven decisions. In addition to offices of institutional research at most institutions, a growing number of student affairs divisions have their own research and assessment units, particularly at large universities. These offices may coordinate the institution's participation in large, national studies.

Student Affairs Assessment Leaders holds an annual meeting that rotates between ACPA and NASPA national conferences and maintains an active e-mail list for members. Assessment professionals may also present their research findings at a variety of academic conferences such as the Association for the Study of Higher Education and publish in refereed journals such as the *Journal of Higher Education.*

Auxiliary Services Functional Areas

A variety of programs and services may operate as auxiliaries and follow business practices to generate revenue and cover expenses. Varying from cam-pus to campus, some areas may report to student affairs and others to business affairs. Housing, bookstores, dining, health services, student unions, and con-ference and event programs are common auxiliaries. These areas offer many on-campus student employment opportunities. The National Association of College Auxiliary Services publishes *College Services Magazine;* specific auxilia-ries also have their own organizations and publications.

Campus Security

Campus police or security officers work to provide a safer campus environment by protecting the community and enforcing laws and policies. Sworn police officers who are employees of the institution or a local law enforcement agency or contracted security personnel may provide these services. This office typically reports to business affairs or student affairs. Campus officers work closely with student affairs on education and prevention efforts, particularly for students who reside on campus. The International Association of Campus Law Enforcement Administrators publishes the *Campus Law Enforcement Journal*.

Career Services

In addition to aiding students and alumni in their job searches, career services professionals develop relationships with employers to secure job, internship, and co-op placements for students. They offer an array of programs and services including résumé workshops, career advising, networking opportunities, and career fairs. The office may be part of student or academic affairs, perhaps a unit of enrollment management. Career services may be centralized operations or decentralized and run by individual schools or colleges within a university. The National Association of Colleges and Employers publishes the *NACE Journal*. The National Career Development Association publishes *Career Development Quarterly*.

Civic Engagement and Service-Learning Programs

Offices of civic engagement and service-learning work with faculty members to develop syllabi and community partners for service-learning courses, help students engage in community service, and connect community agencies with volunteers and interns. Service-learning typically takes place within a credit-bearing academic course. A variety of professional organizations supports these programs including Campus Compact and International Association for Research on Service-Learning and Community Engagement. The *Journal of Higher Education Outreach* and the *Michigan Journal of Community Service Learning* are two of the publications.

College Union and Campus Activities

The union acts as the living room of the campus, a gathering place for students and faculty, staff, and community members. Unions offer cultural, educational, social, and recreational programming in addition to for-profit services such as a bookstore, bank, full-service and fast food restaurants, and game rooms. Campus activities professionals, often operating within the college union, endeavor to promote student learning by helping them engage actively in campus life. Campus activities may have a program dedicated to developing student leaders. The Association of College Unions International and the National Association of Campus Activities are the major professional organizations in these areas. ACUI publishes *The Bulletin* and NACA produces the *Campus Activities Programming* magazine.

Commuter and Off-Campus Student Services

The vast majority, 86.8 percent, of undergraduate students reside off campus. At four-year public institutions, 22.5 percent live on campus compared to 43.8 percent at four-year private nonprofits. Most off-campus students do not reside with their parents (Skomsvold, 2013). Many are traditional-age undergraduates who reside close to campus in apartments and houses and others commute by car, public transportation, bicycle, or foot. Many work full-time and may have multiple jobs. Some campuses have programs and services specifically for commuter students and assist them to find suitable housing, work with property owners, live peaceably with neighbors, and engage in the campus community. The National Clearinghouse for Commuter Programs assists professionals in this area and publishes *Commuter Perspectives* for its members.

Counseling Services

Many students on campus face substantial mental health concerns; 34.5 percent reported feeling so depressed it was hard to function at least once in the previous twelve months (American College Health Association, 2015). A key source of support for students' personal development and psychological health comes from the counseling center. Counselors typically have graduate degrees in counseling psychology, clinical psychology, mental health, counselor education, and related fields. Many are licensed or certified. Counselors see students in individual and group therapy, do outreach programming, provide consultation to the community, work with students in crisis, and consult with staff members on risk assessment and intervention strategies. Counseling services may be a unit within student affairs, affiliated with the health center, or (less commonly) be contracted with local service providers. There are many professional organizations including the American Counseling Association and its division, the American College Counseling Association; ACA publishes the *Journal of College Counseling*.

Dean of Students Office

The office of the dean of students often encompasses several functional areas such as student conduct, learning assistance programs, and parent and family programs. These staff members play a key role in crisis management, especially those related to students. They respond to student issues and concerns raised by students, faculty and staff members, parents, and community members and play complex roles in helping and supporting students while also holding them accountable to campus policies and procedures. Primary professional organizations for the dean of students are ACPA and NASPA. Key publications are ACPA's *Journal of College Student Development* and *About Campus* and NASPA's *Journal of Student Affairs Research and Practice* and *Net Results*.

Disability Services

Authorized by the Rehabilitation Act of 1973 and the Americans with Disabilities Act of 1990 (amended in 2008), staff members in disability services secure access and accommodation for students with disabilities. Located in student affairs or academic affairs, they arrange a variety of services depending on students' needs such as note takers, sign language interpreters, and test administration. The Association on Higher Education and Disability publishes the *Journal of Postsecondary Education and Disability*.

Education Abroad and International Student Programs

In 2014–2015, 304,467 US students studied abroad for academic credit (Institute of International Education [IIE], 2015), a number that continues to increase. Education abroad works with domestic students and faculty members to help them study and teach in other countries. Students and faculty members may participate in the institution's programs located in other countries, enroll in other US institutions' programs abroad, use a private company's international program, or enroll directly in foreign universities.

International student programs works with students and faculty members coming to the United States from other countries to study and teach. In 2014–2015, 293,766 international students enrolled in US colleges and universities, an 8.8 percent increase from the prior academic year. They comprise 4.8 percent of college students in the United States (IIE, 2015). As budgets tighten and the number of high school graduates shrinks, many institutions look to international students to boost enrollments and diversify their campuses. Staff members in international student programs often help recruit international students; work with them to obtain necessary passports, visas, and other required paperwork; and help them acclimate to the campus and community.

Education abroad and international student programs may operate out of the same or different departments. These offices may report to student affairs but are often located within academic affairs. The helping skills critical to both program areas are a strong match to graduate preparation in higher education and student affairs.

NAFSA: Association of International Educators is a major professional organization for these areas. The Association for Studies in International Education, a group of international education organizations, including NAFSA, publishes the *Journal of Studies in International Education*.

Enrollment Management

Enrollment management coordinates important functions related to the recruitment, retention, and graduation of students. Offices of admissions, the registrar, the bursar, financial aid, orientation, academic advising, marketing, institutional research, and career services may report to enrollment management; even if they do not, they must work closely together to achieve enrollment goals. Given its importance to institution, enrollment management may report directly to the provost or the president. The American Association of Collegiate Registrars and Admissions Officers hosts an annual conference on strategic enrollment management and publishes *College & University*. Specific functional areas within enrollment management also have their own professional organizations and publications.

Fraternity and Sorority Programs

Professionals in fraternity and sorority (FS) programs work with individual members, chapter leaders, the campus FS system, alumni, local and national FS headquarters, and national organizations devoted to fraternities and sororities to advance chapter and system goals and to promote community, leadership, scholarship, and philanthropy. The National Multicultural Greek Council is a coalition for multicultural Greek-letter organizations. The National Panhellenic Conference is composed of twenty-six sororities. The National Pan-Hellenic Council is an organization of the nine historically African American fraternities and sororities. The North-American Interfraternity Conference represents seventy-four national and international men's fraternities. Campuses may also have local rather than national fraternities and sororities.

Housing for fraternities and sororities may be located on or off campus and be owned by the university, a local chapter, or a housing corporation. FS staff members may be involved in management of those facilities. Steeped in traditions, it can be difficult to change chapter cultures that run contrary to campus and organization values and promote hazing, alcohol abuse, and other problematic behaviors. FS programs may be located within a unit of campus activities. The Association of Fraternity | Sorority Advisors publishes *Oracle: The Research Journal* of the Association of Fraternity/Sorority Advisors and *Perspectives* magazine.

Fund-raising and Development

As state support for higher education decreases, reliance on contributions from alumni and other donors increases. A growing number of student affairs divisions have their own development officers who seeks support for programs, services, scholarships, and more from alumni, particularly those who were very engaged in student affairs as undergraduates. Staff members in alumni affairs work closely with development officers. The Council for Advancement and Support of Education publishes *CURRENTS* magazine. The *Chronicle of Philanthropy* is another important publication for development professionals.

Graduate and Professional Student Programs and Services

Programs and services for graduate and professional students are a growing trend on campuses. Often housed in the graduate college or in professional programs such as law or medical schools, staff members in these units work closely with program faculty members and administrators to provide support services for students. Functions may include recruitment and admissions, orientation, advising, professional development, graduate council, and scholarship and fellowship programs. Staff members may also advocate for university-wide attention to graduate student issues, distinct from those of undergraduates.

These staff members may affiliate with a variety of organizations, including the Council of Graduate Schools, National Association of Graduate-Professional Students, Association of American Law Schools, and National Association of Graduate Admissions Professionals, each producing a variety of publications and reports.

Health and Wellness Programs

Efforts to promote the health and wellness of the campus community come from a variety of programs and services that may be in the same or different organizational units. Small campuses may have a health clinic on campus to provide basic services such as immunizations, physicals, and routine care for minor illness or injury. Medical staff members may be available for limited hours. Larger campuses may have full-service medical clinics with several doctors, nurses, and other medical professionals along with laboratories and in-patient treatment. Increasingly, outside vendors, perhaps in conjunction with a local hospital, provide these services. Other campuses have full hospitals, particularly those with medical schools, and campus health services may fall under that umbrella.

Other efforts toward health and wellness include promotion of healthy lifestyles including exercise, nutrition, weight management, and sexual health. Campuses may also have units dedicated to alcohol, tobacco, and other drug programs. This unit may run workshops for students sanctioned for violation of those policies and provide educational sessions during orientation and for campus organizations and residence halls. The American College Health Association publishes the *Journal of American College Health*.

Housing and Residence Life

Most four-year institutions offer on-campus housing for undergraduate students and many larger universities have housing for graduate students and families as well. Residence halls—typically staffed by undergraduate resident advisors, graduate students, and full-time professional staff members—are primary sites for co- and extracurricular programming intended to promote student engagement and development. On a growing number of campuses, academic affairs and student affairs collaborate through living-learning communities to enhance student learning. Housing and residence life may report through student affairs, business affairs, or both. Some campuses have public-private partnerships in which private companies own or operate campus residence halls or manage functions such as dining or maintenance.

The Association of College and University Housing Officers–International publishes *The Journal of College and University Housing*. ACUHO-I also runs a large summer internship program for graduate students and recent college graduates.

Intercollegiate Athletics

As noted, athletics at Division I schools are big business and may report directly to the president. At small colleges and community colleges, athletics often report to student affairs. The portfolio of programs at many institutions has shifted to comply with Title IX requirements prohibiting sex discrimination. Intercollegiate athletics work closely with the National Collegiate Athletic Association among other organizations. The NCAA conducts research but does not sponsor a journal.

Lesbian, Gay, Bisexual, Transgender, and Queer (LGBTQ) Student Programs and Services

LGBTQ offices provide programs, services, and advocacy to promote a campus climate welcoming to LGBTQ students and staff and faculty members. Institutional mission and type strongly influences this functional area. There may be no dedicated program at some religiously affiliated colleges, for example, or a multicultural affairs office may include these programs. The Consortium of Higher Education Lesbian Gay Bisexual Transgender Resource Professionals is a primary professional organization that offers a variety of publications and resources online.

Multicultural Student Programs and Services

Staff members in multicultural student programs and services (MSPS) work to promote a culture of inclusion in which all students can thrive. They may offer academic support programs, promote social justice, advocate for students, and much more. They may focus on a broad range of identities including race, ethnicity, gender and gender identity, sexual orientation, disability, religion and spirituality, and social class. Specific programs such as a women's center or LGBTQ student services may fall within MSPS or work collaboratively from separate programs.

The National Coalition Building Institute is one of many professional organizations for professionals in multicultural affairs. They offer a variety of publications and resources online.

Orientation and First-Year Programs

Orientation programs should introduce the academic life of the campus as well as support services and campus life. There are many models for orientation including one-day sessions, programs lasting several days to a week, and off-campus immersion programs. Orientation must also attend to the particular needs of transfer students. Many programs include sessions for parents and family members. Orientation may also include first-year experience programs, such as semester-long seminars, to help students acclimate to college and build skills to succeed. Orientation may be a unit of student affairs, enrollment management, or academic affairs. Regardless of structure, faculty and staff members must collaborate to achieve critical goals of orientation.

NODA: Association for Orientation, Transition, and Retention in Higher Education is a primary professional organization that publishes the *Journal of College Orientation and Transition*. NODA also runs a large summer internship program for graduate students and college graduates.

Parent and Family Programs

Parent and family programs collaborate with those stakeholders to support student success and promote their learning and development. This office may sponsor sessions during new student orientation, provide information and resources so parents and families can help their student, and offer programming to engage parents and families. The Association of Higher Education Parent/ Family Programming Professionals publishes the *AAHEPPP Journal*.

Recreational and Fitness Programs

Recreation and fitness programs promote physical activity, wellness, and social interaction. Many campuses have state-of-the-art recreation centers with swimming pools, indoor tracks, cardio and weight machines, climbing walls, yoga classes, and more. Intramural sports programs create opportunities for teamwork and fitness. National Intramural-Recreational Sports Association (NIRSA) publishes the *Recreational Sports Journal*.

Student Conduct Programs

Often situated in the dean of students' office, student conduct programs exist to enforce the rules and regulations detailed in the student handbook, contribute to a positive ethical climate, and maintain academic integrity in the campus community. Most systems are designed to be educational versus punitive, although serious incidents may result in suspension or expulsion. Conduct professionals are vigilant in protecting the rights of students and the health and safety of the community. Conduct administrators work closely with residence life, campus police, faculty members, community leaders, and local courts. This office is very involved in handling allegations of sexual assault. Mishandling complaints may lead to a violation of Title IX of the Education Amendments of 1972, which prohibits gender discrimination at schools receiving federal support. The major professional organization for this functional area is the Association for Student Conduct Administration. ASCA publishes the *Law and Policy Report* most weeks of the year.

Student Veteran Support Services

Veteran coordinators and advisors work with student veterans, reserve and active duty military members, and their benefit-eligible family members. Professionals connect these students to institutional resources, oversee compliance with regulations, help the institution deal with military mobilization, and more. The National Association of Veteran Program Administrators and Association of Veterans Education Certifying Officials are two professional organizations for this functional area. Student Veterans Association works to establish student organizations on campuses.

TRiO and Other Educational Opportunity Programs

Federal TRiO programs provide grants to identify and provide support services for low-income students, first-generation students, and students with disabilities to help them enroll in and graduate from postsecondary institutions. Upward Bound and the Ronald E. McNair Post-baccalaureate Achievement program are two examples of TRiO programs. The Council for Opportunity in Education produces various publications and sponsors the Pell Research Institute.

Women Student Programs and Services

Women's centers support women and advocate for gender equity. They may be a unit of women's studies or gender studies academic programs and target faculty and staff members in addition to students. They typically sponsor a wide range of programming targeted to students, faculty and staff members, and the surrounding community. The National Women's Studies Association sponsors the *NWSA Journal*.

Issues and Recommendations for Practice

Higher education faces myriad challenging issues. Editors and reporters at *The Chronicle of Higher Education* (2015) identified ten key shifts in higher education. Two of them—retention and career competence—are particularly important for student affairs and discussed in the following sections. Additionally, outsourcing, reorganization, and government regulations present difficult challenges for student affairs.

Retention

Detailed in chapter 15, retention is critically important to colleges and universities. To the extent that retention affects the financial bottom line of every college and university, there is no functional area untouched by it. Enrollment management and related areas including admissions, financial aid, academic advising, and assessment are focused each day on direct recruitment and retention efforts. Furthermore, there is strong evidence that student engagement correlates positively to retention and other important outcomes. Student organizations, leadership experiences, campus programming, residence halls, recreational sports, and other programs and services designed and directed by student affairs professionals to support student learning and development contribute to student success, retention, and degree completion. Retention must be a campus-wide priority; it requires collaboration between student and academic affairs and many other campus offices. By carefully mining data, faculty members and administrators can target proven interventions for students at the highest risk of attrition.

Career Competence

Career competence is another trend identified in the report. There are growing demands from stakeholders—students, parents, legislators, taxpayers, employers—that college degrees will lead to gainful employment. This can be a particular challenge for liberal arts institutions where tuition may be extremely expensive but the institution's mission is not squarely focused on career preparation and placement. In addition to partaking in career center offerings (for example, résumé critiques, mock interviews, internships), engagement in student affairs programs helps students develop noncognitive skills attractive to employers such as leadership, group work, and presentation skills; creativity; grit; and self-awareness. There are countless opportunities for career center professionals to collaborate with faculty members and other student affairs professionals to help prepare students for employment and lives as engaged citizens.

Outsourcing and Reorganization

Outsourcing and reorganization are two other critical issues facing student affairs. Outsourcing may save the institution money by eliminating staff members and reducing investment in new facilities. However, it can also remove control of decisions from university officials and may increase costs to students. Reorganization can shift key areas out of student affairs, taking with it the human and financial resources of those programs. Demands for fiscal accountability will continue to increase, regardless of their status as outsourced or internally run programs and services. Programs and services must be able to demonstrate that they are fiscally viable and contribute to intended outcomes.

Government Regulations

Government regulations have also changed the nature of student affairs work. For instance, the Jeanne Clery Disclosure of Campus Security Policy and Campus Crime Statistics Act requires extensive reporting. Many campuses are under investigation for alleged violations of Title IX, particularly related to handling reports of sexual assault. The USA PATRIOT Act has added many new requirements for international students. Some states now permit concealed carry of weapons on campus and more are debating such legislation. ADA rules permit emotional support and psychiatric support animals, creating many new issues for residence life programs. Although handling crises has always been part of the student affairs portfolio, high-profile incidents and fear of terrorist attacks have increased scrutiny of campus policies and procedures. Very often, student affairs professionals are trying to do more work with fewer staff members, which can stretch them to the limit.

Conclusion

The placement of student affairs on the organization chart and the functional areas comprising the division are important. Much more important, however, is the commitment, dedication, and skills of student affairs professionals throughout the campus who develop strong relationships with students, advocate for them as important decisions are made, and design programs and services to promote their learning and development. They must think critically about their work, provide evidence that their programs and services contribute to clearly articulated outcomes, and collaborate across the campus to achieve them.

Discussion Questions and Activities

1. Locate the college or university and student affairs division organization charts for your undergraduate institution and another school at which you might like to work. Join a small group of peers from different institutional types and sizes. Compare and contrast patterns in your organization charts. To whom does the SSAO report? How many direct reports does the SSAO have? Is the structure very hierarchical or rather flat? How do institutional mission and culture shape organizational structures and functions? What are the advantages and disadvantages of the student affairs division reporting to the president versus the provost?

2. Facing increasing pressures to generate revenue and reduce costs, student affairs professionals have employed a variety of strategies to reach financial goals. Consider one of those strategies on your campus (for example, outsourcing the operation of residence halls or the campus health center) and discuss the benefits and challenges of that arrangement.

3. Choose a functional area in which you have little or no experience. Review the CAS standards and interview a professional who works in that area to increase your knowledge of the specific programs and services they offer and the challenges they face. Locate an article in *The Chronicle of Higher Education* or *Inside Higher Ed* related to the functional area, share it with classmates in advance, and prepare to lead a short class discussion on that topic. How does institutional type and culture influence this functional area?

4. Identify a major issue or challenge facing your campus. What role does student affairs have in addressing it? What role *should* it have?

References

American College Health Association. (2015, Spring). *American College Health Association National College Health Assessment II: Reference group executive summary.* Hanover, MD: American College Health Association. Retrieved from http://www.acha-ncha.org/reports_ACHA-NCHAIIc.html

Bok, D. (2013). *Higher education in America.* Princeton, NJ: Princeton University Press.

Campbell, J. (2015). *Behaviors, attitudes, skills, and knowledge for senior student affairs officers: Perceptions of leadership success.* Doctoral dissertation. Bowling Green State University, OH. Retrieved from https://etd.ohiolink.edu

Chronicle of Higher Education. (2015, March 9). The trends report: 10 key shifts in higher education. Retrieved from http://chronicle.com/specialreport/The-Trends-Report-10-Key/7

College and University Professional Association for Human Resources. (2015). *Administrators in higher education salary survey executive summary for the 2014–15 academic year.* Retrieved from www.cupahr.org/

Council for the Advancement of Standards in Higher Education. (2015). *CAS professional standards for higher education* (9th ed.). Washington, DC: Author.

Heida, D. (2006). The student affairs portfolio in small colleges. In S. B. Westfall (Ed.), *The small college dean* (New Directions for Student Services, no. 116, pp. 15–29.) San Francisco: Jossey-Bass.

Hirt, J. B. (2006). *Where you work matters: Student affairs administration at different types of institutions.* Lanham, MD: United Press of America.

Institute of International Education. (2015). *Open Doors 2015 "Fast facts."* Retrieved from http://www.iie.org

Lindsay, K. R. (2014). *Senior student affairs officers' perceptions of critical professional competencies.* Doctoral dissertation. Bowling Green State University, OH. Retrieved from https://etd.ohiolink.edu

Manning, K., Kinzie, J., & Schuh, J. H. (2014). *One size does not fit all: Traditional and innovative models of student affairs practice* (2nd ed.). New York: Routledge.

National Association of Student Personnel Administrators (NASPA). (2014). *The chief student affairs officer: Responsibilities, opinions, and professional pathways of leaders in student affairs.* Washington, DC: Author. Retrieved from http://www.naspa.org/

Sandeen, A., & Barr, M. J. (2006). *Critical issues for student affairs.* San Francisco: Jossey-Bass.

Skomsvold, P. (2013). *Web tables: Profile of undergraduate students: 2011–12.* (NCES 2015–167). US Department of Education. Institute of Education Sciences. Washington, DC: National Center for Education Statistics. Retrieved from http://nces.ed.gov/pubsearch/pubsinfo.asp?pubid=2015167

Tull, A., & Kuk, L. (2012). *New realities in the management of student affairs: Emerging specialist roles and structures for changing times.* Sterling, VA: Stylus.

CHAPTER 18

STRATEGIC PLANNING AND FINANCE IN STUDENT AFFAIRS

Brian A. Burt and John H. Schuh

A mong the most vexing challenges facing contemporary leaders in higher education are developing strategic plans and managing fiscal resources. These tandem activities provide a foundation for offering programs, services, and activities in student affairs. Institutional leaders develop plans to secure financial resources in the short and long term so that expenses can be met. But traditional plans for developing a financial base no longer work. The halcyon days of simply resorting to increasing tuition and fees to meet proposed expenses are in the past; for public institutions, receiving annual increases in appropriations from state legislatures are yesterday's story. As costs have escalated, doubts and concerns about college costs have been raised (Finley, 2013); state funding has been surpassed as the primary funding source for public higher education by tuition, according to the United States Government Accountability Office (2014). From 1961 through 2014, the Higher Education Price Index, a measure of inflation specifically calibrated to the costs experienced by institutions of higher education, increased at a rate greater than the consumer price index in forty-five of the fifty-four years of data (Commonfund Institute, 2014, table A). Moreover, "the reality is that students are leaving school with more debt than their counterparts five or ten years ago" (Baum, Elliott, & Ma, 2014, p. 7).

This chapter describes how principles of strategic planning can be applied to student affairs, provides a conceptual way of thinking about the costs of higher education, and then moves into sources of revenue and expenditures in student affairs. It includes approaches to managing financial resources through various methods of budgeting. A number of books and other resources have been written about student affairs strategic planning and higher education finance; these resources are highlighted in the chapter. The reader is encouraged to consult with these materials for a more in-depth treatment of these topics.

Because so many different units can be part of a division of student affairs, we have used the definition of the Integrated Postsecondary Education Data System (IPEDS) for student services:

> A functional expense category that includes expenses for admissions, registrar activities, and activities whose primary purpose is to contribute to students [sic] emotional and physical well-being and to their intellectual, cultural, and social development outside the context of the formal instructional program. Examples include student activities, cultural events, student newspapers, intramural athletics, student organizations, supplemental instruction outside the normal administration, and student records. Intercollegiate athletics and student health services may be included except when operated as self-supporting auxiliary enterprises. Also may include information technology expenses related to student service activities if the institution separately budgets and expenses information technology expenses related to student services activities (otherwise these expenses are included in institutional support). Institutions include actual or allocated costs for operation and maintenance of plant, interest, and depreciation. (IPEDS, 2015, n.p.)

It is important to note that we are not suggesting through the organization of this chapter that strategic planning and financial planning are mutually exclusive, nor that the process of strategic planning should necessarily take place before financial planning. Realistically, we acknowledge that most units have a general sense of their budget prior to the start of a strategic plan based on trends from previous fiscal years. Understanding the financial confines first may help shape some of the goals within the strategic plan. Alternatively, a strategic plan created before knowing the exact budget could help to determine how much capitol will be needed to achieve the unit's goals. In the ideal case, however, the strategic planning and financial planning processes take place simultaneously and are deliberately linked. Conneely (2010) describes the misalignment that can occur when these processes are not linked: "Where a student affairs organization with a strategic plan puts its resources dictates its priorities. If the financial plan and the strategic plan are not linked and managed together, they can move out of alignment" (p. 57).

Strategic Planning

The process of strategic planning has been widely covered in fields ranging from organizational management to student affairs. Some commonalities across fields are the concerns that strategic planning is a waste of everyone's time, creates unrealistic and unachievable goals, is boring and not engaging, and results in a document that does not get used. These common concerns highlight the anxiety and angst individuals have for creating strategic plans. This is important to acknowledge up front because those who volunteer—or those who are appointed—may not be totally into the process based on previous experiences. It is important to acknowledge this as a legitimate challenge of the process. Several strategies can be implemented to help positively mediate the planning process. One in particular is that the facilitator must create a culture or understanding that your unit's planning process likely will be different than what one might have experienced at other institutions, it will be engaging, everyone will contribute in valuable ways, and the final document will establish a plan of action that will benefit the unit. Another useful strategy is to ask planning members for feedback on what elements or information should be included in the document that would increase the likelihood that the document will be used. Other practical strategies and elements should be considered, for example, who should be included in the development and execution of the strategic plan.

This section is not intended to be a how-to guide for strategic planning. Rather, we cover much broader—yet equally important—topics that would be of use to professionals new to the task of strategic planning. In particular, we start with a broad discussion of what strategic planning is, what it can be, and why it is important for units to have—and engage in the process of—strategic planning. Next, we offer broad ideas about how strategic planning should work to maximize its usefulness to the unit. Finally, we offer ideas about how the strategic plan relates to and interacts with financial budgeting. By the conclusion of this section, we hope that you will have a better understanding of how to create and implement an effective strategic plan and process, one that is deemed valuable and is consistently used within your unit.

What Is Strategic Planning?

The process of strategic planning is slightly different than the product that results from strategic planning. Because we briefly discuss them both in this section, some attention to differences is warranted. The strategic plan itself is a product. A strategic plan is not a report card of the unit's past performance. Rather, it is a guide detailing the shared vision of what the unit aspires to become and a plan for how to get there. Similarly, Atkins (2010) describes the process as "an organization's process of defining its strategy or direction and making decisions on how its resources will be used to pursue this strategy" (p. 19). This plan should be dynamic by design; that is, it should be broad enough to enable evolution but defined enough to provide direction for stakeholders. As new information is gathered, the unit should be positioned to adjust accordingly. The process of strategic planning should be interactive and inclusive. Although it is true that different stakeholders have different needs and perspectives, and the more individuals involved in the process can make the experience complicated, the final product will have included "honest conversations . . . dreaming, creating, strategizing, and implementing" (Ellis, 2010b, p. 8). The result of engaging in this planning process has the potential to "lead [your unit] into the future with foresight, flexibility, and purpose" (Ellis, 2010a, p. 1).

How Should Strategic Planning Work?

There is no one-size-fits-all strategy for how a unit should engage in strategic planning. We offer, however, several suggestions to help you get started. Because setting the course for future direction may require a bounded amount of ideas and opinions, you may want to start by forming a committee to begin the initial work. The committee may want to start by thinking about the following questions: who are we and what is our current status, who or where do we want to be in the future, and what steps do we need to take to get there (Ellis, 2010b; Whitney, 2010)? Answering these questions may be challenging because it will force committee members to abstractly think about the unit's future directions, irrespective of where the unit currently is. Committee members should be reminded to think aspirationally, without confines of budget, personnel, political structures, and so on, at least during the brainstorming phase. Answers to these questions should help to get the committee on track to seeing where there is a common vision for the unit.

Other necessary items the committee members will want to consider are which stakeholders will be included, in what capacities these stakeholders will contribute to, and when will stakeholders be invited to aid in later parts of the plan. In formulizing the initial ideas of the strategic plan, the committee will want to make sure that the plan aligns with the larger goals of the institution (Bresciani, 2010). This can be done by consulting the institution's—and the unit's—mission and value statements (Conneely, 2010).

Although we encourage a committee to get the planning process underway, we also believe it to be essential for the committee to think early on about opportunities for communicating to the wider campus community the steps being taken throughout the duration of the strategic planning process. This may not always be the case and will depend on the unit doing the planning. For example, a judicial affairs unit may not want to communicate its strategic plan to the wider community, whereas the larger student affairs division might. Nonetheless, these strategies for transparency provide access to stakeholders to engage in various phases of the process. It can also help stakeholders feel a part of the process before they are formally invited to participate.

After getting the initial items of the strategic plan going, adequate time should be devoted to discussing who and how a broader constituency will be invited to participate in later phases of the plan. Recall that in the beginning phases we recommended a smaller working group to get the plan underway and organized; in the later phases of the plan—especially when it is time to execute the plan across the unit—a larger variety of stakeholders will need to be and feel included in the contributions toward the plan, especially because the final project should consist of shared goals and a shared vision. Some items you may want to consider for discussion when defining future participants: what role will initial committee members play in later phases of the plan (for example, is it expected that some committee members fizzle out, and an entire new group of participants come in to help implement the plan; is participation restricted to a small group or is any and everyone welcome; if others will be involved in implementation of the plan, how might you get them involved in earlier stages of the process?).

When considering future participants, do not limit yourself into thinking only about individuals internal to the unit; also consider individuals external to the unit. There are those on campus who possess expertise that could lend itself to a robust strategic plan (or design to execute the strategic plan). For example, Whitney (2010) reminds us that faculty members may have certain expertise and talents that can be useful to the development of a strategic plan:

> The diversity of talent, expertise, and perspective available on campus provides energy for powerful partnerships and programs . . . Including faculty in the process can provide additional perspectives, research interests, expertise, as well as committee members and additional energy to complete the process . . . This partnership provides a more holistic approach and draws on the natural talents and resources waiting to be tapped on campus. (p. 63)

As Whitney suggests, faculty members could help conceptualize the assessment strategy, research questions, or theoretical framing used to guide the plan, assuming the plan needs to be theoretically guided. Similarly, there might be those with less direct expertise with the vision your unit is creating and a less direct connection to the unit. But these individuals may have a vested interest in the betterment of the unit, which could be helpful to the unit. Again, you will want to define the boundaries of future participants. The key is to understand that everyone contributes differently, and importantly, and their contribution may not span the duration of the project.

Similar to starting the process with a smaller group of committee members, adding additional ideas and voices can also pose challenges. Newer individuals added at a later phase may express dissatisfaction with previous decisions made by the committee, or dissatisfaction at not being included in the initial committee work group. It will be important that at this phase, all individuals interested in working toward moving the unit forward feel welcome and appreciated for their contributions. It will also be necessary for the initial committee members to diminish feeling like gatekeepers and sole owners of the strategic plan; sharing the strategic plan, and the tasks to reach the unit's goal, will take many committed people working together.

Assessment in Strategic Planning

An important component of strategic planning is incorporating an assessment plan. Assessment should take place early and throughout the entire strategic planning process. Bresciani (2010) defines assessment as the "systematic process that gathers programmatic outcomes-based assessment data and merges those data with trend, forecast, and capacity data, as well as institutional goals and vision" (p. 39). Assessing the unit at the beginning of the strategic planning process will help you to deeply understand the unit's needs. Ellis (2010b) goes a step further to suggest that the assessment should evaluate not only the presence of resources but also their "effectiveness" in serving the unit's students: "[It's important to conduct an assessment of the] needs of current and future students and an assessment of the effectiveness of people, programs, and services in meeting them"(p. 8). As a starting point, take into consideration the various contextual factors that have influence on the unit; these contexts may be local (for example, institutional departments) or even external (for example, market and stakeholders outside of the institution and unit). Remember, however, the goal of the strategic plan is to create a forward-thinking plan. Do not completely allow the various contextual factors that bear on the unit to diminish the creative vision of the strategic plan.

After broadly thinking about contexts, next, take inventory of what resources are already available. Then, consider what resources will be needed to execute the plan, or as Ellis (2011b) describes, "determining the priorities and allocation of time, money, and expertise" (p. 8). After taking stock of the needs of the unit—in efforts to help guide the direction of the plan—incorporate incremental goals that will help to guide evaluation of progress; some call these *performance indicators* (see, for example, Ellis, 2010b). To ensure that assessments take place, establish dates for additional formal assessments throughout the duration of the strategic plan. At the minimum, a specified yearly date should be set when the committee can perform a type of audit trail on the progress of the strategic plan's execution. With the new information that arises from the assessment, what minor changes will be needed to the strategic plan to help keep the unit on track to achieving its goals? Depending on your unit's goals and strategic plan, some examples of performance indicators might be "first-year retention rates, graduate rates, student satisfaction, at-risk student persistence and graduation rates, financial aid distribution, and staff-to-student ratio" (Ellis, 2010b, p. 13).

Engaging in assessment early in the process is important because it enables the planning committee to understand the undertaking that will be needed during the strategic planning and implementation phases. In addition, by assessing early in the process, the committee can identify potential barriers to achieving the vision of the plan and make appropriate changes (Bresciani, 2010). The need to provide early assessments, however, may generate some anxiety for those working on the strategic plan, especially if there are not people in the planning committee who are experts in assessing data. This is a great example of why involving others in the planning process is important and beneficial to the creation and execution of the strategic plan.

Concluding Thoughts about Strategic Planning

Before concluding this section, we return to the critiques that strategic planning is a "waste of time" or "serves no real purpose but to collect dust." We previously mentioned the importance of including incremental assessments of the progress the committee is making toward the development and implementation of the strategic plan. By consistently revisiting the strategic plan, you ensure that the document is used in an intentional way. In addition, as each new fiscal year approaches, and new goals are being discussed, use the strategic plan as a guide for all new policies and procedures; new goals within the unit should align with and address needs specified within the strategic plan (Cherrey & Castillo Clark, 2010).

It is likely that those new to engaging in strategic planning are asking, "How long should the whole process of developing and executing the plan take?" The realistic answer is that it depends, in part, on how extensive the needs are of the unit. That is, if a major new direction is required, it may be important to take more time developing and implementing the plan. However, under emergency situations in which time is of the essence, a finite scope of time may need to be set to ensure that the plan is ready to be executed, based on the existing information at that time. For an example, see Cherrey and Castillo Clark (2010), who describe the need for a solid strategic plan during the aftermath of the Hurricane Katrina tragedy at Tulane University in New Orleans, Louisiana. In some instances, a swifter plan might be best to give stakeholders a sense of security in the wake of emergencies, tragedies, or circumstances that require quick action. For other aspirational instances, a well-thought-out visionary plan may take more time to assure stakeholders that the committee was thorough.

Given these caveats, we encourage readers to consider the strategic planning process not as the blueprint to solving all of the unit's issues, but as a living document that charts the unit on the course to achieving its goals in fiscally responsible ways.

Thinking about Finance Conceptually

Bowen (1996) identified certain "laws" that govern higher education costs. Among Bowen's laws are that institutions of higher education have virtually no limit on the amount of money they can spend on "seemingly fruitful education ends" (p. 123); that each institution raises all the money it can; and that each institution spends all it raises. As a consequence, these systemic "laws," which illustrate the fiscal environment in which higher education operates, are an approach to explaining why higher education has experienced rapidly increasing costs.

Another approach posited by Archibald and Feldman (2008) has to do with rapidly increasing costs of services provided by highly educated workers, among them health care providers, lawyers, statisticians, actuaries, and faculty members in higher education (pp. 285–286). The underlying concept is that higher education is no different from industries that rely on highly educated people who deliver services and consequently, "cost per student in higher education follows a time path very similar to the time path of other personal service industries that rely on highly educated labor" (Archibald & Feldman, 2008, p. 289). Regardless of which approach one subscribes to, the fact is that the cost of attendance for students has increased rapidly and pressure is being put on students and their families to cover the costs of attendance particularly at private for-profit institutions as depicted by Baum and Ma (2014, figure 15B).

In the final analysis, those who have budgetary responsibilities in student affairs will have to make sure that their organizations are efficient, use resources wisely, and be able to demonstrate to stakeholders that their interests are central in financial decisions. Sandeen and Barr (2006) described the situation this way: "If student affairs leaders are to achieve their goals on their campus, it is essential that they become expert fiscal managers, articulate advocates for their programs, creative resource procurers, and knowledgeable contributors to their institution's overall budget processes" (p. 106). For that to occur, a good place to start is with an examination of the sources of revenue and categories of expenditures in student affairs.

Revenue Sources

Revenue for student affairs comes essentially from three sources: the institution's general fund, student fees, and fees for service. Although this observation may seem simplistic, it represents the sources of the vast preponderance of revenue that supports student affairs operations. The commentary that follows is very general nature and makes no attempt to cover the universe of institutions of higher education. Many colleges and universities have different approaches to funding student affairs that are idiosyncratic because of their institutional mission, history, culture, custom, or for other reasons. The examples given in the following are designed to be illustrative only and are not representative of any specific institution.

General Fund Revenue Depending on an institution's form of governance, general fund revenue will represent different categories of revenue. Institutions are either "public," meaning that they are "an educational institution whose programs and activities are operated by publicly elected or appointed school officials and which is supported primarily by public funds" (IPEDS, 2015, n.p.), or they are private. A private, not-for-profit institution is defined as "an institution in which the individual(s) or agency in control receives no compensation, other than wages, rent or other expenses for the assumption of risk. These include both independent not-for-profit schools and those affiliated with a religious organization" (IPEDS, 2015, n.p.). A private for-profit institution is defined as "a private institution in which the individual(s) or agency in control receives compensation other than wages, rent or other expenses for the assumption of risk" (IPEDS, 2015, n.p.).

Student Fees Some institutions charge some, or perhaps many, fees for student services that are mandatory and are paid as part of the student's semester (or quarter) bill. Examples of mandatory student fees are student health fees, campus recreation fees, and computer fees. These are fees assessed to students whether they use the facility or service or not. The primary difference between mandatory student fees and tuition is that the proceeds from the collection of mandatory fees typically are assigned directly to the operation they support.

Other student fees may be optional. That is, the student does not have to pay the fee but may choose to do so when paying the institutional bill for tuition and mandatory fees. Examples of these fees could be a subscription to the campus newspaper or parking fees if students are permitted to keep a car on campus.

Fee for Service   Finally, fees for service may fund some student services. These are fees that are paid for the use of various services, often using a metric of use, such as a monthly meal pass or rental of an apartment on campus for a month. Examples of these could include day care centers, student housing, dining services, and tickets to campus entertainment and sporting events. And, of course, a blended approach often is used. For example, student fees might fund recreational services' facilities, but then users might pay a fee to rent a locker or to participate in a specific activity such as a camping or sailing trip.

Expenditures

The categories for expenditures will range widely in student affairs. All student services are likely to have expenditures for personnel costs (salaries and fringe benefits), for office operations (such as office supplies and communications devices including telephones and computing services), and perhaps support for hourly employees including students. Units may also spend money on travel for staff members and in some cases students, and for capital items, such as furniture, computing equipment, and other, nonconsumable goods such as buildings or infrastructure. The definition of *capital* will vary from institution to institution, but often a specific expenditure amount will define what a capital item is. For example, this amount might be purchases of $500 or more for some institutions, and at others the minimum expenditure might be $1,000 or even $5,000.

Besides personnel and basic operational costs such as office supplies and telecommunications, the cost of operations will vary considerably from unit to unit. For example, some student services are strictly office operations, such as judicial affairs, and others have significant commitments to supporting facilities. Housing, student unions, and recreational services are examples of facilities-intensive operations in which the cost of operations including utilities, maintenance, and housekeeping can be significant. In addition, some units have facilities that have been financed through a borrowing program in the form of bonds. In these cases the unit is responsible for repaying the bonds through periodic payments to bondholders. Student housing and student unions are examples of operations that can include significant expenditures dedicated to repaying their debt.

Institutional Differences in Funding Student Affairs

There are two common ways of measuring institutional support of student affairs: the amount of revenue per student that is devoted to student affairs and the percentage of institutional budget that is devoted to student affairs. Regardless of the measure used, public institutions tend to devote less funding to student affairs than private, not-for-profit institutions (Snyder & Dillow, 2015). The current taxonomy of expenditure categories for private, for-profit institutions is such that it is not possible to draw conclusions about the level of support at such institutions (see Snyder & Dillow, 2015).

As reported in the *Digest of Education Statistics, 2013* (Snyder & Dillow, 2015), in the most recent year reported, academic year 2011–2012, two-year public institutions devoted 8.38 percent (down from 9.21 percent in 2005–2006) of their budgets to student services and spent $1,091 per full-time equivalent (FTE) student on student services in 2011–2012, down from $1,184 in 2005–2006 in constant dollars (table 334.10). Four-year public institutions allocated 3.83 percent of their budgets and spent $1,455 per FTE student on student services in 2011–2012, up from 3.71 percent and $1,402 per FTE student in constant dollars in 2005–2006 (table 412). Private, not-for-profit institutions spent more on student services. Two-year private not-for-profits spent 14.60 percent of their budgets on student services, or $2,671 per FTE student in 2011–2012 (table 334.30). Four-year private not-for-profit institutions spent 8.03 percent of their budgets or $3,964 per FTE student (table 414).

Budgeting Approaches and Financial Management

Institutions have budgets for several reasons. Budgets provide a guide to unit leaders so that they can track their revenues and expenditures over the course of a fiscal year, which commonly, but not always, runs from July 1 through June 30. With real-time budgeting, unit managers can access information at any time to determine the relative status of the revenues and expenditures for which they are responsible and make adjustments accordingly. Budgets also serve as planning documents informed by the institution's or unit's strategic plan. Over the course of several years, unit managers can provide additional funds to support initiatives that are aligned with the unit's strategic plan. For example, if the housing department has set a goal of expanding learning communities, over time the department's budget officer can dedicate additional funds to the learning communities program. Or, in times of fiscal stress, the budget may be reduced in ways that are consistent with the strategic plan. Finally, budgets also provide a transparent tool for describing the priorities of the department for the reasons that are previously described. A useful way to determine a unit's priorities is to review budgets over time, say for a period of five years. Over that period of time one can learn the unit's priorities because where resources are allocated clearly represent organizational priorities.

This section begins with a brief discussion of the concept of line items. Line items are a common way of depicting revenue sources and expenditures. Then, several budgeting approaches are introduced, including incremental, performance, and responsibility-centered budgeting. Most institutions of higher education use one or a combination of these approaches. Formula budgeting, zero-based budgeting, and planning programming and budgeting systems (PPBSs) are not discussed because they not used commonly. Readers seeking more information about these approaches should consult Woodard and von Destinon (2000). We conclude with a brief discussion of capital budgets, common accounting methods used in higher education, preparing budgets, and budgeting in auxiliary services.

Line Items

Line items are used to depict revenue sources and expenditures categories in budgets and can be found in a wide variety of budgets. Often, line item expenditures are divided into personnel and nonpersonnel categories. Personnel categories can be as detailed as having a line for every salaried position funded by a budget, along with fringe benefits, and wages for hourly employees. Nonpersonnel items may include office supplies, telecommunications, equipment rental, utilities, and others depending on the nature of the expenditures of the department or program funded by the budget. In some institutions expenditures for travel and capital items also are discrete categories.

Why, then, are line items used? First, they are easy to understand. It does not take much of an accounting background to understand the concepts underlying line item budgets. Second, they are easy to construct. New resources are added to a department's budget whenever possible, perhaps without serious questions being raised about the efficacy of the programs and activities the department provides. Third, they provide for good budgetary controls, in that the budget manager can determine literally on a line-by-line basis the extent to which revenues are meeting projections and expenditures are in line with expectations.

Incremental Budgeting

In this model, central administrators allocate incremental revenues based on the specific needs of individual academic and service units (Szatmary, 2011). It is the most commonly used approach to budgeting in higher education (Gibson, 2009). This type of budget often is depicted by line items. Put simply, this approach takes the previous year's budget and makes a percentage or incremental change to it. For example, the total amount of money allocated to salaries may be increased by 3 percent or funding for supplies is cut by

2 percent. "An incremental approach to budgeting is based on the assumption that both needs and costs vary only a small amount from year to year" (Barr, 2002, p. 37). In the end, budget managers adjust their budgets accordingly, and the work of budgeting is accomplished.

Incremental budgeting has some disadvantages. "The weakness with this approach is that it maintains the status quo and does not encourage planning. It also does not require any connection between allocation of resources and institutional goals" (Gibson, 2009, pp. 35–36). Remember that strategic planning challenges an institution to develop a vision of what it might become, and thus it may require dramatic changes in organization and programs. Incremental budgeting does not lend itself well to making major changes in an institution's educational program and services.

Performance Budgeting

Another form of budgeting evolves from performance funding, an approach that has been adopted by a number of states designed to encourage institutions to achieve specific objectives. "Performance-based funding is a system based on allocating a portion of a state's higher education budget according to specific performance measures such as course completion, credit attainment, and degree completion, instead of allocating funding based entirely on enrollment" (Miao, 2012, p. 1). Using this approach, a state legislature might indicate that if certain objectives are reached, say a larger percentage of students who are enrolled in a university graduate in four years, that funding will be increased, or if graduation rates decline, appropriations will be reduced. This approach requires a long-term commitment, because many goals in higher education take years to measure. Examples are persistence rates, graduation of students who complete certain majors to alleviate labor shortages (engineering or nursing, for example), or increased enrollment of in-state residents.

Responsibility Center Management (RCM)

Responsibility center management (RCM) is a relative newcomer to the budgeting scene in higher education. It many respects it approaches budgeting using principles that have been associated with budgeting for auxiliary services. "RCM delegates operational authority to schools, divisions, and other units within an institution, allowing them to prioritize their academic missions. Each unit receives all of its own revenues and income, including the tuition of its enrolled students. In this way, units effectively compete for students. Each unit is also assigned a portion of government support (where applicable). However, units are also responsible for their own expenses, as well as for a portion of expenses incurred by the university's general operations" (Hanover Research, 2015, n.p.). Institutions can define "unit" in a variety of ways. In student affairs, for example, a "unit" could be the office of the dean of students, judicial affairs, or career services. Each unit is responsible for generating sufficient revenues to sustain its expenditures. Sources of revenues could be the institution's general fund, student fees, fees for service, or a combination of these sources.

This approach to budgeting is significantly different than the traditional approach of incremental budgeting. It blends principles from zero-based budgeting and budgeting for auxiliary services. About this form of budgeting, Strauss, Curry, and Whalen (2001) observe, "Can responsibility center budgeting work at a public institution of higher education? Of course, it can. What are required are leadership and the ability of an institution to earn income and retain unspent balances. And of the two, leadership is by far the most important" (p. 607). It is highly likely that this approach to budgeting will be adopted by more institutions of higher education in the future because of its emphasis on flexibility. Retaining unspent balances, in particular, affords a unit head to plan for major expenditures such as a renovation project that cannot be done using more traditional budgeting approach.

Capital Budgets

One other form of budgeting that student affairs units may be engaged in on an occasional basis is capital budgeting. Capital budgets are designed for facility development or renovation or other major expenditures that may extend over several years and may be paid for through the issuance of bonds. The renovation of a student union is an example of a capital project. Typically, institutions have guidelines for this type of budgeting and the process will involve the senior officers of the institution as well as its governing board in the approval process. Barr (2002) provides an excellent framework for understanding capital budgeting and Price (2003) describes facility development projects in detail.

Accounting Methods

Depending on the kinds of accounts a student affairs office manages, two different forms of accounting—cash or accrual—commonly are used. Cash accounting is defined as a form of bookkeeping in which "revenue, expense, and balance sheet items are recorded when cash is paid or received" (Finney, 1994, p. 174). Accrual accounting is a system in which "revenue is recorded when earned and balance sheet account charges are recorded when commitments are made" (p. 173), regardless of when funds are actually received or disbursed. "In other words, the accrual basis attempts to determine the real economic impact of what has occurred during a given period of time rather than simply determining how much cash was received or disbursed" (Meisinger & Dubeck, 1996, p. 469).

One other concept of importance in understanding accounting procedures is the difference between unrestricted and restricted accounts. Unrestricted accounts essentially mean that funds in the account can be spent in any way that is allowed by the institution. An example of an unrestricted account might be one that is supported by a public institution's general fund (tuition and state appropriation). In this case, the division's senior budget officer might be able to transfer funds from one office supported by the general fund (for example, the office of the dean of students) to pay for office supplies in the office of student activities (also supported by the institution's general fund). But a restricted fund means that the resources in this fund may be used only to support the purposes for which the funds were received. An example could be fees to the office of career services to support an online résumé system. Typically, these fees could not be transferred to the department of recreation to pay for repairs to the campus swimming pool. Restricted accounts commonly are found in scholarship programs in which, for example, donors have made restricted gifts to support a specific scholarship, for example, such as a scholarship to an outstanding sophomore to study abroad during the junior year. Assuming appropriate restrictions are in place, the scholarship funds could not be used for any other purpose.

Preparing Budgets

Student affairs staff members need to pay close attention to the budgeting process. They need to avoid what Woodard, Love, and Komives (2000) asserted: "*student affairs professionals do not place a premium on understanding the financial and budgeting structure and processes of their institutions*" [emphasis added] (pp. 71–72).

Woodard and von Destinon (2000) offer some additional budgeting recommendations, including determining the contribution of the unit to the divisional and institutional mission, measuring the workload of staff in individual units; trying to provide measurable outcomes for a unit; determining if most activities help students do things for themselves; protecting services designed to maintain ethical, health, and safety standards; and identifying new sources of revenue. To this list, the Pew Higher Education Research Program (1996) recommends that across the board cuts be resisted. Pew concludes, "Democratic [budget] cutting represents not just a failure of will, but, more significantly, a failure to understand that maintaining quality in some areas will require a reduction or elimination of others" (p. 515). For example, if an institution downsizes one unit and assigns a number of its activities to another unit that does not have adequate staff members or expertise to take on the additional responsibilities, institutional decision makers are engaged in self-deception. Funds might be saved, but students will be poorly served. Little good will result. The reader is referred to Woodard and von Destinon (2000) and Barr (2002) for additional discussions of the budget development process.

Budgeting for Auxiliary Services

Auxiliary services, according to Ambler (2000, p. 131), can represent "as much as eighty percent or more of a chief student affairs officer's fiscal responsibility" and can include units such as student housing, student unions, health services, food services, and bookstores. Indeed, the size of auxiliary budgets can be enormous. For example, the auxiliary enterprises operating budget at Indiana University–Bloomington in 2014–2015 was more than $277 million, or approximately 18.8 percent of the university's total budget of more than $1,470 million. The university defines auxiliary expenditures as those for "dormitories, varsity athletics, bookstores, parking operations" (Indiana University, 2015, n.p.).

Auxiliaries must include additional factors such as changes in debt service, utilities, and institutional overhead charges in the development of their budgets. Auxiliary budgets are segregated from other institutional budgets and are designed to be operated without institutional subsidy, meaning that they must generate sufficient revenue to fund their operations. In fact, Lennington (1996, p. 87) asserts that auxiliary enterprises "provide an opportunity to generate revenues that can be used to subsidize" the institution's academic mission.

Auxiliary unit heads should heed the same advice given for other unit heads regarding personnel expenditures. The director of the student union typically cannot award employees 4 percent raises, even if the money is available, if the average increase for all staff members at the institution is 2 percent. Nor can fringe benefits be adjusted differently, such as providing a better retirement package for auxiliary unit staff members or more vacation days. Auxiliaries generally function within the budgeting framework of their institution, even if they must generate their operating revenue.

Selected Trends in Finance and Budgeting

In this section we identify several trends in financing student affairs related to the contemporary financial environment in which student affairs operates.

Outsourcing or Privatization

One strategy related to downsizing—outsourcing or privatization—involves entering into contracts with enterprises outside the institution to provide services that have become quite expensive for the institution to offer itself. Food service operations, for example, have been outsourced for years. One institution went from losing about $100,000 per year when the college operated its own food service to an annual rebate from a contractor of $168,000 (Angrisani, 1994). Although such savings are not always the case, outsourcing represents one alternative for senior administrators looking for ways to cut expenditures.

Increasing Revenues

Although outsourcing and downsizing are used to reduce costs, two recent trends have emerged in higher education to help raise additional revenues. One is to apply substantial overhead charges such as a percentage of gross revenue to auxiliary units for services provided by general administrative units on campus, such as purchasing, accounting, security, and the like. Auxiliaries at public institutions typically are expected to pay their way without subsidies from the campus general fund and at some private institutions are designed to subsidize the institution's general fund. At some institutions, contributions from auxiliaries actually exceed the value of the services provided by the institution. Situations exist in which some units, such as health services, are charged rent for the space they occupy in a campus building. In other circumstances, charges are assessed for custodial and maintenance services without the auxiliary service being given the option of hiring its own staff or contracting with a private firm. The consequence of levying overhead charges is that additional funds are provided for other needs on campus, such as faculty member salaries, library support, and other activities charged to an institution's general fund.

Another option is to charge students dedicated fees or activity fees for student affairs units, as discussed. These might include a special fee to pay the debt on student affairs buildings (such as the student union) or a dedicated health services or counseling fee. Quite obviously, dedicated, mandatory fees represent additional costs to students. Sandeen and Barr (2006) state that "critics of the student fee approach to funding student services may assert that it may cause resentment toward student affairs because of its 'privileged funding position' and may even result in accusations that student affairs leaders manipulate students in order to obtain their support for new or increased student fees" (p. 101). Nevertheless, given the lack of fiscal health in higher education over the past decade, more fees quite possibly will be charged to students.

Grants and Contracts

Still another source of funding that is likely to play an increasingly important role in the future is external grants or contracts. Grants can be sought from not-for-profit sources for activities such as supporting start-up costs for new programs or for support for students. An example of this might be finding support to develop a resource center for historically underrepresented groups of students. The grant would support the development of the program and securing appropriate space. In turn, the institution would have to promise to sustain the program once it is up and running.

Fund-raising

One other fairly recent development in the area of generating additional revenue is that of fund-raising. Annual giving, such as the yearly fund-raising drive that focused on gifts from alumni and institutional friends, can be concentrated on routine operations, whereas campaigns are designed to secure larger gifts, often for specific purposes such as scholarship programs or to provide seed gifts for the development of new facilities or significant renovation of facilities that are becoming obsolete. Barr (2002) and Jackson (2000) provide additional details about the nature of fund-raising efforts.

Conclusion

This chapter has provided foundational information about strategic planning and financing student affairs. We addressed these two topics in the same chapter because they are central to the development of the services, program, and learning experiences that typically are part of a student affairs portfolio. Furthermore, they are inextricably related; one cannot exist without the other in our opinion. A student affairs' unit's strategic plan lays out priorities and aspirations that often require resources. The financial plan will provide a framework in terms of what financial resources will be available to support the strategic plan. In short, one informs the other, so we think it makes intellectual and practical sense to explore both topics in the same chapter. Clearly, these subjects are more complex and detailed than space allows. We urge our readers to do additional reading on these topics as well as explore the following questions.

Discussion Questions

1. How important is it for student affairs educators to have a strong understanding of strategic planning? Budget development?
2. What are your reservations for participating in strategic planning, and what can you do to minimize your concerns?
3. How should one new to a unit engage in the strategic planning process?
4. In addition to the concepts introduced in this chapter, are there other sources of revenue that might be available to student affairs?
5. What would it take for public colleges and universities to be less reliant on tuition and fees as revenue sources? How likely is it that such ideas will occur?

References

Ambler, D. A. (2000). Organizational and administrative models. In M. J. Barr, M. K. Desler, & Associates, *The handbook of student affairs administration* (2nd ed., pp. 121–134). San Francisco: Jossey-Bass.

Angrisani, C. (1994). Students' needs dictate contract decision. *On-Campus Hospitality, 16*(4), 22–26.

Archibald, R. B., & Feldman, D. H. (2008). Explaining increases in higher education costs. *Journal of Higher Education, 79*(3), 268–295.

Atkins, K. (2010). Strategically planning to change. In S. E. Ellis (Ed.), *Strategic planning in student affairs* (New Directions for Student Services, no. 132, pp. 17–25). San Francisco: Jossey-Bass.

Barr, M. J. (2002). *Academic administrator's guide to budgets and financial management.* San Francisco: Jossey-Bass.

Baum, S., Elliott, D. C., & Ma, J. (2014). *Trends in student aid.* New York: The College Board.

Baum, S., & Ma, J. (2014). *Trends in college pricing 2014.* New York: The College Board.

Bowen, H. R. (1996). What determines the cost of higher education? In D. W. Breneman, L. L. Leslie, & R. E. Anderson (Eds.), *ASHE reader on finance in higher education* (pp. 113–127). Needham Heights, MA: Simon & Schuster.

Bresciani, M. J. (2010). Data-driven planning: Using assessment in strategic planning. In S. E. Ellis (Ed.), *Strategic planning in student affairs* (New Directions for Student Services, no. 132, pp. 39–50). San Francisco: Jossey-Bass.

Cherrey, C., & Castillo Clark, E. (2010). Strategic planning: Renewal and redesign during turbulent times. In S. E. Ellis (Ed.), *Strategic planning in student affairs* (New Directions for Student Services, no. 132, pp. 63–74). San Francisco: Jossey-Bass.

Commonfund Institute. (2014). *2014 HEPI (Higher Education Price Index).* Wilton, CT: Author.

Conneely, J. F. (2010). Strategic planning and financial management. In S. E. Ellis (Ed.), *Strategic planning in student affairs* (New Directions for Student Services, no. 132, pp. 51–6). San Francisco: Jossey-Bass.

Ellis, S. E. (2010a). Editor's notes. In S. E. Ellis (Ed.), *Strategic planning in student affairs* (New Directions for Student Services, no. 132, pp. 1–4). San Francisco: Jossey-Bass.

Ellis, S. E. (2010b). Introduction to strategic planning in student affairs: A model for process and elements of a plan. In S. E. Ellis (Ed.), *Strategic planning in student affairs* (New Directions for Student Services, no. 132, pp. 5–16). San Francisco: Jossey-Bass.

Finley, A. (2013, Aug. 28). Richard Vedder: The real reason college costs so much. *Wall Street Journal.* Retrieved January 6, 2015, from http://www.wsj.com/articles/SB1000142 4127887324619504579029282438522674

Finney, R. G. (1994). *Basics of budgeting.* New York: AMACOM.

Gibson, A. (2009). *Budgeting in higher education.* Silver Spring, MD: Education Department of the General Conference of Seventh-day Adventists.

Hanover Research. (2015). *6 alternative budget models for colleges and universities.* Retrieved January 28, 2015, from http://www.hanoverresearch.com/insights/6-alternative-budget-models-for-colleges-and-universities/?i=higher-education

Indiana University. (2015). *IU fact book.* Bloomington: The Trustees of Indiana University. Retrieved January 29, 2015, from https://www.iu.edu/~uirr/reports/standard/factbook/2014–15/University/Finance/Operating_Budget

Integrated Postsecondary Education Data System (IPEDS). (2015). *Glossary.* Washington, DC: National Center for Education Statistics. Retrieved January 29, 2015, from http://nces.ed.gov/ipeds/glossary/index.asp?id=507

Jackson, M. L. (2000). Fund-raising and development. In M. J. Barr, M. K. Desler, & Associates, *The handbook of student affairs administration* (2nd ed., pp. 597–611). San Francisco: Jossey-Bass.

Lennington, R. L. (1996). *Managing higher education as a business.* Phoenix, AZ: ACE/Oryx.

Miao, K. (2012). *Performance-based funding of higher education.* Washington, DC: Center for American Progress.

Meisinger, R. J., Jr., & Dubeck, L. W. (1996). Fund accounting. In D. W. Breneman, L. L. Leslie, & R. E. Anderson (Eds.), *ASHE reader on finance in higher education* (pp. 465–491). Needham Heights, MA: Simon & Schuster.

Pew Higher Education Research Program. (1996). The other side of the mountain. In D. W. Breneman, L. L. Leslie, & R. E. Anderson (Eds.), *ASHE reader on finance in higher education* (pp. 511–518) Needham Heights, MA: Simon & Schuster.

Price, J. (Ed.). (2003). *Planning and achieving successful student affairs facilities projects* (New Directions for Student Services, no. 101). San Francisco: Jossey-Bass.

Sandeen, A., & Barr, M. J. (2006). *Critical issues for student affairs.* San Francisco: Jossey-Bass.

Snyder, T. D., & Dillow, S. A. (2015). *Digest of education statistics, 2013* (NCES 2015–011). Washington, DC: National Center for Education Statistics, Institute of Education Sciences, US Department of Education.

Stocum, D. L., & Rooney, P. M. (1997, Sept./Oct.). Responding to resource constraints: A departmentally based system of responsibility center management. *Change, 29*(5), 51–57.

Strauss, J., Curry, J., & Whalen, E. (2001). Revenue responsibility budgeting. In J. L. Yeager, G. M. Nelson, E. A. Potter, J. C. Weidman, & T. G. Zullo (Eds.), *ASHE reader on finance in higher education* (2nd ed., pp. 591–607). Boston, MA: Pearson.

Szatmary, D. P. (2011). Activity-based budgeting in higher education. *Continuing Higher Education Review, 75*, 69–85.

United States Government Accountability Office. (2014, Dec.). *Higher education state funding trends and policies on affordability.* Washington, DC: Author.

Whitney, R. (2010). Involving academic faculty in developing and implementing a strategic plan. In S. E. Ellis (Ed.), *Strategic planning in student affairs* (New Directions for Student Services, no. 132, pp. 63–74). San Francisco: Jossey-Bass.

Woodard, D. B., Jr., Love, P., & Komives, S. R. (2000). *Leadership and management issues for a new century* (New Directions for Student Services, no. 92). San Francisco: Jossey-Bass.

Woodard, D. B., Jr., & von Destinon, M. (2000). Budgeting and fiscal management. In M. J. Barr, M. K. Desler, & Associates, *The handbook of student affairs administration* (2nd ed., pp. 327–346). San Francisco: Jossey-Bass.

CHAPTER 19

ASSESSMENT AND EVALUATION

Ann M. Gansemer-Topf and Lance C. Kennedy-Phillips

How do you know your work is effective? If we eliminated your position, what would be the consequences? Students like your program, but what do they learn as a result of participating in your programs?

Included within this book are discussions of the profession's philosophical and theoretical foundations, organizational structures, and functional areas and competencies; this chapter focuses on assessment and evaluation and changes the questions from "What do we do and believe?" to "How do we know that what we do and believe are effective or important?" This chapter's intent is to raise awareness of the importance of asking these questions and to provide information that can assist student affairs professionals in answering these questions. We intend to accomplish this through a brief overview of the history of student affairs assessment, discussing the purposes and definitions of assessment and evaluation, illustrating key components of and skills needed for assessment, identifying different types of assessment, and describing strategies for building a culture of evidence.

History of Student Affairs Assessment

Student affairs professionals entered the assessment scene in the early to mid-1990s and focused primarily on assessing student needs, satisfaction, campus environments, student cultures, program and service outcomes, and organizational performance comparisons. Toward the late 1990s the American Association for Higher Education (AAHE), the American College Personnel Association–College Student Educators International (ACPA), and the National Association of Student Personnel Administrators–Student Affairs Administrators in Higher Education (NASPA) put forth a joint statement to define good practice in the profession that defined student affairs professionals as educators responsible for engaging students in active learning (AAHE, ACPA, & NASPA, 1998). This new definition of good professional practice expanded the dimensions of student affairs assessment to include student learning.

Since the turn of the century, a series of foundational documents have been written to help guide assessment in student affairs. Publications, such as *Learning Reconsidered* (Keeling, 2004), redefined learning as a holistic student experience and thus an institutional responsibility for which all areas were accountable, including student affairs. In 2007 College Student Educators International (ACPA) published standards designed to "articulate the areas of assessment skills and knowledge (ASK) needed by student affairs professionals in all functional areas" (p. 1). ACPA and NASPA (2010) created a joint task force to develop a set of professional competencies for the field of student affairs, including competencies in assessment, evaluation, and research.

During this same period, the Council for the Advancement of Standards (CAS) in Higher Education continued to revise outcomes for units within student affairs and published a book titled *Frameworks for Assessing Learning and Development Outcomes* (CAS, 2006). Although CAS promoted outcomes for specific units, *Learning Reconsidered 2* (Keeling, 2006) was published to provide examples of how individual campuses successfully "developed and assessed student learning outcomes, found points of collaboration across campus or identified new ways to link their work to learning activities" (p. vii).

Definitions of Assessment

Assessment activities currently permeate the postsecondary environment, focusing on student learning, program effectiveness, and organizational efficiencies. Because of the variety of purposes assessment serves, definitions of assessments have also varied.

Palomba and Banta (1999) define assessment as "the systematic collection, review, and use of information about educational programs undertaken for the purpose of improving student and learning" (p. 4). Viewing assessment from a student learning lens Suskie (2009) defines assessment as a process involving the development of learning outcomes, providing opportunities to achieve outcomes, collecting and analyzing data to determine if students met the learning outcomes, and then using results to improve student learning. In their seminal book, *Assessment in Student Affairs*, Upcraft and Schuh (1996) define assessment as "any effort to gather, analyze, and interpret evidence which describes institutional, divisional or agency effectiveness" (p. 18). In their work on outcomes-based assessment, Bresciani, Moore Gardner, and Hickmott (2009) define assessment as a "systematic and critical process that yields information about what programs, services, or functions of a student affairs department or division positively contribute to students' learning and success and which ones could be improved" (p. 16).

These multiple assessment definitions may cause frustrations for new student affairs professionals wanting to have *the* definition. However, the scope and breadth of the student affairs profession makes any one definition limiting. Palomba and Banta (1999) and Suskie (2009) emphasize assessing educational programs and remind student affairs professionals of their need to focus on how they contribute to the educational mission of the institution, specifically student learning. Upcraft and Schuh's (1996) definition focuses on the need to assess the effectiveness at all levels of the institution—within individual units as well as institution-wide. Their definition also implies that the assessment efforts at each level should complement and integrate one another. Bresciani and other's (2009) definition acknowledges the role of student affairs in providing services that, although they may not contribute to student learning, should contribute to student success.

Despite differences, the definitions illustrate that assessment is a formalized process that involves collecting, analyzing, and acting on the results of the data. The nuances in definitions mirror the scope and breadth of student affairs work and, therefore, should be viewed as a positive illustration of student affairs' critical role within higher education.

Assessment, Evaluation, and Research

The ACPA/NASPA Joint Committee (2010) recognized assessment, evaluation, and research as one of the ten competencies needed for effective student affairs work. The combining of these three into one competency symbolizes the overlap and distinctions among these three entities. This section provides a brief overview of the similarities and differences among the three.

Assessment and evaluation are often seen as interchangeable and, as a consequence, explaining the distinctions can be confusing. Evaluation has been defined as "the identification, clarification, and application of defensible criteria to determine an evaluation object's value (merit or worth) in relation to those criteria" (Fitzpatrick, Sanders, & Worthen, 2010, p. 18). Assessment and evaluation involve a process of data gathering, analysis, and using the data to make decisions. "To determine an evaluation object's value" against a set of standards differentiates evaluation from assessment. Student affairs assessment activities, such as those using CAS standards to assess program effectiveness, may fit the criteria of evaluation: programs are being evaluated on specific criteria and a judgment is made about the performance. In this instance assessment and evaluation may be used interchangeably. However, not all assessments require a judgment to be made. For example, assessing what students learn as a result of participating in a community service project involves gathering and analyzing data, but these assessments are conducted to understand the impact on student learning, not to judge the individual students. Program evaluation would require examining the community service project and making a judgment regarding its worth; assessment of student learning would examine what students learn—in the aggregate—by participating.

Differences between Research and Assessment and Evaluation

Assessment and evaluation are distinct from research in several ways. In developing research projects, the researcher has autonomy in deciding what and whom to study. Assessment activities are influenced by a variety of institutional stakeholders—internally and externally. These stakeholders play a significant role in determining what is assessed, what standards are used, and if the assessment was useful, effective, or important (Fitzpatrick & others, 2010; Upcraft & Schuh, 1996).

Whereas research is conducted to generate new knowledge or test a theory and focuses on relationships and exploration of new phenomena, assessment is conducted to examine program effectiveness or student learning and is primarily descriptive (Fitzpatrick & others, 2010; Schuh, 2009). Because assessment is usually conducted within a specific context for a specific purpose, the results are usually applicable only to that context and purpose; results from research projects have broader implications for a discipline. As Upcraft and Schuh (1996) succinctly summarized, "assessment guides good practice while research guides theory or conceptual foundations" (p. 21).

Despite these differences, assessment and research activities do overlap. Student affairs educators as scholar-practitioners illustrate this connection. Research can inform assessment activities by illustrating what could or should be assessed or by providing an understanding of assessment results. Similarly, a comprehensive assessment project can provide insights that are generalizable. Projects that may have been started as assessment can be turned into manuscripts for publication.

The overlap and confusion among assessment, evaluation, and research should be recognized but not used as an excuse for conducting assessment and evaluation. We suggest that student affairs professionals not get hung up on the nebulousness of these three concepts but rather understand how these terms could be used and interpreted across the institution. For instance, faculty members are familiar with the research process. This understanding will aid in their understanding of the assessment process. However, faculty members may quickly critique any assessment, as they would critique research, by pointing out small sample sizes, low response rates, or lack of generalizability. In these instances, it is helpful for student affairs to articulate how these assessments, despite limitations, are still useful and informative. It is also critical that, although you may be focused on a small group of students, methodological rigor is not compromised. Demonstrating your knowledge of quantitative and qualitative methods will garner respect and trust among faculty colleagues.

Understanding context is critical in doing effective student affairs assessment and evaluation. Similarly, before beginning any assessment or evaluation, we recommend that you define these terms for your audience and stakeholders. Will you focus on student learning or program effectiveness? Will you be making judgments about the efficiency of a service or examining its impact? We believe that articulating your purpose, process, what you hope to accomplish, and the importance of the project is more critical than debating if the project is an assessment or an evaluation.

Purposes of Assessment

As the history of assessment illustrates, reasons for engaging in assessment have evolved to meet the needs of higher education's external and internal constituents. As Ewell (2009) articulates, the two primary purposes of assessments have been accountability and improvement. These purposes, often in conflict with one another, have been evident since the beginning of the formal assessment movement and remain strong catalysts for assessment activities (Ewell, 2009). A third purpose, transformative action, highlights how assessment can be used to further the professions' values of social justice and equity.

Assessment for Accountability

The accountability movement has permeated all aspects of American higher education. On college and university campuses across the country, there is a growing need for a shared responsibility for student learning and success. Student learning takes place at the intersection of three factors: the curricular environment, the cocurricular environment, and the student's motivation. Colleges and universities must be able to demonstrate that student learning occurs at this intersection and that all actors—academic affairs divisions, student affairs divisions, and students—are contributing to the learning process.

Internal and external constituents demand results backed by clear and convincing evidence. Parents, legislators, employers, and students want assurances that the higher education environment will be a pathway to employment on graduation. They want to believe the university is providing students with the skills they need to be successful in their career pursuits and as citizens in a global society. Student affairs offices have a responsibility to contribute to this skill development by creating environments and opportunities that enhance student learning and development (ACPA, 1996). Subsequently, student affairs professionals also need to document this learning.

Assessment for Improvement

As student affairs administrators begin to realize a need to collect research and assessment data, they need to consider another question that emerges regarding how to use the data; more specifically, student affairs educators need to know how to use data to inform program improvement. Some professionals may ask how to use data to align with institutional priorities and others may ask how to use data to demonstrate the cocurricular impact on student learning. A growing number of student affairs practitioners are asking how to use data to tell their organization's story. These questions are centered on the ideas and principles of organizational learning. Student affairs professionals, similar to most higher education professionals, are asking the question, "How can data be used to demonstrate organizational effectiveness?"

Assessment as Transformative Action

Mertens (2009) describes a transformative paradigm approach to research and evaluation that values social justice and diversity in evaluation work and recognizes the relationships among discrimination, oppression, and evaluation. The transformative paradigm challenges assessment professionals to focus on those populations and voices that may be traditionally underrepresented in higher education and to examine the broader institutional contexts that contribute or impede the success for all students. This approach calls on student affairs professionals to examine how student affairs activities and approaches can be vehicles for social justice and equity efforts and requires that these activities and processes be assessed to determine their influence on students and their environments.

Key Elements to Effective Assessment

Maki (2004) developed a systematic cycle of assessment to illustrate the key elements to effective assessment. Viewed as an iterative process, this cycle provides a template that can be used to design assessment projects. This assessment process is applicable for all student affairs areas, and it can be used for an individual program or to develop an institution-wide assessment plan. The scale of the assessment may differ but the process is the same.

Start with the Mission and Goals

Before undertaking an assessment project is it necessary to determine if the goals of the assessment and the results you hope to gain are aligned with the mission and goals of the institution, department, or unit. If there is no connection to the broader mission and goals, time and money on assessment are wasted.

Develop a Purpose and Goals for the Assessment

After determining that the assessment aligns with the broader institutional goals and purpose, it is important to articulate a purpose and learning outcomes for your specific assessment. What is the purpose of your assessment? What do you hope to accomplish? Although seemingly simple, this task is the most critical because subsequent decision about whom to assess, methods to use, and how to analyze the data are defined by the purpose.

Goals of the assessment may be called *learning outcomes, evaluation questions,* and *assessment objectives.* Regardless of their title, these goals serve to identify the scope of the assessment. Goals should be clear, usable, and measurable (Suskie, 2009; Walvoord, 2004).

Gather Evidence: Articulate Assessment Methods

Using the purpose and goals of the assessment as a guide, articulate your assessment methods. Similar to research methods, assessment methods should identify the sample and participants (who will you assess?); data collection methods (survey, focus groups, or document analysis?); and data analysis procedures (descriptive or inferential statistical techniques, coding for themes?). Once established, the process of collecting and analyzing data begins.

Interpret Evidence and Implement Change

Unfortunately, most assessments stop after the data have been collected. Maki's (2004) cycle of assessment requires that the data be interpreted and that changes are made based on this. Interpreting evidence goes beyond reporting results. For example, you reported that students who used tutoring services had a grade point average (GPA) of 3.23 and students who did not use tutoring had a GPA of 2.99. One interpretation is that students who use tutoring have higher GPAs than those who did not. Although you cannot determine a cause-and-effect relationship, you may interpret the data to suggest that tutoring does improve students' academic performance. With this information, you may then decide to expand your tutoring program to benefit more students.

Begin Again

Continuous assessment efforts are needed to build a culture of evidence in student affairs. Maki's (2004) cycle of assessment acknowledges the iterative aspect of assessment. Using the previous tutoring example, assessment on tutoring services must continue after changes have been made to again assess differences in students' GPAs. Assessment activities may be expanded to examine differences among students who use tutoring or examine specific tutoring services. Assessment should be viewed as a continuous, rather than one-step, process, and effective assessment closes the loop by using data to inform future programs, decisions, or assessments.

Skills Needed to Do Effective Assessment

Doing assessment effectively involves technical skills and soft skills. It requires an awareness of the assessment process as well as the institutional context in which assessment is conducted. It involves having the confidence and ethical principles in making recommendations and suggestions that may not be popular while simultaneously acknowledging and working within the political contexts so recommendations can be implemented. Following are a list of some of the primary skills needed to conduct assessment.

Knowledge of the Assessment Process

To do assessment effectively, it is necessary to have a foundational knowledge of what assessment is (and is not) and the types of assessment that can be conducted. Often, individuals ask, "What is the best type of assessment to do?" Effective assessment professionals respond, "It depends on the purpose of your assessment" and then assist individuals in choosing the assessment type that will best address the purpose and assessment questions (Schuh, 2009).

Communication Skills

A common frustration with assessment is that work is done to gather and analyze data but seldom do results get acted on. Good communications skills can improve chances that assessment results will be used. Communication skills are necessary throughout the entire assessment process. Before the assessment is conducted it is important to articulate your assessment plan to stakeholders, communicate its importance, and demonstrate why the results are necessary. Strong oral communication skills are needed in working with stakeholders, participants, and in presenting results. Written skills are necessary in writing proposals, reports, and executive summaries. Last, strong visual communication skills are needed to be able to create effective charts, figures, and tables that present data efficiently and accurately (Fitzpatrick & others, 2010).

Research Methods Skills

Although research is not the same as assessment, doing assessment requires a foundational knowledge of research methods. Identifying a population, sample, or participants and articulating a research design, data collections methods, and analyses is necessary (Cooper, 2009; Gansemer-Topf & Wohlgemuth, 2009). Many times entry-level student affairs professionals may shy away from assessment, thinking they lack the skills to carry out complex qualitative and quantitative analysis. Although some projects use these methods, the majority of assessments require the ability to complete descriptive statistics such as averages, percentages, and frequencies and simple coding of qualitative data analysis. Partnering with colleagues in departments such as institutional research or statistics can be useful when more complex data analysis is required. So, for instance, if you would like to go beyond reporting frequencies to engaging in more advanced statistical techniques, such as hierarchical regression or wanting the ability to approach qualitative data analysis using critical race theory, reaching out to institutional researchers, statisticians, and faculty members and graduate students with extensive training in these advanced research methods may be an effective strategy.

Understanding Institutional Context and Culture

Assessment is critical because it enables one to understand what is happening within one's institution. To be useful, assessment results should interpreted within one's institutional context; recommendations also should be tailored to fit the needs of a particular context and culture. For example, factors that contribute to students' leaving an institution may be significantly different at a community college than at a highly selective university; policy recommendations at a small liberal arts institution may not be applicable at a large, public institution.

Recognizing and Navigating Politics

In addition to context and culture, good assessment requires recognizing and navigating the politics of the institution (Fitzpatrick & others, 2010; Schuh, 2009). As student affairs professionals, understanding the political context is critical. Who makes decisions? Who can influence decisions? Are their key issues or concerns that will elicit strong responses? Navigating these political realities while maintaining integrity and ethics can be challenging. Unfortunately many of these political realities are not outlined in any handbook or training session. Therefore, to conduct assessment effectively, it is important for student affairs professionals to ask questions from others at the institution and to observe how the institution functions. Do you have buy in from upper level administration? Who is interested in the results and how will they be used? The question is not "Are there political situations I should be aware of?" but rather "Please tell me the institutional politics that may affect this assessment."

Skill Development Resources

At first glance, the list of skills needed to do assessment may seem overwhelming, but they are attainable. Many graduate programs require course work in research methods and more programs are requiring course work on assessment. NASPA and ACPA highlight assessment sessions during their regional and national conferences, and both organizations have a conference specifically devoted to assessment. Blogs, e-mail lists, and social media sites provide assistance in assessment skill development.

Types of Assessment

University College, a public, regional institution, has seen a decline in the retention rate of first-year students for the past five years. Although enrollment of new students has remained the same or even increased these same five years, more students are leaving between their first and second year of college. This decline has caught the attention of the state legislature, local and regional news outlets, and the most recent college rankings guides. The university has estimated that, on average, the institution loses approximately $50,000 in tuition revenue and other income such as room and board fees when a student leaves. More important, this monetary figure does not account for the adverse effects on the student such as accrued student loan debt, a negative institutional experience, and frustrations with the university specifically and higher education in general.

The president has formed a university-wide retention committee to examine why retention may be declining and make recommendations for improving retention. The first task of this committee is to conduct a comprehensive assessment to examine factors that may contribute or enhance retention at the institution. You have been asked to serve as a member of a university-wide retention committee representing the Division of Student Affairs. Your division includes a dean of students office; academic advising; enrollment services (student financial aid, admissions, registrar); new student orientation; residence life; and affinity group support services (such as the women's center, multicultural student services, and LGBTQ). You have worked with your staff to complete a variety of assessments that will inform the work of the larger committee.

As mentioned previously, there are different purposes for doing assessment. There are also many different types of assessment that can be done to meet these purposes. This section discusses some of the most common types of assessments and will provide an example of how each of these types of assessment can be used in the case study just described.

Utilization Assessment

This assessment, perhaps the least complex type of assessment, involves collecting data on the number and types of students who use specific services (Upcraft & Schuh, 1996). Although it is difficult to make the connection between participation and other outcomes, such as learning and retention, it can be useful a place to begin assessment.

Example Utilization assessment would include counting the number of students who chose to live in campus residence halls, participate in orientation, or attend a session on time management and then analyzing these data by major and student demographics.

Needs Assessment

Needs assessment, as the name suggests, is gathering data to determine the needs of a certain population (Schuh, 2009). Needs assessment often is done before a program or intervention is developed, although it also can be conducted to improve a program or make a decision to cut a program. A needs assessment is done often before new building such as a residence hall is designed to assess what amenities students would prefer. Students may also be asked what information they would want included in certain programs such as in new orientation or academic advising sessions.

Example   Plans are being developed to remodel a residence hall for new students. Current residents are surveyed and asked to list the top five improvements they would like to see in their residence halls.

Program Assessment

Program assessment focuses on the effectiveness of a specific program (Fitzpatrick & others, 2010). Student affairs divisions develop and implement a multitude of programs ranging in size and scope from a one-time time management program for students on one residence hall floor to a division-wide, year-long training program for new staff members. Formative program assessment could be done as a way to improve a program, and summative program assessment could be conducted to determine if the program should continue or be cut.

Example   The new student orientation program was developed to ease the transition from high school to college by exposing students to campus resources, connecting them with new students, and providing information on their curriculum and classes. Focus groups and surveys were conducted to determine if the new student orientation program achieved these goals.

Student Learning Assessment

Student learning assessment seeks to understand what students learned as a result of participating in a certain program or experience. Whereas a program assessment would focus on the effectiveness of a program meeting its intended goals, student learning assessment focuses on what students have learned.

Example   The Division of Students Affairs offers many leadership opportunities for students within clubs and organization. An assessment of presidents and vice presidents of each campus organization was conducted to determine what students learned about leadership and how they developed their leadership skills as a result of being president or vice president.

Satisfaction Assessment

Satisfaction assessment measures serve an important function in the work of student affairs professional as they gauge student's perspectives on their experience. Professionals should not depend solely on satisfaction measures to assess student learning or evaluate program effectiveness, but they can be used to understand the student experience and make improvements to programs or policies.

Example   Based on previous student complaints, new dining options were offered for on- and off-campus students. The plans offered students more flexibility in meal options and pricing structures. At the end of the fall semesters, a survey was given to assess students' satisfaction with the new dining options.

Key Performance Indicators (KPIs)

Key performance indicators (KPIs) and metrics are the essential functions of the department and division that lead to fulfillment of the division's mission. It is critical for each department of the division to clearly articulate KPIs and the measures that demonstrate progress toward fulfilling those activities. This process could result in the development of an annual report of KPIs by each department, which contributes to the identification of divisional outcomes and goals. The KPIs represent the everyday management processes for the department. A vast majority of the division's data-driven evidence is captured in the measurement of KPIs.

Example   The residence life department identified a series of KPIs to measure departmental effectiveness. They have decided to track their KPIs on a term basis and aggregate the measures annually for review. The department made a deliberate effort to map the KPIs back to the divisions' and departments' goals and outcomes. The KPIs included housing capacity, student-to-staff ratios, students served per square foot, number of experiential activities offered per term, residential students' retention, and graduation rates. The department acknowledges that these measures are descriptive in nature and one part of the overall assessment process.

Campus Environment and Culture Assessment

Campus environment assessments seeks to "evaluate how the various elements and condition of the college campus milieu affect student learning and growth" (Upcraft & Schuh, 1996, p. 167). Strange and Banning (2001) identified four primary aspects of the campus environment: physical, human aggregate, organizational, and constructed. The physical environment is focused on the physical location and design of the campus; the human aggregate focuses on the types of students and faculty and staff members in an institution; organizational focuses on how the institution is organizationally structured, such as the degree of centralization, stratification, and formalization; and the constructed environment involves the meaning that individuals attribute to certain symbols, events, and so on. Campus environmental assessments may also focus on student cultures and their impact on the overall campus environment or the impact of these cultures on certain populations of students and the influence of cultures on student success.

Examples   A campus audit of computer labs illustrated that because most students had their own computers, theses spaces were no longer used. Plans for renovating these spaces to accommodate personal computers and enable more group work were developed. An assessment of students participating in Greek organizations was conducted to determine how these student cultures affected retention. Policies such as those regarding academic probation, dropping classes, and changing majors were analyzed to understand how these policies contributed to student retention. An analysis of the campus climate for women, ethnic, and LGBTQ students was conducted to determine students' views on campus community and safety.

◆ ◆ ◆

This section provided examples of different types of assessments. The type of assessment conducted depends on the purpose of your assessment and the type of information you are seeking to gain. Some assessments will use multiple types of assessment. For example, in a focus group you may be looking to assess students' satisfaction as well as their perceptions of campus cultures. Used together, these types of assessment will provide a comprehensive overview of the effectiveness of student affairs work.

Creating a Culture of Evidence in Student Affairs: The Four Cs

A culture of evidence is the shared belief within an organization that the use of data to inform decision making is vital to the organization's success and effectiveness. A strong and sustained culture of evidence is vital to any student affairs organization and does not happen without hard work and intervention. In a student affairs context, there are four components necessary to creating and sustaining a culture of evidence in student affairs. First, there must be commitment at all levels of the organization to assessment and data collection. Second, the organization must be consistent in all aspects of its assessment processes. Third, a strong culture of evidence is connected to goals and outcomes internally and externally to the division. Finally, communication is key to developing a positive and sustained culture of evidence.

Commitment

For any culture of evidence to be sustained and successful, it needs executive support and it needs ownership from all levels of the division. The culture will not be successful without a charge from the senior student affairs officer (SSAO). The SSAO sets the tone for the division. If the SSAO provides only casual support for assessment and data collection, the effectiveness of these actions diminishes immediately. The executive charge legitimizes the process, which is needed when you are attempting to devise and establish a culture that cascades to all levels of the division.

The clearest way to show commitment to creating a culture of evidence is by providing the financial and staffing resources necessary to maintain and build the culture. For example, at larger institutions, there should at least be one full-time professional designated to lead the assessment function. At smaller institutions, there should be designated staff members across the division who can conduct assessment and research. These staff members would be assessment "champions" who could be a part of a division-wide assessment council.

Building staff member capacity to do assessment is key element of sustaining a strong culture of evidence.

Consistency

Assessment and evidence gathering must become part of the institutional process. Just as we develop budgets and content for our programs and services, we must also develop clear outcomes and the method for assessing those outcomes. Building a culture is more than just designating "the year of assessment" or conducting disparate assessments throughout the year. The assessment process should remain as consistent as possible and fit the unique needs of the institution. Developing a consistent process minimizes the burden for staff members who are responsible for collecting data each year.

A consistent and reliable assessment and evidence-collection process can yield strong trend data for the organization that can also be used for KPIs and benchmarking. Student affairs professionals can see changes over time and make adjustments to programs and services when necessary. Demonstrating that data are consistently being collected and reported bolsters a culture of evidence.

Connection

A strong and sustained culture of evidence is connected to the larger university mission and goals. Student affairs divisions must be able to demonstrate that their work aligns with university values so that senior staff members can secure monetary and personnel resources, participate in institutional accreditation, and help students develop the skills necessary to achieve career success. Student affairs divisions contribute to all of these aspects of the university; by aligning and mapping a division's data and evidence with the larger institution, the story, or evidence, is clear, strong, and persuasive.

Connection is also important for increasing staff motivation and momentum to assess programming and services and to gather data. Staff members want to know that their work is connected to the larger university narrative; assessment does not take place in a vacuum. For example, we know there is no single measure for student success. Showing staff members how their work connects to the achievement of university outcomes may help connect the various touch points that lead to student learning and success. Demonstrating these connections to staff members may make them more interested in collaborating across the institution and provide support that these collaborations will lead to increased student learning and success.

Communication

Without transparent, clear, and frequent communication, a sustained and strong culture of evidence is not possible to develop or implement. Communication regarding the division's assessment process should involve all layers of the organization. Failure to clearly articulate the assessment process may lead to confusion and frustration. The language describing the process should be clear. We advocate for divisions to develop a glossary of assessment terms (such as *outcome* versus *goal*). This is helpful to prevent unnecessary barriers regarding participation in the process. Having consistency in language is key to any culture, and it is especially necessary for a culture built on evidence.

It is important to communicate results of assessments and research regularly to all members of the community. Sharing evidence with senior administrators and board members puts the division in charge of narratives on key issues regarding cocurricular experiences. Proactively sharing data with faculty members sends the message that student affairs is an active participant and contributor to student learning. Finally, sharing assessment results with students demonstrates that their voices are being heard. By communicating data in this way, the division establishes a reputation for providing regular and reliable reports and lays the foundation and establishes expectations for receiving evidence in this form from the division.

Conclusion

This chapter focused on assessment and evaluation within student affairs. Given the recent past and the foreseeable future, assessment and evaluation activities are here to stay. Student affairs professionals can no longer can claim that "we don't have time to do assessment," but instead they must ask, "how can we create and sustain a culture of evidence?" Our profession has evolved through our passion for educating students and our efforts in supporting student success for all students. Through assessment we can demonstrate that our passion and efforts are worthwhile.

Discussion Questions and Activities

1. Develop one purpose statement and two assessment outcomes for a student affairs unit, program, or service.
2. Based on the learning outcomes you created, develop a communication plan to share assessment results with other students.
3. Given the skills needed to conduct effective assessment, identify skills you currently possess and skills you need to gain.
   a. (Optional). Create a plan outlining how you plan to gain the needed assessment skills.
4. Discuss the role accountability has played in the assessment movement in higher education.
   a. (Optional) Explain how has this affected student affairs.
   b. (Optional) Do you think conducting assessment for student affairs is more or less difficult than conducting assessment for academic programs? What assessment data are needed to demonstrate accountability in student affairs?

5. Identify three ways you can celebrate assessment in a division of student affairs.

6. This chapter focused specifically on conducting assessment for student affairs. How is assessment in student affairs similar to or different from assessment in other areas of higher education, such as in academic departments, business units (such as the treasurer's or bursar's office), athletics, or alumni relations and fund-raising?

References

American Association for Higher Education (AAHE), College Student Educators International (ACPA), & Student Affairs Administrators in Higher Education (NASPA). (1998). *Powerful partnerships: A shared responsibility for learning.* Retrieved from http://www.opt.uab.edu/retentioncouncil/Exhibits/JTFSL_Principles.htm

Bresciani, M. J., Moore Gardner, M., & Hickmott, J. (2009). *Demonstrating student success: A practical guide to outcomes-based assessment of learning and development in student affairs.* Sterling, VA: Stylus.

College Student Educators International (ACPA). (1996). *The student learning imperative: Implications for student affairs.* Washington, DC: Author.

College Student Educators International (ACPA). (2007). *ASK standards: Assessment skills and knowledge content standards for student affairs practitioners and scholars.* Washington, DC: Author.

College Student Educators International (ACPA) & Student Affairs Administrators in Higher Education (NASPA). (2010). *ACPA and NASPA professional competency areas for student affairs practitioners.* Retrieved from http://www2.myacpa.org/img/Professional_Competencies.pdf

Cooper, R. M. (2009). Planning for and implementing data collection. In J. H. Schuh (Ed.), *Assessment methods for student affairs* (pp. 51–76). San Francisco: Jossey-Bass.

Council for the Advancement of Standards in Higher Education (CAS). (2006). *Frameworks for assessing learning and development outcomes.* Washington, DC: Author.

Ewell, P. T. (2009, Nov.). *Assessment, accountability, and improvement: Revisiting the tension.* (NILOA Occasional Paper No.1). Urbana: University of Illinois and Indiana University, National Institute for Learning Outcomes Assessment.

Fitzpatrick, J. L., Sanders, J. R., & Worthen, B. R. (2010). *Program evaluation: Alternative approaches and practical guidelines* (4th ed.). New York: Longman.

Gansemer-Topf, A. M., & Wohlgemuth, D. (2009). Selecting, sampling, and soliciting subjects. In J. H. Schuh (Ed.), *Assessment methods for student affairs* (pp. 77–105). San Francisco: Jossey-Bass.

Keeling, R. (Ed.). (2004). *Learning reconsidered. A campus-wide focus on the student experience.* Washington, DC: National Association of Student Personnel Administrators & American College Personnel Association.

Keeling, R. (Ed.). (2006). *Learning reconsidered 2: Implementing a campus-wide focus on the student experience.* Washington, DC: American College Personnel Association, Association of College and Housing Officers–International, Association of College Unions–International, National Academic Advising Association, National Association of Campus Activities, National Association of Student Personnel Administrators, & National Intramural–Recreational Sports Association.

Maki, P. L. (2004). *Assessing for learning: Building a sustainable commitment across the institution.* Spokane, VA: Stylus.

Mertens, D. M. (2009). *Transformative research and evaluation.* New York: Guilford.

Palomba, C. A., & Banta, T.W. (1999). *Assessment essentials: Planning, implementing, and improving assessment in higher education.* San Francisco: Jossey-Bass.

Schuh, J. H. (2009). *Assessment methods for student affairs.* San Francisco: Jossey-Bass.

Strange, C. C., & Banning, J. H. (2001). *Education by design: Creating campus learning environments that work.* San Francisco: Jossey-Bass.

Suskie, L. (2009). *Assessing student learning: A common sense guide.* (2nd ed.). San Francisco: Jossey-Bass.

Upcraft, M. L., & Schuh, J. H. (1996). *Assessment in student affairs: A guide for practitioners.* San Francisco: Jossey-Bass.

Walvoord, B. E. (2004). *Assessment clear and simple: A practical guide for institutions, departments, and general education.* San Francisco: Jossey-Bass.

CHAPTER 20

LEFT BEHIND: HOW THE PROFESSION OF STUDENT AFFAIRS IS UNDERPREPARED TO MEET STUDENTS WHERE THEY (DIGITALLY) ARE

Jeffrey Rokkum and Reynol Junco

Social media, as they are understood today, started around 1997 with the founding of "Open Diary" by Bruce and Susan Abelson, which was an early social networking site which brought people together to write in an online diary that other people could comment on (Richmond, 2009). Ten years after its inception, more than five million diaries had been posted by the more than 517,000 members (*Journaling a tool for writers,* 2007). Other websites were influenced greatly by opendiary.com because of the introduction of reader comments and the idea of public and private favorites pages (Richmond, 2009). The term *weblog* was invented around this time and was then shortened within a year to *blog* (Blood, 2000). One of the promises of the early Internet was that everyone would have a voice and be able to communicate; however, in the early days, only those who knew how to code a website could make their voice heard. Then when people were able to comment easily through blogs they were able to connect with each other without the same skills-based barrier (Blood, 2000). With increasing access to high-speed Internet, the concept of social networking with websites such as MySpace (2003) and Facebook (2004) was popularized, which in turn led to the coining of the term *social media* and has contributed greatly to the prominence of the term today (Kaplan & Haenlein, 2010). There are six overarching types of social media (Grahl, 2015) that encompass most of the currently existing websites:

Social networks enable connections among people with similar interests and similar backgrounds. They consist of a profile, user-to-user interaction, as well as many other aspects that allow one-to-one and one-to-many connections.

Bookmarking sites enable people to save, organize, and manage different websites that they like to visit on the Internet. Then after organizing them they can be "tagged," which enables easy searching and sharing. Two popular websites within this category are Pinterest and StumbleUpon.

Social news services enable members to vote on the provided outside links and news items; however, in this method the voting aspect is important because the items with the most votes are featured most prominently. Therefore, the items that are deemed more important or interesting are decided on by the community as a whole before they are shown. Two popular websites within this category are Reddit and Digg.

Media-sharing websites have services that enable visitors to upload and share media such as videos and pictures. Additionally they contain the ability to comment, like, and have a profile. Popular websites within this category are YouTube and Flickr.

Microblogging is a newer activity with services that focus on publishing short updates to anyone who is subscribed to receive them, with Twitter being the most popular in the United States.

Blogs are platforms that enable publishing of entries that often include a comments section so that readers can have conversations by posting messages back and forth. Blog comment sections are similar to forums except they focus on the blog post instead of a forum topic. There are many popular blogging platforms with WordPress, Medium, and Tumblr being popular ones in the United States.

There are some websites that overlap among these areas; for instance, Facebook has the features of a microblogging site through their "status updates" and Flickr and YouTube have comment systems similar to those found in blogs (Grahl, 2015).

We are constantly being bombarded by the message that the Internet is a dangerous place for our children; however, children are being limited in their abilities to roam in the offline world, so their roaming has gone digital. "Parents, teachers and schools worry about teenagers posting their lives (romantic indiscretions, depressing poetry and all), leaking passwords and generally flouting social conventions as predators, bullies and unsavory marketers lurk. Endless back-and-forthing over how to respond effectively—shutting Web sites, regulating online access and otherwise tempering the world of social media for children—dominates the P.T.A. and the halls of policy makers" (Paul, 2012, p. 5). Children, however, congregate on social media sites so they can have conversations, flirtations, social exchanges, and engage in the humor that they are increasingly unable to access in the offline world. However, parental attitudes toward the Internet and social media take the form of moral panics. The most common misconception about Internet-centric communication is the idea we have of sexual predators: "The model we have of the online sexual predator is this lurking man who reaches out on the Internet and grabs a kid. And there is [sic] no data that support that. The vast majority of sex crimes against kids involve someone that kid trusts, and it's overwhelmingly family members" (Paul, 2012, p. 19). Indeed, this statement is partially supported by data from the Crimes Against Children Research Center, whose research shows that acquaintances are most often the perpetrators of sexual violence toward children followed by family members (Finkelhor, 2008). When a child does not feel safe communicating with adults offline, he or she could greatly benefit through communication with counselors, like-minded peers, and other helpers online. For instance, online counseling has been shown to have a similar impact and replicates the conditions of a face-to-face counseling session (Richards & Viganó, 2013).

Other fears that are spread about social media include (1) Facebook is giving us a narcissistic outlook (Chowdhury, 2013); (2) Facebook causes depression and isolation (Jimenez, 2013); (3) Facebook use lowers grades (Choney, 2010); and (4) using Facebook can lead to your child to being bullied (Gayle, 2013). Higher education has been driven by fear-mongering myths about youth use of social media based on "inadequate or miscontextualized research" (Junco, 2014, p. 5). The myths about the use of social media are inconsistent with the reality of social media use. Children and students use social media as a reflection of their social lives: the transgressions, friendships, gossiping, flirting, as well as hiding the good and bad from their parents. Teenagers use the Internet for the same reason that many adults do: they have a desire to feel connected, supported, and loved, just through a different medium than adults are used to.

In a survey of over one thousand thirteen- to seventeen-year-olds conducted by Common Sense Media, a child advocacy group, it was found that 20 percent of children reported that social media made them feel more confident, with 4 percent reporting that it made them feel less confident. This trend continues across multiple avenues of social media use with 28 percent reporting that they feel more outgoing on social media compared to 5 percent who felt less so, and 29 percent who said it made them feel more extroverted with 3 percent who felt more introverted. Fifty-two percent of teens indicate that social media have actually made their friendships and relationships better compared with the 4 percent who reported that the relationships had worsened because of social media (*Social media, social life*, 2012).

Because of the relatively new emergence of the mind-set that social media are used for positive psychosocial development, there is acceptance from some people and pushback from others. These cultures of acceptance or pushback can be organized using the adult normative and youth normative dichotomy (Gasser, Cortesi, Malik, & Lee, 2012). Those engaging in an adult normative perspective harbor the view that social media are a negative influence on all aspects of youth development and student engagement, and because of these ideas adults may be unwilling to use or engage youth through social platforms, whereas the youth normative perspective embraces social media and integrates it into daily activities. Many student affairs professionals, especially those in upper-level positions, either knowingly or unknowingly have adopted an adult normative view that does not take into account students' lived experiences with social media, which removes a great tool for professionals to use to support students. For years, research has shown that students learn from computers—when technology can be used as a tutor, to increase basic skills and knowledge, and to develop higher-order thinking, creativity, and research skills (Reeves, 1998; Ringstaff & Kelley, 2002). There is a broad swath of research on social media and results range from positive to negative student impacts; however, when they are used in educationally relevant ways, social media have demonstrated to affect student growth and learning significantly and positively (Junco, 2014).

The profession of student affairs has been struggling with a crisis of assessment—student affairs practitioners have spent little time documenting how what they do leads to improved student outcomes (Schuh & Gansemer-Topf, 2010). Generally, this is traceable to the value system of the profession—that our mission should be to serve students. Student affairs professionals do not typically enter the profession because they have strong skills in or desire to conduct outcomes assessment. However, recent calls for educational accountability will soon be affecting student affairs practitioners. The cost of higher education has skyrocketed in recent years and with this increase in the cost of attendance has come an increased scrutiny on what institutions are doing to add value to students' lives. Politicians and society have taken note and want to know that institutions are delivering on their promise to educate and prepare students for the future. Various government bodies are calling for accountability checks to verify that the programs are working (De Vise, 2012), and because of the way that social media can keep track of all interactions, the interactions themselves can be retained as examples of various successes and as a stepping stone toward developing a plan that can be used almost automatically. The use of social media can help resolve this long-standing student affairs issue and help provide data to support the effectiveness of our interventions.

From Research to Practice

The question may arise, "Is it really valuable to focus on social media use in the area of student affairs?" This question is nearing uselessness with the uptake of technology among the population, especially among the younger population. Cellphone ownership is near universal with 90 percent of adults owning a cell phone in 2014 (Pew Internet, 2015). This trend cuts across all ethnicities, ages, education levels, income levels, and community types, so much so that it can be said that owning a cell phone is ubiquitous in the United States (Pew Internet, 2015). Technology has become a staple of daily life for most people: as of 2014,

29 percent of cell phone owners reported that they could not imagine living without their cell phone (Pew Internet, 2015). Some smartphone owners, specifically younger adults, lower-income Americans, and those from minoritized racial and ethnic backgrounds, rely on their smartphone for Internet access (Pew Internet, 2015). The Internet has become such an important place that in 2011 the United Nations declared that disconnecting people from the Internet is a human rights violation and against international law (United Nations, 2011).

Technology is continuing to take over the most mundane tasks in our lives; one of the most abundant examples of technology replacing a service job is ATMs replacing the need for bank tellers; additionally, self-checkouts at grocery stores are becoming more prolific and cars such as the Tesla are being developed with the ability to drive (almost) autonomously. The software update that will be released in late 2015 will enable the Tesla to autosteer to keep you in a lane, and if it cannot see the lane lines on the road it will beep at you until you take hold of the wheel again. The Tesla will change lanes automatically when simply indicating with a turn signal, and the car will wait and automatically change lanes for you when it is safe. The most anticipated addition might be the autopark feature, in which the car will notify the driver when it finds a parking space and will then park the vehicle (even parallel parking).

This autopilot idea can be applied to student affairs quite simply: technology is able to aid drivers of a Tesla in the mundane and everyday tasks that they engage in; in the same way, social media communications enable student affairs practitioners to be more able to focus on student goals and desires instead of the unremarkable aspects of student affairs. Through the use of various forms of social media, results have shown that Facebook time is positively correlated with time spent on campus activities (Heiberger & Harper, 2008; Junco, 2013), creating and RSVPing to Facebook events is a positive predictor of student engagement (Junco, 2013), and students' natural use of Facebook promotes social and academic integration by enabling reflection on experiences, exchanging academic information, seeking information about new friends, and so on (Ellison, Steinfield, & Lampe, 2007, 2011; Junco, 2014; Junco & Mastrodicasa, 2007). Facebook also has a direct impact on students' performance proficiency, self-esteem, and self-reported satisfaction with university life (Yu, Tian, Vogel, & Kwok, 2010).

Social media use has been shown to lead to higher retention rates. For instance, students who use social networking sites to learn about on-campus activities end up participating more in face-to-face activities that then lead to improved retention (Ward, 2010). Introducing these ideas to an ingrained system might seem daunting; however, with proper monitoring of student social media for keywords and phrases, the appropriate help and support can be provided. If a student tweets about money issues, such as "I hate being broke," the financial aid office can respond with helpful information about scholarships or information about an upcoming budget management workshop (Junco, 2014). This would provide another route for students to have their questions answered, if the answer cannot be easily found online. Another use could be for community building by linking together RAs, residents, and staff members within residence halls. This enables students to cooperate and more easily learn the new social and cultural norms of their environment, which would enable further academic and social engagement.

Psychosocial Tensions and Resistance

Whenever new technology or methods are suggested, there is pushback against them (Foot, 2014), and the integration of social media into student affairs is no different. A change in thinking must be accomplished to relieve the tensions and resistance that are sure to spring up. Many traditional student affairs professionals are more interested in what they know that works for them, and they come at social media from a similar perspective. Avoiding using new technology or dismissing new technology as a fad is a dangerous pitfall that many older practitioners will fall into, because it will leave their students unaware of how to manage their online presence or how to appropriately conduct themselves or their activities when using these platforms. Abstinence-only education does not work for sexual and reproductive health, and it does not work for helping students approach and use social media in ways that are psychologically and developmentally beneficial. A new wave of student affairs practitioners who are aware of the importance of a professional online appearance for employees is already rising, especially on sites such as LinkedIn and Twitter.

Having a social media presence in a professional capacity is important for many reasons. Students will look to educational professionals as examples and as sources of inspiration, which enables the student affairs practitioner to be a model for positive social media use. Using social media to engage students promotes education outside of required curricula, because most students have difficulty navigating the gulf between how they use social media and what is expected of them professionally on social media. This lacuna provides an opportunity for student affairs professionals to showcase their profiles as a way to demonstrate the use of social apps and websites as well as to share timely and educationally relevant information. Consider, for instance, an advisor who uses social media to communicate important class registration deadlines or to help advisees engage in peer learning about the advising process. One important benefit of using social media to support student education is that once connections have been established between students and student affairs professionals, community engagement drastically increases. For instance, Junco, Heiberger, and Loken (2011) found that students who used social media with their first-year seminar instructors were much more engaged and socially and academically integrated.

Use of Social Media and Related Technologies in Student Affairs

How students develop their identities using social media is an often-overlooked, yet important, area. Social media are crucial for helping college students explore and develop a stable sense of self that is externally validated and internally consistent (Chickering & Reisser, 1993; Erikson, 1968; Junco, 2014). Once students start tying their opinions and statements online to their real name, they start developing a "brand." The personal brand that a student develops creates an impression about who they are in the minds of the people with whom they interact. If students create an account with their real name and start providing help to other people, they can begin to accrue a positive reputation within a community. Additionally, when students use a real name it enables others to search for the person online and see postings in other settings. Such online participation encourages the accrual of social capital—the psychological and physiological benefits gained from networked connections. When people have higher degrees of social capital, they are more connected to their communities and are often physically and psychologically healthier (Adler & Kwon, 2000; Helliwell & Putnam, 2004). Research has demonstrated that when people use social media for communication purposes their social capital increases (Burke, Kraut, & Marlow, 2011; DeAndrea, Ellison, LaRose, Steinfield, & Fiore, 2011; Ellison, Vitak, Gray, & Lampe, 2014). When using one's real name on social media platforms, one's social distance—the extent to which individuals are removed from participating in someone else's life—will decrease, which increases connections when one is offline.

The online disinhibition effect is when people are more likely to say something online than they are in face-to-face interactions. Disinhibition online enables students to test multiple facets of their personality and their identity with the idea that the online sites are safer places to test it. It is safer to test one's identity online because there is less ego investment by the students and by the audience themselves; there is also a greater opportunity for the individual to take creative risks and to explore aspects of their personality that they simply would not be able to explore offline. Eventually young people adopt a personality that is a stable sense of their online persona, which can be seen through the consistency of their postings, their behaviors, and their reactions toward others. The extent to which college students can successfully develop their identity is demonstrative of their interpersonal and academic success. When identity is not developed properly, the student won't possess the strong interpersonal connections needed for a sense of connection to the institution, which then reduces the ability to develop academic and social integration, which in turn reduces their motivation to be social (Tinto, 1993). After building a social network, students then are able to develop greater social capital and have a support network of their peers for when they require assistance (Ellison, Steinfield, & Lampe, 2007, 2011). Therefore these students who have not engaged in identity formation have a significantly harder time adapting to college environments (Kroger, 2008). Learning about oneself online transfers to the offline environment, the content and environment might be different, but they take away information about how others react to those facets of their identities, and they could build significant interpersonal bonds. Through this online identity formation students can build true intimacy offline as well (Erikson, 1968). One of the ways that students construct identities online is through the creation of an idealized-self profile (Junco, 2014), often created in high school to fool potential colleges or employers, which contains only positive attributes, pictures, and posts that are sanitized for a working environment. Sometimes students post false status updates about volunteer activities to make themselves appear in a more positive light.

Geolocation data act as excellent trace—seemingly irrelevant data collected through natural uses of technology—and can be used to measure student involvement on campus. This will enable student affairs professionals to understand student involvement and maintain a connection with students. Evaluating geolocation data may help student affairs professionals to identify those students who are uninvolved and take steps to help with their social and academic integration. Geolocation data can also help with predictive analytics; for example, economics students might perform better on their economics tests when they spend more time in the library. Aggregation of geolocation data with additional trace data, such as digital textbook use, texting, or phone calls, could serve to bolster the identification of students who are at risk of poor exam performance before they even take any exams. These early alerts for faculty members, advisors, and student support professionals can help the educators address the needs of students, and affect course outcomes. In the past, at-risk students were identified through generalized methods; mainly low-SES or first-generation college students were aggregated into at-risk categories. Categorical groupings are good for a place to begin to provide assistance; however, they have the potential to encompass many more students than those who truly require help. With the introduction of trace analytics these wide categories can be refined to the students who are truly at risk based on their behavior patterns. Trace data and predictive analytics can be used in even more ways than that: a residence advisor can use the data to see if any of the students within their hall will become disengaged, and because disengaged students are less likely to persist, the director might choose to intervene directly to improve the engagement for the student and therefore increase the student's overall persistence. Another use would be through digital textbook reading on a week-by-week basis. High school GPA is a strong predictor of college success (Belfield & Crosta, 2012), but another stronger predictor is how often students read and use their digital textbooks (Junco & Clem, 2015). Because that variable can change constantly, student affairs educators can take advantage of monitoring the variable in real time, thereby increasing the potential for effective interventions.

Privacy concerns are a major issue when it comes to blanket data collection, especially when people believe that their data can be used to identify them. In order to address concerns with data collection, the student's name needs to be disaggregated from personal data, and an ID number should be used instead. The data need to be encrypted when sent out for analyses. Once the outside analyst is chosen, all care needs to be taken to ensure that the analyst follows FERPA regulations and requirements. Students become much more comfortable with data acquisition plans when there is complete transparency about what the data will be used for, how it is being collected, and once the experiment ends, how the data will be disposed safely.

Professional development consists of educational activities that happen outside of the usual work schedule and outside the typical duties ascribed to a position. By engaging in professional development activities student affairs professionals are able to participate in lifelong learning experiences. By building a professional social and support network, healthy work practices and attitudes can be promoted. Burke, Noblet, and Cooper (2013) noticed that emotionally intense work—such as the kind performed in student affairs—can lead to burnout. This, in turn, can lead to decreased effectiveness, increasingly staff member turnover rates, substance abuse problems, and can result in an increase of health and psychological problems (Alarcon, 2011; Swider & Zimmerman, 2010). The professional support network that can be built through social media can assist in alleviating the psychological stressors that can lead to burnout in student affairs work (Bährer-Kohler, 2013). Previously, sharing resources, information, and support was difficult for student affairs for a variety of reasons including a lack of adequate professional development funds. Lack of these funds often correlates with diminished institutional and divisional resources, which signals a need for increased professional development. Professionals are able to use personal learning networks (PLNs) to maintain a connection with a network of their professional peers, which will enable professionals to reap the benefits of having those relationships. When student affairs professionals build PLNs they are able to seek and receive help from the other professionals that can help to maintain a positive work-life balance. Additionally educators would be able to use their PLN to find information about effective learning outcome evaluation interests.

Twitter has become a popular tool used by professionals in higher education to build and maintain PLNs (Veletsianos, 2012). Twitter enables educators to build communities, which is especially necessary when their field of focus is exceptionally specialized or unusual. Veletsianos (2012) found that Twitter is used by academics for primarily seven activities. Information, resource, and media sharing was the primary activity of higher education scholars, with 39 percent of all tweets being about research and other items related to their professional activities. Twitter also is used to expand learning opportunities outside of the classroom, with scholars using Twitter to make activities and content available outside of the classroom while also helping students to form connections with individuals outside of the usual classroom environment. The PLNs developed also enable individuals to ask for help and assistance through their Twitter networks, while improving their own knowledge and practices. Twitter enables scholars to share their personal lives in a socially acceptable way: day-to-day activities are shared, as well as likes, dislikes, personal lives, and their profession, while additionally providing important social commentary. A scholar's personal image can be developed and maintained through Twitter, and eventually it can be used to build and promote his or her professional image. Through Twitter, scholars connect to others within their fields and serve as a bridge to connect their students to others interested in similar topics. Twitter then enables the bridging of multiple social networks, because scholars are able to share content from their own sites with a broader audience than their sites would usually be able to reach. Scholars' "networked participation is a complex and multifaceted human activity where personal and professional identities blend, and where participatory digital practices meet individual reflections, fragmented updates, and social interaction" (Veletsianos, 2012, p. 345).

Evidence has shown that when scholars and students alike focus on sharing professional work on social media, it leads to positive career outcomes. Social technologies can then be used to create professional networks, which will enable building social capital that can support and facilitate career development while sharing with a broader audience. Because it is no longer acceptable to not have an online presence, student affairs professionals will need to practice promoting their online image as professionals, and using social media is the ideal way to do so. The appropriate use of social media can be used to showcase their skills, literacy, and professional interests. Communication skills will inherently be highlighted when it is demonstrated that the person is able to communicate easily and fluidly within his or her area of expertise and across institutions. Information literacy can be illustrated by the evaluation of shared content with a critical eye and thereby only sharing content that has passed quality screening. Collaboration skills can be demonstrated quite simply by highlighting how student affairs professionals work with others within their networks; then they will be able to showcase their technology skills by demonstrating the creative way that they use technology.

Other Aspects of Social Media and Student Affairs Practice

"It is becoming clear that the Internet is not destroying community but is resonating with and extending the types of networked community that have already become prevalent in the developed Western world" (Wellman, 2001, p. 2032). It is clear that even though the concept of social media, as it is known today, is a more recent phenomenon, the Internet itself has been used for social connections since its inception. Because this drive for connection has always been present, and will outlive our current idea of social networks, what will be coming next?

Social media have enabled us to establish connections that in the past would have been nearly impossible. Now people can meet and know each other solely in an online environment but never meet face-to-face. However, this form of interaction can lead to issues as well. Society keeps moving along the social media adoption curve and new tensions can arise along the entire path. Social media are becoming a massive driving force throughout the world, but in many schools and K–12 environments almost all technology use by students in school is banned. This philosophy frames social media from the adult normative perspective and does not coincide with youths' lived experiences. Most news stories and reporters focus on the negative aspects of social media, because that appears to be the topic that appeals to the lowest common denominator. Because reporters are not scientists, they have no desire to seek evidence that might contradict the theory they believe; moreover, they have little or no concept of how to judge the scientific merit of any of the stories they are reporting.

It is important to look for contradicting information. Confirmation bias is the tendency to dismiss ideas that go against preexisting beliefs, which makes it simpler to stick with a worldview that a person may already possess and less likely to seek out disconfirming evidence. If the concept one holds is that social media is a "bad" thing, then are we willingly allowing ourselves and our children to engage in a negative activity on a daily basis even though these technologies are woven into the fabric of everyday life and are promoted by the same news sources that are denouncing them? Student affairs professionals do not have the choice to go with the flow; they must search for and engage in personal and professional soul-searching to help support and challenge their students. All of the aspects about social media are not positive; however, if students are approached from an adult normative perspective instead of the youth normative perspective, student affairs educators will be unable to communicate with the students effectively.

Student affairs professionals need to understand how the technologies around them are being used by students in terms of what is normative and beneficial and how some technologies can and do hurt the students. Their overarching goal should be to help students with the positive aspects of technology while minimizing the negative impacts. "Only by understanding the biases of the media through which we engage with the world can we differentiate between what we intend, and what the machines we're using intend for us—whether they or their programmers even know it" (Rushkoff, 2010, p. 21). Knowing where to spend one's energy is crucial; not every new social medium is going to become Facebook or Twitter. However, if student affairs educators engage with students only from their adult perspective, they might miss out on what the youth are using and how it aids in their psychosocial development. Social media can be used by student affairs to promote informal learning, but only if the student affairs officers themselves are aware of the methods that can be used.

Retaining accountability in the ever-changing world of social media is a difficult and challenging prospect but one that is key to maintaining relevancy in our students' lives. Some websites enable users to vote when other users do "good." An example of this practice is DailyFeats, which enables users to give other users badges when they have done well. The badges are aggregated into an overall "life score." These badges help people to stay accountable to themselves, and it adds value to their credibility because it demonstrates the goals that they have set and then achieved and also indicates how long it took for them to achieve those goals. With the shift into the virtual realm, a person's value within an area is becoming more measured by the real-world impact on one's colleagues and fellow scholars. In the long term these scores could become adopted by multiple companies, which could enable companies to see the real-world impact that employees have on their company, rather than basing judgments about employees on their title within a company.

In order to promote the goals of the student affairs profession, professionals need to develop a social currency that will encourage users to promote their brand. Social currency can move social initiatives and campaigns beyond basic marketing to affecting and changing people's lives. By increasing the social currency of student affairs, students will benefit because they will participate more in social platforms and use more social technologies. Social currency at its core is another way for students to engage with the world around them, so it should be used as another way for student affairs to assist students.

An important thing to consider moving forward is which forms of social media are important to use and which are unimportant for student affairs. Facebook, Twitter, Instagram, and LinkedIn are almost necessities, but should there be others that can encourage students to participate in events on campus? Accountability is not a lofty goal; it just calls for scientific rigor and for supporting evidence for new modes of education. Other institutions—such as Harvard and Berkeley—are constantly trying new things such as massive open online courses (MOOCS), and the incorporation and integration of the validated and working methods along with new methods to try is the key to success.

The classroom of the future might be nearly unrecognizable today. A movement that is gaining momentum is called *flipping the classroom,* in which the content is delivered outside of the classroom—through technologies—and work conducted through active learning occurs inside the classroom. The idea of lectures is going by the wayside and will be replaced by a more interactive format. If this movement manages to take hold, the classroom of the future could become a highly engaging space, where vigorous conversations and debates are encouraged while students collaborate, communicate, and build a sense of community with their classmates. With the induction of social media into the mainstream classroom, student expectations are likely to shift. More faculty members might use social media as a replacement for the current discussion platforms (that is, learning and course management systems), and Twitter could be used to extend classroom discussions while enabling students to build a community, as well as including other technologies in novel ways to promote positive student outcomes.

Conclusion

Student affairs practitioners will need to use social media to an even greater extent in the near future, and with time there will come more ingenious ways to use social media in their efforts. More rigorous examination on the use of social media likely will occur, which will enable dissemination of better techniques that have been scientifically tried and tested. Because student affairs individuals are in a unique position of being able to use geolocation data to actively engage students, new methods using such data can be developed to accomplish this important activity. The future is an exciting prospect with so many current opportunities to increase student involvement and development, and these opportunities should continue to expand as the technology available evolves. Using social media properly will help those working in the field of student affairs to grow in previously unthought-of ways and will enable us to assist our students more thoroughly.

Discussion Questions

1. There are six main types of social media listed within this chapter: social networks, bookmarking sites, social news services, media-sharing websites, microblogging, and blogs themselves. Is this list all-encompassing? Which other sites and services might you include in your own definition of social media?

2. Is the Internet really a dangerous place, or is this an idea perpetuated by popular media outlets? Many people have referred to the Internet now as being in the Wild West of our time. Why would it be seen this way?

3. What new interventions might you implement using current technology that can help you promote student development and psychological outcomes?

4. Which social media sites and services are congruent with your personal style? Which ones do you feel are best suited for the ways in which you want to connect with students?

5. What are some arguments for and against the use of social media in student affairs?

6. How can current calls for accountability be answered through the use of social media? How might social media help you automatize such data collection and assessment?

References

Adler, P. S., & Kwon, S. W. (2000). Social capital: The good, the bad, and the ugly. In E.Lesser (Ed.), *Knowledge and social capital: Foundations and applications* (pp. 89–115). Boston: Butterworth-Heinemann.

Alarcon, G. M. (2011). A meta-analysis of burnout with job demands, resources, and attitudes. *Journal of Vocational Behavior, 79*(2), 549–562.

Bährer-Kohler, S. (2013). *Burnout for experts: Prevention in the context of living and working.* New York: Springer.

Belfield, C., & Crosta, P. M. (2012). *Predicting success in college: The importance of placement tests and high school transcripts.* Retrieved Sept. 16, 2015, from http://hdl.handle.net/10022/AC:P:13086

Blood, R. (2000, Sept. 7). *Weblogs: A history and perspective.* Retrieved Sept. 16, 2015, from http://www.rebeccablood.net/essays/weblog_history.html

Burke, M., Kraut, R., & Marlow, C. (2011). Social capital on Facebook: Differentiating uses and users. *Proceedings of the SIGCHI Conference on Human Factors in Computing Systems* (pp. 571–580). New York: ACM.

Burke, R. J., Noblet, A. J., & Cooper, C. L. (2013). *Human resource management in the public sector.* New Horizons in Management Series. Northampton, MA: Edward Elgar.

Chickering, A. W., & Reisser, L. (1993). *Education and identity* (2nd ed.). San Francisco: Jossey-Bass.

Choney, S. (2010). Facebook use can lower grades by 20 percent, study says. *NBC News.* Retrieved August 24, 2015, from http://www.nbcnews.com/id/39038581/ns/technology_and_science-back_to_school/t/facebook-use-can-lower-grades-percent-study-says/

Chowdhury, A. (2013). Is Facebook leading to narcissist outlook? *CoolAge.* Retrieved Aug. 24, 2015, from http://www.coolage.in/2013/05/13/is-facebook-leading-to-narcissist-outlook-top-3/

DeAndrea, D. C., Ellison, N. B., LaRose, R., Steinfield, C., & Fiore, A. (2011). Serious social media: On the use of social media for improving students' adjustment to college. *The Internet and Higher Education, 15*(1), 15–23.

De Vise, D. (2012, March 16). *College accountability: A closer look.* Retrieved Sept. 4, 2015, from https://www.washingtonpost.com/blogs/college-inc/post/college-accountability-a-closer-look/2012/03/16/gIQAECG7GS_blog.html

Ellison, N. B., Steinfield, C., & Lampe, C. (2007). The benefits of Facebook "friends": Social capital and college students' use of online social network sites. *Journal of Computer-Mediated Communication, 12*(4), 1143–1168.

Ellison, N. B., Steinfield, C., & Lampe, C. (2011). Connection strategies: Social capital implications of Facebook-enabled communication practices. *New Media & Society, 13*(6), 873–892.

Ellison, N. B., Vitak, J., Gray, R., & Lampe, C. (2014). Cultivating social resources on social network sites: Facebook relationship maintenance behaviors and their role in social capital processes. *Journal of Computer-Mediated Communication, 19*(4), 855–870.

Erikson, E. H. (1968). *Identity: Youth and crisis.* New York: Norton.

Finkelhor, D. (2008). *Childhood victimization: Violence, crime, and abuse in the lives of young people.* Oxford, UK: Oxford University Press.

Foot, K. (2014, Aug.). The online emergence of pushback on social media in the United States: A historical discourse analysis. *International Journal of Communication,* pp. 1313–1342.

Gasser, U., Cortesi, S., Malik, M., & Lee, A. (2012). *Youth and digital media: From credibility to information quality.* Berkman Center for Internet & Society. Retrieved Sept. 16, 2015, from http://ssrn.com/abstract=2005272

Gayle, D. (2013). Facebook is the worst social network for bullying with 19-year-old BOYS the most common victims. *Daily Mail.* Retrieved Aug. 24, 2015, from http://www.dailymail.co.uk/sciencetech/article-2294023/Facebook-worst-social-network-bullying-New-survey-shows-youngsters-targeted-online-else.html

Grahl, T. (2015). *The 6 types of social media.* Retrieved Aug. 15, 2015, from http://timgrahl.com/the-6-types-of-social-media/

Heiberger, G., & Harper, R. (2008). Have you Facebooked Astin lately? Using technology to increase student involvement. In R. Junco & D. M. Timm (Eds.), *Using emerging technologies to enhance student engagement* (New Directions for Student Services, no. 124, pp. 19–35). San Francisco: Jossey-Bass.

Helliwell, J. F., & Putnam, R. D. (2004). The social context of well-being. *Philosophical Transactions of the Royal Society of London, 359*(1449), 1435–1446.

Jimenez, F. (2013). Social envy—Study finds Facebook causes depression and isolation. *World Crunch.* Retrieved Aug. 24, 2015, from http://www.worldcrunch.com/culture-society/social-envy-study-finds-facebook-causes-depression-and-isolation/zuckerberg-social-network-health-depression-fb/c3s10718/

Journaling a tool for writers. (2007, Aug. 13). *Washington Times.* Retrieved Sept. 16, 2015, from http://www.washingtontimes.com/news/2007/aug/13/journaling-32a-tool-for-writers/

Junco, R. (2013). Comparing actual and self-reported measures of Facebook use. *Computers in Human Behavior, 29*(3), 626–631.

Junco, R. (2014). *Engaging students through social media: Evidence-based practices for use in student affairs.* San Francisco: Jossey-Bass.

Junco, R., & Clem, C. (2015). Predicting course outcomes with digital textbook usage data. *The Internet and Higher Education, 27,* 54–63.

Junco, R., Heiberger, G., & Loken, E. (2011). The effect of Twitter on college student engagement and grades. *Journal of Computer Assisted Learning, 27*(2), 119–132.

Junco, R., & Mastrodicasa, J. (2007). *Connecting to the net generation: What higher education professionals need to know about today's students.* Washington, DC: NASPA.

Kaplan, A. M., & Haenlein, M. (2010). Users of the world, unite! The challenges and opportunities of social media. *Business Horizons, 53*(1), 59–68.

Kroger, J. (2008). Identity development during adolescence. In G. R. Adams & M. D. Berzonsky (Eds.), *Blackwell handbook of adolescence* (pp. 205–226). Oxford, UK: Blackwell.

Paul, P. (2012, Jan. 21). Cracking teenagers' online codes. *New York Times.* Retrieved Aug. 24, 2015, from http://www.nytimes.com/2012/01/22/fashion/danah-boyd-cracking-teenagers-online-codes.html

Pew Internet. (2015, April 1). U.S. smartphone use in 2015. Retrieved Aug. 24, 2015, from http://www.pewinternet.org/2015/04/01/us-smartphone-use-in-2015/

Reeves, T. C. (1998). The impact of media and technology in schools. *A research report prepared for the Bertelsmann Foundation.* Retrieved, Aug 24, 2015, from https://www.researchgate.net/profile/T_Reeves/publication/237429044_The_Impact_of_Media_and_Technology_in_Schools_A_Research_Report_prepared_for_The_Bertelsmann_Foundation/links/004635331a32c56d65000000.pdf

Richards, D., & Viganó, N. (2013). Online counseling: A narrative and critical review of the literature. *Journal of Clinical Psychology, 69*(9), 994–1011.

Richmond, S. (2009, Jan. 22). What is a blog? How the technology shapes the medium. *Telegraph Blogs.* Retrieved Sept. 16, 2015. blogs.telegraph.co.uk/technology/shanerichmond/8173527/What_is_a_blog_How_the_technology_shapes_the_medium/

Ringstaff, C., & Kelley, L. (2002). *The learning return on our educational technology investment: A review of findings from research.* San Francisco: WestEd.

Rushkoff, D. (2010). *Program or be programmed: Ten commands for a digital age.* New York: Or Books.

Schuh, J. H., & Gansemer-Topf, A. M. (2010). The role of student affairs in student learning assessment. *NILOA Occasional Paper, 7,* 1–14.

Social media, social life: How teens view their digital lives. (2012, June 26). Retrieved Sept.16, 2015, from https://www.commonsensemedia.org/research/social-media-social-life-how-teens-view-their-digital-lives#

Swider, B. W., & Zimmerman, R. D. (2010). Born to burnout: A metaanalytic path model of personality, job burnout, and work outcomes. *Journal of Vocational Behavior, 76*(3), 487–506.

Tinto, V. (1993). *Leaving college: Rethinking the causes and cures of student attrition* (2nd ed.). Chicago: The University of Chicago Press.

United Nations. (2011, May 16). *Report of the special rapporteur on the promotion and protection of the right to freedom of opinion and expression, Frank La Rue.* Retrieved Aug. 24, 2015, from http://www2.ohchr.org/english/bodies/hrcouncil/docs/17session/A.HRC.17.27_en.pdf

Veletsianos, G. (2012). Higher education scholars' participation and practices on Twitter. *Journal of Computer Assisted Learning, 28*(4), 336–349.

Ward, T. H. (2010). *Social network site use and student retention at a four-year private university.* Doctoral dissertation. The Claremont Graduate University, Claremont, CA.

Wellman, B. (2001). Computer networks as social networks. *Science, 293*(5537), 2031–2034.

Yu, A. Y., Tian, S. W., Vogel, D., & Kwok, R. C.-W. (2010). Can learning be virtually boosted? An investigation of online social networking impacts. *Computers & Education, 55,* 1495–1503.

CHAPTER 21

ACADEMIC AND STUDENT AFFAIRS PARTNERSHIPS

Elizabeth J. Whitt

Only when everyone on campus—particularly academic affairs and student affairs staff—shares the responsibility for student learning will we be able to make significant progress in improving it.

AAHE, ACPA, AND NASPA

Not all partnerships are virtuous.

KATHLEEN MANNING, JILLIAN KINZIE, AND JOHN H. SCHUH

Both of the chapter-opening quotes—one asserting that academic and student affairs collaborations are necessary for fostering student learning and the other a caveat about such collaborations—are relevant to the topic of creating and sustaining academic and student affairs partnerships. This chapter examines the context for calls for such partnerships, considers evidence of their advantages and disadvantages, and offers some practical suggestions for academic and student affairs staff members and leaders who seek to form effective partnerships for student learning. Offering advice to leaders facing complex and unpredictable challenges within and outside their organizations, psychologist Karl Weick said, "Refuse to simplify reality . . . [and] leap while looking" (as cited in Coutu, 2003, pp. 86,88). A similar request is appropriate for the reader of this chapter: do not approach this text seeking a recipe for creating academic

This chapter is based on the substantial contributions of Becki Elkins Nesheim, Melanie Guentzel, Angela Kellogg, William McDonald, and Cynthia Wells.

and student affairs partnership programs or simple answers to questions about how to create and sustain effective partnerships. Do approach it with a sense of your context and culture and how they might influence using the information provided here to facilitate partnerships on your campus.

Partnerships for Learning

Critiques from outside and within the academy have been a consistent feature of the landscape of higher education in the United States for more than three decades (see also AAC, AASCU, & APLU, 2015; AAC&U, 2002; ACPA, 1994; Blumenstyk, 2015; Byrne, 2006; Carey, 2015; Craig, 2015; NASULGC, 1997, 1999, 2000; Study Group on the Conditions of Excellence in American Higher Education, 1984; US Department of Education, 2006). Themes from these critiques have been consistent: increasing costs and declining funding, inadequate responses to shifting student (and national) demographics, new competitive economic demands, complex technological advancements, globalization, and increasing public skepticism that colleges and universities provide a quality return on investment. Yet, in the second decade of the twenty-first century, challenges to American higher education seem to be more insistent and more consequential than ever: "Higher education is most assuredly in crisis . . . A restless reform movement, inspired by the promise of new technology and backed by powerful political and financial might, is growing more insistent that the enterprise spend less, show better results, and become more open to new kinds of educational providers" (Blumenstyk, 2015, p. 2).

At the same time, the importance of higher education increases as undergraduate education verges on a "requirement of a fully expressed citizenship" in contemporary society (Shapiro, 2005, p. 8). In a 2009 address to the Congress, President Barack Obama called on every American "to commit to at least one year or more of higher education or career training . . . But whatever the training may be, every American will need to get more than a high school diploma . . . That is why we will provide the support necessary for you to complete college and meet a new goal: by 2020, America will once again have the highest proportion of college graduates in the world" (Speech to the Joint Houses of Congress, February 24, 2009).

Five years later, President Obama announced "an ambitious new agenda" (The White House, 2013) to widen access to higher education by increasing affordability. This agenda was aimed at increasing institutional accountability for successful student outcomes by, among other things, establishing a ratings system that was intended to tie federal financial aid to institutional performance (for example, graduation rates, community college transfer rates, earnings of graduates, student debt, and enrollment rates of low-income students) (Blumenstyk, 2015).

Among the perceived barriers to achieving the purposes of higher education is fragmentation of campuses and curricula. For many years, reformers have charged that colleges and universities have become too divided by organizational structure, disciplinary priorities, and competing missions to educate students effectively. "The lack of good integration . . . of the intellectual and social, emotional, physical, and spiritual dimensions of students . . . undermines real, rigorous learning and obstructs the achievement of desired learning goals" (Keeling & Hersh, 2011, p. 66).

Indeed, research on college impact is unequivocal: student success (learning, development, persistence) is associated with seamless learning environments, which are characterized by coherent educational purposes and comprehensive policies and practices designed to achieve those purposes (Kuh, 2008; Kuh, Kinzie, Schuh, Whitt, & Associates, 2005/2010; Kuh & O'Donnell, 2013; Pascarella & Terenzini, 1991, 2005).

Research on the impact of college also points to student engagement as the primary means by which students learn, develop, and persist to graduation (Kuh & others, 2005/2010; Pascarella & Terenzini, 1991, 2005). Engagement has two key components: (1) the amount of time and effort students put into their studies and other education-related activities and (2) the allocation of institutional resources for services and learning opportunities that encourage students to participate in and benefit from such activities (Astin, 1993; Kuh & others, 2005/2010; Pascarella & Terenzini, 1991, 2005). Summarizing thirty years of research on college impact, Pascarella and Terenzini (2005) noted that "the greatest impact [of college] appears to stem from students' total level of campus engagement, particularly when academic, interpersonal, and extracurricular involvements are mutually reinforcing. [Therefore], the holistic nature of learning suggests a clear need to rethink and restructure highly segmented departmental and program configurations" (p. 647).

Partnership programs between academic and student affairs units have been advocated as one means to create seamless learning environments and foster student engagement. Academic and student affairs partnerships have the potential to create such environments by calling on those who work most closely with students—in class and out of class and in curricular, cocurricular, and extracurricular activities—to collaborate in designing, implementing, and improving student learning.

The benefits of academic and student affairs partnerships for addressing concerns about fragmentation and effective undergraduate education have been extolled widely and repeatedly in student affairs literature for many years (AAHE, ACPA, & NASPA, 1998; Arcelus, 2011; Blimling, Whitt, & Associates, 1999; Cook & Lewis, 2007; Engstrom, 2004, 2008; Kezar, 2001, 2003; Kuh & Banta, 2000; Kuh & others, 2005/2010; Kuh, Schuh, Whitt, & Associates, 1991; Manning, Kinzie, & Schuh, 2014; National Association of Student Personnel Administrators [NASPA] & American College Personnel Association [ACPA], 2004; Schroeder, 1999a, 1999b, 2004; Schuh & Whitt, 1999). In 2007, for example, Cook and Lewis compared fully developed academic and student affairs partnerships to Dante's ninth circle of heaven and asserted that "student affairs leaders tend to be collaborators and risk takers by nature" (p. 167).

Two aspects of most of this body of literature—with a few exceptions (for example, Kezar, 2001, 2003; Kuh & Banta, 2000; Kuh & others, 1991,

2005/2010; Manning, Kinzie, & Schuh, 2014)—are notable for our purposes. First, the literature is mainly exhortative rather than based on research; most assertions about the effectiveness of partnerships for learning are made without reference to empirical evidence. Second, it seems to assume that partnerships between academic and students affairs are—almost always and almost everywhere—an appropriate response to challenges in facilitating undergraduate success. One could argue that academic and student affairs partnerships have become an all-purpose response to a wide variety of campus issues and student concerns, an end—"Let's create a partnership"—rather than a means—"Let's address our students' needs for meaningful community involvement by a sustained programmatic collaboration between academic and student affairs" (Bourassa & Kruger, 2001; Kezar, 2001; Kezar & Lester, 2009; Magolda, 2005). The next section provides a brief overview of the limited research about academic and student affairs partnerships.

Research about Academic and Student Affairs Partnerships

This section provides an overview of research about partnerships between academic and student affairs units and personnel. Specific foci of the overview include a discussion about the benefits of, and challenges to, developing such partnerships.

Benefits of Partnerships

As noted, many examples of the value of academic and student affairs partnerships are based on anecdote and hope rather than on evidence. A considerable body of literature has emerged, however, on how partnerships are enacted (that is, how they are created and maintained, rather than how they influence student success). Although most of this work is based on descriptions—rather than studies—of examples of partnerships, when examined holistically, it illustrates some of the salient issues that partnerships are intended to address, including improving student access and retention, providing evidence of learning outcomes, coping with financial constraints, and meeting the needs of changing student populations. Examples of the uses of partnerships include assessment and research on students (Gansemer-Topf & Tietjen, 2015; Kuh & Banta, 2000); early academic warning systems (Kuh, & others, 2005/2010; Schroeder, 1999a, 1999b); first-year experiences (Kezar, 2001, 2003; Rieske & Benjamin, 2015; Schroeder, Minor, & Tarkow, 1999); learning communities (Engstrom, 2004, 2008; Fink & Hummel, 2015; Inkelas & Weisman, 2003; Pike, 1999); service-learning (Jacoby, 1999); and sexual assault prevention (Yeater, Miltenberger, Laden, Ellis, & O'Donohue, 2001).

One of few examples of research focused on the creation of academic and student affairs partnerships was a national study conducted by Kezar (2001, 2003). Her survey in 2000 of senior student affairs officers asked about the role of student affairs in collaboration; structural models facilitating collaboration;

successful strategies for collaboration; and obstacles to, and outcomes of, collaboration. The respondents to the survey noted that collaborative initiatives were occurring on each of their campuses and identified cooperation, student affairs attitudes, common goals, and personalities as important factors in creating effective partnerships. These data provided insights into the use and success of cultural and structural strategies in developing and maintaining academic and student affairs partnerships. Cultural strategies included cross-institutional dialogue, staff development, common vision development, common language development, communication strategies, cooperation, faculty member attitudes, personalities, redefining mission, student affairs attitudes, and generating enthusiasm. Structural strategies included combined fiscal resources, changes in promotion and tenure requirements, reassignment of duties, modified reward systems, and changes in alignments and expectations within units. The student affairs leaders involved in the study preferred cultural strategies but asserted that structural strategies were similarly effective. Kezar (2003) concluded that partnership development was complex, multifaceted, and somewhat context dependent.

Moreover, recent research on educational effectiveness has fueled the notion that forming partnerships might be a productive strategy. For example, the Documenting Effective Educational Practices (DEEP) project, a comprehensive study of educationally effective colleges and universities (Kuh & others, 2005/2010), identified six conditions common to these institutions. One of those conditions was shared responsibility for educational quality and student success. The authors noted, "The collaborative spirit and positive attitude that characterize DEEP campuses are evident in the quality of working relationships enjoyed by academic affairs, which operate on many other campuses as functional silos" (Kuh & others, 2005/2010, p. 172).

Among the examples used to highlight the importance of shared responsibility for student success on DEEP campuses was the first-year experience (FYE) initiatives at Miami University (OH), which were described by Miami community members as founded on a shared commitment to undergraduate student success. Student life staff members at Miami were commended for their role in implementing that commitment through their belief that "their fundamental mission is the intellectual mission of the university, and student life programs and policies emphasize intellectual growth and challenge" (Kuh & others, 2005/2010, p. 165). Partnerships might, therefore, have a positive impact on learning and the educational climate.

Not All Partnerships Are Virtuous

Although the results of an academic and student affairs partnership might be positive, and although the intentions of parties entering into an academic and student affairs partnership are generally honorable, partners face many challenges to developing and sustaining an effective partnership. Partnerships can fail as a result of competing assumptions about student learning (Kezar, 2001; Schroeder, 2004), as well as differing cultural assumptions of faculty and staff members (Arnold & Kuh, 1999; Kuh & Whitt, 1988; Magolda, 2005).

The historical separation within colleges and universities between the formal curriculum, provided by faculty members, who address the in-class cognitive development of students, and the informal curriculum, provided by student affairs professionals responsible for the out-of-class and psychosocial development of students, has also contributed to the barriers that limit collaboration (Manning & others, 2014). Enhancing these difficulties are organizational characteristics of institutions of higher education, including distinct governance structures for academic and student affairs (Kezar & Lester, 2009).

This historical focus on separate aspects of student life has enabled the formation of divergent perspectives on student learning. Amid calls to bridge the gaps between academic affairs and student affairs, and to refocus their mutual work as educators on student learning, these divisions continue (Keeling & Hersh, 2011; Manning, Kinzie, & Schuh, 2014; NASPA & ACPA, 2004; Task Force on the Future of Student Affairs, 2010; Tinto, 2012).

In a 2005 *About Campus* article about academic and student affairs partnerships, Peter Magolda queried, "Is collaboration inherently a good deed?" (p. 17). He answered his question, in part, by noting, "I remain unconvinced that all such efforts to reorganize the way individuals and offices work together are worthwhile. 'Just because' does not meet the prima facie test" (p. 17). In Magolda's view, the "all-important question [is] 'Is collaboration a good idea?'" (p. 17). He asserted that academic and student affairs partnerships have, instead, become "a bandwagon . . . because it is fashionable and sounds right, [adopted] often without purposefully and carefully considering whether a particular partnership has merit" (p. 17).

Kezar and Lester (2009) posed a similar question: "Is collaboration always necessary?" Their answer was no. "There is nothing worse than people forcing collaboration on a situation that simply does not require it" (p. 7).

Boyer Partnership Assessment Project

As noted, research about the effectiveness of academic and student affairs partnerships is in its infancy. Whereas literature advocating their use—even asserting their benefits—is easy to find, research about the extent to which they are "a good idea," and in what forms, under what circumstances, in what ways, and for which students, is scarce. Little empirical guidance exists for persons or institutions interested in deciding if a partnership program is a good idea in their particular contexts. The promise of partnerships is clear but empirically grounded, comprehensive assessment of the outcomes of specific partnership programs—for students, educators, and institutions—is required. The Boyer Partnership Assessment Project sought to address this need.

The Boyer Partnership Assessment Project (BPAP) was a Fund for the Improvement of Postsecondary Education (FIPSE)–funded study coordinated by the Ernest L. Boyer Center at Messiah College and conducted by the author of and contributors to this chapter. The study used qualitative research methods to examine academic and student affairs partnership programs at eighteen institutions: four community colleges and fourteen four-year institutions, including six public universities, three private universities, and five private colleges (see the following list). Types of partnership programs represented were first-year transitions, service-learning and community service, living-learning communities, academic support, interdisciplinary courses, cultural programming, and leadership development.

Boyer Partnership Assessment Project Institutional Participants

- Barnard College (NY): In-Residence Seminar
- Brevard Community College (FL): Center for Service Learning
- Carson-Newman College (TN): Boyer Laboratory for Learning
- DePaul University (IL): Chicago Quarter
- DePauw University (IN): DePauw Year One
- George Mason University (VA): New Century College
- Messiah College (PA): External Programs
- North Carolina State University: First-Year College Living-Learning Community
- Portland Community College, Cascade Campus (OR): Multicultural Awareness Council
- Prince George's Community College (MD): Developmental Math Program
- Saint Mary's College (CA): Catholic Institute for Lasallian Social Action
- Siena College (NY): Franciscan Center for Service and Advocacy
- University of Arizona: Faculty Fellows and Student-Faculty Interaction Grants
- University of Maryland: College Park Scholars
- University of Missouri: Freshman Interest Groups
- Villanova University (PA): Villanova Experience
- Virginia Tech University: Residential Leadership Community
- William Rainey Harper College (IL): Learning Communities

Data were collected via site visits to each institution by teams of researchers (Whitt & others, 2008). The primary data-collection method was individual and group interviews with institutional and partnership program leaders as well as student and faculty and staff member program participants. We also reviewed relevant institutional documents and attended program events. Following each site visit, we prepared a detailed report of the partnership program. To ensure trustworthiness (Lincoln & Guba, 1985; Merriam, 1998), we sent the initial site report to the institution for wide distribution and review. These reports formed the basis for inductive analysis of data across the sites.

We began this research with the goal of discovering and describing the elements of effective partnership programs. Could we identify practices common to these programs? Did they, in fact, create seamless learning environments? What learning, what outcomes—for students, for educators, for institutions— occurred as a result of the partnership programs? What, as we looked across our sample, accounted for those positive outcomes? And what might others take from these elements in thinking about creating effective partnership programs? The following sections offer brief responses to these questions about student outcomes and common—what we called "good"—practices.

Student Outcomes

The BPAP research yielded information and insights about outcomes of partnership programs for students, educators, and institutions. Detailed descriptions of these outcomes and the conditions associated with them are provided elsewhere (Elkins Nesheim, Guentzel, Kellogg, Whitt, & Wells, 2006; Elkins Nesheim, Guentzel, McDonald, Wells, & Whitt, 2007; Wells, Kellogg, Elkins Nesheim, Guentzel, McDonald, & Whitt, 2007). What follows is a brief summary of the results about partnership program outcomes for students (Elkins Nesheim & others, 2007).

As a result of involvement in the BPAP partnership programs, students became acclimated to college life and to their particular colleges or universities and engaged in meaningful ways in a variety of academic and nonacademic experiences. Participation in the programs facilitated students' adjustment to the academic and social demands of postsecondary education, in part by helping students acquire the sense that they were important members of a community of students and faculty and staff members. Participation also facilitated involvement in educationally purposeful activities on and off campus, which also assisted in acclimation to college. Effective transitions, in turn, facilitated persistence.

Perhaps most important, involvement in partnership programs yielded a wide range of learning outcomes, encompassing curricular and cocurricular experiences as well as in-class and out-of-class endeavors. Educators and students noted a variety of student learning outcomes, including helping students to (1) make connections between in-class and out-of-class experiences, (2) think critically, and (3) understand themselves and others.

Students involved in freshman interest groups (FIGs) at the University of Missouri, for example, noted that "what happened on the floor tied into every aspect of your life" and commented that FIGs include "all the aspects of what directly affect your life once you come to college—where you live and your classes" (personal communication). The FIGs also provided an academic foundation for student interactions in the dorm. A hall coordinator said, "I hear them in the bathrooms in the morning talking about what they had to do for class that day . . . It's really neat."

Good Practices for Academic and Student Affairs Partnerships

One of the purposes of the BPAP was to identify good practices in academic and student affairs partnerships. To do so, we analyzed data across the sites inductively. At the end of this process, we had identified seven "good practices" and created operational definitions of each that were consistent with and reflected the weight of evidence from the eighteen sites. Note that we do not characterize these as "best practices." One of the overarching results of the study was an emphasis on the significance of institutional context in determining whether particular approaches to creating and sustaining partnerships were effective. To describe a practice as "best" is to assert its usefulness across contexts, an assertion that cannot be accurate when it comes to academic and student affairs partnerships. What follows, then, is a brief description of good partnership practices, based on the BPAP study (more information can be found in Whitt & others, 2008).

1. **Good practice for partnership programs reflects and advances the institution's mission.** Effective partnership programs are grounded in and extend the institution's mission in their purpose, design, implementation, and assessment. In the process, the partnership programs demonstrate and enhance institutional commitments to students and their learning. The importance of clear connections between institutional mission and institutional policies, practices, and programs for creating educationally effective opportunities for students has been well established in other research about college impact (see Kuh & others, 1991, 2005/2010; Pascarella & Terenzini, 2005; Tinto, 2012).

At the time of the BPAP, the mission of George Mason University (GMU), a public research university in Virginia, focused on interdisciplinary research and teaching and the restructuring of the institution interdisciplinarity required. One example of GMU's commitment to interdisciplinary teaching and rethinking traditional structures was New Century College, an interdisciplinary academic unit that integrated academics with experiential learning focused on real-world challenges. An academic administrator at GMU commented that, as the research mission of the institution expanded, "[our] challenge is to make sure that we continue to develop emphases on and rewards for-high quality and innovative teaching . . . New Century fits solidly in here. They contribute greatly to our educational climate" (personal communication).

2. **Good practice for partnership programs embodies and fosters a learning-oriented ethos.** Effective partnership programs foster learning, in and out of classrooms, in formal and informal settings, and for students as well as educators. This principle from the BPAP echoes Schroeder's (2004) assertion that effective partnerships focus on things that matter to the partners and to the institution, including student success. Florida's Brevard Community College (renamed Eastern Florida State College in 2012) developed the Center for Service Learning (CSL) in 1988 to involve students systematically in educational and public service experiences. The mission of CSL was to make service an integral part of students' educational experiences and to prepare students to be lifelong learners, responsible community members, and productive citizens. Service activities were credit- and non-credit-bearing and aimed to link community service and academic study.

3. **Good practice for partnership programs builds on and nurtures relationships.** Effective partnerships grow out of existing relationships between and among academic and student affairs professionals. Such relationships—often based on mutual interests or shared experiences—cross organizational

and cultural boundaries to blur distinctions between academic and student affairs. In every case, the partnership programs we studied evolved from informal and formal relationships based on common interests. This underscores the importance of taking advantage of existing relationships, rather than starting from scratch with strangers, in creating partnerships.

Relationships were essential to the success of the Developmental Math Program at Prince George's Community College in Maryland. Counselors from the College's Student Development and Counseling Office were paired with faculty members who taught developmental mathematics. An advisor described her partnership with a faculty colleague: "We were cooperating right from the very beginning. He comes down and gives me a list of students who miss his class . . . I visit class and we've done several workshops with students in class on goal setting, learning styles, study skills, that kind of thing. I see our work as a partnership" (personal communication).

4. Good practice for partnership programs recognizes, understands, and attends to institutional culture. Recognition of the institutional culture in which the partnership program exists is paramount to success. Partnerships comprehended and heeded institutional subcultures, organizational structures, and the unique characteristics of students, faculty and staff members, and administrators. The Multicultural Awareness Council (MAC) at the Cascade Campus of Portland Community College (PCC) in Oregon is a committee of academic and student affairs staff members and students that develops creative programs for student populations typically underserved by campus activities. The council was developed "to create a multicultural event calendar that will honor the diverse cultures, perspectives, and ethnicities of the PCC student body and community"; "to emphasize the immigrant experience in the United States"; and "to provide PCC students, faculty, and staff with a forum to discuss multicultural issues" (personal communication). A number of faculty and staff members and students described the culture of PCC as "a family." One educator affirmed, "We are very tight-knit. We're all part of the Cascade family—it's a culture that's been there since the beginning [requiring] conversations about values and our relationships. When it's nurturing, people want to be together no matter what it takes. People can put up with a lot of stress if they're in a supportive environment" (personal communication). And a student noted that MAC is "a partnership—that's what it is. It brings together the key components of the college, like a marriage" (personal communication).

5. Good practice for partnership programs values and implements assessment. Whether responding to an external funding application or institutional concern, effective partnership programs have a clear understanding of what they intend to accomplish and identify means to evaluate their accomplishments. Multiple assessment strategies and data (for example, participation rates, retention rates, satisfaction, and learning outcomes) are used to guide, alter, and improve the program.

One of the benefits of assessment for Virginia Tech University's Residential Leadership Community (RLC) was its very existence. During one of many rounds of budget cuts, the vice president for student affairs made "an early decision [to] preserve the programs that were most effective." "How did we know [what was effective]? We had assessment processes in place. We knew what we were doing well and we could continue the things we knew we were doing well" (personal communication). The RLC "survived the budget cuts [because] we had evidence of its effectiveness" (personal communication).

6. Good practice for partnership programs uses resources creatively and effectively. Effective partnership programs thrive in resource-rich and resource-limited contexts. They capitalize on existing financial, human, and environmental resources and generate additional resources as necessary. The programs we studied differed in size and resources, but they shared a willingness to think creatively about using resources to support student learning.

One example of this principle in a limited-resource context was the FIG partnership program at the University of Missouri. An administrator noted, "We are right now operating kind of on a budget that we proposed last year for which none of the funds have been allocated. We're kind of running full speed ahead but on empty" (personal communication). It is to the FIG's advantage, then, that it was a relatively inexpensive program to run and had a fairly tight budget from the beginning. One way the program has managed to be "successful on a shoestring" and "both inexpensive and effective" was by establishing partnerships with campus units beyond academic and student affairs. For example, "Campus Dining is another partner that has been supportive. They have provided dining cards for [FIG faculty members] and feed all the FIG students a day early"—that is, a day before the regular dining contract begins for residence hall students (personal communication).

7. Good practice for partnership programs demands and cultivates multiple manifestations of leadership. Effective partnership programs not only require strong organizational leadership but also draw on and foster principles of shared leadership. For example, from the beginning, the Chicago Quarter (CQ) at DePaul University had "the full support of University leaders. They were visionary people who saw that the people involved were really committed" to the program (personal communication). As a consequence, CQ "was very much top-down in its inception." "[Leaders in Liberal Arts] said 'let's go for it.'" Program founders asserted "we were in the right place at the right time. We had all the right people and it was the right thing to do. You can do amazing things with the right combination of people" (personal communication). They also believed it was "unlikely that a program of this scope could come from a grassroots effort." The early leaders "had a collective vision—and authority—that made it practical to go ahead with sweeping change" (personal communication).

Conclusion

We embarked on the Boyer Partnership Assessment Project (BPAP) with the assumption that academic and student affairs partnerships are a good idea. In fact, five years of study and interaction with the partnership program sites taught us that such collaborations can be a wonderful idea, yielding positive outcomes—anticipated and unanticipated—for students, educators, and institutions. At the same time, we have modified our initial assumptions to acknowledge that partnerships are a good idea when they reflect and respect their contexts. In addition, partnerships can be a good idea if they are created for reasons and in ways that serve the interests of students and the partners. Most important, they are a good idea if they are consistent with the partners' individual and collective values about learning and teaching and reflect the cultural contexts of the partnership accurately. To be effective and meaningful, then, collaborations between academic and student affairs should be approached "cautiously, purposefully, and honestly" (Magolda, 2005, p. 21).

To facilitate thinking about how to proceed to use all of this information, this chapter concludes with a few lessons or points for you to ponder. They are offered in the hope that they can be instructive to readers who seek to understand or create effective academic and student affairs collaborations.

- Effective partnerships "grow where they are planted." That is, in collaborations, as in so many other aspects of higher education, context is everything. They cannot be created without clear understanding of their cultural roots, including the cultures of the institution, of academic and student affairs, and of students. A corollary to this lesson follows.
- Effective partnerships require cultural *self*-awareness. Typically, partnership literature focuses on understanding the culture of the partner—the "other"— rather than one's own culture. Magolda (2005, p. 20) noted, however, a ". . . lack of self-awareness is a setup for confusion in the collaboration," because to be an effective partner, one must recognize one's own assumptions, values, norms, and expectations and understand the impact they have on one's approach to partnership. In fact, "as we become socialized to student affairs, we are less and less likely to challenge what we know and believe about students, faculty, our roles, and our institutions (Woodard, Love, & Komives, 2000, p. 18).
- Effective partnerships are in the eye of the beholder. In fact, we found that our understandings of the terms *partnership, academic affairs,* and *student affairs* were meaningless in many of the programs we studied. We abandoned attempts to develop a clear and concise definition of *partnerships* early on as we came to appreciate that partners are engaged in a partnership if they think they are.
- Effective partnerships require some planning, quite a lot of nurturing, and a bit of serendipity. The partners we studied gave a great deal of credit for their success to good timing, risk-taking in the face of unexpected opportunities, and fortuitous relationships. At the same time, they acknowledged that partnerships are hard work. Tending to the health of relationships, assessing whether the partnerships are achieving their goals, sustaining the programs despite and in response to changes and challenges—in all cases, two or more individuals made the partnership and the partnership program a priority for time and effort.

- Effective partnerships do not eliminate politics or territoriality. Deciding to collaborate does not constitute the waving of a magic wand that eliminates messiness and conflict. Instead, deciding to collaborate seems to involve creating a sense of community that includes a willingness to stay present in the partnership and dedicated to its goals, despite conflicts within or external to the partnership.

- Effective partnerships are, in many ways, about belief: belief in shared responsibility and shared effort in improving students' learning as well as belief in the capacity of the participants to create and sustain something meaningful. We found little discussion about equal responsibilities, resources, and credit, or who initiated the partnership. We did, however, find a lot of discussion about the importance of communication, openness to change, and willingness to work hard. We found less attention to management of partnership details than we expected and a lot more attention to inspiration and creativity. One of the BPAP respondents provided a fitting conclusion: "It's just so much fun!"

Discussion Questions

1. What surprised you about the information provided in this chapter? Why? How might you use that surprising information in your work?

2. What lessons can you take from this chapter to assist you in deciding whether partnerships you engage in or anticipate are a good idea? How might you make those partnerships a better idea?

3. Among the lessons from the research cited here is "effective partnerships require cultural self-awareness." When you think about academic and student affairs partnerships in your work, what might cultural self-awareness include? What barriers exist to cultural self-awareness? How might you address those barriers?

4. Another lesson noted here is "effective partnerships bloom where they are planted." What potential exists for effective partnership programs in relationships or initiatives already underway?

References

American Association of Community Colleges (AAC), American Association of State Colleges and Universities (AASCU), & Association of Public and Land-Grant Universities (APLU). (2015). *Advancing a comprehensive study of post-collegiate outcomes.* Washington, DC: Authors.

American Association for Higher Education (AAHE), American College Personnel Association (ACPA), & National Association of Student Personnel Administrators (NASPA). (1998). *Powerful partnerships: A shared responsibility for learning.* Washington, DC: American College Personnel Association.

American College Personnel Association (ACPA). (1994). *The student learning imperative: Implications for student affairs.* Washington, DC: Author.

Arcelus, V. J. (2011). If student affairs-academic affairs collaboration is such a good idea, why are there so few examples of these partnerships in American higher education? In P. M. Magolda & M. B. Baxter Magolda (Eds.), *Contested issues in student affairs: Diverse perspectives and respectful dialogue* (pp. 61–74). Sterling, VA: Stylus.

Arnold, K., & Kuh, G. D. (1999). What matters in undergraduate education? Mental models, student learning and student affairs. In E. J. Whitt (Ed.), *Student learning as student affairs work: Responding to our imperative.* Washington, DC: National Association of Student Personnel Administrators.

Association of American Colleges and Universities (AAC&U). (2002). *Greater expectations: A new vision for learning as a nation goes to college.* Washington, DC: Author.

Astin, A. (1993). *What matters in college? Four critical years revisited.* San Francisco: Jossey-Bass.

Blimling, G. S., Whitt, E. J., & Associates. (1999). *Good practice in student affairs: Principles to foster student learning.* San Francisco: Jossey-Bass.

Blumenstyk, G. (2015). *American higher education in crisis? What everyone needs to know.* New York: Oxford University Press.

Bourassa, D. M., & Kruger, K. (2001). The national dialogue on academic and student affairs collaboration. In A. Kezar, D. J. Hirsch, & C. Burack (Eds.), *Understanding the role of academic and student affairs collaboration in creating a successful learning environment* (New Directions for Higher Education, no. 116, pp. 9–38). San Francisco: Jossey-Bass.

Byrne, J. V. (2006). *Public higher education reform five years after the Kellogg Commission on the Future of State and Land-Grant Universities.* Washington, DC: National Association of State Universities and Land-Grant Colleges and W. K. Kellogg Foundation.

Carey, K. (2015). *The end of college: Creating the future of learning and the university of everywhere.* New York: Riverhead.

Cook, J. H., & Lewis, C. A. (Eds.). (2007). *Student and academic affairs collaboration: The divine comity.* Washington, DC: National Association of Student Personnel Administrators.

Coutu, D. L. (2003). Sense and reliability: A conversation with noted psychologist Karl E. Weick. *Harvard Business Review, 81*(4), 84–90.

Craig, R. (2015). *College disrupted: The great unbundling of higher education.* New York: Palgrave Macmillan.

Elkins Nesheim, B. S., Guentzel, M. J., Kellogg, A. H., McDonald, W. M., Wells, C., & Whitt, E. J. (2007). Outcomes for students of student affairs–academic affairs partnership programs. *Journal of College Student Development, 48*, 435–454.

Elkins Nesheim, B. S., Guentzel, M. J., Kellogg, A. H., Whitt, E. J., & Wells, C. (2006, Nov.). *Outcomes for educators of student and academic affairs partnership programs.* Paper presented at the Annual Meeting of the Association for the Study of Higher Education, Anaheim, CA.

Engstrom, C. M. (2004). The power of faculty–student affairs partnerships for promoting integrative learning experiences in learning communities. In S. N. Hurd & R. Freerman Stein (Eds.), *Building and sustaining learning communities: The Syracuse University experience* (pp. 59–75). Bolton, MA: Anker.

Engstrom, C. M. (2008). Curricular learning communities and unprepared students: How faculty can provide a foundation for success. In J. Braxton (Ed.), *The role of the classroom in college student persistence* (New Directions for Teaching and Learning, no. 115, pp. 5–20). San Francisco: Jossey-Bass.

Fink, J. E., & Hummel, M. L. (2015). With educational benefits for all: Campus inclusion through learning communities designed for underserved student populations. In M. Benjamin (Ed.), *Learning communities from start to finish* (New Directions for Student Services, no. 149, pp. 29–40). San Francisco: Jossey-Bass.

Gansemer-Topf, A., & Tietjen, K. (2015). Assessing the "learning" in learning communities. In M. Benjamin (Ed.), *Learning communities from start to finish* (New Directions for Student Services, no. 149, pp. 79–90). San Francisco: Jossey-Bass.

Inkelas, K., & Weisman, J. L. (2003). Different by design: An examination of student outcomes among participants in three types of living-learning programs. *Journal of College Student Development, 44*(3), 335–368.

Jacoby, B. (1999). Partnerships for service learning. In J. H. Schuh & E. J. Whitt (Eds.), *Creating successful partnerships between academic and student affairs.* (New Directions for Student Services, no. 87, pp. 19–35). San Francisco: Jossey-Bass.

Keeling, R. P., & Hersh, R. H. (2011). *We're losing our minds: Rethinking American higher education.* New York: Palgrave Macmillan.

Kezar, A. (2001). Documenting the landscape: Results of a national study on academic and student affairs collaborations. In A. Kezar, D. J. Hirsch, & C. Burack (Eds.), *Understanding the role of academic and student affairs collaboration in creating a successful learning environment* (New Directions for Higher Education, no. 116, pp. 39–52). San Francisco: Jossey-Bass.

Kezar, A. (2003). Achieving student success: Strategies for creating partnerships between academic and student affairs. *NASPA Journal, 41,* 1–22.

Kezar, A., & Lester, J. (2009). *Organizing higher education for collaboration: A guide for campus leaders.* San Francisco: Jossey-Bass.

Kuh, G. D. (2008). *High-impact educational practices: What they are, who has access to them, and why they matter.* Washington, DC: Association for American Colleges and Universities.

Kuh, G. D., & Banta, T. W. (2000). Faculty–student affairs collaboration on assessment: Lessons from the field. *About Campus, 4*(6), 4–11.

Kuh, G. D., Kinzie, J. I., Schuh, J. H., Whitt, E. J., & Associates. (2005/2010). *Student success in college: Creating conditions that matter.* San Francisco: Jossey-Bass.

Kuh, G. D., & O'Donnell, K. (2013). *Ensuring quality and taking high-impact practices to scale.* Washington, DC: Association for American Colleges and Universities.

Kuh, G. D., Schuh, J. H., Whitt, E. J., & Associates. (1991). *Involving colleges: Successful approaches to fostering student learning and development outside the classroom.* San Francisco: Jossey-Bass.

Kuh, G. D., & Whitt, E. J. (1988). *The invisible tapestry: Culture in American colleges and universities* (ASHE-ERIC Higher Education Report No. 1). Washington, DC: Association for the Study of Higher Education.

Lincoln, Y. S., & Guba, E. G. (1985). *Naturalistic inquiry.* Beverly Hills, CA: Sage.

Magolda, P. M. (2005). Proceed with caution: Uncommon wisdom about academic and student affairs partnerships. *About Campus, 9*(6), 16–21.

Manning, K., Kinzie, J., & Schuh, J. H. (2014). *One size does not fit all: Traditional and innovative models of student affairs practice* (2nd ed.). New York: Routledge.

Merriam, S. B. (1998). *Qualitative research and case study applications in education* (2nd ed.). San Francisco: Jossey-Bass.

National Association of State Universities and Land-Grant Colleges (NASULGC). (1997). *Returning to our roots: The student experience.* Washington, DC: Author.

National Association of State Universities and Land-Grant Colleges (NASULGC). (1999). *Returning to our roots: A learning society.* Washington, DC: Author.

National Association of State Universities and Land-Grant Colleges (NASULGC). (2000). *Returning to our roots: Toward a coherent campus culture.* Washington, DC: Author.

National Association of Student Personnel Administrators (NASPA) & American College Personnel Association (ACPA). (2004). *Learning reconsidered: A campus-wide focus on the student experience.* Washington, DC: Authors.

Pascarella, E. T., & Terenzini, P. T. (1991). *How college affects students.* San Francisco: Jossey-Bass.

Pascarella, E. T., & Terenzini, P. T. (2005). *How college affects students: Vol. 2. A third decade of research.* San Francisco: Jossey-Bass.

Pike, G. R. (1999). The effects of residential learning communities and traditional residential living arrangements on educational gains during the first year of college. *Journal of College Student Development, 40*(3), 269–284.

Rieske, L. J., & Benjamin, M. (2015). Utilizing peer mentor roles in learning communities. In M. Benjamin (Ed.), *Learning communities from start to finish* (New Directions for Student Services, no. 149, pp. 67–78). San Francisco: Jossey-Bass.

Schroeder, C. (1999a). Forging educational partnerships that advance student learning. In G. S. Blimling & E. J. Whitt (Eds.), *Good practice in student affairs: Principles to foster student learning* (pp. 133–156). San Francisco: Jossey-Bass.

Schroeder, C. (1999b). Partnerships: An imperative for enhancing student learning and institutional effectiveness. In J. H. Schuh & E. J. Whitt (Eds.), *Creating successful partnerships between academic and student affairs* (New Directions for Student Services no. 87, pp. 5–18). San Francisco: Jossey-Bass.

Schroeder, C. (2004). Collaborative partnerships: Keys to enhancing student learning and success. In J. Gardner & L. Upcraft (Eds.), *Challenging and supporting the first-year student.* San Francisco: Jossey-Bass.

Schroeder, C. C., Minor, F. D., & Tarkow, T. A. (1999). Freshman interest groups: Partnerships for promoting student success. In J. H. Schuh & E. J. Whitt (Eds.), *Creating successful partnerships between academic and student affairs* (New Directions for Student Services, no. 87, pp. 37–49). San Francisco: Jossey-Bass.

Schuh, J. H., & Whitt, E. J. (Eds.). (1999). *Creating successful partnerships between academic and student affairs* (New Directions for Student Services, no. 87). San Francisco: Jossey-Bass.

Shapiro, H. (2005). *A larger sense of purpose: Higher education and society.* Princeton, NJ: Princeton University Press.

Study Group on the Conditions of Excellence in American Higher Education. (1984). *Involvement in learning: Realizing the potential of American higher education; Final report.* Washington, DC: National Institute of Education.

Task Force on the Future of Student Affairs. (2010). *Envisioning the future of student affairs: Final report of the task force on the future of student affairs.* Washington, DC: ACPA & NASPA.

Tinto, V. (2012). *Completing college: Rethinking institutional action.* Chicago: University of Chicago Press.

US Department of Education. (2006). *A test of leadership: Charting the future of U.S. higher education.* Washington, DC: Author.

Wells, C., Kellogg, A. H., Elkins Nesheim, B. S., Guentzel, M. J., McDonald, W., & Whitt, E. J. (2007, Nov.). *Institutional outcomes of academic and student affairs partnership programs.* Paper presented at the annual meeting of the Association for the Study of Higher Education, Louisville, KY.

The White House. (2013). *The president's plan to make college more affordable: A better bargain for the middle class.* Fact Sheet. Washington, DC: Author.

Whitt, E. J., Elkins Nesheim, B. S., Guentzel, M. J., Kellogg, A. H., McDonald, W. M., & Wells, C. A. (2008). "Principles of good practice" for academic and student affairs partnership programs. *Journal of College Student Development, 49*, 235–249.

Woodard, D. B., Love, P. G., & Komives, S. R. (2000). *Leadership and management issues for a new century* (New Directions for Student Services, no. 92). San Francisco: Jossey-Bass.

Yeater, E. A., Miltenberger, P., Laden, R. M., Ellis, S., & O'Donohue, W. (2001). Collaborating with academic affairs: The development of a sexual assault prevention and counseling program within an academic department. *NASPA Journal, 38*, 438–450.

PART FIVE

ESSENTIAL COMPETENCIES

One of the hallmarks of a profession is the identification of competencies that guide the practice, professional development, and preparation of new professionals entering the field. The evolution of student affairs has also prompted stronger scholarly work focused on identifying the professional competencies needed to be in the field. As the research and scope of students affairs expands, so must the competencies that are needed to be a knowledgeable practitioner. This section of the book considers the competencies identified by the *Professional Competency Areas for Student Affairs Educators* (ACPA-NASPA, 2015) and emerging competencies that are necessary as our society and educational expectations change.

Consensus on what competencies are essential for new professionals may elicit multiple responses. Although we acknowledge that it would be desirable for all levels of professionals to have the same competencies, this is not realistic. For this

reason, the focus of the chapters in this section is oriented toward the new professional and the essential competencies needed within his or her graduate preparation and work. We begin this section with chapter 22 by Jan Arminio and Anna M. Ortiz, who frame how all these competencies come together and develop within three levels: foundational, intermediate, and advanced. Some new professionals may have skills at the intermediate level as a result of past experiences or training, and others may be developing these skills at the foundational level. This chapter emphasizes the need to reflect on personal skills as well as contextual influences.

In chapter 23 Raechele L. Pope and John A. Mueller introduce the multicultural competence model that consists of awareness, knowledge, and skills necessary to work with diverse populations. In addition, this chapter includes how multicultural change can take place within our institutions.

John P. Dugan and Laura Osteen follow this with chapter 24 on leadership, which explores the interrelated dimensions of how an individual experiences and enacts leadership: understanding socialization, formal leadership theory, and engaging in leadership development.

A competency most leaders must attain is that of staffing and supervision. In chapter 25 Joan B. Hirt, Tara E. Frank, and Patricia A. Perillo provide an overview of models and current research on the staffing of student affairs departments. The presented model begins with recruitment and includes the separation of an employee from the institution.

The next set of chapters focus on skills necessary in practice. In chapter 26 Stephen John Quaye elaborates on how teaching and facilitation help practitioners guide students and introduces several models that can facilitate how students learn. This chapter also includes how social media needs to be considered when looking at student learning.

Chapter 27 by Amy L. Reynolds frames the student issues we face and the role of the helping relationship. Different than counseling are the skills necessary for advising student groups.

Norbert W. Dunkel and Nancy E. Chrystal-Green elaborate on the skills necessary to align the roles and functions of student organization advisors with the organization's purposes and institutional culture in chapter 28.

Crisis management leads the next set of chapters focused on issues that should influence the kinds of competencies practitioners develop. In chapter 29 Mahauganee D. Shaw and Larry D. Roper pose questions in order to provoke our perspectives and values around how we respond to crisis management.

In chapter 30 Sherry Watt, Cindy Ann Kilgo, and Wayne Jacobson draw connections between programs that deal with difference and how they should be seen as high-impact practices that promote student success.

And finally, Florence A. Hamrick and Jillian Kinzie illustrate how our practice should be influenced by the cycle of applying formal theories and research while also influencing those theories and research through application in practice. In chapter 31 they emphasize that how theories and research are applied in practice is as important as knowing the theories.

Together these chapters frame the essential competencies necessary to perform the work of student affairs. As the reader considers these, it is important to understand that at the forefront of all competencies is self-reflection and assessment. Professional development works best when we know what skills we need to improve.

Reference

ACPA-NASPA. (2015). *Professional competency areas for student affairs educators.* Retrieved from http://www.myacpa.org/system/files/ACPA%20NASPA%20Professional%20Competencies%20FINAL.pdf

CHAPTER 22

PROFESSIONALISM

Jan Arminio and Anna M. Ortiz

Having been employed in student affairs for more than twenty years in the same position after completing a master's degree, Aston directs a student affairs unit in a well-defined, structured way. Aston attends the same association conference year after year but does not adopt "fads." New professionals and graduate students complain that Aston is inflexible. Weekly reports and inventories are due every Monday by 9:00 am regardless of any unexpected campus events or crises the previous day or week. For example an inventory of a campus lounge space, including ping pong table equipment, was expected, though supervisees had been dealing with the aftermath of a campus fight that morning. Moreover, applicants for open positions must have specific experiences—"none of this transferrable skills stuff."

Udo has served in several positions in student affairs over the course of ten years. With each position came increasing and new responsibilities. Contemplating entering a doctoral program, Udo not only attends conferences but also is a leader in a national professional association. Constantly adapting new practices based on what is discussed at conferences and in the literature, Udo appears to others as creative. For example, Udo is implementing a restorative social justice philosophy to student conduct programs. Also, employees in Udo's area have job-swap days to learn more about each other's work.

Aston and Udo are meant to represent different perspectives about being a professional. Often in student affairs, professionals are judged along a continuum similar to Aston and Udo. In what ways are they professional? In what ways might they lack professionalism? How might each of us compare with Aston and Udo? How do our perceptions change if the social identities, age, and other descriptors of these two are revealed? This chapter covers the general characteristics that define a profession and responsibilities of professionals in higher education, including agreed-on competencies and standards. We also offer vital elements of being a student affairs professional along three intersecting contexts: individual, institution, and the profession itself. These elements include lifelong professional development, professional identity, serving one's profession, and mentoring others. Last, to facilitate an understanding among the various sources of professional competencies and standards, we offer a table of where those topics can be found in this book and their intersection with student affairs competency and standards documents. To encourage discussion and reflection, questions about Aston and Udo in relationship to topics of professionalism are integrated throughout this chapter. We close with questions for reflection.

What Is It to Be a Student Affairs Professional?

The word *professional* comes from the root word *profess,* meaning to declare openly or affirm allegiance to knowledge claims (Hoad, 1986). Professionalism characterizes aspirational qualities of a professional. According to Shah, Anderson, and Humphrey (2014) professionalism relays a responsibility to the field and the public. Professionalism "invokes a sense of duty, certainly to other practitioners in the field . . . and often to the public as a whole" (p. 536). Furthermore, a profession is "a discreet group of practitioners who possess a specialized body of knowledge allowing them to engage in a narrow field of work" (Shah, Anderson, & Humphrey, 2014, p. 537). An example of a specialized body of knowledge is offered by Mehta (2013), who compared the accountability movements between K–12 education and higher education. Mehta believed that it is the function of generating new understanding by those who possess specialized analytic knowledge and skills in higher education that has protected higher education from the intense scrutiny that K–12 education has experienced. Moreover, the function of specialized knowledge has enabled higher education professionals greater control in institutions than teachers have in their schools.

Professionalism in higher education "is an interactive process that is continually modified by societal forces that impact upon academia. Because professionalism is at once societal, academic, and personal, it is often assessed locally and situationally" (Bruhn, Zajac, Al-Kazemi, & Prescott, 2002, p. 267). In other words, the current climate influences the characteristics of professionalism. For example, in today's context, maintaining professional boundaries, particularly with students, is an important characteristic of professionalism that may not have been expected several decades ago.

Ibarra (1999) defined professional identity as the "relatively stable and enduring constellation of attributes, beliefs, values, motives, and experiences in terms of which people define themselves in a professional role" (764–765, see also Schein, 1978). Renn and Jessup-Anger (2008) noted that new professionals in student affairs often lament the difficulty in creating a professional identity from that of graduate "student-as-learner" to "professional-as-educator" (p. 325). Two concepts connected with identifying as a professional in higher education are "oughtness" (personal values, beliefs, and feelings) and "obligations" (others' expectations and legitimate demands) (Calvert, Lewis, & Spindler, 2011, p. 29). Hence, professionalism is not only what a professional knows and should do as determined by the profession but also how professionals present themselves as professionals, how they demonstrate values, beliefs, and feelings in meeting professional expectations. The integration of personal ideals with professional ideals reveal professionalism to others and the self (Bruhn & others, 2002) so that in our profession when individuals contemplate important aspects of the self, student affairs professional is one of them. How do Aston and Udo differ in their perceptions of "oughtness" and "obligation"? What are the obligations to which student affairs professionals affirm their allegiance and identity?

Professional Competencies

Chapter 3 of this book covered philosophies and values, and chapter 6 discussed ethical principles and standards. Those certainly are critical obligations professional student affairs educators owe their field and their constituencies. Competencies are also critical obligations. The student affairs profession has identified competencies crucial to effective student affairs practice. These competencies define professional knowledge, skills, and dispositions (attitudes, beliefs, and values) expected of student affairs professionals regardless of their area of specialization. In August 2015, the American College Personnel Association–College Student Educators International (ACPA) and the National Association of Student Personnel Administrators–Student Affairs Administrators in Higher Education (NASPA) endorsed the updated *Professional Competency Areas for Student Affairs Practitioners*. That document described competency areas as follows (in the order listed in the document):

- Personal and ethical foundations
- Values, philosophy, and history
- Assessment, evaluation, and research
- Law, policy, and governance
- Organizational and human resources
- Leadership
- Social justice and inclusion
- Student learning and development
- Technology
- Advising and supporting

In each of these competency areas essential knowledge, skills, and dispositions are listed for three levels: foundational, intermediate, and advanced outcomes. Authors of the competencies urge users to practice a complex perspective in considering the three levels: "it is important to distinguish between meeting the outcome in a singular setting and mastering that outcome in multiple contexts" (ACPA & NASPA, 2015, p. 8). Although all student affairs professionals are expected to meet all foundational competencies in all the listed areas, and although all student affairs professionals are obligated to pursue continuous professional development, some professionals should seek increased competency in certain areas because of increased job responsibilities or to meet specific position expectations. Competency authors noted that "an individual may begin work on several intermediate- or advance-level outcomes before demonstrating full foundational-level proficiency for that competency area (ACPA & NASPA, 2015, p. 8). Furthermore, they noted, "the outcomes should not be viewed as checklists but as sets of indicators mapping in and around each of the competency areas. Viewed this way, progressive development builds on the work of prior levels and moved from foundational knowledge to increased capacity for critique and synthesis, from introductory skills to application and leadership within larger venues and multiple areas, and from attitudes to values and habits of the mind" (p. 8).

Nuanced institutional expectations may also dictate the level of competency required. Clearly, intermediate and advanced outcomes build on foundational knowledge, skills, and dispositions.

Though space restrictions limit the reproduction of the competencies at all levels, in table 22.1 we list the competency areas; offer an example of a basic knowledge, skill, and disposition; and note where these competencies are described in this book. Chapters describing expectations in multicultural competence, leadership, staffing and supervision, teaching and facilitation, counseling and helping skills, advising, crisis management, embracing difference through programming, and applying theories to practice follow this chapter. The full competency document can be found at http://www.myacpa.org/professional-competency-areas-student-affairs-practitioner and at http://www.naspa.org/images/uploads/main/ACPA_NASPA_Professional_Competencies.pdf.

TABLE 22.1.   STUDENT AFFAIRS COMPETENCIES BASIC EXAMPLES WITH CORRESPONDING BOOK CHAPTERS

ACPA/NASPA Competency	Example of a Basic Knowledge, Skill, and Disposition	Where Discussed in This Book	Addressed in CAS?
Advising and Supporting	Know and use referral sources	Chapters 27 and 28	
	Exhibit culturally inclusive active listening skills		
	Seek opportunities to expand one's own knowledge and skills in helping students with specific concerns		
Assessment, Evaluation and Research	Differentiate among assessment, program review, evaluation planning, and research as well as appropriate methods for each	Chapters 19	Yes

ACPA/NASPA Competency	Example of a Basic Knowledge, Skill, and Disposition	Where Discussed in This Book	Addressed in CAS?
	Design program and learning outcomes that are appropriately clear, specific, and measurable, that are informed by theoretical frameworks, and that align with organization goals and values		
	Effectively articulate, interpret, and apply results		
Law, Policy, and Governance	Explain the difference between public, private, public, and for-profit higher education with respect to the legal system and what they may mean for respective students, faculty members, and student affairs professionals	Chapters 4 and 7	Yes
	Act in accordance with national, state and provincial, and local laws and with institutional policies regarding nondiscrimination		
	Encourage and advocate participation in national, state and provincial, local, and institutional electoral processes as applicable		
Leadership	Articulate the vision and mission of the primary work unit, the division, and the institution	Chapters 24	Yes
	Build mutually supportive relationships with colleagues and students across similarities and differences		
	Think critically and creatively and imagine possibilities for solutions that do not currently exist or are not apparent		
Organizational and Human Resources	Explain the basic tenants of personal or organizational risk and liability as they relate to one's work	Chapters 13, 16, 17, 18, 25, and 29	Yes
	Demonstrate effective stewardship and use of resources		
	Advocate for equitable hiring practices		
Personal and Ethical Foundations	Identify ethical issues in the course of one's job	Chapters 2, 3, and 6	Yes
	Demonstrate an understanding for the role of beliefs and values		
	Articulate key elements of one's set of personal beliefs and commitments as well as the source of each		

(continued)

TABLE 22.1 (*continued*)

ACPA/NASPA Competency	Example of a Basic Knowledge, Skill, and Disposition	Where Discussed in This Book	Addressed in CAS?
Social Justice and Inclusion	Identify systems of socialization that influence one's multiple identities and sociopolitical perspectives and how they affect one's lived experiences	Chapters 4, 5, 10, 12, 23, and 30	Yes
	Engage in critical reflection in order to identify one's own prejudices and biases		
	Advocate about issues of justice, oppression, privilege, and power that affect people based on local, national, and global interconnections		
Values, Philosophy, and History	Articulate the history of the inclusion and exclusion of people with a variety of identities in higher education	Chapters 1, 2, and 3	
	Demonstrate responsible campus citizenship and participation in the campus community		
	Model the principles of the profession and expect the same from colleagues and supervisees		
Student Learning and Development	Identity the strengths and limitations in applying existing theories and models to varying student demographic groups	Chapters 8, 9, 10, 11, 12, 14, 15, 21, 26, and 31	Yes
	Construct learning outcomes for daily practice as well as teaching and training activities		
	Articulate one's own developmental journey in relation to formal theory		
Technology	Remain current on student and educator adoption patterns of new technologies and familiarize oneself with the purpose and functionality of those technologies	Chapter 20	Yes
	Model and promote the legal, ethical, and transparent collection, use, and securing of electronic data		
	Critically assess the accuracy and quality of information gathered via technology and accurately cite electronic sources of information respecting copyright law and fair use		

There are a number of uses for the competency document. First, competencies and descriptions of the three levels could be used as a tool to identify strengths and weaknesses for professional development goals, perhaps in consultation with a supervisor. Also, the competencies could be used to guide student affairs graduate programs and offer research and assessment opportunities for faculty members and students.

With the brief descriptions of Aston and Udo at the beginning of the chapter, and noting the basic competencies offered in table 22.1, in what ways do these two student affairs educators meet or fail to meet the basic competencies of the organizational and human resources competency? Aston and Udo believe that what they do is valued by their institutions and that they are competent. How might they find evidence that this is the case?

Professional Standards

Although the *Professional Competency Areas for Student Affairs Practitioners* is a description of competency areas and levels for individual professionals, how can strengths and weaknesses of student affairs units be identified? The Council for the Advancement of Standards in Higher Education (CAS) began publishing standards for student affairs units in 1986 (CAS, 2015). In the most recent publication there are standards for more than forty program and service functional areas. These range from academic advising to women student programs and services. Recently established functional area standards include graduate and professional student programs and services and undergraduate research programs. Each functional program and service standards document includes specialized standards for that particular functional area as well as general standards that are required for all functional areas. For example, general standards include student learning outcomes in knowledge acquisition, cognitive complexity, interpersonal development, intrapersonal competence, humanitarianism and civic engagement, and practical competence. The commuter and off-campus living program would be assessed on evidence of how its programs and services have added to student learning in those areas. Also, according to the CAS standards, it is expected that students involved in the commuter and off-campus living program will relate knowledge to their daily life, establish meaningful relationships, understand and appreciate cultural and human difference, and live a purposeful and satisfying life. In addition to stated student learning outcomes, CAS designates standards related to a program's or service's mission and program offerings as well as the processes units use to accomplish their mission and program. Vital to these processes are meeting general standards related to the following categories:

- Leadership
- Human resources
- Ethics
- Legal responsibilities
- Equity and access; diversity
- Organization and management
- Campus and external relations
- Financial resources
- Technology, facilities, and equipment
- Assessment and evaluation

The CAS self-assessment process requires that current practice be compared with described standards. The CAS standards enable assessment of units as well as an entire student affairs division. Assessment guides (called SAGS, self-assessment guides) with criterion measures of the standards across a four-point scale are available to encourage self-assessment. Returning to Aston and Udo, Aston believes the accountability movement to be a fad whereas Udo is open to exploring individual and unit strengths and weaknesses. How might these attitudes relate to their professionalism?

Being dedicated to student learning, student affairs units also must be engaged in institutional accreditation efforts. Most US institutions aspire to be accredited by one of the Council for the Higher Education Accreditation regional accrediting bodies. Typically, institutions are accredited every ten years, though the process and timing is dependent on the regional accrediting body and weaknesses identified in the previous accreditation cycle. Institutions also typically must submit a mid-cycle accreditation report. Similar to all institutional departments and units, student affairs units must offer documentation attesting to how they add to and encourage student learning and also describe their effectiveness and efficiency. Professionalism in higher education requires that employees be concerned about and engaged in assessment efforts.

◆ ◆ ◆

Now that we have defined professionalism, discussed general notions about professionalism in higher education and student affairs, and identified student affairs competencies and the nature of standards in student affairs, we turn to a more specific discussion about professionalism in student affairs along the individual, institutional, and discipline contexts.

Multiple Levels of Professionalism

Aston and Udo demonstrate their professionalism in different contexts. Aston seems to ground professionalism within the context of the unit served within a specific campus context, whereas Udo expands the context to professional associations and to the field as a whole. They also exhibit different kinds of personal professionalism with Aston's being grounded in doing a job steadily and well for the long term and Udo seeing that personal professionalism involves continued professional development and seeking new challenges.

The Individual Context

Professionalism in the individual context takes on three dimensions: professional identity, a commitment to continual improvement, and disposition toward lifelong learning. There should be an important connection between professionals and their profession. Case study analysis revealed that congruence of who one is, what is valued, and how one works is "paramount to job effectiveness and personal satisfaction" (Ortiz & Shintaku, 2004, p. 167). Ortiz and Shintaku wrote, "Identity and work are intertwined, primarily due to a society that often equates identity with occupation" (p. 163). Congruence between professional and personal identities in which integration of individual background factors, such as family of origin, sexual orientation, socioeconomic status, race, ethnicity, gender, and professional identities (Ortiz, O'Brien, & Martinez, 2015), enables "synergies between who they are personally and their professional actions" (Piskadlo & Johnson, 2014, p. 46). Thus, a connection is drawn between professional and personal identity, as well as values and action (Piskadlo & Johnson, 2014). Collins (2009) further contributed that work-life balance and other important life decisions demonstrate the close connection between professional and personal identity. For example, Aston and Udo likely are involved in work activities, professional association interest groups, scholarship, and mentoring relationships that reflect their salient social identities, such as gender, sexual orientation, race or ethnicity, or an intersection of one or more of these.

Previously in the chapter we discussed professional competencies agreed on by the field's leading professional associations. Although the profession currently has no formal mechanism to assess professional competence through individual certification or accreditation, it is the responsibility of members of the profession to seek continuous improvement through self-evaluation and active participation in institutional evaluation processes. Self-assessment is often a hallmark of what it means to be a professional (Powell, 2000). In various studies self-evaluation or self-assessment has been shown to have many positive outcomes, such as better strategic thinking (Powell, 2000), enhanced collaboration with colleagues (Podgornik & Mazgon, 2015), the development of critical friendships (Day, 1993), and the creation of work environments that are less competitive (Powell, 2000). In fact, Day (1993) found that when staff members share problem-solving strategies and reconstruction of meaning through self-evaluation, senses of autonomy and communal responsibility are established. Thus, he concluded that in organizations in which reflective practice is supported and valued, the benefits extend beyond the individual to the organization.

There are practical benefits in becoming a reflective practitioner. Through self-assessment early career professionals can determine strengths and weaknesses. This matters because knowing one's weaknesses promotes an honest appraisal of competencies, making it more likely that a new professional will either reject interventions or practices that are beyond the current skill set and knowledge base or change course, seek further training and guidance, or make a referral (Eva & Regehr, 2005). Self-assessment also makes it easier to set appropriate learning goals so that new professionals do not "overreach," generating motivation and increased confidence. Intentionally integrating reflection in graduate preparation programs increases the likelihood that professionals use self-reflection in their future careers (Podgornik & Mazgon, 2015).

Self-evaluation, self-assessment, and reflection are present in the ACPA and NASPA professional competencies (2015), specifically in the personal ethical foundations and leadership competencies. Self-assessment throughout one's career is facilitated by attending to the increasing level and sophistication of these competencies, because they are described for foundation, intermediate, and advanced outcomes. Similarly, Janosik (2009) outlined a student affairs professional development curriculum that lays the foundation of history, philosophy, administration, and law; progressing to the next level of assessment and multiculturalism; culminating in student development and learning. The learning orientation that Renn and Jessup-Anger's (2008) participants noted included reflection, observation, and self-correction through trial and error, generally characterizing "that they used their work experience as a laboratory in which consistently to examine and improve themselves as professionals" (p. 327).

There are ample opportunities for student affairs professionals to participate in lifelong learning through professional development opportunities on one's own campus, in numerous professional organizations, and through companies that offer seminars and short courses. Aston and Udo show us that simply participating in professional development does not equate to a disposition toward lifelong learning. Aston simply attends the annual meeting of the professional association, refraining from learning about new strategies and programs; Udo uses what is learned through conferences and published literature to inform practice. Udo is contemplating pursuing a doctorate, further evidence of lifelong learning. The tenants of lifelong learning are well aligned with professionalism. Andragogy (Knowles, 1968) is based on assumptions that adults developmentally move toward self-directed learning, use experience as a resource for learning, seek learning as a result of varying social roles and transitions, and see learning as a long-term investment rather than focusing on immediate application. Thus, there are times in one's professional life when learning through professional development or formal education, such as obtaining a doctorate or other terminal degree, is appropriate and desired.

The Institutional Context

Professionalism in the institutional context is an important dimension because it is the primary place where student affairs professionals interface with other academic professionals. A professional identity grounded in student affairs gives the practitioner the background necessary to bring best practices, the ethic and values of the profession, and the needed preparation to best serve students. Practitioners, in essence, become representatives of the profession on their own campus. How do you think Aston represents professionalism in the institutional context? What might other professionals on campus assume about the profession of student affairs based on how Aston's staff is treated? These are important questions to consider as institutions of higher education count on the expertise student affairs professionals bring to campus especially with regard to critical issues for today's college students, student development, and student success on their campuses.

Learning about institutional culture, policies, politics, roles, and responsibilities should be on the agenda for student affairs professionals as they enter new campuses no matter their career levels. Professionalism pervades these discoveries and interactions with institutional agents and structures. Knowing things such as channels of communication, positional boundaries, and the ways work is accomplished assists in defining professional behavior and expectations. Uncovering more subtle elements such as the politics of campus, how student affairs professionals work with faculty members, or the campus racial climate requires tact, respect, intuitive insight, and persistence. Although employee orientation programs and supervisors should provide information and guidance (Collins, 2009), ultimately the professional is responsible for this learning despite the presence or lack of institutional assistance.

Mentoring is often an informal way in which this learning takes place. A survey of new student affairs professionals found that mentoring was their preferred method of receiving training and professional development on the issues they deemed most important (Henning, Cilente, Kennedy, & Sloane, 2011). However, Janosik (2009) cautions that having a mentoring relationship with one's immediate supervisor can create difficult ethical situations when the requirements of supervision conflict with the support and guidance of mentorship. The new professionals in Renn and Hodges's study (2007) reported that it was difficult for them to build a mentor relationship with their supervisors and realized that it was their responsibility to look to other places in the institution and the field for mentors. In doing this, new professionals posited that they were finding ways to contribute to the development of others as well, demonstrating a key responsibility of professionalism.

The Context of the Profession

According to Henning and colleagues (2011), "Ultimately, after learning about what is expected of them in their position, new student affairs professionals need and want to learn what it means to be a professional staff member within the larger context of student affairs" (p. 29). Part 1 of this book documents the development of student affairs as a profession. All student affairs administrators are a part of the profession, though many may not have the professional identity of a student affairs professional, be trained as a student affairs professional, or participate in professional associations. These are the key dimensions in professionalism in the context of the professional community. Carpenter (1991) identified three roles of a professional community: (1) sharing knowledge, goals and objectives with clarity and coherence so that they can be discussed and examined by members; (2) creating policies regarding professional behavior and enforcing them; and (3) offering means of socializing and regenerating new members. Attending an opening session of a national conference provides ample opportunity to experience the professional community, common identity, and common destiny of student affairs professionals.

There are a number of professional associations within student affairs. In addition to the generalist organizations (ACPA and NASPA), there is one or more for every functional area. Functionalist associations include the Association of College and University Housing Officers–International (ACUHO-I), the National Association for Campus Activities (NACA), the National Orientation Directors Association (NODA), the National Academic Advising Association (NACADA), as well as many others.

Professional associations promote professional socialization, a common sense of identity, and opportunities to build a network. In addition, they advocate on behalf of members on issues such as government policy decisions and collaborate with other higher education professional associations to advance the work of student affairs and policies and programs that benefit students and their institutions. Indeed, there are multiple benefits of involvement in professional associations. Presenting ideas, research, and new practices is an important professional development opportunity, but they also simultaneously enrich the profession through the exchange of information. Building networks across institutions within regions and across the country and internationally, provides for an exchange of perspectives that contributes to the breadth and depth of the profession and enables practitioners to bring new programs and ideas to their home campuses. Connecting with professionals at multiple levels within the profession confers the benefits of colleagueship and mentorship—both in seeking and providing mentorship. Within the larger, generalist professional associations there are smaller working groups, knowledge communities, or commissions that are focused on specific functional areas and social identity groups that enable in-depth involvement and learning in smaller communities. Professional associations are also sought for their workshops on specific topics, especially for new professionals (Henning, Cilente, Kennedy, & Sloane, 2011).

Involvement in these associations range from volunteering at a regional or national convention to the higher-level involvement of holding a national office. New professionals may find that it is most appropriate to locate their involvement at the more local, state, or regional level. In fact, given budget restrictions that often affect all student affairs professionals, involvement at the regional level is a reasonable alternative. Also, connecting to a network at a smaller venue may be more easily accomplished. Regardless of level, it is quite easy to become overinvolved, because the work of the associations depends on member volunteerism. Balancing campus responsibilities with professional involvement is an important goal to achieve. A career in student affairs often includes progressively higher levels of involvement in professional associations as an obligation of being a member of a profession and for the multiple benefits involvement distributes. Mata, Latham, and Ransome (2010) described an involvement trajectory that includes professional association membership, conference attendance, offering presentations, networking, volunteering service, and collaborating, ultimately resulting in improved programs and advocacy, demonstrating that professional involvement benefits the students we serve.

Professional associations are also a key way for members to engage in ongoing professional development so that they remain current with the most innovative programs, research, theoretical perspectives, and legal developments. Indeed, the numerous workshops (traditional and virtual) and conferences are designed to provide lifelong education to members of the profession, making regular attendance and engagement in these activities a hallmark of professionalism. Returning to Aston and Udo, it is evident that Udo uses professional associations to continue further education while contemplating a doctorate. Udo also demonstrates reciprocity and a generative spirit by contributing to the profession through assuming leadership positions.

Summary

We defined being a professional as affirming an allegiance to and demonstrating a commitment to and identification with the profession. This means demonstrating a commitment to its ethical principles, standards, and meeting expected competencies. In this chapter we identified important elements to professionalism in the contexts of the individual and institution as specific to the student affairs profession. These elements include a demonstrated commitment to continual professional development, being mentored and mentoring others, and creating a professional identity. Also, we recognized other chapters in this book and in the professional literature that offer more specifics about the necessary competencies in student affairs. We believe that professionalism is where the personal and professional intersect. This is integrity; the intersection of obligations and "oughtness." Ultimately, the responsibility for professionalism and ongoing professional development falls on the professional, with support from professional associations, institutions, supervisors, and colleagues. Aston and Udo honored their commitment to students, their institutions, and the profession by being involved with their profession, but do they honor this commitment by entering the profession through specialized dedicated training that promulgates values, norms, and conceptions of student affairs? How is an aspect of their identity connected to the profession? How might we answer these questions about ourselves and our colleagues? All of us take responsibility in promoting the profession by how we practice as professionals and to what degree we demonstrate professionalism. Consider how this occurs through the subsequent chapters that examine specific competencies.

Activities

1. Interview a student affairs professional to find out about this person's career trajectory and how professional development played a role in that trajectory.
   a. How does or how might this person define professionalism and professional identity?

    b. How is this person involved in professional associations? Compare and contrast this person's experiences and perspectives to the notions in this chapter. What do you make of any differences?

2. Pretend that you supervise Udo and Aston. Annual evaluations are coming up for both of them.

    a. What would you want them to provide for you to prepare for this meeting?

    b. In preparing for the meeting how might theory discussed previously in the book be useful to you?

    c. What would the goals of this meeting be? Role-play such a conversation.

References

American College Personnel Association–College Student Educators International (ACPA) and The National Association of Student Personnel Administrators–Student Affairs Administrators in Higher Education (NASPA). (2015). *Professional competency areas for student affairs practitioners*. Washington, DC: Authors.

Bruhn, J. G., Zajac, G., Al-Kazemi, A., & Prescott, L. D. (2002). Moral positions and academic conduct. *Journal of Higher Education, 73*, 461–493. doi:10.1353/jhe.2002.0033

Calvert, M., Lewis, T., & Spindler, J. (2011). Negotiating professional identities in higher education: Dilemmas and priorities of academic staff. *Research in Education, 86*, 25–38.

Carpenter, D. S. (1991). Student affairs professional: A developmental perspective. In T. K. Miller, R. B. Winston Jr., & Associates (Eds.), *Administration and leadership in student affairs* (pp. 253–278). Muncie, IN: Accelerated Development.

Collins, D. (2009). The socialization process for new professionals. In A. Tull, J. B. Hirst, S. A. Saunders (Eds.), *Becoming socialized in student affairs administration: A guide for new professionals and their supervisors*. Sterling, VA: Stylus.

Council for the Advancement of Standards in Higher Education (CAS). (2015). *CAS professional standards for higher education* (9th ed.). Washington, DC: Author.

Day, C. (1993). Reflection: A necessary but not sufficient condition for professional development. *British Educational Journal, 19*(1), 83–93.

Eva, K. W., & Regehr, G. (2005). Self-assessment in the health professions: A reformulation and research agenda. *Academic Medicine, 80*(10), S46–S54.

Henning, G., Cilente, K., Kennedy, D., & Sloane, T. (2011). Professional development needs for new residential life professionals. *The Journal of College and University Student Housing, 37*(2), 26–37.

Hoad, T. F. (Ed.). (1986). *The concise dictionary of English etymology*. New York: Oxford University Press.

Ibarra, H. (1999). Provisional selves: Experimenting with image and identity in professional adaption. *Administrative Science Quarterly, 44*, 764–791.

Janosik, S. M. (2009). Professional associations and socializations. In A. Tull, J. B. Hirst, S. A. Saunders (Eds.), *Becoming socialized in student affairs administration: A guide for new professionals and their supervisors*. Sterling, VA: Stylus.

Knowles, M. S. (1968). Andragogy, not pedagogy. *Adult Leadership, 16*(10), 350–386.

Mata, H., Latham, T., & Ransome, Y. (2010). Benefits of professional organization membership and participation in national conferences: Considerations for students and new professionals. *Health Promotion Practice, 11*(4), 450–453.

Mehta, J. (2013). When professions shape politics: The case of K–12 and higher education. *Educational Policy, 28*, 881–915. doi:10.1177/0895904813492380

Ortiz, A. M., O'Brien, J., & Martinez, C. R. (2015). Developing a professional ethic. In M. J. Amey & L. M. Ressor (Eds.), *Beginning your journey* (4th ed., pp. 39–60). Washington, DC: NASPA.

Ortiz, A. M., & Shintaku, R. H. (2004). Professional and personal identities at the crossroads. In P. M. Magolda & J. E. Carnaghi (Eds.), *Job one: Experiences of new professionals in student affairs* (pp. 163–178). Lanham, MD: University Press of America.

Piskadlo, K., & Johnson, C. (2014). Identity and the job one experience. In P. M. Magolda & J. E. Carnaghi (Eds.), *Job one 2.0* (2nd ed.). Lanham, MD: University Press of America.

Podgornik, V., & Mazgon, J. (2015). Self-evaluation as a factor in quality assurance in education. *Review of European Studies, 7*(1), 407–415.

Powell, L. A. (2000). Realizing the value of self-assessment: The influences of the business excellence model on teacher professionalism. *European Journal of Teacher Education, 23*(1), 37–48.

Renn, K. A., & Hodges, J. P. (2007). The first year on the job: Experiences of new professionals in student affairs. *NASPA Journal, 44*(2), 367–391.

Renn, K. A., & Jessup-Anger, E. R. (2008). Preparing new professionals: Lessons for graduate preparation programs from the national study of new professionals in student affairs. *Journal of College Student Development, 49*(4), 319–335.

Schein, E. H. (1978). *Career dynamics: Matching individual and organizational needs.* Reading, MA: Addison-Wesley.

Shah, N., Anderson, J., & Humphrey, H. J. (2014). Teaching professionalism: A tale of three schools. *Perspectives in Biology and Medicine, 51*, 535–546. doi:10.1353/pbm.0.0041

CHAPTER 23

MULTICULTURAL COMPETENCE AND CHANGE ON CAMPUS

Raechele L. Pope and John A. Mueller

Developing multicultural competence is essential for effective college student affairs work. Indisputable demographic shifts and ongoing struggles to effectively address racism, homophobia, sexism, religious intolerance, ableism, and classism on college campuses create opportunities and challenges for student affairs practitioners. Among the opportunities, student diversity generates more positive learning communities, promotes increased interaction with diverse others, has a positive influence on college satisfaction and intellectual and social self-concept (Chang, 2001; Gurin, Dey, Hurtado, & Gurin, 2002), and are positively related to a variety of educational outcomes (Umbach & Kuh, 2006). The challenges arise when student affairs and higher education professionals are ineffective in responding to this diversity.

Dynamic Model of Multicultural Competence

Multicultural competence has become a significant component of the multicultural literature in student affairs. Increasingly scholars have emphasized the importance of developing multicultural competence as an essential step to creating more multiculturally sensitive and inclusive campuses (ACPA & NASPA, 2015; Iverson, 2012; Pope & Reynolds, 1997; Pope, Reynolds, & Mueller, 2004, 2014). However, few practitioners have received adequate training in multicultural issues and even fewer have had their work performance evaluated using multicultural competence as a criteria (Mueller & Pope, 2001; Pope & Reynolds, 1997; Williams, 2013). Failure to recognize multicultural competence as a core requirement for all student affairs professionals and limited institutional support are two significant barriers to effective multicultural training. Despite these barriers, Pope and Reynolds (1997) assert "that multicultural competence is a necessary prerequisite to effective, affirming, and ethical work in student affairs" (p. 270).

The theoretical underpinnings of multicultural competence in student affairs were initially adapted from the field of counseling psychology by Pope and Reynolds (1997). They defined *multicultural competence* as the awareness, knowledge, and skills needed to work with others who are culturally different from one's self.

Multicultural awareness, the first element in the tripartite model, consists of the attitudes, values, beliefs, and assumptions that shape our understanding of others who are culturally different from us. Being aware of the impact that one's upbringing, life experiences, and cultural worldview has on perceptions and interpersonal interactions is central to multicultural awareness. Evaluating stereotypes, biases, or culturally based assumptions is necessary to determine what, if any, inaccurate or inappropriate views we hold of a particular culture or person. In order to be multiculturally sensitive, individuals must be open to challenging any misinformation they have absorbed and unlearning any flawed assumptions and beliefs.

Multicultural knowledge, the second part of the tripartite model, is focused on background information of distinct cultural groups and content knowledge about important cultural constructs. Having cultural group knowledge is essential to multicultural competence, particularly because most individuals are inadequately exposed to the history, experiences, and realities of various cultural groups such as American Indians, Latino/a Americans, African Americans, and Asian Americans. There is also a lack of accurate information shared about other groups whose voices are often lost, such as Jews, Muslims, nonbelievers, people with disabilities, immigrants, and LGBT individuals. Such knowledge can help us contextualize what we observe, deepen our understanding, and enhance our ability to work with others who are culturally different from us. It is important to highlight that there is a potential risk in focusing on group knowledge because it can be used in ways that ultimately stereotype and minimize within-group differences.

In addition, understanding important cultural constructs such as acculturation, identity development, or oppression is vital for developing multicultural competence. Acculturation and identity development underscore that it is not a person's membership in a cultural group that is essential but rather what meaning that membership has for her or him. For example, the values and life experiences of a third-generation Korean American are very different from those of a new Korean immigrant. It is also essential that oppression and its effects be fully understood, whether by realizing the impact that internalized self-hatred might have on a Muslim American or comprehending how the heavy weight of racism and classism limits the opportunities for Native Americans living on the reservation. At times the amount of information that is needed to be multiculturally competent seems overwhelming; it is clearly impossible to know everything. However, it is possible to immerse ourselves in understanding the diverse cultures and communities that are in our immediate environment so that as student affairs professionals we can best serve them.

Multicultural skills are the third component of the tripartite model and consist of the behaviors used to effectively apply the multicultural awareness and knowledge previously internalized. Central to multicultural skills is the ability to effectively communicate across cultural differences and appreciate how culture influences every aspect of verbal and nonverbal communication. How we use silence, humor, touch, physical space, eye contact, as well as the content of our conversations, are highly influenced by our gender, culture, and upbringing. Designing and implementing culturally appropriate interventions, being comfortable with cultural conflict, consulting with cultural experts, and recovering from cultural errors are just a few of the specific skills needed to be culturally sensitive. Many practitioners report that they are less confident in their skills or ability to translate their multicultural awareness and knowledge into practice so it is vital that multicultural skills receive ample attention.

Although the tripartite model of multicultural competence has remained constant, the conceptualization of multicultural competence within student affairs has evolved during the past twenty years and multicultural research critical to the profession has grown and changed. Pope, Reynolds, and Mueller (2004) built on and refined the earlier work of Pope and Reynolds (1997) and developed the dynamic model of student affairs competence to intensify understanding and further integrate the construct of multicultural competence into foundational, theoretical, and applied understanding of the profession (see figure 23.1).

FIGURE 23.1. DYNAMIC MODEL OF STUDENT AFFAIRS COMPETENCE

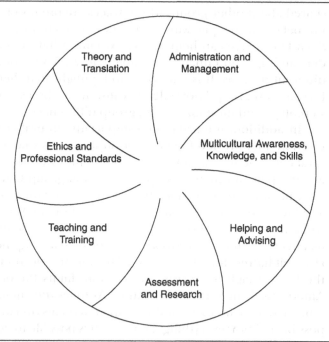

Source: Pope, R. L., Reynolds, A. L., & Mueller, J. M. (2004). *Multicultural competence in student affairs* (p. 10). San Francisco: Jossey Bass.

Pope and Reynolds (1997) asserted that there was limited consensus regarding the specific competencies needed for effective and ethical practice in student affairs. The dynamic model was the first comprehensive framework to suggest core competencies for all practitioners and one that included multicultural competence as central to all competencies. In 2015 The Joint ACPA and NASPA Task Force on Professional Competencies and Standards revised the 2010 document detailing competency areas for student affairs practitioners. Although the focus of the task force was not on multicultural competence, equity, diversity, and inclusion were identified as competency areas for the profession and there was some effort to incorporate multicultural issues into many of the other competency areas.

The dynamic model of student affairs competence offers a comprehensive and multiculturally inclusive conceptualization of the qualities and abilities for efficacious student affairs practice. The visual representation of the model underscores important philosophical assumptions. The open hub at the center of the wheel suggests a dynamic and fluid nature to multicultural competence (see figure 23.1). Proficiency in one area may influence one's competence in another area. The dynamic model conceptualizes multicultural competence as a distinctive category of awareness, knowledge, and skills and as an area that needs to be effectively integrated into each of the other six core competencies. All practitioners need a basic level of competence in all of these areas in order to be effective and ethical professionals; however, some will develop expertise in certain areas depending on their job requirements and personal interests.

The first core competency is administration and management, which incorporates the awareness, knowledge, and skills needed for most practitioner positions such as budgeting, strategic planning, resource allocation, and supervision. Understanding how the core assumptions, theories, and practices of administration have not always effectively incorporated cultural concerns and realities is fundamental to being a culturally competent administrator. Being aware of the limitations of the literature, seeking out alternative literature, such as the work on multicultural organization development (Jackson & Holvino, 1998; Pope, 1993), and understanding how cultural worldview and identity development may influence the interpersonal components of human resource management are some of the necessary competencies in administration and management.

Theory and translation, the second area of competence, incorporates the theory and research that inform the entire field of student affairs. Although many theories are influential, some of the most vital are student development, leadership, organization development, and the process models that prescribe the translation of theory to practice. It is important to challenge the cultural relevance of the core assumptions of these foundational theories such as the view that gaining independence from one's parents is necessary for mature development or the belief that assertion and independence are truly the hallmark of effective leadership.

The third competence, helping and advising, involves the diverse expertise necessary for most student affairs positions, such as communication, crisis intervention, group advisement, and conflict management. In reality, all inter-actions involve diverse worldviews, values, and experiences, so being aware of how cultural similarities and differences can have a significant impact on all relationships is very important. Cultural realities also need to be integrated into our understanding of the fourth component of the model: ethics and professional standards. The multicultural nature of higher education is at the center of many ethical challenges and requires that we make ethical principles more culturally meaningful and appropriate for all individuals.

The fifth area of competence, teaching and training, emphasizes the importance of integrating multicultural awareness, knowledge, and skills into preparation programs and professional development within the field of student affairs. It is essential that we incorporate multicultural issues and dynamics into all types of teaching and training; otherwise, our educational interventions may be incomplete, inaccurate, or irrelevant. Assessment and research, the sixth competence area, require that student affairs professionals infuse multicultural knowledge, skills, and awareness into all aspects of assessment and research. That means being aware of the assumptions and the cultural variables that influence research and assessment and being familiar with culturally sensitive research designs and techniques and diverse instruments.

Finally, the seventh competence area, multicultural awareness, knowledge, and skills, are unique competences to assist student affairs practitioners in creating and sustaining diverse and inclusive campuses. Because all professionals need to be able to provide services, intervene, and address the needs of all students, it is incumbent on them to ensure that they have the insight, knowledge, and tools necessary for multiculturally sensitive practice. And although the field of student affairs is increasingly attending to multicultural issues, it is still necessary for all professionals to take responsibility for the development of their own multicultural competence.

Multicultural Change on Campus

Multicultural competence is important as a theory and construct but, arguably, its greatest value is in its application to everyday work in student affairs. However, multicultural competence is not a panacea to all multicultural challenges confronting campuses today. But it can function as a transformational framework to create multicultural change on the individual, group, and institutional levels. To be clear, multicultural competence is necessary but, by itself, is not sufficient to creating lasting multicultural change on campus. Given the complex nature of change, additional tool, theories, and models are needed to conceptualize and enact multicultural change.

Multicultural organization development (MCOD) theory offers many of the principles, strategies, and models essential to creating multicultural change on campus. Jackson and Holvino (1998) first proposed MCOD as a method for systematic and systemic multicultural change in organizations. MCOD merges organization development (OD) theories, social justice strategies, and a commitment to diversity. Although initial work focused on corporate culture, recent scholars have adapted their framework to higher education settings. MCOD models focused on higher education, such as Pope's (1993, 1995) multicultural change intervention matrix (MCIM) and Ingrid Grieger's (1996) multicultural organizational development checklist, offer tools and planning strategies for creating multicultural change on the individual, group, and institutional levels.

The MCIM is designed for higher education practitioners to conceptualize and plan multicultural change efforts (see table 23.1). The 2 × 3 matrix has been used to codify, understand, and strategically plan the type and range of multicultural activities and interventions on campus. The MCIM is based on two different dimensions. The first dimension focuses on possible targets of multicultural interventions: (1) individual (for example, individual students, staff and faculty members, administrators); (2) group (for example, paraprofessional or professional staff members, faculty members, or student organizations); and (3) institutional (for example, entire college or university, student affairs or academic affairs division). The second dimension categorizes two levels of intervention: first- and second-order changes, which have been adapted from the family systems literature for understanding how change occurs in a variety of contexts and systems (Lyddon, 1990; Pope, 1993; Williams 2013). Pope (1993) described "first-order change as a change within the system that does not create change in the structure of the system. Second-order change is any change that fundamentally alters the structure of a system" (p. 241). Williams (2013) further states, "Whereas *first-order changes* refer to minor adjustments such as developing a new diversity office or establishing a new diversity requirement, *transformative changes* [or second-order changes] by contrast often create new patterns of behavior and assumptions governing organizational life" (p. 16).

Using those two dimensions, the MCIM provides a practical rubric for understanding how first- and second-order multicultural change efforts and interventions occur across the individual, group, and institutional levels within higher education. As shown in table 23.1, the MCIM identifies six ways to codify existing multicultural change efforts and envision new multicultural

TABLE 23.1. THE MULTICULTURAL CHANGE INTERVENTION MATRIX (MCIM)

Target of Change	Type of Change	
	First-Order Change	**Second-Order Change**
Individual	A. Awareness	B. Paradigm shift
Group	C. Membership	D. Restructuring
Institutional	E. Programmatic	F. Systemic

Source: Pope, R. L. (1995). Multicultural organizational development: Implications and applications in student affairs. In J. Fried (Ed.), *Shifting paradigms in student affairs: Culture, context, teaching and learning* (p. 242). Washington, DC: American College Personnel Association.

interventions or programs in order to provide multicultural change agents with more detailed understanding of the various types of activities, strategies, and tools necessary to create multicultural campuses.

Change agents can use cell A (first-order change, individual level) and cell B (second-order change, individual level) interventions, which are typically focused on educating others at the awareness, knowledge, or skill level. Pope (1993) and Williams (2013), despite a difference of twenty years in their work, suggest that most multicultural interventions are targeted at the cell A level. These interventions typically target increasing knowledge or cultural sensitivity, such as coming-out day programs, presentations on the social conditions of a particular cultural group, or an antiracism program. As an alternative approach, cell B change efforts often entail education aimed at deeper understanding that may ultimately lead to cognitive restructuring or an "ah-ha" moment when individuals transform their multicultural worldview. In order to achieve such paradigm shifts, these interventions are often more intensive, interactive, or experiential (Reynolds, 1997), such as in many intergroup dialogue programs, when participants challenge their assumptions and beliefs about the world and themselves. Examples include more extended consciousness-raising workshops or ongoing staff training requiring introspection and self-examination.

Group-oriented change efforts include cell C (first-order change, group level) and cell D (second-order change, group level) and typically create changes in the makeup and structure of the group. Cell C focuses on diversifying the membership of the group without changing the goals or norms of the group even though research has shown that such changes do not necessarily change the experience of underrepresented individuals (Rankin & Reason, 2005). Traditional recruitment efforts, which do not automatically change the interpersonal and structural dynamics of a group or campus, are good examples of first-order change in which a campus increases the number of students of color or when a predominantly male academic program such as engineering admits more female students. Cell D (second-order change, group level) change efforts are typically focused on restructuring groups with new goals and missions. Before actually adding new members, the group examines what changes are needed in order to ensure that new individuals will be invested and will stay. New members should be involved in this examination process rather than creating new norms and then inviting new people to join. A retreat in which a specific group, department, or unit reexamines and reformulates its mission and goals and infuses multicultural values and practices with input and participation from new members is an excellent example of this type of change.

Institution-oriented change efforts include cell E (first-order change, institution level) and cell F (second-order change, institutional level) and typically focus on multicultural interventions targeting the institution or a particular division within an institution. Programmatic efforts at the cell E level often address multicultural issues but do not alter the underlying values or structure of an institution or organization. Creating a new multicultural office or developing a new multicultural in-service for staff members are important multicultural interventions, but they do not necessarily alter the underlying values or priorities of a division or the entire campus. If criteria for evaluating work performance or distributing discretionary funds are not tied to diversity issues, then a paradigm shift is unlikely to happen. For second-order change (cell F) to occur, there needs to be a strategic and systematic exploration of the underlying mission, values, goals, and practices of the campus that links them to multicultural values and initiatives throughout the institution or unit. These interventions are typically more involved and may lead to more extensive dialogue and changes within the organization. Instituting a campus-wide multicultural strategic-planning process would be one example of this type of change. Although top leadership needs to be involved in creating true second-order change at the institutional level, it is essential that all individuals on campus be involved and invested in the process.

With these six cells, the MCIM is a systemic model that incorporates all types of change. First-order change efforts are no more important than second-order changes, and it is vital that interventions targeting all six cells are used. Each cell suggests unique approaches or interventions for multicultural change; however, together they provide a rubric for developing a multicultural strategic plan. Without work on the awareness level, paradigm shifts may not be possible. The dynamic and fluid nature of the MCIM is depicted by the dotted lines between the six cells, which depicts the interconnections among the types and targets of change (Pope, 1993). Multicultural scholars believe that the long-standing reliance on individual educational interventions has made it difficult for many multicultural change efforts to succeed (Pope, Reynolds, & Mueller, 2004; Williams, 2013). According to Reynolds (1997), using systemic planned change efforts such as the MCIM to "create multicultural change may not only assist with the necessary goal setting but also will identify methods of implementation" (p. 220).

Developing Multicultural Competence

Developing multicultural competence means enhancing awareness, expanding knowledge, engaging in new behaviors, and translating those competencies to new and different settings. The process can be exciting, stimulating, provocative, rewarding, and exhausting. Although it is an internal process, an environment that challenges our ways of thinking and behaving and, at the same time, supports the risks we take and the efforts we make can facilitate this process. Given these two dimensions, the internal and the external, developing multicultural competence can occur at the individual level and the professional level.

Individual Level

Developing multicultural competence requires an investment in lifelong learning, a willingness to engage in self-exploration, and a readiness to expand one's multicultural settings and interactions. More specifically, as noted by Pope,

Reynolds, and Mueller (2004), developing multicultural competence is a call to personal action, a process rather than an endpoint, a paradigm shift, a multi-faceted approach to learning, and a deliberate act. By *a call to personal action* we suggest multicultural competence becomes part of our daily experiences, not just at work but in the many spheres of our lives, including our families, neighborhoods, and communities. Developing multicultural competence is *a process* and not an end point that only a few experts will reach. Any activity that involves developing an integrated and complex set of abilities, insights, and understandings will require patience and an appreciation of small accomplishments along the way. It is a *paradigm shift* in that it requires us to seek ways and opportunities to examine and deconstruct our assumptions and worldviews. Developing multicultural competence on the individual level requires tapping into *multiple sources of learning* beyond reading, attending workshops and seminars, and consulting with experts. We enhance our multicultural competence when we legitimize and take advantage of the learning that comes from increased and intentional relationships with our colleagues, supervisors, supervisees, and students. Finally, it is important to think of developing multicultural competence as a *deliberate act* that involves risk-taking, meaning making, crossing borders, and placing ourselves in (sometimes uncomfortable) positions to explore, reflect, examine, and challenge our ways of seeing and being in the world.

Professional Level

Developing multicultural competence needs support and commitment at the professional level of student affairs. Institutions and departments, for example, can establish multicultural competence as a guiding principle and an expectation. Organizational models, such as Pope's (1993, 1995) MCIM, Grieger's (1996) multicultural organizational development checklist, and Reynolds, Pope, and Wells's (2002) student affairs MCOD template, can provide organizational structures that prioritize and support individual efforts to develop one's multicultural competence.

Professional organizations can also be key to enhancing multicultural competence among practitioners. Many student affairs professional organizations, including the National Association of Student Personnel Administrators (NASPA) and the American College Personnel Association (ACPA), have incorporated the essential concepts and principles of multicultural competence into their professional development priorities and initiatives and statements on professional competency areas (ACPA & NASPA, 2015). Professional associations can also enhance multicultural competence by infusing principles of social justice in their governance and leadership structures as well as modeling these principles in policy-making and decision-making activities.

Graduate preparation programs can become a significant starting point for developing multicultural competence among student affairs professionals. McEwen and Roper (1994) were among the first to call for integrating multiculturalism in student affairs preparation programs by incorporating multicultural content into core courses and practical experiences. Pope, Reynolds, and

Mueller (2004) suggested that graduate students develop greater multicultural competence by observing these skills in supervisors and faculty members. Iverson (2012) and Henderson and Kline (2014) made a case for grounding multicultural competence in social justice advocacy: teaching students not just about working with diverse populations but also about fostering social change. Finally, Cooper, Howard-Hamilton, and Cuyjet (2011) offered practical tips and resources for faculty members in graduate preparation programs who teach diversity-related content.

Considerations in Developing Multicultural Competence

As discussed throughout this chapter, developing multicultural competence requires commitment and a supportive environment to nurture that commitment. This begins, arguably, with becoming aware of one's own assumptions, biases, and privileges. This awareness can raise feelings of guilt, shame, discomfort, resentment, and anxiety. In response, some may employ coping strategies to manage these feelings. Watt (2015) describes these strategies as defense mechanisms and urges practitioners and educators to understand and address them in order to become more multiculturally competent. Second, developing multicultural competence involves expanding our circle of multicultural relationships and interactions and the inherent risk of making cultural mistakes. We need to be open to these potential mistakes, lower our defenses when we encounter them, see them as learning opportunities, and make an effort not to make these mistakes again. Third, some of us may find ourselves in work environments that do not support our efforts to become multiculturally competent. This may require that we intensify our efforts to create and sustain new environments by openly supporting the efforts of those who are attempting to make a difference or by identifying those who share similar goals and building alliances with them to create affirming communities of justice and inclusion where none existed before. Fourth, as practitioners in an applied profession, we must resist the desire to find solutions to problems before we fully understand them. As Krumboltz (1966) observed, "The way we think about problems determines to a large degree what we will do about them" (p. 4). Finally, Bula (2000) urges practitioners to consider the many aspects of our multicultural selves—including race, gender, age, socioeconomic status, sexual orientation, religion, abilities, and language—and examine how each influences our beliefs, values, knowledge, and understandings of oppression and privilege. This self-examination can become a strong foundation for multicultural awareness, knowledge, and action.

Creating Multicultural Change

Effecting multicultural change on campus is a rewarding and a challenging process. Its rewards are campus environments that are inclusive and affirming. The inherent challenges are apathy, resistance, and even hostility that may confront and undermine attempts to make meaningful change on campus.

These challenges should not come as a surprise. Change is difficult because it can interrupt and disrupt long-held assumptions, norms, and expectations in individuals, groups, and organizational structures. Multicultural change efforts, then, require courage, vision, assessment, planning, and a marshalling of key resources (Chesler & Crowfoot, 1997; Harper & antonio, 2008; Pope & LePeau, 2012). Numerous principles and considerations gained from the literature can undergird these efforts (Kline, 2013; Nash, Bradley, & Chickering, 2008; Petitt & McIntosh, 2011; Pope, Reynolds, & Mueller, 2004; Watt, 2007, 2015). We discuss several of these in the following.

First, *multicultural change is a long-term effort.* Although there may be immediate and clear successes from short-term interventions, they quickly fade as the long-engrained effects of monoculturalism creep back into the institution. Multicultural change on campus needs to be an ongoing and sustained effort. Second, *multicultural change requires substantial human resources.* When it comes to change on campus, institutions tend to rely heavily on particular individuals to facilitate that change: the most vocal, grassroots-level change agents or those with the most power and influence, namely, the institution's leadership. Pinning hope for change on a small cadre of change agents is unsustainable and must also include and engage the "middle dwellers" (Chesler, Lewis, & Crowfoot, 2005, p. 192). Third, *multicultural change must be infused into the institution,* "right down to the mortar between the bricks" (McTighe-Musil, 2014, p. x). Coordinated multicultural change efforts are most impactful when grounded in strategic planning, with mechanisms to monitor, account for, reward, and evaluate. Fourth, *multicultural change must begin sooner rather than later.* Disrupting business as usual on campus can be unsettling and will likely meet resistance. However, this does not mean that the wheels of change cannot begin to grind, even if it starts with a small and dedicated critical mass of individuals, groups, and organizational units. Finally, *multicultural change cannot occur without open discussion.* These discussions may surface long-held biases, assumptions, and unacknowledged privileges. Professionals engaged in change efforts should expect strong feelings and should prepare for defensive strategies, polarization of positions, and even immobilization, the hallmarks of difficult dialogues. When engaged in these dialogues, Watt (2012) urges us to seek and understand our mutual goals while ensuring mutual respect among all involved.

Assessment

Developing multicultural competence and creating multicultural change on campus are challenging tasks. Assessment of multicultural competence can facilitate the development of an individual's competence, the implementation of effective educational interventions, and the examination of factors that are related to and influence multicultural competence (Reynolds, 2008). Assessment of multicultural change efforts can lead to infusing multiculturalism into the structure and operation of a higher education institution (Pope & LePeau, 2012).

Assessment of Multicultural Competence

Pope, Reynolds, and Mueller (2004) suggested that the dynamic model of multicultural competence, although not a measurement instrument itself, might be used informally in self-assessment, goal setting, and supervision. Professionals are likely to note that they have greater expertise in some areas than in others, although there should be a level of basic competence in each area (Pope, Reynolds, & Mueller, 2004). The characteristics of a multiculturally competent student affairs practitioner (Pope & Reynolds, 1997) and a checklist of more detailed and nuanced descriptions of the multicultural awareness, knowledge, and skills may also be used as an informal assessment device. These informal forms of assessment can be useful in identifying and developing goals to promote multicultural competence in staff evaluation procedures and staff development programs.

More formal and research applications of the characteristics of a multiculturally competent student affairs practitioner (Pope & Reynolds, 1997) are evident in the multicultural competence in student affairs—preliminary form 2 (MCSA-P2) scale, developed by Pope and Mueller (2000), and the multicultural competence characteristics of student affairs professionals inventory (MCCSAPI), developed by Castellanos, Gloria, Mayorga, and Salas (2007). Both self-report instruments operationalize and assess the cultural competence of practitioners and the effectiveness of programs designed to address diversity. Finally, using counseling literature as a guide, student affairs researchers and practitioners may also consider assessment of multicultural competence through use of portfolios (Coleman & Hau, 2003) or observer reports (Ponterotto, Mendelsohn, & Belizaire, 2003).

Assessment of Multicultural Change on Campus

Assessment of multicultural change efforts are best viewed as a measure of change across all individual, group, and institutional levels, what Livingston (2006) called a "systems view" (p. 233). Using the concepts from the MCIM (Pope, 1993), assessment at the *individual level* is a measure of self-awareness and knowledge with respect to diversity-related content (first order) and of one's motivations, cognitive restructuring, or shift in worldview (second order). Assessment at the *group level* might be an examination of the demographics and structural diversity of the group regarding recruitment and retention of its membership (first order) and of the dynamics within the multicultural group, such as group norms, ability to manage conflict, goals, roles, procedures, and interpersonal relations (second order). Assessment of multicultural change at the *institutional level* examines the institution's success at introducing new and needed multicultural programs and positions throughout the campus (first order) and its ability to systematically address core values and practices with respect to budget allocations, hiring practices, policy development, curriculum, and so on (second order).

Beyond these levels of institutional assessment (and to some degree embedded them) is *assessment of campus climate* or the satisfaction, concerns, expectations, and perceptions of students and faculty and staff members regarding "access for, inclusion of, and level of respect for individual and group needs, abilities, and potential" (Rankin & Reason, 2008, p. 264). For a comprehensive and thorough description of potential assessment instruments and protocols across the levels of multicultural organizational change and campus climate, readers are encouraged to refer to Pope, Reynolds, and Mueller (2004).

Conclusion

Multiculturalism is an integral component of student affairs work. Professionals at every level face multicultural issues, concerns, and dynamics that affect their work on a daily basis. By focusing on the concepts of multicultural competence and multicultural change, we ensure that practitioners and institutions have principles and models needed for efficacious and culturally relevant practice. Developing individual multicultural competence and effecting multicultural change are long-term processes that involve establishing goals, taking risks, and changing the way people think and institutions operate.

For practitioners to become multiculturally competent and to create multicultural change on campus, they must address these issues on personal and professional levels. On the personal level, each individual must make multicultural competence a part of his or her daily life. That means making intentional choices to pursue life experiences and professional opportunities to expand multicultural awareness, knowledge, and skills. It is also essential that student affairs professionals consider the importance of integrating multicultural issues into every aspect of their professional lives, from what programs they attend at conferences to the ways in which they address the needs of underserved and underrepresented students on their campuses. Beyond the personal level, professionals must join with others on campus who are committed to multicultural change to build a stronger and more unified effort; collaboration and consultation are the cornerstones of effective multicultural change. Developing systemic and systematic efforts to integrate multicultural issues into every aspect of one's work is essential, from the type of programs offered to what is discussed in supervision; there are endless opportunities every day to embrace multiculturalism in a way that will truly make a difference.

Discussion Questions

1. What is your current level of multicultural knowledge, awareness, and skills?
2. What specific multicultural competencies are needed to do your job effectively?
3. What are your next steps to increasing your level of multicultural competence?

4. Where does your institution, department, or office target most of its multicultural interventions (individual, group, institution, first or second level)?

5. What barriers exist to creating multicultural change on your campus (department or office)?

6. What are the next steps to creating multicultural change on your campus (department or office)?

References

American College Personnel Association (ACPA) & National Association of Student Personnel Administrators (NASPA). (2015). *Professional competency areas for student affairs educators.* Washington, DC: Authors.

Bula, J. F. (2000). Use of the multicultural self in effective practice. In M.Baldwin (Ed.), *The use of self in therapy* (2nd ed., pp. 167–189). New York: Haworth Press.

Castellanos, J., Gloria, A. M., Mayorga, M., & Salas, C. (2007). Student affairs professionals' self-report of multicultural competence: Understanding awareness, knowledge, and skills. *NASPA Journal, 44,* 643–663.

Chang, M. J. (2001). Is it more than getting along? The broader educational relevance of reducing students' racial biases. *Journal of College Student Development, 42,* 93–105.

Chesler, M. A., & Crowfoot, J. (1997). *Racism in higher education II: Challenging racism and promoting multiculturalism in higher education organizations* (Center for Research on Social Organization Working Paper #558). Retrieved from http://141.213.232.243/handle/2027.42/51322

Chesler, M. A., Lewis, A. E., & Crowfoot, J. E. (2005). *Challenging racism in higher education.* Lanham, MD: Rowman & Littlefield.

Coleman, H.L.K., & Hau, J. M. (2003). Multicultural counseling competency and portfolios. In D. B. Pope-Davis, H.L.K. Coleman, W. M. Liu, & R. L. Toporek (Eds.), *Handbook of multicultural competencies in counseling and psychology* (pp. 168–182). Thousand Oaks, CA: Sage.

Cooper, D. L., Howard-Hamilton, M. F., & Cuyjet, M. J. (2011). Achieving cultural competence as a practitioner, student, or faculty member. In M. J. Cuyjet, M. F. Howard-Hamilton, & D. L.Cooper (Eds.), *Multiculturalism on campus: Theory, models, and practices for understanding diversity and creating inclusion* (pp. 401–420). Sterling, VA: Stylus.

Grieger, I. (1996). A multicultural organizational development checklist for student affairs. *Journal of College Student Development, 37,* 561–573.

Gurin, P., Dey, E. L., Hurtado, S., & Gurin, G. (2002). Diversity and higher education: Theory and impact on educational outcomes. *Harvard Educational Review, 72*(3), 330–366.

Harper, S. R., & antonio, a. l. (2008). Not by accident: Intentionality in diversity, learning and engagement. In S. Harper (Ed.), *Creating inclusive campus environments for cross-cultural learning and student engagement.* Washington, DC: NASPA.

Henderson, S., & Kline, K. A. (2014). Critical social dialogues and reflecting in action. In K. A. Kline (Ed.), *Reflection in action: A guidebook for student affairs professionals and teaching faculty* (pp. 51–64). Sterling, VA: Stylus.

Iverson, S. V. (2012). Multicultural competence for doing social justice: Expanding our awareness, knowledge, and skills. *Journal of Critical Thought and Praxis, 1*(1), 63–97.

Jackson, B. W., & Holvino, E. (1998). Developing multicultural organizations. *The Journal of Religion and Applied Behavioral Sciences, 9,* 14–19.

Kline, K. A. (2013). Implications for daily practice and life. In K. A. Kline (Ed.), *Reflection in action: A guidebook for student affairs professionals and teaching faculty* (pp. 155–165). Sterling, VA: Stylus.

Krumboltz, J. D. (1966). Promoting adaptive behavior: Behavior approach. In J. D. Krumboltz (Ed.), *Revolution in counseling.* Boston: Houghton Mifflin.

Livingston, R. E. (2006). Evaluation and termination phase. In B. B. Jones & M. Brazzel (Eds.), *The NTL handbook of organization development and change: Principles, practices, and perspectives* (pp. 231–245). San Francisco: Pfeiffer.

Lyddon, W. J. (1990). First- and second-order change: Implications for rationalist and constructivist cognitive therapies. *Journal of College Student Development, 69,* 122–127.

McEwen, M. K., & Roper, L. D. (1994). Incorporating multiculturalism into student affairs preparation programs: Suggestions from the literature. *Journal of College Student Development, 35,* 46–53.

McTighe-Musil, C. (2014). Foreword. In R. L. Pope, A. L. Reynolds, & J. A. Mueller, *Multicultural competence in student affairs* (pp. ix–xi). San Francisco: Jossey-Bass.

Mueller, J. A., & Pope, R. L. (2001). The relationship between multicultural competence and white racial consciousness among student affairs practitioners. *Journal of College Student Development, 42,* 133–144.

Nash, R. J., Bradley, D. L., & Chickering, A. W. (2008). *How to talk about hot topics on campus: From polarization to moral conversation.* San Francisco: Jossey-Bass.

Petitt, B., & McIntosh, D. (2011). Negotiating purpose and goals. In D. L. Stewart (Ed.), *Multicultural student services on campus* (pp. 201–217). Sterling, VA: Stylus.

Ponterotto, J. G., Mendelsohn, J., & Belizaire, L. (2003). Assessing teacher multicultural competencies, self-report instruments, observer report evaluations, and a portfolio assessment. In D. B. Pope-Davis, H.L.K. Coleman, W. M. Liu, & R. L. Toporek (Eds.), *Handbook of multicultural competencies in counseling and psychology* (pp. 191–210). Thousand Oaks, CA: Sage.

Pope, R. L. (1993). Multicultural-organization development in student affairs: An introduction. *Journal of College Student Development, 34,* 201–205.

Pope, R. L. (1995). Multicultural organizational development: Implications and applications in student affairs. In J. Fried (Ed.), *Shifting paradigms in student affairs: Culture, context, teaching and learning* (pp. 233–250). Washington, DC: American College Personnel Association.

Pope, R. L., & LePeau, L. A. (2012). The influence of institutional context and culture. In J. Arminio, V. Torres, & R. L. Pope (Eds.), *Why aren't we there yet? Taking personal responsibility for creating an inclusive campus* (pp. 103–130). Sterling, VA: Stylus.

Pope, R. L., & Mueller, J. A. (2000). Development and initial validation of the multicultural competence in student affairs—preliminary 2 scale. *Journal of College Student Development, 41,* 599–607.

Pope, R. L., & Reynolds, A. L. (1997). Student affairs core competencies: Integrating multicultural awareness, knowledge, and skills. *Journal of College Student Development, 38,* 266–277.

Pope, R. L., Reynolds, A. L., & Mueller, J. A. (2004). *Multicultural competence in student affairs.* San Francisco: Jossey-Bass.

Pope, R. L., Reynolds, A. L., & Mueller, J. A. (2014). *Creating multicultural change on campus.* San Francisco: Jossey-Bass.

Rankin, S. R., & Reason, R. D. (2005). Differing perceptions: How students of color and white students perceive campus climate for underrepresented groups. *Journal of College Student Development, 46,* 43–61.

Rankin, S., & Reason, R. D. (2008). Transformational tapestry model: A comprehensive approach to transforming campus climate. *Journal of Diversity in Higher Education, 1,* 262–274.

Reynolds, A. L. (2008). *Helping college students: Developing essential support skills for student affairs practice.* San Francisco: Jossey-Bass.

Reynolds, A. L. (1997). Using the multicultural change intervention matrix (MCIM) as a counseling training model. In D. Pope-Davis & H.L.K. Coleman (Eds.), *Multicultural counseling competence: Assessment, education, and training, and supervision* (pp. 209–226). Thousand Oaks, CA: Sage.

Reynolds, A. L., Pope, R. L., & Wells, G. V. (2002, March). *Creating a student affairs diversity action plan: Blueprint for success.* Paper presented at the meeting of the American College Personnel Association, Long Beach, CA.

Umbach, P. D., & Kuh, G. D. (2006). Student experiences with diversity at liberal arts colleges: Another claim for distinctiveness. *The Journal Higher Education, 77*(1), 169–192.

Watt, S. K. (2007). Difficult dialogues, privilege and social justice: Uses of the privileged identity exploration (PIE) model in student affairs practice. *College Student Affairs Journal, 26*(2), 114–126.

Watt, S. K. (2012). Moving beyond the talk: From difficult dialogue to action. In J. Arminio, V. Torres, & R. L. Pope (Eds.), *Why aren't we there yet? Taking personal responsibility for creating an inclusive campus* (pp. 131–144). Sterling, VA: Stylus.

Watt, S. K. (2015). *Designing transformative multicultural initiatives: Theoretical foundations, practical applications and facilitator considerations.* Sterling, VA: Stylus.

Williams, D. A. (2013). *Strategic diversity leadership: Activating change and transformation in higher education.* Sterling, VA: Stylus.

CHAPTER 24

LEADERSHIP

John P. Dugan and Laura Osteen

Cecilia is a second-year student in a higher education and student affairs graduate program and incredibly excited to take a course on leadership because it is a topic she was highly engaged with as an undergraduate. She served as the vice president of student government, president of the Latin@ Student Union, and is actively engaged with her local church. Cecilia also grew up in a family in which her parents pushed her to take responsibility for the things she wanted to change and advocate for herself and others. She sees leadership as the vehicle for doing this in her career. Her first assignment involves developing an Instagram account where she photographs people and asks them to share their definitions of leadership. Cecilia spends an afternoon outside the Student Union doing just that. Following is a representative sample of what she received:

- "Leadership is all about the team dynamic . . . creating an environment where everyone shares responsibility and feels connected to a larger purpose."
- "Leadership? No thanks. Leaders are the reason we have all the problems we do right now. We need fewer leaders."
- "Leadership is about challenging the way things are, getting back up when you or your group gets knocked down, and working collectively to make things better."
- "Leadership is stepping up when others don't want to and making things happen. You have to be strong, fearless, and willing to be unpopular to be a good leader."
- "Leaders solve problems and inspire people. It's about knowing the people you supervise and how to meet goals."
- "I wouldn't have the slightest idea. I'm not a leader. You should talk to my boss."

Cecilia finds herself frustrated. She never expected to encounter such divergent definitions of leadership let alone some that seem so negative. As she prepares for her next class, she realizes that she is disappointed that most people she interviewed saw leadership so differently than she does. She also wonders if she has a skewed perspective and what this might mean for her professional practice.

Leadership is routinely positioned as a critical outcome of college and desperately needed for the delivery, advancement, and success of higher education (Astin & Astin, 2000; Keeling, 2004; Kezar, Carducci, & Contreras-McGavin, 2006). This book and many others situate leadership as a critical professional competency for those working in student affairs (Astin & Astin, 2000; Love & Estanek, 2004; Woodard, Love, & Komives, 2000). Yet, research on professionals working directly with college student leadership programs revealed that over half reported no formal post-baccalaureate study in the area (Owen, 2012). In other words, they were responsible for the design and delivery of educational interventions associated with a knowledge base for which they had little formal course work or intentional study. If this lack of preparation is prevalent among those working directly with leadership programs, it is likely also present among professionals in general who are still expected to engage in the practice of leadership.

The goal of this chapter is to clarify what comprises leadership as a professional competency in student affairs. Note that the chapter is not concerned with the presentation of a universal definition of leadership. Rather, it explores three interrelated dimensions that shape how someone understands, experiences, and enacts leadership: understanding socialization, learning formal leadership theory, and engaging in leadership development. Also included are considerations specific to leadership in student affairs.

Understanding the Role of Socialization

Situating leadership as a professional competency begins by acknowledging that how people understand the concept is largely a function of socialization, which in turn shapes how they experience and enact it. Leadership, by its very nature, is a social construction (Dugan, 2016). It is named, defined, and given meaning based on shared social understandings that are personally, culturally, and contextually derived. This explains at least in part why Cecilia saw such variation in definitions of leadership among her participants.

Because of social construction, individuals develop informal theories about what leadership is and how it operates. These informal theories typically function in the background of our thinking subconsciously guiding how we understand, experience, and enact leadership. They also reflect untested assumptions that may or may not be accurate. Cecilia's surprise at discovering how people's definitions of leadership could vary so widely may indicate that she was operating from her own informal theory. Her example also demonstrates that unless we are compelled to do so, we may never question the accuracy or transferability of informal theories.

Informal theories are not necessarily bad. Cecilia, for example, seems to have a positive understanding of leadership characterized by a commitment to community responsibility. Nevertheless, allowing informal theories to guide leadership is a risky proposition because they often operate implicitly and reflect broader social systems and the social stratifications that come with them.

Implicit assumptions about leadership that go unchallenged typically default to the construction of ideal leader prototypes emphasizing the traits of charisma, dedication, intelligence, sensitivity, and strength while privileging perceptions of attractiveness, whiteness, and masculinity (Eagly & Chin, 2010; Junker & van Dick, 2014; Ospina & Foldy, 2009; Rosette, Leonardelli, & Phillips, 2008). This is advantageous for those who match the ideal leader prototype, but it results in harmful consequences (for example, lower performance evaluations, job satisfaction, general well-being, and perceptions of trust) for those who do not. Thus, when informal leadership theories fail to be made explicit they run significant risk of perpetuating social stratification and injustice engraining them even further into organizational processes and relationships.

Informal theories of leadership are greatly informed by the process of cultural socialization. Given leadership is socially constructed, the cultures in which we hold membership shape how we understand, experience, and enact it. International research examines cross-cultural patterns in how leadership is understood along with areas of convergence and divergence in associated values, attributes, and processes (House, Hanges, Javidan, Dorfman, & Gupta, 2004). Taking these into account plays an important role in the success of global leadership as well as ensuring that US values are not imposed in global contexts.

Similar cultural patterns exist domestically within the United States where affiliations based on social identity (for example, race, class, gender, sexual orientation) frequently play a role in shaping informal theories about leadership as well as reactions to the terms *leader* and *leadership* (Ayman & Korabik, 2010; Dugan & Velázquez, 2015; Fassinger, Shullman, & Stevenson, 2010; Guthrie, Jones, Osteen, & Hu, 2013; Ospina & Foldy, 2009). The sociohistoric and systematic oppression that characterizes US society interacts with unchallenged ideal leader prototypes contributing to a marginalizing effect and potentially distancing people from the concept of leadership altogether. This only serves to reinforce unequal power structures.

Informal leadership theories are also contextually contingent reflecting the environments in which people find themselves. These environmental influences reflect organizational, cultural, and societal levels, each of which has the potential to inform how a person understands, experiences, and enacts leadership (Alvesson & Sveningsson, 2012). This explains why a person may operate from one set of assumptions about leadership in one context but another set altogether in a different context.

Cecilia's assignment in the opening scenario was to collect definitions of leadership. Yet, it seems to be missing a major component, given the importance of cultural and contextual influences on the informal leadership theories from which definitions are derived. How might her interpretation of definitions been enriched had participants also shared salient social identities and the contexts influencing their definitions? For example, one of the participants associated social problems with leadership suggesting we would be better off with fewer leaders. Might this understanding be a function of cultural or contextual factors? Has the person experienced the negative influences of *not* being aligned with ideal leader prototypes? Did the person work in an environment with an abusive leader who caused more harm than good and as a result sees leaders as negative?

The power of socialization lies in its ability to situate one's understanding of a phenomenon, in this case leadership, as natural and normative (Harro, 2013). Thus, leadership as a professional competency necessitates that we move our informal theories from implicit to explicit and unpack how our understandings are influenced by cultural and contextual factors. This is a process of denaturalizing our assumptions. We also have to confront ways in which our informal leadership theories may reflect social norms that systematically privilege and oppress. This is a process of engaging with and challenging normative assumptions. Explicitly understood informal theories have the potential to serve as positive and powerful tools validating one's understanding of leadership rather than simply defaulting to dominant understandings or relying on formal theory alone. Engaging in this process collectively in the organizational teams and units that comprise student affairs is even more critical. It provides a platform to build shared understanding, enrich collaborative work, and foster collective agency for leadership.

Learning Formal Leadership Theory

The second key dimension of leadership as a professional competency emphasizes the importance of studying its knowledge base. This content exposes professionals to essential language, an understanding of how leadership theory has evolved, and points of contention that often differentiate theories and have a direct impact on practice. The goal is not to adopt wholesale any one theory but to construct a more informed understanding of leadership that draws on personal understandings and the component parts of multiple formal theories that resonate and are most useful in a particular context.

Formal leadership theories attempt to explain socially constructed understandings of leadership, how the process of leadership unfolds, and what constitutes leadership. Note, however, that leadership "theory" frequently reflects an umbrella term that includes theories, models, conceptual frameworks, typologies, and heuristics, some of which are empirically tested and others that are not. This means that professionals need to be conscientious learners ensuring a clear understanding of how well a theory has been tested along with constraints associated with how it translates to practice.

Numerous scholars have mapped the terrain of leadership theory attempting to organize evolving understandings (Komives, Lucas, & McMahon, 2013; Rost, 1991; Yukl, 2013). Simple chronological analyses typically begin with early conceptualizations focused on characteristics and traits of those with formal authority in positional leader roles (for example, great man and trait theories). When no universal set of leader characteristics or traits emerged, scholars shifted to exploring the specific behaviors of positional leaders (for example, style theory). Not surprisingly, no single "right" way to lead emerged pointing to the influence of context and the need to adapt behavior to a particular environment (for example, situational and path-goal theories). This, however, did not always capture why a leader succeeded or failed, and a shift occurred emphasizing the didactic relationship between leaders and followers (for example, leader-member exchange theory). Theories then began decentering hierarchical assumptions repositioning leadership as inherently concerned with mutual benefit and the common good (for example, transformational and servant leadership). Contemporary theories have expanded on this offering greater attention to leadership as a reciprocal process (for example, team and relational leadership); social justice (for example, the social change model); personal development (for example, authentic leadership); and complex systems (for example, adaptive leadership).

Although informative, chronological descriptions of the evolution of leadership theory often fail to capture how early theoretical conceptualizations retain influence today despite substantive evidence regarding their limitations. Sometimes this is because they connect so strongly to implicit, socialized understandings of leadership based on cultural or contextual influences. For example, one of Cecilia's participants defined leadership by listing the traits of strength, fearlessness, and willingness to be unpopular. Not only is this a return to a reductionist, trait-based understanding of leadership but also the traits selected reflect dominant cultural values associated with masculinity. It could be that this is a function of unchallenged assumptions that have been adopted into the individual's informal leadership theory. Other times theories retain influence because they are retrofitted, often without empirical testing, to better align with contemporary perspectives (Komives & Dugan, 2010). These theories often fail to capture the complexity of leadership, but they offer enticing prescriptive recommendations. They may also represent the ways in which leadership theory has been commoditized and a greater desire to maintain influence and promote a "product" over genuine interest in advancing the knowledge base and effecting meaningful change (Dugan, 2016).

A central purpose for learning formal leadership theory is to explore variations in how leadership is understood and intentionally integrating those concepts into one's informal theory of leadership. A number of points of differentiation emerge across theories that draw important definitional, philosophical, and pragmatic distinctions. Two of these are worth mentioning here.

The Power-Authority Dynamic

Leadership literature has a love-hate relationship with the concepts of power and authority. This is particularly apparent in formal theory, which initially almost exclusively examined leaders' use of authority, yet now seems to evade the topic altogether. Authority is based on a person having the *right* to direct others or take action in pursuit of a goal (Vecchio, 2007). It typically uses legitimacy associated with a positional role, coercion, and reward to achieve results. Power, however, is the ability to *shape* others' behaviors drawing on more informal means to encourage action. This includes perceptions of expert knowledge or reverence for a person based on a desire for affiliation and acceptance.

Authority and power may be coupled and a person often draws on multiple sources simultaneously (Vecchio, 2007). Student affairs professionals in positional roles have certain degrees of authority to take action, direct others, and pursue organizational goals. Individuals may not feel that they have significant authority comparatively with other institutional agents (for example, president, trustees, deans), but they likely still have the right to make decisions within a particular sphere of influence. It is important to remember, too, that power is often a function of perception, and in the minds of others an individual may be perceived as having substantial power. For example, if a professional working in health and wellness programs serves on an institutional task force addressing alcohol and drug use on campus, colleagues may extend that person significant power based on perceptions of content expertise.

Understanding differences between power and authority as well as attending to how they are addressed in formal theory is critical for leadership as a professional competency. Theoretical insights offer opportunities to learn how power flows in an organization as well as how power and authority can best be leveraged responsibly to achieve goals. Additionally, every individual has a personal relationship to power and authority that frames reactions to it as well as shapes informal theories about leadership (Lipman-Blumen, 2005). Moving these from implicit to explicit enables more effective navigation of leader roles and leadership processes. Thus, raising one's level of power consciousness becomes an essential component of leadership as a professional competency.

Challenging Dichotomies

Leadership studies scholars increasingly challenge the false dichotomies present in formal leadership theories (Alvesson & Spicer, 2014; Collinson, 2014). These dichotomies oversimplify what it means to engage in leadership as well as reinforce power differentials. Three common dichotomies include management versus leadership, leader versus leadership, and leader versus follower.

A long-standing debate in leadership theory explores the degree to which management and leadership are related or conceptually distinct. A number of scholars strongly assert that management reflects something altogether different from leadership and is largely about maintenance of the status quo; others express concern that such stark differentiation diminishes management as a critical aspect of leadership (Rost, 1991; Yukl, 2013). Intriguingly, Heifetz (2010) states the importance of management suggesting that more often than not exceptional management is sufficient for organizational success and that leadership is a much more infrequent phenomenon. So, does this mean that there should be separate professional competencies for management and leadership?

Perhaps not surprisingly, rigid distinctions between management and leadership are just as pragmatically unhelpful as suggesting the terms are synonymous. Task and social coordination usually associated with management is frequently a necessary but insufficient component of effective leadership. Similarly, exceptional managers may also be excellent leaders and vice versa. These terms are neither mutually exclusive nor one and the same. For student affairs professionals, management is typically a nonnegotiable dimension of their work. Routine failures in budget management, supervision, facilities operations, or coordination of events would certainly have an impact on employment. However, positioning leadership as a professional competency suggests that the work of student affairs is simultaneously so much more. It is about cultivating deep learning and personal development, shaping institutions to better reflect the values of social justice, and creating environments in which creativity and innovation can flourish.

A false dichotomy between management and leadership showcases how positional roles (that is, leader, manager) and processes (that is, leadership, management) are also situated either as mutually exclusive or synonymous. Early formal theories focused almost entirely on the traits and actions of formal leaders defined largely by the authority roles they held. These theories often presented leaders and leadership as equivalent terms. Later theories reflect a shift to leadership as a process differentiating the terms. The distinction between leader and leadership is an important one because the knowledge, skills, and attitudes associated with each have areas of overlap as well as uniqueness. For example, working in student affairs places an individual in a positional leader role with a particular set of responsibilities that require individual knowledge and skills. Concurrently, student affairs professionals participate in work teams engaging in the process of leadership to advance shared goals that require collective knowledge and skills.

Too strong a differentiation between leaders and leadership as well as conflating the terms contributes to a problematic overemphasis on leaders. In fact, dominant cultural norms in the United States often translate to leader-centric considerations as a default. Take, for example, the definitions provided by Cecilia's participants. They were asked to define leadership, yet more than half instead defined characteristics of good leaders. Defaulting to leader-centricity results in disproportionate knowledge, research, and training on leaders and leader development at the expense of leadership and leadership development (DeRue & Myers, 2014; Guthrie & others, 2013). It also makes it easier to misattribute leadership outcomes solely to leaders reinforcing heroic myths and co-opting collective contributions in the process (Day & Drath, 2012).

A final dichotomy exists in the differentiation between leaders and followers. This distinction is so strong "the division between leader and follower is usually taken for granted, and the former is believed to be the key agent, while the latter is seen as a more or less passive receiver of influence" (Alvesson & Sveningsson, 2012, p. 205). Leadership theories are notorious for perpetuating the idea that positional power automatically earns labeling as *the* leader while everyone else serve as followers, subordinates, or constituents. This bolsters power differentials as well as clear social roles. The participant in Cecilia's assignment who expressed she was not a leader but to speak with her boss may reflect in her response the negative impact of such staunch distinctions.

Heifetz (2010) expressed frustration that "the term *follower* is an archaic throwback rooted in our yearning for charismatic authorities who will 'know the way,' particularly in times of crisis and distress" (p. 20). This risks reinforcing authority dependence and further alienating people from the concept of leadership altogether (Heifetz, 2010; Lipman-Blumen, 2005). Such strong differentiation fails to acknowledge that multiple "leaders" can coexist in leadership processes as well as how power flows through organizations rather than just in a top-down manner (Alvesson & Sveningsson, 2012). The treatment of leader-follower dichotomies in formal leadership theories provides content from which to challenge understandings and assumptions. Leadership as a professional competency requires that concrete attention be directed to how language as well as organizational culture may perpetuate this false dichotomy marginalizing individuals from leadership and reinforcing authority compliance dynamics.

An unfortunate reality of graduate preparation as well as continuing professional development in student affairs is that educators may never be exposed to formal leadership theory yet expected to routinely take on leader roles and engage in the process of leadership. Doing so without exposure to or continued engagement with the content of formal leadership theory increases the risk of defaulting to implicit informal theories that go unchallenged regarding accuracy and transferability. Formal leadership theory provides content to address informal assumptions and more successfully advance professional and organizational goals.

Engaging in Leadership Development

The third dimension of leadership as a professional competency involves actively engaging in leadership development. All too often students are seen as the sole audience for developmental intervention. However, the meaningful, ongoing work of leadership development must also extend to professionals and cannot end with the earning of a degree. It must unfold over the life span of a person's career responding to evolving understandings of self, changing contextual influences, and shifting social dynamics.

Scholars typically differentiate between leader development and leadership development. Leader development reflects "the expansion of a person's capacity to be effective in leadership roles and processes" (Van Velsor & McCauley, 2004, p. 2) and focuses on the cultivation of human capital or individual knowledge, skills, and attitudes. Leadership development involves "enhancing the capacity of teams and organizations to engage successfully in leadership tasks" (Day, Harrison, & Halpin, 2009, p. 299). This emphasis on interpersonal relationships involves the cultivation of human capital and social capital (that is, beneficial relationships and networks). Scholars routinely position leader and leadership development as directly associated with increases in organizational effectiveness (Day, Harrison, & Halpin, 2009; DeRue & Myers, 2014).

Content of Leader and Leadership Development

The content of leader and leadership development flows directly from informal and formal theories. For example, one of Cecilia's participants defined leadership as "leaders solve problems and inspire people. It's about knowing the people you supervise and how to meet goals." If this reflects the individual's informal theory of leadership, what might a leadership training look like if he or she were asked to create one? It stands to reason that it might default to leader development instead of leadership development based on the person's definition, which may or may not be congruent with the intended purpose. It might also focus on building human capital through training in problem-solving, supervision, and inspirational motivation. These may be helpful skills, but to what extent do they reflect a greater emphasis on management than leadership? Is this what was desired for the session?

Formal leadership theory also directly influences the content of leader and leadership development. For example, let's say a residence life unit has adopted the social change model of leadership to guide its organizational and student leadership initiatives. This theory defines leadership as "a purposeful, collaborative, values-based process that results in positive social change" (Komives, Wagner, & Associates, 2009, p. xii). A leader or leadership development program with this emphasis would look radically different from that of a unit that adopted path-goal theory, which is leader-centric and concerned with how best to motivate followers' performance in the pursuit of organizational goals (Northouse, 2016).

Thus, content and assumptions of a particular informal or formal theory shape the content of leader and leadership development initiatives. Furthermore, the delivery of leader versus leadership development opportunities can easily be confounded when intentions and learning goals are not clearly stated. This further elevates the importance of making informal leadership theories explicit and learning the content of formal leadership theories. Both of these considerations may seem like common sense, but all too often people presume that the principles by which they operate related to leadership are consistent with those of others rather than taking the time to verify and co-construct them together.

Domains of Leader and Leadership Development

Several scholars challenge that leader and leadership development have for too long focused almost exclusively on the development of knowledge, skills, and attitudes without directing sufficient attention to the multiple domains in which development unfolds (Day, Harrison, & Halpin, 2009; DeRue & Myers, 2014; Komives & Dugan, 2014). Four specific domains emerge consistently in the literature and operate at individual and collective levels.

Leadership capacity involves the development of knowledge, skills, and attitudes associated with successfully serving in leader roles and engaging in leadership processes (Day & others, 2009). Most leader and leadership development interventions target capacity building, and the vast majority of scholarship focuses on it. However, just because someone has knowledge, skills, and attitudes does not necessarily mean that it will ever be enacted.

Leadership enactment represents the translation of capacity into practice. It is the manifestation of leader and leadership behaviors. Note that the accuracy of enactment is developed over time and largely dependent on one's capacity as well as ability to match specific capacities with specific environmental contexts (Komives & Dugan, 2014).

Leadership efficacy reflects one's internal beliefs about whether he or she can be successful when engaging in leader roles and leadership processes (Bandura, 1997; Hannah, Avolio, Luthans, & Harms, 2008). Leader and leadership efficacy are among the most potent predictors of capacity as well as critical mediators of whether individuals ever enact capacity, because people rarely make attempts in areas in which they do not feel they can be successful (Bandura, 1997; Hannah & others, 2008). This positions the cultivation of efficacy beliefs as essential to leadership development.

Leadership motivation examines individuals' decisions to participate in learning experiences related to leadership, adopt leader roles, and engage in leadership processes (Chan & Drasgow, 2001; Kark & Van Dijk, 2007). It also plays a powerful role in shaping quality of effort, affective responses, and persistence and is typically influenced by efficacy beliefs. Motivation is developmental and can stem from a variety of sources such as altruistic intentions, naiveté, or social identity associations.

Beyond these four leadership development domains are influences associated with other factors, such as social identity, resilience, cognition, and social perspective taking, all of which play important roles in leader and leadership development. Additionally, just as informal and formal leadership theories dictate the content of leader and leadership development in general, they also dictate the content of leadership development domains. For example, a person might demonstrate significant capacity associated with servant leadership but only minimal capacity associated with leader-member exchange theory. Similarly, a person might hold high leader efficacy when leadership is characterized by principles of collaboration and democratic justice but low efficacy for command and control approaches.

A key dimension to leadership as a professional competency involves the recognition that it is a constantly evolving process. This means engaging in leadership development oneself as well as contributing to an organizational culture that values and provides concrete opportunities for it. Those opportunities should be purposefully structured and avoid oversimplified approaches that fail to address the multiple domains of leader and leadership development.

Considerations for Leadership in Student Affairs

This chapter concludes with several specific considerations for leadership as a professional competency in student affairs.

Alignment with Institutional Mission

Shaping the leadership climate of a campus begins with a clear understanding and alignment with the university mission. College and university mission statements describe the campus's reason for existing. They are maps to institutional values and resources. Student affairs professionals seeking to enact, design, and navigate leadership on their campus should start with a clear understanding of their institution's stated purpose. Often falling into one of three broad categories: economic growth, critical thinking, or engaged citizenry, mission statements are clarion calls for how to align with institutional goals.

In addition to statements of purpose, mission statements are self-portraits of an institution. They are descriptions of culture tailored through institutional characteristics (for example, public or private funding structures, intended and targeted student populations, secular or religious affiliation). All too often, student affairs educators falter by not following Oprah Winfrey's interpretation of Maya Angelou's advice, "when someone shows you who they are, believe them the *first time*" (Winfrey, 2013). Failure to enact organizational leadership and leadership development initiatives aligned with the institutional mission is a guaranteed way to be dismissed or defunded.

Claiming Our Unique Role

Although mission statements in higher education have called for leadership development since the 1600s, it is only in the 1970s that student affairs professionals have claimed our role in this work (Komives, 2011). Student affairs professionals are uniquely prepared to draw on their education in human development, training and evaluation, and diversity and inclusion to create leadership development programs for students and colleagues. Two specific foundational assumptions of this work—the power of failure and relationships—frame our unique professional perspective on the design of leadership development programs.

Leadership that transforms our communities can be aptly defined as a process of disappointing people at a rate they can stand, which typically involves failing repeatedly (Heifetz, 1994). Student affairs professionals accept and create spaces where failure can be a celebrated form of learning. This learning emerges through our relationship with others as relationships serve as the foundation from which collective understanding of leadership are formed (Wheatley, 2006). Student affairs professionals recognize that reality is socially constructed *through* relationships, and drawing on this knowledge they design powerful environments where the campus community comes together to learn and grow. As student affairs professionals, we have the capacity to combine an understanding of the university context with professional skills to create leadership development across our institutions.

Cultivating Access to and Broadening the Content of Leadership

If we expect all, not simply some, of our students to increase their capacity, efficacy, enactment, and motivation for leadership, then we must create universal access to the programs that cultivate it. Through creating ongoing leadership development programs for faculty and staff members, student affairs professionals can cultivate campus partners whose efforts expand and diversify access for students. Centralized offices (for example, leadership development units, human resource units) may have responsibility for coordination, but ultimately they must encourage and advocate for student leadership development efforts across the campus. As clearly as we state all students have capacity, we must ensure all students have access. If leadership is for everyone then it must become a campus-wide endeavor.

In addition to access, the diversity of who is teaching and what theories are being used will shape who sees themselves in this work. Even the language of leader and leadership can feel exclusive, which is an important reminder about its potential impact on students with stories of loss and pain at the hands of leaders who abused power (Dugan & Velázquez, 2015). Without diverse models of people and processes outside of positions of authority, many of our students will not equate their desire for change with the experience of leadership (Guthrie & others, 2013). We must ensure our enactment of leadership and design of learning experiences reinforces philosophical beliefs associated with social justice. As student affairs professionals we can easily point fingers at external hierarchical models and then turn around and replicate them ourselves. For example, how often are our student leadership development training opportunities overwhelmingly directed toward positional leaders in student organizations versus the broader student population?

Conclusion

Leadership is a word with almost infinite meanings, yet in practical use it is rarely defined, often left to hang in the air with a presumption of shared understanding. It simultaneously carries enormous significance and is muted by overuse. And yet, within it lies incredible potential for shaping our experiences, how we relate to one another, and the ability to alter our social systems for the better. Perhaps the greatest challenges associated with leadership begin with unpacking how we have come to understand the term, disrupting assumptions about it, and purposefully co-constructing its meaning as well as how it is manifest in our organizational contexts.

Activity

Interview ten individuals on your campus to learn their informal theories of leadership. At least five interviews should be with students. Each interview will use the questions in part 1 and last no more than twenty minutes. Additionally, to evoke a more personal and symbolic understanding of leadership, ask participants to bring a photo that represents their definition of leadership.

Part 1: Complete the Interviews and Gather Photos
1. How do you define leadership?
2. What experiences have led you to this definition?
3. How do you connect yourself—or any parts of your identity—to this definition?
4. Share a bit about the photo you selected to match your definition of leadership. Why did you select it? What does it mean to you? How is it reflective of your definition?

Part 2: Reflection
Use the following reflection suggestions and questions to analyze your interviews and photos.
1. Describe themes of similarity or difference across responses and photos.
2. How did concepts described in this chapter emerge in the responses and photos?
3. Were there particularly strong influences from informal leadership theories? To what extent and how did social identities influence what surfaced in interviews and photos?
4. What surprised you most from the interviews and photos? What did you learn about your own informal leadership theory from what others shared?
5. How would you assess your own leadership capacity, enactment, efficacy, and motivation? Which domain would you most like to develop? How could you start that work now?

References

Alvesson, M., & Spicer, A. (2014). Critical perspectives on leadership. In D. V. Day (Ed.), *The Oxford handbook of leadership and organizations* (pp. 40–56). Oxford, UK: Oxford University Press.

Alvesson, M., & Sveningsson, S. (2012). Un- and re-packing leadership: Context, relations, constructions, and politics. In M. Uhl-Bien & S. M. Ospina (Eds.), *Advancing relational leadership research* (pp. 203–226). Charlotte, NC: Information Age Publishing.

Astin, A. W., & Astin, H. S. (2000). *Leadership reconsidered: Engaging higher education in social change.* Battle Creek, MI: W. K. Kellogg Foundation.

Ayman, R., & Korabik, K. (2010). Why gender and culture matter. *American Psychologist, 65,* 157–170.

Bandura, A. (1997). *Self-efficacy: The exercise of control.* New York: W. H. Freeman.

Chan, K. Y., & Drasgow, F. (2001). Toward a theory of individual differences and leadership: Understanding the motivation to lead. *Journal of Applied Psychology, 86,* 481–498.

Collinson, D. (2014). Dichotomies, dialectics and dilemmas: New directions for critical leadership studies? *Leadership, 10,* 36–55.

Day, D. V., & Drath, W. (2012). A dialogue on theorizing relational leadership. In M. Uhl-Bien & S. M. Ospina (Eds.), *Advancing relational leadership research: A dialogue among perspectives* (pp. 227–251). Charlotte, NC: Information Age Publishing.

Day, D. V., Harrison, M. M., & Halpin, S. M. (2009). *An integrative approach to leader development.* New York: Routledge.

DeRue, D. S., & Myers, C. G. (2014). Leadership development: A review and agenda for future research. In D. V. Day (Ed.), *The Oxford handbook of leadership and organizations* (pp. 832–855). Oxford, UK: Oxford University Press.

Dugan, J. P. (2016). *Leadership theory: Cultivating critical perspectives.* San Francisco: Jossey-Bass.

Dugan, J. P., & Velázquez, D. (2015). Teaching contemporary leadership: Advancing students' capacities to engage about and across difference. In S. Watt (Ed.), *Transformative multicultural initiatives* (pp. 105–118). Sterling, VA: Stylus.

Eagly, A. H., & Chin, J. L. (2010). Diversity and leadership in a changing world. *American Psychologist, 65,* 216–224.

Fassinger, R. E., Shullman, S. L., & Stevenson, M. R. (2010). Toward an affirmative lesbian, gay, bisexual, and transgender leadership paradigm. *American Psychologist, 65,* 216–224.

Guthrie, K., Jones, T. B., Osteen, L. K., & Hu, S. (2013). Cultivating leader identity and capacity in students from diverse backgrounds. *ASHE Higher Education Report, 39*(4). San Francisco: Jossey-Bass.

Hannah, S. T., Avolio, B. J., Luthans, F., & Harms, P. D. (2008). Leadership efficacy: Review and future directions. *Leadership Quarterly, 19,* 669–692.

Harro, B. (2013). The cycle of socialization. In M. Adams, W. J. Blumenfeld, R. Castañeda, H. W. Hackman, M. L. Peters, & X. Zúñiga (Eds.), *Readings for diversity and social justice* (3rd ed., pp. 45–51). New York: Routledge.

Heifetz, R. A. (1994). *Leadership without easy answers.* Cambridge, MA: Harvard University Press.

Heifetz, R. (2010). Leadership. In R. A. Couto (Ed.), *Political and civic leadership: A reference handbook* (pp. 12–23). Thousand Oaks, CA: Sage.

House, R. J., Hanges, P. J., Javidan, M., Dorfman, P. W., & Gupta, V. (Eds.). (2004). *Culture, leadership, and organizations.* Thousand Oaks, CA: Sage.

Junker, N. M., & van Dick, R. (2014). Implicit theories in organizational settings: A systematic review and research agenda of implicit leadership and followership theories. *The Leadership Quarterly, 25,* 1154–1173.

Kark, R., & Van Dijk, D. (2007). Motivation to lead, motivation to follow: The role of the self-regulatory focus in leadership processes. *Academy of Management Review, 32,* 500–528.

Keeling, R. P. (Ed.). (2004). *Learning reconsidered.* Washington, DC: National Association of Student Personnel Administrators and American College Personnel Association.

Kezar, A. J., Carducci, R., & Contreras-McGavin, M. (2006). Rethinking the "L" word in higher education: The revolution in research on leadership. *ASHE Higher Education Report, 31*(6). San Francisco: Jossey-Bass.

Komives, S. R. (2011). Advancing leadership education. In S. R. Komives, J. P. Dugan, J. E. Owen, W. Wagner, C. Slack, & Associates, *Handbook for student leadership development* (pp. 1–34). San Francisco: Jossey-Bass.

Komives, S. R., & Dugan, J. P. (2010). Contemporary leadership theories. In R. A. Couto (Ed.), *Political and civic leadership* (pp. 109–125). Thousand Oaks, CA: Sage.

Komives, S. R., & Dugan, J. P. (2014). Student leadership development: Theory, research, and practice. In D. V. Day (Ed.), *Oxford handbook of leadership and organizations* (pp. 802–828). Oxford: Oxford University Press.

Komives, S. R., Lucas, N., & McMahon, T. R. (2013). *Exploring leadership: For college students who want to make a difference* (3rd ed.). San Francisco: Jossey-Bass.

Komives, S. R., Wagner, W., & Associates. (2009). *Leadership for a better world.* San Francisco: Jossey-Bass.

Lipman-Blumen, J. (2005). *The allure of toxic leaders.* New York: Oxford University Press.

Love, P. G., & Estanek, S. M. (2004). *Rethinking student affairs practice.* San Francisco: Jossey-Bass.

Northouse, P. G. (2016). *Leadership: theory and practice* (7th ed.). Thousand Oaks, CA: Sage.

Ospina, S., & Foldy, E. (2009). A critical review of race and ethnicity in the leadership literature: Surfacing context, power and the collective dimensions of leadership. *Leadership Quarterly, 20,* 876–896.

Owen, J. E. (2012). *Findings from the multi-institutional study of leadership institutional survey.* College Park, MD: National Clearinghouse for Leadership Programs.

Rosette, A. S., Leonardelli, G. J., & Phillips, K. W. (2008). The white standard: Racial bias in leader categorization. *Journal of Applied Psychology, 93,* 758–777.

Rost, J. C. (1991). *Leadership for the twenty-first century.* Westport, CT: Praeger.

Van Velsor, E., & McCauley, C. D. (2004). Our view of leadership development. In C. D. McCauley, & E. Van Velsor (Eds.), *The Center for Creative Leadership handbook of leadership development* (2nd ed., pp. 1–22). San Francisco: Jossey-Bass.

Vecchio, R. P. (2007). Power, politics, and influence. In R. P. Vecchio (Ed.), *Leadership: Understanding the dynamics of power and influence in organizations* (pp. 69–95). Notre Dame, IN: University of Notre Dame.

Wheatley, M. J. (2006). *Leadership and the new science.* San Francisco: Barrett-Koehler.

Winfrey, O. (2013). *When people show you who they are, believe them* [Video file]. Retrieved from https://www.oprah.com/oprahs-lifeclass/When-People-Show-You-Who-They-Are-Believe-Them-Video

Woodard, D. B., Love, P. G., & Komives, S. R. (2000). *Leadership and management issues for a new century* (New Directions for Student Services, no. 92). San Francisco: Jossey-Bass.

Yukl, G. (2013). *Leadership in organizations* (8th ed.). Boston: Pearson.

CHAPTER 25

STAFFING AND SUPERVISION

Joan B. Hirt, Tara E. Frank, and Patricia A. Perillo

This section of the book is devoted to the competencies that student affairs administrators need to master in order to succeed. Teaching, advising, and conflict resolution are among the skills that enable professionals to manage the broad array of programs and services they provide for students. Rarely, however, do administrators work alone. In most instances, student affairs educators work with others—student and support staff members and professional colleagues—in an administrative unit. In turn, supervisors teach employees new skills, advise those who report to them, and resolve disputes among staff members. In short, supervision is a function that requires professionals to use many of the capacities described in this book.

Supervision goes beyond the daily management of personnel and activities, however. It involves a full spectrum of duties from recruiting and hiring new staff members to training them, providing them with developmental opportunities, and evaluating their performance. Even the separation of employees from an administrative unit is a supervisory responsibility. Collectively, these duties are best described as staffing practices and they form the focus of this chapter.

We start by looking at the guiding principle that informed our thinking on supervision: learning partnerships within a learning community (Baxter Magolda & King, 2004). Then we offer three scenarios that depict common work settings for new professionals. Next, we present models of supervision and staffing practices, including one posited by Winston and Creamer (1997) that forms the nexus of the chapter: recruitment and selection, orientation, supervision, evaluation, professional development, and separation. We describe the responsibilities associated with each element and use the scenarios to illustrate how that element can be enacted in a learning community. We conclude by discussing the role that staffing practices play in the vitality of the student affairs profession.

The Context for Staffing Practices: Learning Communities

At their core, colleges and universities are learning communities. A primary mission of postsecondary institutions is undergraduate education (Thelin, 2011; Urban & Wagoner, 2000) and this shared investment is the thread that links community colleges, liberal arts institutions, master's, and research universities (Hirt, 2006). Producing graduates who are lifelong learners is pivotal in the academy.

In this chapter, however, learning goes beyond the education of students. We embrace the work of Baxter Magolda and King (2004), who described the learning partnerships model: student affairs professionals who partner with faculty members and academic leaders to design learning communities. To promote such learning communities requires professionals to model lifelong learning for students. This can come as a surprise for those who are new to student affairs and who have earned a bachelor's and, likely, a master's degree (Cilente, Henning, Skinner Jackson, Kennedy, & Sloane, 2006; Renn, Jessup Anger, & Hodges, 2007). Many new administrators presuppose that their graduate degree has fully prepared them for administrative life (Liddell, Wilson, Pasquesi, Hirschy, & Boyle, 2014). They may assume that professional practice is all about task management and goal attainment. In reality, nothing could be farther from the truth. Because "student affairs professionals are intentional in their efforts to enhance student learning and development" (Ignelzi, 2011, p. 418), they must also be intentional about their own learning. It is incumbent on student affairs administrators to continually learn about their work in order to improve professional practice and model for students that learning is a lifelong endeavor.

New professionals do not operate in isolation. Most are in units with colleagues and have a supervisor who oversees their work. Many are supervisors themselves, managing the activities of undergraduates, graduate assistants, support staff members, and other professionals. It is essential that supervisors promote learning for those staff members (Ignelzi & Whitely, 2004). In essence, "the complexity of learning-centered practice calls for increased attention to the learning and development of professionals who implement it" (Baxter Magolda, 2014, p. 2). This is what it means to work in a learning community—one that is focused on learning for self, staff members, and students. Supervision in the context of a learning community, then, takes on new meaning.

Common Supervisory Scenarios

To fully appreciate staffing practices in a learning community, we offer three scenarios in which new professionals (those in their first two years in student affairs) might find themselves. We refer back to these scenarios throughout the remainder of the chapter.

Scenario 1: New Student and Family Programs

Maria is embarking on her second year as the assistant director of new student and family programs at a large, public, research university. She supervises three graduate assistants (GAs) who are studying student affairs and higher education. The first is in her second year of graduate study and wants to work in orientation and the second, also in his second year, wants to work in a dean of students office. The third GA is just starting in the graduate program and has no specific career objectives yet. Maria also inherited two administrative assistants. One has been in her position for only a year and the other has worked in the office for more than twenty years and is two years away from retirement.

Scenario 2: Residence Life

Miguel is in his first year as an area coordinator at a midsized regional university. He supervises four hall directors who have bachelor's degrees. Two are considering graduate studies in student affairs or higher education. One is interested in a career in the hospitality industry. The fourth took the job while waiting for his partner to complete her undergraduate degree. A high-performing fiscal technician who handles all budgetary matters and an administrative assistant who coordinates issues related to facilities and operations staff the area office. The administrative assistant's performance in the six months that Miguel has been on the job has not met expectations.

Scenario 3: Campus Engagement

Mei is in her second year at a small liberal arts college. She was hired as the assistant director of campus engagement to advise student government, but after one year her supervisor (who had worked on campus for thirty-two years) suddenly retired for health reasons and Mei was asked to step in as the director. She supervises three assistant directors, each with very different responsibilities. One has a master's degree, was hired at the same time Mei was hired, and manages major events on campus such as homecoming. The second assistant director, Mei's former position (advising student government), is currently vacant. The third is an alumnus of the college, has worked at the college for eight years since earning a BA, and oversees multicultural programs and services. Mei wants to provide specific supervision for each supervisee but also wants to cultivate a greater sense of team among her staff members.

Models of Staffing Practices

Surprisingly, the research on supervision and staffing practices in student affairs is relatively limited (Carpenter, Torres, & Winston, 2001; Cooper, Saunders, Howell, & Bates, 2001; Saunders, Cooper, Winston, & Chernow, 2000) although definitions of supervision are abundant. Some, such as Dalton (2003), adopt a human resource approach and emphasize how supervisors can hone the talents of staff members. Others (for example, Mills, 2000) concentrate on the role of supervision in achieving organizational objectives. In this context the supervisor's job is to harness employee talents to achieve institutional goals. Both of these approaches capture certain elements of supervision but neither addresses the full array of responsibilities associated with personnel management (Janosik & Creamer, 2003).

Winston and Creamer (1997) delineated a comprehensive framework of staffing practices. Their original model consisted of five interactive elements. The cornerstone—recruitment and selection—requires supervisors to analyze the staffing needs of the unit, design a position description that captures the essential duties of the job, conduct a recruiting campaign that attracts candidates from a broad spectrum of backgrounds, and hire the right person for the position. Orientation, the second element of the model, facilitates the transition of the newly hired employee to the position. As such, it often precedes a new hire's first day on the job (Saunders & Cooper, 2009) and may continue throughout the incumbent's first year in the position or longer.

The next three elements in the model include the responsibilities that professionals typically associate with the personnel function. Supervision entails a relationship between manager and staff member that facilitates the attainment of organizational and individual objectives. Performance appraisals serve to evaluate employee performance and identify future professional development needs (Winston & Creamer, 1997). The fifth element, staff development, involves purposefully designed, multifaceted activities that enable staff members to address gaps in their knowledge base and to gain new skills. The original model was modified to include a sixth element—separation— when Conley (2001) pointed out the varied reasons that cause staff members to leave a position. Supervisors have obligations to the person leaving and to other employees in their unit when a departure occurs.

Collectively, these six elements encapsulate the building blocks of staffing practices. We caution readers, however, not to consider these elements as either discrete or sequential. They operate synergistically, at times overlapping and interacting. Supervision, for instance, likely takes place while orientation is occurring. Performance appraisal, done right, uncovers areas that should be addressed even as professional development activities are occurring. The very essence of the model is the evolutionary nature of staffing practices. Individuals and institutions are constantly changing as they adapt to growth and environmental shifts. Staffing, then, must be thought of as an ongoing activity that supervisors routinely engage in (Janosik & Creamer, 2003; Winston & Creamer, 1997). Some further elaboration may illuminate the importance of each element of the model.

Staff Recruitment and Selection

The success of any administrative unit rests in large part on the people who work to accomplish the organization's goals. As Winston and Creamer (1997) note, "There are no equivalent substitutes for talented and professionally competent staff . . . The first commandment for student affairs administrators, therefore, is to hire the right people. The second commandment is to do it the right way" (p. 123). There are multiple reasons why recruiting and hiring are important, but three are most relevant to this discussion. First, selecting the candidate best suited for a position ensures that the incumbent is prepared to carry out the job's responsibilities and increases the probability that the organization can achieve its goals. Second, hiring the right candidate maximizes the potential for employee development. Finally, recruiting is the single most fertile opportunity to expand organizational perspectives by attracting people with diverse backgrounds and skill sets.

To achieve these outcomes recruiting and hiring need to be done correctly (Winston & Miller, 1991). To start, administrators who strive to attract a diverse pool of applicants have to design a diversified recruiting plan. This may entail traditional actions such as listing the job in *The Chronicle of Higher Education* or through placement centers at professional conferences. It should go beyond these efforts, however, to reach out to other potential applicants. For example, advertising jobs in *Diverse Issues in Higher Education, The Hispanic Outlook in Higher Education,* or similar publications might reach some applicants who otherwise might not learn of the vacancy. In the same vein, *how* a position is advertised is as important as *where* it is publicized. Websites, electronic bulletin boards, discussion forums, social network sites, and e-mail lists are all economical and efficient ways to announce job opportunities that also may result in a more diverse applicant pool.

Selected candidates should be interviewed by representative stakeholders, including students, support staff members, and professional colleagues, as well as by the supervisor. Deciding among several competitive candidates is the desired end state in a hiring process: alternative scenarios are troublesome. When the recruiting process fails to produce a pool of qualified applicants or a pool that is not sufficiently diverse, the manager must decide whether to proceed with interviews. Likewise, if candidates are interviewed but none are a good fit for the job, a supervisor must decide whether to make an offer. In either of these eventualities, administrators are advised to remember that hiring a less-than-qualified applicant serves neither the institution's nor the individual's interests. It is almost always better to start the search process anew than to deal with the individual and organizational consequences of hiring someone who is not right for the job.

How can the recruitment and selection process be enacted in a learning community? Consider Mei's situation in the previously described scenario 3. She needs to recruit and hire a new assistant director for the position she formerly held—advising student government. As a supervisor, she should consider what she and others involved in the recruitment and selection process can learn from that process. To start, candidates should learn not only about the position but also about the office, the division of student affairs, the college, and the local community. Second, every college or university has policies and procedures that guide hiring. Those involved in the recruitment and selection process must learn about those parameters. Finally, Mei needs to examine her own potential biases in this situation. She held this position and needs to learn how to allow another person to assume the reins and lead.

Thus, all parties involved in the recruitment and selection process can and should learn about hiring. Employing staff members who are qualified for the job, who stand to benefit personally and professionally from the job, and who can contribute to the organization positions the supervisor to address the second element of the model: orientation.

Staff Orientation

Recent hires and experienced staff members with newly assigned roles need guidance if they are to work effectively on starting the new job (Janosik & Creamer, 2003; Strayhorn, 2009). Supervisors should use orientation to deliver the necessary guidance and knowledge that promotes staff member success. Providing information about the position, unit or division, institution, and surrounding community offers new staff members a sense of history, an understanding of how work gets done, and even practical advice about insurance options and retirement plans. Orientation is important for other reasons, as well. The way in which staff members are oriented influences whether they can manage their personal and professional transitions effectively, whether they will understand the importance of professional development and therefore engage in it regularly, whether they will achieve individual and institutional goals in terms of productivity, and whether they will remain in the student affairs profession (Conley, 2001; Saunders & Cooper, 2003).

Student affairs practitioners, especially those new to the field, cite orientation as critical to their success during the first few years of professional service (Frank, 2013). Yet, all staff members need to learn certain information to carry out their assigned duties. For instance, supervisors should talk with staff members about behavioral norms (what to wear to work, for example), political realities (how shrinking budgets affect travel, for instance), procedures for performance appraisal (including standards by which work will be evaluated), and everyday practices (such as where to find office supplies, how to access e-mail) that affect the nature of work. Doing so will enable professionals to succeed and lessen the chances for role ambiguity or confusion. Effective orientation programs ease concerns about adjustment and reduce, if not eliminate, the trepidation that many new administrators feel about their roles. Additionally, well-designed orientation programs socialize new members to the values, traditions, and culture of an organization, foster their sense of belonging, and build their confidence to carry out job tasks (Saunders & Cooper, 2003).

Responsibilities for orienting new and newly reassigned staff members to the institution, unit, or job function falls to supervisors and experienced staff peers, although supervisors, by virtue of their position, generally assume the lion's share of the work in designing and implementing a formal orientation process. Additionally, contextual factors influence orientation practices because the nature of student affairs work varies by institutional size, racial composition, and mission (Hirt, 2006).

Orientation is inherently about learning, so examining it in the context of a learning community is fairly straightforward. Think about Maria's situation in scenario 1. She has two returning GAs and one new GA. Graduate assistants are employees who will likely transition to another institution in a year or two; hence, creating an immediate connection to campus is important if they are to succeed in their assistantship. Supervisors can shape that connection through effective orientation processes. When designing the orientation for her new GA Maria can identify what the new GA needs to learn. This will likely include gaining knowledge about environments (including the office, the division, the campus, the community); how work is accomplished (the distribution of tasks and the policies and procedures that guide the completion of those tasks); how work is evaluated; and what opportunities for additional learning are available to the GA. Next, she should consider how her returning GAs can contribute to the orientation process and what they can learn from it. For example, having the returning GAs train the new staff member on policies and procedures may enable them to learn how to organize and present information in a cogent manner. Likewise, they may be unfamiliar with some policies and procedures and assigning them the task of teaching those to a new GA offers them the opportunity to learn. Finally, Maria can learn how the orientation process can be used to build a stronger team and cohesive work environment.

Attending to the knowledge, skills, and abilities of staff members early on (during orientation), should enable managers to identify areas where additional supervision may be needed. This is another core element of Winston and Creamer's (1997) model.

Staff Supervision

Supervision may seem like the most straightforward element of staffing practices. After all, most professionals supervise others—paraprofessionals, support staff members, or other professionals—and all college and university administrators report to someone in the organizational hierarchy. However, supervision is far more complex than it appears at first blush (Tull, 2009) and requires an understanding of human dynamics and appreciation for human differences (Arminio & Creamer, 2001). Done right, supervision leads to individual accomplishment, organizational achievement, personal development, and professional advancement.

Good supervision enables employees to accomplish their job tasks, appreciate the responsibilities of others, gain new knowledge, and acquire skills to advance their careers (Amey & Ressor, 2002; Shupp & Arminio, 2012). When individuals thrive in their job, they contribute to the success of the administrative unit in which they work. Achievement at the unit level contributes to the institutional accomplishment (Rebore, 2001). In addition to individual and institutional benefits, supervision serves the profession overall by promoting professional retention. Student affairs administrators routinely cite good supervision as key to their decision to remain in the field (Frank, 2013; Renn & Hodges, 2007).

Because supervision is relatively important, it is surprising that so few administrators are trained in the art of managing people. There is an abundance of literature identifying the characteristics of good supervisors for those interested in the topic to study (Tull, 2006). In general, these characteristics can be conceptualized in three categories. First, supervisors are teachers who instruct staff members about the organizational environment and institutional culture. Second, they are conduits that transmit information to those they manage as well as communicate needs of their staff members to unit and institutional managers. Finally, good supervisors motivate their employees not only through formal rewards but also by modeling leadership on a daily basis (Winston & Hirt, 2003).

Supervision can be meaningful for supervisees and supervisors. Reconsider Mei's situation in scenario 3. She has two assistant directors in addition to the vacancy she needs to fill. Mei was promoted to director over one of those (with oversight for major events) hired at the same time Mei was originally hired. The second has not earned a master's degree but has been at the college far longer than Mei and also has a student's perspective of the institution from his years as an undergraduate there. As she sets about hiring her third assistant director (who will advise student government), Mei wants to provide opportunities for her staff members to learn while simultaneously building a team. For example, both assistant directors need to learn how to report to a new supervisor and a new supervisor who was a peer until this year. The AD who manages multicultural programs does not have a master's degree in student affairs and needs to gain an understanding of the profession. Finally, Mei needs to learn more about the responsibilities of her two ADs so she can best direct the office. Once she identifies what each person may benefit from learning, Mei can create ways to facilitate that learning. For instance, she might design a series of staff meetings led by each AD during which the AD trains others on his or her responsibilities so they can not only learn from one another but develop a sense of camaraderie as well. Effective supervision in a learning community should lead to employee success that, in turn, is at the core of performance appraisal.

Staff Performance Appraisal

By now, the interactive nature of the Winston and Creamer (1997) model is relatively clear. The recruitment and selection process identifies areas that may need to be addressed in the orientation process. The orientation process enables supervisors to assess the assets that staff members bring to the job as well as areas where ongoing direction might be warranted. All these elements would seem to lead up to what is commonly referred to as employee evaluation. The term *evaluation*, however, infers some sort of summative rating. Performance appraisal, rather, is a process in which employee productivity is assessed in light of individual and institutional objectives.

There are eight essential elements that characterize the performance appraisal process (Creamer & Janosik, 2003; Winston & Creamer, 1997). To start, it should lay the groundwork for staff member development. Development efforts may address deficiencies in performance but should also identify a person's strengths. Too often supervisors focus on what needs to be improved and not enough on the employee's strengths (Shushok & Hulme, 2006). Ultimately, the appraisal process should identify ways to acquire the knowledge, skills, and experiences that enable the employee to move forward. Evaluation should be tied to rewards; those who contribute to organizational success should be rewarded for their achievements and underperformers should not. Next, the context must be considered. Jobs tend to change over time, as do employees. Moreover, environmental factors can contribute to the circumstances under which a job is performed. For example, a career services administrator should not be held accountable if the job placement rate for graduates drops precipitously because of an event well beyond the employee's control such as an economic downturn.

The next two elements of the procedure are inextricably linked. Personnel who are affected by the appraisal process should be involved in that process. Staff member engagement links directly to the fifth element—the appraisal process should be transparent, open, and equitable. Although this may appear patently obvious, achieving clarity can be challenging. Transparency is facilitated when appraisal is ongoing (the sixth element of the process) rather than episodic. Ongoing evaluation, however, relies on good leadership (the seventh element). Supervisors should serve as role models for employees and offer praise and constructive criticism in an effort to promote employee growth and organizational success (Creamer & Janosik, 2003; Winston & Creamer, 1997). Finally, the appraisal process should provide for contextual differences in systems. The nature of the administrative unit, the mission of the institution, the type of employee involved, and related characteristics all should be considered when designing a process (Creamer & Janosik, 2003; Winston & Creamer, 1997).

Miguel's situation (scenario 2) illustrates issues of performance appraisal. Recall that he has a fiscal technician whose work is exceptional and an administrative assistant whose performance is less than satisfactory. Regardless of any regular feedback Miguel has offered to either staff member, the formal evaluation process provides learning opportunities for all involved. The staff members should be offered the opportunity to engage in a self-evaluation that examines their strengths and passions. The fiscal technician might use the self-evaluation to identify new aspects of the university's budgetary processes she would like to learn about. The administrative assistant might learn to identify what he is handling well and what elements of his job performance need to improve. For Miguel, the appraisal process provides the opportunity to develop a skill that many student affairs professionals never learn: how to have difficult conversations and hold staff members accountable. Praising staff members is relatively easy for most professionals. Providing the constructive criticism the administrative assistant needs is far more uncomfortable, but, if done well, will yield far greater benefits for the staff member and Miguel. Indeed, a solid appraisal process will inherently identify opportunities for personal and professional development.

Staff Professional Development

Conventional wisdom suggests that great people are not born; they are made. Student affairs practitioners become productive, effective administrators through professional development, an element of staffing practices that centers on the notion of learning and is crucial to increasing performance and enhancing growth of new, newly reassigned, and even experienced staff members (Winston & Creamer, 1997).

Professional development has two primary purposes: professional-personal growth of individual staff members (human development) and facilitation of institutional effectiveness (organization development) (Janosik & Creamer, 2003). Activities that foster individual growth fall along the lines of "talent development" (Dalton, 1996). Participating in workshops and in-service programs; reading recent publications; attending national, state, and regional conventions; and undertaking advanced course work represent widely used strategies for talent development. When all staff members are involved in professional development programs, supervisors can improve functioning across the unit, which in turn enhances overall effectiveness.

DeCoster and Brown (1991) outlined six goals that represent a curriculum for professional development: (1) facilitating interaction among staff peers, (2) learning specific skills and competencies, (3) promoting self-awareness and achievement of predetermined objectives, (4) encouraging staff participation in programs and workshops, (5) nurturing staff renewal, and (6) sharing knowledge based on theory and research. Supervisors in learning communities can use this framework when working with their staff members to design intentional and meaningful development opportunities.

Our scenarios provide ample illustrations of how professional learning and development in a college or university might be enacted. For example, Maria might work with her two continuing GAs to identify activities they can undertake to gain knowledge and skills in the functional areas in which they aspire to work (orientation, dean of students). Her new GA needs to learn more about the full array of professional opportunities in the student affairs profession. The staff member who has been in place for a year might benefit from more information about the policies and procedures that govern university operations. It would be easy for Maria to assume that the staff person who has worked on campus for more than twenty years might not have much to learn, but that would be a mistake. Policies, processes, and personnel change over time and it is imperative that staff members stay current in order to maximize their effectiveness. As for Maria, she needs to learn how to manage organizational effectiveness while also supporting staff members' professional development.

Using the information that emerges for performance appraisal is key to successful professional development programs. Miguel has a real opportunity to work with the administrative assistant who is underperforming to identify training programs, workshops, online tutorials, and other mechanisms that might improve his performance. It is equally important that the staff member has the chance to select activities that are of interest to him in order to ensure that he is invested in learning and the developmental plan. In synergistic supervision, all the elements of staffing practices—recruitment and selection, orientation, supervision, performance appraisal, and professional development—occur interactively and, oftentimes, simultaneously. Regardless of how well the model is enacted, however, separation is likely inevitable.

Staff Separation

Throughout this chapter, we have identified many of the crucial needs of student affairs professionals that also are key elements of Winston and Creamer's (1997) model of staffing practices. Failure to attend to the needs of staff members can undermine job performance, compromise achievement of individual and departmental goals, and lead to dissatisfaction, which is an immediate precursor to departure from the job or *separation* (Burns, 1982; Conley, 2001). Whether measured in time spent training a new hire or actual dollars, a tremendous loss of resources occurs when workers depart prematurely (Frank, 2013). Thus, separation is an important and costly matter for supervisors.

Conley (2001) identified five reasons why staff members leave their positions or the field of student affairs entirely: (1) professional reasons, (2) personal reasons, (3) retirement, (4) involuntary separation, and (5) incapacitation, illness, or death. Subsequently, Hirt and Janosik (2003) reduced these into voluntary and involuntary reasons for employee departure. Voluntary reasons can be further divided into three major groups: professional reasons, personal reasons, and issues related to retirement. Involuntary reasons for employee separation include illness or death and job termination. In all cases, supervisors in learning communities play an important role when staff members separate from an institution or leave a position.

The supervisors in two of our scenarios may need to deal with separation in the near future. Maria has two GAs who will be completing their degrees at the end of the year and a staff person who is close to retirement. The GAs need to learn how to conduct a successful job search and the staff person needs to learn about retirement planning. Maria can use these personnel changes to learn more about the hiring and retirement policies and procedures at her institution. Miguel supervises a hall director who will leave as soon as a partner completes a degree and an underperforming administrative assistant. The hall director may seek information about dual career programs and Miguel may need to educate himself on the personnel policies regarding termination.

In the end, the reasons for separation (voluntary versus involuntary) may drive the learning that employees and supervisors must engage in but learning still occurs. Indeed, many supervisors dread employee turnover. Certainly there is a loss when a staff person departs and the time, energy, and resources consumed in the hiring and orientation of a new employee are costly (Hirt & Janosik, 2003). Separation, however, is part of the supervisory cycle. If supervisors are doing their job well, good employees will grow, develop, and be competitive for promotion to higher ranks. Likewise, supervisors will terminate less-than-stellar employees who are not serving the unit's interests. In this light, separation is simply one more element of staffing practices that supervisors should anticipate and prepare for.

Conclusion

In conclusion, staffing is a synergistic process. The recruiting and selection process lays the groundwork for what should be covered when orienting new staff members. It can reveal areas where professional development may be merited. Ongoing supervision offers employees regular feedback on their accomplishments and enables supervisors to appraise performance as well as note areas for future professional development. When employees are promoted or leave an administrative unit, supervisors have an opportunity to assess the personnel needs of the organization as well as those of the remaining staff members. At every stage of the cycle, learning can and should occur by all involved. New professionals who master the skills associated with staffing practices may need to terminate underperforming employees, but they also are certain to manage individuals who succeed in their personal aspirations. Staff members who achieve their ambitions are more likely to remain in the field and that ensures the viability and vitality of the student affairs profession.

Activities

1. Design the orientation process that Mei should use to train the new assistant director she hires to advise student government. What topics should be addressed and who should deliver that information?
2. In pairs, one of you assume the role of Miguel and the other assume the role of his administrative assistant who is underperforming. Role-play how Miguel might conduct the performance appraisal of this employee.
3. Assume you are Maria. Have a discussion with the administrative assistant in the office who is two years from retirement that lays the groundwork for separation from the office.

References

Amey, M. J., & Ressor, L. M. (2002). *Beginning your journey: A guide for new professionals in student affairs.* Washington, DC: National Association of Student Personnel Administrators.

Arminio, J., & Creamer, D. G. (2001). What supervisors say about quality supervision. *College Student Affairs Journal, 21*(1), 35–44.

Baxter Magolda, M. B. (2014). Enriching educators' learning experience. *About Campus: Enriching the Student Learning Experience, 19*(2), 2–10.

Baxter Magolda, M. B., & King, P. M. (2004). *Learning partnerships: Theory and models of practice to educate for self-authorship.* Sterling, VA: Stylus.

Burns, M. (1982). Who leaves the student affairs field? *NASPA Journal, 20,* 9–12.

Carpenter, D. S., Torres, V., & Winston, R. B. (2001). Staffing the student affairs division: Theory, practice, and issues. *College Student Affairs Journal, 21*(1), 2–6.

Cilente, K., Henning, G., Skinner Jackson, J., Kennedy, D., & Sloane, T. (2006). *Report on the new professional needs study.* Washington, DC: American College Personnel Association. Retrieved Dec. 11, 2006, from http://www.myacpa.org/research/newprofessionals.php

Conley, V. M. (2001). Separation: An integral aspect of the staffing process. *College Student Affairs Journal, 21*(1), 57–63.

Cooper, D. L., Saunders, S. A., Howell, M. T., & Bates, J. M. (2001). Published research about supervision in student affairs: A review of the literature 1969–1999. *College Student Affairs Journal, 20*(2), 82–92.

Creamer, D. G., & Janosik, S. M. (2003). Performance appraisal: Accountability that leads to professional development. In S. M. Janosik, D. G. Creamer, J. B. Hirt, R. B. Winston, S. A. Saunders, & D. L. Cooper, *Supervising new professionals in student affairs: A guide for practitioners* (pp. 123–151). New York: Brunner-Routledge.

Dalton, J. C. (1996). Managing human resources. In S. R. Komives, D. B. Woodard Jr., & Associates (Eds.), *Student services: A handbook for the profession* (3rd ed., pp. 494–511). San Francisco: Jossey-Bass.

Dalton, J. C. (2003). Managing human resources. In S. R. Komives, D. B. Woodard Jr., & Associates (Eds.), *Student services: A handbook for the profession* (4th ed., pp. 397–419). San Francisco: Jossey-Bass.

DeCoster, D. A., & Brown, S. S. (1991). Staff development: Personal and professional education. In T. K. Miller, R. B. Winston Jr., & Associates (Eds.), *Administration and leadership in student affairs: Actualizing student development in higher education* (2nd ed., pp. 563–613). Muncie, IN: Accelerated Development.

Frank, T. E. (2013). *Why do they leave? Departure from the student affairs profession.* Unpublished doctoral dissertation. Virginia Polytechnic Institute and State University, Blacksburg.

Hirt, J. B. (2006). *Where you work matters: Student affairs administrators at different types of institutions.* Lanham, MD: University Press of America.

Hirt, J. B., & Janosik, S. M. (2003). Employee separation: The role of supervisors. In S. M. Janosik, D. G. Creamer, J. B. Hirt, R. B. Winston Jr., S. A. Saunders, & D. L. Cooper (Eds.), *Supervising new professionals in student affairs: A guide for practitioners* (pp. 153–174). New York: Brunner-Routledge.

Ignelzi, M. G. (2011). What forms would supervision take to model inclusive, learning-oriented practice? The case for a developmental supervision model. In P. M. Magolda & M. B. Baxter Magolda (Eds.), *Contested issues in student affairs: Diverse perspectives and respectful dialogue.* Sterling, VA: Stylus.

Ignelzi, M. G., & Whitely, P. A. (2004). *Supportive supervision for new professionals in student affairs* (pp.115–135). Lanham, MD: University Press of America.

Janosik, S. M., & Creamer, D. G. (2003). Introduction: A comprehensive model. In S. M. Janosik, D. G. Creamer, J. B. Hirt, R. B. Winston, S. A. Saunders, & D. L. Cooper, *Supervising new professionals in student affairs: A guide for practitioners* (pp. 1–16). New York: Brunner-Routledge.

Liddell, D. L., Wilson, M. E., Pasquesi, K., Hirschy, A. S., & Boyle, K. M. (2014). Development of professional identity through socialization in graduate school. *Journal of Student Affairs Research and Practice, 51*(1), 69–84.

Mills, D. B. (2000). The role of the middle manager. In M. J. Barr, K. Dessler, & Associates (Eds.), *The handbook of student affairs administration* (2nd ed., pp. 135–153). San Francisco: Jossey-Bass.

Rebore, R. W. (2001). *Human resources administration in education: A management approach.* Boston: Allyn & Bacon.

Renn, K. A., & Hodges, J. P. (2007). The first year on the job: Experiences of new professionals in student affairs. *NASPA Journal, 44*(2), 367–391.

Renn, K. A., Jessup Anger, E. R., & Hodges, J. P. (2007, April). *First year on the job: Themes from the National Study of New Professionals in Student Affairs.* Presented at the American College Personnel Association/National Association of Student Personnel Administrators Joint Meeting, Orlando, FL.

Saunders, S. A., & Cooper, D. L. (2003). Orientation: Building the foundations for success. In S. M. Janosik, D. G. Creamer, J. B. Hirt, R. B. Winston Jr., S. A. Saunders, & D. L. Cooper (Eds.), *Supervising new professionals in student affairs: A guide for practitioners* (pp. 17–41). New York: Brunner-Routledge.

Saunders, S. A., & Cooper, D. L. (2009). Orientation in the socialization process. In A. Tull, J. B. Hirt, & S. A. Saunders (Eds.), *Becoming socialized in student affairs administration: A guide for new professionals and their supervisors* (pp. 109–128). Sterling, VA: Stylus.

Saunders, S. A., Cooper, D. L., Winston, R. B., & Chernow, E. (2000). Supervising staff in student affairs: Exploration of the synergistic approach. *Journal of College Student Development, 4*(2), 181–191.

Shupp, M., & Arminio, J. (2012) Synergistic supervision: A confirmed key to retaining entry-level student affairs professionals. *Journal of Student Affairs Research and Practice, 49*(2), 157–174.

Shushok, F., Jr., & Hulme, E. (2006, Sept./Oct.). What's right with you: Helping students find their extraordinary life. *About Campus, 11*(4), 2–8.

Strayhorn, T. L. (2009). Staff peer relationships in the socialization process. In A. Tull, J. B. Hirt, & S. A. Saunders (Eds.), *Becoming socialized in student affairs administration: A guide for new professionals and their supervisors* (pp. 152–173). Sterling, VA: Stylus.

Thelin, J. (2011). *A history of American higher education.* Baltimore: Johns Hopkins University Press.

Tull, A. (2006). Synergistic supervision, job satisfaction, and intention to turnover of new professionals in student affairs. *Journal of College Student Development, 47*, 465–477.

Tull, A. (2009). Supervision and mentorship in the socialization process. In A. Tull, J. B. Hirt, & S. A. Saunders (Eds.), *Becoming socialized in student affairs: A guide for new professionals and their supervisors* (pp. 129–151). Sterling, VA: Stylus.

Urban, W., & Wagoner, J. (2000). *American education: A history* (2nd ed.). Boston: McGraw-Hill.

Winston, R. B., Jr., & Creamer, D. G. (1997). *Improving staffing practices in student affairs.* San Francisco: Jossey-Bass.

Winston, R. B., & Miller, T. K. (1991). Human resource management: Professional preparation and staff selection. In T. K. Miller, R. B. Winston Jr., & Associates, *Administration and leadership in student affairs: Actualizing student development in higher education* (2nd ed.). Muncie, IN: Accelerated Development.

Winston, R. B., & Hirt, J. B. (2003). Activating synergistic supervision approaches: Practical suggestions. In S. M. Janosik, D. G. Creamer, J. B. Hirt, R. B. Winston, S. A. Saunders, & D. L. Cooper, *Supervising new professionals in student affairs: A guide for practitioners* (pp. 43–83). New York: Brunner-Routledge.

CHAPTER 26

TEACHING AND FACILITATION

Stephen John Quaye

Brandon is a black, male hall director on a campus where 87 percent of the undergraduate students identify as white. The staff members in his hall mirror the larger campus demographics, with five of his six RAs identifying as white women and one as a black man. He has just returned to campus for summer residence life training. Usually, he is excited for the upcoming academic year, but this time, his heart is heavy, and he is dreading the year. Several black men and trans* people were killed by white police officers, which has resulted in a number of protests across campuses and in cities across the nation. Four of the five women on Brandon's RA staff are second-year students, who are all new RAs. Sophia, the fifth white woman, and Newton, the black man, are returning RAs and third-year students. The new RAs are particularly concerned about building community on their floors and mediating roommate conflicts. In the first week of training, they have relied heavily on Brandon to provide them with answers about how to do these tasks; however, Brandon has tried to get them to rely less on him, as Newton and Sophia do. Brandon would like his RAs, especially the two who are particularly resistant, to take more ownership over the training process, share their perspectives, and see the knowledge that they hold.

As Brandon ponders the protests about police brutality, in which he participated in several times, his attention shifts to the present, as Newton approaches him. "Hey, Brandon, how are you? You look deep in thought." "Yes, I'm a bit distracted. How are you, Newton?" "I'm struggling. Can I walk with you before we head to the next session?" "Sure," says Brandon. Newton continues: "Have you been watching the news? I don't know if the other RAs are thinking about these police cases like I am." "Yes, I'm with you on that. I think a lot about us as the only two black men on the staff, and you, in particular, as the only person of color on a staff of six RAs," Brandon says.

This week in RA training, they will be discussing social justice and, specifically, how to engage residents in conversations about privilege, power, and oppression and be allies to their residents of color experiencing racism. Brandon has been thinking of this week with anxiety. Training has been particularly difficult, because his staff members who identify as white women have never thought about privilege. Meanwhile, Brandon has had few opportunities to process these societal events and take time to self-care and heal from the toll of being black and witnessing how he is seen and treated as a problem. The daylong retreat he has planned will focus on building trust among his RAs to engage in dialogues about privilege, power, and oppression with some structured activities to process these issues. He has two learning outcomes for his staff members: (1) to gain awareness that privilege exists and (2) to reflect on their intersected social identities.

◆ ◆ ◆

The opening scenario illustrates a number of complex issues facing student affairs educators in their daily teaching and facilitating. For instance, they must pay attention to the different developmental needs of learners (Berger, 2012); understand how students' social identities affect their learning (Maxwell, Chesler, & Nagda, 2011); and use a diverse array of strategies to respond to the various ways students learn (Phillips & Soltis, 2009). In addition, they must think about their own social identities, what triggers them during teaching or facilitating (Obear, 2007), and be flexible to respond to student needs as they change (Quaye, 2014). In this chapter, I focus on the teaching and facilitating among student affairs educators. Following a broad discussion about teaching and facilitating in student affairs, I shift to teaching and facilitating in practice with models of teaching and facilitating that student affairs educators can use to guide their practice. I then discuss teaching and facilitating about social media, given its proliferation among college students, and conclude the chapter with various questions and activities readers can use in their own work with students.

Teaching and Facilitating in Student Affairs

To lay the groundwork for *teaching* and *facilitating*, in this section, I discuss these two terms, devoting more attention to facilitating, because the kind of work in which student affairs educators engage more frequently calls for facilitation. Traditional notions of teaching imply a teacher in a classroom with students, in which the teacher is responsible for creating a syllabus, an agenda or lesson plans for each class session, and using techniques (for example, lecture, small-group discussion, reflection) to foster student learning (Phillips & Soltis, 2009). Teachers also use various methods (for example, papers, exams, quizzes) to assess student learning of the subject. However, student affairs work typically necessitates progressive forms of teaching (Dewey, 1997, hooks, 1994); thus, I focus solely on this kind of teaching in the chapter.

What Is Teaching?

Progressive, critical notions of teaching are based on the mutual sharing of power between students and teachers. Dewey (1997) explicated this kind of teaching in his book *Experience & Education*. In this text, Dewey established the importance of experience in education. The way experience enters one's teaching is a critical component of more critical, progressive forms of teaching. The role of one's authority in teaching helps exemplify how experience enters the teaching space. As Dewey wrote, "When external authority is rejected, it does not follow that all authority should be rejected, but rather that there is need to search for a more effective source of authority" (p. 21). Rejecting the sole power of external authority in progressive teaching does not mean abandoning authority or adopting an "anything goes" philosophy. Rather, this entails a different kind of teacher-student relationship. "Basing education upon personal experience may mean more multiplied and more intimate contacts between the mature and the immature than ever existed in the traditional school, and consequently more, rather than less, guidance by others" (Dewey, 1997, p. 21). As Dewey noted, progressive forms of teaching mean more guidance from a teacher given that students are socialized in the traditional notion of teaching and may, thus, resist alternative ways of being in a classroom.

As hooks (1994) conveyed, teaching to transgress (that is, subverting power and being critically conscious) entails a way of being as a teacher that supports students in challenging power imbalances and actively reflecting on their lives and the world. "To begin, the professor must genuinely *value* everyone's presence. There must be an ongoing recognition that everyone influences the classroom dynamic, that everyone contributes" (hooks, 1994, p. 8, emphasis in original). hooks's words in the previous quotation connect with Dewey's (1997) notion of the importance of experience in this form of teaching. When one's experience is provided space in the classroom where the teacher regards every student's presence, then students take an active role in also shaping what happens in the classroom—what hooks referred to as the *classroom dynamic*. To exemplify this point even further, in *The Courage to Teach*, Palmer (1998) discussed the idea of embracing paradox in one's teaching. He identified six paradoxes that progressive teachers should consider, one of which involved honoring "the 'little' stories of the individual and the 'big' stories of the disciplines and tradition" (p. 76). This means not ignoring the role of facts, information, and knowledge from teachers and the discipline as prioritized in traditional ways of teaching but also reserving space for students' stories and experiences while also placing those stories in a larger context to see how they are tied to larger themes and ideas from the disciplines under study.

What Is Facilitating?

Building off ideas from critical, progressive notions of teaching, facilitating primarily involves taking a less-directive approach and working to support students' learning through reflection, guided activities, asking important questions, and paying attention to the voices in the space (Nagda & Maxwell, 2011; Quaye, 2014). One type of facilitating I discuss in this chapter is grounded in a critical-dialogic framework, which embodies the intergroup dialogue model (discussed in greater depth in the next section). Some student affairs educators (for example, those in multicultural affairs, women's centers) are tasked with engaging students in dialogues about privilege, power, and oppression. Facilitation using the critical-dialogic framework will help these educators in their work. Student affairs educators also work in, for example, student activities, student conduct, residence life, orientation and first-year programs, or academic advising. They need to learn how to train staff members, manage group conflict or confrontations, adjudicate student conduct cases, set expectations for groups and hold them accountable, and work on building community. These roles do not necessarily entail a focus on privilege, power, and oppression. I begin with discussing the critical-dialogic framework as a basis for facilitating dialogues about privilege, power, and oppression and then address facilitation for working with college students on issues beyond these kinds of dialogues.

Facilitating in Diversity Affairs   The critical-dialogic framework combines adopting a critical approach as well as a dialogic one (Nagda & Maxwell, 2011). The critical part means facilitation involves attending to the larger systems that create inequitable conditions and oppression for many people and dominance and power for some. Some of these larger systems reflect how racism, sexism, classism, and heterosexism, for instance, are embedded in laws, schools, policies, the judicial system, and other larger systems in society. Being critical of these systems means the facilitator poses questions and develops activities that enable students to have space to name these systems and understand their own roles in maintaining them or dismantling them. Facilitation, thus, is inherently based on students' experiences and stories and weaving these with knowledge introduced by facilitators or other students (Nagda & Maxwell, 2011).

The dialogic part of the framework entails using students' stories as a vehicle for understanding these larger systemic issues. "Participants learn to listen to others, share their own perspectives and experiences, reflect on their learning, and ask questions to more fully explore differences and commonalities within and across social identity groups" (Nagda & Maxwell, 2011, p. 5). Facilitators, therefore, adopt an approach that supports students in their own learning while guiding the process as needed. The notion of a guide is important in facilitation. Because issues of privilege, power, and oppression are complex with no easy solutions, addressing them means acknowledging one's role in the process, which can come with feelings of guilt, anger, hopelessness, and shame. A facilitator, therefore, must guide the process of students coming to know by incorporating appropriate readings, reflection activities, questions, and be attuned to the process of learning. This essentially involves paying attention to the classroom dynamic, as Palmer (1998) conveyed, and working to support students in taking ownership over their learning.

Facilitating in Other Student Affairs Settings   Student affairs educators working in other functional areas need to engage students in different ways. For example, working with RAs to mediate roommate conflicts is a common task entry-level professionals in residence life perform. Using the concept of multipartiality, educators work to see how their social identities intersect with power as they work to resolve conflicts (routenberg, Thompson, & Waterberg, 2013). When mediating conflict, one might presume that taking a neutral stance is the best. In reality, however, neutrality often ignores power differentials between parties in conflict. Multipartiality also necessitates recognizing one's biases and assumptions in the mediation process. "Applying multipartiality in facilitation is a delicate balance between impartiality and partiality; it entails navigating this liminality and validating numerous perspectives rather than showing preference for one over another" (routenberg, Thompson, & Waterberg, 2013, p. 175).

Facilitation is also necessary as educators work to build community in residence halls, in orientation and first-year programs, or with staff members. Helping students see themselves as peer facilitators is a useful strategy given their work with their undergraduate peers. As Wilhelm and routenberg (2013) noted, "Students are the most intimately knowledgeable about the campus climate, and although seen differently from faculty, peer facilitators can be equally credible because of their ability to relate and establish trust with fellow students" (p. 216). Knowing how to work with peer facilitators can be an effective strategy for building community and trust among undergraduate students in various settings (for example, orientation, residence halls, student organizations).

As a final example, student affairs educators know that student conduct is an issue with which they must deal. Rather than using only punitive measures, restorative justice is a way to hold those responsible accountable to the community they harmed. Student affairs educators can use restorative justice as a facilitation strategy for working with student conduct issues (Clark, 2014). Because facilitation is grounded in sharing power and authority, restorative justice principles enable those who violated community norms to take ownership over repairing the community (Kitchen, 2013). Facilitators in student conduct settings can work to support students in understanding their violation, how it affects others beyond themselves, and developing ways to restore trust in the community (Clark, 2014).

Teaching and Facilitation Models

Having laid the groundwork for teaching and facilitating, in this section, I concentrate on seven teaching and facilitation models new student affairs professionals and graduate students might employ to foster student learning. I divide these models into three that focus on facilitation with general student affairs tasks (for example, student training, mediating conflict, setting expectations, and building community) and four geared toward facilitating dialogues about privilege, power, and oppression. Although I make this division for ease of understanding, there is overlap in the models and most can be applied to general facilitation and facilitation about privilege, power, and oppression. In describing these models, I weave in examples from the opening case study to ground my ideas in a specific context.

General Facilitation Models

Chickering and Gamson's (1987) seven principles of good practice in undergraduate education, Baxter Magolda's (2004) learning partnerships model, and Lave and Wenger's (2006) communities of practice and legitimate peripheral participation are three models of teaching and facilitation that student affairs educators can employ in their work with college students.

Principle 1 of Chickering and Gamson's (1987) seven principles for good practice in undergraduate education encourages contact between students and faculty members as a way to improve student learning. Principle 2 is about developing reciprocity and connection among students. This principle is based on the sharing of ideas, which is an important component of facilitating. In encouraging active learning, the third principle, Chickering and Gamson noted that "students do not learn much just by sitting in classes listening to teachers, memorizing prepackaged assignments, and spitting out answers" (p. 4). This principle encourages active reflection, a core component of students internalizing what they know. Principle 3 is also emblematic of situating learning in students' experience tenet of the learning partnerships model (LPM) (Baxter Magolda, 2004). When teaching and facilitating are grounded in students' stories and experiences (hooks, 1994; Palmer, 1998), students are better able to actively reflect on and apply what they learn.

Brandon needs to consider how to build community among his staff. One reason he is dreading going into training is that he does not believe his white RAs have reflected on their social identities. He will need to validate them as knowers (Baxter Magolda, 2004), a second principle in the LPM, which means asking his RAs to identify the knowledge they hold and deem this knowledge worthy of sharing. Although Chickering and Gamson's first principle is about faculty member and student relationships, this principle can be applied in Brandon's case, as the person who is deemed the authority figure on the staff. Brandon will need to develop a different kind of relationship with his staff members that reflects a partnership, which will enable him to facilitate their learning during RA training, as they begin to see themselves as holders of knowledge and also authority figures. This practice is consistent with Baxter Magolda's third LPM principle of defining learning as mutually constructing meaning. Rather than Brandon relying on only his expertise, he can invite his RAs to share their own expertise in order to mutually construct meaning with him. For example, Newton might have ideas to share with his peers about what he is processing with police brutality and racism, which might enable his white peers to see a different perspective. Although this sharing can tax Newton further in potentially having to educate his white peers, sharing from his own experiences might be a welcomed way to see his knowledge and experiences as valuable sources, which in turn, encourages ownership over his learning (Baxter Magolda, 2004).

In their communities of practice model, Lave and Wenger (2006) articulated the notion of learning as a situated activity, which involves how newcomers, or novices, become full participants in a community. Specifically, they wrote that "learners inevitably participate in communities of practitioners and that the mastery of knowledge and skill requires newcomers to move toward full participation in the sociocultural practices of a community" (p. 29). Lave and Wenger's ideas, at times, resemble that of apprenticeship, in which a novice student engages with an expert working alongside this person, increasingly taking on more complex responsibilities to master a trade. What is different in Lave and Wenger's approach is the notion of legitimate peripheral participation. The use of "peripherality" implies that there are "multiple, varied, more- or less-engaged and inclusive ways of being located in the fields of participation defined by a community. Peripheral participation is about being located in the social world. *Changing* locations and perspectives are part of actors' learning trajectories, developing identities, and forms of membership" (p. 36, emphasis in original).

If there are varied and more- or less-engaged and inclusive ways of participating in a community, that means that there are ways of participating that will be more or less empowering for learners. When a practitioner prevents a student from becoming a full member of a community, it can be disempowering; whereas, when students feel they are contributing members of a community, it is an empowering experience that can foster deeper learning.

Take, for example, Brandon's RA staff. Brandon is struggling with how to help his RAs feel empowered in their jobs. His new RAs rely on Brandon's guidance to the point that, at times, they cannot make a decision without his approval. His expectation is that they build community among their residents and manage conflict that occurs in the hall. And yet, some of his RAs do not take steps to build this community. Brandon is trying to determine how to hold them accountable when they do not meet his expectations. Two of his RAs, in particular, are resisting taking steps to build community, because they believe they do not have access to Brandon's ideas of what community means. The more opportunities Brandon, as a teacher or facilitator, provides for his RAs to see themselves more fully as contributors to the staff, the more empowering this experience can be. Lave and Wenger are quick to assert that one should not confuse their ideas with *complete participation,* because this would suggest "a closed domain of knowledge or collective practice for which there might be measurable degrees of 'acquisition' by newcomers" (p. 36). Lave and Wenger's beliefs provide possibilities for considering how Brandon might scaffold learning opportunities for RAs to move from being newcomers to gaining fuller participation as they take more ownership over their learning and see their expertise in the learning process. Brandon could ask his RAs what community means and looks like to them, which would situate this idea in their own experiences (Baxter Magolda, 2004). He could also ask his RAs to think of community on a smaller scale, perhaps, between two roommates, which could make this larger expectation feel more manageable to his RAs. Brandon can also use his staff members as an example of community to ground this community-building expectation in a group in which they are all participants.

Giving prompt feedback and emphasizing time on task, principles 4 and 5 (Chickering & Gamson, 1987), respectively, underscore the importance of giving students timely feedback in ways that enable them to reflect on what they are learning, what they are missing, and knowing how to see ideas differently, as well as the importance of allowing sufficient time for students to learn. Training RAs to support college students in their growth and development and build community among residents result in expectations that can be difficult for new RAs to achieve, and yet, such goals are critical for students' learning. Therefore, educators must provide prompt and timely feedback to RAs on their work. The next principle, communicating high expectations, means offering students adequate support to meet expectations. Finally, the last principle is about respecting diverse talents and ways of learning. This principle encapsulates the role of teaching and facilitating in using a variety of strategies to respond to learners' diverse needs.

Privilege, Power, and Oppression Dialogue Facilitation Models

Those wishing to teach about privilege, power, and oppression can use the four-stage intergroup dialogue model (Zúñiga, 2003), navigating triggering events (Obear, 2007), the privileged identity exploration model (Watt, 2007), and Quaye's (2012, 2014) preparing for and facilitating difficult dialogues ideas in their practice. In the following, I weave these four models together, pointing out their nuances at times and integrating the opening case study to apply these models to practice.

In the previous section, I discussed the critical-dialogic framework for facilitating intergroup dialogues. Zúñiga's (2003) model, based on this framework, takes participants through four stages of engaging in dialogues about privilege, power, and oppression, moving from building trust to engaging in action to promote social change. In stage 1, facilitators and participants create an environment for dialogue by working to build trust among participants. This might involve setting ground rules for dialogue, engaging in low-risk activities designed to get to know participants' various stories, and seeking to find ways to trust that dialogue can occur. Lasting usually two sessions, the main goal of this stage is to set the foundation for being able to engage more difficult topics later. This stage complements the work of Quaye (2012), who found that facilitators of difficult dialogues needed to prepare for the dialogue by thinking through how their roles as facilitators differed from being a teacher, classroom dynamics, ground rules, and students' readiness for dialogue. Brandon is working with a staff composed of mostly white RAs who have not thought about race previously. A training experience on social justice, therefore, will require that Brandon provide space for his RAs to discuss their hopes and fears for participating in this training. Brandon might even invite his RAs to practice talking to each other about lower-risk topics before discussing hard topics, such as privilege, power, and oppression.

Stage 2, lasting between two to three sessions, is about situating the dialogue (Zúñiga, 2003). Participants work to learn more about their commonalities and differences. During this stage, participants might meet in homogeneous identity groups in order to spend time with people who share similar identities; this practice is consistent with Quaye's (2014) study, in which he found the importance of students first meeting in smaller groups to gain more confidence discussing racial issues. These smaller groups can be homogenous along various social identity dimensions, thereby enabling participants to discuss shared issues prior to interacting across differences. In Brandon's predominantly white staff of RAs, the five white women could spend time together learning more about whiteness, white privilege, racism, and how these issues manifest in their work with students of color, such as Newton.

Participants spend about four to five sessions in stage 3 when they begin to discuss hot topics that can cause much consternation (Zúñiga, 2003). Participants might work to understand how oppression and privilege function in society and see their own complicity in maintaining certain systems despite their opposition to them. Brandon, for example, can support Newton in looking at intersected identities during this stage. Given Newton's black racial identity, he is astute at recognizing how racism happens in society; however, he might have trouble seeing how his maleness intersects with his blackness to produce a complex interplay of privilege and oppression. Finally, in stage 4, participants move from dialogue to action (Zúñiga, 2003). This stage usually lasts two sessions and involves facilitators working to help participants engage in different actions for social change. Because action can take many forms (for example, challenging a friend who makes an offensive joke, writing an editorial in the student newspaper about oppression, protesting), facilitators support students in identifying what action looks like to them and how they might form coalitions with others invested in similar issues. This is consistent with Quaye's (2014) work in which participants worked to apply racial concepts to their lives. This application process was a way of engaging in action toward racial justice. In the case study in this chapter, Brandon can support his RAs in not only learning about social justice but also seeing examples in which social justice is not happening locally on their campus and consider steps they might take to address this problem.

One of the major issues that can occur while facilitating dialogues about privilege, power, and oppression is a facilitator feeling triggered by a comment made by a participant. A trigger causes an emotional response (for example, anger, annoyance, frustration) in facilitators when they feel unable to respond in a way that will not make participants shut down, resist, or retreat. Because the goal of intergroup dialogues is to open up participants to engaging in difficult topics, if facilitators are not aware of their triggers and how to respond, their actions can have the unintended consequence of shutting down dialogue. Obear (2007) described a seven-step triggering cycle that offers facilitators ways of noticing when they feel triggered, processing the triggering moment, and determining how to respond:

Step 1: Stimulus occurs.
Step 2: The stimulus "triggers" an intrapersonal "root" (a memory, past trauma or experience, fear, prejudice).
Step 3: These intrapersonal issues form a lens through which a facilitator creates a "story" about what is happening.
Step 4: The story a facilitator creates shapes the cognitive, emotional, and physiological reactions s/he experiences.
Step 5: The intention of a facilitator's response is influenced by the story s/he creates.
Step 6: The facilitator reacts to the stimulus.
Step 7: The facilitator's reaction may be a trigger for participants and/or another facilitator. (Obear, 2007, p. 2)

This cycle is important because facilitators may not even be aware that they feel triggered. Another important component of the process Obear (2007) identified is that the comment made by a participant may not be the actual cause of the trigger. Rather, the comment conjures up a "root," which is a past experience a participant has had that is the source of the trigger. This process is synonymous with how racial microaggressions (that is, small, subtle daily racial assaults against people of color) (Sue, 2010) work. It may not be the tenth racist comment, for example, that is the trigger, but rather the combination of the previous nine comments that then triggers the response from the facilitator. Consequently, being aware of the notion of a trigger, in and of itself, is a much-needed experience to gaining awareness of when they happen. Also, the story the facilitator creates is important. Obear (2007) wrote, "If facilitators interpret the silence of dominant group members as resistance, then their reactive self-talk may include: 'They are so typical . . . so arrogant, privileged and clueless . . . These are "our future leaders" . . . What a joke! I'm so tired of all these white people who don't get it . . .' As a result, they may feel angry, judgmental, tense and 'ready to fight'" (p. 5).

However, if facilitators create a story about students' silence because they are afraid or lacking experience in engaging these issues, their reaction will be a more empathetic response and, thus, the response in the dialogue space will be different. The final important point Obear makes is that how the facilitator responds to a trigger may prompt another trigger for participants or the co-facilitator, and then the cycle continues.

Brandon is struggling with the police brutality that is happening regularly in society. As a black man, he enters RA training with these deaths on his mind. Facilitating training on social justice issues has potential to be triggering for Brandon, particularly if his predominantly white staff members make comments that are harmful. Brandon's trigger may prompt him to think about an intrapersonal root, which is a past trauma. For example, Brandon may be empathizing with Newton and thinking about Newtown's struggles as the one black man on his RA staff. This memory may trigger other examples of racism Brandon has experienced from his past or memories of the black men and trans* people who have been killed this year. If Brandon is unaware of how these memories may be triggers, he has the potential to respond to one of his RA's comments in a way that shuts down the dialogue. Although Brandon is justified in any anger he harbors given the emotional weight of these cases of police brutality, as a facilitator he needs to consider how his triggers may prompt triggers for participants (step 7) (Obear, 2007). Given the role that triggers can play in difficult dialogues, it is important for facilitators to provide adequate time for students to debrief at the conclusion of the dialogue (Quaye, 2014). Debriefing may be especially important for facilitators who experience triggers during dialogues and may not be able to name the source of the trigger.

Although the triggering cycle is useful for facilitators, readers also need to consider the experiences of participants during difficult dialogues. Watt's (2007) privileged identity exploration (PIE) model is useful for identifying eight defense modes that people from privileged groups maintain when confronted with exploring their privilege during dialogues about social justice issues. Watt placed these modes into three categories of when participants *recognize, contemplate,* and then *address* their privileged identities. Recognizing is when one gains awareness about privilege for the first time and the emotions that ensue from this process. Contemplating involves the person beginning to reflect on what that privilege means. Addressing is when the person takes steps to do something concrete with that awareness.

Under recognizing, defense modes one might exhibit are *denial, deflection,* or *rationalization.* Denial involves ignoring or displaying resistant attitudes toward recognizing new stimuli. Deflection means shifting attention away from one's responsibility in order to minimize the effects of privilege. When people use rationalizing, they try to provide logical explanations for why inequitable systems work in the ways that they do in order to resolve their feelings of guilt or anxiety, for example. In contemplating one's privileged identity, *intellectualization, principium,* and *false envy* are defenses. Intellectualization means making sense of dominance and oppression in abstract ways, taking a distancing stance from these issues. "A principium defense can be identified by behaviors where one is avoiding exploration based on a religious or personal principle" (Watt, 2007, p. 121). When people express appreciation for someone different from them or wish to identify similarly, they are displaying false envy. The last status, addressing privileged identity, contains two defense modes—*benevolence* and *minimization.* Benevolence is when people engage in charity as a way to display how magnanimous they are in addressing social injustices without really understanding how their very actions work to maintain systems and dominance. Finally, minimization "can be identified by comments that reduce the magnitude of a social and political issue down to simple facts" (p. 122). Understanding the different defense modes that students might display during difficult dialogues helps to normalize these behaviors and assist facilitators in recognizing them when they see students employing them. Much akin to Obear's (2007) triggering cycle, the PIE model can help facilitators be mindful of their own reactions to these defenses by being able to name them as they occur. As Brandon works with his five white RAs, knowing the defense modes they might employ during training will be helpful in naming the modes when they happen and asking his RAs to process the experiences and feelings underneath the mode.

◆ ◆ ◆

The ideas provided in this section help readers see various models they might use to teach and facilitate. What the seven models in this section illustrate is the planning needed to teach and facilitate, because teachers and facilitators need to consider their own social identities; their strengths and limitations; who the learners are (that is, their own stories, experiences, strengths, limitations, and learning preferences); as well as the philosophies that undergird their approaches. Attending to these ideas will provide teachers and facilitators with the necessary grounding for the approaches they use.

Teaching and Facilitating about Social Media

I close this chapter with attention to social media, because students are using social media (for example, Facebook, Twitter, Tumblr) to engage about issues happening within their campuses locally and society at large. The reason, for example, that Brandon and Newton are so attuned to police killings of black people is that students are recording these deaths as they happen and then posting them to social media. Student affairs educators should work with students to understand how they use social media. I discuss three challenges for new professionals in engaging students in their social media use: (1) student activism, (2) being critical consumers of social media, and (3) when students exhibit shame and defensiveness.

Social Media and Activism

Students' use of social media continues to be ubiquitous within higher education. Social media can be a way students engage in activism, drawing attention to key issues happening. Twitter, for example, is a place where new professionals, graduate students, and undergraduate students can tweet about key events. For instance, #MichaelBrown began trending on Twitter during August 2014 following his death at the hands of Darren Wilson, a white police officer. #BlackLivesMatter is also a hashtag many people use, #SayHerName refers to trans* women of color being killed, and #ItsOnUs has been used to point out domestic abuse and violence. Even though students might view social media activism as important, others comment that those using social media for activism are engaged in "slacktivism" (that is, only posting comments on social media without actually engaging in actions to make change in society) (Rosmarin, 2015). Thus, slacktivism is seen as a lazy form of activism, which does not require much effort, risk, or time. New professionals working with college students should help students make sense of their social media activism and connect this activism to local issues happening on campus or in society and resist the urge to merely label social media activism as slacktivism or trivialize the significance of this form of activism.

Social Media and Critical Consumers

New student affairs professionals and graduate students should think about their social media use and work to become critical consumers of social media and strive to develop these skills within college students as well. Because college students use social media often, it is important for new professionals and graduate students to develop their own consciousness of social media and work to engage college students in this platform. Brandon and Newton have been paying attention to how police brutality cases are discussed in the media, and this has affected the ways they engage with each other and the RAs. During the training, Brandon might ask his RAs to note how they use social media and the ideas they are consuming in this venue. This works to situate the learning in his RA's experiences as well as validates their collective capacities as knowers (Baxter Magolda, 2004). It also invites students to actively reflect on social media, a practice consistent with one of Chickering and Gamson's (1987) good practices in undergraduate education principles.

Social Media and Defensiveness and Shame

A common occurrence in social media use is that a person will post or tweet something that someone else finds offensive. Then, several users will heavily critique the original poster, which can result in the person feeling shame (that is, "I am a bad person") for those actions. And when someone is feeling shame, a defense mode they will employ is often denial, rationalization, minimization, or deflection (Brown, 2012; Watt, 2007). Therefore, facilitators need to work with those feeling shame in ways that invite them to continue engaging rather than retreating. In Brandon's case, he can work to support his RAs in understanding these different defense modes, normalize them, and be able to name them when they see them happening (or when they are feeling them).

What makes social media tricky is often the anonymity or inability to build a trusting relationship with the person. This makes engaging the person to keep sharing difficult. #SAChat is a venue on Twitter where student affairs professionals engage in dialogue about current issues in the field. Often, a moderator notes ground rules for dialogue, which helps to create an environment for dialogue (Quaye, 2012; Zúñiga, 2003). Brandon can invite his RAs to observe the online chats happening in this space and then engage in face-to-face exchanges with his RAs to identify what they observed, what troubled them, and what positive outcomes they witnessed. These practices offer ways for his RAs to start seeing themselves as contributors to a community of practice by moving from novices to fuller members (Lave & Wenger, 2006).

Conclusion

In this chapter, I have discussed student affairs professionals' roles in teaching and facilitating learning among college students. The role of a teacher or facilitator is complex and involves not only paying attention to students' needs and their differences but also one's social identities and preparedness for fostering student learning. As seen from the case study, Brandon has many areas to attend to in working with his RAs. Similarly, readers may be working with students at different developmental places and with diverse needs. The models used throughout this chapter provide readers with possibilities for working with students within their own contexts. Ultimately, teaching and facilitating necessitate continually reflecting on one's practices, paying attention to one's biases and assumptions, and thinking of ways to engage students as active participants in the learning process.

Discussion Questions

1. What are your assumptions about how students learn? How do those assumptions translate into how you see yourself as a teacher or facilitator?
2. Think of your learning preferences. When have you felt at your best in a classroom setting? When have you felt challenged in your learning? What could a teacher or facilitator have done in that moment to foster your learning?
3. Of the seven models described in this chapter, which resonates with you the most? Why? What is missing?
4. Imagine you are Brandon. What learning goals would you develop for this retreat? What activities are important for helping students learn about privilege, power, and oppression?

References

Baxter Magolda, M. B. (2004). Learning partnerships model: A framework for promoting self- authorship. In M. B. Baxter Magolda & P. M. King (Eds.), *Learning partnerships: Theory and models of practice to educate for self-authorship* (pp. 37–62). Sterling, VA: Stylus.

Berger, J. G. (2012). *Changing on the job: Developing leaders for a complex world.* Palo Alto, CA: Stanford University Press.

Brown, B. (2012). *Daring greatly: How the courage to be vulnerable transforms the way we live, love, parent, and lead.* New York: Gotham Books.

Chickering, A. W., & Gamson, Z. F. (1987). *Seven principles for good practice in undergraduate education.* Washington, DC: American Association for Higher Education & the Wingspread Foundation.

Clark, K. L. (2014). A call for restorative justice in higher education judicial affairs. *College Student Journal, 48*(4), 707–715.

Dewey, J. (1997). *Experience & education.* New York: Simon & Schuster.

hooks, b. (1994). *Teaching to transgress: Education as the practice of freedom.* New York: Routledge.

Kitchen, S. E. (2013). Restoring the professor and the students: A circle process and contemplative practices in a restorative justice seminar. *Contemporary Justice Review, 16*(1), 28–42.

Lave, J., & Wenger, E. (2006). *Situated learning: Legitimate peripheral participation.* New York: Cambridge University Press.

Maxwell, K. E., Chesler, M., & Nagda, B. A. (2011). Identity matters: Facilitators' struggles and empowered use of social identities in intergroup dialogue. In K. E. Maxwell, B. A. Nagda, & M. C. Thompson (Eds.), *Facilitating intergroup dialogues: Bridging differences, catalyzing change* (pp. 163–177). Sterling, VA: Stylus.

Nagda, B. A., & Maxwell, K. E. (2011). Deepening the layers of understanding and connection: A critical-dialogic approach to facilitating intergroup dialogues. In K. E. Maxwell, B. A. Nagda, & M. C. Thompson (Eds.), *Facilitating intergroup dialogues: Bridging differences, catalyzing change* (pp. 1–22). Sterling, VA: Stylus.

Obear, K. (2007). Navigating triggering events: Critical skills for facilitating difficult dialogues. *Generational Diversity, 15*(3). Retrieved from http://www.mauracullen.com/wp-content/ uploads/2009/11/Navigating-Triggers.pdf

Palmer, P. J. (1998). *The courage to teach: Exploring the inner landscape of a teacher's life.* San Francisco: Jossey-Bass.

Phillips, D. C., & Soltis, J. F. (2009). *Perspectives on learning* (5th ed.). New York: Teachers College Press.

Quaye, S. J. (2012). Think before you teach: Preparing for dialogues about racial realities. *Journal of College Student Development, 53*(4), 542–562. doi:10.1353/csd.2012.0056

Quaye, S. J. (2014). Facilitating dialogues about racial realities. *Teachers College Record, 116*(11), 1–42.

Rosmarin, A. (2015, July 6). I get it. You don't like slacktivism. Now shut up. Only don't. *Huff Post Gay Voices.* Retrieved from http://www.huffingtonpost.com/abby-rosmarin/i-get-it-you-dont-like-sl_b_7727110.html

routenberg, r., Thompson, E., & Waterberg, R. (2013). When neutrality is not enough: Wrestling with the challenges of multipartiality. In L. M. Landreman (Ed.), *The art of effective facilitation: Reflections from social justice educators* (pp. 173–197). Sterling, VA: Stylus.

Sue, D. W. (2010). *Microaggressions in everyday life: Race, gender, and sexual orientation.* Hoboken, NJ: John Wiley & Sons.

Watt, S. K. (2007). Difficult dialogues, privilege and social justice: Uses of the privileged identity exploration (PIE) model in student affairs practice. *College Student Affairs Journal, 26*(2), 114–126.

Wilhelm, H., & routenberg, r. (2013). Training and supporting peer facilitators. In L. M. Landreman (Ed.), *The art of effective facilitation: Reflections from social justice educators* (pp. 215–230). Sterling, VA: Stylus.

Zúñiga, X. (2003). Bridging differences through dialogue. *About Campus, 7*(6), 8–16.

CHAPTER 27

COUNSELING AND HELPING SKILLS

Amy L. Reynolds

Maria has been a hall director for more than five years, and the relationships she forms with her resident advisors (RAs) is one of her favorite parts of the job. This year is different because of one RA, Sheila, who always seems to keep her distance. Today during their weekly one-on-one meeting, Maria notices that Sheila has some fresh bruises on her wrists. She remembers that a few months ago she noticed some bruises on Sheila's arms and face and when she asked about it, Sheila dismissed her questions and said she fell. She begins to wonder if there was something troubling going on in Sheila's relationship. Maria realized that maybe she should have been more assertive in reaching out to Sheila and getting her to open up. Now she isn't sure what to do. How should she approach her and ask questions about the bruises and her overall well-being? What if Sheila is defensive and withdraws? Maria decides that she will call the counseling center the next day to consult.

Attending to the needs of the whole student has been at the core of the values, philosophy, and literature of the student affairs profession from the very beginning. And although student affairs has become highly specialized (for example, first-year programs, residence life, career services, counseling center), student affairs practitioners act first and foremost as caretakers, educators, and helpers to actively assist students with the emotional and academic demands of college life and to promote personal development (Creamer, Winston, & Miller, 2001). Student affairs professionals have endless opportunities to support, advise, and help students on a daily basis from responding to students in acute crisis who come to the counseling center to supporting those who struggle with developmental issues that affect them in social and academic arenas. The visibility of student affairs practitioners on campus make them accessible and approachable to students with a wide range of problems and concerns (Pope, Reynolds, & Mueller, 2004). Increasingly, student affairs professionals are spending time attending to students who are in distress (Reynolds, 2009). However, many student affairs professionals are not specifically trained as counselors and seldom possess the skills, experiences, or desire necessary to provide therapy to students (Reynolds & Altabef, 2015). Yet, given the changing needs of students, it is important that all student affairs practitioners be able to respond to the personal needs and concerns of students with sensitivity and effective helping skills.

Okun (2002) used the term *helper* to describe people who help others understand, cope, and deal with their problems. She suggested *helper* as an umbrella term to include professional counselors, generalist human service workers, and paraprofessional counselors who differ in terms of their formal training in theory, communication, and assessment skills. Most campuses have counselors or psychologists who work in counseling centers and can be conceptualized as professional helpers. They have received more advanced training in counseling knowledge and skills and are well equipped to deal with the more serious psychological concerns that many college students experience. In Okun's framework, student affairs practitioners fall within the second category of generalist human service workers who have specialized human relations training at the college level, a team of colleagues and supervisors to consult with, and access to professional development and more routine day-to-day contact with their clients (students). As helpers, they need to fully understand the limits of their counseling expertise and use their well-developed and practiced helping knowledge and skills in their direct interactions with students.

The primary purpose of this chapter is to examine the specific and unique awareness, knowledge, and skills necessary for student affairs practitioners to be effective and ethical in their roles as helpers and caregivers. Incorporating counseling theory, models of helping, and approaches to assessment and conceptualization of student needs are addressed as part of the core competencies of student affairs professionals. This chapter also will explore some key concerns and challenges facing helpers such the importance of self-awareness, ethical demands, and multicultural competence. Finally, I will reconceptualize and expand the role of student affairs practitioners as helpers on campus to include their work as change agents and advocates who assist in the creation of campus communities that truly value and understand students.

Prevalent Mental Health Issues and Concerns on Campus

Given that "college student mental health problems are becoming more common, more problematic and a much larger focus on college and university campuses" (Benton, 2006, p. 4), it is vital that all student affairs practitioners understand these concerns and what influence they have on the academic, social, and psychological well-being of students. However, it is not uncommon for practitioners, who are helpers and not professional counselors, to feel unsure and unprepared to face the mental health concerns of students (Williams, 2005).

Research has shown that mental health problems impair functioning in major life domains, such as family, work, social, and school, for many college students (Soet & Sevig, 2006). These problems create additional barriers and may make it difficult for students to integrate academically and socially into campus life. Every year the American College Health Association (ACHA) collects data on the significant mental health concerns of all college students, not just those using counseling services. The most recent data from spring 2014 analyzed the results of more than seventy-nine thousand students and found that almost 12 percent experienced depression and 14 percent reported being anxious (ACHA, 2014). When asked about how they felt during the last twelve months, 24 percent of students felt very sad, 21 percent felt hopeless, and 18 percent felt overwhelmed by all they had to do. Almost 6 percent of students surveyed seriously considered suicide during that year and many more (33 percent) stated that it was difficult for them to function at times (ACHA, 2014). A study by Reynolds (2013) identified the most challenging mental health issues faced by student affairs practitioners included anxiety, depression, and suicidal ideation or behavior. Other significant mental health problems for college students include substance abuse, violent behavior, bipolar disorders, family problems, sexual victimization, eating disorders, personality disorders, sleep disorders, impulsive behavior (including sexual promiscuity and self-mutilation) (Grayson & Meilman, 2006; Kadison & DiGeronimo, 2004). Such serious student mental health concerns have consequences. In a study by Soet and Sevig (2006) almost 30 percent of college students either had been or currently were in counseling, 14 percent had taken psychotropic medications, and 6.8 percent were currently using such medicine. In the ACHA survey, the reported issues that were most difficult to handle in the last year were academics (47 percent), finances (33 percent), intimate relationships (31 percent), and family problems (28 percent).

There are many possible explanations for this increase in college student mental health concerns, including increased financial pressure and parental expectations; early experimentation with drugs, alcohol, and sex; reduced stigma; divorce or family dysfunction; physical or sexual abuse; unique needs of millennials; availability of earlier and more sophisticated intervention; and poor parenting (Kitzrow, 2003; Watkins, Hunt, & Eisenberg, 2011). It is also important to note that 75 percent of lifetime mental health conditions start before the age of twenty-four (NIMH, 2005). Regardless of the why, some college students will need treatment, medication, consultation, relapse prevention, and support in order to be successful in college. Because the mental health and well-being of college students "is not the sole responsibility of those with titles such as counselor, psychologist, or advisor" (Benton, 2006, p. 19), it is vital that student affairs professionals expand their awareness, knowledge, and skills to work effectively with students with psychological difficulties and concerns.

Helping Awareness, Knowledge, and Skills

Exploration of the core principles, knowledge, and skills of the student affairs profession occurred over many decades, and a variety of conceptualizations exist (see Lovell & Kosten, 2000). Waple (2006) and Pope, Reynolds, and Mueller (2004) recommended using a competence-based approach within student affairs–preparation programs. Several empirical studies have highlighted the importance of helping skills for student affairs professionals (Burkard, Cole, Ott, & Stoflet, 2005; Reynolds, 2011; Waple, 2006) with some suggesting that student affairs practitioners are not adequately prepared or trained for their roles as helpers. According to Burkard and others (2005), professionals are expected to have "counseling skills that extend well beyond the basic skills often taught in graduate programs" (p. 298). Counseling courses typically focus on individual counseling and microcounseling skills, giving little attention to more advanced helping skills such as supervision, group skills, or crisis intervention and management. Reynolds and Altabef (2015) implore, "It is important that student affairs professionals are prepared to supervise and mentor, to intervene and manage crises, and respond appropriately to challenging student concerns such as suicidality, eating disorders, self-harm, and substance abuse" (p. 229).

There are some essential helping skills that student affairs professionals need to address these challenging issues and effectively do their job. Having well-developed microcounseling skills, such as active listening, reflecting, demonstrating empathy, and asking challenging questions, can help practitioners be more responsive to their students (Roe Clark, 2009). With such skills, advisors of student groups can ask more probing questions and judicial officers can help students be less defensive. These microcounseling skills can increase trust, create more open communication, and enhance relationships with students and colleagues. Developing crisis management and conflict resolution skills can assist student affairs practitioners with many of the challenges they face. To help the advisors of Greek organizations who have to address a crisis in one of their fraternities or sororities or a hall director who has a suicidal student in his hall, these skills are vital to ensuring the well-being of all the students involved in these crises. Many student affairs professionals work with paraprofessional staff members, who may experience conflict and discord, which is why competencies in conflict management are so important. For example, student government advisors or coaches must learn how to manage the conflict that inevitably occurs among students in their various groups in order to achieve the goals of the groups they are advising or coaching. Likewise having effective group skills to build meaningful working relationships is a necessity for any practitioner who works with student groups, such as orientation and residence hall staff members or student judicial panels.

When it comes more directly to working with students with mental health concerns, having more advanced helping skills can be truly valuable in ensuring they get the help and support they need. Whether it be the career counselor who is working with a student on her résumé and notices that she seems depressed or the residence hall director who talks with a student who fears his roommate is suicidal, student affairs practitioners across campus need to feel confident in their helping skills. Knowing how to talk with students and ask questions to determine if they need to be referred for counseling is crucial. That entails being immediate, listening, showing empathy, and asking probing questions. Yet many student affairs practitioners do not have the training they need to develop these more advanced helping skills (Burkard, Cole, Ott, & Stoflet, 2005; Reynolds & Altabef, 2015).

In order to understand the levels and types of competence required to effectively help students, several areas will be briefly addressed in this section: the role of counseling and helping theories, the centrality of the helping relationship, models for helping interactions, conceptualizing student issues, and being a multiculturally competent helper. It is important to highlight that student affairs practitioners are often the first contact with students who are troubled, upset, or unsure, and thus they need to be able to respond in supportive and constructive ways.

Role of Helping and Counseling Theory

Theory has always been fundamental to the student affairs profession, and the field is largely interdisciplinary in its use of theories (for example, organization development, leadership, and student development). Helping and counseling theories are varied and serve different purposes when being used by professional counselors and therapists. There is rich diversity among psychodynamic, cognitive-behavioral, humanistic, feminist, and multicultural theories; however, these theories are not always appropriate or effective for student affairs helping relationships. Nevertheless, they may still offer ways to conceptualize the concerns of college students. For example, humanistic theories such as client-centered or gestalt approaches focus on the potential for growth and the need for self-awareness and responsibility, which is very consistent with the values of the student affairs profession (Mueller, 2009). However, the psychodynamic perspective, as postulated by Sigmund Freud, Carl Jung, and others, is not typically relevant in a student affairs context. These theories still offer insight into the role of the early childhood influences on the development of young adults.

Counseling and helping theories provide student affairs practitioners with insight into human nature and mechanisms for change and growth. Although some student development theories address this issue as well, in that context the interventions are not helping or counseling oriented. By understanding the philosophies, key concepts, goals, and techniques of counseling and helping theories, we can more effectively determine their value for student affairs practice. Once practitioners have a strong understanding of helping theories, they can develop their own philosophies and integrated theories that will guide their helping efforts. According to Mueller (2009), cultivating a personal theory can guide our actions and behaviors in interpersonal relationships; however, these individualized theories are affected by our cultural and social identities (for example, race, gender, sexual orientation); family background; life experiences; education level; socioeconomic status; and other significant variables.

Centrality of the Helping Relationship

Most counseling theories support the notion that the helping relationship is central to the success of those important interactions (Mueller, 2009). Rogers (1995) is best known for his emphasis on building a trusting relationship as the key to successful counseling. Through his client-centered counseling theory, he suggested that there were several key conditions for therapeutic change: contact, empathy, client and counselor congruence, and unconditional positive regard. Making direct personal contact and empathy can help students feel important and reassure them that they are not alone. Such connection encourages them to be more open. The helping relationship is more effective when helpers and students are fully present; are aware of their thoughts, feelings, and beliefs; and express these in ways that are genuine, consistent, and appropriate. When a helper is real, the relationship is strengthened. Without a doubt, unconditional positive regard, or the genuine acceptance of the student's feelings, behaviors, experiences, and attitudes, is a necessary condition for trust and connection. If students are worried about being judged, they hold back and are unable to benefit from the helping relationship. Conversely if students believe that their helpers will accept them even when they have made bad choices or are struggling, then they will be more open and able to grow in self-awareness. When students experience "genuine acceptance and empathy, therapeutic change is most likely to occur" (Mueller, 2009, p. 102).

Helping Models

Within the counseling field there are many models that describe the helping process; however, many experts agree that helping is typically a multistage process. Roe Clark (2009) offered a three-phase model of helping for the student affairs practitioner primarily based on the work of Okun (2002) and Hill and O'Brien (1999). The three phases are (1) establishing rapport with the student and exploring the dilemma, (2) gaining insight into the dilemma and focusing, and (3) taking action. Each phase suggests particular skills needed for the helper to be successful.

The first phase highlights the importance of building rapport. Student affairs practitioners often enjoy ongoing relationships with the students they help. Through those connections, professionals have multiple opportunities to reach out to students. Being welcoming, learning background information, initiating contact, and spending time together are just some of the ways that practitioners build rapport and help students feel safe and comfortable. This initial bonding becomes the foundation for the rest of the working relationship (Okun, 2002). Using the opening scenario of the chapter with Maria and

Sheila, it would be important for Maria to actively reach out to Sheila and ask her how she has been doing. The conversation can begin casually and eventually build to asking more personal questions. If a positive relationship has already been established, this initial phase is much easier. Another goal during this initial phase is to help students express themselves so helpers can listen for the dilemmas or problems often embedded in students' stories. The specific micro skills to enhance rapport and encourage student openness typically emphasized during this phase include listening, reflecting, and summarizing.

With the second phase of helping, helpers center attention on the core of the students' concerns. Many individuals who seek help may need support in sharing their true concerns, because they often begin by discussing concerns that are less central. During this phase student affairs practitioners can reframe students' dilemmas or encourage them to explore how they contribute to their dilemma. Through ongoing deeper conversations students can uncover their true thoughts and feelings. Similarly, by gently asking probing questions about Sheila's life and what parts of her life are going well and what areas are creating stress, Maria may be able to help Sheila open up and confide in her. Sometimes just shining a different light on a problem can help a student see it in a new way and access alternative solutions and approaches to her or his concerns. According to Roe Clark (2009), the helper is more active during phase 2, and several new skill clusters are added: questioning, clarifying, interpreting, and confronting.

In the final phase of helping, helpers assist students in setting goals and making action plans. Insight without action is unlikely to have much effect on a student's life so this phase is quite important. Using the opening scenario, the action step may involve encouraging Maria to reach out to others if she is struggling and to consider counseling to help her with her problems. Action can occur on the inside (changing one's self-image or worldview) or on the outside (altering specific behaviors). This phase tends to be the more concrete of the three in that the helper encourages the student to act in measurable ways. It is essential to follow up with additional support to help the student implement and maintain any changes. As the helper gathers more information and has a greater understanding of the student's underlying concerns, it may become clear that the student should meet with a professional counselor. In these circumstances, an appropriate referral must be made. Making referrals and developing goals and action plans are the skill clusters commonly used in this final phase of helping.

The three phases of helping as proposed by Roe Clark (2009) can occur in a one-time interaction or across several meetings and can be initiated by the student or helper. Each phase has its own unique challenges, such as learning to be patient with silence, helping a student get unstuck, or dealing with intense emotions. Developing the necessary skills to be an effective helper will take time and practice. New helpers, in particular, who have minimal training will struggle with some temptations and fears as identified by Roe Clark: excessive questioning and fact finding, premature problem-solving, and worrying about saying the "right" thing. According to Roe Clark (2009), "Effective helping is not accidental, but rather the intentional result of a skilled and structured interaction intended to foster rapport, self-understanding, and positive action" (p. 167).

Conceptualizing Student Issues

When working with college students with mental health and other personal issues, it is important to consider how we conceptualize their concerns. Being in treatment or having emotional or psychological issues may or may not be relevant to our interactions with students. Some students may be depressed or anxious but have learned how to manage their mood disorders through psychotherapy, medication, or social support. In general, if a student's behavior or performance is not problematic, then her or his diagnosis or mental health history is not relevant. Acting in ways that show bias toward someone with mental health difficulties may be discrimination, based on the Americans with Disabilities Act (Dickerson, 2006). Undoubtedly, some students are not able to effectively manage their mental health and create difficulties for other students. However, it is important to state that even in those circumstances it is their behavior, not their diagnoses, that should be considered and addressed.

The AISP (assessment-intervention of student problems) model offers a way of viewing problematic students in multidimensional ways to provide more just, effective, and appropriate services and interventions (Delworth, 1989/2009). Being able to distinguish between behaviors that have a negative effect on others compared to those that result from serious underlying psychological issues is essential to effective helping. Student affairs practitioners may not always know if a student has underlying psychological issues or whether he or she is simply immature. However, by identifying specific problematic behaviors and consulting others, including professional counselors, helpers can determine the most appropriate and necessary response. In order to accomplish this, student affairs professionals need active and collaborative relationships with health staff members, counselors, and other staff members from the students with disabilities office.

In order to ascertain which students need what type of assistance, it is important to be able to effectively conceptualize students' concerns. Many practitioners spend a lot of time addressing the needs and concerns of a few students who have negative effects on the larger campus community; however, it is also important to reach out to those students who are not extremely distressed or who do not disturb the campus environment. Spooner (2000) suggested that campuses evaluate what impact the environment is having on students and their behavior, rather than assuming that all difficulties come from students themselves. When the campus is experienced as being distressing or oppressive, for example, it can create psychological difficulties or intensify ones that already exist. This has become increasingly important because many campuses struggle with policies and procedures regarding students with mental health issues and behavioral problems.

Being a Multiculturally Competent Helper

It is essential that multicultural competence be viewed as a core competence necessary for all helpers. Pope, Reynolds, and Mueller (2004) described *multicultural competence* as the awareness, knowledge, and skills needed to ethically and effectively work with others who are culturally different and similar. Multicultural scholars suggested that important values, worldviews, and realities of many individuals are ignored, minimized, or viewed as irrelevant (Sue & Sue, 2003). Therefore, the unique experiences and perspectives of individuals from diverse cultural, religious, racial, social class, and sexual orientation backgrounds need to be integrated into helping theories and practices. Student affairs professionals who are unable to fully comprehend, for example, the struggles that many Native American students feel when they enter a predominantly white campus or the centrality of family to many Latino/a students may not be able to help those students succeed. If practitioners interact with students based on the assumption that all students are heterosexual or identify as either male or female, they will undoubtedly hurt or disempower LGBT students and increase their isolation. It is vital that student affairs practitioners increase their multicultural helping competence in order to provide the most affirming, effective, and ethical services possible.

Concerns and Challenges for Helpers

The role of counselor and helper is challenging and demanding. Personal and ethical concerns and challenges may emerge to which the helper must attend and draw on his or her own skills and talents. An important part of being a helper is having the tools and insights to handle the complex issues that come the way of student affairs practitioners.

Personal Concerns and Challenges

Personal concerns or challenges need to be considered by student affairs practitioners when acting in the role of helper. One challenge is for helpers to be continually engaged in the process of self-awareness. Effective helpers are insightful and self-critical. Being in touch with their feelings and comfortable with themselves are ways that helpers can set positive examples for students. This does not mean that helpers need to be fully self-actualized; however, it is vital that they are engaged in their own development and self-improvement. A second potential challenge to those who want to be helpers is avoiding burnout. Dealing with students' strong emotions, hearing their painful stories, and setting appropriate boundaries can make helpers feel drained and emotionally overwhelmed. Corey and Corey (1998) explored the effect of stress on helpers. Individual sources of stress includes self-doubt, perfectionism, emotional exhaustion, or taking on too much responsibility for those being helped. Environmental challenges include having too many demands and not enough time or resources to deal with them, leading to frustration that sometimes makes it difficult to help others. To be effective helpers it is necessary to attend to our own needs and ask for help when needed.

Ethical Concerns and Challenges

There are many complex and demanding ethical challenges inherent in the helping role (see also chapter 6 in this book). According to Janosik, Creamer, and Humphrey (2004), despite the availability of professional codes of ethics to address ethical dilemmas, many practitioners are unsure about how to respond to ethical challenges. Because many ethical issues grow out of helping relationships, it is crucial that student affairs professionals understand the unique dilemmas and circumstances that arise when engaged in helping or counseling relationships. Being aware of potential ethical dilemmas is the first step to becoming an ethical student affairs professional.

 Among the primary ethical issues that affect helpers are competence, dual relationships, confidentiality, and duty to warn. Competence means not practicing outside our area of expertise. Well-meaning helpers must not be so overtaken by the desire to help that they forget that they are not therapists. The number one ethical guideline is to do no harm and when practitioners work outside their areas of competence, it is possible to do more harm than good. A second ethical area pertains to the dual relationships that often occur on college campuses. It is not uncommon for student affairs professionals to serve multiple roles with students (supervisor-friend, counselor–committee member), which can lead to a conflict of interest for either the students or the helpers. Sometimes, through the course of helping, practitioners can learn information about which they may feel some pressure to report or act on. Although there are legal requirements protecting the privacy of students' educational records (for example, the Family Education Rights and Privacy [FERPA] Act of 1974), the primary reason for helpers to maintain confidentiality is that it increases students' trust in the helping process. However, this can become complex based on the policy, procedures, or expectations of a particular campus. Professional codes for counselors state that they are unable to break confidentiality unless their clients are threatening suicide, homicide, or are endangering the well-being of a child. Although these guidelines are not relevant for student affairs practitioners, it is likely that students will not disclose to practitioners if they do not believe that their confidentiality is being protected. Furthermore, students' expectations can be complicated at times. A student may disclose to her hall director that she is being stalked yet still want to have control over that information. Although a student does not have to file a police report in such circumstances, sometimes residence hall policy or other state or federal regulations require that reports be made to protect the safety and well-being of the residents. In order to effectively manage such ethical dilemmas, it is essential that student affairs practitioners anticipate and discuss how to address some of these prominent ethical challenges before they occur.

The issue of suicidal and homicidal ideation and behavior has become a heightened concern in recent years. What is the liability for practitioners who learn of a student's feelings of despair or rage? The mandate of doing no harm is still central to the responsibility of professionals but balancing the rights of individual students with the safety and well-being of the larger campus community is typically an ethical dilemma with no right or wrong answers (Fried, 2011). Student affairs professionals need to be prepared to directly deal with and respond to these types of issues on a regular basis.

Dickerson (2006) suggested that institutions review relevant laws and ethical codes, train staff members, and provide adequate information and informed consent to all students. There are many resources available to assist campuses in these efforts. For example, the Bazelon Center for Mental Health Law (2007) has created a model policy in its efforts to "help colleges and universities navigate these complex issues and develop a nondiscriminatory approach to a student who is in crisis because of a mental health problem" (p. 2). Ultimately, learning how to navigate this balancing act will help student affairs professionals manage the complicated ethical demands of being a helper and an administrator.

Helpers as Change Agents on Campus

Typically helping is conceptualized in the context of a one-on-one relationship in which one helper (student affairs professional) assists one college student. Although often very important, these interactions are only a small subset of the actual and potential opportunities for helping. Further, such interventions rarely focus on addressing how the larger environment (family, campus, community, or society) may contribute to a student's difficulties. Many multicultural experts view this type of individualistic helping as not always culturally relevant and meaningful (Sue & Sue, 2003). The role of helper may be expanded to include that of change agent and advocate.

Expanding the Helping Role

The need for student affairs practitioners to act as helpers and guide students through their college experience is unquestioned. Every day provides new opportunities for student affairs professionals to listen, give support, and offer feedback to students who are struggling to understand themselves, others, and their futures. And although most of these interactions are not therapy, providing challenge and support to students can be therapeutic and increase the likelihood of their personal and academic success.

Embracing the role of helper as central to the mission and goals of student affairs enables practitioners to not only contribute to the growth, development, and well-being of students but also to benefit the larger community. By espousing a helping orientation and broadening our conceptualization of the helping role, we, as professionals, not only honor our past but also create additional opportunities to build more responsive campuses that can benefit everyone. Recent and ongoing campus events have demonstrated that the emotional and psychological concerns of students are having an impact on our communities. Through our role as helpers we can make significant contributions to our campus. Our knowledge of student development and insight into who college students are and what they need to learn, grow, and develop as students and human beings can only help humanize our institutions. In order to achieve such lofty goals, it is essential that the profession, through its preparation programs and professional development efforts, effectively train all student affairs professionals to be helpers.

Importance of Social Change and Advocacy

Many in the counseling profession are giving increased attention to the value of social advocacy conceptualizing helping as occurring in the broader realm. Lewis, Arnold, House, and Toporek (2003) suggested that helpers should view student or client empowerment and community collaboration as essential to all helping interactions. Identifying the strengths and resources of students and assisting them with self-advocacy fits with a commitment to social justice based in the historical and philosophical foundations of the field (Evans & Reason, 2001). According to Reynolds (2009),

> By making a commitment to advocacy and placing it as a primary goal of the helping enterprise, we are able to help others twice. Once, by addressing their individual concerns and needs, and twice by encouraging the development of self-advocacy skills whereby they are empowered to make meaning of their own world and create changes that will benefit them and the larger world around them. This speaks to the larger professional imperative of incorporating multicultural competence so that we are fully able to help all students. Advocacy, empowerment, and community collaboration are the tools of tomorrow; they are the gifts that keep on giving because they create the strategies and tools in individuals to affect their environment and create change. (pp. 260–261)

By developing compassionate and affirming environments, student affairs professionals—in their helping role—will better serve their campuses acting as change agents to ensure students' personal and academic success.

Conclusion

Student affairs professionals are frequently placed in the role as helpers; many students rely on them for compassion, support, and guidance. In order to be effective helpers, practitioners need to develop essential awareness, knowledge, and skills that guide their efforts. Being self-aware, developing an understanding of counseling or helping theories and models for helping, and cultivating important skills and interventions are necessary for ethical practice. Furthermore, reconceptualizing and expanding the helper role to focus on a broader range of helping skills and opportunities to act as student advocates is truly needed in order to create campus environments that value and understand students.

Discussion Questions and Activity

1. How would you describe your current level of helping competence?
2. What are the most important helping skills you use when working with students?
3. What knowledge and information is needed to enhance your helping skills?
4. What are the most challenging student concerns you face?
5. Identify a scenario in your job in which helping skills were required and describe how you effectively used your competence to address the situation.

References

American College Health Association (ACHA). (2014). *Reference group executive summary.* Retrieved Aug. 10, 2007, from http://www.acha-ncha.org

Bazelon Center for Mental Health Law. (2007). *Supporting students: A model policy for colleges and universities.* Retrieved Aug. 12, 2007, from http://www.bazelon.org/pdf/SupportingStudents.pdf

Benton, S. A. (2006). The scope and context of the problem. In S. A. Benton & S. L. Benton (Eds.), *College student mental health: Effective services and strategies across campus* (pp. 1–14). Washington, DC: National Association of Student Personnel Administrators (NASPA).

Burkard, A., Cole, D. C., Ott, M., & Stoflet, T. (2005). Entry-level competencies of new student affairs professionals: A Delphi study. *NASPA Journal, 42,* 283–309.

Corey, M. S., & Corey, G. (1998). *Becoming a helper.* Pacific Grove, CA: Brooks/Cole.

Creamer, D. G., Winston, R. B., & Miller, T. K. (2001). The professional student affairs administrator: Roles and functions. In R. B. Winston, D. G. Creamer, & T. K. Miller (Eds.), *The professional student affairs administrator: Educator, leader, and manager* (pp. 3–38). New York: Brunner-Routledge.

Delworth, U. (1989/2009). *The AISP model: Assessment-intervention of student problems* (New Directions for Student Services, no. 128, pp. 11–21). San Francisco: Jossey-Bass.

Dickerson, D. (2006). Legal issues for campus administrators, faculty, and staff. In S. A. Benton, & S. L. Benton (Eds.), *College student mental health: Effective services and strategies across campus* (pp. 35–120). Washington, DC: NASPA.

Evans, N. J., & Reason, R. D. (2001). Guiding principles: A review and analysis of student affairs philosophical statements. *Journal of College Student Development, 42,* 359–377.

Fried, J. (2011). Ethical standards and principles. In J. H. Schuh, S. R. Jones, & S. R. Harper (Eds.), *Student services: A handbook for the profession* (5th ed., pp. 96–119). San Francisco: Jossey-Bass.

Grayson, P. A., & Meilman, P. W. (2006). (Eds.). *College mental health practice.* New York: Routledge.

Hill, C. E., & O'Brien, K. M. (1999). *Helping skills: Facilitating exploration, insight, and action.* Washington, DC: American Psychological Association.

Janosik, S. M., Creamer, D. G., & Humphrey, E. (2004). An analysis of ethical problems facing student affairs administrators. *NASPA Journal, 41,* 356–374.

Kadison, R., & DiGeronimo, T. F. (2004). *College of the overwhelmed: The campus mental health crisis and what to do about it.* San Francisco: Jossey Bass.

Kitzrow, M. A. (2003). The mental health needs of today's college students: Challenges and recommendations. *NASPA Journal, 41,* 167–181.

Lewis, J., Arnold, M. S., House, R., & Toporek, R. (2003). *Advocacy competencies.* Retrieved April 22, 2008, from http://www.counseling.org/Publications

Lovell, C., & Kosten, L. (2000). Skills, knowledge, and personal traits necessary for success as a student affairs administrator: A meta-analysis of thirty years of research. *NASPA Journal, 37,* 553–572.

Mueller, J. A. (2009). Underlying and relevant helping theories. In A. L. Reynolds, *Helping college students: Developing essential support skills for student affairs practice* (pp. 75–108). San Francisco: Jossey-Bass.

National Institute on Mental Health (NIMH). (2005, June 6). *Mental illness exacts heavy toll, beginning in youth.* Retrieved from http://www.nimh.nih.gov/science-news/2005/mental-illness-exacts-heavy-toll-beginning-in-youth.shtml

Okun, B. F. (2002). *Effective helping: Interviewing and counseling techniques* (6th ed.). Pacific Grove, CA: Brooks/Cole.

Pope, R. L., Reynolds, A. L., & Mueller, J. A. (2004). *Multicultural competence in student affairs.* San Francisco: Jossey-Bass.

Reynolds, A. L. (2009). *Helping college students: Developing essential support skills for student affairs practice.* San Francisco: Jossey-Bass.

Reynolds, A. L. (2011). Helping competencies of student affairs professionals: A Delphi study. *Journal of College Student Development, 52*(3), 362–369.

Reynolds, A. L. (2013). College student concerns: Perceptions of student affairs practitioners. *Journal of College Student Development, 54*(1), 98–104.

Reynolds, A. L., & Altabef, D. (2015). Addressing helping competencies in student affairs: Analysis of helping skills course syllabi. *Journal of Student Affairs Research and Practice, 52,* 1–12. doi:10.11080/19496591

Roe Clark, M. (2009). Microcounseling skills. In A. L. Reynolds, *Helping college students: Developing essential support skills for student affairs practice* (pp. 131–167). San Francisco: Jossey-Bass.

Rogers, C. (1995). *A way of being.* New York: Mariner Books.

Soet, J., & Sevig, T. (2006). Mental health issues facing a diverse sample of college students: Results from the College Student Mental Health Survey. *NASPA Journal, 43,* 410–431.

Spooner, S. E. (2000). The college counseling environment. In D. C. Davis & K. M. Humphrey (Eds.), *College counseling: Issues and strategies for a new millennium* (pp. 3–14). Alexandria, VA: American Counseling Association.

Sue, D. W., & Sue, D. (2003). *Counseling the culturally diverse: Theory and practice* (4th ed.). New York: John Wiley & Sons.

Waple, J. N. (2006). An assessment of skills and competencies necessary for entry-level student affairs work. *NASPA Journal, 43,* 1–18.

Watkins, D. C., Hunt, J. B., & Eisenberg, D. (2011). Increased demand for mental health services on college campus: Perspectives from administrators. *Qualitative Social Work, 11,* 319–337. doi:10.1177/1473325011401468

Williams, L. B. (2005, March/April). My medicated students: I'm not that kind of doctor. *About Campus, 10,* 27–29.

CHAPTER 28

ADVISING STUDENT ORGANIZATIONS

Norbert W. Dunkel and Nancy E. Chrystal-Green

After years of research it is clear. Students who engage in purposeful activities benefit and receive a return on the time they invested in ways that their noninvolved peers do not (Astin, 1985, 1993; American College Personnel Association, 1994; National Survey of Student Engagement, 2012; Pascarella & Terenzini, 2005). Student involvement has been a long-standing focus for practitioners and scholars in higher education as a means of ensuring the quality of the student experience and skill development. Student organizations consistently have been outlets of involvement and for the most part have existed and persisted because of the effort students make to ensure their success. Student organizations also have had a prominent place in the history of their institutions, and although student organization advisors have been present and active since the beginning, there is a renewed focus on advising. This increasing importance of organization advising is in part because of the increasing emphasis on accountability, the changing legal landscape, the complexity of student events, and the push for colleges to provide opportunities for students to develop relationships with faculty members.

Advising students and groups of students is an important competency in a student affairs practitioner's toolkit. The skills used to advise student organizations and groups are wide ranging, and a proficient advisor needs to be adept at matching the necessary skill to the situation at hand. For example, an advisor who is working with a newly elected student senator will employ different skills than one who is advising the programming board's annual homecoming week events. Advising is also an important skill set because, whether you are a new or seasoned professional, if you work with individuals or groups of students, no matter the functional area within student affairs, you will regularly use these skills. Therefore, being familiar with and working to improve these skills are paramount not only to the success of college students but also the success of the student affairs field.

This chapter will provide an overview of advising student organizations, discuss the roles and functions of an advisor, share current issues and considerations with advising organizations, and offer suggestions on how to ensure quality within the advising experience.

Most colleges and universities also have academic advisors, career planning and placement advisors, and counselors who work with students who have mental health concerns. The authors recommend that student organization advisors refer students to the appropriate academic advisor for issues related to required and elective course selection, academic major and minor selection, and graduation requirements. Additionally, advisors frequently will be asked about career guidance. Similarly, advisors should refer students to the campus career planning and placement center for issues related to career preparation (for example, cover letters, résumés, interviewing, dressing for success), and internships. The advisor almost certainly will be asked to write letters of recommendation and reference for students they have worked closely with, but for all other academic advising inquiries, we recommend referral. Students with challenging developmental or mental health issues need to be referred to appropriate staff members, typically found in the institution's counseling center or student health service.

Although this chapter focuses on advising student organizations, the reality is that an advisor really does not have a relationship with an organization; rather, the relationship is with the students who comprise that organization. There are two main reasons why advising student organizations are topics onto themselves. First, advisors must practice many of the same skills they would with individual students, but they have to apply them to a group context that becomes more complex. Also, advisors must prioritize the organization's mission and goals above those of any particular individual member. This can lead to conflict when goals of individuals do not align with that of the organization. This chapter provides the foundational elements for a student organization advisor to perform his or her responsibilities.

Overview

Advising has been defined in numerous ways but examples of the common terms used in any definition include one who gives guidance and advice, counsels, and shares ideas and insights. The basic skills used in advising students, whether in the context of academic advising, career coaching, financial aid, student activities, and student conduct, are universal, and it would be prudent for all student affairs practitioners to develop strong advising skills because they will be used for the duration of their career.

The Council for the Advancement of Standards in Higher Education (2012) has standards specific to campus activity programs. Those who serve as advisors to student organizations would do well to keep these standards in mind:

- Be knowledgeable of student development theory and philosophy to appropriately support students and also to encourage learning and development.
- Have adaptive advising styles in order to be able to work with students with a variety of skill and knowledge levels.
- Have interest in the students involved in the organization.
- Have expertise in the topic for which the student group is engaged.
- Understand organizational development process and team building. (p. 95)

Additionally, there are a number of standards found in the section on academic advising that are relevant to advising student organizations (CAS, 2012):

- Assist students in assessing their interests and abilities, examining their educational goals, making decisions and developing short-term and long-term plans to meet their objectives.
- Discuss and clarify educational, career, and life goals.
- Assist students to understand the educational context within which they are enrolled.
- Reinforce student self-direction and self-sufficiency.
- Direct students with educational, career, or personal concerns, or skill/learning deficiencies, to other resources and programs on the campus when necessary.
- Make students aware of and refer to educational, institutional, and community resources and services. (p. 39)

There is no one specific profile of student organization advisors. They come from different disciplines and have a variety of interests, experiences, and skill sets. Campuses have set their own standards and requirements based on the individual needs of the institution. Many campuses require registered student organizations to have an advisor although there are differences in who can serve. Some institutions require student organization advisors to be full-time employees (either faculty or staff members); others will allow graduate assistants or campus affiliates (such as campus ministers) to serve. Sometimes advisor eligibility is dictated by the purpose of the organization. For example, some sport clubs will allow a part-time or volunteer coach to serve or Greek letter organizations will accept a volunteer alumnus/a. Regardless of their affiliation, institutions have the responsibility to ensure that advisors have a basic understanding of their responsibilities, be aware of campus resources including where they can go for support, and a general understanding of university policies that will affect their success as an advisor and the success of the student organization.

The current climate on college campuses, including the competitiveness of the job market, a consumer-oriented approach to higher education, and the increasing number of choices for entering students, has put a greater emphasis on the college experience. For those who work closely with students, this means developing conditions that motivate and inspire students to devote more time and energy to educationally purposeful activities (Dunkel, Schuh, & Chrystal-Green, 2014). "Activities with a purpose" can translate into a plethora of things that takes the context of each college campus into consideration. The popularity of involvement in student organizations enables a natural linkage in which students can benefit from activities that are not only enjoyable but also at the same time are developing career-readiness skills, such as sharpening communication competencies, understanding and practicing community values, or learning how to work in a multicultural environment. And, student organization advisors are probably the best equipped and positioned to ensure that students are connected to the purpose behind their activities of choice. It is during the transformative years of college life that students develop a set of values and beliefs and learn to make meaning of the world around them and their place in it. As students develop a sense of self and, therefore, a sense of purpose, effective advisors support this growth. Being familiar with two significant areas of individual development—leadership development and student learning—will help an advisor continue to promote involvement with a purpose.

The perspectives about leadership and the dynamics between the members of a group have evolved and changed so much over time (Komives, 2011). What was once an obvious explanation of leadership—the leader is the person in the highest ranking position and if one was not in that position one could not lead—has evolved to be more about influence and relationships, that leadership can be a shared experience (Dugan & Komives, 2011). Although there are a multitude of leadership theories, models, and styles, there are a few that work especially well with student leaders. The concept of servant leadership, introduced in the 1970s by Robert Greenleaf, describing the desire of the positional leader to serve the group and the concept of empowering individuals to contribute, develop, and lead themselves, has become the interest of scholars and gives advisors a framework to discuss the responsibilities student leaders have to the rest of the group (Dugan & Komives, 2011). James Kouzes and Barry Posner identified five exemplary practices of ordinary leaders at peak performance and an easily applied inventory to measure the leadership practices of student leaders (Kouzes & Posner, 2012). The social change model of leadership development posits that leadership is tied to social responsibility. Student leaders will benefit from understanding the social change model as it is intended to increase an individual's level of self-knowledge and ability to work with others (Dugan & Komives, 2011). The relational leadership model offers an approach to leadership in organizations by reflecting "how the organization's purpose influences the components of being inclusive, empowering, and ethical" (Komives, Lucas, & McMahon, 2013, p. 96). It is imperative to remember that leadership is a constantly evolving phenomenon that is not demonstrated by a one-size-fits-all mentality (Komives, Lucas, & McMahon, 2013). Advisors can use any of these theories, models or styles quite easily to develop a framework in which to assist student leaders in operationalizing the leadership development they are experiencing.

Student organization advisors are also uniquely positioned to connect the curricular and cocurricular learning by viewing cognitive and affective leaning as parts of one process (King & Baxter Magolda, 2011). King and Baxter Magolda (2011) assert that it is the responsibility of higher education to provide students with opportunities to experience the world and make meaning of these experiences. Advisors can facilitate this transformative learning process with students by using tools such as the learning partnerships model developed by Baxter Magolda, which helps students learn through their experiences, promoting self-authorship, and is grounded in the constructs of challenge and support (Baxter Magolda & King, 2004). Perhaps the simplest way for advisors to consider the concept of student learning is to think about how to enrich the learning environment a student organization already provides by encouraging hands-on experiences, the opportunity to be introduced to unfamiliar persons and places, and the opportunity to understand community standards (King & Baxter Magolda, 2011).

The greatest influence advisors can have on student learning is through reflection. It is very rare for student organizations to build time into any of their activities to reflect but by having students share their reactions to experiences, reflect on their interactions with others, and apply what they have experienced to other situations, advisors can feel comfortable that learning opportunities have been provided. Exhibit 28.1 provides an example of reflective questions in the context of a service-learning project, although the questions can be applied to other activities.

Exhibit 28.1. How to Make Reflection Meaningful

The president of the student organization you advise asks you to help the organization to reflect on the service-learning project they just participated in. You use the "What? So what? Now what?" framework that is based on Kolb's experiential learning cycle.

What? (happened; report the facts and events of an experience):

- What happened?
- What did you observe?
- What issue is being addressed?
- What were the results of the project?
- What events or critical incidents occurred?
- What was of particular notice?

So what? (does it mean to you; analyze the experience):

(a)   The Participant

- Did you learn a new skill?
- Did you hear, feel, or smell anything that surprised you?
- What feelings or thoughts seemed the most strong today?
- How was your experience different than what you expected?
- What do the critical incidents mean to you? How did you respond to them?
- What did you like or dislike about the experience?

(b)   The Recipient

- Did the service empower the recipient to become more self-sufficient?
- What did you learn about the people or community we serve?
- What might affect the recipient's views or experiences of the project?

(c)   The Community

- What are some of the pressing needs or issues in this community?
- How does this project address those needs?
- How has the community benefited?
- What is the least impact you can imagine for the project?
- With unlimited resources, what is the most impact on the community you can imagine?

(d)   For Group Projects

- In what ways did the group work well together?
- What does that suggest to you about the group?
- How might the group have accomplished its task more effectively?
- In what ways did others help you today? How did you help others?
- How were decisions made? Were everybody's ideas heard?

Now what? (are you going to do; consider the future impact of the experience on you and the community):

- What seems to be the root cause(s) of the issue or problem addressed?
- What kinds of activities are currently taking place related to this project?
- What contributes to the success of projects like this? What hinders success?
- What learning occurred for you in this experience? How can you apply this learning?
- What would you like to learn more about, related to this project or issue?
- If you were in charge of the project, what would you do to improve it?

Adapted in part from http://www.servicelearning.umn.edu/info/reflection.html#Ideas at the Service-Learning Center at the University of Minnesota. Based on the University of Florida's Center for Leadership and Service training guide for Gator Plunge. Kolb, D. A. (1984). *Experiential learning: Experience as the source of learning and development.* Englewood Cliffs, NJ: Prentice Hall.

Roles and Functions

Advisors are cheerleaders and helpers. They serve as the moral conscience and keeper of institutional memory. They give reminders and ask critical questions. There is no doubt that advisors are a critical component to any student organization's success. However, when advisors stop to think about all the hats they wear when working with students and student organizations, they might find the list to be overwhelming. Not only that, many advisors enter into the advising relationship thinking they will have one set of responsibilities only to find they are serving a completely different role. This section will discuss three common roles—mentor, supervisor, and educator—an advisor has when advising students. Two roles an advisor will have when working with the student organization as a whole will be discussed as well: those of facilitator and preservationist.

The scope of this chapter will not include a discussion on advising students from either the career coaching or academic perspectives. However, it is important for advisors to be able to discuss, in broad terms, that involvement in student organizations helps students develop career-readiness skills and what those skills may be as it related directly to activities within the organization, as well as the opportunity to link in-class learning to organizational activities. As it has been stated before, relationships with advisors are often the most significant, if not the only one, a student has with a university employee (Dunkel, Schuh, & Chrystal-Green, 2014). Being able to connect students to the campus career services and academic advisors is essential.

Dunkel, Schuh, and Chrystal-Green (2014) offer a discussion of three roles frequently used by advisors in situations with individual students. The first of these roles is that of a *mentor*. DeCoster and Brown (1982) discuss mentoring as a one-to-one learning relationship between an older and a younger person based on modeling behavior and on an extended, shared dialogue. Although many mistakenly view a mentor as someone who has the responsibility to offer advice, Love and Maxam (2011) state that "providing advice is a unidirectional relationship" (p. 413) that runs counter to the concept of a shared dialogue. Therefore, when mentoring students, advisors need to be cautious when giving advice. Instead advisors can demonstrate the following characteristics of good mentors: (1) enthusiasm for the mission of the organization; (2) a genuine interest in the professional and personal development of students; (3) a warmth and understanding in relating to students; (4) a high, yet achievable, standard of performance for self and others; (5) an honest emotional rapport; (6) the available time and energy to give freely to the organization; (7) the initiative to expose students to a network of professionals; (8) the care to guard students from taking on too much too soon in their career (adapted from Dunkel & Schuh, 1998). For many advisors, the ability to mentor students from within the organization they are advising is difficult. This is in part because of the stage of development either the students or the organization is in does not enable this mentoring role. The timing may just not be right. However, an advisor may help identify students who would benefit from a mentoring relationship and assist students in seeking professionals from within the campus, within the field of the organization, or from the surrounding area who could serve in this capacity.

The second frequently played role is that of *supervisor*. Unlike a supervisor who has ultimate responsibility for the outcome of an organization, an advisor's responsibility rests more in the process the organization took to arrive at a particular outcome, such as a decision about how to hold a specific event. However, there are components of the supervisor role that are transferable to effective advising (Dunkel, Schuh, & Chrystal-Green, 2014). There are six components of the supervisory cycle: team building, performance planning, communication, recognition, self-assessment, and formal evaluation (Dunkel, 1996). An effective advisor will use these components to support the work of the group. Here is an example of how one of these components can be applied. Performance planning is one aspect of the supervisory role that may require the advisor to work with individuals within the organization. Performance planning starts with members in key leadership positions understanding their unique responsibilities and the linkage of achieving those responsibilities to the success of the organization. Advisors often need to have students review or develop a job description and hold them accountable to that job description. Student leaders do well when they have clearly determined expectations and have set goals for their personal performance. Discussing performance indicators for success goes a long way toward members and officers understanding their responsibilities and taking the initiative to reaching organizational goals.

The third role advisors have with individual students is that of an *educator*. At the very basic level the reason advisors exist is the fundamental responsibility of educating students and contributing to learning or the purpose of higher education. Creamer, Winston, and Miller (2001) list advising as a behavioral characteristic of educators that is described as "listening to interests and concerns; aiding in identification of available resources; explaining institutional rules and procedures; initiating cooperative problem solving; challenging unexamined assumptions, beliefs and prejudices; providing emotional support" (p. 14). An advisor should be committed to the educator role before agreeing to advise a student organization.

In addition to roles and functions advisors have when working with individual students from within an organization, there are also roles that take on a bit more breadth and serve more as oversight to the organization as a whole. Two such roles are facilitator and preservationist.

Although the concept of *facilitator* can be applied to an individual and group, it is within the later context that student organization advisors will spend more of their time. A *facilitator* is described as someone who "helps bring about an outcome by providing indirect assistance or guidance" by helping make something run more smoothly or effectively (http://www.merriam-webster.com/dictionary/facilitator) and who encourages the discussion of ideas, critical thinking, and enables democratic decision making (Creamer, Winston, & Miller, 2001).

The facilitator role is an important one and has a few different meanings. Sometimes advisors are facilitating a retreat or a meeting as a function of the performance planning mentioned previously. Advisors will focus on the process. Sometimes being a facilitator means spending a significant amount of time on issues of group dynamics. Saunders and Cooper (2001) defined group dynamics as "the study of behavior in groups and includes research about the interrelationships between individuals and groups, how groups develop over time, the ways in which groups make decisions and the roles that individuals play within a group context" (p. 318). Advisors are constantly observing group dynamics and working with student leaders to solve problems, developing methods to be a more inclusive organization, and helping

to resolve conflict. Johnson and Johnson (2013) point out that group development explains the reasons why one group is productive and another is
not. They indicate that an effective group will perform three core activities:
"achieve its goals; maintain good working relationships among members;
and adapt to the changing conditions in the surrounding organization, society and the world" (p. 23). Advisors in the facilitator role will do well to focus
the organization on these activities because performing only one does not
necessarily equate to success.

A second role of an advisor related to the student organization as a whole is
that of *preservationist*. According to Merriam-Webster.com (http://www.merriam-
webster.com/dictionary/preservation), the goal of a *preservationist* is "to keep
something in its original state or in good condition." This definition describes
what student organizations often ask of their advisors. Frequently, advisors are
relied on to maintain a sense of the organization's history. For example, an
advisor may need to explain the context of certain actions the organization
took in relation to the institutional landscape at the time or remember key
officers and what they accomplished during their tenure. Advisors also often
play a key role in officer transitions and the annual registration process that is
directly linked to preserving the integrity of the organization.

One of the most rewarding aspects of being an advisor to a student organization is the growth and development of the advisor him- or herself.
Considering all of the roles and functions listed previously, coupled with the
complexity of institutional issues, the organization itself, and that of the membership, advisors are always facing situations that challenge their skills and
abilities. They are developing new roles and responsibilities that expand their
professional competencies. All student affairs practitioners should seek out
the opportunity to advise a group of students. The benefits students receive by
having the opportunity to engage in a meaningful relationship with an advisor
during college are balanced with the sense of accomplishment and professional development achieved by the advisor.

Issues and Considerations

Perhaps one of the most productive ways to discuss the art and science of
advising is to talk with professionals who work with student organizations
on a regular basis. These professionals possess a wealth of knowledge that
needs to be regularly tapped. A survey of student organization advisors
provided interesting results regarding the current issues facing advisors of
student organizations (Chrystal-Green & Dunkel, 2015). The majority of
respondents included advising within their current job responsibilities. In
addition to the requirements of their job, a few professionals volunteer their
time to advise an organization that is of a particular personal interest. A few
of the respondents advised on a volunteer basis only. There was an equally
distributed range of advising experience among respondents between two
and more than twenty years.

When asked what they spend the majority of their time working with students on, the following tasks received the highest number of responses:

- Event planning including risk management
- Explaining university policy or enforcing compliance with policy
- Leadership development
- Funding and budget issues
- Conflict resolution

This list probably is not surprising to most, especially because those new to the profession and seasoned professionals answered in many of the same ways. What is interesting to note, however, is that many advisors discussed how the most time-consuming tasks may be different if advising is a primary responsibility or if they were serving as advisors on a voluntary basis. For example, one professional mentioned that enforcing compliance with university policy is the responsibility of an advisor whose main job responsibility is to advise, such as a staff member in the student activities office, but is not necessarily the responsibility of volunteer advisors. This type of thought process has implications for those who train volunteer advisors because all advisors need to have a working knowledge of policy to aid in compliance efforts. This response demonstrates that clear expectations need to be set regarding who is responsible for enforcement and, ultimately, any type of sanctioning for noncompliance.

Although there was consistency among our advisors on the tasks that are the most time consuming, when asked about new issues facing advisors of student organizations some intriguing themes emerged. The following three themes were the most widely commented on:

- The role of social media
- Enforcing university policy and the increasing institutional liability for behavior
- Younger members serving in leadership roles

Understanding the value of social media as a communications tool is in the best interest of every advisor. Today's students receive so much of their information through social media that it is important for any organization to communicate in that space. Marketing events, services, and projects through Facebook, Twitter, Snapchat, and Instagram is cost effective and can reach a diverse audience of students. Organization members can quickly communicate brief messages and make group decisions on applications such as GroupMe and Listly. As good as social media are, advisors would be well served to talk with the student organizations about expectations for the use of social media. Some best practices for the use of social media should be discussed regularly. For example, an organization should be using social media only as a means to improve the reach and reputation of the group. Therefore, no personal information should be shared on a student organization's social media presence, accurate information must be consistently posted, and someone should regularly review comments and respond appropriately in a timely manner. One advisor pointed out that an effective method to understand the participant experience at events is to check the reactions to the event on social media. This is an example of how social networking works to the benefit of the organization. Waters, Burnett, Lamm, and Lucas (2009) discuss how social networking enables organizations to develop relationships with stakeholders, but they found that most sites do not do enough to stay current and share the breadth of their activities to cultivate relationships and recruit supporters. It is also a best practice for an advisor to "follow" an organization's social media presence, and in some occasions it may make sense for student leaders to have access to their advisor's social media sites because it can facilitate building trust and rapport, but only if the advisor is prepared to role model appropriate use of social media on a regular basis.

Many advisors, new as well as seasoned, discussed how a new conversation is emerging about the liability the institution may incur when a student organization is negligent or demonstrates significant poor behavior. On the face of the issue, many institutions feel as if they have separated themselves from liability by using descriptors such as "registered at" instead of "recognized by" or not allowing an organization to use the institution's tax-exempt status. But the current reality is that institutions are linked, certainly by public perception, to the actions of the student organizations found at on their campuses.

The third theme discussed by advisors has to do with the trend that younger students are finding themselves in positions that more seasoned students would historically hold. For example, some advisors commented that they are observing more and more rising sophomores being elected as president of a student organization. This development has a number of implications, especially when one considers what is known about the current generation of college students. Students, in general, are overcommitted, fear failure, and have high anxiety. By virtue of having fewer life experiences, younger student leaders also may lack some of the necessary skills, such as conflict management and program planning, to be a successful president. This potential deficit can be overcome by providing these presidents with some extra training and additional support. Advisors should be prepared to spend more time with younger presidents to ensure the health of the organization and the success of the individual student.

One of the best things about those who work with student organizations regularly is that they are all quick to share wisdom with others. One piece of wisdom is to *be present*. For many advisors, as time permits, this starts with attending a few meetings and events so the organization becomes familiar with their advisor's presence. It also means trying to find ways to be involved with the individual students such as knowing students' majors and their hometowns. One advisor said to look, learn, and listen. The effort it takes to be present helps develop the trusting relationship an advisor needs with the students in the organization.

Another popular tip heard from advisors is to *talk about expectations*. Dunkel, Schuh, and Chrystal-Green (2014) discuss setting expectations as part of performance planning advisors must do when adopting the supervisory role mentioned previously. Although institutions will more than likely have a long list of expectations, it is imperative that an advisor and the students in the organization have a conversation about the expectations they have of one another. The following is a selection of questions that can be used to open a dialogue with the organization's leadership about expectations.

- How often does your organization meet and how often should the advisor attend those meetings?
- What events does the organization have on an annual basis and which of those should the advisor attend?
- What do individual members and the advisor need from the advising relationship?
- How available does the organization expect the advisor to be and what does availability look like?
- How available does the advisor expect student leaders to be?
- What behaviors does the advisor expect student members to exhibit?

Another valuable piece of advice is to remind yourself that the *advisor is not the president*. Often, advisors are so invested in the student organization that they get caught up in the output instead of remembering that their impact is really made throughout the process. Advisors are not necessarily supposed to solve problems; rather, their role is to work with students through the students' problem-solving process. There is a big difference in these approaches. The first may have immediate results and ensure a problem is solved quickly and appropriately. The latter ensures that students learn through the process, take action, and possess responsibility for finding a solution. It takes longer but it has lasting effects on the students.

Quality

Although you may not have received any training or preparation prior to assuming your role as a student organization advisor, it is likely that you will have an interest in knowing if you are being an effective advisor. Additionally, you probably will want to know how well your student organization is functioning. Using proper assessment strategies will provide you with the information you need to better understand yourself and your organization's effectiveness. This type of assessment will lead to improvement (Ewell, 2009). We understand the complexity of assessment and there are quite a number of publications on this topic. For purposes of this chapter, we will use the following definition of *assessment:* "any activity designed to determine the effectiveness of the organization or its advisor" (Dunkel, Schuh, & Chrystal-Green, 2014, p. 256).

For smaller student organizations with little or no budget and a small membership base you may ask a series of questions to the executive board or membership at various times of the year or at the end of the year regarding you, the executive board, and your organization's effectiveness. The following are some questions you could ask:

- Have I provided you with the information you need to make good decisions?
- Have I been available to you when you needed me?
- Do you feel that I support you and the organization? How?
- What is the most important thing you need from me? Have I provided that for you?
- Have you accomplished your goals?
- What has changed since the beginning of the year?
- What skills have you learned since taking office?
- What areas could the organization improve on for next year?

For large, complex student organizations with budgets exceeding tens of thousands or millions of dollars and a membership in the hundreds or thousands, you will need a more formal approach to assessment.

You may want to first conduct a self-evaluation in your role as an organization advisor. The advisor's self-evaluation checklist (exhibit 28.2) is a good form to use at any time of the year (Dunkel, Schuh, & Chrystal-Green, 2014).

Exhibit 28.2. Advisor's Self-Evaluation Checklist

Please answer the following questions as they relate to your role as an organization advisor:

Item	Yes	No
I actively provide encouragement to members.		
I know the goals of the organization.		
I know the organization's members.		
I attend regularly scheduled executive board meetings.		
I attend regularly scheduled organizational meetings.		
I meet regularly with the officers of the organization outside of formal meetings.		
I assist with the orientation of new members and participate as needed.		
I attend the organization's special events.		
I assist with the orientation and training of new officers.		
I help provide continuity for the organization.		
I confront the negative behavior of members.		
I understand principles of group development.		
I understand how students grow and learn.		
I understand the principles that lead to orderly meetings.		

Item	Yes	No
I have read the organization's constitution and bylaws.		
I am knowledgeable about the organization's history.		
I recommend and encourage without imposing my ideas and preferences.		
I review the organization's financial records with its financial officer.		
I understand the principles of good fund-raising.		
I understand how issues of diversity affect the organization.		
I attend conferences on and off campus with the organization's students.		
I know the steps to follow in developing a program or event.		
I know where to find assistance when I encounter problems I cannot solve.		
I can identify what members learn by participating in the organization.		
I work with the organization's members in conducting assessments.		

The advisor's evaluation checklist (exhibit 28.3) can be used by the organization's officers and members. This checklist can be administered at any time during or at the end of the year (Dunkel, Schuh, & Chrystal-Green, 2014). Once completed you can summarize the information and meet with the officers to share the information. The information will provide you with an excellent opportunity for open conversation about your advising role and effectiveness.

Exhibit 28.3. Advisor's Evaluation Checklist

Please answer the following statements regarding your advisor:

Item	Yes	No
The advisor provides encouragement to members.		
The advisor knows the organization's goals.		
The advisor knows the organization's members.		
The advisor attends regularly scheduled executive board meetings.		
The advisor attends regularly scheduled organizational meetings.		
The advisor regularly meets with the officers of the organization outside of formal meetings.		
The advisor participates in the orientation of new members.		
The advisor attends the organization's special events.		
The advisor assists with the orientation and training of new officers.		
The advisor helps provide continuity for the organization.		
The advisor confronts the negative behavior of members.		

(continued)

Exhibit 28.3 (*continued*)

Item	Yes	No
The advisor understands principles of group development.		
The advisor understands how students grow and learn.		
The advisor understands the principles that lead to orderly meetings.		
The advisor has read the organization's constitution and bylaws.		
The advisor knows the organization's history.		
The advisor provides advice and encouragement without imposing his or her ideas and preferences on the organization.		
The advisor reviews financial records with the organization's financial officer.		
The advisor understands the principles of good fund-raising.		
The advisor understands how issues of diversity affect the organization.		
The advisor attends on- and off-campus conferences with the organization's students.		
The advisor knows the steps to follow in developing a program.		
The advisor can identify what members have learned by participating in the organization.		
The advisor works with the organization's members in conducting assessments.		
Other items specific to your organization:		

To assess the overall organization's functioning, reviewing the organization's stated goals and objectives is an excellent way to consider the organization's work over the course of the year. Many student organizations are formed to provide programs, services, and activities to member students. You can measure the effectiveness of the organization against its goals and objectives through reviewing the individual events by having members complete the generic statements for program evaluation (exhibit 28.4) for each event (Dunkel & Schuh, 1998). The information from this form can be used by your students in a discussion to improve their program.

Exhibit 28.4. Generic Statements for Program Evaluation

Please indicate the extent to which you agree or disagree with the following statements:

Item	Strongly Agree	Agree	Neutral	Disagree	Strongly Disagree
The purpose of the program was clearly identified.					
The purpose of the program was achieved.					

Item	Strongly Agree	Agree	Neutral	Disagree	Strongly Disagree
My expectations for this program were met.					
I have learned new skills as a result of attending this program.					
I can apply what I have learned from the program.					
I anticipate that my behaviors will change because of the program.					
I have greater knowledge of the organization because of this program.					
Different points of view were encouraged during the program.					
The material presented in the program was well organized.					
The presenters were well informed about the material presented.					
I found the presenters to be interesting.					
The information presented was communicated well.					
The handouts were well done.					
The visual aids enhanced the program.					
The facilities were adequate for the program.					
Other statements:					

Source: Adapted from Dunkel, N. W., & Schuh, J. H. (1998). *Advising student groups and organizations* (p. 220). San Francisco: Jossey-Bass,

Conclusion

This chapter has been designed to provide the foundational elements to perform your work as a student organization advisor. The various roles and functions of mentor, supervisor, and educator have been shared. Issues and considerations from student organization advisors across the United States have been provided to ensure that you understand how advisors spend their time working with students and organizations, the legal liability assumed when advising a student organization, and how younger students are assuming key leadership roles within the organization—roles that in the past were held by junior and senior students.

This chapter also encourages you to consider how maintaining quality will help you to effectively advise the student organization. Your engagement in and understanding of the students and the organization will go far in assisting the students to achieve their individual and organizational goals.

Advising student organizations comes with a long list of challenges and a longer list of rewards. These can be categorized by the community, institution, organization, advisor, and individual student (Dunkel, Schuh, & Chrystal-Green, 2014). Challenges include shrinking resources, a moving target on legal issues, complex mental health issues, a well-connected population through which information travels faster than ever before, and how to motivate and keep students engaged while balancing their time. Although some of the challenges that come with advising student organizations can be daunting, this can also be one of the most rewarding professional experiences. Advisors stay connected to students, energized, and young at heart. Advisors directly affect the health of an organization and a healthy organization can have a positive impact on the reputation of the institution. Being instrumental in the success of students, being a part of the moment when a student gets it, developing trust with students to challenge them to be better and do better, being remembered by students long after they graduated are tremendously gratifying. Advising student organizations provides student affairs practitioners with the opportunity to directly influence student learning and development and is a reminder of why the field of student affairs is important and necessary work.

Discussion Questions

1. What should an advisor do when faced with no returning students willing to serve on the organization's executive board?
2. What are some considerations that advisors should consider prior to the beginning of the academic year regarding how and when to set expectations of the executive board and the advisor?
3. Who should be involved in the evaluation of a program developed and held by the student organization?
4. How involved should an advisor be in the regularly scheduled student organization meeting?
5. Your students are struggling to keep up with their academic loads and fulfilling their responsibilities as the organization's executive board. What do you do?
6. What is the advisor's role when you realize that the organization is discussing involvements outside of their organization's constitutional mission?
7. Should the advisor question the organization's financial or legal issues as part of their work? Why or why not?
8. What would you do as an advisor to maintain your energy and interest in the student organization?

References

American College Personnel Association. (1994). *The student learning imperative.* Washington, DC: American College Personnel Association.

Astin, A. W. (1985). *Achieving educational excellence: A critical assessment of priorities and practices of higher education.* San Francisco: Jossey-Bass.

Astin, A. W. (1993). *What matters in college? Four critical years revisited.* San Francisco: Jossey-Bass.

Baxter Magolda, M. B., & King, P. M. (2004). *Learning partnerships: Theory and models of practice to educate for self-authorship.* Sterling, VA: Stylus.

Chrystal-Green, N. E., & Dunkel, N. W. (2015). *Survey of current issues in advising student organizations.* Unpublished manuscript.

Council for the Advancement of Standards in Higher Education (CAS). (2012). *CAS professional standards for higher education* (8th ed.). Washington, DC: Author.

Creamer, D. G., Winston, R. B., & Miller, T. K. (2001). The professional student affairs administrator: Roles and functions. In R. B. Winston, D. G. Creamer, T. K. Miller, & Associates, *The professional student affairs administrator: Educator, leader, and manager* (pp. 3–38). New York: Brunner-Routledge.

DeCoster, D. A., & Brown, R. D. (1982). Mentoring relationships and the educational process. In R. D. Brown & D. A. DeCoster (Eds.), *Mentoring-transcript systems for promoting student growth* (New Directions for Student Services, no. 19, pp. 5–17). San Francisco: Jossey-Bass.

Dugan, J. P., & Komives, S. R. (2011). Leadership theories. In S. R. Komives, J. P. Dugan, J. E. Owen, C. Slack, W. Wagner, & Associates, *The handbook for student leadership development* (2nd ed., pp. 35–58). San Francisco: Jossey-Bass.

Dunkel, N. W. (1996, July 15). *Supervision: Creating a relationship for advancement, progressivity, and education.* Presentation at the annual meeting of the Association of College and University Housing Officers-International, Providence, Rhode Island.

Dunkel, N. W., & Schuh, J. H. (1998). *Advising student groups and organizations.* San Francisco: Jossey-Bass.

Dunkel, N. W., Schuh, J. H., & Chrystal-Green, N. E. (2014). *Advising student groups and organizations* (2nd ed.). San Francisco: Jossey-Bass.

Ewell, P. T. (2009). *Assessment, accountability and improvement: Revisiting the tension.* Champaign, IL: National Institute for Learning Outcomes Assessment.

Johnson, D. W., & Johnson, F. P. (2013). *Joining together: Group theory and group skills* (11th ed.). Boston: Pearson.

King, P. M., & Baxter Magolda, M. B. (2011). Student learning. In J. H. Schuh, S. R. Jones, S. R. Harper, & Associates. *Student services: A handbook for the profession* (5th ed., pp. 207–225). San Francisco: Jossey-Bass.

Komives, S. R. (2011). Leadership. In J. H. Schuh, S. R. Jones, S. R. Harper, & Associates, *Student services: A handbook for the profession* (5th ed., pp. 353–371). San Francisco: Jossey-Bass.

Komives, S. R., Lucas, N., & McMahon, T. R. (2013). *Exploring leadership* (3rd ed.). San Francisco: Jossey-Bass.

Kouzes, J. M., & Posner, B. Z. (2012). *The leadership challenge: How to make extraordinary things happen in organizations.* San Francisco: Jossey-Bass.

Love, P., & Maxam, S. (2011). Advising and consultation. In J. H. Schuh, S. R. Jones, S. R. Harper, & Associates, *Student services: A handbook for the profession* (5th ed., pp. 413–432). San Francisco: Jossey-Bass.

National Survey of Student Engagement (NSSE). (2012). *Promoting student learning and improvement: Lessons from NSSE at 13.* Bloomington: Indiana University Center for Postsecondary Research.

Pascarella, E. T., & Terenzini, P. T. (2005). *How college affects students: A third decade of research: Volume 2.* San Francisco: Jossey-Bass.

Saunders, S. A., & Cooper, D. L. (2001). Programmatic interventions: Translating theory to practice. In R. B. Winston, D. G. Creamer, T. K. Miller, & Associates, *The professional student affairs administrator: Educator, leader, and manager* (pp. 309–344). New York: Brunner-Routledge.

Waters, R. D., Burnett, E., Lamm, A., & Lucas, J. (2009). Engaging stakeholders through social networking: How nonprofit organizations are using Facebook. *Public Relations Review, 35,* 102–106.

CHAPTER 29

CRISIS MANAGEMENT

Mahauganee D. Shaw and Larry D. Roper

Over the years, campus crises have become more regular occurrences, resulting in crisis management skills being an expected competency for student affairs professionals. New professionals on the front line of student services quite often find themselves as the first responders when emergencies arise. This reality has led to this new chapter being added to this edition. This chapter provides an overview of crisis and conflict; reviews definitions and classification schemes, strategies, and skills for addressing and responding to campus crisis and conflict; and describes theories that aid the process of working through these incidents. Throughout the chapter we pose questions to challenge readers to consider personal and professional perspectives and values and how those inform crisis management.

Understanding Crisis and Conflict

Crisis and *conflict* are words used frequently to describe incidents that threaten personal, institutional, or reputational safety and create high-stakes decision-making environments. Several definitions of these words have been offered over the years. Here, we present the definitions and terminology that will be used throughout this chapter. The following definitions highlight the nuances among situations that arise in student affairs work and introduce language that is appropriately suited for managing challenging scenarios.

Defining Crisis and Conflict

Researchers studying crisis management on college campuses generally identify a crisis situation by the element of surprise. Combining pieces of several previous definitions, Zdziarski (2006) provides a definition of crisis specific for those in higher education and student affairs: "A campus crisis is an event, often sudden or unexpected, that disrupts the normal operations of the institution or its educational mission and threatens the well-being of personnel, property, financial resources, and/or reputation of the institution" (p. 5). This definition leaves a wide variety of potential incidents, on and off campus, which can be classified as crises. To help provide some order to this variety of incidents, researchers have offered varying levels of crisis (Quarantelli, 2006; Zdziarski, Rollo, & Dunkel, 2007). From smallest to largest, these levels include the following:

Critical incidents—crises that are isolated to a particular section of campus or have an impact that is confined to a particular segment of the campus population

Campus emergencies—crises that affect the life of the campus but are confined within the borders of the campus

Disasters—crises that permeate campus borders and extend into the surrounding community

Catastrophes—more severe forms of disasters, with increased and long-lasting damage to the affected area

Given the focus of this text on new professionals, the chapter will emphasize critical incidents, the types of crises most likely to arise in daily student services work. Although it is quite possible that new professionals may be called on to assist in the institutional response to a campus emergency, disaster, or catastrophe, those situations are less likely to arise in a given academic year. By contrast, critical incidents are certain to arise throughout every semester. The information and techniques described in this chapter are helpful to new and emerging professionals who are honing crisis management skills and seeking to apply their personal leadership philosophy to their work with students.

In addition to levels of crisis, there are different types of crisis: human, facilities, and environmental. These types are based on how a crisis begins and where it originates. The focus of this chapter is on human crises, "any event or situation that originates with or is initiated by humans, whether through error or conscious act" (Zdziarski & others, 2007, p. 41). The most common crisis and conflict management challenges faced by new professionals are human critical incidents. Therefore, this chapter has been dedicated to exploring this type and level of crisis and how conflicts and crises intersect. Human critical incidents may result from interorganizational or interpersonal conflicts that arise between people or campus constituencies with disparate interests and objectives.

Most organizations are divided into subgroups of people who share interests or responsibilities (Bolman & Deal, 2013; Morgan, 2006). This is true regardless of organizational size; that is, whether the organization is an entire postsecondary institution, one office or division within an institution, or one student club on a campus, the organization is a conglomeration of people, some of whom cluster together around particular purposes or points of interest. Competing interests or needs between subgroups within one college or university setting can lead to conflict. Examples could be two roommates in a campus residential facility arguing over common space, two student clubs or Greek-letter organizations that are vying for something as simple as programming space or something as abstract as respect and reputation, or two campus offices debating over which office should own and control a particular function on campus. In all of these examples, conflict is a result of the tension caused between different campus units, employees, or students who are in competition for scarce institutional resources and likely harming each other in the process of competing. Although each of these examples focus on two competing parties, it is possible for conflict to arise with three or more parties involved.

Theories, Skills, and Strategies for Approaching Crisis

As described previously, campus crises may arise in multiple forms. Although there is no universal approach to resolving group, interpersonal, or intergroup crises, there are particular strategies recommended and skills needed by student affairs professionals to be effective in resolving the types of crises that arise in day-to-day campus life. Those strategies include establishing effective working relationships with the parties involved in the crisis that engender trust in the third party, establishing a cooperative problem-solving attitude toward the crisis or conflict between the conflicting parties, developing a creative group process, and developing sufficient background on the issues involved to function as a viable resource (Deutsch, 1991). This list of skills requires that certain behaviors become a usual part of a professional's work life prior to the occurrence of a crisis. For instance, effective working relationships must be developed over time and thus established prior to the time that a crisis or conflict occurs. Attempting to mediate an escalated situation between parties without an established rapport may be possible, but it will be a more difficult task.

In responding to crises and resolving conflicts, student affairs professionals may adopt a variety of roles: mediator, conciliator, process consultant, facilitator, or counselor. These roles are easier to embody when one has an understanding of guiding theories and has worked to build the skills and competencies that are most useful in addressing crises. In the following section, we briefly describe crisis management strategies that are useful for identifying how to approach a developing crisis. Next, we outline theories on justice that may be applied when mediating, consulting, facilitating, or counseling parties involved in a conflict. Finally, we describe the skills and competencies needed to manage and work through the high-stakes situations presented by crisis.

Organizing the Approach to a Crisis Response

Understanding how to identify a crisis situation is a prerequisite to the process of managing a crisis. The ability to distinguish among the different types and levels of crisis is important to enacting a successful response. Determining the type and level of a crisis helps to identify the proper resources and response strategies. As noted previously, this chapter focuses on human critical incidents. Designating a crisis as a human critical incident provides a few parameters that help to identify starting points. First, a human crisis involves people. Second, the impact of the critical incident is isolated to a smaller subgroup within the campus population. Therefore, a response can begin by identifying which specific people are involved in the conflict and which portions of the campus community may be affected by the developing or ongoing conflict.

Once the people who should be the focus of any response efforts have been identified, it is possible to begin constructing a plan for how to approach the situation. Knowing which portions of the campus population are affected by a conflict can help to determine which administrators should be involved in the response effort. Reason and Lutovsky (2007) provide an overview of the resources and information to which various functional areas have access. Although this list is intended to help senior student affairs officers identify which colleagues are most useful when responding to different crises, it can also help those who work in different functional areas to consider what resources they have to offer to a crisis response process. It is important for early-career and mid-level student affairs professionals to know what resources and information they have to offer in times of crisis, because more senior administrators may not always be aware of how each office can assist.

Understanding Nuances of Justice: Distributive, Social, and Restorative

When conflict arises because of values and perspectives concerning justice, it may be important to understand some of the ways that "justice" can be understood. Three particular views of justice may be relevant to engaging conflict, specifically by understanding some of the tensions among these concepts. Focusing too narrowly on any single conception of justice is unlikely to resolve conflict in a manner consistent with creating and sustaining community. Conflicts concerning justice, then, may be more carefully navigated by taking a nuanced understanding of these different paradigms and using them as frameworks for analyzing individual, group, and community interests when engaging conflict.

Distributive Justice Distributive justice is arguably the most common construct influencing a majority of people. In a campus context, distributive justice is viewed in terms of the distribution of goods and resources, such as space, support, money, and supplies. Although attention to quantifiable disparities is important, this emphasis on material solutions is incomplete without addressing intangible matters of human dignity that are important matters of justice (Young, 1990).

Social Justice Social justice is often discussed with regard to material disparities, yet as Young (1990) argues, social justice also accounts for self-respect, dignity, recognition, rights, and opportunities—real social patterns that are impossible to quantify. Social justice can be viewed as a process and a goal to address institutions that are assumed to have embedded oppression. Leaders concerned with social justice will not only be conscious of the equitable distribution of resources but also with creating environments in which campus community members will be physically and psychologically safe and secure (Bell, 2013). Social justice has emerged as a dominant frame through which student affairs leadership and decision making is evaluated. Watt, Jacobson, and Kilgo give a fuller description of the practice of social justice in student affairs in chapter 30.

Restorative Justice   Models of restorative justice address conflict as matters of harm or wrongdoing (Sue, 2006; Zehr, 2002). Adherents to principles of restorative justice point out that many conflicts emerge from a sense of injustice. Therefore, responding to conflict involves acting to restore a state of justice in interpersonal and institutional contexts. When people believe that a person or group has committed a harmful or unjust act, theories of restorative justice encourage those involved to view conflict surrounding wrongdoing and harm with an immutable commitment to conflict transformation and peacebuilding. This is quite different from most conventional models of justice that view offenders or perpetrators as inherently flawed and beyond repair; that kind of "lock them up and throw away the key" method falls within a framework called *retributive justice*. On the contrary, restorative methods see all persons as deserving of humane treatment and healing. Those who have been identified as acting to cause conflict or harm are primarily responsible for the healing response, but they are not alone in their responsibility. Restorative justice requires that we acknowledge one another as sharing in common social and community processes that give rise to the actions of individuals. Our social and communal influences may prohibit or permit, discourage or encourage, or diminish or enhance the likelihood that certain individuals or groups will commit just or unjust acts.

Engaging conflict through a restorative approach literally involves work to restore the dignity of those who have been victims or survivors of wrongdoing, *as well as* restoring the humanity of those who carried out harmful acts. Zehr (2002) explains at least three guiding principles that can provide practical reference points for addressing conflict: (1) there must be opportunities for a wrong to be articulated by victims and acknowledged by offenders; (2) through an apology, often involving work to make restitution, equity needs to be restored to all persons involved. This often requires empowering people by compensating for disparities of power and influence; and (3) there must be a creative plan for the future, addressing key questions surrounding commitments to the future of the community. Young, Ehrhart, and Meyer (2012) shared their experience with integrating principles of restorative justice into their institutional judicial process for students who violate the student code of conduct. This process led them to create a more equitable focus on the victim and overall campus community, in addition to focusing on the offender.

Applying Justice as a Framework

Writing about the application of justice in organizational settings, Bolman and Deal (2013) provide advice that translates to the role of student affairs professionals in helping to resolve conflict between two parties: "The key gift that leaders can offer in pursuit of justice is sharing power. People with a voice in key decisions are far more likely to feel a sense of fairness than those with none . . . The gift of power enrolls people in working toward a common cause" (p. 402).

When mediating conflict or facilitating dialogue between two competing people, groups, or campus entities, it is important to not assume a position of power and authority that ignores the power and perspectives of the conflicting parties. Addressing a crisis will be made easier if the student affairs professional acknowledges from the outset that each party has a perspective, that there is validity in those perspectives, and that everyone shares the power to influence the conflict-resolution process. Setting these expectations models the behavior that is desired from each party: to interact cordially, focus on understanding one another, and move toward a solution.

LeBaron (2003) suggests that because all conflict is relational, finding effective ways to relate to each other is our primary task during attempts at resolution; this must be the focus regardless of the issues present or the precipitating events. The goal of the conflict-resolution leader is increased relationship effectiveness through implementation of the appropriate process. The success of the process is influenced by four activities: *naming*, what we call the conflict; *framing*, giving the conflict boundaries by defining where it begins and ends; *blaming*, assigning shared responsibility and accountability in a way that does not put the burden of solution solely on one party; and *taming*, bringing the conflict to some kind of closure. Although the process and framework applied during conflict resolution are important, there are certain skills and competencies that enable one to better navigate this process. We turn now to a discussion of those.

Skills and Competencies for Approaching Crisis

Conflict-competent leaders will manifest skills and apply appropriate strategies to help their organization address the types of conflict situations associated with their area of professional responsibility (Runde & Flanagan, 2007). It has been noted that "theory and research about what constitutes effective crisis leadership characteristics are less abundant than opinion and advice about the same thing. Nevertheless, much of the theory and research is promising and often supports opinion, advice, observation, and practice" (DuBrin, 2013, p. 3). Therefore, if you were to pause reading right now and make a list of the characteristics you believe are necessary for effective crisis leadership, it might match much of what we have included in this section.

Effective crisis leadership has been evaluated in many ways, including the personal traits of leaders, their behaviors, and their skill sets. Given that traits have long been dismissed as an accurate measure of leadership capacity

(Rost, 1993), we have focused this section on the behaviors and skills that lead to competent leadership in times of crisis. Wooten and James (2008) have identified leadership competencies that are important for different stages of managing a crisis. Although that list is more extensive, we present the skills and competencies that are most likely to be needed during human critical incidents. These include effective communication, perspective taking, acting with integrity, and a learning orientation.

The *effective communication* skills that lead to successful crisis intervention require good listening, the ability to appropriately reframe, and the ability to observe while suspending judgment (Ting-Toomey & Oetzel, 2001). These skills heighten the crisis mediator's personal capacity to successfully engage those involved in conflict at a level that engenders trust and willingness to participate in the crisis-resolution process (Wilmot & Hocker, 2007). Ting-Toomey and Oetzel (2001) suggest that successful mediators will possess the ability to manage their personal judgments in a way that will enable all parties to feel respected; possessing mindfulness and "giving face" to those involved will support the creation of a respectful environment (p. 187).

Although communication can help to engender trust in the conflict-resolution process, *perspective taking*—the ability to assume and identify with the perspective of another for the purposes of understanding all sides to a situation—can help provide a broader view of the underlying issues. Exercising personal *integrity* in this process leads to ethical decisions and helps to strengthen one's personal leadership style. Finally, approaching crisis response with a *learning orientation* acknowledges the opportunities presented by crises—opportunities for personal, as well as organizational, growth and development. Crisis leadership is an intentional act; combining the skills and competencies previously outlined with the frameworks described in the next section will lead to successful outcomes in times of conflict.

General Strategies for Effective Crisis Management

In addition to the theories, skills, and strategies previously outlined, student affairs professionals should be equipped with a professional outlook that will enable them to approach conflict and crisis from a healthy, educational perspective. It is especially important for a professional to be discerning with regard to the philosophical frameworks and perspectives that can guide one's engagement with crisis. The next sections provide examples of frames that are applicable to the educational missions of colleges and universities and thus are helpful when engaging in the mediation of a crisis. These frames include hospitality, critical thinking, emotional intelligence, charity—the principle of fairness—and dynamic tension. Each of these frames provides optional approaches that a student affairs professional might adopt to engage the task of crisis management. Following, we explain each of these frames and offer questions to consider when applying each frame to a crisis response. Different crises and conflicts will require different approaches. Thus, it is not likely that anyone would use all these frames simultaneously; instead, certain frames may be more appropriate for particular situations. It is up to the student affairs professional to discern and determine which frame is most appropriate.

Hospitality

Emerging from the study of ethics through personal narratives, Hallie (1981) describes an important tenet of moral philosophy for a world that struggles with conflicts. He suggests that within our institutions there are many forms of cruelty and many forms of kindness. He argues that leaders make a mistake when they assume that peace is the opposite of hate and war—peace is only the absence of hostility, violence, and harm. Instead, Hallie (1981) asks us to think about our capacity to demonstrate hospitality, which he calls "unsentimental efficacious love" (p. 27). Freedom from a hostile, negative, or degrading relationship is not the opposite of harm; it is merely the absence of harm. Hospitality refers to actions that not only remove harm but also that seek to heal the harms that have been done and, most important, prevent further harms from occurring. The nature of the college experience should involve promoting health and well-being and positive self-concept, which requires a safe and welcoming campus environment. Questions to consider when using hospitality as a frame include the following:

1. In the midst of conflict and crisis, how can you show hospitality in the ways described by Hallie?
2. What is your capacity to help foster healing among conflicting parties?
3. Recognizing that conflict will continue to occur, what can you do to help create the kinds of relationships and communities in which conflict does not involve the degradation of one's humanity?
4. What can you do to foster hospitality amid conflict that enables creativity and interpersonal insight into one another to flourish?

Using hospitality as an operational frame in one's work and encouraging our students and colleagues to do the same can create the type of environment that mitigates interpersonal or intergroup harm and the types of conflict that arises from such harm.

Critical Thinking

Throughout postsecondary education, the phrase *critical thinking* is widely used, though it is rarely defined with any practical import. What does critical thinking mean, and what does it have to do with conflict? Critical thinking as a practical philosophy emerged out of the writings of Karl Marx and was later advanced by theorists at the Institute for Social Research, sometimes called the Frankfurt School, founded in 1923 in Frankfurt, Germany (Bronner & Kellner, 1989). Critical thinking is an important skill for academic study and research but also for application in daily life outside of the classroom environment. A substantial amount of academic and social learning emphasizes three general perspectives for thinking about subjects and issues: (1) how a relationship or situation has been (in the past); (2) how a situation or relationship is right now (in the present); and (3) how a particular situation or relationship will likely be (in the future) (Matheis, 2006).

Critical thinking as a mode of operation encourages consideration of at least two additional perspectives on a given subject or situation. In addition to the three perspectives just mentioned, thinking critically means that we also consider (4) how society or issues could be (potentially) as well as (5) how a relationship or situation should, or ought to, be (ethically, morally, and practically) (Matheis, 2006). This level of insight requires that persons provide substantial arguments for why a given relationship or situation should be one way as opposed to another. The student affairs professional must effectively cultivate critical thinking skills and create a critical frame when confronted with crisis situations. Specifically, professionals may ask questions based in critical thought, such as these:

1. How should we understand a particular situation or relationship, and why?
2. How should we treat people who are involved in a conflict, and why?
3. What should we do in order to foster and sustain the kinds of relationships in which conflict is positively and effectively engaged, and why?

Emotional Intelligence

Individuals and groups have capacities for emotional intelligence (Druskat & Wolff, 2001; Goleman, 1998). Operating in an emotionally intelligent manner requires one to be aware of one's emotions and to regulate those emotions when interacting with others. Regulating emotion does not mean that one should attempt to appear stoic but that the emotions present are recognized and controlled. In addition to being aware of one's own emotions, exercising emotional intelligence requires that one also be aware of others' emotions and make an attempt to understand the origin of those emotions.

The four-branch model of emotional intelligence includes the abilities to perceive emotion, use emotion to facilitate thought, understand emotions, and manage emotions (Mayer, Salovey, & Caruso, 2004). The capacity to master each of these four branches is useful to engaging with those involved in campus conflict. A student affairs professional who works to understand the perspectives of everyone involved in a conflict is better able to recognize and understand the emotions of those people and to regulate one's own reactions to others' displays of emotion. The following questions can help one tune in to one's own level of emotional intelligence, as well as that of other people, in the midst of a conflict:

1. What events, words, or actions are serving as trigger points for the individuals involved?
2. Which emotions are interfering with the goal of resolution, and how can we bypass those?
3. What can I do to model emotional intelligence and help people to see perspectives that are opposite of their own?

Charity—The Principle of Fairness

The principle of fairness, sometimes also called the *principle of charity*, is not only important for effectively engaging conflict but also for building and sustaining healthy relationships and for making effective judgments (Kiersky & Caste, 1995). Adhering to this principle means that the conflict mediator chooses to interpret others with the most generous assumptions—about their motives, interests, ideas, and so on. It is easy to diminish the arguments and character of another person by attributing flawed premises to their ideas. However, in order to think clearly and make valid judgments, one must be willing, if not eager, to attribute the assumptions that will provide the greatest ideological strength one would expect from another critical thinker. To be able to successfully criticize or evaluate the views of another person, one must be willing and able to understand and defend that person's point of view to its fullest extent prior to attempting to critique it. Otherwise, one risks criticizing a weakened version of an idea that they have subconsciously contrived solely for the purposes of discrediting the other person.

Charity also involves a self-critical willingness to recognize where your perspectives are accurate and where they may need to be modified as more information is learned. Charity may mean taking away from an experience those things that you find to be useful and leaving the rest—rather than seeing any particular idea or approach as entirely good or entirely bad; charity means discerning positive qualities from negative qualities in a careful and critical manner. Some questions to help one apply charity in the midst of conflict include these:

1. Are you motivated by charity in giving the strongest interpretations to another person's meaning and intentions? If not, how might you adjust your approach?
2. Are you able to be generous toward those who may arouse negative feelings within you? If not, what will it take for you to be able to do so?
3. Are you making thoughtful evaluations or are you applying broad and sweeping judgments without care? How can you trend toward the former?
4. What does it mean to role model charity and the principle of fairness for others who are observing and learning from your leadership?

Charity may be easier to apply in the midst of navigating a conflict in which one can truly serve as an impartial third party. When loyalties are aligned with different parties involved in a conflict, exercising charity becomes a more trying task.

Dynamic Tension

Conflict cannot be resolved through avoidance of the inherent tension that accompanies difficult situations, which are natural and important elements of the life of a student affairs leader. Dynamic tension refers to ongoing changes in comfort and discomfort experienced by people to the extent that some positive response or reaction may be evoked or provoked as an intended or unintended result (Matheis, 2006; Matheis & Sue, 2007). In other words, tensions experienced in a safe environment can positively influence our abilities to work and think creatively. For example, on many occasions classroom discussions in postsecondary education will focus on or touch on historical and contemporary approaches to addressing and resolving important social issues, such as racism, sexism, heterosexism, ageism, ableism, socioeconomic disparities, religious persecution, and so on. It is reasonable to assume that differences of opinion will arise as people think through these topics.

With an understanding of the value of dynamic tension, professionals can facilitate conversations in which conflicts, mistakes, and inevitable divergence in thoughts and ideas do not place relationships in jeopardy. With this in mind, conflict can be engaged such that tension can exist between and among people with different perspectives without fear of losing substantial access to equitable rewards and fair support from instructors, administrators, and peers (Matheis & Sue, 2007; Rankin, Roosa-Millar, & Matheis, 2007). Dynamic tension can be difficult to embrace. As professional staff members, student affairs administrators may be inclined to avoid the uncertainty that exists within the experience of dynamic tension; the inclination to shy away from tension may be amplified when working with students as a new professional, sometimes struggling to be viewed as an authority figure. As you think about your ability to comfortably welcome and experience dynamic tension, consider the following:

1. What is your capacity to facilitate and guide others through challenging conversations?
2. How does your awareness of dynamic tension affect your ability to support those involved in crisis situations?

Comfort with dynamic tension is something that develops over time, with experience navigating various levels of conflict. If this is an area of discomfort, it may be helpful to seek advice or training on facilitating dialogue either on difficult topics or between differing perspectives.

Engaging with Crisis Situations

New professionals may benefit from carefully considering each of the five frames we outline in the preceding section, personal comfort levels with using each of those frames, and a plan for developing familiarity with any frames that are personally uncomfortable to engage. This final section offers an opportunity to contemplate how one might work through an instance of conflict. Two scenarios are presented next, followed by discussion questions. The discussion questions encourage reflection on the information contained in the previous portions of this chapter.

Scenario 1

A homeless man, who was rummaging through a campus dumpster (in search of recyclable bottles and cans) in an alley behind several fraternity houses, was shot and injured by a pellet gun. Because the assailant was not immediately identified, the occupants of the three fraternity houses nearest the dumpster were pursued as possible perpetrators. During the investigation it was determined there had been a history of individuals from one of the fraternities shooting at the homeless, as well as targeting the homeless with name-calling and thrown objects. The responsible person was eventually identified and charged. This incident generated attention and opinions from on- and off-campus audiences, including calls for closing the fraternity and expulsion of its members.

Scenario 2

A group of residents from your university's Social Justice Living Learning Community is walking back to campus following an off-campus dinner to celebrate a very successful week of events to promote justice and equity in education. As the group walks through a neighborhood close to campus they are verbally taunted from the window of a house. Among the comments made toward the group were "no niggers or fags allowed here," "go back to Mexico where you belong," and "we know where you live and we will visit you some night."

News of the incident very quickly spreads through social media. Students respond by organizing a rally and march to protest the house, which is inhabited by a group of students from the university. There are calls for a strong administrative response.

Through your role you will have the responsibility and opportunity to meet with the parties involved in each of these incidents. As you prepare for the conversations, consider the following questions.

Related to the Incident

- What information should be gathered first?
- Which individuals and groups may be affected in this situation?
- In what ways is the incident at odds with institutional values and policies?
- Who "owns" the issue(s) at the heart of this incident?
- Who should be involved in conversation prior to individual administrative response?
- What is the role of your functional area in the conversation and response?
- What are the major factors involved in the incident?
- What competencies are needed to effectively provide leadership to respond to this crisis?
- What are some appropriate models or frameworks to use as reference points in thinking and acting to engage with this conflict?

Related to Your Personal Leadership

- What strengths and competencies do you bring to the conversation?
- What are your personal perspectives and feelings of which you must be aware?

- What biases might you bring to the interaction?
- What challenges will you confront in demonstrating openness to all parties with whom you will meet?
- Through what personal philosophical perspective will you approach the conversation?
- What is your institution's stated student conduct philosophy and how will you integrate it with your personal values and philosophy?
- What are some appropriate models or frameworks to use as reference points in thinking and acting to engage with this conflict?
- How will you address the concerns of those most immediately involved as well as the broader community?
- How can you ensure your role adds value to the conversation?
- Creatively, how might problem-solving become a shared responsibility for all parties involved?
- How will you determine whether a successful outcome has been achieved?

Conclusion

The ability to address and respond to campus crises and conflicts has become an essential skill for student affairs professionals, as evidenced by adding this new chapter to this edition. Yet, many available resources on crisis management focus on managing large-scale institutional crises and overlook the day-to-day experiences of new professionals who are often responsible for addressing the smaller emergencies that regularly arise in our work. In this chapter, we have focused on the new professional and the process of addressing issues related to conflict. Integrating principles of justice and campus crisis management, we have offered tips on how to approach a crisis and five frameworks (hospitality, critical thinking, emotional intelligence, charity, and dynamic tension) that can assist with mediating conflicts and deescalating evolving crises.

The chapter ends with an activity that can be used by new professionals or with graduate students who are preparing to enter the field of student affairs. The activity is intended to help readers digest, synthesize, and practice implementing the information provided in the chapter. Although crises carry an element of unpredictability (Zdziarki, Rollo, & Dunkel, 2007), this does not preclude one from preparing to respond if, and when, crisis occurs. Working through the scenarios provided at the end of this chapter, and engaging the reflection questions provided along with the earlier presentation of the five frames, is a solid first step toward developing this new essential competency within our field. Collectively, the information in this chapter encourages readers to consider their personal and professional perspectives and values, how they overlap, and how to remain true to those perspectives and values when engaging with situations that are likely to challenge that foundation. Considering these questions in the safeness of these pages and the practice scenarios are certain to prove helpful when crises emerge in one's work environment.

References

Bell, L. A. (2013). Theoretical foundations. In M. Adams, W. Blumenfeld, C. Castaneda, H. W. Hackman, M. L. Peters, & X. Zúñiga (Eds.), *Readings for diversity and social justice*. New York: Routledge.

Bolman, L. G., & Deal, T. E. (2013). *Reframing organizations: Artistry, choice, and leadership* (5th ed.). San Francisco: Jossey-Bass.

Bronner, S., & Kellner, D. (1989). *Critical theory and society*. New York: Routledge.

Deutsch, M. (1991). Subjective features of conflict resolution. In R. Vayrynen (Ed.), *New directions in conflict theory: Conflict resolution and conflict transformation* (pp. 26–56). London: Sage.

Druskat, V. U., & Wolff, S. B. (2001). Building the emotional intelligence of groups. *Harvard Business Review*, March, 80–90.

DuBrin, A. J. (2013). Personal attributes and behaviors of effective crisis leaders. In A. J. DuBrin (Ed.), *Handbook of research on crisis leadership in organizations* (pp. 3–22). Northampton, MA: Edward Elgar.

Goleman, D. (1998). *Working with emotional intelligence*. New York: Bantam.

Hallie, P. (1981). From cruelty to goodness. *The Hastings Center Report, 11*(3), 23–28.

Kiersky, J., & Caste, N. (1995). *Thinking critically*. Belmont, CA: West.

LeBaron, M. (2003). *Bridging cultural conflicts: A new approach for a changing world*. San Francisco: Jossey-Bass.

Matheis, C. (2006, Oct. 17). *Who needs hierarchy? Revolutionary leadership for diverse groups*. Presented at the Pennsylvania College Personnel Association annual conference in Stroudsburg, PA.

Matheis, C., & Sue, R. (2007). Difference, power, and discrimination and graduate education: Earning an advanced degree in a fragmented curriculum. In J. Xing, J. Li, L. Roper, & S. M. Shaw (Eds.), *Teaching for change: The difference, power, and discrimination model*. Lanham, MD: Lexington Books.

Mayer, J. D., Salovey, P., & Caruso, D. R. (2004). Emotional intelligence: Theory, findings, and implications. *Psychological Inquiry, 15*(3), 197–215.

Morgan, G. (2006). *Images of organization*. Thousand Oaks, CA: Sage.

Quarantelli, E. L. (2006). *Catastrophes are different from disasters: Some implications for crisis planning and managing drawn from Katrina*. Retrieved from http://understandingkatrina .ssrc.org/Quarantelli/

Rankin, S., Roosa-Millar, L., & Matheis, C. (2007). Safe campuses for LGBTQA students: Systemic transformation through re(A)wakened senior leaders. In M. Terell (Ed.), *Creating and maintaining safe college campuses: A sourcebook for evaluating and enhancing safety programs*. Sterling, VA: Stylus.

Reason, R. D., & Lutovsky, B. R. (2007). You are not alone: Resources for college administrators. In J. L. Jackson & M. C. Terrell (Eds.), *Creating and maintaining safe college campuses: A sourcebook for evaluating and enhancing safety programs* (pp. 241–260). Sterling, VA: Stylus.

Rost, J. C. (1993). *Leadership for the 21st century*. Westport, CT: Praeger.

Runde, C. E., & Flanagan, T. A. (2007). *Becoming a conflict competent leader: How you and your organization can manage conflict effectively*. San Francisco: Jossey-Bass and Center for Creative Leadership.

Sue, R. (2006). *Sexual harassment and restorative justice: A transformational approach to addressing sexual harassment claims*. Unpublished master's thesis. Oregon State University, Corvallis.

Ting-Toomey, S., & Oetzel, J. G. (2001). *Managing intercultural conflict effectively*. Thousand Oaks, CA: Sage.

Wilmot, W. W., & Hocker, J. L. (2007). *Interpersonal conflict*. Boston: McGraw-Hill.

Wooten, L. P., & James, E. H. (2008). Linking crisis management and leadership competencies: The role of human resource development. *Advances in Developing Human Resources, 10*(3), 352–379.

Young, I. M. (1990). *Justice and the politics of difference.* Princeton, NJ: Princeton University Press.

Young, W., Ehrhart, C., & Meyer, G. (2012). Big change through small action. *About Campus, 17*(5), 20–26.

Zdziarski, E. L., II. (2006). Crisis in the context of higher education. In K. S. Harper, B. G. Paterson, & E. L. Zdziarski, II (Eds.), *Crisis management: Responding from the heart* (pp. 3–24). Washington, DC: National Association of Student Personnel Administrators.

Zdziarski, E. L., II, Rollo, J. M., & Dunkel, N. W. (Eds.). (2007). *Campus crisis management: A comprehensive guide to planning, prevention, response, and recovery.* San Francisco: Jossey-Bass.

Zehr, H. (2002). *The little book of restorative justice.* Intercourse, PA: Good Books.

CHAPTER 30

DESIGNING PROGRAMS FOR ENGAGING DIFFERENCE

Sherry Watt, Cindy Ann Kilgo, and Wayne Jacobson

The purpose of this chapter is to discuss the use of high-impact practices in concert with programs that engage cultural diversity in ways that will increase student's competency for engaging difference. Saunders and Cooper (2001) define a *programmatic intervention* as "a planned activity with individuals or student groups that is theoretical based and has as its intention the promotion of personal development and learning" (p. 310). Programming efforts on college campuses aimed at systematic ways to engage and retain students are beneficial. Additionally, a focus on diversity and global that explore "difficult differences" (as cited on www.aacu.org/leap/hips) are important components to developing students to be good citizens of a rapidly changing and increasingly more diverse world. Postsecondary institutions play an important role in advocating for social change in the areas of racial and gender inequality and other human rights issues by designing and implementing programmatic interventions to promote self-awareness, understanding across difference, civic engagement, and social justice. College campuses exist within a larger society where social oppression exists. An important part of the college experience is not only teaching students the skills to exist in a diverse society with honor, respect, and dignity but also to expand their knowledge about how to deconstruct social inequity. In order to do that, postsecondary institutions have to expose students intentionally to difference through programmatic interventions. Watt and Linley (2013) define *difference* as "having dissimilar opinions, experiences, ideologies, epistemologies and/or constructions of reality about self, society, and/or identity" (p. 6).

The Ernest L. Boyer Commission (1995) calls on research-intensive higher education institutions to expand opportunities for students to "interact with people of backgrounds, cultures, and experiences different from the student's own and with pursuers of knowledge at every level of accomplishment, from freshmen students to senior research faculty" (p. 13). Watt (2011, 2015a, 2015b; Watt & Linley, 2013) builds on this idea by suggesting that campuses focus on making changes in the environment whereby the engagement with *difference* does not solely depend on the introduction of people from a minority group (that is, students of color, nonheterosexuals, non-gender binary) to a majority (white, heterosexual, cisgender) student but also includes a shift in focus on the individual engaging in an authentic exploration of self in relation to otherness.

Many college campuses have implemented high-impact practices to engage students in the college experience. However, these practices provide general guidelines for engagement and are not specifically designed to strengthen student's skills for *engaging difference* unless applied with that intention. High-impact practices are a set of practices commonly seen as beneficial to undergraduate college students from all backgrounds that increase the likelihood that they will engage in and be retained in college (Kuh, 2008). The traditional high-impact practices such as first-year seminars and programs, capstone courses, common core curriculums, learning communities, writing-intensive courses, internships, and undergraduate research are a specific set of teaching and learning practices that are assumed to benefit students and enhance their experiences in college (Kuh, 2008). In addition to those traditional high-impact practices, researchers have delineated some strategies that specifically intend to support development in the area of diversity experiences (for example, Bowman, 2011, 2012; Gurin, Dey, Hurtado, & Gurin, 2002; Hurtado, Milem, Clayton-Pederson, & Allen, 1999). There are three categories of these types of practices:

1. Structural diversity or the representation of students of color within a larger group
2. Classroom diversity including diversity-related courses, but also structured cocurricular activities
3. Informal, interactive diversity experiences outside of curricular and cocurricular activities

When incorporated with intentionality, the traditional and added delineations of high-impact practices have great potential to encourage the development of college students, build their skills for working across *difference*, and assist them in preparing to be good citizens.

This chapter discusses ways that high-impact practices can be intentionally applied to engage across *difference*. We describe and critically analyze the traditional high-impact practices and further delineations as they relate to engaging *difference*. In addition, we share practical ways college educators can implement campus-wide programming using high-impact practices in ways that can strengthen the student's ability to be in a community and authentically consider the self in relation to otherness. This chapter begins by describing the characteristics of an inclusive community and practices that engage students in authentic explorations of *difference*.

Inclusive Community Characteristics

Systemic oppression is in the social fabric of this country. Oppression constitutes interrelated attitudes and behaviors that position dominant (for example, white, male, heterosexual, and cisgender) and oppressed (for example, people of color, gay, lesbian, gender-nonconforming) groups in relation to each other (Hardiman, Jackson, & Griffin, 2007; Pharr, 1997). The nature of systemic oppression is that it exists within an overall system of power embedded in social structures that dehumanize marginalized individuals, which cause psychological, physical, and economic harm to its citizens. These behaviors and attitudes consciously and unconsciously invade and inform how people interact on college campuses.

In 1990, American Council on Education (ACE) and the Carnegie Foundation collaborated to conduct a study on campus life. The special report entitled *Campus Life: In Search of Community* (1990) implored that every college campus needs strive for six qualities of community, namely, that college and university communities intentionally create community that "1. Is an educationally purposeful place where learning is the focus; 2. Is an open place that affirms civility and diversity is valued; 3. Is a just place that honors persons and aggressively pursues diversity; 4. Is a disciplined place where group obligations guide behavior; 5. Is a caring place where individuals are supported/services encouraged; and 6. Is [a] celebrative place where rituals embrace both traditions and change" (McDonald & Associates, 2002, p. xviii).

Fundamentally, these six practices of community are inspired by the legacy of Ernest Boyer and are ideals for *valuing difference* (McDonald & Associates, 2002). As Palmer (1998) says, knowing and learning are communal acts. Productive communities are ones that not only have different identity groups, ideologies, and opinions connected by a set of shared values but also they commune in ways that depend on the strengths of *difference* to maximize the betterment of individuals within and the community as a whole.

Making campus programs high-impact experiences for students involves teaching students the skills to enter into the social change process constructively. In this increasingly more diverse world, it is essential that college students strengthen their ability to engage with *difference* (Watt, 2011, 2015a, 2015b; Watt & Linley, 2013). Intentionally designing programs with an underlying structure that determines the values of inclusive communities as defined by Boyer (in *Campus Life: In Search of Community*, 1990) and Watt (2011, 2015a, 2015b; Watt & Linley, 2013) will support the skill development of students for working together productively across *difference*. In developing skills for engaging across *difference*, the characteristics associated with high-impact experiences provide a valuable set of guiding principles.

Overview of Traditional and Delineations of High-Impact Practices

Kuh, O'Donnell, and Reed (2013) describe high-impact practices as a set of educational programs and activities commonly characterized by the following:

- Educationally purposeful activities
- High degree of student-mentor interaction
- Substantive feedback to students on their learning and development
- Integrating, extending, or deepening knowledge beyond the setting in which students first encountered it
- Meaningful engagement with people who don't share the student's knowledge, background, or experiences

Using these practices increases the involvement and engagement of students with the campus and members of the college community (for example, student affairs professionals, other students, and faculty members). The authors note that this set of characteristics is not necessarily comprehensive and that a particular experience need not share all these characteristics to have high impact. The traditional high-impact practices vary in nature, scope, purpose, and contexts in which they are situated, but we have come to recognize them as similar in their contributions to enriching the undergraduate experience. It has been useful to give a name to this set of experiences and examine their effects across institutional settings, but for people designing educational programs, it is important to note that the label emphasizes what individual participants experience, and not campus environment in which they occur.

To illustrate how these characteristics shape particular practices on an individual level, consider the example of a practice commonly thought of as high impact: undergraduate research. A campus program that invites undergraduates to be a part of research projects might include student-mentor interactions signified by individualized guidance that undergraduates receive from faculty members and other research team members as they contribute to a research effort. The student might be asked to apply the knowledge gained from the research project to a real-world problem and present it at a conference or conduct a community service project informed by the findings. Substantive feedback woven throughout this experience is an indicator of a high-impact practice. In fact, without feedback, it may be difficult to justify this as a learning experience. High-impact practices require students extend their learning from an experience by making meaning of what they learned and requiring in a structured way that they apply it to other situations. This may be an effective high-impact practice that focuses on engaging and retaining students using individual attention. At the same time, by focusing on the individual-level impact of this experience, this type of practice ignores the larger campus climate as a potential protagonist.

Campus climate as a protagonist is not necessarily a new concept. Researchers have long suggested that the environment plays an essential role in students' growth and development (see Renn & Arnold, 2003). As the protagonist, campus climate takes the leading role and focus off the student. Delineating from the traditional high-impact practices, centering campus climate as the protagonist requires that institutions move toward intentionally designing programs to value *difference*, as Bowman (2010) highlights through the use of diversity experiences.

High-impact practices that specifically relate to diversity experiences include programs such as structured curricular and cocurricular experiences as well as informal interactive activities outside of the classroom (Bowman, 2010). Typically, these types of experiences include a focus on teaching about *difference* by helping students to gain knowledge, skills, and awareness (Pope, Reynolds, & Mueller, 2004). The tripartite framework highlights the importance of infusing into these experiences an awareness of a student's own assumptions, biases, and values, an understanding of the worldview of others as informed by various cultural groups, and attending to developing the skills for appropriate intervention strategies and techniques to bring about social change because of inequities in society. However, everyday opportunities need to be created through intentional programming that can support student's skill development to engage across *difference*. Service-learning, for example, has been suggested to positively benefit student learning through the diversity experiences and positive interactions with diverse peers within the programmatic facilitation of the high-impact practice (Kilgo, 2015). By creating opportunities for engagement in communities that are often outside of students' familiar experiences, service-learning provides one example of intentionally centering of the campus environment as protagonist. Research reveals many characteristics of traditional and delineated high-impact practices that can have positive developmental impact on college students. And yet, there are limitations to implementing these practices without tailoring them to specific campus environments. The next section summarizes the research on high-impact practices and the delineations specifically for engaging *difference*.

Research on High-Impact Practices for Engaging Difference

This section discusses the research related to the types of diversity experiences, such as multicultural courses, workshops, and general, informal exposure, to how *difference* contributes positively to cognitive and psychosocial development of college students. Using aspects of the traditional set of high-impact practices (for example, first-year seminars, learning communities, and so on) along with the delineations (for example, increases in structural diversity, diversity curricular and cocurricular initiatives, and so on) can potentially strengthen the skill set of college students to engage *difference* effectively if diversity is a central feature of intentional programmatic interventions in higher education. Yet, there are some cautions and limitations to broadly applying high-impact practices and important delineations to improve effectiveness of programming to engage *difference*.

Overall Outcomes of High-Impact Practices

The effects of these high-impact practices, specifically the programmatic ones, have been well documented. In particular, the following high-impact practices appear to positively influence cognitive development: collaborative experiences (Astin, 1993; Kilgo, Sheets, & Pascarella, 2015); undergraduate research (Bauer & Bennett, 2003; Kilgo, Sheets, & Pascarella, 2015); service-learning (Vogelgesang & Astin, 2000); and internships (Kilgo, Sheets, & Pascarella, 2015). Psychosocial growth and development is also influenced by high-impact practices. In particular, collaborative experiences (Kilgo, Sheets, & Pascarella, 2015); study abroad and diversity and global learning (Laird, Engberg, & Hurtado, 2005; Salisbury, An, & Pascarella, 2013); and service-learning (Astin & Sax, 1998; Engberg & Fox, 2011; Jones & Abes, 2004; Kilgo, 2015). Retention and persistence are also noted as being positively influenced by undergraduate research (Kilgo & Pascarella, 2016).

Kilgo, Sheets, and Pascarella (2015) explored high-impact practices as a collective set of practices, with their study looking at the net and unique effects of these high-impact practices on cognitive and psychosocial student learning outcomes. Their work used data from the NSSE and the Wabash National Study of Liberal Arts Education (WNS). They found that several of the high-impact practices led to cognitive learning and development as unique effects (high-impact practices entered into analytic models without controlling for the other high-impact practices), including participation in learning communities, active and collaborative learning activities and experiences, undergraduate research, internships, and capstone courses or culminating experiences (Kilgo, Sheets, & Pascarella, 2015). Their findings indicate that even more of AAC&U's ten high-impact practices led to growth in psychosocial and affective domains, including participation in learning communities, writing-intensive courses, active and collaborative learning experiences, undergraduate research, study abroad, service-learning, internships, and capstone courses or culminating experiences (Kilgo, Sheets, & Pascarella, 2015).

Delineations of High-Impact Practices for Engaging Difference

Diversity experiences are consistently associated with positive outcomes in college. The quality of interpersonal interaction and engagement with *difference* has a high impact on how students experience college. Bowman's (2010) research diverges slightly from the traditional literature on high-impact practices. In particular, Bowman's (2010) work focuses on the environment as an essential component and as the protagonist within the effectiveness of educational practices. His work has investigated the experiences students have with purposeful engagement with diversity. The caveat, however, of his research was the finding that sustained engagement was critical for positive benefits to students (Bowman, 2010). This finding and the rest of Bowman's (2010) work go beyond the traditional high-impact practices literature in which a checklist of experiences is posited as the only necessary component.

The environment acts as a protagonist. Therefore, engaging with differences needs to not only be facilitated in ways that are intentional but also sustained over time. This has implications for practice and the current limitations associated with high-impact practices. Many of these practices are one-time experiences (Kuh, 2008), which is in contrast to the environment that Bowman (2010) suggested as essential for student learning.

Cautions and Limitations of High-Impact Practices

The literature on high-impact practices is limited mainly to studies examining these educational practices monolithically (that is, not examining high-impact practices as a unit but instead focusing on one specific educational practice), based on a single institution, or with limiting research and survey design. Much of the practical facilitation and empirical evidence examines students' participation in these high-impact practices in a dichotomous way comparing participation to nonparticipation using a checklist reporting format. This disproportionate amount of research on the effectiveness of the practices is limiting. This research, although beneficial, does not reach the level of impetus that these practices have on college campuses. Essentially, in some ways, these practices are touted as "high impact" anecdotally and used quite liberally. And yet, the complexities of the application of these practices are important when designing programs to strengthen the skills of students for engaging difference.

The studies mentioned in the previous section constitute the majority of empirical explorations examining the set of high-impact practices that AAC&U put forth as a collective set of educational practices for student success. The evidence suggests that these types of practices contribute to student success within college and university settings for the individual and most likely for those with dominant identities (for example, cis-male, cis-female, white, heterosexual). Emerging research suggests that the effect from participation in high-impact practices varies by student subpopulations (Brownell & Swaner, 2010; Kilgo, Sheets, & Pascarella, 2014; Kuh, 2008; Parker, Kilgo, Sheets, & Pascarella, 2016). Further, marginalized students do not consistently participate in high-impact practices (Brownell & Swaner, 2010; Kilgo, Sheets, & Pascarella, 2015). This disparity in participation rates by identity makes it difficult to determine the effectiveness for marginalized subpopulations.

These marginalized identity groups include racial and ethnic minorities; students from low-socioeconomic status backgrounds; first-generation college students; women; transgender and gender-nonconforming students; lesbian, gay, bisexual, and queer-identified students; and students with poor precollege academic preparation.

Further, campus environment and climate is a factor in student engagement and involvement. A few recent studies have suggested that, for high-impact practices in particular, a negative or hostile climate can lead to decreased benefits and lessened participation, oftentimes by students who could benefit the most from these educationally enriching practices (Brownell & Swaner,

2010; Kilgo, Sheets, & Pascarella, 2014; Kuh, 2008; Parker, Kilgo, Sheets, & Pascarella, 2016). One study suggested that students of color and female-identified students had decreased gains in cognitive and affective learning outcomes compared to their white and male-identified peers (Kilgo, Sheets, & Pascarella, 2014). The negative impact increased for high-impact practices, which are classroom-based, such as first-year seminars, writing-intensive courses, and capstone courses, suggesting a possible hostile classroom climate for these students. Further, students' perceptions of social acceptance for sexual and gender identity as well as their level of outness on campus (and subsequently their level of comfort being out on campus) appear to lead to lessened likelihood of participation in several high-impact practices (Kilgo, Sheets, & Pascarella, 2015).

Given that we exist in a society where dictated dominance and marginalization by social identities is perpetuated, these programs are likely facilitated in ways that preserve privilege and further decentralize oppressed groups. Although it helps empirically to see the effects of participation, these findings do not ascertain the quality of facilitation and implementation. These high-impact practices are most effective when tailored to meet the needs of students within the context of the particular campus environment. High-impact practices are a quick way for practitioners to facilitate these practices on a large scale, but practitioners must take care to identify the specific components and characteristics within these high-impact practices, which might be mediating the effects of these ten educational practices on student learning and development. This missing piece is essential for practitioners to consider as they continue to examine and implement these high-impact practices. The participation of any educational practice without thoughtful and intentional facilitation can not only deter student growth and development but also can lead to harmful or negative effects. It is important to attend to not only infusing various types of high-impact practices into programming on campus but also to be intentional about how the programs are implemented and facilitated. This next section illuminates guideposts for using high-impact practices in strengthening student's skills for engaging *difference*.

Guideposts for Programmatic Interventions for Engaging Difference

The Ernest L. Boyer Commission (1995) concluded that a key element of learning and becoming a good citizen is expanding the skills of college students to engage effectively with difference. Higher education institutions maintain systems of oppression perpetuated by the larger society whereby "diversity exclusion is the act of centralizing dominant culture value, which dehumanizes, downplays, and shifts to the margins individuals and groups with noncentralized worldviews" (Watt, 2015a, p. 14). Changing macro-level environmental aspects of engaging *difference* include increasing the number of required diversity courses, improving efforts to diversify the student body, and fostering opportunities for diversity workshop experiences (Bowman, 2010), simultaneously addressing the micro-level aspects of engaging difference, which are the interpersonal commitments that shape how campus community members relate to one another. The macro-level environmental aspects shaped by organizational structures and leadership paired with the micro-level skills of interpersonal interaction combined can create the ideal conditions to support student's development of cultural competency skills and the perspectives needed to be a good citizen in an increasingly diverse society.

Campus programming that aims to shift the dynamic whereby otherness is explored on an interpersonal level that examines the self in relation to the other invites deeper exploration and skill development for engaging *difference.* In other words, rather than solely focusing on what a majority student can learn from a minority student, Watt (2015a, 2015b) suggests that all individuals explore more in depth the question of "who am I?" in relation to this *difference.* For example, a white, heterosexual, cisgender-male student and a multiracial, lesbian, cisgender-woman can each personally situate the differences between them on individual and societal structural levels. Each can explore how these social and political identities play out in their lives, gaining a deeper understanding by examining the full context and what factors influence their reactions to these differences. Together these two individuals can deconstruct the campus environment's practices of exclusion. Through various authentic dialogues they might explore the ways in which gender, race, and sexual orientation shape the way they interact with each other, with others, and how it influences what they value. This dialogue between two individuals that focuses on deconstructing assumptions concerning these social constructs within the environment is a step toward reconstructing the environment for inclusion. This shifts away from interrogating the other with the goal of acceptance toward monitoring personal reactions to the *difference* and developing the skills to engage respectfully with a person who is different from oneself. At the same time, research has shown that the presence of difference (that is, gender, sexual orientation, race, and so on) improves the effect of the programmatic intervention (Milem, Chang, & antonio, 2005). Therefore, it is important that higher education institutions intentionally create opportunities for interaction with differing experiences, ideologies, and identities by diversifying the student body as well as through programmatic interventions.

High-impact practices that focus on "doing" prioritize outcomes, such as bringing in a speaker or going to service-learning programs. These types of programming interventions can overlook the ways students are "being" in relationship with each other (Watt, 2015b). Increasing the effectiveness of these high-impact practices happens when program designers pay attention to the ways students are being in relationships. The micro-level skill involved in the intentional facilitation of high-impact practices is essential to the effectiveness of programs in higher education and student affairs. Faculty members, higher education administrators, and student affairs practitioners can nurture being skills to support students getting the most out of their experiences. The authentic, action-oriented framing for environmental shifts (AAFES) method provides some guideposts that practitioners can use as they aim to create the environmental conditions that support the development of the skills needed for being amid controversies (Watt, 2015b). The AAFES method process qualities include the following attributes:

- Being authentic by prioritizing self-exploration rather than solely analyzing the other
- Being action-oriented by engaging a thoughtful balance between dialogue and action
- Reframing campus environments by embracing the realities of social oppression and creating spaces for inclusion and not just for surviving dehumanization

The AAFES method describes the skills and ways of being for students and faculty and staff members to use as they interact on micro-levels when exploring *difference*. Improving the environment by attending to the process and skills of being can help to make programming high impact.

Making Programmatic Interventions High Impact for Engaging Difference

For student affairs professionals designing programs to facilitate student learning and development related to embracing *difference*, focusing on characteristics of high-impact practices offers good news and challenges. The good news is that high-impact learning need not be limited to academic settings. At first glance, it might appear that widely recognized high-impact practices are limited to credit-bearing academic experiences. However, it is clear that the defining characteristics of these high-impact practices can be found in academic and student affairs programming. The challenge, however, is that genuinely high-impact experiences can be costly. They require significant investments of time, people, and resources to intentionally design, carry out, and monitor their effects so that we can make the learning apparent to participants and facilitators of the experience. There are no shortcuts to high impact, though the path is clear: it includes educationally purposeful activities, mentoring, feedback, integration or application of learning, and meaningful engagement with *difference*.

The implication of these observations for developing skills for engaging with difference is that program designers need to focus on *how* to engage students in this type of learning and development. It is understandable that program designers need to put considerable effort into determining what students need to learn, but we also need to be educationally purposeful in choosing options (presentations, discussion, guided reflection, hands-on activities, and so on) that are most likely to foster the kinds of learning we hope to facilitate. Taking from the research on high-impact practices, Project DEEP, and the theoretical framing of Watt's AAFES skills for being, this final section of the chapter offers examples of ways to incorporate these types of characteristics into programs designed to develop skills for engaging with *difference*. Using student-mentor relationships as an example, following are some practical considerations for making practices high impact.

Student participants in mentoring programs have reported changes in their sense of belonging on campus similar to those observed by students in other traditionally defined high-impact practices (for example, Gose, 2014). Mentors provide support, challenge, and the wisdom of their own experience through their relationships with students. If mentors are prepared for the role of coming alongside students as they engage with difference, then this sustained interaction with an experienced mentor would be a critically important opportunity for raising the impact of this experience by addressing Watt's (2015b) question, "Does your initiative encourage awareness of one's own racial identity?"

For example, when campuses face the immediacy of highly publicized racial incidents, many react to these events primarily as a crisis to manage, especially when shocking and horrific actions happen such as a murder motivated by racial hatred. Watt (2015b) suggests that in addition, college campuses simultaneously work toward supporting the racial identity development of students by recognizing the centrality of race in society, examining racial inequity as a systemic and societal problem rather than as an individual experience, and by shaping programming that teaches students how to engage across racial difference. To make these educationally purposeful programs and activities high impact, we also consider not only what we want students to learn but also how that type of learning occurs. Mentors can identify what students who are part of a mentoring program might need to see, discuss, reflect on, and experience to guide them into learning these foundational understandings of race.

Student-mentor relationships are also opportunities for providing substantive feedback to students to support their learning and development, another central feature of high-impact practices. Intentional opportunities for feedback in which participants record and reflect on their experiences engaging with *difference*, share them with a mentor, and receive feedback on their learning—will provide much higher impact learning than the experiences alone. Perhaps more important, this level of intentional feedback and assessment suggests that mentors take this goal seriously and realize student learning in this area will not come without effort and practice. Students need feedback so that they can critically reflect on the skills they are developing, pay attention to the effects of their own actions, and realize that they might not get everything right the first time. Indeed, if they don't create opportunities for feedback, mentors may inadvertently suggest to students that they learned all they need to know simply through their own observations. Considering the complexity of learning to engage meaningfully with *difference*, it is important that students learn to value, seek out, and grow through reflection and feedback from trusted mentors.

Feedback also plays a role in how students engage with the community. Through this intensive feedback process, students can explore cognitively and emotionally complex outcomes, such as distinguishing between brave and safe space or learning from the inevitable missteps and offenses across racial lines

(Watt, 2015b). Engaging with difference in these ways is challenging to learn and easy to get wrong. Without feedback from trusted mentors, novice learners may have little basis for examining their own progress or recognizing needs for deeper learning.

Creating opportunities for meaningful interaction across difference can help students to integrate, extend, or deepen knowledge about self and the other. In this case, a mentoring program can be designed to create intentional opportunities that will develop learners' capacity to take their learning farther, because that is itself a capacity that has to be developed. Watt (2015a, 2015b) poses the need to engage participants in dialogue that invites sharing about upbringing and messages learned about race and to prepare participants with the skills to wrestle with the meaning of race as lifelong learners. However, if we do not intentionally create structures to scaffold these broader levels of engagement, we have little reason to believe students will spontaneously apply their learning to their own experiences over time.

Creating opportunities for explorations of race and other social constructs that recognize personal positionality and nurture collective empathy and that allows space for the complexities and ambiguities of social identity to be included in the dialogue (Watt, 2015a, 2015b). However, it is essential to develop programs in ways that demonstrate engaging difference is not just a matter of learning about people but also about engaging with people in significant ways and learning through the discomforts and inevitable missteps that often accompany this kind of learning and development. In some ways these high-impact characteristics encompass all others, because it is difficult to imagine participants learning at this level without well-chosen educational activities, significant mentoring, meaningful feedback, and meaningful structured opportunities to extend their learning across contexts.

Our goal in these examples is to demonstrate that it is not the label that makes initiatives high impact but the extent to which they are educationally purposeful, provide high student-mentor interaction and substantive feedback, extend and deepen knowledge, and provide meaningful engagement with (not just about) difference. These characteristics can define a much wider array of learning and development opportunities than those traditionally defined as high impact.

Conclusion

This chapter focused on the various programmatic efforts that strengthen student's skills to engage *difference* with fidelity. It incorporates Ernest Boyer's seminal ideas on an open and celebrative inclusive community and builds on Boyer's foundation to describe ways to make programmatic interventions high impact by identifying process qualities for engaging *difference* within structured programs. In conclusion, this chapter raises critical questions that will help faculty and staff members, administrators, and student affairs professionals design effective programs for engaging *difference*.

Discussion Questions

This section provides reflective questions for practitioners to consider when incorporating ways to engage difference into programmatic interventions on college campuses. These guiding questions suggest designing interventions for high impact by reflecting on structural, facilitation, and interpersonal skill development aspects for engaging *difference.*

1. How does your campus engage with diversity as an opportunity for high-impact learning and student development rather than solely as compliance with regulations or management of crises?
   a. Who is participating? Who is recruited? How are obstacles to participation identified and addressed (costs, accessibility, location of facilities, inclusiveness of staff members, and so on)?
   b. Who are your partners and allies?
2. How will you facilitate your high-impact programmatic intervention?
   a. Are you creating educational experiences that deliberately incorporate the characteristics that make an intervention high impact?
   b. How are you personally reflecting on your own privilege as you facilitate these practices as tools to engage difference on campus?
3. How are you attending to the campus community members' ways of "being" together within controversy?
   a. Does your programmatic intervention intentionally prepare participants to work together through challenge and discomfort?
   b. How does your programmatic intervention teach individuals to consider their positionality within the context of a larger inequitable society?

References

Astin, A. W. (1993). *What matters in college? Four critical years revisited.* San Francisco: Jossey-Bass.

Astin, A. W., & Sax, L. J. (1998). How undergraduates are affected by service participation. *Journal of College Student Development, 39*(3), 251–263.

Bauer, K. W., & Bennett, J. S. (2003). Alumni perceptions used to assess undergraduate research experience. *Journal of Higher Education, 72*(2), 210–230.

Bowman, N. A. (2010). College diversity experiences and cognitive development: A meta-analysis. *Review of Educational Research, 80*(1), 4–33.

Bowman, N. A. (2011). Promoting participation in a diverse democracy: A meta-analysis of college diversity experiences and civic engagement. *Review of Educational Research, 81*(1), 29–68.

Bowman, N. A. (2012). Promoting sustained engagement with diversity: The reciprocal relationships between informal and formal college diversity experiences. *Review of Higher Education, 36*(1), 1–24.

Brownell, J. E., & Swaner, L. E. (2010). *Five high-impact practices: Research on learning outcomes, completion and quality.* Washington, DC: Association of American Colleges and Universities.

Carnegie Foundation for the Advancement of Teaching. (1990). *Campus life: In search of community* Princeton, NJ: Princeton University Press.

Engberg, M. E., & Fox, K. (2011). Exploring the relationship between undergraduate service-learning experiences and global perspective-taking. *Journal of Student Affairs Research and Practice, 48*(1), 85–105.

The Ernest L. Boyer Commission. (1995). *Reinventing undergraduate education: A blueprint for American's research universities.* Amherst: University of Massachusetts. (Originally written by Ernest L. Boyer)

Gose, B. (2014, Nov. 9). On U.S. campuses, networking and nurturing to retain black men. *New York Times.* Retrieved from http://www.nytimes.com/2014/11/10/education/on-us-campuses-networking-and-nurturing-to-retain-black-men.html?_r=0

Gurin, P., Dey, E. L., Hurtado, S., & Gurin, G. (2002). Diversity and higher education: Theory and impact on educational outcomes. *Harvard Educational Review, 72*(3), 330–366.

Hardiman, R., Jackson, B., & Griffin, P. (2007). Conceptual foundations for social justice courses. In M. Adams, L. A. Bell, & P. Griffin (Eds.), *Teaching for diversity and social justice* (2nd ed., pp. 35–66). New York: Routledge.

Hurtado, S., Milem, J. F., Clayton-Pedersen, A. R., & Allen, W. R. (1999). Enhancing diverse learning environments: Improving the climate for racial/ethnic diversity in higher education. *ASHE-ERIC Higher Education Report, 26*(8). Washington, DC: George Washington University.

Jones, S. R., & Abes, E. S. (2004). Enduring influences of service-learning on college students' identity development. *Journal of College Student Development, 45*(2), 149–166.

Kilgo, C. A. (2015). The estimated effects of service learning on students' intercultural effectiveness. *Journal of College Student Development, 56*(8), 852–856.

Kilgo, C. A., & Pascarella, E. T. (2016). Does independent research with a faculty member enhance four-year graduation and graduate/professional degree plans? Convergent results with different analytical methods. *Higher Education, 69,* 509–525.

Kilgo, C. A., Sheets, J.K.E., & Pascarella, E. T. (2014, April 6). *Do high-impact practices actually have high impact on learning for all students?* Paper presented at the 2014 Annual Meeting of the American Educational Research Association, Philadelphia, PA.

Kilgo, C. A., Sheets, J.K.E., & Pascarella, E. T. (2015). The link between high-impact practices and student learning: Some longitudinal evidence. *Higher Education, 69*(4), 509–525.

Kuh, G. D. (2008). *High-impact educational practices: What they are, who has access to them, and why they matter.* Washington, DC: Association of American Colleges and Universities.

Kuh, G. D., O'Donnell, K., & Reed, S. (2013). *Ensuring quality & taking high-impact practices to scale. LEAP.* Washington, DC: AAC&U. Retrieved from www.aacu.org/leap

Laird, T.F.N., Engberg, M. E., & Hurtado, S. (2005). Modeling accentuation effects: Enrolling in a diversity course and the importance of social action engagement. *Journal of Higher Education, 76*(4), 448–476.

McDonald, W. M., & Associates. (2002). Creating campus community: In search of Ernest Boyer's legacy. San Francisco: Jossey Bass.

Milem, J. F., Chang, M. J., & antonio, a. l. (2005). *Making diversity work on campus: A research-based perspective.* Washington, DC: Association of American Colleges and Universities.

Palmer, P. J. (1998). *The courage to teach.* San Francisco: Jossey-Bass.

Parker, E. T., Kilgo, C. A., Sheets, J. K. E., & Pascarella, E. T. (2016). The differential effects of internship participation on end-of-fourth-year GPA by demographic and institutional characteristics. *Journal of College Student Development, 57*(1), 104–109.

Pharr, S. (1997). *Homophobia: A weapon of sexism.* Berkeley, CA: Chardon Press.

Pope, R. L., Reynolds, A. L., & Mueller, J. (2004). *Multicultural competence in student affairs.* San Francisco: Jossey Bass.

Renn, K. A., & Arnold, K. D. (2003). Reconceptualizing research on college student peer culture. *Journal of Higher Education, 74*(3), 261–291.

Salisbury, M. H., An, B. P., & Pascarella, E. T. (2013). The effect of study abroad on intercultural competence among undergraduate college students. *Journal of Student Affairs Research and Practice, 50*(1), 1–20.

Saunders, S. A., & Cooper, D. L. (2001). Programmatic interventions: Translating theory to practice. In R. B. Winston, D. G. Creamer, & T.K.K. Miller (Eds.), *The student affairs administrator, educator, leader, and manager* (pp. 309–340). New York: Brunner-Routledge.

Vogelgesang, L. J., & Astin, A. W. (2000). Comparing the effects of community service and service-learning. *Michigan Journal of Community Service Learning, 7*(1), 25–34.

Watt, S. K. (2011). Moving beyond the talk: From difficult dialogues to action. In J. Arminio, V. Torres, & R. Pope (Eds.), *Why aren't we there yet: Taking personal responsibility for creating an inclusive campus* (pp. 131–144). Sterling, VA: Stylus.

Watt, S. K. (2015a). Designing and implementing multicultural initiatives: Guiding principles. In S. K.Watt (Ed.), *Designing transformative multicultural initiatives: Theoretical foundations, practical applications and facilitator considerations.* Sterling, VA: Stylus.

Watt, S. K. (2015b). Situating race in college students' search for purpose and meaning: Who am I? *Journal of College and Character, 16*(3), 135–142. doi:10.1080/219458 7X.2015.1057158

Watt, S. K., & Linley, J. L. (Eds.). (2013). *Creating successful multicultural initiatives in higher education and student affairs* (New Directions for Student Services, no. 114, pp. 5–15). San Francisco: Jossey-Bass.

CHAPTER 31

APPLYING THEORIES AND RESEARCH TO PRACTICE

Florence A. Hamrick and Jillian Kinzie

Taylor Smith is a new residence coordinator at Midwest State University (MSU) and oversees Stevens, Harrison, and Robertson buildings. Each is a five-story, coeducational (suite-by-suite) residence hall. Because the MSU director of residence life continues to be consumed with extensive and long-overdue residence hall renovations and construction of new campus housing, the director specifically hired Taylor because of Taylor's experience and expertise with educational programming and student learning in residence halls.

At the director's request, Taylor has begun to work with MSU professors Chris Richards (computer engineering) and Pat Thomas (environmental engineering). For six years, Chris and Pat have collaborated to support a residential learning community in Stevens Hall called CME-LC ("Smelk") for MSU students interested in studying computer, mechanical, or environmental engineering. (The participating mechanical engineering faculty counterpart just retired from MSU, and other faculty members have shown little interest or willingness to be involved.) CME-LC occupies the top three floors of Stevens Hall. Incoming MSU students request to live in CME-LC when they submit housing deposits, and first-year students comprise about 60 percent of CME-LC's membership. Upper-class students make up the remaining 40 percent, and they must be selected in a lottery to remain in CME-LC after the first year.

Both professors acknowledge that CME-LC students, as a group, are much less diverse than students enrolled in either the introductory engineering course or the first-semester math courses required of engineering majors, courses in which enrollments usually have 30 percent or so African American and Latino/a students and about 40 percent women. The group of CME-LC students most resembles enrollments in advanced engineering and math courses—about 85 percent white men.

Two principal goals of CME-LC, according to Chris and Pat, are to increase the numbers of students of color and women who enter and are retained in MSU's engineering degree programs. However, CME-LC student demographics have not changed appreciably over its six years of existence. Shortly before CME-LC started, Stevens underwent extensive renovations, and the director of residence life assured the faculty members that most incoming first-year students would prefer to live in the upgraded residence halls. Engineering classroom and lab buildings surround Stevens on three sides, which Chris and Pat regard as an undeniable attraction for new engineering students.

Taylor has collected focus group data from some current and former CME-LC students. At the next meeting with Chris and Pat, Taylor has offered to present some empirical and theoretical insights to identify ways that CME-LC can more effectively achieve its goals.

Applying theory to practice, applying research to practice, and using practice to advance theory and research are long-standing expectations of and challenges for student affairs professionals (see, for example Evans, Forney, Guido, Patton, & Renn, 2009; Patton & Harper, 2009). Most descriptors of "professional" and "professional practice" feature words such as *knowledge, skills,* and *expertise* to distinguish professionals from amateurs or tinkerers. Student affairs professionals draw on the knowledge and skills gained from their own individual experiences, and this store of resources provides useful reference points for them. Studying formal theories and empirical research is also necessary for effective practice. Through systematic study, professionals understand—among other things—that the sum of their own individual experiences, preferences, and characteristics does not equip them well to help all students thrive. This chapter provides an overview of applying theory and research to practice and presents potential missteps and cautions. We will also return periodically to Taylor's upcoming presentation for illustrations and examples.

Strengths and Limitations of Formal Theory

The chapters in part 3 of this book provide overviews of theories and models central to student affairs practice. Space limitations permit us to provide only a few examples here, and in this section we focus principally on students' cognitive and psychosocial development and environments to enhance students' development. Acknowledging strengths and shortcomings of formal theories is critical to effective application of theory to practice. Formal theories tend to be grounded in analysis and interpretation of empirical data and are tools to provide insights into students' experiences and growth. However, students' experiences and the meanings they make from their experiences are complex and complicated; constructing a formal theory that purports to encompass *all* students' "realities" would be an endless and likely futile undertaking that would ultimately not lend itself to improving professional practice.

To set reasonable parameters for formal theories, Weick (1979) identified *simplicity, accuracy,* and *generalizability* as criteria for judging the quality and worth of theories. He also explained how a single, useful theory may meet one or two of these criteria but never all three. For example, a hypothetical theory that met all three of Weick's criteria *might* be perceived as accurate because of its detail, complexity, and breadth, yet generalizations from such an unwieldy theory would be impossible for the same reasons. And such a theory would be neither simple nor straightforward. Largely because they are social constructions, theories are neither "true" nor "indisputable" but instead subject to challenge and revision. Theorists may subsequently revise and augment (in essence, reconstruct) a formal theory. As only one example, in collaboration with Abes, Jones and McEwen (2007) published a reconceptualization of Jones and McEwen's (2000) model of multiple identities to incorporate attention to meaning making and input filtering. Individually and collectively, theories are partial and incomplete, which makes them—perhaps paradoxically—quite useful resources for professional practice. As examples, new social and cultural identity theories centered on or involving groups of students' college experiences appear regularly in student affairs literature, and the framework of critical race theory is used for theory construction, critique, and redevelopment.

Finally, theories do not provide molds into which students are to be pressed or categories into which students ought to be sorted or labeled. Although the existence of and reliance on a sound theoretical and empirical knowledge base has long been acknowledged as minimal criteria for a profession (for example, Bloland, Stamatakos, & Rogers, 1994; Stamatakos, 1981a, 1981b), *how* the theories and knowledge are used and applied by members of that profession is a vital consideration. Without appropriate cautions, what might seem to be "using" theories can too easily devolve into stereotyping. Such "applications" of theory can contribute to reducing students into "single stories" (Ngozi Adichie, 2009) composed of one or two diagnoses or hunches about theoretical stage, level, or type rather than respecting students as complex, whole human beings. The knowledge of students offered by formal theories must be tempered by comprehension of students as complex, multifaceted individuals who traverse and negotiate multiple environments and cultures— many of which students affairs professionals may never be aware. Accordingly, "applying theory to practice" means that student affairs professionals learn and incorporate theoretical knowledge *into their professional practice* as they work with and on behalf of students. Applying theory *to students* by sorting individuals into particular "stages" or "vectors" can result, even inadvertently, in failures to know and respect students as unique individuals who continually experience, reflect, grow, and understand themselves and their worlds.

Proceeding from this caution, learning and applying theories also entail similar, continual self-exploration and ongoing reflection by practitioners who seek to use theories effectively. These reflective dispositions and acts represent an orientation to "professionalizing" one's practice as a necessary, ongoing process (Young, 1988) rather than regarding "professional" as a role to occupy through achievements such as earning a master's degree.

Theory-to-Practice Models

A broad range of theory-to-practice models supplies professionals with useful frameworks to systematically consider and determine relevant factors, potential action plans, and appropriate implementation strategies. We limit our discussion here to two long-standing models that are frequently used by student affairs professionals: practice to theory to practice, or PTP (Knefelkamp, Golec, & Wells, 1985), and the "cube" (Morrill, Oetting, & Hurst, 1974).

The eleven-step PTP model outlines a relatively linear yet flexible pathway that incorporates design, implementation, and evaluation steps. This model emphasizes the mutual benefits of theory to ground practice and for practice to inform theory development or critique. For many, the PTP steps may be reminiscent of models that, with the incorporation of the "closing the loop" step, convey the ideally cyclical, ongoing nature of assessment and evaluation as part of professional practice. PTP's eleven steps are as follows:

1. Identify concerns that need to be addressed.
2. Determine desired goals and outcomes.
3. Investigate theories that may be helpful in understanding the issue and achieving the desired goals.
4. Analyze relevant student characteristics from the perspective of the theories identified.
5. Analyze characteristics of the environment associated with the issue from the perspective of identified theories.
6. Identify potential sources of challenge and support, taking into account both student and environmental characteristics, and recognizing factors that produce a balance.
7. Reexamine goals and outcomes in light of the theoretical analysis.
8. Design the intervention using methods that will encourage achievement of goals.
9. Implement the intervention.
10. Evaluate the outcomes of the intervention.
11. Redesign the intervention if necessary. (cited in Woodley, 2013, p. 16)

The *cube* is a three-dimensional portrayal for identifying and implementing appropriate, purposeful delivery strategies (Morrill, Oetting, & Hurst, 1974). Although theories per se are not part of this model, the cube assists practitioners with aligning the intended *purpose* (remediation, prevention, or development); *target audience* (individual, primary group, associational group, or institution or community); and *method* for implementation (direct service, consultation and training, or media). Evans (1987) subsequently adapted and illustrated the cube's utility in framing theoretically grounded developmental interventions, specifically moral development, with particular attention to environmental factors and influences.

Applying theory to practice is a dynamic, tailored, if not individualized, process. It does not entail professionals functioning simply as conduits of formal theory or "automated teller machines" to dispense received theoretical knowledge, nor does it mean that professionals rely completely on their own experiences and assumptions regarding students—their "gut" instincts or reactions. Accordingly, theorists and researchers often define, acknowledge, or account for the mediating role(s) of professionals' own informal theory(ies) in theory-to-practice applications. Recent articles have sought to define more specifically what informal theory is and whether individuals' informal theories are sufficiently malleable or evolve with the acquisition of knowledge of formal theories and the accumulation of professional experiences (Evans & Guido, 2012; Love, 2012). Because of the importance of informal theories and their personalized nature, individuals can benefit from ongoing opportunities to surface, test, and revise evolving assumptions and understandings about students. Reflection, role-plays, and supported experimentation are indispensable to effectively applying theory to professional practice. Let's return to Taylor, who is examining focus group data for potential insights and strategies to enhance the CME-LC experience for students. Taylor knows that these data constitute limited, partial information from and about the focus group participants yet also realizes that valuable insights can be gained.

Taylor is reviewing these transcript excerpts in particular:

Jeffrey (first-year MSU and CME-LC student, eighteen years old, Caucasian, in-state resident): "I'm basically in CME-LC because my mother signed me up. My parents want me to major in engineering."

Rosa (second-year MSU student, biology major, spent first year in CME-LC, twenty years old, Latina, in-state resident): "I liked the classes last year, but almost no one in CME-LC could seem to believe that I liked engineering and was good at it. Students in my same engineering class hardly ever spoke to me in the hallways or lounge. Halfway through last year, I found out that they had been holding study group sessions all fall semester and hadn't let me know."

Rich (third-year MSU student, computer engineering major, spent first year in CME-LC, twenty-three years old, African American, out-of-state resident): "I hadn't realized last fall how important it would be for me to be around people who looked like me. CME-LC was fine, but I felt more at home at the African American Center, and then with my fraternity brothers. I'd like to be part of CME-LC now and help mentor the new students, but I can't because I moved out after my first year and once you leave the program, you can't rejoin."

Suzanne (MSU senior, business major, twenty-two years old, Caucasian, in-state student): "I only stayed in CME-LC for one year. Not many women were part of the learning community, and I spent most of my time with friends on the other two floors of Stevens. Otherwise, it was 'all engineering, all the time' with the engineering buildings and labs right next door. When I told friends I was in CME-LC, they would say, 'SMELK?! Eww!' and hold their noses and laugh."

Edward (second-year MSU student, living in CME-LC, nineteen years old, Caucasian, out-of-state): "Last year I saw on the housing website that upper-class CME-LC students tutored and peer-mentored first-year students, but that didn't last long. Two or three weeks after classes started, they disappeared into the labs and we were on our own. At the time, that was frustrating, but I'm really glad that I'll stay in CME-LC. The new first-years can figure things out for themselves, and I can get my work done."

Saying, "It's going to be a long night," Taylor stands up to take a break.

Although the ultimate large-scale intervention will focus on CME-LC redesign, Taylor began to think about the meeting with Pat and Chris as a sort of "intervention" that could be approached strategically. Referring to the cube, Taylor identified the meeting as one with a principally developmental purpose—that of improving CME-LC. Taylor determined the targeted audience to be the primary group of CME-LC faculty coordinators and the principal implementation method to be the consultation and information sharing that Taylor's been asked to provide. Indeed, Taylor had heard most of the perspectives voiced by focus group students during prior experiences in residence life at two campuses. Taylor earned a BA in communications and enjoyed collaborating on programming with two engineering students who were fellow RAs. Taylor was determined to keep in mind that two RAs majoring in engineering on another campus gives very limited insight into MSU undergraduate engineering students—and particularly engineering students of color and women.

Using Research and Evidence to Guide Practice

A wide range of higher education scholarship can productively inform student affairs practice. As the previous section on theory to practice introduced, research has produced a variety of useful theories, including psychosocial and identity development, cognitive development, and environmental theories, essential for practitioner success. Theories can help explain how students define themselves and their relations to others and guide practitioners to deeper levels of understanding about students and the undergraduate experience.

Although there is plenty to celebrate about the utility of a well-researched theory, over the last several decades the field of student affairs has increased its reliance on a wider range of evidence, mainly in the form of *assessment*, and occasionally *evaluation* studies and *evidence-based practice*, to guide student affairs practice. In this section we briefly distinguish these terms, clarify their value to practice, and provide some approaches and examples to illustrate their application.

Assessment, most commonly defined as systematic efforts to "gather, analyze, and interpret evidence that documents institution, division, or program effectiveness" (Schuh, Upcraft, & Associates, 2001, p. 21), with some scholars adding an emphasis on the use of this information to improve (Banta & Palomba, 2015), has evolved almost to the point of being institutionalized in student affairs practice. Assessment is undertaken to respond to specific questions of accountability and quality and to provide information to guide practice, planning, and decision making. Typically, assessment has as its focus particular implications for the institution or program.

Evaluation work is generally considered distinct from, but linked to, assessment (Upcraft & Schuh, 1996). Similar to assessment, evaluation gauges effectiveness but places greater emphasis on the use of information to improve or change and has more to do with rendering judgment. For example, assessment results could be positive, revealing that a program is achieving desired outcomes, yet from a cost-evaluation perspective, the program may be deemed not worth the expense. Evaluation studies are also more typically designed as summative efforts to gauge the overall value of a project or program and to ultimately continue, curtail, or enhance a program or activity.

Taylor's thoughts shift to questions about the availability of information on the effectiveness of the learning community and the extent to which the renovated facility supports the learning community's goals for students. "We have some student data from focus groups, but we should take a step back and also examine CME-LC, its environment, and programs. If upper-class students are advisors and mentors, how have they been trained and monitored? How beneficial have first-year students found that advice and mentoring? How do students use their common spaces? Was increased use of these spaces a goal of the renovation? Had it worked? Is CME-LC really worth the effort? How is that decided? And who decides?"

Another way evidence is being incorporated in student affairs is through the notion of evidence-based practice. This approach, first established in health care to make decisions about patient care by integrating the best available evidence with practitioner expertise and patient characteristics, is a formal way of describing the practice of drawing from accumulated research on a topic and using the findings to inform practice (Sackett, Straus, Richardson, Rosenberg, & Haynes, 2000). For example, evaluations of the effectiveness of various approaches to delivering developmental education and tutoring could help inform modifications to services; or findings about "best practices" in, for instance, new student orientation, may guide the design and implementation of orientation components.

A standard definition of evidence-based practice is the accumulation of practice-relevant research findings and empirical documentation of "what works" in a field that informs practice. The idea is that practice should be grounded in prior empirical findings that demonstrate that certain actions performed with a particular type of student, or student groups, or to achieve a particular outcome, such as student persistence or belongingness, are likely to produce predictable, beneficial, and effective results. For example, evidence on the features and practices that work to support residential learning communities drawn from practical information compiled by organizations including the Association of College and University Housing Officers–International (ACUHO-I) and studies including the National Study of Living-Learning Programs (NSLLP), are resources for practitioners interested in applying evidence-based practice. Organizational, staffing, and programming decisions in CME-LC may or may not be supported by findings from the NSLLP or the promising practice reports produced by national organizations that support engineering programs such as the National Science Foundation (NSF) or the National Academies of Science (NAS). A necessary, but not sufficient, condition for evidence-based practice is that practitioners appreciate the key role that empirical findings play in guiding the selection and application of practice interventions and the importance of remaining current with an ever-growing scholarship.

A Wider Framework for Application: College Impact and I-E-O

To fully appreciate the application of research and other forms of evidence in student affairs, it is helpful to understand two families of theories that frame the work: college impact theories and Astin's I-E-O model (1991). These broad frameworks have proved to be influential in guiding the application of theory, research, and assessment and for considering evidence-based practice by providing a common set of terms and reference points. Because they are so commonly referenced as frameworks in the field, professionals are well served to become familiar with their essential elements.

The family of theories informing the application of research and theory to practice and assessment fall under the broad category of *college-impact models*. College-impact models are distinct in their emphasis on interactions between students and institution environments and their focus on the range of sources of student change, including institutional characteristics, programs and services, and students' experiences and interactions with faculty members and peers, which affect student outcomes. In contrast to developmental theories that draw heavily on psychology and are more often focused on the individual, college-impact models incorporate sociological perspectives and reflect aggregated group effects. Ostensibly, college-impact models assert that during college students encounter a variety of experiences that, when combined with their background characteristics (inputs), shape educational and personal outcomes directly and indirectly (Pascarella & Terenzini, 2005).

In their encyclopedic compendium of college-impact research, Pascarella and Terenzini (2005) concluded that the impact of college is largely determined by student effort and level of involvement in curricular and cocurricular experiences. The family of college-impact theories, including Astin's (1984) theory of involvement, Pace's (1984, 1987) quality of effort, and Tinto's (1975, 1987) student persistence work, are helpful frameworks for making application to practice. Perhaps most comprehensive for assessment and practical application is Pascarella's (1985) general model for assessing change, which incorporates five sets of variables, including student background characteristics, structural and organizational features of the institution, the frequency of contact between the student and campus socializing agents, and students' quality of effort, which exert a direct and indirect impact on student change. These frameworks help articulate how experiences and environments can be manipulated to have an impact on students.

By far the most common framework employed in student affairs assessment and research is Astin's (1991) concept of institutional excellence, which is premised on the idea that "true excellence lies in the institution's ability to affect its students and faculty favorably, to enhance their intellectual and scholarly development, and to make a positive difference in their lives" (p. 7). This concept is the foundation for his input-environment-output (I-E-O) model, which underscores the point that to fully evaluate institutional effectiveness, it is necessary to have an understanding of student qualities and characteristics on entry to an educational institution (inputs), the nature of the educational environments with which they come into contact during college (environment), and their qualities and characteristics as they exit the institution (output). This model is popular for framing student affairs assessment projects because it clearly outlines the need for student input data about what students are exposed to in the environment and student outcomes.

The Importance of Evidence to Student Affairs Practice

In part a response to the US economic recession of the early 1980s and as public funding for universities and colleges steadily declined, assessment and accountability, and their corresponding pressure for student affairs to demonstrate impact, guided by data and defined by outcomes, have become firmly established as priorities in higher education (Bresciani, Zelna, & Anderson, 2004; Hoffman & Bresciani, 2010; Kinzie, 2011). The need to demonstrate the impact of programs and services on student success and, more important, learning have made assessment a compulsory responsibility for student affairs professionals. Aside from the demands for assessment as evidence of effectiveness, the importance of doing assessment and using assessment results is simply stated by Blimling and Whitt (1999) as a principle for effective student affairs practice. Good practice in student affairs includes an integration of theory, understanding of the body of evidence-based practice, a commitment to assessment, and the effective application of this information to practice.

The use of research and assessment results to shape institutional and student affairs policies, programs, and practices has been facilitated by the growing emphasis on assessment and outcomes throughout higher education and also improved professional education in assessment, increase in graduate-level course work in evaluation and research, and the incorporation of assessment, evaluation, and research as a professional competency in student affairs (ACPA & NASPA, 2015). Large assessment and research efforts exemplified by the longitudinal research projects sponsored by the Higher Education Research Institute (HERI), home to the CIRP Freshman Survey, and the National Survey of Student Engagement (NSSE) housed at the Indiana University Center for Postsecondary Research, focus attention on what matters to student learning and success. The projects have also helped foster the use of evidence in student affairs practice by providing participating institutions with information about their students' experiences along with peer comparison results to aid benchmarking and improvement efforts. Quite simply, having data to benchmark performance is an important lever to improve educational quality.

Again, Taylor ponders the availability of data and evidence. "Does MSU participate in national surveys such as NSSE? Could MSU and national peer data on NSSE or CIRP be useful here? What MSU office would have data about entering student characteristics? Does MSU collect exit surveys that ask how graduates rate various experiences or involvements? Does residence life collect any data from residents about living in their respective residence halls?

To illustrate the value of using evidence from large assessment projects in student affairs, and to consider what might help inform the CME-LC program staff members, we can consider NSSE findings related to learning communities. As mentioned previously, the research base on the value of learning communities to support student success, and specifically students in STEM fields, and theories about the many dimensions of student diversity and the factors that support historically underrepresented students provide a sound foundation for guiding action related to the establishment of learning communities. Institutional assessment projects can then be implemented to investigate the particular qualities of learning communities at MSU including CME-LC. NSSE results at MSU could be included in a broad study of entering engineering students' perceptions of the institution, first-year engineering courses, and the quality of the student experience in CME-LC. Additionally, comparing CME-LC student engagement results with non-CME-LC student results could help determine if the educational practices that CME-LC hopes to foster, such as student-faculty interaction or collaborative learning, are experienced by students. These results could contribute to an assessment of the effectiveness of CME-LC and guide efforts to enhance the program.

One of the most beneficial aspects of applying research-guided practice and relying on evidence from assessment and evaluation projects in student affairs is that these approaches can help change practice. By relying on evidence to guide change, student affairs professionals can be more confident about plans to modify practice or implement new programs. Outlining research-guided practice and layering on assessment or evaluation results can provide a firm foundation for action.

Challenges of Application

The effective translation of theory, research, and assessment to practice is an essential goal of student affairs professionals. However, it is not without challenges. Application may most realistically be considered along a continuum (Jacobi, Astin, & Ayala, 1987). One end emphasizes application to everyday practice, including the theory that guides practitioners in routine decisions and interactions on campus; the other end incorporates an intentional, direct identification of relevant theory and research and assessment findings; focuses on a specific practice, problem, or context; and applies and evaluates the evidence to the issue at hand. Between these two ends of the continuum is the general use of theory or evidence to shape policy or program design or to establish new practices. Thinking about application on a continuum should help practitioners realize that theory and research can be applied to different degrees.

One of the foremost challenges to increasing the application of theory and research to practice is overcoming the perception that theory and research are far removed from the practical matters of student affairs (Sriram & Oster, 2012). Theory and research findings can seem remote and inaccessible to busy practitioners with demands that frequently do not allow time to fully contemplate theoretical models and to make the needed translations to their specific situation. To increase accessibility, practitioners must let go of the idea that theory and research is the private language of scholars or something reserved for the classroom. Relevant and well-done research ought to speak to practical implications, and practitioners need to feel empowered to engage with and critique research.

To foster greater engagement with research, student affairs professionals should intentionally build in time to translate research to practice. One approach is for practitioners to build into their professional development plan an approach to reviewing theory and research, and to consider regular journal article or theory review reading and the translation to practice, as important as attending professional conferences. Arranging informal discussions with colleagues to read and share thoughts on theory and research are also ways to make literature more accessible and to build a collective understanding of research. Unfortunately, the busyness of practice can also preclude practitioners from producing or contributing to research. The theory-to-practice and practice-to-theory cycles can be enacted only when practitioners are also raising questions about existing research, exposing knowledge gaps, and contributing to the body of work with their own practical research and application.

In response to the pressure to account for how efficiently and effectively students affairs is performing, and the extent to which programs and services contribute to student learning and other important success measures, most student affairs divisions have stepped up their assessment efforts and increased their reliance on well-researched approaches and evidence of "what works" to justify program investments. The greater use of evidence to demonstrate program outcomes is a productive move for student affairs in that this can provide a strong rationale for sustaining what works to support student success or educational effectiveness. Although the challenge to carve out time to do meaningful assessment and attend to findings is significant, findings are critical to effective practice and can also contribute to scholarly practice.

Another challenge to expanding the application of theory and research to practice is the fact that because research findings are complicated and situational, applying research to local practice is equally if not more complicated. Research findings should be applicable to campus practice and conditions, yet as Pascarella and Terenzini (2005) asserted, research on the impact of college reveals that the influences on students' outcomes can differ, depending on the characteristics of students. In other words, what works for students in general does not necessarily work for particular subgroups of students. The increasing diversity of students in college and the range of conditions and environments in which they participate make it difficult and potentially unwise to generalize and apply research findings. Research must be consulted to understand the conditional effects and to examine whether the implications of research hold equally for all student subgroups. It is critical to understand the processes with which students holding different attributes interact with their institutions. Although claiming that research findings are difficult to apply because of conditional effects is by no means an argument for ignoring them, it is important to acknowledge the complexities.

Professional and Ethical Standards

The professional competencies document (ACPA & NASPA, 2015) and the identification of principles and strategies to foster student learning (Blimling & Whitt, 1999) stipulate knowledge of theory and research and successful applications of theory to practice as central aspects of *effective* professional practice.

Additionally, the NASPA *Standards of Professional Practice* (NASPA, 1990) and the ACPA *Statement of Ethical Principles and Standards* (ACPA, n.d.) stipulate this knowledge and these abilities to be critical parts of *ethical* professional practice (see chapter 6 for more details about ethical professional practice). In terms of services and program areas, the CAS (Council for the Advancement of Standards in Higher Education) standards and guidelines for all functional areas in student affairs identify applications of theory and research to practice as *necessary* to program or unit effectiveness (CAS, 2012).

Not to be confused with CAS *guidelines* (ideal but not mandatory elements), the CAS general *standards* address applications of theory and research in multiple ways. For example, programs and services must be, at minimum, "guided by theories and knowledge of learning and development" and "reflective of developmental and demographics of the student population" (CAS, 2012, p. 29). Additionally, to be CAS compliant, all programs and services must design and implement systematic assessment plans to ensure continued program effectiveness. Using multiple data sources, assessments are to yield information documenting relative achievements of the unit's overall goals as well as evidence of specific student learning outcomes identified by the unit.

The NASPA standards place an obligation on members to continue "enhancing personal knowledge and skills, [and] improving professional practices" (NASPA, 1990, Professional Development standard). Consistent with the CAS standards, NASPA members should also "regularly and systematically assess organizational structures, programs, and services to determine whether the developmental goals and needs of students are being met" (NASPA, 1990, Assessment standard). To be professionally responsible and competent, ACPA members should "conduct their professional activities in accordance with sound theoretical principles" (ACPA, n.d., p. 2). Acknowledging that developing expertise and fluency in applying theory to practice are themselves ongoing, developmental processes, ACPA members are expected to "maintain and enhance professional effectiveness by continually improving skills and acquiring new knowledge" (ACPA, n.d., p. 2). With respect to student learning and development, student affairs professionals should "be sensitive to and knowledgeable about the varieties of backgrounds, cultures, experiences, abilities, personal characteristics and viewpoints evident in the student population and be able to incorporate multiple theoretical perspectives to identify learning opportunities and to reduce barriers to development" (ACPA, n.d., p. 3). Additionally, echoing CAS and NASPA statements, ACPA members' responsibilities to their employing institutions include engaging in systematic assessment and evaluation (ACPA, n.d.).

In light of the centrality of these obligations and expectations, professionals must work to avoid some common pitfalls, one of which is reductionism. Frequently, professionals and aspiring professionals create or rely on bulleted lists of a theory's stages, levels, vectors, types, or other key features, and they note very generalized recommendations for practice relevant to a single theory. Such lists can be very useful as prompts or guides, but overreliance on these can also make it easy to forget the fully developed underlying concepts and dynamics within theories or to separate the bulleted points from their theoretical and practical contexts. Additionally, effectively applying theory to practice entails bringing combinations of theories to bear on situations or decisions at hand. Although professionals tend to identify certain theories or constructs as ones that particularly resonate with them or "ring true" as more useful or more important to their work, student affairs professionals (and ultimately students) are better served when multiple theories are consulted to help reveal multiple relevant dimensions, factors, and complexities at play.

New professionals particularly may be hesitant to experiment and try out their own theory-to-practice applications in real-life situations. By itself, one of Kitchener's (ACPA, n.d.) five ethical principles, "Do no harm," may seem to suggest that inaction is preferable to the uncertainties and potential mistakes that accompany early theory-to-practice attempts. Depending on the situations, however, professionals should understand that inaction, even well intended, may lead to harm. For example, not engaging with students who are telling racist, sexist, or homophobic jokes or posting bigoted messages and graphics can be interpreted as tacit approval or indifference to those acts. In such a case, inaction would deny students of just-in-time opportunities to examine and reflect on rationales, intentions, and potential outcomes of their actions. Inaction also robs professionals of valuable opportunities to meet students "where they are" and challenge the particular judgments and acts while also offering support of students as autonomous, developing persons of worth and value.

The exact words and approaches that new professionals use in encounters such as those described in this chapter will differ, incorporating the professional's own individual preferences and styles as well as reflecting where professionals are in terms of their own development of expertise. Careful study of theories, combined with role-plays and personal experiences, help professionals develop and use their own strengths as well as build a repertoire of approaches from which they can select. Supervisors are particularly critical to professionals' continued development toward effectiveness, because supervisors must decide how to acknowledge staff members' successes, mistakes, or missteps and determine their own availability to supervisees for ongoing reflection, discussion, and learning.

Several thoughts occur to Taylor while preparing for the upcoming meeting, including, "I haven't been in this type of professional situation before—meeting with faculty members. Maybe I should discuss the agenda with my boss beforehand? Should I postpone the meeting until my boss can attend? What are the pluses and minuses here?"

Conclusion

Similar to other applied fields, including health care and psychology, the field of student affairs benefits from integration of theory, research, and evidence from practical assessment and evaluation studies combined with expert practitioner perspectives. Through increased adoption of more integrated approaches, nursing and other fields have demonstrated its positive impact on outcomes. Theories, research, and assessment findings alone do not make or dictate decisions, but when considered together and applied by professionals, they can help support effective student affairs practice. Student affairs professionals must intentionally and thoughtfully select what to draw on to inform practice and to understand the strengths and limitations of source materials.

Greater integration of theory, research, and assessment in student affairs practice is also a key function of the emergent role of student affairs professionals as *scholar-practitioners*. Student affairs professionals are increasingly being called on to engage in research and scholarly endeavors to improve effectiveness of practices while serving in the role of an administrator (Hatfield & Wise, 2015; Jablonski, Mena, Manning, Carpenter, & Siko, 2006). The scholar-practitioner intentionally uses research findings to inform decisions and policies, values data, and regularly engages in empirical work including assessment projects. Professionals become scholar-practitioners by reflecting on how their experiences advance knowledge in the field, applying knowledge of theory and research to everyday practicalities, and disseminating practices that work. In particular, scholar-practitioner skills can be sharpened through assessment work and by using local knowledge when applying theories or research findings to practice.

Discussion Questions and Activities

1. In what ways could CME-LC be structured to be developmentally responsive to the students' expressed concerns from the focus group?
2. What student development theories might you consult to inform your work with CME-LC?
3. What kinds of information and data sources about CME-LC program participants, what aspects of what students experience and their perceptions and what program outcomes might you imagine accessing to inform your efforts to help CME-LC achieve its goals?
4. On your campus, how do you (if you can) access the data and institutional information that Taylor seeks?
5. As Taylor considers RA staffing for the three floors of CME-LC in Stevens, what characteristics would you recommend seeking in applicants? What about for the RAs of the remaining two floors in Stevens?
6. In small groups, examine the set of living-learning community (LLC) outcomes specified in the housing and residential life programs section of the CAS standards (or formulate a list of outcomes relevant to a program or unit of your choice) and identify student development theories relevant to pursuing and achieving these outcomes. Create and describe four activities or environmental features and explain why these would be developmentally appropriate to incorporate into the LLC (or another program or unit). Outline several questions that could be explored to assess the achievement of these outcomes.

7. Invite students to identify a source of evidence-based practice related to learning communities and to evaluate the information for helping to improve CME-LC.

8. List some collaborative opportunities for Taylor, Chris, and Pat to disseminate information regarding CME-LC redesign steps and assessment work to a broader audience of student affairs professionals. What are opportunities to disseminate information to Chris's or Pat's faculty colleagues? Should the presentations be identical? Why or why not?

References

Abes, E. S., Jones, S. R., & McEwen, M. K. (2007). Reconceptualizing the model of multiple dimensions of identity: The role of meaning-making capacity in the construction of multiple identities. *Journal of College Student Development, 48*(1), 1–22.

ACPA. (n.d.). *ACPA statement of ethical principles and standards.* Washington, DC: Author. Retrieved from http://www.myacpa.org/sites/default/files/Ethical_Principles_Standards.pdf

ACPA–College Student Educators International and NASPA–Student Affairs Administrators in Higher Education. (2015). *Professional competency areas of student affairs practitioners.* Washington, DC: Authors. Retrieved from http://www.naspa.org/images/uploads/main/ACPA_NASPA_Professional_Competencies_FINAL.pdf

Astin, A. W. (1984). Student involvement: A developmental theory for higher education. *Journal of College Student Personnel, 40*(5), 518–529.

Astin, A. W. (1991). *Assessment for excellence: The philosophy and practice of assessment and evaluation in higher education.* Washington, DC: American Council on Education/Oryx Press Series on Higher Education.

Banta, T. W., & Palomba, C. (2015). *Assessment essentials: Planning, implementing, and improving assessment in higher education.* San Francisco: Jossey-Bass.

Blimling, G. S., & Whitt, E. J. (1999). Identifying the principles that guide student affairs practice. In G. S. Blimling & E. J. Whitt (Eds.), *Good practice in student affairs: Principles to foster student learning* (pp. 1–20). San Francisco: Jossey-Bass.

Bloland, P. A., Stamatakos, L. C., & Rogers, R. R. (1994). *Reform in student affairs: A critique of student development.* Greensboro: University of North Carolina at Greensboro, School of Education, ERIC Counseling and Student Services Clearinghouse.

Bresciani, M. J., Zelna, C. L., & Anderson, J. A. (2004). *Assessing student learning and development: A handbook for practitioners.* Washington, DC: National Association of Student Personnel Administrators.

Council for the Advancement of Standards in Higher Education (CAS). (2012). *CAS standards and guidelines.* Washington, DC: Author. Retrieved from http://standards.cas.edu/getpdf.cfm?PDF=E868395C-F784–2293–129ED7842334B22A

Evans, N. J. (1987). A framework for assisting student affairs staff in fostering moral development. *Journal of Counseling and Development, 66,* 191–194.

Evans, N. J., Forney, D. S., Guido, F. M., Patton, L. D., & Renn, K. A. (2009). *Student development in college: Theory, research, and practice* (2nd ed.). San Francisco: Jossey-Bass.

Evans, N. J., & Guido, F. M. (2012). Response to Patrick Love's "informal theory": A rejoinder. *Journal of College Student Development, 53*(2), 192–200.

Hatfield, L. J., & Wise, V. L. (2015). *A guide to becoming a scholarly practitioner in student affairs.* Sterling, VA: Stylus.

Hoffman, J. L., & Bresciani, M. J. (2010). Assessment work: Examining the prevalence and nature of learning assessment competencies and skills in student affairs job postings. *Journal of Student Affairs Research and Practice, 47*(4), 495–512.

Jablonski, M. A., Mena, S. B., Manning, K., Carpenter, S., & Siko, K. L. (2006). Scholarship in student affairs revisited: The summit on scholarship, March 2006. *NASPA Journal, 43*(4), 182–200.

Jacobi, M., Astin, A., & Ayala, F. Jr. (1987) College student outcomes assessment: A talent development perspective. *ASHE-ERIC Higher Education Report, 7.* Washington, DC: Association for the Study of Higher Education.

Jones, S. R., & McEwen, M. K. (2000). A conceptual model of multiple dimensions of identity. *Journal of College Student Development, 41*(4), 405–414.

Kinzie, J. (2011). Student affairs in the age of accountability and assessment. In P. Magolda & M. B. Baxter Magolda (Eds.), *Contested issues in student affairs: Diverse perspectives and respectful dialogue* (pp. 201–214). Herndon, VA: Stylus.

Knefelkamp, L. L., Golec, R. R., & Wells, E. A. (1985). *The practice-to-theory-to-practice model.* Unpublished manuscript. University of Maryland, College Park.

Love, P. (2012). Informal theory: The ignored link in theory-to-practice. *Journal of College Student Development, 53*(2), 177–191.

Morrill, W. H., Oetting, E. R., & Hurst, J. C. (1974). Dimensions of counselor functioning. *Personnel and Guidance Journal, 53,* 354–359.

NASPA. (1990). *NASPA standards of professional practice.* Washington, DC: NASPA–Student Affairs Professionals in Higher Education. Retrieved from https://www.naspa.org/about/student-affairs

Ngozi Adichie, C. (2009). The danger of a single story. *TED Talk.* Retrieved from http://www.ted.com/talks/chimamanda_adichie_the_danger_of_a_single_story/transcript?language=en

Pace, C. R. (1984). *Measuring the quality of college student experiences. An account of the development and use of the College Student Experiences Questionnaire.* Los Angeles: Higher Education Research Institute, University of California, Los Angeles. Retrieved from http://files.eric.ed.gov/fulltext/ED255099.pdf

Pace, C. R. (1987). *CSEQ test manual and norms.* Los Angeles: Center for the Study of Evaluation.

Pascarella, E. T. (1985). College environmental influences on learning and cognitive development: A critical review and synthesis. In J. Smart (Ed.), *Higher education: Handbook of theory and research* (Vol. 1, pp. 1–64). New York: Agathon.

Pascarella, E. T., & Terenzini, P. T. (2005). *How college affects students: Vol. 2. A third decade of research.* San Francisco: Jossey-Bass.

Patton, L. D., & Harper, S. R. (2009). Using reflection to reframe theory-to-practice in student affairs. In G. S. McClellan & J. Stringer (Eds.), *Handbook of student affairs administration* (3rd ed., pp. 147–165). San Francisco: Jossey-Bass.

Sackett, D. L., Straus, S. E., Richardson, W. S., Rosenberg, W., & Haynes, R. B. (2000). *Evidence-based medicine: How to practice and teach EBM 2.* London: Churchill Livingstone.

Schuh, J. H., Upcraft, M. L., & Associates. (2001). *Assessment practice in student affairs: An applications manual.* San Francisco: Jossey-Bass.

Sriram, R., & Oster, M. (2012). Reclaiming the "scholar" in scholar-practitioner. Journal of Student Affairs Research and Practice, *49*(4), 377–396.

Stamatakos, L. C. (1981a). Student affairs progress toward professionalism: Recommendations for action: Part I. *Journal of College Student Personnel, 22,* 105–112.

Stamatakos, L. C. (1981b). Student affairs progress toward professionalism: Recommendations for action: Part II. *Journal of College Student Personnel, 22,* 197–207.

Tinto, V. (1975). Dropout from higher education: A theoretical synthesis of recent research. *Review of Educational Research, 45*(1), 89–125.

Tinto, V. (1987). *Leaving college: Rethinking the causes and cures of student attrition.* Chicago: University of Chicago Press.

Upcraft, M. L., & Schuh, J. H. (1996). *Assessment in student affairs: A guide for practitioners.* San Francisco: Jossey-Bass.

Weick, K. E. (1979). *The social psychology of organizing.* Reading, MA: Addison-Wesley.

Woodley, E. (2013). *Building a foundation for higher education case management: From theory to practice.* Retrieved from https://nabita.org/wordpress/wp-content/uploads/2013/11/2013-11-20-NaBITA-Resource-Building-a-Foundation-for-Higher-Education-Case-Management-.pdf

Young, R. B. (1988). The profession(alization) of student affairs. *NASPA Journal, 25*(4), 262–266.

PART SIX

THE FUTURE

The final section of this book includes two chapters that focus on the future. Chapter 32 by Peter Magolda and Jill Ellen Carnaghi (with contributions from Aleidra Allen and Hoa Bui) looks at the continuing professional development of student affairs educators, and chapter 33 by the editors includes our prognostications for the future of student affairs practice.

We trust you will find chapter 32 challenging and thought provoking. The authors have deviated from the typical advice to attend professional conferences and read the literature and have suggested thinking very differently about professional development. They introduce the chapter with contributions from a student and a staff member that form the basis for their discussion about professional development. They provide foundational principles for reenvisioning professional development in student affairs and a multistep model for professional development. They conclude with recommendations for stakeholders in professional development.

In chapter 33 we offer our speculations, guesses, and estimates about what the future might hold. Recall that we described student affairs practice in the preface to this book as working in permanent white water, borrowing from Allen and Cherrey (2003). Accordingly, making predictions is risky, at best. Nevertheless, we believe our thinking about societal trends and student affairs trends as well as what we think will be required for future student affairs practice will provide the basis for discussion and critique as readers contemplate our collective future. We offer our predictions cautiously and encourage alternative points of view.

Reference

Allen, K. E., & Cherrey, C. (2003). Student affairs as change agents. *NASPA Journal, 40*(2), 29–42.

CHAPTER 32

EVOLVING ROLES AND COMPETENCIES: PROFESSIONAL DEVELOPMENT RECONSIDERED

Peter Magolda and Jill Ellen Carnaghi
(with contributions from Aleidra Allen and Hoa Bui)

The Song of a Lonely Bird
by Hoa Bui

When a bird leaves its nest too early, it will realize where its heart is too late.

I left home when I was 18.

Not knowing how big the Pacific Ocean can be

Not knowing how fear can disguise as independence

Not knowing how a box of shiitake, like ice cream, can mean happiness

Not knowing how a five minute phone call can be warmer than a handshake

But I soon learned.

I learned that my name became a group of sounds squeezed together with no meaning attached.

I learned that "That is so cool!!" to come from Vietnam, but it is not cool to act and be Vietnamese.

Or collectivist. Or Communist.

I learned to water down 4000 years of complex history to give an answer that I will regret.

I hide my loneliness behind "cultural barriers" and "cultural differences."

Behind a freezing "I'm fine, thank you" which I top with a chilling smile.

A code for "I can barely breathe. Please don't leave."

I made peace with the fact that my dinner in Frank Dining Hall is more than how much my Dad makes a week.

I made friends; none of them are international students.

I gave up on pseudo-friend, many of them are.

How lonely it is, to look at those who look like you and are apparently supposedly similar to you without seeing your reflection!

We smile and "I'm fine" at each other, because we are afraid that we should not come here in the first place.

And we fake our happiness to our parents, because we have to protect them from our pains.

I leave a part of myself where I came from, but I am not weak. I am not injured.

I am strong because I am here.

I am here, and I am stronger.

I still sing the song, the song of a lonely bird, even when I am not sure if anyone is listening.

Neutral No More
by Aleidra Allen

Michael Brown's death changed me. As an African American woman, and as an educator, remaining silent about race and racism is no longer an option. Growing up, my friends did not always look like me, and it did not seem like a big deal. But between high school and graduate school, my awareness of race increased as I witnessed and experienced microaggressions, blatant acts of racism, and horrific racial injustices. Initially, my naive "solution" was to refuse to be stereotypical and "defy the odds." While I joined the gospel choir and the Black Student Union, I also held officer positions in organizations with mostly white membership, being one of the few people of color involved. I thought these modest actions would help other black students recognize that they, too, could occupy traditional white spaces and slowly "end the segregation." But when I learned about Michael Brown's death while working full-time as a program coordinator at Saint Louis University (SLU), I realized while well-intended, my martyr-like actions masked a much larger issue that needed to be addressed directly—Black lives matter.

I closely followed the Ferguson story long before the shooting became international news. My St. Louis friends posted pictures on social media of Michael's dead body lying in the street. Outside of work, I engaged in protests and meetings and used social media to educate and speak out. However, campus reactions and discussions were dramatically different. Despite Ferguson being in close proximity to SLU, initially the predominately white campus appeared detached from and mute about the incident that engulfed St. Louis. Even my colleagues, members of what I assumed to be a progressive and socially just profession, remained uneasy and too often silent.

When the #OccupySLU movement arrived on campus, colleagues and senior administrators vigilantly monitored the actions of protesters and their impact on the campus. Administratively, the university worked tirelessly to ensure the safety of all students and community members. Morally, the university upheld its Jesuit mission, remained neutral, and justified the continuation of the "demonstrations" because the awareness and dialogue were educational. All the while, parents of students pressured institutional leaders to remove "demonstrators" (both students and community members) while social media sites such as Facebook and Yik Yak scorned activists with hurtful and derogatory posts. With tears in their eyes students approached me, frustrated with peers and parents who failed to understand their concerns and outrage. Despite their frustrations and fears, these activists inspired and offered me hope.

Job responsibilities and priorities changed during #OccupySLU. Student Development staff signed up to answer calls from family members and alumni regarding campus protests. Staff members augmented their existing responsibilities by, for example, facilitating late-night campus dialogues. The university deemed certain staff "essential personnel" and required them to attend meetings on the newly implemented security levels and codes, and mandated many of us to be "on call" during times of potential unrest, such as the night of the Grand Jury announcement. I spent considerable time supporting students who wanted to express their emotions and process their experiences. Then, I reflected on these interactions myself.

The silence of some student development professionals was deafening. The Division of Student Development sponsored professional development programs about race, white privilege, and social justice. Unfortunately too many faculty, staff, and students opted out of these seminars. Fortunately, during these dialogues, I identified supportive staff. We had to find each other and we did. Together, we talked and posed questions that we are still trying to answer. How can we enhance the cultural competence of students and staff? How do we foster learning environments that create welcoming environments for marginalized students and staff? How can we support student activists? How can the campus community better understand its privilege?

Michael Brown's death revealed injustices within the American criminal justice system that need to be fixed. Michael Brown's death also revealed issues that persist in higher education that need to be challenged and changed. The neutral stance of some student development professionals caused black educators and allies to wonder if it was okay to interact with student activists and community protesters. Would colleagues be uncomfortable? Would jobs be in jeopardy? Should we *seek justice or protect our careers?*

Michael Brown's death transformed me into an activist. Since his death, I have involved myself in initiatives aimed at positive change in African American communities in St. Louis. I use social media and blogs to educate others on the #BlackLivesMatter movement. Events in Ferguson redirected my career goals and ignited my passion for uplifting black people. I am more intentional about volunteering to assist with multicultural programs and initiatives hosted by SLU's Cross Cultural Center and Black Student Alliance. I aspire to work in a college multicultural affairs department, which will better align my career goals and passion. Indeed, Michael Brown's death changed me.

Reenvisioning Professional Development

We began this chapter with a poem and the beginnings of a blog post because "maturation or development occurs as people become more capable of articulating and critiquing personal stories, reframing them and reshaping their own lives" (Keeling, 2004, p. 9). Stories are relevant in this context because human interactions, learning, and communication are at the epicenter of effective professional development in student affairs, and stories of student affairs educators are vital to understanding them and to providing the profession with ideas for how to serve students best.

Hoa and Aleidra reveal the unique and wide-ranging challenges student affairs educators encounter each day, such as cultural insensitivity and ideological disputes. They understand the value of reflecting on and making public how these challenges influence others and themselves. Most important, they model ways of affirming, supporting, and learning from "the other," including lonely birds and awakened activists. Similar to participants in Renn and Jessup-Anger's (2008) research study about new professionals in student affairs, Hoa and Aleidra used their work contexts as laboratories to regularly examine and improve themselves and the lives of those with whom they interact.

Hoa expressed her feelings of being alone, caused in part by leaving her family and homeland of Vietnam to attend a university that was neither as empathic nor welcoming as she imagined. Determined and resilient describe her response to cultural differences, indifference, and insensitivity. The increase in international students attending American universities has diversified many historically homogeneous white campuses and exposed cultural differences as well as tensions. Too often, these universities have insufficient, insensitive, or inflexible support mechanisms, wounding marginalized students and confounding student affairs educators' efforts to mediate conflicts and provide support (McIntire & Willer, 1992). The poem reveals ways that universities can encourage lonely birds to sing and others to learn to listen to and harmonize with them (rather than drowning them out or insisting they remain silent).

Aleidra reminds readers that "real-world" incidents, such as a police shooting resulting in a death and removed from higher education's insular ivory towers, have an intense and profound influence on campus life. Her insights about the toxicity of racism suggest that experiencing injustices and remaining silent, to fit in and not make proverbial waves, may be safe in the short term but harmful over time.

Hoa and Aleidra identified issues they care deeply about, and they heeded the advice of Carducci and Jaramillo (2014): "Rather than quickly resolving this cognitive tension by soliciting the expertise and guidance of external authorities, you must grapple with the ambiguity inherent in new experiences and take responsibility for making meaning, thoughtfully reflecting on, questioning, and integrating new perspectives and bodies of knowledge you encounter" (p. 188).

Hoa and Aleidra recognize self-reflection and personal transformation as prerequisites to enacting their activist agendas aimed at holistic transformative learning and public action. In this context, *holistic* refers to efforts aimed at promoting growth in how people understand knowledge and how they understand themselves and their relationships. *Transformative learning* refers to "formulating more dependable beliefs about our experiences, assessing their contexts, seeking informed agreement on their meaning and justification, and making decisions on the resulting insights" (Mezirow, 2000, p. 4).

A primary aim of this chapter is to answer the question, "What types of professional development can foster holistic transformative learning and public action?" This question is applicable to professional development educators and the constituents they serve.

Professional Development Foundational Principles

Hoa's poem and Aleidra's blog contain ideas and actions that are relevant to reenvisioning professional development in student affairs. In this section we introduce and elaborate on five principles we believe should guide professional development opportunities: (1) good intentions are never enough, (2) lifelong learning is essential, (3) embracing change is scary and necessary, (4) difference in and of itself is good (one's unwillingness to face difference is "bad"), and (5) inclusion is essential.

Knowledge must augment good intentions. Having a sincere interest in and concern for collegians, without possessing requisite knowledge (for example, the history of higher education, theories about students' development, or cultural competencies) is risky business (Magolda & Baxter Magolda, 2011). Neither international students such as Hoa nor the African American male students (traumatized by the death of Michael Brown) with whom Aleidra works will benefit from allies or advisors who have a sincere desire to support them but possess minimal knowledge about universities and college students and discount the value of stories as guides for professional development.

The Student Learning Imperative (ACPA, 1996) encouraged student affairs educators to intentionally create conditions that enhance student learning and personal development. It identified hallmarks of a college-educated person, including "(a) complex cognitive skills such as reflection and critical thinking; (b) an ability to apply knowledge to practical problems encountered in one's vocation, family, or other areas of life; (c) an understanding and appreciation of human differences; (d) practical competence skills (for example, decision making, conflict resolution); and (e) a coherent integrated sense of identity, self-esteem, confidence, integrity, aesthetic sensibilities, and civic responsibility" (p. 1).

For student affairs educators to create conditions for fostering learning and development, they, too, must possess complex cognitive skills, knowledge that they can use to solve problems, practical skills, and a sense of self and civic responsibility. *Professional Competency Areas for Student Affairs Practitioners* (ACPA/NASPA, 2015) identified requisite knowledge, skills, and attitudes for student affairs educators, which included advising and helping; assessment, evaluation, and research; equity, diversity, and inclusion; ethical professional practice; history, philosophy, and values; human and organizational resources; law, policy, and governance; leadership; personal foundations; and student learning and development. Hoa's and Aleidra's understanding about culture, politics, and the self (as evident in the poem and blog) were invaluable assets as they grappled with challenges on their respective campuses.

Professional development must be knowledge-driven and based on competencies so that participants can be theoretically informed as they assume roles as administrators, advocates, activists, counselors, assessors-evaluators, advisors, technologists, disciplinarians, free speech experts, public safety officers, referral agents, crisis managers, leadership developers, arbitrators, ethicists, and role models. Professional development based on good intentions that also recognize the value of knowing *and* acting will more likely yield holistic transformational learning for educators and those they serve.

At first glance, lonely collegians and protesters are hardly breaking news stories on college campuses. Yet, a more in-depth examination of these common occurrences reveals the complexities associated with educators resolving issues such as these in light of rapid changes on the political, social, cultural, economic, and pedagogical fronts (Keeling, 2004).

The unique campus challenges require contemporary wisdom that attends to history and context. Hoa's loneliness is not simply a case of homesickness. For advocates to understand and support Hoa, they would need to understand, for example, the history of US-Vietnamese relations as well as the recent efforts of US universities to recruit thousands of international students (with insufficient infrastructures in place to support them). Aleidra understood the history of policing in Ferguson and the university's history of involvement in community matters, which helped her understand and respond to the civil unrest and fears that dramatically upended campus life.

Colleges as well as graduate preparation programs in student affairs are excellent starting places but inadequate ending places for educators to explore ways to address these thorny and ever-changing challenges. Hoa's undergraduate studies in education and rhetoric and Aleidra's graduate studies in student affairs provided them invaluable foundational knowledge to solve real-world problems.

Yet, these real-world challenges are more complex, and knowledge to address these challenges continues to proliferate. Knowledge generated and disseminated at the turn of the century is woefully outdated today. The complexity of contemporary campus issues represents adaptive challenges—those in which neither the causes nor solutions are well known (Heifetz, 1998). Staff development or career-long learning is essential for educators to continue to build on their existing wisdom and cultivate their intellectual curiosities.

As an undergraduate, Hoa encountered theoretical perspectives about race, class, power, and privilege; after graduation she remained intellectually curious and continued to read about and ponder issues such as loneliness and cultural colonization. She wondered why it was so difficult to forge authentic relationships with peers. She questioned why American values and American ways of life seemed to trump Vietnamese values and cultural norms. She scrutinized her economic privilege as a US student (when compared to her family in Vietnam) and questioned her new "good life."

Aleidra's graduate studies provided her a firm theoretical foundation about college student development, organizations, and culture. After graduation, her intellectual curiosities expanded to explore issues such as racism and white privilege. This ongoing learning intensified after the death of Michael Brown. Her intellectual curiosities and her lived experience gave her real-life context and tacit learning to draw on as she conducted cultural analyses of the City of Ferguson and SLU scrutinizing their responses to Michael Brown's death. Cultivating intellectual curiosities benefited Hoa and Aleidra as well as those with whom they interacted.

Unprecedented and ubiquitous change has engulfed the world. Today in the academy multiple and diverse knowledge bases enrich understanding about students, learning environments, and learning, which makes mastery of this knowledge unlikely. These changes have complicated student affairs professionals' efforts to optimally educate and support collegians. Career-long learning is vital and makes ongoing professional development essential because of the vast and ever-changing nature of knowledge about higher education, the diverse career paths of student affairs educators (Tull, Hirt, & Saunders, 2009), and the speed with which knowledge becomes antiquated.

"Knowledge is no longer a scarce—or stable—commodity . . . knowledge is changing so rapidly that specific information may become obsolete before a student graduates and has the opportunity to apply it" (Keeling, 2004, p. 4). Thus, career-long learning, woven into the fabric of student affairs work, is one way to continually and progressively address the aforementioned challenges and changes and ensure holistic transformational learning for teachers and learners.

Responsive and innovative curricula and pedagogies are the exception, not the rule, in the world of professional development for student affairs educators. Predictable professional development programs (for example, white privilege), delivered using conventional pedagogies (for example, a lecture) that target specific audiences (for example, residence hall staff), although beneficial are also limiting. First, familiar and perfunctory staff development programs, educating participants about topics such as "racial stereotyping" (in response to incidents such as Ferguson) are well intentioned, informative, but seldom transformative. Sponsoring staff development programs is difficult to argue against, yet assessing program effectiveness is allusive. Questions persist before, during, and after such programs. What outcomes can an architect or facilitator of a "stereotyping" workshop reasonably expect to achieve? Is it reasonable to assume change will result from a brief, stand-alone program? Making clear the intention and desired outcomes of these programs are modest steps to addressing this concern.

Second, contemporary staff development pedagogies are frequently problematic, as evident in SLU's post-Ferguson professional development offerings. The presentation of conventional topics to student affairs staff members, using tried-and-true modes of delivery, such as lectures and one-time small group discussions—do little to foster meaningful dialogue, transformative learning, and action. Too often, these all-too-familiar pedagogies have a numbing effect on facilitators and participants.

Third, conventional staff development–sponsored programs attracted the proverbial choir or the "believers" yet seldom inspired skeptics or individuals intimidated and scared about the topic to participate.

The stories crafted by Hoa and Aleidra are useful guides in addressing these three professional development concerns: content, pedagogy, and audiences. Hoa's poem blends familiar issues with professional development topics such as the importance of relationships and fitting in with topics off the proverbial "beaten path," such as what counts as "normal" and the influence of the dominant culture's normalizing expectations (respecting the American way of collegiate life while discounting one's cultural past) have on subcultures (for example, new international students). The poem contains personal and powerful insights about what dominant and marginalized subcultures need to do. Aleidra's story blends familiar topic such as "understanding" cultural difference to include progressive and different strategies to address indifference.

Hoa and Aleidra also model ways to reenvision the delivery of professional development programs. Hoa's poem, an alternative pedagogy, is an innovative, unconventional, and a powerful way of introducing perennial issues such as diversity and inclusion. Her poem is a refreshing and offbeat way of "coming to know." Similarly, Aleidra used a blog as a pedagogical device to creatively invite a diverse audience (including individuals beyond her staff) to engage in online dialogues about topics such as why black lives matter and social justice. This pedagogy modeled ways for participants to teach and learn from each other, garnered multiple perspectives, and mobilized participants to act. Soliciting input about "what matters" from participants is a good start to satisfying their professional development needs as well as expanding these audiences.

We doubt that either Hoa or Aleidra would describe their respective poem or blog as "professional development," yet their work contains theoretical-influenced ideas that could improve professional development in unusual and powerful ways. For example, Aleidra developed a professional development program from her blog and social media work using a hybrid workshop model with a more conventional "in-service" workshop format. These innovative ideas delivered using democratic pedagogies do more than simply transmit knowledge from expert to novice. They disrupt binaries, such as teacher-learner and expert-novice, favoring education and professional development that co-creates and co-disseminates knowledge. Their works represent teaching and learning opportunities that emphasize respecting learners' thinking, engaging learners in a mutual exploration of the complexities of knowing, and collaborating to solve problems (Baxter Magolda, 2009). They respected learners' perspectives and encouraged them to make public their experiences. We advocate mixed-methods models and ongoing curricula (not one-shot deals) for the most challenging areas of new learning.

If sponsors of professional development programs follow the lead of Hoa and Aleidra and devise curricula and pedagogies that are meaningful, innovative, collaborative, and responsive to real-world problems, audience size and learning would likely increase. These aspirations align with ideas advanced by Rhoads and Black (1995), who advocated that student affairs educators foster conditions that enable diverse constituents, such as students and educators, to interact together in ways that are participatory and community building.

These change-oriented ideas sound "good" in theory yet are risky in practice. Richelle Mead has said, "throughout history, people with new ideas—who think differently and try to change things—have always been called troublemakers" (Thomsett, 2015, p. xiii). Hoa easily could be branded as an ungrateful international student, critical of a university that offered her an opportunity to gain a college education. Aleidra, similarly, could be pigeonholed as a young rebel, who neither understands the politics of race nor higher education. From our vantage point, sustaining the status quo is a greater threat than trying something new that may be risky but could help professionals in devising transformational learning opportunities that enable them to address adaptive challenges.

Renn and Hodges's (2007) qualitative study about the experiences of new professionals in student affairs and Magolda and Carnaghi's (2004, 2014) *Job One* books (which included stories about new professionals, written by new professionals) showcased the importance of relationships and institutional fit. Senior and seasoned administrators also share these two aspirations. Idyllic and romanticized notions about relationships and fitting in are pervasive. *Job One* contributors confessed that they wanted colleagues to like and respect them . . . supervisors to be "warm and fuzzy" . . . students to be their mentees . . . work environments to be conflict-free. Intellectually, they recognized that these expectations were Camelot-like; operationally, they struggled to modify these expectations. These new professionals also recognized that their supervisors and more seasoned colleagues, too, shared these unlikely aspirations. Professional staff development would be an ideal place to address issues of relationships and fit. "Fit" can be code for "dominant culture"; a better way of determining fit might be to examine the individuals' and institution's values and honest expression of them. Aleidra and Hoa offer insights about ways to challenge these pervasive romanticized and idyllic notions.

Relationships and fit matter to Hoa and Aleidra; yet, acknowledging and celebrating differences are as important as harmonious human relationships and fitting into the university. They grapple with the messiness resulting from clashes involving cultural differences, human relations, and institutional fit.

Hoa's geographic distance from her family and friends in Vietnam strain these interpersonal relationships. Competing cultural norms as well as others' lack of curiosity about her life complicated Hoa's quest to forge authentic relationships with peers and mentors that contributed to her lonely bird feelings. She refused to mask or abandon her core values to form campus friendships and fit in. Aleidra is geographically close to her colleagues, but ideologically she is worlds apart from many peers during the Ferguson campus protests. She resisted urges to compromise her beliefs and sense of self. She actually became more honest and enlightened about herself (reflecting her experiences and those of others in the black community). Her newfound confidence and passion and her deep feelings about injustices mobilized her actions. Balancing loyalty to her university (that is, fitting in) and being true to herself was a formidable challenge. She wanted to identify like-minded colleagues, and she wanted to explore ideological differences with "the other." As her activist inner self awakened, she forged authentic and supportive relationships by blogging, which represented establishing different kinds (that is, online) of relationships with educators broadening what "counts" as fitting in and being part of a community. Blogging was her way of fitting in, being true to her values, and providing opportunities (that is, online responses to her blog) to acknowledge opposing views.

Contrary to professional development opportunities that focus on points of agreement (avoiding contested issues), professional development options such as blogging about privileges and "difference" (for example, blog followers posting reactions) are integral and necessary aspects of all educational communities, including staff development communities. Professional development must provide space for diverse individuals who hold diverse perspectives to make their view public, invite critique, and explore collaborative and mediated problem-solving. Such an atmosphere can be co-constructed by stakeholders and is critical to healthy professional development initiatives. Gamson (1993) spoke to the importance of accepting conflict and difference: "[higher education communities] must develop ways for members to disagree with one another without losing the respect of other members. People in colleges and universities are notoriously uncomfortable with conflict. We run away from it or stomp it into the ground. We deny it or over-dramatize it. . . Dealing with conflict . . . requires respect and civility. It does not ask that parties love or even like each other, just that they continue interacting" (p. 6).

There are, however, very real political aspects that can have very real consequences for expressing views publicly. Professional development requires risk-taking and recognizing that institutions may not be able to provide spaces that shield folks from harm. Professional development should provide space to negotiate realms of meaning, social relations, knowledge, and values, which is no easy task. It needs to include conversations about celebrating difference and accepting conflict as a way of life. As Tierney (1993) noted, dealing with difference is hard work, time consuming, and discomforting. Desiring collaboration necessitates accepting differences and conflict. Hoa and Aleidra make clear their desire for human relationships and fitting in; and they make equally clear that the inability to recognize, accept, and celebrate differences divides us.

In an era when American higher education and global societies are intertwined, educators are keenly aware of their responsibility to prepare themselves and students to thrive in this new world order. Educators aspire to generate and disseminate knowledge and practices that will enable students and themselves, as global citizens, to develop wisdom, competencies, and skills to solve real-world problems.

Again, good intentions and knowledge are insufficient. What is key is developing conditions for educators to come to terms with their own sense of power, privilege, and public voice as social agents of change and examine and frame critically what they learn as part of what it means to live and educate in a global democracy. Aleidra and Hoa valued and modeled this global world-view. For Aleidra, the death of Michael Brown was more than a single tragic event involving a police officer and citizen; it brought up issues of omnipresent prejudices, stereotypes, power, privilege, and politics. It represents long-standing global malaises. She examined her underlying assumptions about these issues and altered her role as a result. For Hoa, being a lonely bird was more than an isolated case of homesickness or a result of an inadequate new student orientation program; it was about ubiquitous cultural assimilation and imperialism, hegemony, and the politics of difference. She also examined underlying assumptions that guided her actions. Aleidra's and Hoa's writings illuminate ways educators can reflect on and be responsible for "their own ideas, take intellectual risks, develop a sense of respect for others different from themselves, and think critically in order to shape the conditions that influence how they participate in a wider democratic culture" (Giroux, 2007, p. 201).

Nowhere is this principle of globalization more clear than in what is commonly called *diversity training*. Often focused on learning about "the other," this training usually gives insufficient attention to learning about oneself. Critically examining one's white privilege, ingrained assumptions one holds that marginalize various populations (for example, heteronormativity), microaggressions—subtle nonphysical insults or oppressive acts that create an unwelcoming environment for individuals already on the margins (Sue, 2010)—one commits, and systems of inequity and oppression in which one participates are necessary to developing an authentic multicultural outlook. Creating citizens with a global view will take more than study abroad and intergroup dialogue experiences; it necessitates reexamining our core assumptions and how they play out in everyday injustices which work for everyone, not just for a few.

The stories of these two young professionals reveal that both women are committed to learning and developing in their work contexts. Their reflections are thoughtful, offer important insights, and expose the crux of the transformational learning demanded of them by their work environments. They also illustrate that no one body of knowledge or skill set is sufficient for facing the adaptive challenges inherent in their work lives. Drawing from their experiences to craft transformational professional development means being purposeful, acquiring knowledge, engaging in career-long learning, cultivating intellectual curiosities, deploying innovative pedagogies, reaching out to underrepresented and marginalized audiences, remaining authentic, acknowledging and negotiating cultural differences, thinking globally and politically, and collaborating with "the other." These are key dynamics to creating holistic transformative learning contexts that benefit educators and collegians.

Learning Partnerships in Professional Development

The adaptive challenges noted throughout this chapter require lifelong—or at least career-long—learning, critical reflection, negotiating difference, and navigating complex systems. Baxter Magolda (2014) argued that in addition to knowledge and skill, student affairs professionals need complex developmental capacities to meet these expectations. Specifically, she advocated self-authorship, or the capacity to internally craft one's beliefs, identities, and relationships, as the minimum capacity for addressing these challenges (see chapter 9 for an in-depth description of self-authorship). Self-authoring persons carefully consider multiple perspectives but do so without being consumed by them, and they are able to act on their internally crafted values in ways that respect differences. Taylor and Baxter Magolda (2015) offer a professional development plan based on the learning partnerships model (Baxter Magolda, 2004) that incorporates the key dynamics described in this chapter. Their plan places the professional as the architect of the plan, draws on the professional's experience, and offers the opportunity for transformational learning by explicitly addressing growth and developmental capacity.

The model involves seven steps. The first step is to identify a context in which you want and need to meet an adaptive challenge. Hoa's adaptive challenge involved integrating her cultural heritage into authentic relationships with others who did not understand or necessarily value it. Aleidra's adaptive challenge was to integrate her social justice values into a work context that appeared to place boundaries on their expression. There are no standard, clear-cut solutions in either of these cases, making them adaptive challenges.

Adaptive challenges can be overwhelming. Thus, an important second step is to identify your learning goals so as to focus on your professional growth. For example, Hoa might choose a learning goal centered on how to communicate her cultural history and values to others with whom she would like to initiate substantive relationships. Aleidra might choose a learning goal centered on how to articulate and express her social justice values within her professional work context.

Part of the significance of identifying learning goals is to examine the developmental capacities they require, which is step 3 of this process. For Hoa to share her cultural history and values when she is aware others may not appreciate them requires that she be able to coordinate, respond, and address others' reactions rather than be silenced by them. The developmental capacity of self-authorship is necessary for her to acknowledge others' perceptions and be able to shape her reactions to them. Similarly, Aleidra will need a self-authored sense of her values to articulate them in her professional role and navigate the boundaries that the context might impose on her. Ideally, both women would strive for self-transformative capacities that would enable them to see multiple ideologies more clearly and integrate their perspectives with those of others more fluidly.

Once one has identified a context, learning goals, and the developmental capacities the learning goals require, step 4 is to identify individualized developmental goal(s). To do so requires reflecting on how you know the world, yourself, and your relationships to identify your current developmental capacities (table 9.1 in chapter 9 is a helpful resource for this purpose). Once an individual has identified current capacity, one must identify the next step toward the identified capacity as required for your learning goals. For example, if Hoa or Aleidra noted that concerns about others' reactions stopped them from enacting their values, they might determine that they have some socializing capacities that hold them back from meeting their goals. If this were the case, they would identify working toward self-authorship as their developmental goal. If they perceived themselves as already self-authoring but still sometimes inhibited by others' reactions, they would instead choose to work on consolidating or strengthening their self-authoring capacity across contexts.

The last three steps of Taylor and Baxter Magolda's (2015) model reflect finding the support needed for tackling learning and developmental goals. The learning partnership model defines support as respecting learners' thoughts and feelings, helping learners sort through their experiences, and collaborative problem-solving (Baxter Magolda, 2009). Step 5 involves supporting your own growth. Because you know your context, learning, and developmental goals, you can shape how you approach your work to find support for your growth. Although Taylor and Baxter Magolda (2015) specify particular supports for each developmental capacity, the key to supporting your own growth is to find venues to express your ideas (such as Hoa's poem or Aleidra's blog) and work through them. Step 6 is finding a learning partner with whom to collaboratively work through your goals. It is important to seek out partners who respect the views, collaboratively explore them further, and help explore multiple perspectives (rather than mandating what to do). Step 7 is finding a community of practice, or a group of people who work collaboratively to meet adaptive challenges. Aleidra's blog community served that purpose for her, giving her a place to explore her perspectives, hear others' perspectives, and collaborate on productive action. Taylor and Baxter Magolda (2015) recommend altering the way existing groups (that is, staff members, organizations) function to make them supportive contexts for working through adaptive challenges and transformational learning.

The key dynamics of our vision of professional development and Taylor and Baxter Magolda's (2015) plan for professional development echo key perspectives articulated by numerous professional associations regarding professional development. For example, *Learning Reconsidered* (Keeling, 2004) and the *Professional Competency Areas for Student Affairs Practitioners* (ACPA/NASPA, 2015) emphasized the inseparable nature of learning and development, the importance of multiple sources of knowledge, intellectual curiosity, placing learning in a broad context, and blending knowledge and action. What we advocate here is reshaping professional development to live out these conceptualizations. This model provides an answer to the question we posted at the outset, "What types of professional development can foster holistic transformative learning and public action?"

Evolving Roles in Student Affairs

Thus far in this chapter, using the stories of Hoa and Aleidra as guides, we have identified five foundational principles for reenvisioning professional development in student affairs, and we introduced a model, centered on learning partnerships, which could be used as a process to achieve this reenvisioning goal. We conclude this chapter with modest recommendations for the four primary stakeholders in professional development to consider, taking into consideration the ideas advanced in this chapter.

Graduate Preparation Faculty Members

For many entering student affairs, graduate preparation faculty members are looked to as not only professors but also students' first confidants, mentors, advisors, and coaches. Carducci and Jaramillo (2014) noted,

> As a professional preparation faculty member, you share responsibility for ensuring that the next generation of student affairs professionals possesses the knowledge, competencies, and dispositions essential for promoting the holistic development and learning of college students. You also are called upon to provide new student affairs professionals with good company on their journey toward self-authorship. Several new professionals featured in this book [*Job One 2.0*] acknowledged the significant cognitive, intrapersonal, and interpersonal development they experienced as graduate students, reflecting fondly on the powerful learning partnerships they forged with their program faculty, peers, and supervisors. (p. 181)

Hoa and Aleidra provide insights into knowledge that matters, and faculty members should use and expose students' broad-ranging knowledge bases (for example, politics, race, cultural assimilation) beyond the traditional curriculum offerings, such as in human development and administration. Curricula need to be fluid to tend to contemporary issues and challenges. Integrating knowledge from multiple sources is critical to continue to adapt to ever-changing campus environments.

Faculty members need to prepare students for the transition from graduate schools and highly structured practica and assistantships to more loosely coupled and autonomous job situations. Students should have an appreciation of what they learned as graduate students and at the same time realize they have so much more to learn as full-time professional educators. Faculty member should use their classrooms as laboratories for learning—experimenting with diverse pedagogies and learning partnerships, soliciting input from students—particularly those who find themselves on the margin. Faculty members have the additional responsibility of fostering a passion for career-long learning as part of students' future responsibilities.

New Professionals

Learn new ways of thinking, doing, and reflecting. "The learning way is about approaching life experiences with a learning attitude. It involves a deep trust in one's own experience and a healthy skepticism about received knowledge. It requires the perspective of quiet reflection and a passionate commitment to action in the face of uncertainty" (Kolb & Yaganeh, 2011, p. 2). Professional development extends well beyond national and international conventions. Some of the most profound and potent professional development opportunities can often occur on college campuses. It is essential for new professionals to identify and seek out meaningful learning opportunities that focus on knowledge that matters.

Similar to Hoa and Aleidra, new professionals should take responsibility for their own professional development and not wait for others to provide content or structure. Following Hoa and Aleidra's lead, forge a professional development plan that draws from graduate course work, one's own readings, cultural audits, and self-reflection. Using one's intellectual curiosity to access, integrate, and apply multiple sources of knowledge will most likely result in greater investments in learning. Staying intellectually curious and committed to continually learning only fosters greater curiosity for exploring the unknown and pushing oneself to be invigorated by learning more and different content and ways of knowing. Learning from others without being self-reliant and deferential to others is an art form that may take some practice. There is not always a happily ever after to every experience, and those are times when it is crucial to reflect on the mismatches, the missteps, and to embrace the dissonance—even when painful—to the benefit of one's personal and professional growth.

Seasoned Professionals: Mentors, Coaches, Advisors, and Supervisors

Seasoned professionals need to know and understand the issues that matter most to new professionals. Some of these issues were clearly articulated by the new professionals who shared their stories in *Job One 2.0* (Magolda & Carnaghi, 2014), such as building relationships, exploring professional and organizational fit, developing competence and confidence, managing differences between expectations and lived realities, the value of risk-taking, exhibiting courage, cultivating resiliency, and integrating personal and professional identities. Seasoned professionals should be wholly invested in new professionals' success from the time of recruitment.

Hoa and Aleidra inferred that they valued elders and wanted relationships with them but struggled. Supervisors, with more power, need to reach out to make the initial relationships work. One-on-one supervision meetings represent untapped professional development opportunities. The synergistic supervision model (Winston & Creamer, 1997) is a complete model of supervision and begins with creating the appropriate job description and continues with recruitment and selection, orientation to the position, supervision, staff development, performance appraisals, and separation. If a supervisor operates with a mind-set based on the various components of synergistic supervision, then every interaction is open to the possibility of professional development. And, there is always, always time for the individual meetings, teachable moments, appropriate challenge and support, as well as time for reflection. Individual and staff meetings should be considered as curriculum and pedagogy, not simply as another administrative task. Supervisors have the ability to create learning partnerships that respect supervisees' perspectives, while at the same time, promote collaborative problem-solving.

Professional Development Architects

Really just about anyone could be, and often is, responsible for professional development opportunities and just not the one-time, content-specific, present-the-material, question-and-answer type, and then it is done. Who is, or is not, responsible for professional development says a lot about the organization and its values and culture. Is professional development part of one individual's portfolio? Is there a committee who is charged with professional development from orientation activities to social events to awards to good-byes? There is no one way to do" professional development but much thought should be given to identifying desired outcomes and audiences.

After reflecting on Hoa's poem and Aleidra's blog, professional development architects should consider the content, pedagogy, and audience(s) to foster continued reflection and growth around the thornier topics that have no answers but that require holistic transformative learning. Being open to change and not viewing staff members on the margins as troublemakers may lead to high-impact professional development experiences focused on assessment, evidence-based discovery teams, and bright idea grants to name a few.

Some student affairs organizations have not had the privilege of choosing topical areas, but rather they have had to respond and provide training after a crisis has befallen the institution—bias incidents, sexual assaults—which can be too little too late. By being proactive and thinking about holistic transformative learning as a basis for professional development, the year's agenda can focus on programs of difference such as race, gender, power, and politics with time for follow-up conversations and even field trips. The power of a lived experience is often the catalyst or prompt for "readiness." Placing learning in a broader context (what one knows, one's identity, one's values, ways one contributes to society) can be powerful for all members of an organization and shows that all are valued and have a role to play. The multiple layers of professional development also must be acknowledged and addressed—including knowledge, skills, and developmental capacity.

Conclusion

Student affairs educators must situate professional development at the epicenter of their practices and work on a daily basis to forge learning partnerships with colleagues. Career-long learning must be embedded in their values and their work; the world is changing too fast to think that the knowledge acquired at the beginning of one's career will sustain one's effectiveness over one's professional lifetime. Every member in the organization must contribute to the knowledge base to serve students the best they can. Finally, they should recognize the political struggles associated with individuals and groups and engage in campus political processes to continually define and redefine what it means to teach and learn.

Discussion Questions

1. How do you define professional development?
2. Within your organization, who is or who should be responsible for professional development?
3. Which of the five principles resonates with you and your current situation?
4. What are the components of an effective learning partnership for your growth and development?
5. What is your most pressing adaptive challenge?

References

American College Personnel Association (ACPA). (1996). *The student learning imperative.* Washington, DC: Author.

American College Personnel Association (ACPA) & National Association of Student Personnel Administrators (NASPA). (2015). *Professional competency areas for student affairs practitioners.* Washington, DC: Authors.

Baxter Magolda, M. B. (2004). Learning partnerships model: A framework for promoting self-authorship. In M. B. Baxter Magolda & P. M. King (Eds.), *Learning partnerships: Theory and models of practice to educate for self-authorship* (pp. 37–62). Sterling, VA: Stylus.

Baxter Magolda, M. B. (2009). *Authoring your life: Developing an internal voice to navigate life's challenges.* Sterling, VA: Stylus.

Baxter Magolda, M. B. (2014). Enriching educators' learning experience. *About Campus: Enriching the Student Learning Experience, 19*(2), 2–10. doi:10.1002/abc.21150

Baxter Magolda, M. B., & Magolda, P. (2011). Intellectual curiosity and lifelong learning. In P. Magolda & M. B. Baxter Magolda (Eds.), *Contested issues in student affairs: Diverse perspectives and respectful dialogue* (pp. 3–14). Sterling, VA: Stylus.

Carducci, R., & Jaramillo, D. (2014). Job one: Continuing the journey toward self-authorship. In P. Magolda & J. E. Carnaghi (Eds.), *Job one 2.0: Understanding the next generation of student affairs professionals* (pp. 162–191). Lanham, MD: University Press of America.

Gamson, Z. (1993). The destruction and re-creation of academic community: A personal view. *ASHE Open Forum, 6,* 4–7.

Giroux, H. A. (2007). *The university in chains: Confronting the military-industrial-academic complex.* Boulder, CO: Paradigm.

Heifetz, R. (1998). *Leadership without easy answers.* Cambridge, MA: Harvard University Press.

Keeling, R. P. (Ed.). (2004). *Learning reconsidered: A campus-wide focus on the student experience.* Washington, DC: National Association of Student Personnel Administrators, American College Personnel Association.

Kolb, D., & Yaganeh, B. (2011, Sept. 13). *Deliberate experiential learning: Mastering the art of learning from experience* (WP-11–02). Cleveland, OH: Case Western Reserve University, Weatherhead School of Management. Retrieved from http://weatherhead.case.edu/departments/organizational-behavior/workingPapers/WP-11–02.pdf

Magolda, P. M., & Baxter Magolda, M. B. (Eds.). (2011). *Contested issues in student affairs: Diverse perspectives and respectful dialogue.* Sterling, VA: Stylus.

Magolda, P. M., & Carnaghi, J. E. (Eds.). (2004). *Job one: Experiences of new professionals in student affairs.* Lanham, MD: University Press of America.

Magolda, P. M., & Carnaghi, J. E. (2014). *Job one 2.0: Understanding the next generation of student affairs professionals* (2nd ed.). Lanham MD: University Press of America.

McIntire, D., & Willer, P. (1992). *Working with international students and scholars on American campuses.* Washington, DC: National Association of Student Personnel Administrators.

Mezirow, J. (Ed.). (2000). *Learning as transformation: Critical perspectives on a theory in progress.* San Francisco: Jossey-Bass.

Renn, K. A., & Hodges, J. P. (2007). The first year on the job: Experiences of new professionals in student affairs. *NASPA Journal, 44*(2), 367–391.

Renn, K. A., & Jessup-Anger, E. R. (2008). Preparing new professionals: Lessons for graduate preparation programs from the national study of new professionals in student affairs. *Journal of College Student Development, 49*(4), 319–335.

Rhoads, R., & Black, M. (1995). Student affairs practitioners as transformative educators: Advancing a critical cultural perspective. *Journal of College Student Development, 36*(5), 413–421.

Sue, D. W. (2010). *Microaggressions in everyday life: Race, gender, and sexual orientation.* Hoboken, NJ: Wiley.

Taylor, K. B., & Baxter Magolda, M. B. (2015). Building educators' capacities to meet 21st century demands. *About Campus: Enriching the Student Learning Experience, 20*(4), 16–25.

Thomsett, M. C. (2015). *Getting started in stock analysis.* Singapore: Wiley.

Tierney, W. G. (1993). *Building communities of difference: Higher education in the twenty-first century.* Westport, CT: Bergin & Garvey.

Tull, A., Hirt, J. B., & Saunders, S. A. (2009). *Becoming socialized in student affairs administration: A guide for new professionals and their supervisors.* Sterling, VA: Stylus.

Winston, R. B., & Creamer, D. G. (1997). *Improving staffing practices in student affairs.* San Francisco: Jossey-Bass.

CHAPTER 33

SHAPING THE FUTURE

Susan R. Jones, John H. Schuh, and Vasti Torres

Predicting the future can be difficult at best and potentially can result in missteps, inaction, or an occasional on-target projection. Our history is full of examples of predictions that turned out to be completely wrong. Notable among the wildly inaccurate was the prediction of *Literary Digest* that Alf Landon would win the 1936 presidential election (actually, he received eight electoral votes), which resulted in the demise of the magazine. However, the model structure that Ursula Delworth and Gary Hanson presented for the student affairs profession in 1989 is still contemporary (Delworth & Hanson, 1989, figure 1). Although less a prediction of what will be and more of an analysis of what is, Delworth and Hanson's thinking about student affairs has stood the test of time very well. We hope that we are as prescient as they were, and in this concluding chapter we incorporate several contemporary issues and dynamics facing higher education and student affairs that we think will contribute to shaping our work with students today and into the future.

We are not alone in making predictions about higher education. For example, Blumenstyk (2015) revisits predictions made in the *Chronicle of Higher Education* in 2005 about 2015. Some of the predictions were correct (a slowdown in the growth of colleges in the private sector), and others, such as increasing state appropriations for higher education or student financial aid keeping pace with the cost of higher education, missed the mark. Such is the life of forecasters—some predictions turn out to be accurate and others are not.

One of the strategies that can be used in predicting the future is to examine what experts identify as current issues and use them as a point of departure in terms of the extent to which these issues are likely to have a long-term dimension to them. An excellent example, in our view, of identifying current issues in student affairs was the study reported by Whitt, Roper, Porterfield, and

Carnaghi (2016), who identified issues that caused concern for a group of senior leaders in student affairs as well as those issues that created excitement for the same group. We recommend this book as a thoughtful report of current and future issues as seen through the eyes of a group of very experienced, highly attentive leaders in our profession.

In this chapter we offer some thoughts about what we think the future will hold for higher education in general and our profession in particular. We do not claim to be soothsayers, prognosticators, or have access to crystal balls that allow us to be clearer than anyone else. So, with these caveats, let's take a look at our educated guesses for the future.

Societal Trends

We begin by identifying several selected societal trends that have a direct effect on higher education and how we deliver services, programs, and learning experiences. These trends tend to be more external and imposed on institutions of higher education or reflect larger societal issues to which higher education must respond.

Debate about the Purpose of Higher Education

Our country is in the throes of a vigorous debate about the nature and value of a college education and the future of higher education altogether. This debate has moved beyond whether education is a public good or a private good; instead, it has shifted to scrutinizing the values associated with the outcomes of higher education. Members of the public seem to think of higher education as a necessary step in preparation for employment (Northeastern University, 2013). Others, exemplified by novelist Marilynne Robinson (a Pulitzer Prize recipient who received the 2016 Library of Congress Prize for American Fiction and is on *Time*'s list of one hundred most influential people), see higher education very differently and are critical of those who see it as utilitarian training (Goldman, 2015). Whether consensus will be achieved on this matter in the foreseeable future is unknown, but clearly the cost of attendance contributes to the question as to whether attending college is worth the cost. A study reported by Fischer (2011, n.p.) concluded, "Public anxiety over college costs is at an all-time high. And low-income college graduates or those burdened by student-loan debt are questioning the value of their degrees, or saying the cost of college has delayed other life decisions." Because attending college, in the mind of some, has been framed as job training (see, for example, Botkin, n.d.), the debate, essentially, is that unless a college degree prepares one for a well-paying job, attending college may not be in the best interests of potential students. We will leave the argument to others, but we do want to point out that the debate is unlikely to go away given the costs incurred by those who choose to enroll in our institutions and, in many cases, incur significant debt to pay the cost of attendance. That leads to the next trend.

Oversight

Serious concerns have been expressed about the extent higher education is accountable to its various constituencies in this century. For example, Leveille (2006) observed, "Accountability in higher education has been an increasingly significant national issue over the past decade or more, spurred by rising college costs, disappointing retention and graduation rates, employer concerns that graduates do not have the knowledge and skills expected in the workplace, and questions about the learning and value that higher education provides to students" (p. 5). More recent examples of concern about the extent to which institutions of higher education are accountable and receive sufficient oversight can be found on both coasts. Examples of activist legislative actions at the state level that influence higher education institutions in various ways are plentiful. Although these legislative initiatives may be made at the state level, they tend to infiltrate to other states once enacted. Examples include the following (some are proposed legislation and others are enacted):

- Focus on performance metrics to fund institutions that reflect a return on investment philosophy rather than a developmental or learning orientation (Maryland)
- Streamlining or dictating general education requirements as well as other curricular requirements (for example, nonrequirement of developmental courses for underprepared students) (Florida)
- Questioning of tenure and shared governance principles (Wisconsin)
- Selection of institutional leadership from outside higher education (government, military, or business) (Indiana, Iowa)
- Unfunded mandates concerning compliance issues (federal initiatives by the Department of Education and the Department of Justice)
- Use of data analytics to drive decisions about institutional policies (Grush, 2014)
- Requiring institutions to allow concealed guns to be carried on campus (Texas, Kansas)
- Mandating individuals to use bathrooms that correspond to their gender identities on birth certificates (North Carolina)

These recommendations illustrate the tenor of the times. Critics would say that higher education has charted a course that is self-serving and independent of the wishes and needs of the citizens who support it. However, these activities have resulted in potentially costly mandates as well as represent intrusion into daily activities that are actually quite limited in importance relative to student learning and development. We do not expect that this element of the external environment will change. What it will require is for higher education institutions, and their faculty and staff members, including those in student affairs, to be aware of the needs of the constituencies they serve and do the best they can to address those concerns within the context of the mission of their institutions and good professional practice. This approach to our work will not be easy but we think it is an element of the future of higher education that cannot be ignored or dismissed. Although we think that some of higher education's critics may not be in touch with issues critical to student learning and development, we also recognize that in any number of cases they have been able to influence educational policy in ways that have a direct impact on higher education, such as mandatory Title IX reporting, influencing policy related to transgender students, concealed carry, teaching loads, and so on. On the surface, this level of involvement may result in an abundance of minutiae for institutions to manage, but we also recognize that these critics are serious in their views and through legislative mandates expect institutions to change in order to meet their expectations.

Demographic Trends

We believe that many of our institutions will continue to grow in terms of the size of their enrollments and, second, they will become more diverse in terms of their students. That does not mean that all institutions will grow at essentially the same pace, because we believe that public institutions (especially community colleges) are likely to grow at a faster rate than private, not-for-profit colleges and universities. In making these predictions, we rely heavily on Hussar and Bailey (2013).

Enrollments in postsecondary, degree-granting colleges and universities grew dramatically between 2000 and 2012 according to data included in the *Digest of Education Statistics* (National Center for Education Statistics, 2015). Over twenty million students were enrolled in 2012 (table 304.10) at 4,726 institutions (table 303.90), an increase from more than fifteen million enrolled at 4,056 institutions in 2000 (table 303.90). In a dozen years five million more students enrolled at just about seven hundred more institutions.

By 2022 enrollment in postsecondary degree–granting institutions is projected to be twenty-four million (Hussar & Bailey, 2013, figure 16). By age, 13.6 million students will be between eighteen and twenty-four, 5.8 million between twenty-five and thirty-four, and 4.3 million students will be thirty-five years of age or over (Hussar & Bailey, 2013, figure 17). By race-ethnicity (Hussar & Bailey, 2013), enrollment is expected to increase by 7 percent between 2011 and 2022 for Asian/Pacific Islanders, by 7 percent for white students, by 26 percent for African Americans, and by 27 percent for Latino/Latina students (figure 21). In spite of the growth in access to higher education for African American and Latinos, these groups continue to be underrepresented and have lower completion rates. Enrollments for American Indian and Alaska native students are not likely to change much according to these estimates.

In rough terms, the proportion of students who enroll in two- and four-year institutions will be about the same—about a third of the students will enroll in two-year public institutions, and about 37.5 percent will enroll in four-year public institutions. More than a third of all undergraduates will enroll on a part-time basis. The proportion of students who will enroll at public and private institutions (for-profit institutions as well as not-for-profit institutions) will be about the same as today.

If these projections are correct, we will find colleges and universities more diverse than ever before—by sex, race, and enrollment status. In addition to these enrollment increases, the pathways that students take will not be linear. Rather, students will swirl between institutions in hopes of completing requirements with convenient course-taking patterns. This approach may not serve the student or our efforts at retaining students and promoting student learning.

If past is prologue, more international students than ever also will enroll in postsecondary institutions in the United States. The number of these students has more than doubled from 1990–1991 to 2013–2014 (National Center for Education Statistics, 2015, table 310.20), and we suspect the number of international students will continue to grow, following the pattern over the past several decades. The largest percentage of foreign students, in recent years, has come from China (over a quarter of all international students), India, and Taiwan, whereas the percentage from the Middle East has declined (table 310.20). Global political events are likely to shape international enrollments in the future.

What this means for student affairs professionals is that they will need to be prepared to work with ever-increasingly diverse students with these characteristics and perhaps others. In addition, division of student affairs leaders will need to evaluate why the work force does not reflect the student populations we serve. The diversification of our own field has not kept pace with the diversification of the student population. Student affairs educators need to understand who enrolls in their institutions and develop programs, services, and learning experiences for these students, not the ones who used to enroll or who student affairs would like to enroll in their colleges and universities. Consider this statistic: Hussar and Bailey (2013) predict that there will be more part-time students enrolled in higher education in 2022 than were enrolled on a full-time basis in 2000 (table 20).

Economic Trends

Economic trends related to higher education were well established over the past several decades and are not favorable toward higher education. In short, higher education increasingly has to look inward to generate sufficient resources to deliver the programs and services that are expected by various stakeholders. Trend data support this conclusion.

Public institutions increasingly receive a smaller percentage of their revenues from the states, whether two-year or four-year institutions. This requires that institutions increasingly rely on tuition and fees paid by students rather than state funding (National Center for Education Statistics, 2015, table 333.10). Similarly, private, not-for-profit colleges and universities increasingly are relying on student tuition and fees as the largest source of revenue, and this reliance has grown from 1999–2000 to 2012–2013 (table 333.40). Private, for-profit institutions have relied more heavily on tuition than public institutions or private, not-for-profit institutions over the years. The most recent data (table 333.55) indicates that about 90 percent of their revenues are from tuition and fees.

The largest expenditure category for public institutions is instruction, and that has been the case over the years (National Center for Education Statistics, 2015, table 334.10). Four-year public institutions devote about a quarter of their expenditures and two-year public institutions specify more than a third to instruction, though four-year institutions spend more than twice as much on instruction as two-year institutions do in terms of actual dollars. Similarly, four-year private, not-for-profit institutions spend more on instruction than any other expenditure category, though they devote about a third of their expenditures to instruction, and, in actual dollars, spend considerably more than four-year public institutions (table 334.30). The percentage of expenditures of private, for-profit institutions devoted to instruction has declined in this century, and the actual expenditures in constant dollars have decline for four-year institutions but increased for two-year institutions (table 334.50).

Expenditures for student services at public institutions remained relatively flat in this century, increasing just a bit for four-year institutions ($49 per student over seven years in constant dollars) and declining a bit for two-year institutions ($75 per student in constant dollars over seven years) (National Center for Education Statistics, 2015, table 334.10). Expenditures on student services at private, not-for-profit institutions have increased as a percentage of budget and in constant dollars in this century (table 334.30). These institutions continued to spend more on student services than their public counterparts. Data are not available for dedicated expenditures for student services at private, for-profit institutions. Student services expenditures are aggregated with other expenditures at these institutions.

Clearly, young adults are concerned about college costs and loans. A recent Gallup Poll (Saad, 2014) reported, "Paying tuition or college loans far exceeds other money matters as the top financial challenge young adults in the U.S. say they face today" (n.p.). We have no reason to believe that this pressure on higher education in general or student affairs in particular will change. Tough economic times, and the attendant debate about the value of higher education, will be with us for years.

We see no ray of sunshine in this gloomy trend. Governments, be they state or federal, appear to have no appetite for increasing their support for higher education to past levels. Tuition and student fees have increased dramatically over several decades and in many situations institutions simply cannot charge more even though their costs are increasing at a rate faster than the generally accepted rate of inflation (see Commonfund, 2015, for additional information about higher education inflation). Endowments have grown significantly over the years for some institutions, but not all. The consequence is that income from endowments can provide a cushion against increasing costs for only a few institutions, but many simply do not have an endowment that can generate sufficient income to cover cost increases and realistically cannot raise sufficient funds to add to their endowments to head off future financial obligations. Our view is that the challenging financial situation that institutions in general face in contemporary times will not change in the future. Budgets will not increase fast enough to match cost increases and student affairs will not be immune from the resulting challenges faced by higher education. At least two potential changes may affect student affairs. One is that programs or services increasingly may be treated, for budgetary purposes, as auxiliary services, meaning that they will be responsible for generating their own sources of revenue. The other is that units may be outsourced to private companies that will provide services through a contractual relationship with the college or university.

Supposed Post-Racial Era

After the election of an African American president in the United States many individuals purported that society had moved beyond racial discrimination and into what is called a post-racial era. According to the Cooperative Institutional Research Program's (CIRP) freshman survey, 25 percent of incoming students at four-year institutions indicated that they believed racial discrimination is no longer a major a problem in the United States (Hurtado & Ruiz, 2012). This idea that society has overcome historically ingrained negative beliefs, attitudes, and behaviors concerning race, gender, and ethnicity is a major issue for student affairs practitioners.

The need to promote student success among all students requires that practitioners recognize that not all students have the same access to educational opportunities (Torres, 2015). This makes the catch-phrase "I treat all the students the same" a contradiction, because not all students have the same opportunities. The inequality of educational opportunities in secondary education settings limits the type of access some students have within higher education (Ladson-Billings, 2006). Because college campuses are a microcosm of the greater society, issues of inequality and discrimination are reflected on our campuses in a variety of ways.

Student protest about issues of inequality and discrimination on the basis of race, gender identity, and ethnicity are as prevalent today as they have been for the past fifty years. The ability of students to organize using social media outlets such as Twitter and Facebook enables a quick response to incidents that highlight inequity (#blacklivesmatter; #occupywallstreet; #wejustneedtopee). Social media also enable students to make anonymous posts (Yik Yak) that are racist, disrespectful, and damaging. The use of electronic devices to capture beatings of citizens who appear to be cooperating or officials making comments that illustrate racist or sexist beliefs enables these incidents to be spotlighted quickly and on a national level. Although attitudes about tolerance may have changed over time, there continues to be evidence that beliefs and behaviors are not changing at the same rate. In essence, to believe that we are in a post-racial era is ignoring the voices of the growing population of students who experience these inequities every day and highlights the ineffectiveness of higher education to advance real change in the direction of inclusion and equity.

Technology

Predicting the future of technology can be risky at best. Although previous editions of this book addressed technology, much of the information had to do with technological applications in student affairs that we take for granted in contemporary student affairs practice, such as communication, data-based management systems, developing websites, and the use of personal digital assistants such as smartphones or tablets. Where technology will take us is not entirely clear, and student affairs, as Jeffrey Rokkum and Reynol Junco point out in chapter 20, will need to develop new and more effective ways of engaging students through technology. We are certain that students enrolling in postsecondary education will be increasingly facile with the use of technology, perhaps more so than faculty members and administrators. Staying contemporary in the use of technology will be an ongoing challenge for student affairs educators because new applications and other forms of technology seem to be rolled out on a weekly, if not daily, basis. Our best advice is to keep talking with students about technology, how they use it, and how it can best facilitate their educational experiences. They know more about technology than many of us!

Technology also influences the pace of work and expectations for how student affairs practitioners do their work. Today, a Twitter feed may send out information about a situation before a professional even knows it has occurred. The expectations of getting an immediate response to a question prompts new professionals to think they must be glued to their technology devices—thus affecting the balance of one's personal and professional lives. In addition, the ability to videotape behaviors and post those videos on public sites adds additional pressures to how our work is done on a daily basis. Use of Yik Yak to make anonymous posts brings hateful and disrespectful sentiments into the day-to-day routine of campus life. These aspects of our professional lives bring new challenges and need to be negotiated with supervisors and colleagues—it is unrealistic to think they can be ignored.

Trends in Student Affairs

We offer predictions about several trends that we think will apply to student affairs, realizing that this book is full of observations from experts about the future of various aspects of student affairs.

Student Affairs' Identity and Role

Of the three units that typically are found on college campuses (academic affairs, business affairs, and student affairs) student affairs has the shortest longevity and least stable role in higher education. Fundamentally, academic affairs has centered on the curriculum, faculty members, and scholarship. Students take courses, earn grades, and receive degrees, all under the supervision of the faculty members who determine course and degree requirements. Staff members in business affairs provide everything from landscaping and building repairs to utilities, business services, human resources, and myriad other support activities. Rarely have we found the services offered by units in business affairs coveted by those associated with academic or student affairs.

The mission of student affairs has evolved over the years and even today is viewed differently from campus to campus. The portfolio under the oversight of student affairs can vary widely (see Manning, Kinzie, & Schuh, 2014), and the purposes of student affairs will be different from campus to campus as Kathleen Manning, Jillian Kinzie, and John H. Schuh describe in chapter 16. As Maureen E. Wilson reports in chapter 17, student affairs will have a range of units included in it, often determined by mission, tradition, and culture.

We think that student affairs educators will be well served if they focus on how they can add value to student learning within the context of their institution's mission and goals. Of course they will need to provide assessment data to affirm their contributions, but it is very difficult to argue with the efficacy of a unit that adds value to the education of students. Without question, some units, such as the production of identification cards that might be a function of student affairs on some campuses, provide services, and they should not be trivialized. But in the main we think student affairs units, through the students they serve, should stay focused on student learning, as has been asserted by the American College Personnel Association (1996, 2008) and the National Association of Student Personnel Administrators (Keeling, 2006). The mission of the institution in which the units that comprise student affairs will frame the nature of this learning typically occurs outside the formal curriculum.

Mental Health and Physical Health Concerns

Students, as we pointed out in the fifth edition of this book, have a variety of health concerns that have only increased over the past few years. Useful data are compiled by the American College Health Association (2008, 2015), which conducts annual studies of college students' physical and mental health issues. For the purposes of this chapter, we have compared the results of a sample of students from fall 2008 and a different sample of students from spring 2015. Though the results of these surveys are similar, a smaller percentage of the 2015 student sample described their health as good, very good, or excellent when compared with the 2008 sample (86.5 percent in 2015 compared with 92.1 percent in 2008). The 2015 sample also reported to be more affected than the 2008 sample by anxiety (21.9 percent compared with 18.2 percent), depression (13.8 percent compared with 11.2 percent), sleep difficulties (20.0 percent compared with 19.3 percent), and stress (30 percent compared with 27.2 percent).

Although the differences of the data are not dramatic, they do point to concerns about the health of students that require the attention of student affairs educators. The data also suggest that the presenting problems of students may be more complex than in the past. This trend may require that the new professional be more informed about legal and compliance aspects of students' health regulations as well as being attuned to students' emotional well-being.

Intercultural Engagement

As our institutions become increasingly diverse, which based on the data provided by Hussar and Bailey (2013) will likely continue, we anticipate that multicultural competence will be an absolutely essential skill set for student affairs educators. Increasingly diverse students are likely to have increasingly diverse needs that will have to be met, but in addition to meeting student needs, student affairs staff members will need to develop strategies and programs so that members of diverse groups can learn to work together and learn from each other.

This trend will also affect professional staff members working with each other. The campus climate is set by a combination of behaviors between permanent staff members and students. How we treat each other on campus has been the foci of many student protests in 2015 (for example, Black Lives Matter) and is likely to continue in the future. The idea that higher education is color-blind is far from the reality that many students face—student affairs will likely be asked to take an even greater lead in addressing the campus climate and how diverse students are treated. Real intercultural engagement will not be successful unless deep-seated attitudes and behaviors regarding racism and sexism (and other isms) are addressed.

New Programs

Predicting what new programs might be implemented in divisions of student affairs can be a difficult assignment, but we are certain that parental involvement in the lives of students is likely to continue for the foreseeable future for the reasons identified by Carney-Hall (2008) including "changing structures of families and campus environments, consumerism, and increased communication through technology" (citing Merriman, 2007). As a consequence, we anticipate that relationships that institutions have with the parents of students will continue to evolve and likely will require additional attention in the future. We also think the press on institutions of higher education from external forces will result in the development of programs designed to improve student retention and graduation rates. A good start has been implemented through learning communities (see Benjamin, 2015), but more will need to be done to assist students in achieving their educational goals. One other area of programming deserves mention—helping students secure employment or achieving other goals they have set for themselves after they graduate. Clearly, many programs and support systems are in place, as is evident from McClellan and Parker (2012) and Smith (2014), but more will need to be done to provide support for students as they strive to achieve their postgraduation goals. Our perception is that colleges and universities will be held accountable if students can't achieve their goals, and we believe that student affairs will be on the front lines in terms of developing approaches to help students achieve their educational aims.

Without question one of the challenges faced by student affairs staff members is determining what programs, services, and experiences will need to be retained, and what will need to be discontinued. Our view is that student affairs staff members have been very good at taking on additional tasks but not as adept at determining what not to do. This problem is not new to student affairs or higher education for that matter (Kuh, Kinzie, Schuh, Whitt, & Associates, 2005/2010), but given the economic scenario for most institutions, simply adding things to staff portfolios will result in staff member overload and create the potential for erosion of existing services and programs. As new programs and services are added, presumably without additional staff members or resources, decisions will have to be made about what to discontinue.

Accountability

We wrote of increasing unease being expressed by legislators and other higher education stakeholders about the lack of responsiveness of higher education institutions to their concerns, although disagreement appears to exist among these stakeholders about specifically what they seek from higher education. Nevertheless, institutions will be asked to increasingly provide evidence that they are achieving their stated purposes. We think this emphasis will include student affairs educators. As performance metrics become a part of funding systems, student affairs will need to provide evidence for how their programs influence student success measures in order to receive a portion of these funds.

We are not alone in expressing this concern that student affairs leaders must provide more and better evidence of the effectiveness of the work of student affairs educators. Roper and Whitt (2016), in their study of the perceptions of student affairs leaders, concluded, "Some noted that student affairs, as a field and on campuses, still appears to be struggling to capture and represent the powerful learning that occurs outside the classroom and appropriately and to have those data included in the institutional national discourse on the value of higher education" (p. 33). This concern has been expressed in various forms for more than three decades, going back to the monograph *Involvement in Learning* (Study Group on the Conditions of Excellence in American Higher Education, 1984). Our view is that student affairs educators must understand the importance of being able to demonstrate how their work advances their institutions in general and student learning in particular.

Moreover, as Ann M. Gansemer-Topf and Lance C. Kennedy-Phillips have pointed out in chapter 19, assessment for accountability and improvement are crucial aspects of student affairs work. We believe that student affairs educators will continue to be asked (even required) to conduct assessments for accountability and improvement purposes. Failure to do so will result in potentially negative consequences for them and their areas of responsibility.

Future Directions

We conclude this chapter, and the book, with observations about future directions of student affairs.

Violence

In 1998 Schuh observed, "No one can predict with absolute assurance where violence will rear its ugly head next" (p. 361). Decades later, that observation, unfortunately, is still true. Whether violence occurs in communities, such as Aurora, Colorado, or Paris, France, on a military installation as Fort Hood, Texas, or on college campuses such as the University of California–Merced, Virginia Tech, or Umpqua Community College, there appears to be no aspect of our society that is immune from violence. Whether the number of these incidents is increasing or we are simply more aware of them is not entirely clear. What we can be sure of is that student affairs educators will be on the front lines preparing their institutions to deal with such incidents should they occur, and they will certainly be asked to deal with the aftermath within their communities. One approach to increasing violence that has been implemented in some states is legislative action that allows individuals to carry weapons on campus (see National Conference of State Legislatures, 2015). The efficacy of this approach is unknown at the time of this writing but as administrators and faculty members in higher education for decades, we are not convinced that having students and others carry firearms on college campuses will lead to less violence. On campuses, for example, campus police routinely facilitate violent incident response training (such as active shooter training) for faculty, staff members, and students, designed to provide strategies to help members of the campus community survive a violent incident on campus. This training is very important to help ensure safety on campus but that it is necessary speaks volumes about how college campuses have changed during our careers in higher education.

Clearly one aspect of violence that has received much more attention in recent years is sexual violence. The American College Health Association (ACHA, 2011) has observed the following about sexual violence: "Students cannot learn in an atmosphere where they do not feel safe" (p. 1). ACHA went on to recommend that "efforts to prevent sexual violence should be multifaceted and include but not be limited to such strategies as classroom discussions, health promotion programs, media campaigns, peer education, and discussions during student health and counseling services visits" (p. 2). Without question this approach would involve student affairs educators. Sexual violence is a significant problem on many campuses. Efforts need to be redoubled to reduce and ultimately eradicate this sexual violence from our campuses. The significance of this issue prompted greater scrutiny from the Office of Civil Rights by using Title IX as the mechanism to ensure institutions do more about sexual harassment and violence. We think student affairs educators need to be in the forefront of these efforts.

Adaptation to Change

Student affairs educators, in our view, will need to continually adapt to change brought about by external factors, whether it is having an increasingly large number of veterans enroll in higher education or internal factors including a challenging budgetary environment. How student affairs will be organized and how it will respond to the challenges of the day will illustrate the adaptability of the field to respond to the ever-changing societal trends that influence higher education. We can be certain, we believe, that change will be ever present and often will occur as a result of unforeseen circumstances. Accordingly, student affairs will be affected.

Our opinion is that student affairs educators will need to realize that their environment is fluid, that they cannot expect conditions to remain static over a period of time, and that they need to conceptualize their work as adding value to the contemporary student experience. This environment has been described as permanent white water (Vaill, 1996). That is, problems happen with increasing rapidity, change is omnipresent, and it occurs at a faster pace than ever before. This environment, for example, might mean offering services and learning experiences for students who, historically, have not enrolled in higher education or may be enrolling on a part-time basis when they might have been full-time enrollees in a different era. Most important, student affairs educators need to be ready to offer their programs, services and experiences in an environment that is marked by continuous change at an increasingly faster pace.

Collaboration

In chapter 21 Elizabeth J. Whitt makes an excellent case for the efficacy and potency of partnerships that are created by student affairs and academic affairs units under the right conditions. The right conditions include factors such as mutual interest in the initiative, shared goals, shared leadership, shared resource commitment by units from each area, and a willingness to contribute time to create the conditions that will give the initiative the potential to be successful. Even then, not all partnerships result in success.

As the chapter indicates, simply collaborating for the sake of collaborating will not necessarily result in success. Our recommendation is that collaborations be developed cautiously and stay focused on the goal of the collaboration. Clearly, great strength can result from multiple units bringing their resources together to accomplish a shared goal, such as projects that focus on retaining students will need to bring together resources such academic advising, enrollment services, financial aid, and student housing. A multifaceted approach, in this case, has the potential to develop a richness that may well result in students being retained and ultimately achieving their educational goals.

We think in the future more pressure will be brought to bear on various units to collaborate, and this is likely to involve student affairs. But it does not mean, from our point of view, that student affairs should contribute the staff members and other resources to achieve goals established by academic affairs' units. In reality, it is likely that student affairs may do a bit more of the work on a project, but it also means that student affairs and academic affairs collaborators agree on the purposes and desired outcomes and initiatives that they develop jointly.

Preparation of Student Affairs Educators

As the field of student affairs matures and expectations for how we serve students increases, it is clear that the preparation of student affairs educators will need to consider more formalized criteria to ensure that professionals have the necessary competencies. Historically, multiple pathways into student affairs have provided great diversity of educational backgrounds, yet as our professional associations look to formalize the competencies needed to be effective practitioners, so must the criteria in hiring decisions. We see many reasons that support the efficacy of the professional preparation of student affairs staff members. We also recognize that for many reasons, among them institutional culture and history, in some circumstances those who enter the profession of student affairs will not have the professional preparation that we advocate. In those circumstances we urge that those who enter student affairs professional roles are committed to student learning and are centered on students (see Kuh, Kinzie, Schuh, Whitt, & Associates, 2005/2010). For such staff members, we hope that institutions cultivate a robust professional development program so that the services, programs, and experiences that they develop have a level of effectiveness that will facilitate student learning and growth.

Personal and Professional Development

The demands from technology along with the increased diversity within the student population will require more specialized professional development. Though many of the professional associations offer a multitude of professional development activities, ever-changing demands will require reconsideration of delivery modes for these offerings. To hold on to old delivery modes and status quo content will only diminish the effectiveness of practitioners in the field.

There is also the pressing need to evaluate the effectiveness of the field in providing a value added to the educational mission of our institutions. The accountability movement within higher education will require that the field be more specific about what contributions are being made toward student success.

This will require that practitioners be much more invested in evaluation and assessment of outcomes associated with student affairs areas.

All of these future directions in the area of professional development will require personal self-reflection about how we do our work and if we are truly serving students or doing the same old thing for students with a completely different set of expectations. The idea of self-reflection is embedded within the professional competencies, yet it is an extremely personal developmental process. Because the focus of student affairs work is on getting things done, we seldom take the time for self-reflection. Change in the workplace is not likely to occur without significant reflection on our practice; therefore, we must ask which is more important—sustaining the status quo or reflecting on necessary changes?

Conclusion

As a reader of this book we hope you have been challenged to think about the student affairs profession differently and have been supported in your ideas of serving students. This balancing act is one that is not easily achieved in our ever-changing environment. As editors of this book we wanted to bring forth new ideas while valuing the traditions of the field we have personally chosen for our careers. It is our sincere hope that there will be generations of student affairs professionals who will see the "green book" as a powerful resource to assist them in their work in student affairs.

References

American College Health Association. (2008, Fall). *American College Health Association–National College Health Assessment II: Reference group data report.* Baltimore: American College Health Association.

American College Health Association. (2011, Dec.). *Position statement on preventing sexual violence on college and university campuses.* Hanover, MD: Author.

American College Health Association. (2015, Spring). *American College Health Association–National College Health Assessment II: Undergraduate students reference group data report.* Hanover, MD: American College Health Association.

American College Personnel Association. (1996). *The student learning imperative.* Washington, DC: Author.

American College Personnel Association. (2008). *The student learning imperative: Implications for student affairs.* Washington, DC: Author.

Benjamin, M. (Ed.). (2015). *Learning communities from start to finish* (New Directions for Student Services, no. 149). San Francisco: Jossey-Bass.

Blumenstyk, G. (2015, Oct. 25). A decade ago, the *Chronicle* envisioned higher education in 2015. How'd we do? *Chronicle of Higher Education.* Retrieved October 30, 2015, from http://chronicle.com/article/A-Decade-Ago-The-Chronicle/233874

Botkin, K. (n.d.). Is a college degree valuable without job skills? *Money Crashers.* Retrieved from http://www.moneycrashers.com/is-college-degree-valuable-without-job-skills/

Carney-Hall, K. C. (2008). Understanding current trends in family involvement. *Managing parent partnerships* (New Directions for Student Services, no. 122, pp. 3–14). San Francisco: Jossey-Bass.

Commonfund. (2015). *About Higher Education Price Index®*. Wilton, CT: Author. Retrieved from http://www.commonfund.org/CommonfundInstitute/HEPI/Pages/default.aspx

Delworth, U., & Hanson, G. R. (1989). Future directions: A vision of student services in the 1990s. In U. Delworth, G. R. Hanson, & Associates, *Student services: A handbook for the profession* (2nd ed., pp. 604–618). San Francisco: Jossey-Bass.

Fischer, K. (2011, May 15). Crisis of confidence threatens colleges. *The Chronicle of Higher Education*. Retrieved May 6, 2015, from http://chronicle.com/article/Higher-Education-in-America-a/127530/

Goldman, C. (2015, Nov. 3). Novelist Marilynne Robinson warns Stanford audience against utilitarian trends in higher education. *Stanford News*. Retrieved May 6, 2015, from https://news.stanford.edu/2015/11/03/robinson-humanities-lecture-110315/

Grush, M. (2014, May 28). Big data: An evolution in higher education's technology landscape. *Campus Technology*. Retrieved Dec. 28, 2015, from https://campustechnology.com/articles/2014/05/28/the-big-data-evolution-in-higher-ed.aspx

Hurtado, S., & Ruiz, A. (2012). *The climate for underrepresented groups and diversity on campus*. Higher Education Research Institute UCLA. Retrieved May 12, 2016, from http://heri.ucla.edu/briefs/urmbriefreport.pdf

Hussar, W. J., & Bailey, T. M. (2013). *Projections of education statistics to 2022* (NCES 2014–051). US Department of Education, National Center for Education Statistics. Washington, DC: US Government Printing Office.

Keeling, R. P. (Ed.). (2006). *Learning reconsidered 2: Implementing a campus-wide focus on the student experience*. Washington, DC: American College Personnel Association (ACPA), Association of College and University Housing Officers–International (ACUHO-I), Association of College Unions–International (ACUI), National Academic Advising Association (NACADA), National Association for Campus Activities (NACA), National Association of Student Personnel Administrators (NASPA), and National Intramural-Recreational Sports Association (NIRSA).

Kuh, G. D., Kinzie, J., Schuh, J. H., Whitt, E. J., & Associates. (2005/2010). *Student success in college: Creating conditions that matter*. San Francisco: Jossey-Bass.

Ladson-Billings, G. (2006). From the achievement gap to the education debt: Understanding achievement in U.S. schools. *Educational Researcher, 35*(7), 3–12.

Leveille, D. (2006). *Accountability for higher education: A public agenda for trust and cultural change*. Berkeley: Center for the Study of Higher Education, University of California, Berkeley.

Manning, K., Kinzie, J., & Schuh, J. H. (2014). *One size does not fit all: Traditional and innovative models of student affairs practice* (2nd ed.). New York: Routledge.

McClellan, G. S., & Parker, J. (Eds.). (2012). *Stepping up to stepping out* (New Direction for Student Services, no. 138). San Francisco: Jossey-Bass.

National Center for Education Statistics. (2015). *Digest of education statistics, 2013*. Washington, DC: US Department of Education. Retrieved from http://nces.ed.gov/programs/digest/d13/

National Conference of State Legislatures. (2015, Oct. 5). *Guns on campus: Overview*. Retrieved December 29, 2015, from http://www.ncsl.org/research/education/guns-on-campus-overview.aspx

Northeastern University. (2013, Sept. 17). *Innovation imperative: Enhancing higher education outcomes*. FTI Consulting.

Roper, L. D., & Whitt, E. J. (2016). What troubles you? What keeps you up at night? In E. J. Whitt, L. D. Roper, K. T. Porterfield, & J. E. Carnaghi (Eds.), *Angst and hope: Current issues in student affairs leadership* (New Directions for Student Services, no. 153, pp. 19–37). San Francisco: Jossey-Bass.

Saad, L. (2014, April 21). *Young adults cite college costs as their top money problem*. Washington, DC: Gallup World Headquarters. Retrieved December 15, 2015, from http://www.gallup.com/poll/168584/young-adults-cite-college-costs-top-money-problem.aspx?version=print

Schuh, J. H. (1998). Conclusion. In A. M. Hoffman, J. H. Schuh, & R. H. Fenske (Eds.), *Violence on campus* (pp. 347–361). Gaithersburg, MD: Aspen.

Smith, K. K. (Ed.). (2014). *Strategic directions for career services with the university setting* (New Direction for Student Services, no. 148). San Francisco: Jossey-Bass.

Study Group on the Conditions of Excellence in American Higher Education. (1984). *Involvement in learning.* Washington, DC: US Department of Education.

Torres, V. (2015). Access to college is about equality of opportunity. In T. C. Ream & J. M. Braxton, (Eds.), *(Ernest L. Boyer: Hope for today's universities* (pp. 169–206). Albany: State University of New York Press.

Vaill, P. (1996). *Learning as a way of being.* San Francisco: Jossey-Bass.

Whitt, E. J., Roper, L. D., Porterfield, K. T., & Carnaghi, J. E. (2016). *Angst and hope: Current issues in student affairs leadership* (New Directions for Student Services, no. 153). San Francisco: Jossey-Bass.

NAME INDEX

Page numbers in italics refer to illustrative material.

A

Abelman, R., 63, 69
Abelson, B., 344
Abelson, S., 344
Abes, E. S., 121, *126, 127, 129,*
    135, 136, 137, 140, 143, 147,
    150, 151, 153, *156,* 162–163,
    164, 167, 168, 171, 186, 187,
    200, 202, 206, 208, 209, 210,
    211, 212, 214, 217, 218, 261,
    266, 504, 512, 516, 528
Adams, H., 9, 17
Adams, H. L., *127*
Adler, P. S., 350, 356
Alarcon, G. M., 352, 356
Alexander, L., 262, 263, 264
Al-Kazemi, A., 378, 390
Allan, E. J., 81, 85
Allen, A., 531, 532, 533–535,
    535–536, 537–538, 539, 540,
    541, 542, 543, 544, 545, 546,
    548
Allen, K. E., xxvii, xxx, 531

Allen, W. R., 74, 76, 77, 86, 500,
    512
Altabef, D., 453, 455, 456, 465
Altbach, P. G., 29, 37
Alvarado, A. R., 189, 202
Alvarez, C. L., 77, 86
Alvesson, M., 410, 413, 414, 415,
    420
Ambler, D. A., 321, 324
Amey, M. J., 429, 434
An, B. P., 504, 513
Anderson, J., 378, 391
Anderson, J. A., 522, 528
Anderson, M. L., *124*
Andrews-Guillen, C., 80, 88
Angell, J., 21
Angelou, M., 264, 418
Angrisani, C., 322, 324
antonio, a. l., 75, 77, 85, 87, 402,
    405, 507, 512
Anzaldúa, G., 214, 217
Appell, E., 169, 181, 182
Aragon, M. C., 84, 86
Arbelo-Marrero, F., 64, 69

Arcelus, V. J., 361, 372
Archibald, R. B., 314, 315, 324
Arellano, L., 77, 86
Arminio, J., 141, 151, 218, 375,
    377, 429, 434, 436
Armstrong, E. A., *132*
Arnett, J. J., *124,* 153, 167
Arnold, K., 185, 200, 364, 372
Arnold, K. A., 47, 54
Arnold, K. D., 503, 513
Arnold, M. S., 463, 465
Arseneau, J. R., *127*
Asker, E. H., 257, 267
Astin, A. W., 62, 69, *132,* 228,
    234, 241, 249, 258, 264, *280,*
    282, 361, 372, 409, 420, 466,
    482, 483, 504, 511, 513, 521,
    523, 528, 529
Astin, H. S., 409, 420
Atkins, K., 310, 324
Avolio, B. J., 417, 421
Axtell, J., 5, 17
Ayala, F., Jr., 523, 529
Ayman, R., 410, 420

567

SUBJECT INDEX

Page numbers in italics refer to illustrative material.